D1364511

# MODERN RETAILING:

# PRINCIPLES AND PRACTICES

# MODERN RETAILING:
# PRINCIPLES AND PRACTICES

**Melvin Morgenstein**
**Harriet Strongin**
*Nassau Community College*

**John Wiley & Sons**

New York • Chichester • Brisbane • Toronto • Singapore

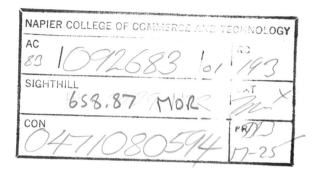
**COVER DESIGN: Joan A. Willens**
**BACKGROUND PHOTO: Steve Sint**
**COMPUTER PHOTO: TRS-80® Model II Computer,**
  **courtesy of Radio Shack, a division of Tandy Corporation**

*Library of Congress Cataloging in Publication Data:*

Morgenstein, Melvin.
  Modern retailing.

  Includes bibliographical references and index.
  1. Retail trade   I. Strongin, Harriet.
II. Title.

HF5429.M598        658.817        82-7063
ISBN 0-471-08059-4                AACR2

Printed in the United States of America

10 9 8 7 6 5 4 3 2 1

# preface

This is perhaps the most exciting time in history to write a book about retailing. With so much change resulting from sociological and technological developments, it is no wonder that merchants continue to devise new forms and techniques for satisfying consumers. To cite just two examples; on the horizon is an altogether new way for consumers to shop—right from their own living rooms! Called Videotex, the shopper receives product information via a TV hookup and orders merchandise through an in-home computer terminal. Another innovation, already operating on a small scale in California, allows a consumer to shop without the use of cash *or* a credit card. Amounts purchased are automatically deducted from the shopper's bank account by way of computer terminals.

We have written this book for students who intend to develop careers in retailing or marketing as well as for those seeking an introduction to the field of retailing. Without burdening you with complex theoretical approaches, we examine the major concerns and practices of retailers in realistic fashion. We have included numerous examples of actual situations to acquaint you with retailing as it exists today. In order to demonstrate the wide variety of retail institutions, we examine both large and small businesses.

The book is divided into six major parts. Part One contains an overview of retailing—from the development and growth of retailing to an analysis of the consumer. Along the way, we study the impact of innovation and competition on retail institutions as well as the influence of fashion, computers, and consumerism on retailing.

Part Two is concerned with the structure of retailing. It examines retail businesses in three ways: type of ownership, type of merchandise sold, and store versus nonstore selling methods. In addition, we study the human and physical sides of store management.

Part Three is devoted to a study of merchandising. We look at the buying function by analyzing how, what, and how much a retailer should buy. We also learn how merchants determine prices and how they handle and protect merchandise.

Part Four deals with promotion; that is, the ways in which retailers communicate with customers. It explores the techniques of personal selling, visual merchandising, advertising, sales promotion, and public relations.

Part Five demonstrates the importance of controls in the operation of a retail business. We study basic accounting procedures and financial reports, inventory control systems, and credit practices.

Part Six deals with the nature and scope of retail decision making. It is concerned with the place of research in the field of retailing as well as the details and problems of going into a retail business. We also identify trends in retailing as we head toward the final decade of this century.

In addition to the in-depth, easy-to-read subject matter, each chapter contains the following features:

- A set of learning objectives
- A list of Key Terms
- Highlights that summarize the chapter
- Questions for discussion
- Field Projects to provide actual application of retail principles
- Cases that test an understanding of retail principles

The book also contains a complete Glossary, with each term identified by the chapter in which it is defined. And Chapter Appendixes supplement the material where appropriate.

The comprehensiveness of the book enables the instructor to adapt it to the students' needs. For institutions requiring full treatment of retailing principles, the material is of sufficient depth for that purpose. For those with other objectives, the chapters are arranged for flexible selection to meet specific course requirements.

Accompanying the book is a Retail Laboratory Manual that supplies students with additional study questions and enlarged practical retailing projects and problems. The Manual is coordinated with the book and includes actual retail situations involving the design of store layouts, the completion of in-store and nonstore forms, the development of courses of action, the computation of decision figures, and so forth.

There are many who have contributed to this book. We are indebted to the following people for their incisive reviews of the manuscript:

Dr. Jerry Boles, Western Kentucky University
Dr. Jack Crespin, Bergen Community College
Prof. Albert T. Fragola, Warrant County Junior College District
Prof. Myron Gable, Shippensburg State College
Prof. John W. Lloyd, Monroe Community College
Prof. Robert L. Walker, Thomas Nelson Community College
Ms. Pam Phillips, Retailing and Marketing Consultant

We also thank the following faculty members at Nassau Community College for their helpful comments and suggestions for the Instructor's Manual and Lab Manual:

Prof. Nancy Bloom
Prof. Marguerite Ehlen
Prof. Noreen Ford

Prof. Mary Ellen Frank
Prof. Patricia Highland
Prof. Tanya Lowenstein
Prof. Noreen Sohm
Prof. Eleanor Smiley

In addition to Dr. Leonard B. Kruk who provided much needed inspiration and guidance and Alan Lesure who encouraged this undertaking, we also are grateful to the following people at John Wiley & Sons who assisted us at various stages in our work:

Kathy Bendo
Maria Colligan
Malcolm Easterlin
Pat Fitzgerald
Dennis Gibbons
Joan Knizeski
Stella Kupferberg
Robert Osman
Claire Thompson
Joan Willens
Cindy Zigmund

We hope that those who read this book will derive as much pleasure from it as we have had in writing it.

March 1982

*Melvin Morgenstein*
*Harriet Strongin*

# contents

# MODERN RETAILING:
# PRINCIPLES
# AND PRACTICES

**part one**
OVERVIEW

**R**etailing touches the lives of many people—consumers, workers, entrepreneurs. The myriad activities in which we engage bring us into almost daily contact with a variety of retail functions: shopping, buying, selling, returning, or paying for goods; working in a retail store; checking the latest fashions; dealing with door-to-door vendors; using a department store's catalog; and so on.

This book consists of six parts. In Chapter 1 of Part One we view the development and growth of retailing from ancient times to the present. We also see how retail outlets emerged to meet the demands of changing societies and the needs of consumers.

In Chapter 2 we study the impact of innovation and competition on existing retail institutions and examine the status of retailing on an international level. We also learn about the economic importance of retailing and the diverse career opportunities it generates.

Chapter 3 deals with some major factors that influence retailing: fashion, computers, and consumerism. We see how each of these maintains retailing as a dynamic force in our economic and social lives. We also identify laws that help consumers, and explain the functions of government and business agencies that affect consumer affairs.

Chapters 4 and 5 analyze several aspects of consumer behavior. In Chapter 4 we look at consumer behavior in terms of buying motives based on emotion, rational thinking, biogenic and psychogenic factors, and patronage appeal. Next we examine consumer behavior with regard to the specific order in which consumers satisfy their needs. We then see how consumer learning takes place, and identify the concepts that are used to understand personality. Finally we study the steps in the buying process and identify their implications for retailers.

In Chapter 5 we analyze two basic factors in the buying process: demographics and lifestyles. This includes a study of changes in groups based on age, education, sex, occupation, income, household type, and marital status. The implications of those changes for retailers are discussed. Lifestyles are then examined as they pertain to social classes. Finally we see how reference groups, such as opinion leaders and families, combine with cultural influences to shape consumers' buying habits.

# chapter 1
# THE DEVELOPMENT AND GROWTH OF RETAILING

After completing this chapter, you should be able to:

1   Identify the three main types of businesses that deal with goods and services.
2   Recount the history of ancient and early European retailing.
3   Identify early and later types of American retailing institutions.

This book is about people who buy goods and services. It concerns students who purchase books and supplies; homemakers who buy food and other household items; workers who pay to get to and from their jobs; and sports fans who purchase tickets to games.

This book is also about the businesses that sell goods and services to people. It deals with large companies like Sears, Roebuck and F. W. Woolworth, and with small neighborhood stores like your local grocer and jewelry shop; with supermarkets like A & P and Safeway; and with businesses that sell services, such as hairdressers and auto body shops.

In one way or another we all play a part in this business of goods and services, the business called retailing. It provides some people's livelihood, while others depend on it for the things they need. Let's take a closer look at the retailing field.

# THE NATURE OF RETAILING

Definition of retailing

**Retailing** consists of the selling of goods and services to their ultimate consumers, that is, individuals who buy something for personal or household use. Someone who purchases a toaster or chair for use in the home is an ultimate consumer.

Three main types of businesses are usually involved in getting goods and services to consumers: *manufacturers, wholesalers,* and *retailers*. **Manufacturers,** such as General Motors and Jordache Jeans, make the products that people buy. **Wholesalers,** or middlemen, purchase and distribute manufactured products to retailers. **Retailers** sell goods and services directly to the ultimate consumer.

How goods and services reach the consumer

The path that a product takes to reach the consumer is called a channel of distribution. Figure 1-1 indicates that manufacturers may sell directly to consumers. The Avon Products Company, which sells cosmetic products from door to door, is an example of this type of manufacturer. So is Electrolux, a company that manufactures vacuum cleaners. Companies like the Thom McAn Shoe Company manufacture goods and sell them directly to consumers in their own retail stores.

Manufacturers often sell their goods to retail operations like R. H. Macy & Company or Montgomery Ward Company. The retailer then sells the product to the consumer for a profit. In some cases manufacturers sell their goods to wholesalers in large quantities. The wholesalers, in turn, sell the goods to retailers in smaller quantities. For example, General Electric sells one of its products, light bulbs, to various wholesalers. The wholesalers then sell the bulbs to a variety of retailers, such as hardware stores and supermarkets, for final sale to consumers.

# THE DEVELOPMENT OF RETAILING

To appreciate the present state of the retailing business, it is helpful to know how it evolved. In the following pages we will show how modern retailing institutions emerged from early European and American practices.

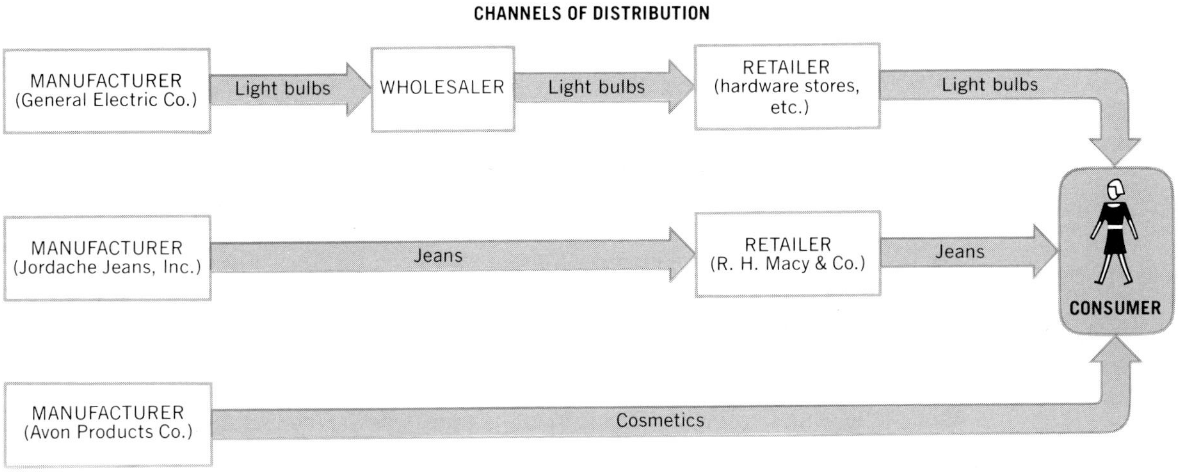


**FIGURE 1-1**
Channels of distribution.

## Ancient Retailing

History of retailing

Retailing probably had its origins in the Mediterranean area, where Crete, the center of Minoan civilization, traded such products as olive oil and wine to neighboring peoples in exchange for handmade goods. During this period, around 2000 B.C., the Greeks developed their own trading practices through contact with the Cretans. They imported the grain they needed, and exported such items as silver and handmade goods.

The next major traders were the Phoenicians, who traveled farther to reach other lands in the Mediterranean region. Proficient sailers, they traded in Italy, Spain, and as far away as the Azore Islands and Britain. The Phoenicians traded glass, dyes, cloth, and oil in return for raw goods.

The last of the traders of the ancient world were the Romans. Within the Roman Empire, food and goods were transported and sold by merchants. From distant lands like Arabia, India, and China, traders returned with valuable products, including perfumes, ivory, and silk. In turn, the Romans exported such products as pottery, building materials, glassware, and excellent wines. Besides engaging in this import–export trade, the Romans built centrally located shops for simple retail trade.

## Early European Retailing

Retailing by peddlers, at fairs, in shops

### Peddlers

After the downfall of the Roman Empire in the fifth century A.D., retailing wa ied on primarily by **peddlers** who traveled on foot. Though this personalized servi material benefits to villagers, it had its drawbacks. Unfortunately, the peddl cheated their customers, and as a result peddling developed a poor rep

### Fairs

The growth of populations during the fifth century stimulated the which people either **bartered** (traded) their goods for other go fairs of Champagne in France, for example, were highly esteemed during the 1200s. Fairs usually functioned under charters issued by kings or local rulers with regulations to ensure honest dealings. Today fairs are still found in many parts of the world.

### Retail Shops

By the twelfth century retail shops had developed on the European continent. Like the earlier Roman shops, they offered townspeople a variety of goods. Peddlers could not compete successfully with them. Peddling entered a permanent decline, and the foundation was laid for the emergence of more advanced retail institutions.

## American Retailing

### Trading Posts

One of the earliest forms of retailing in this country was the **trading post,** where bartering was the accepted mode of exchange. At the post such items as trinkets and knives were sold to Indians in exchange for hides and furs. Farmers visiting the post traded farm products for European manufactured goods. To this day trading posts can be found in the southwestern United States. Of course cash, rather than barter, is the usual method of exchange at these posts.

### Itinerant Peddlers

Emulating their European counterparts, itinerant peddlers, on foot or with horse and wagon, carried a variety of merchandise. They sold knives, pans, scissors, sewing needles, tea, and coffee. Some specialized in particular types of merchandise, such as housewares or spices, or even carried a line of bulkier items, including sewing machines and furniture.

Much of a peddler's trade was conducted through barter because customers frequently had no other means of exchange. As a result, the peddler returned home laden with farm products and handmade furniture for sale to merchants.

In this country, as in Europe, peddlers were a mixed blessing to their customers, for while they satisfied the customers' material needs, they were not always honest. Because the settlers hungered for material items and were unsophisticated about retail practices, they were frequently overcharged. It was not uncommon, for example, for peddlers to make profits in excess of 100 percent. It should be remembered, however, that they were exposed to physical danger when they traveled through sparsely settled areas.

Peddlers served a positive social function by bringing much-welcomed news to people living on the frontiers. They were also one of the few links between frontier families and suppliers seeking outlets for their products. The founders of three well-known department stores, Adam Gimbel, Morris Rich, and Joseph Goldwater, all began their careers as peddlers.

### General Stores

The first authentically American retailing institution was the **general store.** In it the storekeeper maintained a limited but varied stock of merchandise ranging from foodstuffs to manufactured goods. Catering to both townspeople and rural customers, the general store sold for credit as well as for cash and functioned as a social gathering place.

The merchant was largely ignorant of the changes that were taking place in the

An early itinerant peddler selling goods to frontier customers.

The emergence of the general store

development and manufacture of merchandise. Relying on information from traveling salespeople, storekeepers learned little beyond what the salespeople themselves knew or cared to tell them. Consequently, their customers also had little knowledge about the merchandise.

One of the reasons that general stores succeeded was the lack of competition. Restricted as they were by the difficulty of transportation, people relied heavily on the general store for basic as well as luxury goods. Without any competition beyond that provided by peddlers, the store could charge whatever prices it liked.

The helter-skelter arrangement of merchandise in general stores made for inefficiency and waste. By paying little attention to store organization, storekeepers were unknowingly slowing their own progress and stimulating others to develop more efficient forms of retailing.

## Mail Order Retailing

Mail order retailing encroaches on the general store

Another factor that made general stores vulnerable to more sophisticated retailing methods was the advent of the railroad. Freed from the hazards, slowness, and unreliability of wagon-drawn transportation, a new type of retail institution, the **mail order house,** entered the retailing scene. Pioneered by Aaron Montgomery Ward in 1872 mainly as a means of selling to farmers, buying by mail started modestly with merchandise featured in a one-page catalog. The idea caught on quickly as customers found that they could rely on Ward for honesty and low prices. In 1886 Richard W. Sears started a mail order business that sold watches, and was immediately successful. In 1887 he hired Alvah Curtis Roebuck to service and repair watches, and the association of these two men resulted in the establishment of Sears, Roebuck and Company in 1893. At that time the firm's catalog contained almost 200 pages; by 1895 it contained more than 500. Despite Richard Sears' occasional hucksterism, by 1900 the company had surpassed Montgomery Ward as the nation's leading mail order house. Today Sears' annual catalog sales total over $3 billion and the company caters to almost 30 million customers.

Both Montgomery Ward and Sears profited tremendously, as did other mail order houses, from the start of rural free delivery at the end of the nineteenth century and the introduction of parcel post mailing just prior to World War I. By this time mail order catalogs routinely ran to hundreds of pages and displayed a wide variety of merchandise.

Today mail order selling occupies an important place in retailing and is still dominated by Montgomery Ward and Sears, Roebuck. The original concept of a wide, varied

A page from an early J. C. Penney mail order catalog. Notice the prices!

catalog offering has been augmented by mail order companies that specialize in certain types of merchandise, such as outdoor sporting wear (e.g., L. L. Bean of Maine); retail stores that sell by mail (e.g., J. C. Penney); and manufacturing concerns that mail goods directly to customers (e.g., Roots of Toronto, Canada, which makes and sells shoes).

## Specialty (Limited-Line) Stores

The specialty store carries a particular type of merchandise

Along with the development of the general store and the mail order house came the **specialty** or **limited-line store.** As the industrial revolution of the 1800s gathered momentum, the variety of goods manufactured for retail sale increased enormously. The general store, with its limited outlook, stocked only a small amount of the available merchandise. The mail order house, successful though it was, could not satisfy consumers who wanted immediate contact with and delivery of new products. Since the specialty store carried a particular line of merchandise, such as hardware, shoes, or food, it stocked that product fully. It also offered a greater variety of items within the same line. And unlike the owners of general stores, who knew little about the goods they carried, the owners of specialty stores had a thorough knowledge of a limited line of products.

The J. C. Penney Company, which today operates over 2100 department stores, started as a specialty store in Kemmerer, Wyoming, in 1902. Known as the Golden Rule to symbolize James Cash Penney's belief that an ethical yardstick should apply in business as well as personal life, the store carried apparel and novelty goods for men, women, and children.

## Chain Stores (Food)

Food chains emerge

In the late 1800s some of the more aggressive specialty store owners opened additional outlets. This was the start of the phenomenal growth of the modern food **chain store,** exemplified by such companies as Safeway, A&P, and Winn-Dixie Stores. Most people think of a chain organization as having two or more retail outlets under common ownership. However, the Bureau of the Census now defines a chain as having at least eleven outlets.

Although retail chains had existed in the orient and Europe for many years, it was not until 1859 that the first well-known chain in this country had its start. George F. Gilman and George Huntington Hartford opened a tea business in New York City that eventually became the Great Atlantic & Pacific Tea Company (A&P). Other food merchants joined the chain phenomenon; among them were the Jewel Tea Company, Grand Union Company, Lucky Stores, and Kroger's. The westward movement of the frontier and an expanding population gave impetus to the opening of large numbers of chain units, with some of the chains opening as many as 200 new stores per week.

## Chain Stores (Variety)

Variety chains emerge

Another type of chain store that developed in the late 1800s was the **variety store,** which sold novelty items at low prices. This type of outlet was popularized by Frank W. Woolworth, who sold such goods as combs, pins, pencils, and thread for five or ten cents. Capitalizing on the theory that cut-rate (but still profitable) prices would attract customers, Woolworth opened so-called Five and Dime stores in large numbers. Within a short period he had established a giant nationwide chain whose name was known by all.

The A&P food chain opened thousands of stores such as the ones shown here.

Woolworth's wasn't the only variety chain that prospered. Others included H. Kress & Company, a Tennessee-based store; S. S. Kresge; and McCrory's. However, the chains' low-price policy caused them to compete aggressively for customers, and frequent price wars resulted. In addition, the chains had to expand their merchandise lines constantly in order to keep pace with their competitors.

## Department Stores

The great department stores develop

Along with the development of chain stores, the last half of the nineteenth century witnessed the emergence of the **department store.** This form of retailing was totally different from the general store. Instead of a hodge-podge arrangement of stock, the department store offered carefully selected merchandise in specific departments. As a result, customers could make quick purchases of a variety of goods and services under one roof (one-stop shopping). Thus, the department store also differed from the specialty store by selling several types of goods: clothing, hardware, furniture, and so forth.

The first American department store was probably opened in New York City by Alexander Stewart in 1848. Unlike most retailers of the period, who haggled over prices, Stewart instituted a one-price policy. In other words, he charged all customers the same

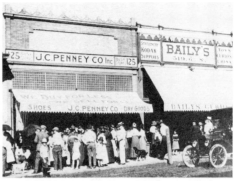

How the stores operated by today's giant chains looked years ago.

price for a particular product. The success of this policy made it possible for him to build a far larger store in another part of the city.

Stewart's experience led to the entrance of other people into the department store business. Rich's, which operates stores in Georgia, got its start in Atlanta shortly after Stewart's second store was opened. Out west, Brigham Young opened a store in Salt Lake City. Simon Lazarus started a business in Columbus, Ohio, that today is the well-known F & R Lazarus. Rowland Macy's early success with competitive pricing policies resulted in the establishment of the famous R. H. Macy's stores. In Philadelphia, John Wanamaker advertised extensively and offered refunds to dissatisfied customers. His innovations were so successful that he is often referred to as the father of retailing. Adam Gimbel's original store in Vincennes, Indiana, grew from an early trading post into a large business with stores in New York, Milwaukee, and Philadelphia. Others who pioneered successful enterprises were William Filene (Filene's of Boston), Marshall Field of Chicago, Joseph Hudson (J. L. Hudson Company in Detroit), Mary Ann and John Magnin (I. Magnin & Company of San Francisco), and A. L. Neiman and Herbert Marcus (Neiman-Marcus in Dallas).

By and large, department stores are credited with raising the level of retailing practices. Abandoning the old ways of bargaining, the stores instituted a one-price system. Offering their customers quality merchandise, attractive surroundings, and personal services, they captured the loyalty of a large part of the public. To this day department stores account for a significant portion of total retail sales.

## Supermarkets

At the beginning of this century, but particularly from 1930 to 1940, the **supermarket** became the dominant type of retail food outlet. Stressing low prices and self-service, supermarkets like A&P and Safeway quickly overtook local grocers in sales volume. Since their emergence as a major force in retailing, supermarkets have expanded their product lines to include housewares, drugs, and other nonfood items.

To understand the phenomenal success of the supermarket, one has to appreciate the limitations of the small food stores operated by A & P and other food merchants in earlier days. Their stores were generally cramped, with few eye-catching displays to attract customers. Catering to consumers who lived within walking distance of their stores, they saw little need to do much more than provide food products and personalized services.

In 1916 Clarence Saunders opened a store in Memphis that brought new selling techniques to the retailing of food. He introduced the self-service concept to the retail food business and augmented it with a cash-and-carry policy and low prices. Though it took time for these radical changes to be accepted, by the 1920s they were well entrenched in food merchandising. In fact, Saunders' ideas were so sound that large food chain organizations like A&P eventually adopted them.

Supermarkets began to sprout up across the country. Opening stores in low-rent areas, people in the East and Midwest like Michael Cullen (King Kullen) and B. H. Kroger (Kroger Company) pushed the cash-and-carry and self-service principles vigorously. In California, enterprising individuals based their new stores on Saunders' methods and found a responsive public.

Perhaps the two most significant reasons for the explosive growth of supermarkets in the 1930s were the mobility provided by the automobile and the severe economic drepression that prevailed in the early years of the decade. No longer relying on local food stores, consumers traveled to more distant supermarkets where they could sample a wider selection of merchandise at lower prices. No longer were they confined to small, dingy stores for their grocery needs. Instead, they had access to bright, modern establishments that carried produce and meat items as well as groceries.

One of the chief outcomes of the supermarket concept has been the elimination by chain organizations of their small stores. Recognizing that they can make more money in larger outlets, the companies now operate in quarters that can accommodate a variety of food and nonfood products in large quantities. In fact, many supermarkets present so diversified an assortment of merchandise that they bear a strong resemblance to a set of specialty store organizations under one roof.

In connection with the movement toward larger quarters, it's interesting to note that A&P once had over 15,000 stores with more than $1 billion in annual sales. Though it had fewer than 1600 outlets by 1980, its sales were over $8 billion. The experience of other chain supermarkets parallels A&P's, and the trend is still toward larger outlets.

## Discount Stores

To complete our brief history of the development of American retailing, mention should be made of the **discount store.** This form of retailing started after World War II as a way of meeting consumer demand for such **hard goods** as home appliances, cameras, and jewelry. Discount stores offered few services, but their low-price policy quickly gained favor with the public. Early discounters like Korvette's (now defunct) and Masters were joined by other chain discount companies like Woolco (F. W. Woolworth) and K mart (formerly S. S. Kresge). All offered a wide variety of merchandise at highly competitive prices.

The first discount houses were small, threadbare stores that cut costs—and also prices—to a minimum. They offered few, if any, customer services, concentrated on selling name brands, and appealed to price-conscious consumers. Their stores were open long hours to accommodate working people, and were located close to large population clusters. From a profit point of view, every attempt was made to sell stock quickly or, as retailers say, "to have a high merchandise turnover."

Though discount stores started with the sale of hard goods, they quickly extended their product lines to include **soft goods** (apparel). As the discount concept took hold, department and specialty stores adopted discount policies of their own. Today few people speak of a "discount store" as such. Instead, we find discounting in virtually every aspect of retailing: There are discount department stores, discount chains, and so forth.

The growth of discount operations has given rise to some serious problems. Touting a cut-rate policy, some discounters have engaged in misleading advertising while others have deceived consumers about the nature of their products. While these practices

---

### Aristede Boucicaut
## AN EARLY INNOVATOR IN RETAILING

Although no one knows for sure when the world's first department store was established, it is generally agreed that today's department stores stem from Bon Marché, the Paris emporium started by Aristede Bouçicaut in the first half of the nineteenth century. At first Bouçicaut sold only piece goods, but he subsequently extended his product line to include clothing, shoes, and hardware.

Bouçicaut introduced a number of novel retailing practices, including money-back guarantees, a one-price policy, and relatively low profits on sales. Depending on large sales volume for success, he encouraged consumers to shop at Bon Marché by forbidding sales clerks to harass customers over prices, a common procedure in those days.

Bouçicaut was disliked by many contemporary retailers because of his departure from conventional practices. However, his persistence in developing innovative policies eventually proved the wisdom of his ideas and caused competitors to adopt the same policies.

The early American department store retailers—Marshall Field, John Wanamaker, Rowland Macy, A. T. Stewart, and others—were greatly influenced by Bouçicaut. As these merchants transformed their stores from specialty shops or dry-goods stores (stores selling piece goods) to department stores, they borrowed liberally from Bouçicaut's ideas. The end result was the impressive department stores that are so familiar to us today.

are not restricted to discount operations, the U.S. Senate and House of Representatives have conducted inquiries into abuses by discounters, and retail trade journals have cited specific discount practices that bilk the consumer. Despite the problems, however, discounting continues to appeal to an increasingly price-conscious public.

**NEW TERMS**

| | |
|---|---|
| barter | peddler |
| chain store | retailer |
| department store | retailing |
| discount store | soft goods |
| general store | specialty store |
| hard goods | supermarket |
| limited-line store | trading post |
| mail order house | variety store |
| manufacturer | wholesaler |

# CHAPTER HIGHLIGHTS

1 Retailing consists of the selling of goods and services to their ultimate consumer.

2 Manufacturers, wholesalers, and retailers are the main types of businesses involved in getting goods and services to consumers.

3 Ancient retailing started in Crete and was continued by the Greeks, Phoenicians, and Romans.

4 Early European retailing was carried on by peddlers, by merchants at fairs, and by retail shops.

5 Early American retailing developed through the trading post, the itinerant peddler, and the general store.

6 As this country grew, new retailing institutions emerged: mail order houses, specialty stores, chain stores (food and variety), department stores, supermarkets, and discount stores.

# QUESTIONS

1 What are the main types of businesses that provide goods and services to consumers?

2 What purpose do wholesalers serve for retailers and consumers?

3 What factor stimulated the development of fairs in early European retailing?

4 Why do we sometimes speak of the itinerant American peddler as serving two purposes?

5 What caused the general store to be replaced by mail order houses as a main source of purchasing by consumers?

6  In what ways does a specialty store differ from a general store?

7  Who were some well-known American retailers involved in the development of food and variety chain stores?

8  What features popularized the department store as a major type of retail institution?

9  What changes do you think will occur in supermarkets in the next ten years? Why?

10  Why has the government investigated the practices of discount stores?

# FIELD PROJECTS

1  Listen to the radio or watch TV to determine the number and types of retailers that advertise their products or services through those media.

2  Listed below are some famous names in American retailing. Read about one of them at your library and list the highlights of his or her career.

| | |
|---|---|
| Lena Bryant (Himmelstein) | Lane Bryant |
| Marshall Field | Marshall Field |
| Margaret Getschell | Macy's |
| Adam Gimbel | Gimbel Bros. |
| Sebastian Kresge | K mart |
| Mary Magnin | I. Magnin |
| Hortense Odlum | Bonwit Teller |
| James Cash Penney | J. C. Penney |
| Richard Sears | Sears, Roebuck |
| Dorothy Shaver | Lord & Taylor |

# CASES

1  The Sagaponack General Store in Sagaponack, New York, recently celebrated its 100th anniversary. Originally it was a grocery store, but now it carries a variety of household and food items. Located in a resort area, it caters to customers with old-fashioned tastes as well as those who desire higher-priced, fancier merchandise.

    The present owners still pump gas outside the store and maintain close ties with year-round residents. They create the atmosphere of early general stores by greeting customers in a casual and friendly way. They appeal to tourists by selling tasty refreshments to beachgoers.

    a  The Sagaponack General Store's prices are higher than those in supermarkets. Why do consumers continue to patronize the store?

    b  How successful might a store like the Sagaponack General Store be in your community? Why?

2  Woolworth's, a giant variety store chain, has sold a limited collection of soft goods for many years. Though many people do not think of this chain as specializing in clothing,

it has managed to satisfy customers' needs for a variety of apparel items. Until recently, however, its windows have not featured clothing significantly.

In 1979, in a calculated move, management decided to test a broadening of its wearing apparel by maintaining full-window clothing displays in several of its large stores. In effect, it was entering the field as a major clothing retailer. At the same time, it was anxious to maintain its status as one of the nation's preeminent variety store retailers.

    **a** What problems in Woolworth's strategy do you foresee?
    **b** Why might Woolworth's management have decided to abandon its image as exclusively a variety store chain?

**3** Gage and Roth, partners in a shoe and clothing mail order business, recently became aware of a national survey showing that the potential mail order market for shoes and clothing is close to saturation. The findings indicated that though these two areas are among the top five product categories in mail order selling, the opportunities for significant increases in their sales levels are limited. As further evidence of this limitation, the survey found that more than 10 percent of the people who buy shoes and clothing by mail do so only because these items are unavailable in their communities in sufficient variety and quality.

In examining the survey statistics, Gage and Roth noted that the total estimated market for direct-mail selling of shoes and clothing is a little less than 30 percent of the total national population. They were disturbed by the fact that this percentage has almost been reached already.

In planning their future, the owners were impressed by the survey's discovery of a large potential market for the sale of sports equipment through mail orders, and by the fact that high-income families are much more likely to buy sports equipment by mail than low-income consumers. With regard to other product categories, however, such as home furnishings, cosmetics, toiletries, and hi-fi equipment, Gage and Roth learned that the potential market is close to being fully tapped.

As aggressive retailers, the two merchants were anxious to develop a strategy for the expansion of their business. They considered both enlargement of their product lines and movement into other forms of retailing.

    **a** What are the arguments for and against the owners' adoption of a mail order sports equipment line?
    **b** What other types of retail outlets should Gage and Roth consider in order to expand their sales of shoes and clothing?

# REFERENCES

Carson, G., *The Old Country Store* (New York: E. P. Dutton, 1965).

Golden, H., *Forgotten Pioneer* (Cleveland: World, 1963).

Groner, A., *The American Heritage History of American Business and Industry* (New York: American Heritage, 1972).

Harris, L. A., *Merchant Princes* (New York: Harper & Row, 1979).

Hendrickson, R., *The Great Emporiums* (New York: Stein & Day, 1979).

Hoyt, E. P., *That Wonderful A&P!* (New York: Hawthorn Books, 1969).

Mahoney, T., and L. Sloane, *The Great Merchants* (New York: Harper & Row, 1966).

Nelson, W. H., *The Great Discount Delusion* (New York: David McKay, 1965).

Peak, H. S., and E. F. Peak, *Supermarket Merchandising and Management* (Englewood Cliffs, N.J.: Prentice-Hall, 1977).

Purtell, J., *The Tiffany Touch* (New York: Random House, 1971).

Scull, P., *From Peddlers to Merchant Princes* (Chicago: Follett, 1967).

Weil, G. L., *Sears, Roebuck, U.S.A.* (New York: Stein and Day, 1977).

# chapter 2
# PRESENT-DAY RETAILING

After completing this chapter, you should be able to:

1 Define the "wheel of retailing" concept and indicate how innovators affect traditional retail institutions.

2 Discuss the status of international retailing.

3 Discuss the economic importance of retailing.

4 Identify career opportunities in retailing.

The retailer's continued success and, at times, survival depend on the ability to adjust to consumer behavior, legal developments, technology, competition, and the changing demands of the consumer. A retailer must accommodate to changes that take place in the social, political, and economic environment.

Retailers must adapt

For example, until recently a long-established stationer was located in a commercial section of a large city. In addition to selling office supplies and stationery to nearby businesses and factories, the store sold consumer products like greeting cards and small gift items. Many of the factories in the area manufactured mens' dress hats. As fashions changed, the hats became less popular and the demand for them decreased. When this happened, most of the factories went out of business. Some of the buildings were torn down and replaced with large apartment houses.

As the character of the area shifted from commercial to residential, the stationer realized that instead of selling primarily to businesses and their employees, he was now selling largely to students and homemakers. In order to buy the right merchandise and remain profitable, he had to recognize the different needs of the "new" customers. As more families moved into the area, new stores opened, including gift shops and card stores, and the stationer found that they carried many of the same items he did. To his chagrin, the retailer found himself confronted with new competition, a changed area, and different consumers.

The stationer was facing a situation that is not uncommon in retailing. Because retailing involves unlimited competition and an endless demand for new products and services, it is in a constant state of change. Some of these changes can be explained by the **"wheel of retailing"** concept.

# THE WHEEL OF RETAILING

Malcolm P. McNair of Harvard University has attempted to explain the institutional changes that take place in retailing by his "wheel of retailing" theory. In this theory a symbolic wheel turns with every retail innovation. New retailers start as low-priced, low-status, **low-margin** (low-profit) **operators.** They offer little in the way of services or glamour and compete with higher-priced traditional retailers. Because of their price appeal, they gain consumer acceptance and have a significant impact on the retailing scene. As they become popular, other retailers enter the field and imitate them. Faced with growing competition, the innovators gradually upgrade their services, merchandise, facilities, and so forth. Owing to increased operating costs, they show lower profit margins and their growth slows. This cycle comes to an end when the innovators reach maturity and become higher-priced operations open to the challenge of newer, low-priced innovators. A new cycle begins and the wheel is ready for another turn.

This concept can be illustrated by the now defunct discounter Korvette's (Figure 2-1). When this company entered the retailing scene after World War II, it was a low-margin, low-price discount store. It drew customers from traditional department stores that maintained higher prices but offered many services. As discounting made an impact, other discounters entered the field. To meet the competition, Korvette's upgraded its operations and expanded its services. Consequently, its overhead increased, rendering

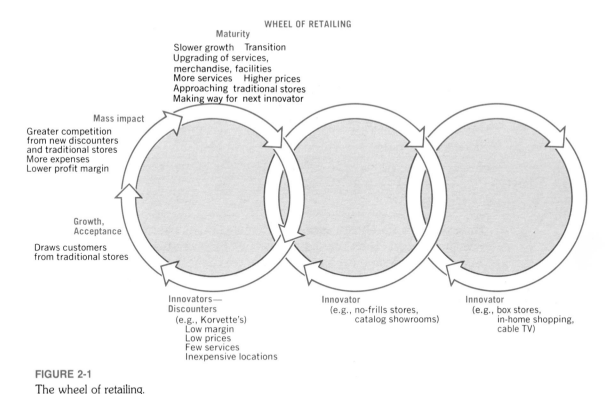

WHEEL OF RETAILING

Maturity
Slower growth   Transition
Upgrading of services,
merchandise, facilities
More services   Higher prices
Approaching  traditional stores
Making way for  next innovator

Mass impact
Greater competition
from new discounters
and traditional stores
More expenses
Lower profit margin

Growth,
Acceptance
Draws customers
from traditional stores

Innovators—
Discounters
(e.g., Korvette's)
Low margin
Low prices
Few services
Inexpensive locations

Innovator
(e.g., no-frills stores,
catalog showrooms)

Innovator
(e.g., box stores,
in-home shopping,
cable TV)

**FIGURE 2-1**
The wheel of retailing.

it vulnerable to the emergence of a new class of innovators. Because Korvette's was unable to operate successfully as a traditional retailer, it was forced to close all fifty-five of its stores by 1981.

## No-Frills Operators

*Flea markets are no-frills operators*

The current innovators in retailing are the so-called **no-frills operators,** that is, retailers whose surroundings or decor are minimal and whose prices are low. For example, **flea markets** once offered merchandise that is not generally found in retail stores, such as old furniture, used clothing, and handmade crafts. These markets have expanded their offerings to include practically all types of merchandise, old and new, and now compete with most retail stores. Since many consumers are willing to trade attractive surroundings, gift wrapping, and credit options for bargains, flea markets have gained in acceptance. Once considered transient and found in such places as parking fields and vacant lots, they are now locating in more permanent sites. Some of the vendors even accept credit cards. Are we perhaps witnessing another turn of the wheel?

Another example of a no-frills operation is PLUS, a discount grocery store where the consumer bags the groceries and pays cash. PLUS, which stands for Priced Low U Save, is a subsidiary of the giant A&P chain; it was introduced to A&P by its new European investors. In 1979 there were 30 PLUS stores in New York, New Jersey, Pennsylvania, and Virginia, and the company expected to expand to 100 stores in 1980. The PLUS approach to merchandising does not call for elaborate displays. Instead, the shelves are stocked with the cartons in which the groceries are delivered. Coupons are not accepted, and the assortment of groceries, produce, and meat is limited. However, the selection is greater with nonperishables and canned goods. At PLUS, lower labor and overhead costs can mean 20–30 percent discounts compared with standard supermarket prices.

Other limited-assortment stores like PLUS have opened in different parts of the country. Several hundred operate in such places as Florida (Jewel T), Ohio (Bi-Lo), and Atlanta (Way-Lo). These stripped-down stores exemplify the new approach to discount food merchandising.

## Box Stores (Warehouse Stores)

**Box stores** or **warehouse stores** are a cross between the limited-assortment store and the supermarket. There are more than 1000 of these stores in the United States. In a warehouse store groceries are displayed in cut-open shipping cartons. Customers pay a monthly membership of 50¢ or more and bag their own items.

## In-Home Shopping

Still another innovative approach to food retailing involves **in-home shopping.** In-home food purchasing goes back to the chicken farmer with an egg route and the local grocer who took—and delivered—telephone orders. Of course, these merchants disappeared after low-cost supermarkets came on the scene in the 1930s. Today in-home shopping on a large scale is possible utilizing closed-circuit television, in-home computer equipment, and automated warehouses. Changes in consumer lifestyles, the increased number of dual-career families, a dearth of free time, and the desire for convenience may very well make this approach to food shopping commonplace. This suggests that traditional food retailers may be vulnerable to a new system of retailing.

## Multilevel Malls

An example of an innovative shopping environment that may turn the wheel of retailing is the new multilevel mall in Northwest Chicago. Called Off Center, this vertical shopping

A box store where customers save by bagging their purchases.

Consumers can now shop from their own homes using closed-circuit television.

complex, formerly a spaghetti factory, features discounted merchandise from some of Chicago's most exclusive retailers. The tenant mix emphasizes women's apparel, but accessories, children's wear, and menswear are also carried. Linens, giftware, and fine wines round out the merchandise offering at Off Center, with all shops selling goods at least 20 percent off their regular retail price.

Off Center's approach is to offer bargains with finesse. The renovated complex was tastefully designed to create a unique shopping environment. There is a center court on every level, and the mall contains a sit-down restaurant for weary shoppers. If the new concept proves a success, it is sure to be copied in other lofts or factories that are conducive to this type of renovation.

# Manufacturer-Owned Factory Outlets

Other innovators

Other innovators are moving ahead under different formats. For example, we are witnessing the beginning of manufacturer-owned factory outlets grouped together in enclosed malls either as divisions of large retail chains or as independent operations. Two such malls, known as Outlets Ltd., opened in Murfreesboro, Tennessee (near Nashville), and Jacksonville, Florida. Each mall was to house some 25 to 27 stores. The shops stock apparel, and most of them are operated by manufacturers.

According to financial analysts at a seminar on off-price retailing sponsored by Donaldson, Lufkin & Jenrette Securities Corporation, off-price retailing is the single fastest-growing segment of the retailing industry.[1] As no-frills operations continue to emerge, other innovators will undoubtedly enter the arena and the wheel will be ready for another turn.

[1]*Women's Wear Daily,* June 9, 1980.

A manufacturer-owned factory outlet, an example of off-price retailing.

# INTERNATIONAL RETAILING

**American and European retailing are similar**

Up to this point our discussion has centered on retailing in the United States. Yet European countries have pioneered some interesting innovations, some of which have been copied by American retailers. In addition, retailing has become truly international, with famous-name retailers functioning both here and abroad.

Inasmuch as living styles in Western Europe are fairly similar to those in the United States, we would expect retail practices and experiences to be similar, too. In fact, this is so. Let's examine two of these similarities.

First of all, individual retailers in Europe are just as vulnerable to changing business conditions as their counterparts in this country. Owing to economic pressures and new forms of retailing, many of them have been forced out of business. Others have joined voluntary chains or buying groups (see Chapters 6 and 13). In other cases they have had to develop creative retail strategies in order to compete with the larger firms. For example, independents (see Chapter 6) have jointly designed pedestrian malls based on a boutique concept. The malls are actually collections of small stores (boutiques), with ownership in the hands of the independents.

Second, like those in the United States, mass retailers in European countries rely on self-service, price appeal, and advertising. With both food and nonfood products in stock, such stores carry between 20,000 and 50,000 brand name items. Operating in a similar fashion to U.S. discounters, they offer low prices and little service.

A distinctive feature of European retailing is the food discount practice followed by many small stores. These outlets carry a small number of the popular items featured in supermarkets, concentrating on high turnover and high volume.

**The internationalization of retailing**

Many large European and American retailers have extended their operations into other countries. This trend has given retailing a distinctively international coloring. For example, J. C. Penney has an interest in European companies, while Sears has established its own stores in Europe. Several American franchise companies have gone international, including the Tandy Corporation (Radio Shack), McDonald's, Wendy's, Kentucky Fried Chicken, Holiday Inn, and Burger King. On the other hand, well-known European firms have established successful operations in this country through franchises and conventional stores. Of particular note are Gucci, known for its leather goods; Charles Jourdan (shoes); Liberty of London (silks); and Cartier, a retailer of fine jewelry. Retailers

Selling shirts in a foreign country.

have been able to transport their images to other countries successfully because international travel has become so common and the media have made their names familiar to consumers.

In some cases foreign companies have purchased major interests in American firms, including A&P, Ohrbach's, and the Saks chain. How much of an impact these investments will have on American retailing remains to be seen.

# THE ECONOMIC IMPORTANCE OF RETAILING

## Sales

In recounting the development of retailing, we have described its major institutions. There are, of course, additional types of operations that will be discussed in later chapters. Before leaving this introduction, however, let's examine the economic significance of modern retailing.

To judge the importance of retailing in our economy, we have only to note some statistics about retail sales. Table 2-1 indicates that sales rose from approximately $503 billion in 1973 to more than $942 billion in 1980, an increase of about 87 percent. These figures indicate that while retailing involves very large sales volumes, its sales growth is also significant.

The gross national product (GNP) is the total market value of all the goods and services produced annually in the United States. Table 2-1 shows that the relationship

**TABLE 2-1**  Retail Trade Sales and Gross National Product in the United States—Summary, 1973–1980

| Year | Total Sales (billions of dollars) | Gross National Product (trillions of dollars) | Total Sales as Percent of Gross National Product |
|---|---|---|---|
| 1973 | $503.3 | $1.3 | 39% |
| 1974 | 536.3 | 1.4 | 38 |
| 1975 | 584.8 | 1.5 | 39 |
| 1976 | 655.2 | 1.7 | 39 |
| 1977 | 724.0 | 1.9 | 38 |
| 1978 | 800.9 | 2.1 | 38 |
| 1979 | 886.0 | 2.4 | 37 |
| 1980 | 942.5 | 2.6 | 36 |

*Sources:* U.S. Department of Commerce, Bureau of the Census, *Statistical Abstract of the United States* (Washington, D.C., 1980), and *Survey of Current Business,* January 1981.

between annual retail sales and the GNP from 1973 to 1980 was significant, ranging from 39 percent in 1973 to 36 percent in 1980.

## Employment

Another indication of the crucial place retailing occupies in our economy is the number of people it employs. Table 2-2 shows that employment in the retail trade went from 13,808,000 in 1977 to 15,324,000 in 1980, an increase of almost 11 percent. Of the total labor force of approximately 107,000,000 people, about 14 percent, or one out of every 7 workers, is gainfully employed by a retailing institution.

## Large Retailing Companies

To appreciate the dimensions of retailing in this country, it helps to examine some statistics about leading retailing companies. Table 2-3 lists the 1980 sales and **assets** (the things a business owns) of the ten largest retailers. With regard to both sales and assets, Sears, Roebuck was the undisputed leader, ranking first in both categories. Safeway Stores ranked second in sales but sixth in assets, while K mart was third in sales and second in assets.

**TABLE 2-2**  Employment in Retail Trade in the United States, 1977–1980

| Year | Employment |
|---|---|
| 1977 | 13,808,000 |
| 1978 | 14,573,000 |
| 1979 | 15,066,000 |
| 1980 | 15,324,000 |

*Source: Survey of Current Business,* January 1981.

**TABLE 2-3** The Ten Largest Retailing Companies in the United States, Fiscal Year Ending January 31, 1981

| Rank | | | | Assets | |
| '80 | '79 | Company | Sales (thousands of dollars) | Amount (thousands of dollars) | Rank |
| --- | --- | --- | --- | --- | --- |
| 1 | 1 | Sears, Roebuck (Chicago) | $25,194,900 | $28,053,800 | 1 |
| 2 | 2 | Safeway Stores (Oakland) | 15,102,673 | 3,338,832 | 6 |
| 3 | 3 | K mart (Troy, Mich.) | 14,204,381 | 6,102,462 | 2 |
| 4 | 4 | J. C. Penney (New York) | 11,353,000 | 5,863,000 | 3 |
| 5 | 5 | Kroger (Cincinnati) | 10,316,741 | 1,997,545 | 11 |
| 6 | 7 | F. W. Woolworth (New York) | 7,218,176 | 3,171,894 | 7 |
| 7 | 6 | Great Atlantic & Pacific Tea (Montvale, N.J.) | 6,684,179 | 1,230,522 | 23 |
| 8 | 8 | Lucky Stores (Dublin, Calif.) | 6,468,682 | 1,400,601 | 18 |
| 9 | 14 | American Stores Co. (Salt Lake City) | 6,419,884 | 1,292,992 | 20 |
| 10 | 9 | Federated Department Stores (Cincinnati) | 6,300,686 | 3,575,513 | 5 |

*Source:* Courtesy of *Fortune* Magazine, Copyright © 1981 Time, Inc.

Five of the ten companies had sales of over $10 billion, and none had less than $6 billion. All ten companies listed assets of more than $1 billion.

With regard to comparative 1979–1980 sales rankings (1979 sales are not shown), the only changes involved F. W. Woolworth, which moved ahead of Great Atlantic and Pacific (A&P) to sixth place; Federated Department Stores, which dropped one rank, to tenth place; and American Stores Co., in ninth place, which had not been among the top ten the year before.

# CAREERS

A number of retailing consultants feel that the biggest problem retailers have today is the lack of competent people. According to one leading retailing recruiter, fifteen years ago the retail industry made the mistake of not placing enough emphasis on recruitment and management training. Consequently, there is a dearth of competent employees in the middle and upper management levels. This shortage has increased the tendency to hire executives who have already had significant success in retailing. Because of this scramble for people, some companies have started training programs to "grow" their own people.

# Aspects of Retail Careers

Retailing possesses characteristics that appeal to many job seekers; these include job opportunities, employee mobility, and a broad selection of retail institutions in which to work.

## Job Opportunities

Demand for retail personnel remains high

Several retail consultants and economic analysts have predicted continued growth and opportunities in sales and merchandising, despite slowdowns in the economy. In fact, during the recession of 1974–1975 retailing employment declined less than employment in other industries. Stores (and alternative methods of acquiring goods and services) are always in demand because people need merchandise to satisfy their needs. Therefore, it is likely that the demand for retailing personnel will continue. As evidence of this trend, a recent Michigan State University survey indicated that large retailing stores like Dayton-Hudson, Carson Pirie Scott, Marshall Field, and Bloomingdale's were stepping up their efforts to recruit college graduates. Another indication of the growth of opportunities in retailing is cited in a report by the Department of Labor of the State of New York.

The growth rate of retail trade employment will exceed that of total employment. An additional 110,000 jobs are expected in the retail sector between 1974 and 1985, somewhat less than one-third of total employment growth. In the State as a whole (with New York City as a major exception where declines are seen), significant expansion is expected in eight of the nine segments of retail trade, with general merchandise stores (primarily department stores), eating and drinking places, food stores, and auto dealers and service stations all recording rises of at least 10 percent. . . .[2]

Technology aids retailing careers

Technological changes have created or expanded career areas in large retailing firms. Continued emphasis on self-service and computerized systems (discussed in Chapter 3) have increased the demand for employees with knowledge of computers. According to Arnold H. Aronson, chairman of the board of Saks Fifth Avenue (a specialty chain), department and major specialty stores must do two things simultaneously; take care of today's business and plan for tomorrow's needs. To accomplish these ends, electronic data-processing systems (computer-generated information) provide a wide spectrum of merchandise information. For Saks, which has stores throughout the country, each of which has its own unique characteristics, technology is a major aid.

The computer has also been a direct cause of the tremendous growth in direct-mail and catalog retailing. The increase in **armchair shopping** or in-home shopping, which was made possible by computers, has increased the number of letters, brochures, fliers, and catalogs being mailed to consumers. These publications offer all types of merchandise, from clothes to greeting cards. Consequently, the need for people to prepare this material has increased. The increased number of women in the labor force,

[2]State of New York, Department of Labor, *Occupational Projections, New York State, 1974–1985.*

the high cost of gasoline, and the convenience of shopping at home have made this a strong employment area for people with ability and skills in art, writing, and computers.

The increase in consumer awareness has expanded customer relations departments in many large retail stores. Training in human relations and psychology is an asset in this area, and public relations trainees are often hired to fill these jobs. Some college background is advisable if one hopes to qualify for these positions.

## Employee Mobility

Since retail shops exist in all communities, people who want to relocate can usually find employment in their new surroundings. In fact, opportunities are always available in retailing because of the constant demand for goods and services.

## A Broad Selection of Retail Institutions in Which to Work

Basically, there are two main categories of employment in retailing.

1   Going into one's own business.
2   Working for a retail employer.

*The dream of starting a business*

1   **Going into One's Own Business**   Many people dream of owning their own business. Virtually all large retailers started out as small retailers. Among them were J. C. Penney, Abraham Abraham (of Abraham & Straus), Richard Sears, and R. H. Macy. Today approximately 80 percent of all small retailing establishments are owned by individuals. Although the dream is not impossible to fulfill, a great deal of knowledge and planning are essential in order to diminish the risks. Starting one's own business will be treated in greater detail in Chapters 25 and 26.

2   **Working for a Retail Employer**   The diversity of retail institutions results in attractive and varied job opportunities in large, medium, and small businesses. More than eighty different types of retail institutions are listed by the *U.S. Census of Business.* Department stores, mail order houses, food stores, apparel stores, home furnishings stores, and eating and drinking places are only part of the selection.

# Jobs with Large Retail Organizations

Jobs with large retailers include buying, merchandising, public relations, research, warehouse management, advertising, display, consumer relations, store design, site selection, and personnel. Most job opportunities are in the areas of merchandising, operations, personnel, control, and sales promotion.

**Merchandising** consists of buying and selling goods. Executive training programs are open to graduates of two- and four-year colleges. The training period varies from three months to four years. Trainees, especially in department stores (Figure 2-2), generally work in a merchandise area, handling goods and records. In addition, they supervise salespeople and help with merchandise displays. The trainee is in contact with vendors and attends lectures and seminars. In addition, he or she analyzes computer records, does fashion forecasting (predicting), assists in administering store policies, and learns about other areas of the store, such as advertising. This is typical of a training program leading to the job of **assistant buyer** or **assistant department manager.**

**STEP 1 ASSISTANT BUYER (ASSISTANT DEPARTMENT MANAGER)**

Major responsibilities:

1. Works with buyer; operates a merchandise department
2. Learns merchandise planning, pricing, and presentation

**STEP 2 DEPARTMENT MANAGER**

Major responsibilities:

1. Supervises a merchandise department in a branch store
2. Supervises service and merchandising activities
3. Accountable for operating a profitable area
4. Supervises sales help

**STEP 3 BUYER**

Major responsibilities:

1. Operates a profitable department
2. Develops overall plan for department
3. Buys merchandise and plans for distribution of goods:
    Pricing
    Sales promotion
    General presentation
4. Develops good vendor and public relations

**STEP 6 BRANCH STORE GENERAL MANAGER**

Major responsibilities

1. Total operation of branch store; accountable for growth, sales, and profits
2. Involved with establishing good relations with the community

**STEP 5 DIVISIONAL STORE MANAGER**

Major responsibilities;

1. Directs buyers with merchandise programs and sales goals
2. Plans storewide promotions
3. Plans advertising for division and sometimes whole store

**STEP 4 ASSISTANT BRANCH STORE MANAGER**

Major responsibilities:

1. Assists branch store general manager
2. Supervises department managers
3. Helps develop sales goals

**FIGURE 2-2**
Career pattern in merchandising (department store).

The next step in training involves working under the direction of a **department manager** or **buyer,** and carries with it greater responsibility. The trainee studies sales reports, purchases goods, reorders merchandise, assists with displays and sales promotion, learns store operations, and supervises personnel. The extent of the trainee's responsibility generally depends on how flexible the buyer or department manager is. After one or two years in this position, promotion to department manager is possible. After one has served as a department manager, the next step is generally a promotion to buyer. As indicated in Figure 2-2, further advancement is also possible.

The **operations** department is responsible for maintaining the store's physical plant and receiving and protecting merchandise. This division is also in charge of the physical distribution of merchandise after it has reached the store. It provides many of the store's customer services.

Executives in this area must be skilled in organization and supervision. The trainee begins his or her job either in a sales-supporting function or in selling. He or she then becomes involved in supervisory store functions on a rotation basis. These positions include acting as a service manager on the selling floor, supervising the receiving of merchandise, handling store security, or participating in warehouse management.

Jobs in operations include those of warehouse manager, customer service manager, store superintendent, security manager, and receiving manager.

The **personnel** department is responsible for effective staffing of the store. It is involved in employee selection, training, advancement, and employee welfare. Training takes place within the personnel department under the supervision of its director and staff. The trainee learns the techniques of employment and recruiting, the process of evaluating employees, and the store's training methods. Advanced training involves the study of labor laws, union negotiations, and management of employee benefits (e.g., hospitalization). Jobs in this division include those of recruiter, interviewer, and training director. Retail personnel executives must acquire experience in both operations and personnel.

The **control** department is responsible for protecting the store's finances. The trainee must have a knowledge of accounting principles. He or she is concerned with all the financial aspects of the business, including accounting procedures, sales tallies, customer and supplier bills, credit, and the processing of information. Top executive jobs in this area are generally filled by people with management experience. The computer has created additional job opportunities in the control division and provides positions for people with training in electronic data processing.

**Sales promotion** is concerned with communicating the store's message to the public through advertising, displays, and public relations. Planning and implementing a store's efforts in this area require specialists. These include copywriters, artists, window and interior display people, special-events coordinators, and mail order experts.

The career ladders for sales promotion are varied. For example, an artist or layout specialist might begin his or her training by preparing rough advertising layouts. A copywriter might start by assisting a copywriter. A display specialist might begin training as a display assistant or window trimmer.

Public relations is concerned with promoting good will through community activities, such as supporting local causes and groups (e.g., civic associations) and making the store's premises available for fashion shows, meetings, and the like. Trainees who understand advertising and other techniques for reaching the public often climb the success ladder in this area. The prestigious jobs of advertising manager and sales promotion director, however, are reached only after years of participation in successful programs.

In large specialty chains training is an important element in the development of effective store managers. Even though the individual stores are generally smaller than large department stores, the retailing functions are similar. Consequently, management training includes on-the-job experience in merchandising, sales promotion, operations,

| Job Title | Functions | Training Period |
|-----------|-----------|-----------------|
| Sales Assistant | Basic operations: sales and stock | 6 months |
| Junior Assistant Manager | Merchandising, promotion, customer service | 12 months |
| Assistant Manager | Buying, merchandising, control, personnel | 12 months |
| Senior Assistant Manager | Overall store operations—emphasis on planning | 12 months |
| Store Manager (trial period) | Complete operation of store—under supervision | 6 months |

**FIGURE 2-3**
Sample four-year executive management program–specialty store.

and control. Figure 2-3 illustrates the job titles, functions, and training periods leading to the position of store manager in a specialty chain.

## Jobs with Medium and Small Retail Stores

*Small retail stores offer varied job experiences*

More than 2 million retailers are classified as medium or small. They have few employees and offer informal training, in contrast to the formal programs found in large retail organizations. For the employee who eventually wishes to own his or her own store, this kind of training often provides comprehensive experience in a short period. The intimacy of a small firm can help the individual learn how to deal with customers on a personal level. All the facets of buying, selling, display, and store operations are readily apparent because they are all conducted within a comparatively small area. However, if one is not planning to own a business, advancement is limited unless one becomes a part owner of the firm.

### NEW TERMS

| | |
|---|---|
| armchair shopping | in-home shopping |
| asset | low-margin operator |
| assistant buyer | merchandising |
| assistant department manager | no-frills operator |
| box store | operations |
| buyer | personnel |
| control | sales promotion |
| department manager | warehouse store |
| flea market | wheel of retailing |

## CHAPTER HIGHLIGHTS

1 If they are to thrive, retailing institutions must adapt to social, political, and economic changes.

2  The wheel of retailing demonstrates the institutional changes that take place when innovators enter the retail arena.

3  Box stores and warehouse stores are innovators that are currently turning the retailing wheel.

4  Changes in consumer lifestyles make in-home food shopping a challenge to traditional food retailers.

5  Utilizing a variety of formats, off-price retailing is a fast-growing segment of the retailing industry.

6  International retailing reveals well-known American firms functioning in European countries, and vice versa. Some European retailing practices have been copied in this country.

7  In 1980 retail sales volume stood at $942.5 billion and the number of people employed in retailing was 15,324,000.

8  In 1980 Sears, Roebuck had the highest sales and assets of all retailers. It was followed by Safeway Stores, K mart, J. C. Penney, and Kroger.

9  The field of retailing offers expanding job opportunities, employee mobility, and a broad selection of institutions in which to work. Self-service and computerized retailing systems have spawned new career patterns for aspiring workers. The two main categories of employment in retailing are going into one's own business and working for a retailing institution.

10  The diversity of retail institutions offers attractive and varied job opportunities. Most job areas are in merchandising, operations, personnel, control, and sales promotion.

## QUESTIONS

1  Define the "wheel of retailing" concept and indicate how retail innovators affect traditional retail institutions.

2  Why have no-frills operations become popular?

3  What indications are there that traditional food retailers may lose some of their patronage to in-home shopping systems?

4  What are the implications for traditional retailers as more manufacturers sell directly to consumers, as in manufacturer-owned outlets?

5  In what ways is European retailing similar to retailing in this country?

6  What was the total volume of retail sales in this country for the period from 1975 through 1980?

7  Which of the ten largest retailing companies (as of 1980) have stores in your community?

8  What percent of the labor force in this country is employed in the retail industry?

9  Why might a person going into retailing prefer to work in a large retail organization?

10  For someone who is contemplating a career in retailing, what are some of the advantages of working in a small store?

# FIELD PROJECTS

1 The advertisements on page 37 were taken from a newspaper's "Help Wanted" section. They describe job openings in the retail trade. Check your local newspaper and list ten different types of retail jobs that are available.

2 There are no-frills retail outlets in most sections of the country. They carry a wide variety of merchandise and attempt to sell goods at lower prices than those found in traditional stores. Visit a no-frills operation in your community. Write a brief report on the following items.
   a Types of merchandise carried.
   b Physical appearance of the premises.
   c Number of employees in the selling areas.

# CASES

1 Some flea markets have changed from "flea-by-night" operators to permanent, reliable vendors. Flea markets not only sell old knick-knacks but are well stocked with new items sold at 20 to 80 percent savings. According to one article, the popularity of flea markets is causing them to develop into large outdoor department stores.

   a If you were a traditional retailer in the same trading area as a flea market, how would you compete?
   b Are flea markets going through a transitional period that might make them vulnerable to some other innovator? Explain.

2 Fred Turner works in a small specialty store that sells women's dresses and coats. He has been with the store for three years and has received a satisfactory pay raise each year. The owner likes Fred's work and has given him increased responsibility. At present Fred handles incoming merchandise, waits on customers, processes merchandise returned by customers, prepares sales receipts, operates the cash register, and assumes other miscellaneous duties.

There are two other employees, one of whom has been with the store two years longer than Fred. The three employees get along well with each other and with the owner. On occasion Fred has gone out socially with one of his co-workers.

The store's sales have increased steadily over the last five years, and the owner has discussed the possibility of expanding the business. He has indicated that the three employees could expect promotions and salary increases in the event of an expansion. Fred, of course, is pleased by the owner's confidence in him.

However, Fred is concerned that his advancement may be limited if he stays with the store. He has heard from friends that large retail organizations offer employment and promotion opportunities that smaller ones cannot. He also feels that if he decides to leave, he should do so while he is young. He has received conflicting advice from relatives and friends, and is finding it difficult to make a decision.

   a What are the advantages and disadvantages to Fred of remaining in his present position? Of switching to a large retail organization?
   b If you were in Fred's position, what would you do? Why?

RETAIL

# DEPARTMENT MANAGERS

Is your career standing still when it should be moving ahead?

Do you need a new challenge?

Join Our Winning Team!

As one of New York's leading Department Stores, Macy's New York is constantly seeking to add depth to its starting line up.

Excellent opportunities available for career-oriented college graduates or MBAs with 1-2 years of retail management experience.

Start in one of our 15 stores with rapid growth and advancement to our Flagship Store

If you have the communication skills, motivation to succeed, and growth potential we're looking for, we'll offer you: Rapid Advancement in Merchandising, Competitive Salary, Comprehensive Benefits & Liberal Shopping Discount.

NOW is the time to send your resume including salary history, in strict confidence, to: Executive Personnel-Room 1602DM

---

## RETAIL

**STORE MGR**          to $30,000
Major hardlines co seeks store mgr

**MDSE HANDLING**  to $30,000
Top NY store seeks director of materials handling for RTW

**AREA MGR**          to $25,000
Top fashion NY store seeks manager with quality RTW experience

**TRAINING MGR**     to $20,000
NJ firm seeks training manager with retail training experience

**DEPT MGRS**          to $18,000
Quality NY store seeks dept mgrs for fashion areas or mens

**ASST BUYERS**       to $17,000
Major department store seeks asst buyers with dept retail exp

**TRAINEES**             to $13,000
Major drug chain seeks mgmt trainees with retail drug or supermarket exp

---

**Help Wanted**

Retail

# Sales People
# Cashiers
## Full Time      Part Time
## Seasonal

Hours: 9:45AM to 6:00PM
Monday thru Saturday
1 DAY OFF MIDWEEK

20% Merchandise Discount!
One of America's leading specialty gift stores is currently seeking full & part-time seasonal employees. CONVENIENT MIDTOWN MANHATTAN LOCATION

## Apply In Person
Personnel Department
10:00AM to 1:00PM

---

Retail

Christmas temporary positions available for experienced individuals in:

# Sales
# Clerical
# Stock
# Packing

Interviews:

Tuesday -Friday
10AM -1PM ONLY

---

## RETAIL

**STORE MGR**          to $30,000
Major hardlines co seeks store mgr

**MDSE HANDLING** to $30,000
Top NY store seeks director of materials handling for RTW

**AREA MGR**          to $25,000
Top fashion NY store seeks manager with quality RTW experience

**TRAINING MGR**    to $20,000
NJ firm seeks training manager with retail training experience

**DEPT MGRS**          to $18,000

---

RETAIL

# ASSISTANT BUYER

Expanding discount chain seeks an aggressive, dynamic and hardworking individual for this newly created Assistant Buyer position in our Mens and Boys Division. We require a minimum of 2 years experience as a softwear assistant buyer; chain store experience is preferable. This is a great opportunity for the right individual.

Excellent medical benefits including dental; pension plan.

---

RETAIL

## FASHION COORDINATOR MANAGER

If you love beautiful clothes and have had fashion experience, wear clothes well, have outgoing warm personality and can coordinate women's high fashion wardrobes, we have an excellent job managing a name designer shop in the 50's.

## TOP SALARY & BENEFITS

---

RETAIL

## ASST MANAGERS

Ladies & childrens apparel chain in Brooklyn. Excellent opportunity. Good salary + incentive bonuses. For appt call

---

# Christmas Merchandise Assistants

We offer attractive starting salaries, an excellent benefit program and liberal employee discounts. W1 Please send resume in complete confidence to: PERSONNEL MANAGER.

---

**ASST BUYERS**       to $17,000
Major department store seeks asst buyers with dept retail exp

**TRAINEES**             to $13,000
Major drug chain seeks mgmt trainees with retail drug or supermarket exp

**3**   Caldor, Inc., is a chain that operates more than sixty stores in southern New England and the Hudson River Valley. The chain combines some of the features of department stores with the techniques of discount chains. Apparently this formula has been successful, for even when economic conditions have caused a slowdown in consumer spending elsewhere, Caldor has attracted consumers who are compelled to shop more carefully.

Retail experts view Caldor as a very fine upscale discounter that appeals to both the blue-collar worker and the middle-class white-collar shopper. The store offers first-quality, brand name merchandise in attractive surroundings, with knowledgeable, trained personnel available to help. According to Carl Bennett, chairman and president, Caldor's clientele consists of middle- to upper-income customers who want better-quality merchandise, a pleasant atmosphere, and efficient service. By providing these features, the chain has developed a fine reputation and a certain chic.

Caldor's merchandising flair is matched by its efficient control of inventories and expenses. The company's president claims that its strength is its regional base. This geographic concentration has made it easier for Caldor to create and maintain tight management controls and to keep its "shrinkage rate" (losses due to theft and defects) down by means of effective security programs.

Caldor is now considering several changes. First, it is pursuing an aggressive expansion program in which it will open stores in several new states by 1983, a move that may test its image as a tightly managed regional retailer. The plan is to open eight to ten stores a year through 1983. This involves moving away from the chain's regional market by expanding into the New Jersey, upstate New York, Massachusetts, Pennsylvania, Washington, and Virginia markets. Second, Caldor plans to change its merchandise mix by expanding the sale of soft goods, such as clothing and accessories, and moving away from hard goods, such as appliances and cameras. (The company currently is basically a hard-goods operation.) The plan calls for a shift from a merchandising mix consisting of 30 percent soft goods and 70 percent hard goods to a 40:60 ratio. Third, Caldor plans to advertise on television to reinforce its regular program of newspaper advertising.

   **a**   What are some of the risks that Caldor faces in undertaking its expansion program?
   **b**   Considering that it is no easy task for a retailer to clearly stamp its fashion image on the mind of the consumer, what do you think of Caldor's plan to shift its merchandising mix by increasing the sale of soft goods?
   **c**   How might Caldor's character change as its territory grows?
   **d**   Some of the planned new markets (e.g., New Jersey and Pennsylvania) are more competitive and less robust economically than Caldor's New England markets. What difficulties do you think the company faces as it ventures into unfamiliar markets?

# REFERENCES

Adler, F., "The Chic Shops in Le Forum Des Halles," *Stores*, October 1980, pp. 46, 49.

Barmash, I., "How They're Selling Name Brands Off-Price," *Stores*, March 1981, pp. 9–14, 55.

Bergmann, J., "The 'New York' Store in Singapore," *Stores*, January 1981, pp. 69–74.

Chaiken, D. G., "A Renaissance for Covent Garden," *Stores*, October 1980, pp. 42–45.

Dolber, R., "Opportunities in Fashion," Skokie, Ill.: *VGM Career Horizons*, 1980.

Dubbs, E. S., "No. 1: Macy's NY," *Stores*, July 1981, pp. 9–11, 14–15.

Lulow, J., *Your Career in the Fashion Industry* (New York: Arco, 1979).

Ringel, L., "Buyer Training," *Stores*, April 1981, pp. 47–48, 62.

Rothman, M. B., "Montreal's Place Bonaventure: Beneath It All!," *Stores*, October 1980, pp. 51–54.

Williams, J. R., "President's Letter," *Stores*, October, 1980, p. 64; November 1980, p. 56; December 1980, p. 62.

# chapter 3
# FACTORS INFLUENCING RETAILING

After completing this chapter, you should be able to:

1 Identify the reasons that retailers study fashion trends and theories.
2 Identify and define the following fashion theories: fashion cycle, trickle-down, trickle-across.
3 Indicate how computers have influenced retailing.
4 Recount the background of the consumer movement and describe its effects on retailing.
5 Identify consumer laws dealing with products, advertising, and credit.
6 List government and business agencies that affect consumer affairs.

In Chapter 2 we examined the significance of the "wheel of retailing" concept and stressed its importance in retail planning. We also studied the impact of retailing on the economy and the varied opportunities available to people seeking careers in retailing.

We now turn our attention to some factors that influence retailing. First we look at the fashion area and the dynamic ways in which it shapes retail strategy. Next we explore the application of computer techniques to retail operations and list the ways in which computers influence retailing. Then we trace the history of consumerism and examine the effects of consumer legislation on various aspects of retailing. Finally we see how federal regulatory agencies, private business groups, and state and local governments affect retailers.

# THE INFLUENCE OF FASHION

Communication of
fashion news

Fashion expressions and ideas are beamed all over the world via satellites, television, radio, and the press. New ideas and trends move so quickly that it is increasingly difficult for the retailer to keep up with the constantly shifting moods and movements of fashion. Designers are influenced by the nostalgia of bygone days, the excitement of the present, and the challenge of the future. New thinking, new music, new interiors, new lifestyles, and new garments are continually transmitted to us by mass communication techniques. Modern dissemination of fashion news has been the impetus for rapid acceptance or rejection of new ideas, making it more difficult for the retailer to gauge the fashion picture correctly.

It is critical for the retailer to understand the why, how, and when of fashion changes because the salability of most merchandise is affected by fashion. In an attempt to meet the needs of consumers, retailers study fashion terminology, trends, and theories.

## Fashion Terms

**Fashion** is how people live, dress, work, and "play" at a given time and place. What is fashionable in the 1980s might not be accepted in the 1990s. Although many people confuse the terms *fashion* and *style,* and even use the words synonymously, they mean different things.

A **style** of a product has a distinct feature or concept that makes it different from others within a particular category. For example, a skirt can be made in several styles, including pleated, flared, and straight. A double-breasted jacket is a style of jacket. A ranch house is the style of house. When a style is accepted or adopted, it becomes a fashion, or fashionable. Therefore, the fashions at any given time include consumer acceptance of certain styles in clothing, houses, lifestyles, and recreation.

Fashion and style
are different

A style that remains in fashion for a long period is considered a **classic.** It is generally simple in design and remains in demand year after year. Examples of classics are blazer jackets, shirtwaist dresses, and loafer shoes. A fashion that is adopted and discarded in a short period is known as a **fad.** Fads are generally accepted by small segments of the consumer market. For example, among the fads for juniors and teens in the late 1970s were disco and roller disco items. At the time, one retailer said, "The

*Fads are in and out quickly*

strongest thing disco outfits have going for them is their ability to make those wearing them feel like they belong to a certain special 'in' crowd regardless of whether they ever dance or attend a disco."[1]

A **fashion trend** is the direction in which different styles move in response to consumer demand. Many trends may exist at the same time. Trends are defined as either incoming or outgoing. **Incoming trends** are on the upward curve of popularity, whereas **outgoing trends** are on the downgrade curve of consumer demand.

Among the theories used to explain the mystery and flow of fashion acceptance are the fashion cycle, the trickle-down theory, and the trickle-across theory. In order for retailers to sell fashion at a profit, they must understand and study the fashion adoption process. By doing so, they can develop greater insight, which can be used in planning merchandise strategy.

# Fashion Theories

*The fashion cycle and fashion adoption process*

A **fashion cycle** is the movement of a style from introduction to acceptance, peak of popularity, and then decline. In the early stages of the fashion cycle, the style attracts individuals who buy because it is something new. These people are sometimes referred to as the avant-garde or pace setters. They are usually found in the higher socioeconomic groups and are confident enough to risk being different. At the introductory stage of the cycle, expensive, exclusive stores carry the style for a wealthy clientele. As the style is accepted, other fine shops and department stores begin to stock the item. Although the style is still expensive, it is less costly than the original models. As the style moves to the peak of popularity, it is more widely accepted and is copied by the mass merchandisers and budget shops. As the item is sold to customers in lower socioeconomic groups and featured in low-end stores, the style is considered to be in the decline stage. At this point the original buyers have already discarded the style and started on something new (Figure 3-1).

It should be noted that the fashion cycle has no definite time period because it is consumer demand that keeps the cycle going. For example, the fashion cycle for menswear historically has been longer than that for women's wear. Also, the fashion cycle for infants' clothing is longer than that for teens' clothing.

The **trickle-down theory** is another concept that begins with the higher socioeconomic levels. Once again, a style is introduced with the upper class and passed down to the masses (Figure 3-2). In the first phase it is adopted by the pace setters, people with enough money and daring to try it. As it gains impetus, it is taken up by other

*The trickle-down theory begins with the upper class*

consumers, those who follow the innovators, and finally by the masses. When the style is generally adopted, it is considered to be in fashion. Both the fashion cycle and the trickle-down theory were widely accepted prior to World War I. At that time Paris was considered the fashion capital of the world, and everyone followed its lead. Adoration of high society, especially European royalty, was the inspiration for the copying of original creations. In America it was the wealthy who adopted the styles that in time were copied by manufacturers for the lower classes.

After World War II America started to create its own designs rather than imitate

[1]"Disco: More Than Music," *Retail Week,* April 15, 1979, p. 39.

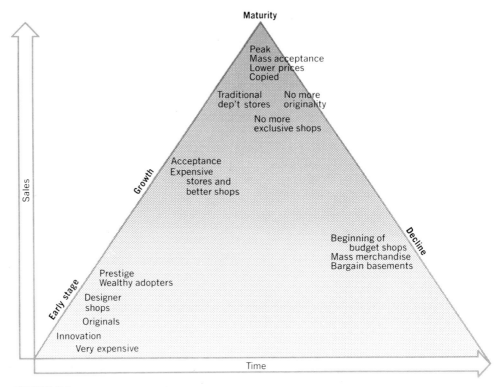

**FIGURE 3-1**
The fashion cycle.

Today's fashion innovators

Paris. The social scene changed. Hollywood, theatre, politics, royalty, and the middle class found themselves drawn together. Money, rather than family background, became all-important in celebrity status. The inspiration for styles was now drawn from various groups. Changes in society, the media, and mass production challenged the accepted theories that held that style innovations begin only with the upper class.

Successful businesspeople, designers, actors, and people in the news developed into the new fashion leaders. The media helped create celebrities, who became very important to retailers. Merchants who promoted celebrities such as Gloria Vanderbilt, Johnny Carson, and Diane Von Furstenberg, honed a competitive edge by selling "exclusive" merchandise at affordable prices. Johnny Carson licensed his name to Hart, Schaffner and Marx to be used in menswear. Diane Von Furstenberg married a prince and became a royal celebrity overnight; as a result, her name in clothing and accessories made millions of dollars for manufacturers and retailers. The marketing of Gloria Vanderbilt is one of the most dramatic of business success stories. With the popularity of "name labels" established in the public mind, this well-known society name on jeans gave retailers a strong product to sell. The scene was now set for a new concept of fashion adoption.

The **trickle-across theory** maintains that innovation can begin with any social class. According to this theory (Figure 3-3), each class has opinion leaders who can

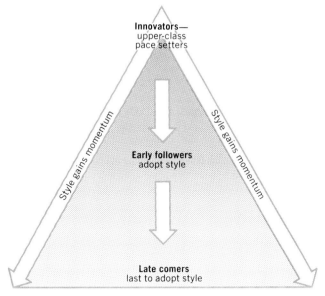

**FIGURE 3-2**
The trickle-down theory.

influence others to buy and accept new styles. In other words, in every class or walk of life there are people who are emulated and followed by others within that class. Furthermore, within a class there are different groups with their own leaders. For example, on a college campus one group might emulate a sports figure, another a scholar, and still another an artist. It is likely then, that the style adopted by a leader will be adopted by others in the group. Thus, the style moves across, rather than down, to another class.

It is also possible to have the same style in different price ranges adopted by more than one class at the same time. For example, when "designer jeans" (e.g., Calvin Klein,

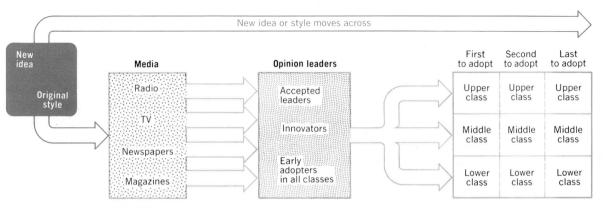

**FIGURE 3-3**
The trickle-across theory.

Sassoon, Jordache) were introduced, the "label" concept was adopted by members of more than one class. However, jeans were manufactured in different price lines for different groups.

# Creating a Fashion Image

**The media create fashion awareness**

Media coverage, extensive advertising, and customer mobility have created fashion awareness in all classes and market segments at the same time. Because of media coverage, consumers in the most remote areas are aware of the latest fashions. Suburban and urban, rich and poor are all alert to fashion. Under these conditions the fashion cycle has become somewhat shorter, causing changes in the adoption process. Planning was different in the days when merchants were familiar with a style that was passing from one group to another. Today, however, style acceptance by all types of customers at essentially the same time has made merchandise planning more difficult for the retailer.

**Customers and the fashion adoption process**

The retailer needs a clear picture of how the store's customers fit into the fashion adoption process. Is the store's clientele made up of innovators, the avant-garde who buy only in the early stages? Or are its customers the latecomers who wait for the style to become established? A retailer who buys too soon or too late for the store's customer base will have difficulty selling the merchandise. Since the salability of merchandise is dependent on the extent to which it meets the customer's desires, a vital aspect of the merchant's job is assessing the customer's "taste" requirements.

By understanding fashion theories, the retailer is in a better position to relate fashion innovation to store image and competition. Through merchandising strategy and product assortment, the retailer can choose to be a known leader in fashion, that is, the first to carry a new item or develop a more conservative fashion stance.

**The importance of creating a fashion image**

A firm fashion image means that the consumer recognizes what the store stands for and to whom it appeals. When the image is clearly established in the public mind, the store attracts customers who respond to that image. For example, Loehmann's, Inc., a specialty chain founded by Frieda Loehmann in 1921, received high marks for creating a quality fashion image at reduced prices. Loehmann developed an unusual atmosphere for shoppers by transforming a former automobile showroom into an artistic "happen-

Shoppers respond to a store's fashion image. (Left) Loehmann's. (Right) Bloomingdale's.

ing." The furnishings were beautiful, and the store boasted many valuable antiques and works of art. The store's image became firmly established: quality merchandise at low prices.

The Bloomingdale's chain is another example of a store that has established a distinct fashion image. "Bloomie's" is known for fashion excitement and has developed strong customer loyalty. It is apparent that a store's success is directly linked to its understanding of customers and their fashion appetites. Retailers must decide whom the store will represent in terms of fashion, and then develop the appropriate merchandise strategy.

# THE INFLUENCE OF COMPUTERS

No discussion of the factors that influence retailing would be complete without reference to computers. These remarkable machines, which have been with us for less than thirty years, enable retailers to conduct a variety of operations quickly and accurately. They are used in sales, purchasing, inventory control, advertising, payroll, and other operations.

The features of computers that make them such powerful tools are their ability to amass large quantities of information at different locations simultaneously, process the data at electronic speeds, make instantaneous decisions, and turn out useful reports quickly. As you can see, the common element in all of these features is speed. The use of computers is often referred to as **electronic data processing** or **EDP.**

To understand how computers are used in retailing, it helps to examine several operational techniques as well as some specific applications. A comprehensive treatment of the merchandising applications of computers in large retail organizations is contained in the appendix at the end of this chapter.

## Computer Techniques in Retailing

### Point-of-Sales (POS)
Many stores are equipped with specially designed cash registers that do much more than merely ring up sales. Called **point-of-sales (POS),** this system provides store executives with a wide range of reports on products sold, cash and charge sales, current stock levels, and other vital statistical needs. Since the registers are connected electronically to computers, the information is processed and made available quickly. A more detailed treatment of POS is contained in Chapter 24.

### Optical Scanning
Optical scanners use the universal product code

Similar to point-of-sale cash registers, and of particular value to supermarkets, are the devices known as optical scanners. This equipment is located at checkout counters and is part of a computerized cash register system. The scanner may be a stationary device or a wand handled by a cashier. Here is how it works.

Point-of-sale cash registers in action. Notice the scanners and screens on the top of the registers.

1  Every package in the store is labeled with sensitized lines that represent the manufacturer, type of product, weight, and size. The lines are symbols for numbers that can be "read" by a scanner. The symbols are part of a standard **universal product code (UPC)** that was introduced in the early 1970s. You have probably seen UPC lines on items that you have purchased.

2  The cashier runs the package across the scanner, which recognizes the UPC symbols.

3  The scanner transmits the symbol information to an in-store computer in which the price of the product has been stored. At the same time, the information is shown on a screen for the customer's benefit.

4  The computer calculates the sale (including the tax, if any) and the register prints a sales receipt for the customer.

The use of optical scanning equipment reduces checkout time, gives the store better control over inventory, and reduces checkout errors. Although the system encountered some consumer resistance at first, it has gained wide acceptance across the country.

### Electronic Funds Transfer (EFT)

EFT is on the horizon

Associated with point-of-sale transactions, but still in its infancy, is a system called **electronic funds transfer** or **EFT**. Its purpose is to eliminate most of the paperwork involved in sales and banking transactions. Here is how it works.

1 An employee's pay is deposited electronically by the employer in the employee's bank account.

2 When the employee purchases merchandise in a store with an EFT installation, he or she uses a bank card (much like a credit card) to record the purchase.

3 After the salesperson has keyed in appropriate sales information, the bank card triggers a computer to automatically deduct the sales price from the customer's bank balance and add it to the store's balance.

This pioneering attempt to create a cashless retail society has its drawbacks. For example, the government has to design careful regulations for everyone's protection. Also, a customer can make a purchase through EFT *only* when his or her bank balance is sufficient to cover the purchase. Though EFT is now used in a limited number of stores, these and similar problems will have to be solved before EFT becomes commonplace in retailing.

## Computer Terminals

*Salespeople can communicate with computers*

Soon to be seen in retail stores are computer terminals, devices that will allow salespeople to communicate with a computer. By keying in certain information, the salesperson will be able to supply immediate answers for such customer questions as Why is this product better than competitive models? How soon can the merchandise be delivered? How does this product differ from similar but differently priced in-store products?

# Computer Applications in Retailing

## Sales Forecasting

*Computers can "predict" sales*

On the basis of current sales figures and information from other sources, such as manufacturers, wholesalers, accountants, economists, and bankers, retail firms use computers to estimate future sales volume. This is known as **sales forecasting.** The aids to decision making provided by computers enables retailers to plan both short- and long-term sales policies.

## Consumer Services

Airlines, hotels, and motels have been using computers for some time to provide customers with instant reservations long in advance of actual use of the accommodations. For example, airlines can provide customers with immediate information about available seats on scheduled flights that are months away. Hotel chains like Hilton can do the same with regard to rooms anywhere in their far-flung network of hotels.

## Advertising

With a computer, retailers can select potential customers for special sales. For example, if a store wants to conduct mail advertising directly to people in a certain income category, a computer will compile the list quickly from stored data. It will do the same for other customer characteristics, such as frequency and volume of previous purchases, family or marital status, and education level.

## Accounting

Accounting consists of the classification, recording, analysis, and interpretation of financial data. It is of great importance to merchants because of the large quantity of financial information involved in retail operations. Following are several common accounting functions handled by computers.

Computers help in collections

**Accounts Receivable** The term *accounts receivable* refers to the amounts owed by customers to a business. Since selling on credit is such a large part of retail sales, it follows that credit sales records should be computerized. This is actually the case in many retail organizations.

In a typical accounts receivable system, customers are issued credit (charge) cards for use in making purchases. When making a purchase, the customer presents the credit card to the cashier, who inserts it into the cash register or some other piece of equipment for processing. The customer's credit card number is recorded, along with details of the purchase.

A central computer that contains information about the customer's account receives the data and updates the balance. The computer prints customer charge statements at required intervals, daily and monthly sales totals, sales by departments, and similar reports. It also handles sales returns and customer payments.

The advantages of computerized accounts receivable systems are the timeliness of customer accounts, the ready availability of sales figures, and the reduction of delinquent customer accounts.

**Purchasing** For large retailers, such as department stores and chains, buying merchandise in the right quantity at the right time is essential to efficient management. Nothing so irks a customer as to have a store clerk say, "Sorry, we're out of it!" In order to avoid such embarrassments, computers are used to maintain up-to-the-moment information about inventory items.

At this writing, many stores have checkout equipment with electronic ties to a computer. The computer uses sales details to keep current records of inventory, and prints out purchase orders when stock gets low. In this way every item in inventory can be maintained at a desired level and customers can be assured of delivery.

**Additional Accounting Applications** Other accounting applications of the computer include payroll and accounts payable. For payroll, the computer prepares payroll records, prints checks, computes taxes, and records payroll entries. For accounts payable, which refers to a retailer's unpaid bills, the computer maintains records of suppliers' invoices and purchase returns, prints checks in time for the retailer to take advantage of suppliers' discounts, and updates amounts owed to suppliers.

# RETAILING INFORMATION SYSTEMS

When some or all of the computer applications available to retailers are integrated to form a cohesive process within an organization, the result is called a **retailing information system** or **RIS.** Put another way, RIS is an ongoing computer-based process for collecting both internal and external data. Internal data are collected from company records, files, and computerized cash registers, while external data are collected from such sources as customers, competitors, and publications. The entire system is designed to prevent as well as solve problems, and it aids management in making profitable decisions and plans. Retailers with RIS are able to conduct useful research regarding customers, merchandise selection, and advertising. A planning aid for an RIS is discussed in the appendix at the end of this chapter.

# THE INFLUENCE OF CONSUMERISM

Today's retailer must deal with a better-educated and more sophisticated customer than was the case in earlier times. Consumers are wiser in their buying decisions and more vocal in fighting for their interests. They are more concerned about inflation, pollution, and the quality of life. They have filed lawsuits against manufacturers, boycotted firms, picketed stores to protest certain business practices, and exerted numerous pressures on business. This increased activism may have come about because of social and economic changes in consumers' lives. Consumers are more affluent, more mobile, and less loyal to local and neighborhood stores. These changes pose additional difficulties for the merchant in the 1980s.

*Consumers exert pressure on business*

The progressive retailer, who acts as the consumer's buying agent, must be responsive to this consumer activity. Not only are merchants expected to sell goods and services, but it is assumed that they will do business in a legal, responsible manner. This section deals with the consumer protection movement, legislation to protect consumers, the agencies involved, and the influences of this movement on the retailer.

## Background

The relationship between the consumer and the retailer has become much more complex than it used to be. The change from small neighborhood shops to large chains has taken away some of the consumer's ability to communicate directly with the producer or seller. For example, in the past, if a customer had a problem with clothing made by a local tailor, he or she knew exactly where to go for satisfaction. At that time the ethics of the merchant were regulated by the marketplace. If a seller wronged a buyer, he or she risked losing a customer and acquiring a bad reputation. Small merchants could not afford a loss of good will or customers, so they generally attempted to settle complaints without interference from others.

*Consumer dissatisfaction*

Today buyers are confronted with a more complicated situation. With changing markets and technology, consumers hardly ever meet the actual producer of a product. Manufacturers are not always visible, and furthermore, their distributors are not always willing to assume responsibility for complaints. The consumers' difficulties become apparent when they are faced with shoddy products, inadequate warranties, late deliveries, unsafe products, and the like. It is no wonder that consumers' faith in business has eroded and that their skepticism has increased. According to Satenig S. St. Marie, more than 70 percent of consumers feel that business is more concerned with profit than with consumer satisfaction, while more than half feel that they are vulnerable in the market-place.[2]

The growing volume of consumer complaints and dissatisfaction prompted the **consumer movement.** This led to a demand for laws protecting the public from unfair trade practices. The term **consumerism** refers to all the activities involved in safeguarding the buyer from mistreatment and exploitation.

## Consumer Advocates

Three distinct periods can be identified in which consumerist groups have attempted to make American business more responsible to the public. There periods are (1) before 1900, (2) 1930–1960, and (3) after 1960. Each was sparked by well-known individuals, authors, and researchers who, through their writing and research, gained political awareness and support for consumer causes. Many of these individuals have acquired national recognition and are known as **consumer advocates.**

### Before 1900

Upton Sinclair's novel *The Jungle* made the public aware of the unsanitary methods used in processing meats. The novel created such a sensation that President Theodore Roosevelt investigated the meat-packing industry. That investigation resulted in improved conditions and such regulations as the Meat Inspection Act (1907).

### 1930–1960

In the 1930s efforts were made to secure protection against harmful products and false advertising. Books like *100,000,000 Guinea Pigs* (1933) and *Your Money's Worth* (1934) helped enlighten politicians. One result was the passage of the Pure Food and Drug Act in 1938.

### After 1960

During the 1960s consumer discontent was aroused by Vance Packard's *The Hidden Persuaders,* first published in 1957, and *The Waste Makers* (1960). Packard accused advertisers of manipulating consumers and condemned manufacturers for planned obsolescence, that is, intentionally producing a product that will wear out within an unreasonably short period. For example, a hair dryer that could be made to last many years might be designed to fail in less time.

In 1962 President John F. Kennedy's consumer address listed the following four rights of consumers.

1  The right to safety.
2  The right to be informed.
3  The right to choose.
4  The right to be heard.

His statement laid the foundation for later legislation, such as truth in packaging and safety laws.

[2]Address by Satenig S. St. Marie, Divisional Vice-President, J. C. Penney, at the annual meeting of the National Retail Merchants' Association, New York City, January 11, 1977, p. 2.

In 1965 a young attorney, Ralph Nader, launched a strong drive for consumer protection through his sensational book, *Unsafe at Any Speed,* which condemned General Motors' Corvair car. The book was widely publicized and hastened the passage of federal standards for automobile safety. Nader is credited with organizing the Public Interest Research Groups, which investigate and watch over a multitude of products and services. These and other groups have subjected business and government to a great deal of public scrutiny. Because they have shown that our economic system does not always serve the best interests of the public, they have prompted additional federal, state, and local legislation to protect the consumer.

Many federal laws have been enacted to protect consumers against fraud and other unfair practices. The philosophy behind these laws and their effects on retailers will be treated in the following section. Basically, the legislation falls into two main categories: (1) laws that regulate business to promote competition and (2) laws that protect consumers.

# Laws That Regulate Business to Promote Competition

These laws were enacted to ensure choice in the marketplace.

## Philosophy

The assumption that competition is the natural regulator of the marketplace—and that it results in fair practices and pricing—is what prompted the laws that guard against monopolistic practices. Basically, they curb the abuse of power by business by preventing large companies from smothering smaller firms in the same industry. Without these restrictions, large firms could stifle smaller competitors and bilk the consumer by charging unfair prices. The major laws in this area are

Sherman Antitrust Act (1890)

Clayton Act (1914)

Federal Trade Commission Act (1914)

Robinson-Patman Act (1936)

Miller-Tydings Act (1937)

Consumer Goods Pricing Act (1957)

## How Laws to Promote Competition Affect Retailers

Retailers cannot join in a conspiracy to control prices. The Clayton and Robinson-Patman acts make it unlawful for any person to knowingly induce or receive a discriminatory price. It is vital, therefore, for the retailer to exercise caution in negotiating prices. If a supplier indicates that a requested price or special service is discriminatory, it violates the act if the vendor agrees to the merchant's request.

When a retailer undertakes to buy and price merchandise, it is important that he or she have a broad knowledge of the laws that affect buying and pricing. However, these laws change from time to time. For example, the Miller-Tydings Act, also known as the Fair Trades Act, allowed manufacturers to obtain agreements from distributors not to sell certain products below a minimum stated price. These laws have since been repealed because consumers and dealers were prohibited from offering and receiving better prices in the marketplace. The laws were designed to protect the manufacturer's brand against price cutting by retailers. They were also intended to shield the small merchant from unfair competition by large chains. In effect, however, they served to prevent consumers from buying at lower prices.

Other ways in which laws that promote competition affect retailers are the following.

1 Retailers cannot force suppliers not to sell to competitors.
2 Retailers cannot cut prices with the intent of forcing small merchants out of business.
3 Retailers must be able to substantiate their advertising claims or else advertise a correction.

# Laws to Protect Consumers

These laws were enacted to safeguard consumer interests with regard to products, advertising, and credit.

## Philosophy

The consumer protection laws were designed to protect the consumer against unfair selling practices, unsafe merchandise, and deceptive information. Although buyers have the right *not* to buy, consumerists claim that buyers cannot make intelligent decisions when they are influenced by promotion and advertising. The laws in this category are of the following types.

1 Laws that require minimum standards for product safety and performance, for example, standards for food, drug, and cosmetic products. Safety standards for automobiles are also in this group.
2 Laws that require the consumer to be provided with necessary information concerning a purchase, for example, information about credit and warranties.
3 Laws that strengthen communications between manufacturers/retailers and consumers, for example, laws requiring honesty in labeling and advertising.

## Major Laws Related to Products

The main consumer protection laws related to products are the following.

Federal Meat Inspection Act of 1907
Federal Food, Drug, and Cosmetic Act of 1938
Wool Products Labeling Act of 1939
Fur Products Labeling Act of 1951
Flammable Fabrics Act of 1953
Textile Fiber Products Identification Act of 1959
Hazardous Substance Act of 1961

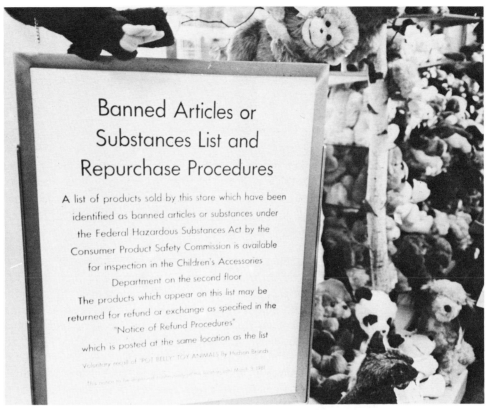

A store poster showing its compliance with the Hazardous Substance Act.

Fair Packaging and Labeling Act of 1966

Consumer Products Safety Act of 1967

Poison Prevention Packaging Act of 1970

Magnuson-Moss warranty section of the Improvements Act of 1974

## Major Laws Related to Advertising

Laws dealing with advertising include the following.

Federal Trade Commission Act of 1914

Federal Communications Act of 1936

Wheeler-Lea Act of 1938

Cigarette Labeling and Advertising Act of 1961

## Major Laws Related to Credit

Among the laws dealing with consumer credit are the following.

Consumer Protection Act of 1968 (Truth-in-Lending)

Fair Credit Reporting Act of 1970

Fair Credit Billing Act of 1974

Equal Credit Opportunity Act of 1975

# How Laws Related to Products, Advertising, and Credit Affect Retailers

*caveat venditor*

Because retailers act as buying agents for consumers, they are responsible by law for selling safe products and can be sued for selling defective ones. The Latin expression **caveat venditor,** "let the seller beware," sets the tone for all consumer legislation. So in the case of unsafe or faulty products the laws make the retailer, rather than the consumer, responsible for notifying the producer.

The various food, drug, and cosmetic acts require accurate labeling and truthful advertising. Labels should indicate exact weight, ingredients, preservatives, and other chemicals. Because the law requires that drugs and cosmetics be proven safe before they are sold, the retailer must remove a product from the selling floor when its safety is questioned by a responsible agency. Retailers selling **store brands**—that is, merchandise sold only in their stores—must abide by the same requirements as manufacturers with regard to labeling, packaging, and pricing.

Retailers should be concerned with quality specifications and guard against selling unsafe and unsanitary products. The law requires that **warranties** (written guarantees of a manufacturer's or retailer's responsibility) be made available to the consumer *before* the purchase. This involves prominent display of warranties at the point of sale.

In the case of a credit transaction, the Truth-in-Lending Law requires the retailer to inform the customer fully regarding credit terms and charges. The Fair Credit Billing Act cautions and regulates the retailer with regard to billing disputes. The Equal Credit Opportunity Act further cautions the retailer in extending credit fairly to all groups.

Finally, in order to advertise a special price, the retailer must have sufficient stock to sell or else must give the customer a "rain check."

# Federal Regulatory Agencies

Listed here are the federal "watchdog" agencies that monitor legislation regarding consumer needs and rights.

## The Federal Trade Commission (FTC)

Federal watchdogs

This agency was established by the Federal Trade Commission Act of 1914 to prevent practices that are in restraint of trade and to promote competition. The Commission's jurisdiction has been increased by subsequent laws to include advertising, labeling, and unfair practices in commerce. It investigates complaints from consumers, business, and other government agencies. In addition, it identifies and investigates situations that are in need of study.

### The Consumer Products Safety Commission

This commission is empowered by the Consumer Products Safety Act to set safety standards for products that could be hazardous to consumers. It handles drugs, cosmetics, and some other products that were originally under the jurisdiction of the Food and Drug Administration.

### Office of Consumer Affairs

This office advises the Department of Health and Human Services and the President on consumer matters and coordinates federal activities for consumer protection.

### The Department of Agriculture

This agency works with the FTC to enforce various laws. For example, a recent controversy involved "junk food" sold in school vending machines. The Department changed its regulations in 1980 to ensure that food sold in schools makes a nutritional contribution to the student's diet.

### The Department of Health and Human Services (Food and Drug Administration)

The agency was established by the Food and Drug Act to protect consumers against impure and unsafe foods, drugs, cosmetics, and other potential hazards.

## Business Regulators

In addition to the federal regulators, there are other institutions and organizations that are literally looking over the shoulders of retailers.

### The Better Business Bureau

This nonprofit association has offices in approximately 150 markets around the country and is financed and supported by private businesses. The purpose of the Bureau is to promote truth in advertising and ethical selling practices, and to protect the public against fraud. Its offices investigate complaints, warn merchants, and, if necessary, turn records over to authorities. For example, in 1979 the Bureau reported that problems with deliveries by mail order businesses topped the list of consumer complaints. As a result, the Federal Trade Commission developed regulations to deal with this problem. Consumers now have the right to know when an order will be shipped, and if there is no time limit the goods must be mailed within thirty days.

### Consumers Union and *Consumer Reports* Magazine

These publications are noted for their testing of consumer products and their furthering of consumer interests.

## Consumerism at the State and Municipal Levels

In addition to the federal laws, many states and municipalities have enacted their own consumer protection laws and have organized consumer bureaus and agencies. State

This product

contains foam.

Avoid contact

with open flame

and smoldering

cigarettes.

Regulations for municipalities

statutes generally cover misleading advertising, deceptive sales techniques, unfair credit policies, and unethical door-to-door selling practices. Some states have regulations regarding product performance and safety. For example, California lawmakers did not consider federal standards for bedding safe enough. They passed a law requiring that a permanent warning label be attached to all bedding containing cellular foam.

Many municipalities have regulations to protect consumers against dishonest weights and measures, contests that do not offer equal opportunities to win, and **bait-and-switch advertising** (luring a customer into the store with the intention of selling something else). There are also laws requiring food dating and a cooling-off period for door-to-door sales. (This allows the customer to cancel a contract within a certain length of time, such as one to three days.)

At all levels of government, a great deal of literature has been published by various agencies in an attempt to educate the public regarding their rights and how to guard themselves against being cheated. Since the laws act as a warning to business, many producers and retailers have attempted to avoid additional regulations by improving or correcting any irregularities in their practices.

## Self-Regulation by Retailers

Three out of four of the nation's major corporations now have a written code of ethics. Large retailers like Sears and J. C. Penney have programs that pretest merchandise before it reaches the selling floor. Other merchants have developed their own consumer relations departments to answer customer questions and complaints. Stores have developed training programs to inform their salespeople regarding product information, thereby preparing them to answer customer questions. Food processors have joined the Food and Drug Administration's Cooperative Quality Assurance Program to ensure the adequacy of their quality standards. In fact, communicating with the various agencies has become so important that some large retailers, such as Penney, have government relations departments in Washington.

Some fast-food restaurants have begun to respond to consumer demand for nutritional data by making information available in a way that resembles the nutritional

J. C. Penney's Merchandise Center pretests products before they are offered for sale.

information on supermarket packages. For example, Pizza Hut distributes cards at its outlets with the complete nutrient breakdown of each of its pizzas, while Arby's offers booklets containing a nutrient analysis of its sandwich combinations.

Today retailers are under constant surveillance. Daily advertisements are checked; special offers are investigated; and most consumer transactions are eligible for public hearings or lawsuits. Class action suits (in which an attorney general sues on behalf of a large group) have become quite common, and many retailers have received negative publicity or been fined. A typical example was the case against Saks Fifth Avenue, Bergdorf Goodman, and Bonwit Teller in 1974. These stores were found guilty of conspiring to raise, fix, stabilize, and maintain the retail prices charged for women's clothing in the New York metropolitan area.

A new law in New York, Private Right of Action, allows consumers to sue businesses for false ads and misleading practices, without the aid of the attorney general.

Retailers who respond positively to the consumer movement will undoubtedly increase good will and fare better than their competitors. The better-educated consumers of the next decade will be willing to pay for long-term quality and have less interest in short-term bargains. The retailer that provides quality and responsibility and advertises intelligently will be ahead of the competition.

## NEW TERMS

| | |
|---|---|
| bait-and-switch advertising | classic |
| *caveat venditor* | consumer advocate |

| | |
|---|---|
| consumer movement | point-of-sales (POS) |
| consumerism | retailing information system (RIS) |
| electronic data processing (EDP) | sales forecasting |
| electronic funds transfer (EFT) | store brand |
| fad | style |
| fashion | trickle-across theory |
| fashion cycle | trickle-down theory |
| fashion trend | universal product code (UPC) |
| incoming trend | warranty |
| outgoing trend | |

## CHAPTER HIGHLIGHTS

1 New ideas and trends in fashion appear so quickly today that it is difficult for the retailer to keep pace with the changes.

2 In order to meet the challenges of fashion change, the retailer should study fashion trends and theories.

3 Class and celebrity status affect the acceptance of fashion.

4 The process of fashion adoption is explained by the fashion cycle, the trickle-down theory, and the trickle-across theory.

5 Because of the media explosion, fashion awareness reaches all segments and classes at the same time.

6 Retail success is dependent on establishing and communicating a store's fashion image.

7 Computers enable retailers to conduct a variety of operations quickly and accurately.

8 Because retailers must deal with better-educated and more sophisticated consumers, they must be responsive to pressures for a "fair deal."

9 The consumer movement developed during three distinct periods, each sparked by well-known individuals called consumer advocates.

10 Aside from regulating business to promote competition, the federal government has enacted legislation to protect consumers in several areas: foods, drugs, cosmetics, safety, credit, warranties, and labeling.

11 Federal and business regulators are among "watchdogs" that monitor consumer legislation.

## QUESTIONS

1 Why is it important for retailers to study fashion trends and theories?

2 Why is the fashion cycle becoming shorter? How does this affect retailers?

3 How does understanding the fashion adoption sequence aid the retailer in developing a fashion image?

4 List some of the functions for which retailers utilize computers.

5 How do consumer lifestyles affect a retailer's merchandise strategy?

6 What is the background of the consumer movement? How have consumer laws affected retailers in everyday practice?

7 How have consumer advocates affected the consumer movement?

8 Explain how the concept of *caveat venditor* affects a retailer's responsibilities to consumers.

9 What are some of the measures to which retailers have resorted in order to avoid additional regulation?

10 How have minorities been protected by the consumer credit laws?

## FIELD PROJECTS

1 During the course of one week, clip any articles in your daily newspaper that are related to consumer protection or consumer problems. From these articles, list the areas of concern and explain how regulations might affect the retailer.

2 Contact or visit your local Office of Consumer Affairs or Better Business Bureau. Find out the major consumer complaints in your locality. Ask for published information on local consumer laws. Are there any laws that are unique to your town?

## CASES

1 During the early years of retailing in this country, there was little government regulation of the retail industry. Though abuses did exist, not much was done to correct them.

With the enormous growth of retail outlets, however, consumers and legislators began pressuring for the correction of such abuses as misleading advertising and product deception. The investigation of discount houses by Congress cast the federal government in the role of a consumer protector.

Some people agree that the government should pass legislation for the protection of consumers. Others believe that the retail industry should regulate itself. Still others think that while some government involvement is necessary, it should be held to a minimum.

a As a consumer, how do you feel about the government's acting as a watchdog for consumers?

b If you owned a store, what would your views be?

c If you were an executive of a large chain organization, would you favor self-regulation by retailers? Why?

**2**   According to some retail analysts, it is essential for retailers to develop uniqueness in order to be successful in the 1990s. Many merchants have already established policies to achieve this aim. For example, specialty chains and department stores rely on nationally promoted products to draw customers into their stores. Calvin Klein, Pierre Cardin, Yves Saint Laurent, and many other American and European designer products are sold at these stores.

When designer labels were first introduced, they were found on distinctive products that offered the stores that carried them a competitive edge. Recently, however, this edge has begun to evaporate because of the proliferation of outlets that sell designer labels at prices significantly lower than those of conventional retailers.

   **a**   In the face of increased competition, how large a part should designer labels play in the merchandise mix of fashion image specialty chains and department stores?

   **b**   What other policies might store executives adopt in order to develop a unique image and carve out a competitive niche?

**3**   Two enterprising men from Dallas recently opened a specialty store in the heart of New York City that features genuine Texas boots. Named To Boot, the shop sells authentic western boots exclusively.

The customers are greeted by a colorful display of boots lined up toe-to-heel against the walls. The boots are designed by one of the owners and manufactured by authentic western bootmakers.

The store features an unusual merchandising concept in which the boots are sold to customers of either sex in a complete range of sizes and colors. Prices start at $160 for a pair of basic boots and have reached $1200 for a pair of alligator skin boots.

To Boot's popularity has led the owners to take some innovative measures to compensate for the small store space and to avoid an overcrowded store. For example, they have placed a sign outside the store that reads, "Capacity 10." Because there are always three salespeople present in addition to the two owners, some customers must wait outside until they are ready to be serviced. On cold days coffee is served to customers waiting outside. According to the owners, the system works well for customer service, maintains traffic control, and cuts down on shoplifting.

The success of To Boot motivated the owners to add another store, called Clothes to Boot, that features western wear and sells mainly suits, shirts, and accessories. The clothing represents western wear as a way of life rather than as a costume. According to the owners, "People who see the clothes begin to reevaluate this western wear, which is a crafty mixture of the West and Ivy League or eastern sportswear. We're just getting them to broaden their closets." And they add, "Men and women feel a little 'sexier' in western clothes, and the popularity of western cowboy hats is certainly indicative of some kind of trend." To augment its unique selling approach, the store's personnel is trained to advise customers on developing a total look in order to feel comfortable with the clothes.

Both stores are doing so well that the owners are considering the start of a wholesale division to accompany their retail operation.

a What do you think about the prospects of wholesaling the western apparel operation?

b Is the popularity of western wear a trend or fad, or might it become something more permanent? Explain.

# REFERENCES

Anderson, J. M., *For the People: A Consumer Action Handbook* (Reading, Mass.: Addison-Wesley, 1977).

"Asbestos Is Blowin' in the Wind," *Retailweek,* April 15, 1979, pp. 18–19.

Baxter, W. F., and P. H. Cootner, *Retail Banking in the Electronic Age: The Law and Economics of Electronic Funds Transfer* (Totowa, N.J.: Allanheld, Osmun, 1977).

"Caveat Venditor," *Clothes Etc.,* February 1, 1978, pp. 23–24.

*Consumer Reports Guide to Consumer Services* (Boston: Little, Brown, 1979).

*Consumers Digest Guide to Discount Buying* (Homewood, Ill.: Dow Jones-Irwin, 1980).

Contini, M., *5000 Years of Fashion* (New York: Chartwell Books, 1979).

Cross, J., *The Supermarket Trap* (Bloomington, Ind.: Indiana University Press, 1976).

DePaola, H., and C. S. Mueller, *Marketing Today's Fashion* (Englewood Cliffs, N.J.: Prentice-Hall, 1979).

*EDP Conference for Retailers, 9th, 1967* (National Retail Merchants Association, Retail Research Institute, 1968).

Ende, J., and C. J. Earl, *Buy It Right! An Introduction to Consumerism* (New York: E. P. Dutton, 1974).

Gorey, H., *Nader and the Power of Everyman* (New York: Grosset & Dunlap, 1975).

Grace, E., *Introduction to Fashion Merchandising* (Englewood Cliffs, N.J.: Prentice-Hall, 1978).

Haskins, J., *The Consumer Movement* (F. Watts, 1975).

Hocker, W. G., *Computerizing the Credit–Accounts Receivable Operation* (National Retail Merchants Association, 1965).

Jelley, H. M., and R. O. Herrmann, *The American Consumer: Issues and Decisions,* (New York: McGraw-Hill, 1973).

Nader, R., C. Ditlow, and J. Kinnard, *The Lemon Book* (Aurora, Ill.: Caroline House, 1980).

Pommer, M. D., E. N. Berkowitz, and J. R. Walton, "UPC Scanning: An Assessment of Shopper Response to Technological Change," *Journal of Retailing,* 56 (summer 1980), pp. 25–44.

Ringel, L., "Fashion or Fad: Western Wear," *Stores,* January 1981, pp. 40–41.

Rothman, M. B., "MIS Understood," *Stores*, June 1980, pp. 44–46.

Rothman, M. B., "New Uses, Threats, and Solutions via POS," *Stores*, June 1979, pp. 41–43.

Rothman, M. B., "Retail Technology: Making It Work," *Stores*, October 1980, pp. 36–40, 58.

"Shopping by Computer," *Sales and Marketing Management*, December 8, 1980, p. 10.

# APPENDIX

## Merchandising Applications of Computers*

**The Challenge** The task of managing a retail company has become as complex and challenging as any in industry today. Many factors contribute to the complexity of the task. Among them are the following.

* Inflation
* Rapidly increasing labor costs
* Increasing costs to construct new store and service facilities
* Increasing costs to maintain existing store and service facilities
* Increasing governmental regulation at all levels—city, county, state, and federal
* Increasing competition from traditional competitors and new forms of retailing (i.e., catalog stores, limited-classification specialty stores, etc.)
* Consumers who are more perceptive, independent, and vocal
* The cost and availability of energy
* The cost and availability of capital

Retailers can exercise little or no control over many of the factors that can impact profit. Therefore, they must concentrate on things that they can influence and control.

In interviews with hundreds of retailers at every level of management, one point becomes very clear: Retailing is a "people" business. A retailer employs thousands of people in dozens of locations, and serves literally millions of customers. To prompt these customers to come into their stores, hundreds of classifications representing millions of dollars of inventory must be maintained. The challenge in today's environment is to improve the productivity of these people, facilities, and inventories so as to produce a profit margin that provides for continued growth and a reasonable return on investment for stockholders.

The core of the retail business is buying and selling merchandise. Therefore, in meeting today's challenges a retailer must focus on improving performance in this critical area. Customer demand must be quickly assessed so that the retailer can offer the merchandise they want, when and where they want it. With millions of items and transactions involved, this is not an easy task. Thus, at a time when customer demand must

*Reprinted by permission from *Planning Aid for Retail Information System, Executive Overview.* Copyright © 1981 by International Business Machines Corporation.

be assessed and met more quickly and accurately than ever before, the task of providing management with an understanding of what is happening in the business, and ultimately providing customers with the merchandise they want, has become even more difficult.

In response to the need for more detailed, accurate, and timely merchandising information, many retailers have begun to install point-of-sale terminals and store systems. This has been a major undertaking and has provided much more information to aid in the merchandising decision-making process. However, while point-of-sale terminals address one of the most important areas of the business (i.e., sales), there are many other areas that must provide information if the merchant is to effectively manage inventory so as to satisfy customer demand. If we look at the retail business process, this becomes very apparent.

*The Retail Business Process* As shown in Figure 1, the process begins with management setting sales, gross margin, expense, and profit goals. Once these goals have

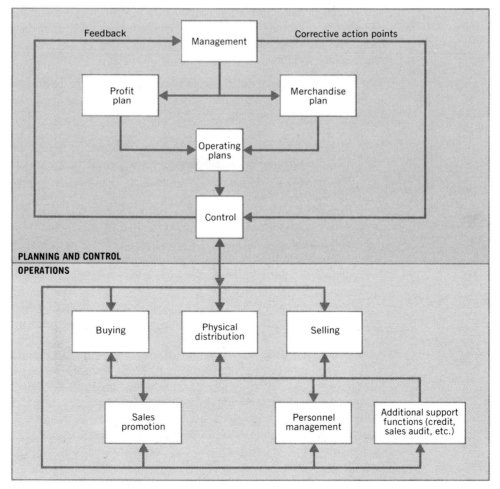

**FIGURE 1**
The retail business process. (Courtesy of International Business Machines Corporation.)

been established and set forth in the profit plan, detailed merchandise and operating plans are developed. Implicit in the planning and control phase is that controls and feedback mechanisms are put in place to monitor actual performance against the plan and to alert management to problems that require corrective action.

In the operations phase, the plans are implemented and become the day-to-day operation of the company. The merchandise and operating plans must be communicated to successively lower levels of management to provide the detail they require, in keeping with their assigned responsibilities and accountability. Again, information must be provided so that performance may be monitored against the plan.

The figure also shows that the process is integrated, interactive, interdependent, and continuous. Each area gives information to and receives information from each other. The merchants are just as dependent on complete, accurate, and timely planning and distribution information as they are on sales information if they are to manage inventory effectively.

Much of the information required by the functional areas shown in the figure is common to all or many of them. The timing, form, and level of detail will differ, but the basic data are essentially the same. Herein lies one of the fundamental problems that retailers face today.

**The Problems**  It is generally acknowledged by retailers that the information provided to merchants in the past is inadequate in today's environment. Among the problems that retailers believe must be solved are the following.

- More merchandising information must be provided than is available today.
- The accuracy and completeness of reports must be improved.
- Information must be available faster to enable merchants to detect problems and opportunities faster.
- Detailed data must be available, but exception reporting must be maximized so that the amount of information presented to merchants is realistic, manageable, and usable.
- Assistance in the planning process is required for the development of the plan and communication of the plan (at the level of detail required) to anyone with responsibility for any part of it.
- Senior management requires better performance-tracking mechanisms for the elements of the profit plan and a way to measure merchants' effectiveness.

These problems can be attributed in part to the fact that many of today's retail systems were installed to address a specific problem or the requirements of one area of the business. Over time, as additional systems were installed, there was considerable redundancy in systems, both in function and in information provided. Each system was designed to stand alone, and little attention was given to the relationship of one system to another or to the total retail business process. The retail business process is an integrated, interactive, interdependent, continuous process, but systems did not address this fact.

The task is to define the information requirements of the retail business process and the systems required to support the process. The PARIS system is intended to help retailers address this problem.

**A Solution** Effective management requires facts, and these facts must be up to date, in a useful form, and available when and where they are needed in the decision-making process. Information that is inaccurate, not current, or not available when and where it is needed is likely to result in less effective decision making.

When information is not available, decisions are based on assumptions or intuition. In today's complex retail environment, these methods, which may have been adequate in the past, are no longer acceptable. If retailers are to cope successfully with the magnitude of the problems facing them today, they must have a methodology, or technique, that provides them with the kinds of business data they can use to help them understand the true status of a situation before making decisions.

To help provide a solution to these problems, IBM initiated a comprehensive study of the information needs and problems associated with the retail business process. The study team explored various avenues that might lead to satisfying the many and diverse interests of everyone from the chief executive officer to the buyer, store manager, and distribution center manager. The result of this study is a general design for a fully integrated retail information system and the data bases required to support the system—a planning aid for retail information system (PARIS).

**PARIS' Objectives** The overriding objective of the design effort for PARIS was to create the framework for a system to provide retailing managers at all levels with current business information at the time and in the form required. PARIS provides a road map for retailers to use as an aid in addressing their particular business problems, their priorities, and the status of application development in their companies.

The conceptual design of the fully integrated PARIS system views the retail process from the top down. It encompasses activities pertaining to development of the company's sales and profit plan, the merchandise and operating plans developed from the profit plan, and the implementation and monitoring of the plans.

The conceptual design of PARIS includes "one set of books" for financial and merchandise records that is up to date and available to all managers who need it and are authorized to have it.

The PARIS design takes full advantage of the technological achievements of the 1970s, eliminating manual operations where possible. It is designed to support retailing managers and to assist them rather than infringe on their prerogatives in the exercise of judgment and performance of their duties.

**System Overview** PARIS is designed to be a data base terminal-oriented system with the ability to record transactions one time at the lowest level of activity. From this single entry, the posting of all merchandising and financial records in the data base at all levels is accomplished. Thus, all records at whatever level of responsibility reflect the same status at the same point in time. Consequently, through terminal access, management personnel at all levels can retrieve and review merchandising and financial records with the assurance that they are reviewing information with the same degree of current status.

The integrated PARIS system is viewed as having the following major functions.

- To provide a managerial tool for use in developing the company's profit and merchandising plans
- To provide a mechanism to assist in tracking performance against plan

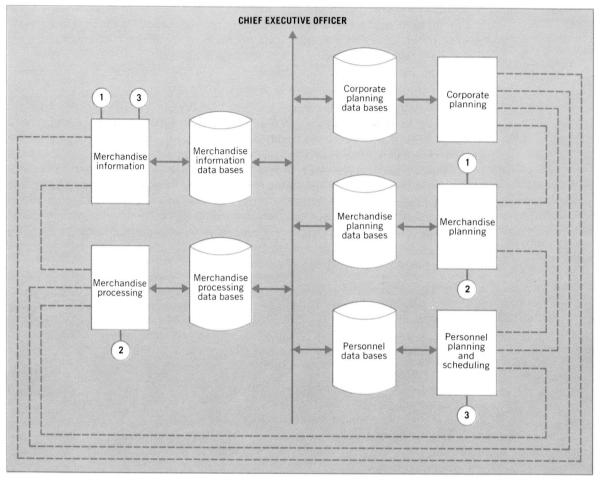

**FIGURE 2**
The PARIS system. (Courtesy of International Business Machines Corporation.)

- To support merchandising and operational personnel in day-to-day functions
- To maintain merchandising and financial information in a current state

As previously stated, the design objectives of PARIS are to provide for the entry of transactions at the lowest level of activity and to record those transactions at all other levels that are affected. Therefore, all records in the system reflect the same level of activity; duplication of records is minimized; duplicate processes are eliminated; and the movement of paper documents is reduced.

*Modular Subsystems* PARIS is organized into five modular subsystems. It addresses selected application areas that are regarded as keys both to the retail business and to the development of an integrated retail information system. The PARIS subsystems are as follows.

- Corporate planning
- Merchandise planning
- Personnel planning and scheduling
- Merchandise processing
- Merchandise information

Each subsystem is modular and is designed to operate independently of the other subsystems. Therefore, implementation of subsystems can proceed in the sequence, and at the pace, required by retailers with differing priorities. In one company a PARIS merchandise planning subsystem may interface with an already installed computerized "batch" merchandise information system, while in another a PARIS merchandise information subsystem may interface with a manual merchandise-processing system.

PARIS provides a framework that ties together the subsystems and the applications within the subsystems with the information they require. A retailer can use this framework, or road map, to develop a base to which other applications may be added in an orderly fashion.

*Integrated Design* A schematic of the total PARIS system is shown in Figure 2. Each of the major subsystems is shown, and the interrelationships among the subsystems are shown by the broken connecting lines. These lines represent the exchange of common merchandise or financial data or the flow of transactions from one subsystem to another. For example, a transaction originating in the merchandise-processing subsystem would cause an interaction with other subsystems, such as the merchandise information subsystem and the personnel planning and scheduling subsystem.

While each subsystem may be implemented independently of the others, and the benefits of each may be obtained, it is important to recognize that the subsystems have been designed to use an integrated data base. Therefore, though they can be implemented in a phased manner, each can be integrated with the ones implemented before so that ultimately a fully integrated system, with its associated benefits, may be achieved.

# chapter 4
# THE
# CONSUMER–I

After completing this chapter, you should be able to:

1 Identify the influences and factors that affect consumer behavior.
2 Identify the factors that motivate consumers to buy.
3 List and illustrate the five levels of needs in Maslow's hierarchy of needs.
4 Identify the ways in which consumer learning takes place.
5 Explain the connectionist and cognitive theories of learning as they pertain to consumer behavior.
6 Identify the concepts used to understand personality.

Most retailers will succeed or fail according to their ability to attract customers. To do this, they must have a clear-cut understanding of how, where, what, and when consumers buy. Merchants must be concerned with all the factors that influence the customers, such as merchandise, prices, salespeople, store atmosphere, and customer services. In addition, they must understand the customer's psyche, emotional needs, habits, and motives for buying.

Understanding why one store is "comfortable" for a shopper —that is, makes him or her feel at home—while another makes the shopper feel ill at ease is part of the difficulty of analyzing the customer. For example, a store that encourages the "just looking" customer to examine merchandise without feeling pressured indirectly invites that customer back to the store.

Images are communicated to the customer by the store's atmosphere, location, displays, and salespeople. Customers make decisions about stores on the basis of the services offered, the merchandise and price lines carried, customer conveniences, and their general feelings about the store personnel, decor, and so forth.

People tend to shop at the types of stores that they feel fit their personalities. A person may subconsciously ask, "What is the status of this store? Is it compatible with the image I have of myself?"

Retailers must appeal to the customer in many ways because buying behavior is complicated by psychological, social, and economic factors. Buying behavior and spending patterns are influenced by income, age, location, social situations, and the like. A merchant's ability to develop a sound strategy for pleasing the customer therefore requires constant study of the consumer and the influences on consumer behavior.

# ANALYZING AND UNDERSTANDING THE CONSUMER

The process whereby consumers decide whether, what, where, when, and how to buy goods and services is known as **consumer behavior.** Outside influences complicate this behavior before as well as during the buying process. A study of consumers' needs and motives helps us understand *why* they buy.

*Consumers' needs and motives determine their buying behavior.*

The study of consumer behavior involves an understanding of **motivation,** the force that causes people to behave the way they do. Motivation is defined as an inner drive resulting from some stimulus that causes a person to act in some fashion. The stimulus may be a psychological or physical need that drives (motivates) a person to satisfy (act) the need. Motives that cause consumers to act or buy have been classified in several ways; there are emotional, rational, biogenic, psychogenic, and patronage motives. These motives are the reasons that people buy, and are called **buying motives.**

## Emotional and Rational Motives

*Buying motives*

**Emotional motives** are those that are developed without logical thinking, such as love and vanity, while **rational motives,** such as security and durability, involve judgment and logical thinking. Retailers generally base their advertising and promotional appeals on these motives when communicating with their customers. While the product benefits

Consumer purchases can be based on emotional (women's hats) or rational (stoves) motives.

of economy, quality, durability, and performance appeal to the consumer's sense of reason, products that touch their inner feelings, such as pride, vanity, and desire for romance, are appealed to on the basis of emotion. The following list of products contains examples of both types of motives.

| EMOTIONAL | RATIONAL |
|---|---|
| cosmetics (vanity) | insurance (security) |
| jewelry (prestige) | fine woven fabrics (durability) |
| furs (status) | compact car (economy) |
| trip (romance) | alarms (protection) |
| social club (keeping up with neighbors) | vitamins (health) |

In recent years the classification of rational and emotional buying motives has been criticized as too simple. Those who have voiced such criticism claim that many products sold through emotional appeals can also be marketed in rational ways. Listed below are several products that can be handled both rationally and emotionally.

| PRODUCT | APPEAL | MOTIVE |
|---|---|---|
| cosmetics | vanity, romance | emotional |
| | improved personal appearance; better job | rational |
| expensive jewelry | impressing others; sign of success | emotional |
| | good investment | rational |
| furs | social status; look successful | emotional |
| | durability; warmth | rational |
| compact car | "everyone" is switching to a smaller car | emotional |
| | economy | rational |

## Biogenic and Psychogenic Motives

**Biogenic motives** are related to physical needs, such as the need for food, sex, drink, and comfort. **Psychogenic motives** stem from psychological needs, such as the need to satisfy, protect, or enhance the ego. To satisfy the ego, individuals are motivated to become involved with experiences and relationships that make them feel wanted and accepted. For example, they may join a club for these reasons. To protect the ego, people avoid experiences that may embarrass them; make them lose face, prestige, or status; or expose them to ridicule. This is why many people avoid entering contests. To enhance the ego, people are motivated to achieve, gain recognition, and work hard. For example, they may work long hours or attend school at night.

*A person's ego must be satisfied, protected, and enhanced*

An understanding of biogenic and psychogenic motives provides useful insights for retailers because these motives affect consumer selection of products, brands, and stores.

## Patronage Motives

Understanding specific buying motives helps the retailer appeal to consumers for their patronage. **Patronage motives** are the reasons that consumers choose one place to shop rather than another and include special brands, attractive facilities, personal services, convenience, good values, attentive salespeople, and a good store image.

A Mother's Day advertisement appealing to the emotions.

## MASLOW'S
## HIERARCHY OF NEEDS

A well-known theory that is used to explain why consumers are motivated to satisfy their needs and desires is **Maslow's hierarchy of needs** (Figure 4-1). According to Dr.

Abraham Maslow, there are several levels of needs.[1] At each level the individual is motivated to act in order to satisfy his or her needs before going on to the next level. The specific need levels are listed here, beginning with the most important at Level I.

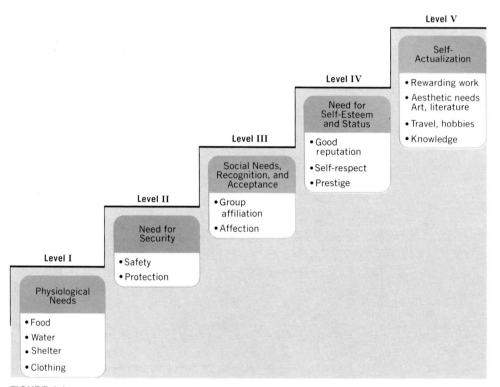

**FIGURE 4-1**
Psychological influences: Maslow's hierarchy of needs.

People's basic needs

**Level I.   Physiological Needs.**   The basic needs, such as water, food, and shelter, must be satisfied first, and they have the highest priority. Consumers satisfying these needs are motivated rationally.

**Level II.   The Need for Security.**   The need to feel safe and secure stimulates rational motives and leads to such purchases as insurance, brand name products, and safety and health devices. At this level there is little experimentation with new products or stores.

**Level III.   Social Needs, Recognition, and Acceptance.**   At this level the urge for emotional security and acceptance is so strong that many purchases are made to impress others. There is also a great deal of emotional purchasing. Romance, love, and family stimulate purchases of jewelry, cosmetics, and the like.

**Level IV.   The Need for Self-esteem and Status.**   Many products are purchased to enhance the individual's self-image and satisfy his or her need for distinction. The purchase of status symbols like expensive cars is emotionally motivated.

**Level V.   The Need for Self-actualization.**   The need to be independent is the last and highest level of needs. People who reach this level are generally affluent, successful in their careers, and concerned with aesthetics. Egoistic (emotional) motives are evident in purchases of designer fashions, hobbies, travel, and the like.

| Consumer ↔ | Stimulus → | Response = | Reward |
|---|---|---|---|
| Associates stimulus with benefit or reward | Physical or mental thing desired by the consumer | Action on part of consumer to obtain the physical or mental goal; response based on positive associations | given for correct action; constant reinforcement or rewards lead to "learned" behavior |

**FIGURE 4-2**
The Stimulus–Response–Reward learning pattern.

# LEARNING

*Motivation studies* on consumer behavior have helped retailers select appropriate means of appealing to consumers. *Learning theories* involving consumer behavior, on the other hand, have aided merchants in the development of store services, product assortments, pricing, and advertising campaigns.

*Learning defined*    **Learning** is generally considered to be any change in an individual's response or behavior resulting from practice or experience.[2] While we cannot observe the learning process in action, changes in consumer attitudes and behavior are observable in purchasing habits. According to James A. Bayton, learning

- Is goal oriented.
- Involves associations that may lead to habitual responses.
- Requires reinforcement of responses.[3]

The goal might be to acquire some object or to satisfy some physical or mental need. The object is the stimulus that arouses desire in the consumer.

The response is the action the consumer takes to obtain the object. When the response involves pleasant associations with the stimulus (object), it may lead to repeated action (habit).

To be learned, responses must be repeated; consequently, reinforcement is necessary. Reinforcement involves some reward, pleasant association, or satisfaction for correct responses. Figure 4-2 shows the relationship of the stimulus–response–reward combination to a consumer's learning pattern.

All consumer behavior is learned through repeated purchase performance. Therefore, retailers attempt to reinforce these purchase patterns through their advertising by repeating information about the store's services, product offerings, and special promotions. In fact, consumers tend to forget information unless retailers and manufacturers use "reminder" strategies in their displays, advertising and other means of communi-

[1]Abraham H. Maslow, *Motivation and Personality* (New York: Harper & Row, 1954), pp. 80–98.

[2]C. Glenn Walters, *Consumer Behavior: Theory and Practice*, 3rd ed. (Homewood, Ill.: Richard D. Irwin, 1974).

[3]James A. Bayton, "Motivation, Cognition, Learning—Basic Factors in Consumer Behavior," *Journal of Marketing*, 22 (January 1958), pp. 282–287.

cations. Because a consumer might forget, there is always an opportunity for competition and for change in consumer purchasing patterns. This accounts for the constant reinforcement found in slogans, store logos, brands, and commercials.

Consumer learning occurs on either a physical or a mental level. Physical behavior involves learned attitudes that result in an action or reaction to a stimulus in order to satisfy a desire. For example, a consumer learns

- That one store is easier to travel to than another.
- That one store provides special services and comfort.
- That one store makes the shopping experience pleasant.

On the mental level, consumer learning involves feelings, opinions, beliefs, and mental associations. For example, a consumer learns

- To prefer the service at one store over that at another.
- To associate a sexy look with Jordache jeans.
- To associate economy with a small car.
- To associate crowded stores with holidays.

Both levels of learning take place for most types of consumer behavior. Attitudes toward certain products or places must develop before some purchasing action can happen. For example, new attitudes toward Sunday shopping must be formed before a consumer considers going to a store on that day of the week.

## Learning Theories

Consumer attitudes are shaped by learning, and because consumers learn in different ways we will examine the two major groups of learning theories: the connectionist and cognitive theories.

**Connectionist theories** involve the stimulus–response approach. Learning takes place by the repeated action and rote experience of association of a stimulus and a response. The individual learns by being rewarded for correct responses or penalized for incorrect ones. It is basically a matter of conditioning, and ignores perception and insight. Pavlov's well-known experiments with dogs, in which the animals associated the ringing of a bell with food, demonstrated the importance of conditioned responses.

Retailers rely on consumers' conditioned responses to communicate their messages. By the association of some benefit or reward with patronage, the merchant can get the consumer into the habit of buying a particular product or shopping at a particular store. For example, one food merchant reduces all perishables by 50 percent one hour before closing the store for the weekend, since this is a slow time for shopping. He finds not only that he stimulates business but that some customers wait to shop at that particular hour.

Pleasure and gain involve the concept that people (consumers) seek pleasurable experiences and relationships while avoiding those that involve pain. By association, individuals learn which activities produce pleasure and which situations produce pain. Consumers may avoid the "pain" of inconvenience and poor service by shopping at certain stores despite their higher prices.

**Cognitive theories** are founded on the individual's ability to learn by using a thought process based on logic to arrive at a solution. The individual's attitudes, beliefs, perceptions, and past experiences are combined to produce some insight and problem-solving techniques. Learning through experience is cognitive in nature when insight is applied to experience.

**Perception,** which is a personal interpretation of information, is part of the cognitive theory. It is how an individual perceives an event or situation. In retail terms, a consumer's perceptions of a product, a store's advertising, and its displays influence the buying action. Since perception is directly related to a consumer's background, a single stimulus or appeal will be perceived differently by different consumers.

## Personality

Personality
defined

The elements that contribute to an individual's perception are type of stimulus, the individual's background, and his or her personality. **Personality** has been used by retailers as another factor in understanding consumer behavior. It is the totality of an individual's characteristics, that is, the sum of attributes that cause an individual to behave in a distinctive manner (Figure 4-3). In short, it makes a person what he or she is.

TELL ME, BAKER, DOES THE PREPPY
LOOK HAVE AN AGE LIMIT ?

**FIGURE 4-3**
This cartoon exhibits our "need" to identify with a group.

The study of personality has been approached in many ways. The following are some of the major concepts used to understand personality.

- The **psychoanalytic concept,** also known as the Freudian theory, views personality as controlled by the mind.
- The **trait concept** views individuals in relation to such characteristics as seriousness, aggressiveness, sociability, and adaptability.
- The **type concept** places individuals in groups according to physical or psychological characteristics or basic or social values. Personality types and traits are used by retailers in their appeal to customers.
- The **Gestalt concept** views personality as the total outcome of an individual's interaction with his or her environment. It holds that attitudes, perceptions, self-concepts, motivation, and so forth are all part of the explanation of personality.
- The **self-concept** involves individuals' perceptions of themselves. The elements in this concept are the real self, the ideal self, the self-image, and the apparent self.

The **real self** is what the consumer is as a person, that is, the individual's physical, mental, and emotional characteristics (Figure 4-4). The **ideal self** is what the individual would like to be. Contained in the ideal self is a consumer's desire to improve. The **self-image** is how the consumer views himself or herself. The individual's perception includes the real self and the ideal self, that is, the person's understanding of what he or she is and would like to be. The **apparent self** is how others see the individual. Generally, what others see is a combination of the real self, the ideal self, and the self-image.

The application of the self-concept theory has been helpful to retailers. For example, consumers act to protect or improve their self-image by purchasing goods that meet those needs. In addition, consumers tend to avoid products and services that are not compatible with their self-image or that of the group to which they belong.

Astute retailers are aware of consumers' self-images through the latter's actions, for example, the brands they buy or the price ranges they prefer.

## THE BUYING PROCESS

Another way of understanding the consumer is through the buying process. This process consists of the steps the consumer goes through when deciding what, when, where, and how to buy. Understanding this process can provide the retailer with the tools for developing an appropriate strategy for attracting customers. The steps in the buying process are as follows.

*Steps in the buying process*

1 **Recognition of a need** An advertisement, a suggestion, or some other stimulus makes the consumer aware of a need. For example, an invitation to a costume party might stimulate the need to buy a costume.

2 **Search for information** Once a need has been recognized, the consumer gathers information to satisfy the need. In the case of the costume, the consumer can check the yellow pages, ask a friend, or search his or her memory for past shopping experiences.

**Real Self**
    What the consumer is
**Ideal Self**
    What the consumer would like to be
**Self-Image**
    How the consumer views himself or herself
**Apparent Self**
    How others see us

**FIGURE 4-4**
Self-concept theory.

3  **Evaluation** The consumer makes selections or choices at this stage. The criteria measured are (among others) price, quality, and service.

4  **Decision making** On the basis of the evaluation, the consumer makes a buying decision. The product is purchased or rejected. From the retailer's point of view, this is the most important stage.

5  **Cognition** After purchasing a product an individual thinks about the decision. At times the consumer is not convinced that the purchase was a wise one. This is called **cognitive dissonance.** In trying to justify the purchase, the consumer searches for

Consumer decision making is a crucial stage in the buying process.

additional facts or ads to prove to himself or herself that the purchase was correct. **Cognitive consonance** exists when the consumer has continued satisfaction after the purchase.

## LOOKING AHEAD

Having examined the way retailers attempt to interpret and act on consumer behavior, we now extend our study to the buying habits of consumer groups: the elderly, working women, ethnic groups, and so forth. With our understanding of motivation, learning theories, and personality, we are in a better position to appreciate the complexity of consumer–retailer relationships and the dynamics of retail strategy.

### NEW TERMS

| | |
|---|---|
| apparent self | motivation |
| biogenic motive | patronage motive |
| buying motive | perception |
| cognitive consonance | personality |
| cognitive dissonance | psychoanalytic concept |
| cognitive theory | psychogenic motive |
| connectionist theory | rational motive |
| consumer behavior | real self |
| emotional motive | self-concept |
| Gestalt concept | self-image |
| ideal self | trait concept |
| learning | type concept |
| Maslow's hierarchy of needs | |

## CHAPTER HIGHLIGHTS

1   The process whereby consumers decide whether, what, when, and how to buy the goods they use is known as consumer behavior.

2   The study of consumer behavior involves an understanding of motivation and its effect on purchasing patterns.

3   An analysis of consumers' needs and motives helps retailers understand why consumers buy.

4   Maslow's theory of needs has been used to explain how consumers are motivated to satisfy needs in a specific order.

5   Motivation studies and learning theories help retailers decide how to appeal to consumers.

6   Consumer attitudes are shaped by learning. Two learning theories are known as connectionist and cognitive.

7 The theories used by retailers to analyze consumer personalities include the following: psychoanalytic, trait, type, Gestalt, self-concept.

8 Understanding the various steps in the buying process is another way of understanding the consumer.

## QUESTIONS

1 What are the influences and factors that affect consumer behavior?

2 List and explain the five levels of needs in Maslow's hierarchy of needs.

3 How would you relate the order of needs in Maslow's hierarchy to consumer purchases?

4 What kinds of products are purchased because of emotional and rational buying motives?

5 Explain how psychogenic and biogenic motives influence consumer purchases.

6 What are the implications for retailers when consumers attempt to enhance their egos?

7 How does an understanding of learning theories and motivation studies contribute to the development of retail strategy?

8 List some examples of consumer learning that occur on the physical and mental levels.

9 Using specific examples, show how retailers rely on consumers' conditioned responses to communicate their messages.

10 List and explain the various steps that a consumer goes through during the buying process.

## FIELD PROJECTS

1 Examine a daily newspaper and find ten advertisements that use emotional or rational appeals. List the products and the types of appeals, for example, vanity, durability, and so on.

2 It appears that the traditional roles of men and women both at home and at work are becoming blurred. This means that changes are occurring on the job as well as in the retailing of goods and services. It is apparent that
   - Women are in the work force to stay.
   - Women and men are sharing child-rearing and home-related jobs more equally.
   - Financial decisions are also shared.

   Try to determine the attitudes of ten of your schoolmates regarding the sharing of household chores and purchasing by asking the following questions.
   
   a In the new sharing of home-related decisions and chores, how would you divide the shopping for
      - Food

- Household supplies
- Hardware materials
- Clothing

**b** What kind of store would you shop at for each item?

## CASES

**1**   A small retailer in a prestigious shopping mall began to feel the competition of many discounters. He sold quality clothes and accessories, and provided such services as knowledgeable salespeople, custom alterations, charge accounts, and return privileges. The store owner feared that he would lose many of his good customers if he maintained full prices. As a result, he placed the following advertisement in newspapers.

---

## CLOTHESTIQUE

The Mall at Greenvail

Announces . . . starting today

## New Store Policy

# DISCOUNT PRICING

Dear Friends and Customers
Being aware of skyrocketing costs in all of the necessities, we have decided to change our entire store pricing policy. So, as of today, our store will reflect a
**20% DISCOUNT**
while our services remain the same.

That's the change!! What stays the same?
- Our carefully selected quality clothes and accessories
- Our knowledgeable and friendly salespeople
- Our alterations
- Our charge, refund, and return privileges

Mon.-Fri. 10-9:30 Sat. til 6

---

    **a** How might this ad change consumer attitudes?
    **b** How do you think this ad affected consumers who had been shopping at discount stores?
    **c** What types of appeals did the retailer use in his ad?

**2** Even though individuals may consider the practical aspects of a purchase, buying decisions involve other factors.

Several prominent women were asked what item they would purchase as the ultimate in extravagance for their fall wardrobes (assuming unlimited funds). Some chose an exciting seasonal wardrobe, others "exotica," and still others items from present-day primitive cultures. For example, Diana Vreeland, consultant to the Costume Institute at the Metropolitan Museum of Art (New York), selected white silk shirts to be made by the finest shirtmaker available. Estee Lauder, head of the famous cosmetics firm, selected a printed street length dress with a matching jacket. Kim Carnes, the pop singer, decided on clothes designed by the well-known designer Georgio Armani. Paloma Picasso, an artist and the daughter of Pablo Picasso, wanted something whimsical—trouser boots that rise from heel to waistline in one piece. Mary McFadden, the fashion designer, selected one ornament of gold—a Greek necklace. Another fashion designer, Norma Kamali, wanted something handcrafted from an African or Indonesian culture.

    **a** In your opinion, what factors were involved in the "buying decision" for each woman?
    **b** From a retailing point of view, how would a retailer evaluate this information?

**3** Datsun's plans to change the name of its cars and trucks from Datsun to Nissan caused some retail analysts to predict uncertainty and confusion among consumers. Nissan, the parent company, explained that its cars are called Nissan in Japan (where half of its sales are made), and that its auto dealerships around the world are known as Nissan. In an attempt to make its name and image uniform throughout the world, the company proposed the name change in the United States.

For more than ten years Nissan had poured advertising and promotion money into the Datsun name at a rate that reached $70 million in 1980. Since 1976, $250 million had been spent in the United States alone. Experts claimed that Nissan would have to double its advertising expenditure because of the change. For example, all dealer signs and other material might require adjustments if the company were to avoid the "cost" of bruised consumer relations. Furthermore, the consumer might wonder if there was something wrong with Datsun.

Even though the name change would give Nissan worldwide uniformity, some people questioned the strategy for American consumers. They reasoned that this was especially so because Datsun had achieved successful brand association.

    **a** How do you think consumers might view the new dealership signs and advertising? (The former ads read, "Datsun is good for you.")
    **b** Considering the conditioned-response aspect, how do you think consumers might react to the name change?

# REFERENCES

Berkman, H. W., and C. G. Christopher, *Consumer Behavior: Concepts and Strategies* (Belmont, Calif.: Dickenson, 1978).

Block, C. E., and K. J. Roering, *Essentials of Consumer Behavior: Concepts and Applications* (Hinsdale, Ill.: Dryden, 1979).

Britt, S. H., *Consumer Behavior and the Behavioral Sciences* (New York: Wiley, 1966).

Cannel, E., *How to Invest in Beautiful Things Without Being a Millionaire: How the Clever Consumer Can Outthink the Tastemakers* (New York: David McKay, 1971).

Engel, J. F., R. D. Blackwell, and D. T. Kollatt, *Consumer Behavior* (Hinsdale, Ill.: Dryden, 1978).

Farley, J. U., J. A. Howard, and L. W. Ring, *Consumer Behavior* (Boston: Allyn & Bacon, 1974).

Ferguson, M., and M. Ferguson, *Champagne Living on a Beer Budget* (New York: Scribner's, 1968).

Hansen, F., *Consumer Choice Behavior: A Cognitive Theory* (New York: Free Press, 1972).

Jenkins, J. R. G., *Marketing and Customer Behavior* (Elmsford, N.Y.: Pergamon, 1972).

Kassarjian, H. H., *Perspectives in Human Behavior* (Glenview, Ill.: Scott, Foresman, 1981).

Lambert, Z. V., "Consumer Alienation, General Dissatisfaction, and Consumerism Issues: Conceptual and Managerial Perspectives," *Journal of Retailing,* 56 (Summer 1980), pp. 3–24.

Loudon, D. L., and A. J. Della Bitta, *Consumer Behavior: Concepts and Applications* (New York: McGraw-Hill, 1979).

Myerson, B., *The Complete Consumer Book* (New York: Simon & Schuster, 1979).

Stossel, J., *Shopping Smart: The Only Consumer Guide You'll Ever Need* (New York: Putnam, 1980).

Walters, G. C., *Consumer Behavior: Theory and Practice,* 3rd ed. (Homewood, Ill.: Richard D. Irwin, 1978).

# chapter 5
# THE CONSUMER–II

After completing this chapter, you should be able to:

1 Identify the demographic categories and explain their impact on consumer behavior.
2 Identify special consumer markets.
3 List the categories in Warner's class system.
4 Identify the factors that influence lifestyles.
5 Explain the impact of reference groups and cultural influences on consumer behavior.

In the last chapter we studied consumer behavior by examining some of the concepts related to consumer motivation and habits and how they contribute to the buying process. In this chapter we continue our examination of the forces affecting the decision-making process. We will study the various consumer segments, which are based on demographic characteristics and lifestyles.

## DEMOGRAPHICS

Population characteristics are important to retailers

**Demographics** is the breakdown of the population into statistical categories: age, education, sex, occupations, income, households, and marital status. This information is particularly helpful for the retailer who wants to reach a special segment of the market. For example, in developing its merchandise offerings a store might be interested in the fact that many senior citizens frequent its premises. Or perhaps a store might want to develop a program to attract the singles group. Information regarding age groups and their spending patterns helps the retailer devise an appropriate retail strategy.

A great deal of demographic information is available from the Department of Commerce, the U.S. Bureau of the Census, and the Bureau of Labor Statistics. In addition, data may be secured from trade associations, professional organizations, and research groups.

In 1978 the Census Bureau projected an 11 percent increase in the U.S. population by 1990. Since a larger population results in more people buying goods and services,

Retailers rely on demographics in developing their strategy.

retailers need to know how the composition of the population will change in order to plan effectively. Let's analyze some of the projected changes and indicate their probable implications for retailers.

# Age

The age groups that are expected to be affected most by the population increase are the following: the elderly (65 and over), middle-year adults (35–44), teens and young adults (14–24), and a possible "baby boom."

## The Elderly

This group will account for an increasingly larger share of the market. The 65–74-year-old segment will expand by 19 percent, while the 75-and-older group will increase by 32 percent. Both groups will probably have larger incomes and more education than similar groups in the past.

**Implications for Retailers** The more affluent and better-educated senior citizens, constituting an increasingly larger segment of the senior-age market, will probably extend their middle-age lifestyles into their later years. Already reflecting this trend, we find retirement communities containing golf, tennis, swimming, cultural, and spa facilities. To match these new activities, older people are dressing differently than they did twenty-five years ago. As the saying goes, "Grandmothers and grandfathers are jogging, not rocking."

Retailers, of course, must evaluate merchandise assortments in departments that cater to senior citizens. The merchandise mix is crucial because this group, though advanced in age, is still fashion conscious and financially sound. Retailers who cater to in-home shoppers will find additional opportunities with the elderly because they are well educated and convenience oriented.

## Middle-Year Adults

This group will expand by 50 percent, by far the largest percentage increase of all age segments. In terms of actual numbers, there will be approximately 6 million more people in this category by 1990 than there were at the beginning of the decade.

**Implications for Retailers** Since the 35–44 age group ranks high on the income and spending scale, retailers who cater to these consumers can expect significantly higher sales because of their growing numbers. In addition, retailers are aware that this group is one of the most lavish spending segments, doling out 27 percent more on goods and services than the average household.

## Teens and Young Adults

*The youth group is getting smaller*

Not too long ago this age group represented a generation that created mass markets for goods and services. It was the largest spending segment in American society. However, because of the decline in birthrates since the late 1950s, the numbers of teens and young adults will decrease dramatically. The 14–17-year-old group will suffer a population loss of approximately 3.9 million between 1980 and 1990. The 18–24-year-olds will record a similar drop, approximately 3.8 million, by 1990.

**Implications for Retailers** The shrinking numbers in these groups will soften the demand for youth-oriented products. Consequently, merchandise planning should reflect this change. For example, McDonald's, which sells approximately 35 percent of its hamburgers to consumers under the age of 19, may have to consider sales strategies that appeal to an older population.

Specialty and similar stores that cater to this age group may need to add more items and services to attract this market.

## A New "Baby Boom"

There will be more women reaching childbearing age in the 1980s. This will reflect an increase from 19.6 million women in the 18–36 age group in 1960 to 33.9 million by 1985. It is estimated that the fertility rate will rise slightly, from 1.8 births per woman in 1976 to approximately 2.1 in 1985.

**Implications for Retailers** If a "baby boom" develops, retailers who cater to the under 5 age group can expect significantly higher sales. Stores will probably expand both their facilities and their merchandise offerings to meet the demand.

## Education

The decade of the 1970s recorded an increase of more than 8 percent in college exposure among people above the age of 25. This significant change is even more dramatic for people who will be middle-year adults in the 1980s. For this group, the increase is an astounding 15 percent!

Education and income are key factors in buying behavior

**Implications for Retailers** The college-educated segment differs in its buying behavior from other workers with similar incomes. While the better educated tend to be more independent in their search for merchandise information, the less educated are more likely to seek such information from friends. Because the former group responds positively to ethical, informative advertising, retailers who are interested in selling to this group would be wise to stress quality, performance, and other rational buying motives.

## Sex

It is obvious that information regarding the number of men and women in the market is crucial for retailers who are targeting (i.e., aiming at) certain populations. For example, a buyer in a men's and boy's department is certainly interested in the size of the potential men's market. In fact, there is currently a trend toward stores catering to specific male and female markets, such as the Athlete's Foot for men and the Winning Woman shops.

Men and women exhibit different buying patterns. For example, women are more likely than men to shop for food and most small household items. In addition, they do much of the shopping for men. On the other hand, today's couples make many joint decisions regarding high-priced items, and shop together more often.

**Implications for Retailers** Communicating to the right target market is important. Since women often select and purchase articles of clothing for men, retailers must be careful where they advertise and how their products are displayed. And because more couples are shopping together, store hours should provide the time they need.

Retailers should cater to people who enjoy shopping. The more enjoyable a shopping spree is, the more often they will shop.

# Occupations

*Changes in the work force*

How people earn a living influences the size of their income as well as their purchasing behavior. Workers are classified as either **white-collar** or **blue-collar.** White-collar jobs are found among professionals, in offices, and in service occupations. Blue-collar jobs include those of factory workers and laborers. Growth rates among these groups have differed markedly, as shown in Figure 5-1. Once a small proportion of the total labor force, white-collar workers now represent about half of the total. The number of service workers also has risen rapidly, while the blue-collar work force has grown slowly and the number of farm workers has declined. Technological advances have so changed employment needs that since 1970 an increasing percentage of the work force has been employed in white-collar jobs while the percentage of blue-collar workers has decreased. Figure 5-2 indicates the changes among the occupational groups that are expected to have occurred by 1990.

**Implications for Retailers**  An understanding of occupational types provides insights into consumers' needs. White-collar consumers have a better understanding of buying sources. They are also more information minded than blue-collar workers, who rely to a greater extent on advice from others.

Occupational shifts cause changes in purchasing behavior, and as workers change jobs they present new challenges to retailers. Better-educated white-collar workers have different product preferences and tastes than factory workers.

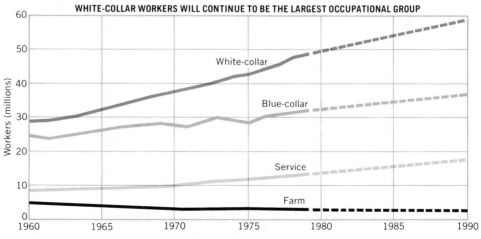

FIGURE 5-1

Occupational groups, 1960–1990. (U.S. Department of Labor, Bureau of Labor Statistics, *Occupational Outlook Handbook, 1980–81 Edition*, Washington, D.C., March 1980.)

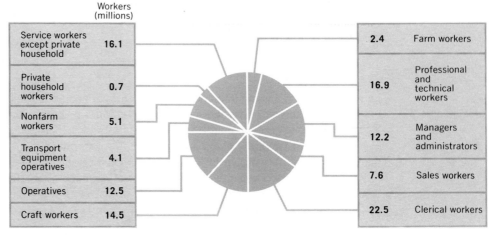

PROJECTED DISTRIBUTION OF EMPLOYMENT BY OCCUPATION IN 1990

Workers (millions)

| | |
|---|---|
| Service workers except private household | 16.1 |
| Private household workers | 0.7 |
| Nonfarm workers | 5.1 |
| Transport equipment operatives | 4.1 |
| Operatives | 12.5 |
| Craft workers | 14.5 |

| | |
|---|---|
| 2.4 | Farm workers |
| 16.9 | Professional and technical workers |
| 12.2 | Managers and administrators |
| 7.6 | Sales workers |
| 22.5 | Clerical workers |

**FIGURE 5-2**

Distribution of employment, 1990. (U.S. Department of Labor, Bureau of Labor Statistics, *Occupational Outlook Handbook, 1980–81 Edition*, Washington, D.C., March 1980.)

## Income

According to the Bureau of Labor Statistics, disposable income (money available for spending after taxes) per person is expected to rise from $4300 in 1977 to $5500 in 1985 and $6300 in 1990. The median household income is expected to increase from approximately $15,000 in 1978 to $32,500 in 1988, while the proportion of consumer households with incomes over $25,000 will probably increase from 5.3 percent in 1972 to 7.3 percent in the 1980s.

The reason for this expected growth is the number of households with more than one wage earner. Dual incomes will lift more families to affluent-household status, so that by 1990 they could account for one of every three households.

**Implications for Retailers** More people moving into higher income brackets means an increase in buyers for luxury goods and services. Retailers who deal in high-fashion items like jewelry and furs will have added opportunities for sales. (An analysis of income and a discussion of Engel's laws regarding the manner in which a family spends its income are contained in the appendix at the end of this chapter.)

## Household and Marital Status

A household may be a family unit, a single person, or a nonfamily unit (unrelated people living together). It is expected that in the next decade the number of nonfamily households will grow faster than that of family units. Within the family structure, the number of one-spouse homes will grow more than three times as fast as that of traditional husband–wife units, increasing to one out of five family units.

Despite the increase in nonfamily households, it is expected that the family will remain the dominant market in the United States, reaching 68 million buying units. However, government projections see a smaller average family size because married couples prefer to have fewer children than previously and more young adults are postponing marriage. The decrease from 3.3 people per household in 1978 to 3.0 in 1990 indicates the magnitude of the expected change.

**Implications for Retailers** The trend toward individually run households indicates that consumer shopping patterns may undergo changes. Store hours may require adjustment to conform to the needs of nonfamily household wage earners as well as single people. The anticipated smaller family size will probably shift merchandise strategies toward young and older adult groups. However, despite the projected decrease in the percentage of family units, the purchasing done by married couples for such expensive items as home furnishings, equipment, and appliances will still be based on joint decisions by the spouses, requiring more information from retailers.

# Demographics and Special Consumer Markets

Retailers who are interested in reaching special populations are concerned with **market segmentation** (the process of dividing the total market into smaller sections, each having a community, e.g., teenagers, veterans). The more important segments consist of

- Working women.
- Consumers with special needs.
- Minority groups.
- Urban, suburban, and rural consumers.

Married couples frequently make joint decisions when buying high-priced merchandise.

## Working Women

The number of women in the work force will continue to escalate. According to Census Bureau projections, this group could swell its ranks by an additional 30 percent by 1990. Working women will account for annual earnings of $128 billion by 1981. One study indicated that 55 percent of American women over the age of 16 will be working by 1990, compared to 48 percent in 1977. It also showed that approximately 25 percent of the 44 million married mothers with intact marriages will be full-time homemakers.[1]

**Implications for Retailers** Studies indicate that the interests and needs of working and nonworking women differ. Working women are concerned about outside interests, appearance, and convenience in doing household chores. Consequently, retailers who deal in fashionable items, convenience products, recreation, and the like should devise strategies to attract this segment of the market.

Although working women have additional purchasing power, they are "time poor." Therefore, merchants who help reduce the number of stops required for shopping, offer more conveniences, and provide additional facilities (e.g., banking) will undoubtedly benefit. Creative retailers who are action minded have already targeted this group for special treatment. J. W. Robinson grouped business attire and accessories in its Career Shop in Los Angeles, while Abraham & Straus created The Office for its working consumers in New York. Others with a similar approach are Marshall Field & Company in Chicago, Filene's in Boston, and Sanger-Harris in Dallas. These stores concentrate on the working woman's need for quick shopping, good value, and special services. Women who shop there have courier service for deliveries to home or office within 24 hours, and are able to charge on long-term accounts. This special merchandising captures the working woman's loyalty.

Catalog shopping and in-home shopping services should benefit working women because they save shopping time. In-home computer terminals are expected to become widespread by the 1990s.

## The Consumer with Special Needs

There are approximately 36 million people for whom shopping is not a routine experience. Members of this group, a sizable market segment, suffer physical and sensory disabilities. Included among them are 20 million in the 18–64 age bracket.

**Implications for Retailers** This is a potentially lucrative market for sensitive merchants. Through physical improvements and service accommodations in their stores, some retailers have already taken steps to "welcome" this special group. For example, Sears recently installed an experimental teletype ordering system that allows deaf customers in the Los Angeles area to place catalog orders. In another instance, Braille menus have been built into counters at selected McDonald's locations.

## Minority Groups

Ethnic and religious backgrounds are somewhat influential in consumers' preferences for different stores and products. Although race and religion are difficult to use as a

---

[1]"Sales and Significant Trends," *Marketing Management,* August 20, 1979, p. 120.

It is estimated that more than half of American women over the age of 16 will be working by 1990.

means of predicting consumer behavior, they are factors to observe. A reasonable forecast regarding minority groups in the 1980s is that the market will be more lucrative and more diverse. It is expected that the increase in the black population will be significantly higher than the increase for the total population. (Blacks represent approximately 12 percent of the population.) In addition, the black population may be sharply segmented into a small, growing, higher-income group and a much larger low-income group. Moreover, the tremendous growth of the Hispanic population may soon rival that of the blacks.

**Implications for Retailers** The growing size of the affluent black market segment represents an opportunity for retailers to satisfy this market's demand for upgraded merchandise. Similarly, merchants who are interested in reaching the growing Hispanic group will consider bilingual store signs and specially designed promotion materials.

## Urban, Suburban, and Rural Consumers
The location of consumers very often affects how they buy. City dwellers have briefer but more frequent shopping experiences than rural and suburban shoppers. The latter groups generally "stock up" more and tend to buy in a more organized fashion (shopping lists, coupons, etc.).

Knowing the type of dwelling in which consumers live is also helpful to retailers. People who live in apartments do not spend heavily on certain items that homeowners purchase, such as window treatments, fixtures, and so forth. Apartment dwellers buy items that are more fashionable, trendy, and movable, whereas homeowners spend more time shopping and are more interested in guarantees and durability.

**Implications for Retailers** Every shift of consumers has strong implications regarding where expenditures for new household products, durables, and nondurables will be made. Retailers located in urban areas might capitalize on the more frequent shopper by offering special in-store promotions and setting up displays for various impulse items.

# LIFESTYLES

Our lifestyles are changing radically

**Lifestyles** are affected by demographic background because age, income, and education have a great deal of influence on the way a person chooses to live. By definition, lifestyle is the unique way in which a particular group sets itself apart from others. A comprehensive study of an individual's lifestyle involves an understanding of the following influences: social class, reference groups, and cultural influences.

## Social Class

**Social classes** are homogeneous divisions within a society into which familes and individuals can be classified for comparative purposes. In some societies, these groups may be so clear-cut that movement between them is not permitted. In others, the dividing lines are not so definite and movement may be easier. Nevertheless, divisions always exist. Consequently, it is important to understand the concept of social class and how it applies to consumer behavior.

Warner's class system

A social class division involves a structure for ranking individuals in the United States according to occupation, source of income, education, family background, dwell-

Consumer purchases reflect different lifestyles.

ing, and other factors. According to Lloyd Warner, the class system is divided into six levels.[2]

1 Upper-upper      4 Lower-middle
2 Lower-upper      5 Upper-lower
3 Upper-middle     6 Lower-lower

The following are some of the characteristics of each class.

**Upper-upper:**
1 percent of population[3]

This group possesses "old wealth" and is composed of second- and third-generation families. Because of their great affluence, its members are secure in their status and reside in exclusive areas. Their children attend prestigious schools and are graduated from some of the best-known institutions in the world. People in this group are active in charities and the arts. Money is not a factor in their purchasing activities.

**Lower-upper:**
$1\frac{1}{2}$ percent of population

This group is sometimes called *nouveaux riche,* French for "new rich." Its members are high-income earners who are usually educated for professional careers in private schools. Active in community work, they are socially aggressive and value possessions highly. As with the upper-upper class, money is not a factor in their purchasing activities.

**Upper-middle:**
10 percent of population

This class contains both professional and business people. It relates its social status to money, attempting to "mirror" an upper-class style of living. It is a highly educated group, with a substantial number of members who attend prestige schools. The group values quality possessions—and purchases accordingly.

**Lower-middle:**
30 to 35 percent of population

This is essentially a white-collar group that reflects middle-class values. Its members are conscientious workers with steady incomes who place great value on higher education for their children. They shop often, with price an important factor in their purchasing activities. Their possessions are related largely to their occupations.

**Upper-lower:**
40 percent of population

While this group is generally involved in blue-collar occupations, individual members' incomes are sometimes higher than those of members of the lower-middle class. Members of this group have limited education, seek job security, and are family oriented. They are not socially active outside of their own circle, and their living style is highly routinized. While status image is unimportant in their purchases, they do show brand loyalty. Money is a strong factor in their purchasing activities.

**Lower-lower:**
15 percent of population

This group has low incomes and unsteady employment. With poor education and depressed living conditions, its members are uninformed and often in need of public or private subsidization. They have limited ability to purchase goods other than necessities and use credit whenever possible.

[2]W. Lloyd Warner, *Social Class in America* (New York: Harper & Row, 1960).
[3]1980 estimate.

Blue-collar workers still comprise an important target market for retailers.

Some retail firms operate effectively with particular social classes by planning merchandise and service offerings for those classes. For example, retailers recognize that when upper-income people shop for fashion items they feel uncomfortable in bargain basements, while a wage earner with ample money to spend may be hesitant about going into a quality store for fear of possible humiliation. Retailers also know that middle-class customers are generally self-confident and willing to explore different types of stores. Since lower-class people are risk conscious and very much concerned with security, they hesitate to buy something brand new or to shop in new environments. Upper-class people, on the other hand, are more confident and are not concerned about money. As a result, this group has a wider product choice. Another contrast lies in the fact that whereas the upper class uses charge accounts for convenience, the lower class uses credit cards to defer payments. Figure 5-3 indicates shopping preferences and merchandise appeals for each social class.

## Reference Groups

Lifestyles are affected by people whose status, achievements, or activities cause others to emulate them. They are also influenced by the manner in which particular groups function. In the former instance, we are dealing with reference groups; in the latter, with cultural influences.

Groups that are influential in shaping attitudes and opinions have an impact on the lifestyle an individual chooses. Known as **reference groups,** they include opinion leaders and the family.

| Social Class | Shopping Preference | Merchandise Appeal |
|---|---|---|
| Upper-upper | Prestige stores | Expensive jewelry, antiques, expensive homes, elegant and conservative clothes |
| Lower-upper | Prestige stores | More ostentatious, less conservative, original designer clothes |
| Upper-middle | Department stores for furniture and fashion goods (goods others would notice), discounters for goods not easily noticed by others | Spending on mass market designer labels, better furniture and clothing |
| Lower-middle | Discounters, department stores, small shops | Do-it-yourself products, modest housing and clothing |
| Upper-lower | Neighborhood stores that extend credit, discount stores | Sports products, outdoor equipment, do-it-yourself products; spend less on clothing, late-model cars |
| Lower-lower | Stores extending credit, neighborhood stores | Buy primarily to provide necessities |

**FIGURE 5-3**

Social classes: shopping preferences and merchandise appeal.

## Opinion Leaders

Opinion leaders exist in all groups

Members of a group who exert influence on consumer decision making are called **opinion leaders.** They are generally the avant-garde and are regarded as a source of information and advice. They have a very strong impact on the decision-making process involving purchases of conspicuous goods and services. These people are particularly important in fashion retailing. They are the first to adopt new styles and are instrumental in having those styles accepted more widely. For example, Walt "Clyde" Frazier, ex-basketball star and former member of the Cleveland Cavaliers and the New York Knickerbockers, popularized flashy and colorful garments that caught the fancy of many young basketball fans. Opinion leaders are found on all social levels and are selected by their followers for several reasons: They are considered important, possess recognized expertise, and are highly visible to the group. These leaders have the ability to promote sales through their consumption patterns.

## The Family

Most of our attitudes are probably shaped by family influences. Consequently, the family is considered one of the most influential of all reference groups. Since attitudes toward stores and products are developed within the household, individuals remember the countless articles used in their first homes. These include types of cars, brands of food, toothpaste, and much more.

Young married women often buy the brands that were used in their early households. Similarly, parents sometimes influence the spending patterns of young married couples.

## Cultural Influences

*Culture and lifestyles are inseparable*

According to Webster's dictionary, culture is "behavior typical of a group or class." Culture and values affect the types of lifestyles individuals choose, as well as their buying patterns. For this reason merchants should be sure that their product offerings and services do not conflict with the cultural values of a targeted group. The social meaning attached to a product within a culture is critical in assessing how the product might be accepted. For example, in some countries higher-status people do not engage in any form of manual labor because it is considered demeaning. Consequently, it is common for members of this group to hire laborers. It follows, then, that the introduction of do-it-yourself products would meet with social resistance. Another example is the varied selling approaches taken by McDonald's restaurants in different countries. In the United States, McDonald's has used the familiar theme, "Nobody can do it like McDonald's can"; in Holland, known for its frugality, the theme is "McDonald's restaurants—unusually good for your money."

We are concerned primarily with several key aspects of American culture: religion, economic relations, status, and grouping. Religious beliefs in American culture affect consumer behavior in many ways. For example, religious groups prohibit the use of products ranging from certain foods to birth control devices; others frown on Sunday business hours; still others ban the consumption of alcoholic beverages.

Economic relations and status have a powerful influence on consumers' buying preferences and habits. They include work achievement, the work ethic, the need for security, and striving for better things. The motivation to achieve sparks the competitive drive to purchase products that identify with success, such as big cars and other expensive items.

Grouping or conforming is an aspect of American society that prompts people to dress like, act like, and follow the trends or fads of their group. Attempts to retard the aging process are another reflection of American culture. Progressive retailers respond to these behavior patterns by supplying products and services that are in demand.

Some of the changing American values that have implications for retailers are the stress on instant gratification as opposed to postponement of pleasure, naturalism in foods versus preservatives and artificial additives, and gender equality instead of male dominance. In addition, the greater emphasis on individualism and the improved status of the aging have influenced lifestyles significantly. Merchants who recognize these changes fare better by integrating new ideas into their sales strategies.

### NEW TERMS

| | |
|---|---|
| blue-collar worker | market segmentation |
| constant dollars | opinion leader |
| demographics | personal income |
| discretionary income | real income |
| disposable income | reference group |
| Engel's laws | social class |
| lifestyle | white-collar worker |

# CHAPTER HIGHLIGHTS

1  Two major factors that influence consumers' buying decisions are demographics and lifestyles. Demographics is the breakdown of a population into statistical categories based on age, education, sex, occupation, income, household, and family status. Lifestyle is the unique way in which a particular group sets itself apart from others.

2  Social class is the ranking of individuals according to occupation, source of income, education, family background, dwelling, and so forth.

3  Warner's class system is divided into six levels: upper-upper, lower-upper, upper-middle, lower-middle, upper-lower, and lower-lower.

4  Through market segmentation retailers can reach special markets, such as the elderly, teenagers, and working women. These market segments provide retailers with important information for store promotions.

5  The social class structure has many implications for retailers regarding the purchasing behavior of each class.

6  Reference groups, including opinion leaders and the family, affect the attitudes, opinions, and actions of consumers.

7  Culture and values play an important part in the lifestyles that individuals choose.

8  Alert retailers benefit from the recognition of changing social values.

# QUESTIONS

1  List and explain how any three of the demographic categories outlined in this chapter affect the retailer's strategy.

2  What is meant by the social class structure, and how are retailers affected by it?

3  Describe how an opinion leader can stimulate sales of a particular product.

4  How do values affect the choice of a lifestyle?

5  Identify special consumer segments that are not listed in the text and explain why they are important to retailers.

6  How do members of the upper and middle classes differ in their buying needs?

7  What are some of the characteristics of the lower-lower class?

8  What are some of the different lifestyles that we see today?

9  How do altered lifestyles affect retailing strategy?

# FIELD PROJECTS

1  Read your local newspaper and clip advertisements that are targeted to special groups. List the market segments that retailers are attempting to attract.

2  On the basis of your own experience and involvement with clubs, sports, work, and other groups, identify opinion leaders within those groups. List the main characteristics of each and plan to discuss why they are leaders and not followers.

# CASES

1 "*Lifestyle merchandising* is a matter of putting it all together for one customer type. When it comes to home furnishings, customers should be able to single out their preferences by contemporary, traditional, rustic, etc., and find everything they could want for their homes within each 'lifestyle' " (*Retailweek,* May 15, 1979).

    a To what other merchandise areas or departments would lifestyle merchandising apply?

    b How can small retailers adopt this approach?

2 Working women will spend approximately $12 billion on work apparel by 1983. The statistics are impressive and certainly warrant retailers' notice. However, the retailer should be aware of the differences among women in the working segment. For example, career women are generally better educated and more affluent than women who consider their work "just a job." Career women are self-assured, well read, and better informed regarding new products, fashions, and the like.

    a How should the retailer communicate with both groups?

    b What are the implications for merchandise assortments and services arising from the differences between the two groups of working women?

3 For the first time in the company's history, Marks & Spencer, Britain's largest retailer, has recorded a decline in sales. The store, a dowdy retailer that the British affectionately call "Marks & Sparks," is a victim of bad timing. Meeting stiff competition from retailers of less expensive lines, such as British Home Stores, Marks & Spencer had been trading up for some time. Traditionally known as the place to go for solid, no-nonsense goods of undisputed quality at unspectacular prices, the store changed its merchandise policy and shifted to "spiffier," higher-priced merchandise, including silk blouses, cashmere coats, and $235 wool suits for men.

    "The customer just didn't want it," said Lord Sieff, the chairman of the board. "We had neglected our traditional market."

    Back went the owners to their original policy. Though the stores may have carpet and other trimmings, merchandise once again is piled on open tables under plain, bright lighting. The no-dressing-room tradition is maintained (no questions asked on refunds), and signs around the store put renewed stress on "lower prices/quality maintained."

    Marks & Spencer claims that it is neither the cheapest nor the most fashionable retailer. The company's very British, very stolid image is so strong that the prime minister, Margaret Thatcher, once posed at M&S butchers' stalls in order to identify herself as a typical thrifty homemaker looking for a good product at a sensible price.

    The store's merchandising changeover received a great deal of publicity. The consumer affairs minister called the price cuts "a perfect example of free enterprise in a competitive marketplace." Financial analysts also praised the move by noting that "Marks corrects its mistakes very quickly."

    a Why couldn't Marks & Spencer, founded in 1917 and considered one of Britain's largest retailers, change its merchandise concept?

    b  What factors contributed to a decline in sales?

    c  Why was "store image" part of the problem with regard to loss of sales?

    d  If Marks & Spencer were to open in America, to what class of shoppers would it appeal? Explain. Name a large American store that would be comparable to M&S.

# REFERENCES

"Babies: Back in Style?," *Sales and Marketing Management,* July 9, 1979, p. 16.

Bearden, W. O., and J. B. Mason, "Elderly Use of In-Store Information Sources and Dimensions of Product Satisfaction/ Dissatisfaction," *Journal of Retailing,* 55 (Spring 1979), pp. 79–91.

Caplovitz, D., *The Poor Pay More: Consumer Practices of Low-Income Families* (New York: Free Press, 1967).

Caplovitz, D., *The Poor Pay More* (New York: Free Press, 1963).

"College Survey Part II: Intimate Apparel and Accessories," *Clothes Etc,* May 15, 1978.

Fullerton, H. N., Jr., "The 1995 Labor Force: A First Look," *Monthly Labor Review,* 103 (December 1980), pp. 11–21.

Lambert, Z. V., "An Investigation of Older Consumers' Unmet Needs and Wants at the Retail Level," *Journal of Retailing,* 55 (Winter 1979), pp. 35–57.

Leezenbaum, R., "The New American Woman and Marketing," *Marketing Communications,* 298 (July 1970), p. 22.

"Lifestyle Furniture Survey: Putting the Pieces Together," *Retailweek,* April 15, 1979, pp. 58–66.

Polk, P., "Today's Customer," *Retail Directions,* 129 (March-April 1975), p. 19.

Ringel, R., "Making a Firm Statement About Career Dressing: Streets & Co.," *Stores,* 63 (February 1981), pp. 30–31, 57.

Taylor, T. C., "Targeting Sales in a Changing Marketplace," *Sales and Marketing Management,* July 27, 1981, pp. A6–A16.

Witt, R. E., *Group Influence on Consumer Brand Choice* (Austin: University of Texas at Austin, Bureau of Business Research, 1970).

# APPENDIX

## The Analysis of Income

The analysis of income and how it is spent has great meaning for retailers. Income is best understood by breaking it down into the following divisions: personal, disposable, discretionary, and real.

- **Personal income** includes all moneys that an individual receives from wages, salaries, investments, interest, and dividends.

- **Disposable income** is the amount of money a person has to spend after taxes have been deducted. It is the portion of income that is available for *essential* household and personal use (rent, mortgage payments, insurance, utilities, health care, etc.).
- **Discretionary income** is money that a person or household has available to spend or save freely after payments for fixed commitments have been deducted. It is the portion of income that an individual is free to spend after paying for essential items.
- **Real income** is the figure that determines the actual dollars available in measuring an individual's purchasing power. Basically, it measures what one dollar will buy in one year as compared to another time. Real income is obtained by measuring all dollar figures according to an index that has been adjusted for the shrinking value of the dollar (inflation). Real-income figures are sometimes called **constant dollars** because they refer to a base year. For example, a 1982 income might be restated in "1978 dollars."

As household income increases, there are decided shifts in the way a family spends its money. In 1857 Ernst Engel, a German economist, made some generalizations about consumer expenditures that are known as **Engel's laws.** Engel observed that as a family's income increases,

- Percentage spent for food decreases.
- Percentage spent for clothing tends to increase.
- Percentage spent on housing and household operations remains constant.
- Percentage spent on discretionary products and services increases.

Although Engel developed his generalizations about income expenditures more than a century ago, they are still valid today.

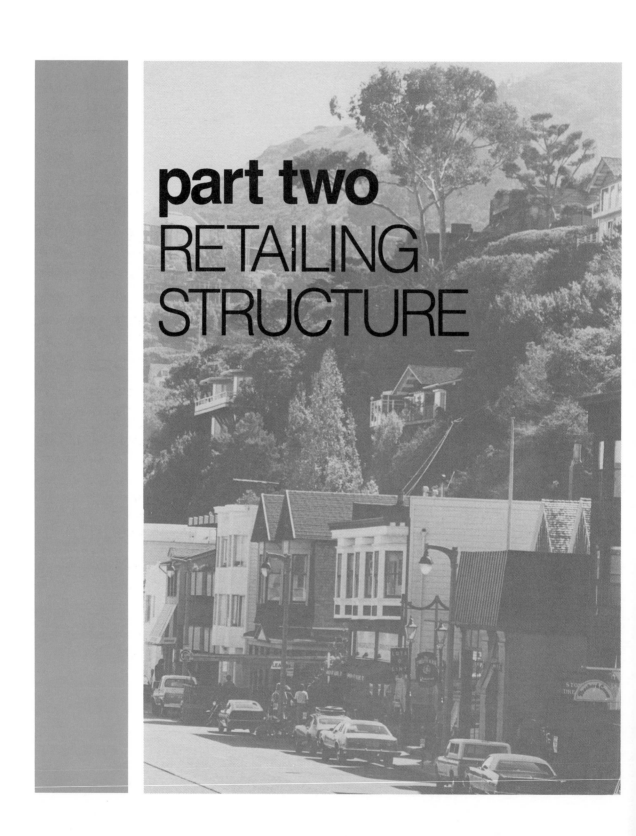

# part two
# RETAILING STRUCTURE

**H**aving read about the development and growth of retailing, we turn our attention to how retail institutions are structured. Chapter 6 identifies retail businesses by type of ownership. After studying the general characteristics of business organizations, we examine specific forms of retail ownership, which range from chains to consumer cooperative associations.

Chapter 7 continues the discussion of the structure of retail institutions by identifying them according to the type of merchandise they sell. We then study the characteristics of general-merchandise and limited-line stores. The discussion includes a description of new types of general merchandise stores.

Chapter 8 concludes our discussion of the structure of retail institutions, focusing on nonstore selling methods. An in-depth treatment of door-to-door selling, party plans, vending machines, mail order retailing, and electronic retailing gives an idea of the variety of nonstore selling arrangements in use today. We also identify services sold by retailers.

In Chapter 9 we study store organization by analyzing line and line-and-staff structures. The material includes organizational arrangements for small retailers, department stores, branch stores, and chain stores. It also outlines the differences between store centralization and decentralization. The last topic covers the organization of store communication in both informal and formal modes.

In dealing with the management of human resources in Chapter 10, we cover the recruitment, hiring, and training of new employees. We also examine problems associated with the transfer, promotion, and discharge of employees. Finally, after studying the establishment of wage and compensation scales and fringe benefits, we determine what retailers should know about labor unions and the law.

Chapter 11 is concerned with the very important topic of store location. We look at the major factors in determining location and identify the types of shopping areas available to retailers. Next we analyze the criteria used in site selection and canvass the alternatives of buying or renting a retail outlet. The chapter closes with a listing of trends in store location.

Chapter 12, the last chapter in Part Two, deals with the physical aspects of a store's exterior and interior. We discuss the physical structure, visibility, entrances, and parking facilities of stores, as well as aspects of lighting, modernization, and layout. We also see how air conditioning, in-store transportation, and customer services contribute to a store's success. Finally, we explore several aspects of store functions that are essential to smooth operations, namely, customer safety and conveniences, store security, and storage.

# chapter 6
# RETAIL INSTITUTIONS, BY OWNERSHIP AND ORGANIZATION

After completing this chapter, you should be able to:

1. Identify business and governmental groups that use retail statistics.
2. Identify the six categories that are used to analyze retail institutions.
3. List the important characteristics of sole proprietorships, partnerships, and corporations.
4. Identify the types and characteristics of retail store ownership.

Because retailing is so important to various segments of our economy, it receives much attention in newspapers, periodicals, and government publications. Hardly a day goes by without some reference in the media to retail statistics regarding sales volume, merchandise lines, and employment. These data are studied by various groups for information about retailing trends, and they provide facts to be used in intelligent decision making.

Among the groups that use retail statistics regularly are retailers, retail suppliers (manufacturers and wholesalers), government agencies, and lending institutions. Retailers use the information for a variety of purposes, including the updating of current plans and the formulation of new ones. Retail suppliers develop production and distribution schedules on the basis of the latest data. Some governmental units study retail sales for estimates of sales tax receipts, while others are concerned with employment figures. Banks analyze the statistics for clues about the extent of borrowing by retailers and the levels of consumer credit.

## RETAIL CATEGORIES

In order to compile useful retail information, it helps to classify retail institutions in understandable categories. This is not easy to do because some retail organizations fall into more than one category. For example, while A&P is a supermarket, it is also a chain operation. Again, while Sears, Roebuck maintains department stores, it also conducts a mail order catalog business.

Basically, retail organizations can be arranged in six categories.

*Six categories of retail institutions*

- **Ownership** This refers to the way control of an organization is exercised. Such control may range from independent ownership to corporations.
- **Types of merchandise sold** This category consists of stores arranged by the types and variety of merchandise they carry. Included are general and limited-line stores.
- **Extent of nonstore selling** This includes retailers who contact consumers in other ways than through stores.
- **Types of services offered** In this category, stores are arranged by the extent to which services are offered to customers. While some stores make available a full line of services, such as delivery, credit, and sales assistance, others are on a self-service, cash-and-carry basis.
- **Extent of departmentalization** This category involves the degree to which stores are departmentalized. Although most small stores are not arranged this way, department and large specialty stores show an astonishing variety of departmental organization.
- **Location of outlets** This category identifies stores by their location: central-city shopping districts, suburban malls, neighborhood locations, and so forth.

In this chapter we analyze retail institutions by form of ownership, an arrangement that permits us to structure retail statistics for easy and useful reference.

# TYPES OF BUSINESS ORGANIZATION

*Three types of business organization*

Before discussing specific types of retail store ownership, mention should be made of the three ways in which a business may be organized (Table 6-1). First, it may be started as a **sole proprietorship.** This means that one person owns the business, investing both money and time. The owner makes decisions about the business and assumes personal responsibility for its debts. Most small retail establishments, and some moderate-sized ones, are sole proprietorships.

A business may also start as a **partnership,** a form of organization in which two or more people invest their money and time. On the basis of a partnership contract, the partners agree on how the business is to be operated, the amount of time each partner is to devote to it, and how profits and losses are to be shared. The partners are personally liable for the debts of the partnership. As with sole proprietorships, most retail partnerships are small establishments.

The third way in which a business may be organized is as a **corporation.** The owners who invest in the company are called stockholders, but they do not necessarily share in its management. Instead, major decisions are made by a board of directors, while day-to-day operations are conducted by executives and other employees. A major advantage of owning stock in a corporation is that stockholders have limited personal responsibility for the company's debts, being limited to the amount of their investment. Virtually all large retail organizations are corporations, and some small retailers are family-owned corporations with few stockholders.

Table 6-2 contains a breakdown of retailing firms in 1977 by type of business organization. It also lists business receipts for each type. It is interesting to note that while sole proprietorships accounted for 75.7 percent of all retail firms, their share of total receipts was only 15.7 percent. On the other hand, corporations, with 17.6 percent of the total number of retail businesses, had 80.3 percent of the receipts. Obviously, sole proprietorships dominate the field of retailing in number of enterprises while corporations garner the lion's share of sales volume. The table also indicates that partnerships, with 6.7 percent of the total number of firms, registered only 4.0 percent of the receipts.

**TABLE 6-1**  Types of Business Ownership

|  | Sole Proprietorship | Partnership | Corporation |
|---|---|---|---|
| Ownership | Single owner | Two or more partners | Stockholders |
| Investment | Money and time | Money and time | Money |
| Decisions made by | Owner | Partners | Board of directors and executives |
| Owner responsibility for debts | Unlimited | Unlimited | Limited to amount of investment |

**TABLE 6-2**   Single (Sole) Proprietorships, Partnerships, and Corporations in the Retailing Industry— Number and Receipts, 1977

| Type of Business Organization | Number | Percent of Total | Business Receipts (billions) | Percent of Total |
|---|---|---|---|---|
| Single proprietorship | 1,862,000 | 75.7% | $123.6 | 15.7% |
| Partnership | 164,000 | 6.7 | 32.0 | 4.0 |
| Corporation | 433,000 | 17.6 | 634.1 | 80.3 |

*Source:* U.S. Bureau of the Census, *Statistical Abstract of the United States: 1980* (Washington, D.C., 1980).

# TYPES OF RETAIL STORE OWNERSHIP

Ownership of retail businesses may take any of the following forms.

1   Chain
2   Ownership group
3   Manufacturer–retailer
4   Independent
5   Leased department
6   Franchise
7   Consumer cooperative association

## Chain Ownership

As indicated in Chapter 1, a chain organization consists of multiple retail outlets under common ownership. Some chains have only a few outlets, while others have hundreds or thousands. The major functions of a chain (buying, advertising, hiring, record keeping, and planning) are controlled by a central headquarters.

### Advantages

Since a chain store sells identical merchandise in all its outlets, it buys in large volume and, thus, can sell at lower prices than smaller retailers. The volume of its purchases gives a chain organization important competitive advantages in establishing selling prices for its merchandise, and enables it to deal with manufacturers and wholesalers from a position of strength.

Because of their economic power and centralized management, chains have a distinct advantage in advertising their products. Specialists design advertising campaigns for the organization and have access to all forms of national and regional media. While a chain can afford to send its message to the consumer through newspapers, periodicals, radio, and television, a retail organization with less economic strength has fewer options.

Chain ownership includes a variety of institutions.

Chain organizations maintain personnel departments that are responsible for hiring and training employees for their stores. Specialists in personnel management outline employee responsibilities so that store procedures are standardized. Potential employees are attracted to chains by the availability of fringe benefits and the possibilities for advancement.

*Advantages and disadvantages of chains*

Owing to their financial strength, chains can utilize sophisticated computers for record keeping and other purposes. The most modern equipment and techniques are used for inventory control, customer records, payroll data, sales forecasting, and credit analysis. The availability of up-to-date information from the computer enables chains to make critical decisions quickly.

Chains recognize the lessons to be learned from failure to adapt to new conditions. They maintain planning departments, employing specialists to analyze economic events, people's habits, and emerging lifestyles. As a result of their long-range planning, they are better prepared than most retailers to meet future needs.

### Disadvantages

It is ironic, but true, that the organizational structure of chains, which gives them competitive advantages, also results in disadvantages. For example, the centralization of control makes it difficult to respond quickly to local changes in customers' desires and needs. Centralization also places severe pressure on top management to respond quickly to problems and inefficiency in dispersed branches. Finally, the very large investment needed to locate, outfit, and stock new branches and maintain existing ones ties up significant sums of money.

## Ownership Group

*The "parent" retail corporations*

Some of the best-known department stores in the country are now owned by parent corporations. While the stores maintain their own names and basic functions, the parent corporations exercise control in the areas of long-range planning, financing, and data sharing. However, unlike chain organizations, in which individual stores have little to do with policy formulation, stores (known as divisions) in **ownership groups** conduct business almost as though they were self-owned. In fact, the public is largely ignorant of the existence of the parent corporation.

The Jarman Shoe chain is a division of the Genesco, Inc., ownership group.

Among the larger ownership groups are the following.

1 Allied Stores Company (Bon Marché, Donaldson's, and other divisions)
2 Carter Hawley Hale Stores, Inc. (Bergdorf Goodman, Nieman-Marcus, and other divisions)
3 Federated Department Stores (Bloomingdale's, Bullocks-Magnin, and other divisions)

## Manufacturer–Retailer

In this type of ownership, which includes only large companies, the manufacturer operates its own retail stores. This eliminates the need for involving wholesalers in the distribution process, and gives the manufacturer–retailer absolute control of the distribution of its products. On the other hand, the high investment costs and operational difficulties discourage many retailers from engaging in manufacturing, and vice versa. The retail outlets in this type of ownership arrangement are usually specialty stores. They include such well-known companies as Firestone Tire & Rubber Company, Kinney Shoes, and The Gap.

## Independent

The most prevalent type of retail ownership is the **independently owned store.** Although this type of business may be a sole proprietorship, a partnership, or a corporation, it usually has only one outlet. Unlike a chain store, which is controlled by a parent company, the independent has its own management.

Independents can be found in every community in the country, and are located wherever people need the convenience of shopping outlets. You can find them on Main Streets and in movie theatres; in office buildings and at roadsides; on busy city streets and in village squares.

An independent store has one outlet

A characteristic feature of the small independent is the personal service it offers to consumers. Unable to compete in price with chains, the independent makes up for this disadvantage by providing customers with personal contact, frequently on a first-name basis.

Because most small independents are owner managed, the proprietors devote much energy and time to the business. Though the store may have one or more employees, the owner tries to control all aspects of the operation. This absolute control may work to the owner's advantage because he or she can make decisions and judgments when they are needed. However, with so many responsibilities— purchasing, selling, advertising, and bookkeeping, to name just a few—the owner sometimes finds the burden too heavy to carry alone. Furthermore, limitations in the owner's managerial skills may affect the business adversely. It is no accident, therefore, that new independent retailers have a high failure rate. It is generally accepted that almost one out of every five new independents will fail within the first year. These failures are usually due to insufficient investment funds, lack of business experience, and poor management.

Though independents have the advantages of relatively low start-up costs and direct control over operations, they are at a disadvantage with regard to the prices they pay for merchandise. This is so because they usually buy in small quantities and cannot secure the favorable price terms accorded to chains and other large retailers.

In order to strengthen their bargaining position with manufacturers and wholesalers, some small independents form associations for purchasing their merchandise. In some cases they combine their orders so as to secure volume discounts. With this arrangement, they can compete more favorably with larger retailers while maintaining their independence. In other cases they organize their own wholesale business as a **cooperative chain.** Each cooperating store receives the benefit of discounted prices

Independent retailing is the most common type of ownership.

while maintaining its individuality. Finally, some independents have arrangements with a wholesaler whereby they agree to sell the latter's products and to use the wholesaler's name instead of their own. This **voluntary chain,** exemplified by Associated Food Stores and Independent Grocers Alliance, gives the independents price advantages as well as help in such matters as advertising and financing. Here, too, the stores operate as independent entities.

There are a growing number of people who believe that independently owned retail establishments will face difficult financial problems in the years ahead. Howard L. Davidowitz, head of the retail consulting services group of Ernest & Whinney, a large accounting firm, maintains that "independents will be severely beset in the 1980's because they'll have to depend upon their own ability to produce cash since banks are getting less and less interested in financing independents."[1] If such predictions come true, many people who plan to enter retailing as independent owners may have to do so in some other way, for example, leased department or franchise.

## Leased Department

Leased departments are found in discount, department, and specialty stores

Some discount, department, and specialty stores rent space to other retailers (lessees), who maintain their own departments in the stores. These are called **leased departments.** This arrangement enables the store (lessor) to widen its product or service line without assuming the necessary expertise or investment responsibilities. It also provides the store with additional revenue through rent collection, which sometimes includes a percent of the lessee's sales. Among the most frequently found leased departments are fur storage, photo studio, shoes, and millinery lines departments.

Many leased departments are operated by chains, which sell standardized products or services in their various leased outlets. Like individually run leased departments, the chains are responsible for all activities in their areas.

To the lessee, the advantages of leasing a department are lower investment costs, access to the store's other traffic, and availability of the store's physical services (parking, etc.). The renting store, of course, counts on the leased department to attract additional customers.

## Franchise

Although the term *franchise* may not be known by many people, names like Howard Johnson, Dunkin Donuts, and H & R Block usually bring instant recognition. In fact, each of these companies is involved in a form of ownership known as franchising.

In a **franchise,** a manufacturer, wholesaler, or service company (the **franchisor**) gives a smaller company or an individual (the **franchisee**) the right (i.e., the franchise) to conduct a retail business in a certain way and within a specified period. Though there are a variety of possible franchise arrangements, let's examine a typical situation.

Suppose you want to start a retail fast-food business but don't possess the necessary skills and experience. You may be reluctant to open an independent store for fear of possible failure and loss of your investment. In that case you may try to secure a franchise from a company like Burger King or McDonald's. The advantage to you is that you will be able to rely on a large company for guidance and help.

[1] I. Barmash, "The Storekeeper's Bookkeeper," *New York Times*, June 8, 1980, p. 9 (Sec. 3).

Leased departments can offer services as well as merchandise.

As the franchisee, you might pay the franchisor a one-time franchise fee for the right to conduct business under the franchisor's name. Depending on the popularity of the franchisor and the cost of equipping the franchise, the fee could run from a few thousand dollars to well over $200,000. For example, it could cost as much as $300,000 to start a McDonalds franchise, whereas you might secure one from H & R Block for a few thousand dollars. In addition, you would probably pay the franchisor a monthly royalty fee based on a stipulated percentage of gross sales. In return, you would receive some or all of the following services from the franchisor.

1   Assistance with planning, financing, and securing a location and store.

2   Training for operating the store. Most franchisors provide several weeks of initial instruction plus continual assistance as needed. For example, Hardee's Food Systems give five weeks of training prior to opening an outlet and ten additional days upon opening. Lum's Restaurant Corporation starts with three weeks of training and stations a consultant at the franchisee's restaurant for two weeks after it has opened.

3   A supply of written materials to help with operations and sales. This includes advertising and bookkeeping aids, newsletters, and forms.

4   Managerial assistance from the parent company's representative. Periodic on-site visits and company meetings are common.

5   Assistance with record-keeping and bookkeeping activities. In some cases, such as Coast to Coast Stores, which sell a variety of hardware and appliance items, the franchisor offers to help with tax accounting, inventory control, and preprinted price tickets.

6   The benefit of the franchisor's national and/or regional advertising and promotional campaigns. This is extremely important when you consider the enormous impact of TV and radio advertising.

7   The benefit of improved methods and products developed by the franchisor.

There are some disadvantages to being a franchisee. Among them are

Pros and cons of a franchise

1   The possibility that the franchisor's services may be of poor quality.

2   The possibility that too many outlets may be franchised in your geographic area, cutting into your sales and income.

Radio Shack is an example of a popular electronics franchise.

3   The possibility that a particular decision by the franchisor may benefit the franchisor but not you. For example, the franchisor might discontinue a low-selling item that is selling well in your outlet.

4   The possibility that your franchise period may be too short to allow you to reap long-range benefits from the hard work you put into the franchise. You may find that renewal of the franchise is unavailable or too costly.

5   The possibility that the franchisor may exercise rigid control over your operations. This could damage your sense of independent ownership.

The advantages of franchising to the franchisor are

1   The ability to create franchises quickly at relatively lower costs than prevail with other types of ownership. The 1960s and 1970s saw very large increases in the number of franchised outlets.

2   The likelihood that franchisees, because they invest their own funds, will work hard to ensure the success of their franchises.

3   The continuance of income through monthly collections of royalty fees.

4   The assumption of operating expenses by the franchisees, which reduces overall costs.

5   In some situations, the immediate payment by the franchisee for delivered goods, which eliminates the need to extend credit.

Franchisors may be faced with the following problems.

1   Difficulty of finding suitable locations for new outlets. Fast-food franchisors have been experiencing this problem lately.

2   The possibility of damage to the franchise's name and reputation caused by inefficiently run franchises.

**3** The reduced resale value of poorly run outlets.

**4** Involvement in costly legal controversies with franchisees because of disagreements over the franchise contract.

**5** The high cost and effort required to secure responsible and competent franchisees.

Common franchise arrangements

The most common franchise arrangements involve

**1** Manufacturers (franchisors) that contract with retailers (franchisees). Car dealerships and gasoline service stations are the largest groups in this category. The next time you pass a Chevrolet dealer or a Mobile station, you will probably be looking at a franchise.

**2** Wholesalers (franchisors) that contract with retailers (franchisees). Radio Shack and Western Auto are in this category.

**3** **Licensors** (franchisors) that contract with retailers (franchisees). This category contains some of the most recently developed and best known of the franchises, such as Thrifty Rent A Car Corporation, International House of Pancakes, and Baskin-Robbins, Inc.

A recent trend in the franchise field is the acquisition by some franchisors of their franchised outlets. This has happened for two reasons: (1) because the success of some franchise companies has enabled them to reap greater profits from wholly owned units, and (2) because adverse court rulings have stripped franchisors of some of their power over franchisees. For example, most franchisors can no longer insist that franchisees purchase goods exclusively from the parent company.

With regard to types of business organization, all franchisors are incorporated. You read and hear about General Motors *Corporation,* Century 21 Real Estate *Corporation,* and Hertz *Corporation*—all franchisors. Unless it is restricted by the franchise contract, however, a franchisee's outlet may be a sole proprietorship, partnership, or corporation.

# Consumer Cooperative Association

A store owned by consumers

In **consumer cooperative associations** consumers own shares in a retail store. Though the owners decide store policy, actual operations are maintained by a managing retailer. The store's products and services are available to all customers, whether owners or not. Each consumer–owner has one vote no matter how many shares he or she owns, and membership is open to all. Yearly profits, called patronage dividends, are distributed on the basis of a member's purchases, not the number of shares owned. In addition, members may also earn low interest on their investments in the association.

Though consumer cooperatives have not had a significant impact on total retail sales in this country, they continue to function in the farm supply, grocery, cafeteria, and bookstore fields. The basic cost of doing business affects "co-ops" in the same way that it affects other businesses. As a result, the early expectation of some cooperatives that consumer members would benefit significantly from lower co-op prices did not materialize. With other cooperatives, prices are set at competitive levels to avoid conflict with privately run stores. Co-op members then benefit from the annual distribution of profits.

## Frank Winfield Woolworth
## THE VARIETY CHAIN BUILDER

Not all merchants are successful in their first attempt at retailing. A case in point is that of Frank Winfield Woolworth, the famous variety store innovator, whose first store in Utica, New York, failed in 1879 almost as soon as it opened.

Banking on the idea that the public would respond to a store that sold items at prices no higher than 10¢, Woolworth immediately started another business in Lancaster, Pennsylvania. As this store flourished, he opened additional outlets, so that by 1900 there were fifty-nine "5-and-10" stores.

In 1909 Woolworth went international with the opening of stores in Liverpool, England. Shortly thereafter he consolidated his chain with those of several of his relatives and friends, forming the F. W. Woolworth Co.

The basic merchandising technique exploited so well by Woolworth was this: People would pay "cash on the barrelhead" for what they perceived as a bargain. Woolworth's genius lay in his ability to acquire goods that consumers wanted—that could be sold at low prices (5¢ and 10¢!) and would result in profits. With proper management, he reasoned, those profits would mount considerably as sales volume increased.

The new F. W. Woolworth Co. comprised 611 stores, but the total grew to more than 1000 by 1919. Annual sales were over $60 million in 1909; they reached $119 million in 1919. Judged by the standards of those days, Woolworth's business receipts were remarkable.

In addition to the "5-and-10" concept, Woolworth's success was ascribed to a variety of business practices. These included purchasing goods directly from manufacturers, thereby excluding wholesalers; the absolute reduction of operating costs; the purchase and sale of merchandise for cash; and the development of accessible store displays.

**NEW TERMS**

consumer cooperative association
cooperative chain
corporation
franchise
franchisee
franchisor
independently owned store

leased department
licensor
ownership group
partnership
sole proprietorship
voluntary chain

## CHAPTER HIGHLIGHTS

1 Retail statistics are used regularly by retailers, manufacturers, wholesalers, government agencies, and lending institutions.

2  Retail organizations are classified according to ownership, types of merchandise sold, extent of nonstore selling, types of services offered, extent of departmentalization, and location of outlets.

3  A new business may be organized as a sole proprietorship (one owner), a partnership (two or more owners), or a corporation (owners are called stockholders).

4  Though a great majority of retail institutions are sole proprietorships, more than three-fourths of retail sales are made by corporations.

5  Ownership of a retail business may take the form of a chain, ownership group, manufacturer–retailer, independent store, leased department, franchise, or consumer cooperative association.

6  Chain organizations have several advantages over smaller competitors: Buying in large volume enables them to pay lower prices for goods; their economic strength and centralized management allow them to advertise in all kinds of national and regional media; they employ specialists to hire and train employees; they have the means to utilize sophisticated computers; and they maintain planning departments to prepare for future needs. Chains sometimes suffer disadvantages: the difficulty of responding quickly to customers' needs and to problems in individual stores, and the large investment needed to start new stores and maintain existing ones.

7  Ownership groups own and exercise control over their department stores. However, the stores usually operate as though they were self-owned.

8  Manufacturer–retailers make and sell their own products. Though they control distribution of their products, they have high investment costs and must contend with operational difficulties.

9  Independent retailers usually have personal contact with their customers and devote much energy and time to the business. They have the advantage of relatively low start-up costs and direct control over operations. Because they usually purchase in small quantities, they pay higher prices for goods than those paid by chains and other large retailers. To meet this problem, some independents form associations, cooperative chains, or voluntary chains in order to purchase merchandise at lower prices.

10  A leased department is a rented area in a discount, department, or specialty store. The store receives rent and the lessee sells its products. Many leased departments are operated by chains.

11  A franchise exists when a manufacturer, wholesaler, or service company (the franchisor) gives a smaller company or an individual (the franchisee) the right to conduct a retail business in a certain way within a specified period. In return for a fee, the franchisor usually assists the franchisee with planning, financing, training, and record keeping. The most common franchise arrangements involve manufacturers and retailers (e.g., gasoline stations), wholesalers and retailers (e.g., Radio Shack), and licensors and retailers (e.g., Baskin-Robbins, Inc.).

12  A consumer cooperative association consists of consumers who own shares in a retail store. Though the owners decide store policy, a managing retailer runs the store.

# QUESTIONS

1 Why are retail statistics important to retailers, suppliers, government agencies, and banks?

2 What are the benefits of arranging a store into departments? Why aren't most small stores arranged departmentally?

3 Why are most large retailing companies organized as corporations?

4 Since corporations account for more than 75 percent of retail sales volume, why are most retailers organized as sole proprietorships?

5 What advantages do small retailers have over chains in the operation of their business?

6 What are the advantages of a division in an ownership group (such as Bon Marché of Allied Stores Company) operating as though it were self-owned?

7 Of what advantage is it to a manufacturer–retailer like the Thom McAn Shoe Company to have absolute control over the distribution of its products?

8 What advice would you give to someone who is thinking seriously about opening an independent retail store?

9 What are some advantages of operating a leased department in a department store?

10 What problems sometimes develop between a franchisor and a franchisee?

11 In what ways do franchisors provide services to their franchisees?

12 Do you think that consumer cooperative associations will someday have a larger share of total retail sales than they do today? Explain.

# FIELD PROJECTS

1 Visit three retail outlets in your community. Talk with the owner or manager (be sure to go when he or she is not busy) and find the answers to the following questions.
   a Is the business a sole proprietorship, a partnership, or a corporation?
   b Is the business a chain, an independent, a franchise, or a consumer cooperative?
   c Who is responsible for hiring and training employees (if any)?
   d Does the business advertise its products or services? If so, how?

2 Talk with the owner of an independent store in your community. After your visit, write a brief report that includes the following items.
   a The approximate cost of starting a similar business.
   b The amount of time the owner gives to the business.
   c The owner's responsibilities.
   d What the owner likes about owning the business.
   e The problems that arise in that type of business.

# CASES

**1**  George Daly and Florence Dee own a record store in a small shopping center as equal partners. As a result of their good management, the store has done well and they are thinking of opening two similar stores.

If they expand their operation, they may reorganize the business as a corporation. Since they are unfamiliar with the organization and operation of retail outlets as corporations, they need advice.

   a  What factors should they consider before deciding to expand?
   b  What would you tell them about the advisability of incorporating the business?

**2**  For some time Norman Drew has wanted a retail store of his own. Working for twelve years as the manager of a hardware store, he has saved $20,000 and is willing to invest the money in a promising business. Norman is not sure whether he should own an independent store or a franchise. If he asked for your ideas, what would you advise him to do? Why?

**3**  Bloomingdale's, a department store division of Federated Department Stores Inc. with stores in Boston, New York, Pennsylvania, and Washington, had been trying for some time to open a store in the Old Orchard Center, a regional shopping center in Skokie, Illinois. Located thirteen miles from Chicago, the center already included Marshall Field & Company, Chicago's major department store chain.

In addition to the Skokie store, Bloomingdale's planned the construction of two other stores: one in downtown Chicago on fashionable North Michigan Avenue and the other in the Northbrook Court Center about twenty miles outside of Chicago. Bloomingdale's ostensible reason for planning the three stores was to tap the affluent populations of Chicago and its environs.

As a co-owner and tenant of the Old Orchard Center, Marshall Field objected to Bloomingdale's entry as a tenant. In fact, the center already contained Montgomery Ward, Saks Fifth Avenue, and Lord & Taylor stores.

Negotiations between Federated Department Stores and Marshall Field involved hard bargaining, with one party attempting to establish a foothold in a new retail market and the other maneuvering to retain its strong position in the area. While recognizing the inevitability of compromise in most business situations, each company was determined to derive maximum benefit from the eventual agreement.

Though Marshall Field's main base consisted of the Chicago area, with seventeen department stores, it also had parent ownership of Seattle's Frederick & Nelson stores, Cleveland's Halle Brothers Stores, and the J. B. Ivey stores in Charlotte, North Carolina. In effect, then, the Old Orchard Center negotiations were conducted by two large parent retail organizations.

   a  Considering that the Old Orchard Center already contained three large retailers, what reasons may Marshall Field have had to resist Bloomingdale's entry into the center?
   b  What inducements may Bloomingdale's have offered Marshall Field to secure approval for its opening a store in Skokie?

# REFERENCES

"At Your Service—Outlook for Leased Departments: Brightest and Best in Service Areas," *Stores,* 59 (December 1977), p. 44.

Davidson, W. R., A. F. Doody, and J. R. Lowry, "Leased Departments as a Major Force in the Growth of Discount Store Retailing," *Journal of Marketing,* 34 (January 1970), p. 41.

"Federated: All That Glitters Is Not Gold," *Retailweek,* July 1, 1980, pp. 24–30.

Finn, R. P., *Your Fortune in Franchises* (Chicago: Contemporary Books, 1979).

Friedlander, M. P., Jr., and G. Gurney, *Handbook of Successful Franchising* (New York: Van Nostrand Reinhold, 1981).

James, D. L., B. J. Walker, and M. J. Etzel, *Retailing Today* (New York: Harcourt Brace Jovanovich, 1981), chaps. 1, 6.

"Leased Departments," New York: National Retail Merchants Association, Controllers' Congress, 1965.

Seltz, D. D., *How to Get Started in Your Own Franchised Business* (Rockville Center, N.Y.: Farnsworth, 1980).

"To Lease or Not to Lease," *Retail Directions,* 129 (March-April 1975), pp. 27–28.

Vaughn, C. L., *Franchising* (Lexington, Mass.: Heath, 1974).

# chapter 7
# RETAIL INSTITUTIONS, BY MERCHANDISE SOLD

After completing this chapter, you should be able to:

1  List the reasons for the classification of merchandise.
2  List four major ways of classifying merchandise and explain how they serve to identify stores.
3  Identify retail institutions according to the merchandise they carry.

In Chapter 6 you learned how retail institutions are classified by form of ownership. You saw that retail ownership assumes an astonishing variety of forms. The discussion indicated that large retail organizations are usually corporations and that small retail institutions are owned and operated as sole proprietorships, partnerships, or corporations.

In this chapter we continue our discussion of retail institutions by identifying them according to the types of merchandise they sell; again the diversity of retail outlets will be surprising. You will also be reintroduced to the "moving" wheel of retailing.

# MERCHANDISE CATEGORIES

Scrambled merchandising

One of the most significant phenomena in retailing has been the often successful attempt by merchants to widen their assortments of merchandise. We see evidence of this all around us: Supermarkets, once selling only food products, have branched into nonfood items like housewares; drugstores, traditionally offering prescriptive medicines and drug-related goods, have added an inventory of toys and games; and variety stores, previously restricted to the sale of knick-knacks, have expanded into health food products, such as vitamins. This movement toward increasing the types of goods carried in a store is known as **scrambled merchandising.** We can expect to see a continuation of this trend as merchants seek new ways to maintain or increase their share of sales.

As the variety of available goods has grown, retailers have had to put them into manageable groups for the following reasons.

1 To provide a system for record keeping, including statistics on inventories, sales, and prices.

2 To establish systems for controlling inventories and orders.

3 To organize merchandise so customers can find what they want (or acceptable substitutes).

4 To study customer buying patterns and find ways to increase sales.

The categories that retailers have developed to meet their needs are as follows.

Merchandise categories

1 **General or Limited-Line Merchandise** **General merchandise** consists of a variety of goods (e.g., clothing, home furnishings, appliances), while **limited-line merchandise** refers to goods within a particular line (e.g., ladies' wear).

2 **Staple or Fashion Goods** **Staple goods** are products that are constantly in demand and are infrequently influenced by fashion changes (e.g., pencils, shoelaces, ladders). **Fashion goods** consist of items that are popular at a particular time (e.g., miniskirts, men's vests).

3 **Seasonal Goods** **Seasonal merchandise** is usually in demand at a certain time of the year; examples are skis, bathing suits, surfboards, and Christmas decorations.

4 **Convenience, Shopping, or Specialty Goods** **Convenience goods** are items that consumers buy because of immediate and usually pressing needs (e.g., shampoo,

Scrambled merchandising in a Safeway store.

flashlights, bread). **Shopping goods** are products that consumers buy after spending time and effort to evaluate them (e.g., appliances, cars, clothing). **Specialty goods** are particular brands for which a consumer shops (e.g., Jordache jeans, Ford Mustangs, Estee Lauder perfume).

Retailers do, of course, classify merchandise in other ways, but the additional categories usually apply only to specific, internal store functions. For example, managers and buyers may sort merchandise by department, price line, color, size, or computerized inventory category. Although all of these classifications are useful, only one system can be used in classifying stores: general or limited-line.

# GENERAL-MERCHANDISE STORES

These stores carry a wide selection of goods and attempt to satisfy most of their customers' needs. Some stores, of course, stock a greater variety of merchandise than others. Included among general-merchandise stores are department stores and their offshoots (branches and twigs), discount department stores, variety stores, catalog showrooms, convenience stores, flea markets, barn stores, general stores, and some new types of general-merchandise stores.

## Department Stores

Merchandise carried by department stores

Department stores, as you have seen, consist of a collection of specialty operations under one roof, with one owner. The variety of goods carried by department stores is wider than that carried by any other kind of retail store. Some department stores carry more lines than others, but the Bureau of the Census has specified that in order to qualify as a traditional department store a retail outlet *must* sell merchandise from each of the following lines: (1) furniture, home furnishings, appliances, radio and television sets; (2) general apparel for the family; and (3) household linen and dry goods.

Department stores are run on the principle that the way to increase revenues is through high sales volume. Managers of these stores believe that sales volume depends on meeting as many consumer needs as possible. So far, this principle has been upheld. Even though some retailers believe that computerized in-home shopping may one day challenge the primacy of department stores, these stores are still the giants of retailing. What's more, other types of stores occasionally grow into department stores. This happens when a limited-line store scrambles its merchandise successfully and thereby appeals to a larger number of customers. As the store expands through the addition of more merchandise lines, it casts off its previous image as a variety, dry goods, or apparel store and begins to resemble a small department store. When furniture, large appliances, and other high-priced merchandise are introduced, it qualifies as a full department store.

Certain kinds of merchandise require specific selling methods. Department stores are able to capitalize on the most appropriate selling techniques by varying them from one department to another. For example, many types of goods lend themselves to self-service merchandising, but some goods, such as furniture, fine jewelry, and furs, require a more personalized approach. So, in addition to a wide variety of merchandise and one-stop shopping, department stores offer a variety of services tailored to the goods being sold.

For about 100 years department stores were located primarily in cities, where they catered to large concentrations of people. However, the population explosion and the need for new residential areas in the 1940s and 1950s affected the stores' traditional marketing strategies. Like all perceptive executives, department store managers recognized the need to meet this new challenge, so onto the retailing scene came the kinds of outlets called branches and twigs.

## Branches

When towns and cities grow, their central business districts expand and many inner-city residents eventually move to the suburbs. As growth continues, the distance between new communities and the downtown shopping center increases. Travel between the suburbs and the central city becomes complicated and inconvenient. To avoid this inconvenience, consumers begin to buy at stores in or near their neighborhoods. These stores prosper and expand their lines to meet customer demands, thereby taking more and more business away from the downtown stores.

Although downtown stores stay in business and continue to serve consumers from outlying communities as well as those in the city, they are eventually forced to find a way of following consumers to the suburbs. By observing how new communities and shopping areas develop, department store executives are usually able to identify high concentrations of potential suburban customers in specific areas. When this happens, the downtown store usually opens a **branch store** designed to meet the needs of consumers in that particular area.

Branches are scaled-down versions of department stores

Branch stores are usually scaled-down versions of the main store, but the size of any one branch depends on the population it serves and on the branch's competition. Branch stores generally cater to smaller, local populations of consumers whose needs, lifestyles, and purchasing patterns are similar and readily identified. This allows the store

Branch stores follow consumers to the suburbs.

to tailor its mix of products by concentrating on merchandise that is in frequent demand and limiting or eliminating merchandise that is not.

Because of its size and product mix limitations, a branch generally sells less than a main store; but since there is usually more than one branch, total branch sales usually exceed main store sales. In fact, two-thirds of all department store sales are branch sales.

## Twigs

Twigs are department stores' specialty stores

**Twigs** are small department store branches that stock only one kind of merchandise or perhaps several similar lines. By all rights, they should be classified as limited-line stores, but because they are part of the department store branch network, they are considered extensions of general-merchandise stores. A Sears auto center is an example of a twig.

# Discount Department Stores

Bradlees, K mart, and Caldor are discount department stores

**Discount department stores** like Caldor, Bradlees, and K mart are very much like traditional department stores in the merchandise they carry. However, the quality and price of their merchandise differ, as do the personal services they offer. Discounters sell nationally known brands below the manufacturer's suggested retail price. Like traditional department stores, discounters offer a wide variety of merchandise and one-stop shopping. Until recently discounters had a fairly wide selection of merchandise, with a narrow range of manufacturers or brands from which to choose. This was partly due to the fact

Discount department stores such as K mart offer one-stop shopping.

that some manufacturers would not sell to discount stores. They felt that their product's image would be damaged by association with discount stores, which lacked status because of their locations, the way they sold and displayed merchandise, and their lack of personal services. However, this situation no longer prevails, largely because of federal legislation such as the Sherman Antitrust Act, the Robinson-Patman Act, and the Federal Trade Commission Act. In addition, off-price retailing has grown so that manufacturers cannot ignore it.

Another reason for discounters' narrower selection of brands is rooted in their operating principle. Although discounters believe in providing customers with one-stop shopping, their biggest selling point is the savings they offer. To provide these savings, they buy in large quantities, take advantage of close-outs by manufacturers, concentrate on fast-moving merchandise, and in many instances offer no-frills service.

Because thrift is such a large selling point for discounters, they seek money-saving methods in order to pass on savings to customers. Naturally, this affects the discounter's selling methods and services. At one time discounters offered few, if any, personalized services. In order to save on salaries for salespeople, they used self-service wherever it was practical. To some extent, they still do, but today they all provide some degree of personal services. Examples of these services are gift wrapping and delivery of merchandise to customers. Also, in order to minimize costs discounters once refused to extend credit to customers, but now most discount department stores accept major credit cards like VISA and Mastercard.

Discount department stores are a far cry from the original discount stores described in Chapter 1. Departing from the exclusive sale of appliances and other hard goods, they now carry a wide assortment of general merchandise. In fact, the differences between traditional department stores and discount department stores have become so blurred that it is increasingly difficult to distinguish between the two. This is another instance of how the "wheel of retailing" turns.

An interesting departure from the discount department store's way of doing business was the successful attempt by Caldor to continue its discount practices on selected merchandise only. At the same time, Caldor tried to cast off its discounter image by selling quality brand names of both hard and soft goods. In addition, it upgraded its personal services and provided customers with department store surroundings, that is, attractive interiors, carpeting, good-looking showcases, and the like. Caldor managed to combine high management standards and a shrewd merchandising strategy with its discount operation. Making its stores accessible to small-town populations, it has developed a large number of steady customers.

Though discount department stores have managed to increase sales over the years, their profit rate has not progressed accordingly. Therefore, they must concentrate on cutting costs and investing in carefully planned merchandise assortments. Otherwise other retailers will invade their turf.

## Variety Stores

In Chapter 1 you learned that variety stores sell a wide assortment of merchandise and, according to the Bureau of the Census, carry goods in the low-to-popular price range. Because Woolworth's was probably the most successful of the variety chains, the name "five and dime store" became synonymous with variety-type outlets. As inflation eroded the reality of the name, consumers came to refer to variety stores by their names— Woolworth's, Kress, and so forth.

Though variety stores have always carried general merchandise in limited-price lines, their competition with department and specialty stores rarely extended into more expensive merchandise. However, as they tested the possibility of carrying a wider and more expensive range of goods, they found that consumers responded positively. So, in addition to maintaining loyal customers who continued to buy such low-priced items as cosmetics, hardware, and toys, variety stores were able to induce the same customers to purchase higher-priced goods. This favorable change was not without its drawbacks; the sale of higher-priced merchandise required a larger sales force to assist customers. It must be remembered that variety stores have always counted on self-service, with little or no help from cashiers.

In 1975 W. T. Grant, one of the largest variety store chains, failed and went into bankruptcy. At that time it was the largest bankruptcy in retailing history. Since most other variety stores were also chain operations, Grant's failure caused many variety store owners to reconsider their merchandising policies. In order to survive, some have re-organized and have shifted some of their outlets into discounting. Woolworth's, for example, has expanded into Woolco Department Stores, a string of successful discount operations. K mart, the country's third-largest retailer, is another notable example of this trend.

In many ways the rise and partial decline of variety stores is a classic example of how consumer buying patterns change and how competitive changes encourage or discourage different kinds of retailing and different kinds of stores.

# Catalog Showrooms

A recent addition to the wide array of retail outlets found in many communities is the **catalog showroom.** The showroom is actually a store in which customers order through catalogs. The assortment of merchandise is extensive, ranging from tennis balls to lawn equipment. In general, these stores sell nonclothing, nonfood items that can be taken home immediately upon purchase.

Many catalog showrooms have inventories of almost all catalog merchandise on the premises. Most of the merchandise that is sold is selected, ordered, paid for, and picked up in one trip. The stores have desks at which customers can examine the catalog. In some areas catalogs are mailed to consumers. To help customers, some stores have a limited number of samples on display.

The use of catalogs as a primary selling device benefits the retailer in several ways.

1 It reduces overhead costs.
2 It reduces shoplifting.
3 The catalogs are partially financed by manufacturers and wholesalers.

Catalogs reduce overhead costs by minimizing the space required to store goods for customer inspection, by reducing sales staffs, and by minimizing security needs. All merchandise, except for the samples, is kept in storage areas or stockrooms, which take up the majority of the store's space. Admittance to the stockrooms is limited to employees, so merchandise is out of the public's sight and reach. This feature alone has meant tremendous savings for the catalog store because it virtually eliminates shoplifting.

Further savings derive from the fact that catalogs are heavily financed by manufacturers and wholesalers, who often supply photographs, illustrations, and copy for them.

Though catalog showrooms received their greatest impetus during the 1970s, they started out in the early 1960s as a form of discount retailing. Their main attraction is their claim to offer low prices on housewares, appliances, jewelry, sporting goods, luggage, hand tools, garden equipment, and other medium- to high-priced merchandise.

Even though there are usually samples of some items in the store, the catalogs are heavily illustrated and contain descriptions, specifications, and other information about the merchandise. This is inherent in the nature of catalog selling because the retailer relies on the catalog instead of a salesperson or the merchandise itself to do the selling.

Though catalog showrooms burst onto the retail scene with great expectations of success, their progress slowed during the mid-1970s because of their inability to undersell other discounters consistently. Difficulties in operating the showrooms, caused by inefficient systems for getting goods to customers, also contributed to slowing the growth of these operations. However, toward the end of the decade they managed to lower their overhead below that of other retailers and once again challenged conventional discounters.

Among the many catalog showrooms in operation today are Service Merchandise Company, Best Products Company, and Consumer Distributing Company. Undoubtedly others will enter the field.

## Convenience Stores

Convenience goods are low in cost and easy to obtain

In observing consumers' buying patterns, retailers long ago recognized the special status of convenience goods. They also knew that consumers do not like to waste time shopping for these items or even to go out of their way to buy them.

Catalog showrooms grew spectacularly in the 1970s.

Convenience stores such as 7-Eleven are found in most communities.

A closer examination of these goods reveals that they share the following characteristics.

- They are inexpensive.
- They are consumed daily or frequently.
- They are purchased frequently.
- They are *easy* to sell because no measuring, matching, or trying on is required.

As retailers added line after line of these goods, they developed a special mix of merchandise that they called convenience goods, which led, of course, to the name **convenience,** or **bantam store.**

To qualify as a true convenience store, a retail outlet must be a small neighborhood store whose principal business is the sale of a balanced mix of convenience items from the following lines.

- *Food products,* such as beverages, dairy and bakery goods, frozen foods, groceries, limited produce, and delicatessen items.
- *Health and beauty aids,* such as aspirin, adhesive bandages, cough drops, soap, shampoo, combs, and shaving supplies.
- *Tobacco products* such as cigars, cigarettes, and pipe tobacco.
- *Printed materials,* such as newspapers, magazines, paperback books, and greeting cards.
- *Small housewares,* such as can openers, fuses, drinking glasses, kitchen gadgets, and small hand tools.

Many stores are called convenience stores even though they do not carry all of the items listed here.

Convenience stores operate on the principle that the way to increase profits is to maintain a high volume of sales of low-priced goods by reducing competition through convenient location and extended store hours. This is why many convenience stores stay open most hours of the day and seven days a week.

However, these are not the only means that convenience stores use to increase profits. They sometimes carry unusual items, such as prepared food, to attract customers. As a matter of fact, the addition of fast foods and prepared products like fried chicken appears to be the trend. For example, the Majik Market convenience store chain operates some 1300 units, primarily in the Southeast. Nearly all of the stores sell fast foods cooked in microwave ovens: sandwiches, soups, and stews and a breakfast menu of pancakes, eggs, and sausage. In addition, Fast Fare, Inc., a 340-unit convenience store chain operating in the Carolinas and Virginia, has opened an experimental fast-food chicken operation in Raleigh and plans to open several more. Its take-out operation has an interesting feature: Customers place their orders at the start of a cafeteria-style line and then pass along a series of self-service beverage machines before reaching the cashier.

Convenience stores keep their operating costs low by maintaining small inventories and low labor costs. This means that most of the store is devoted to display and very little space is required for storage. Since the displays are largely self-service or counter, the store can be run by one or two people whose basic job is to act as cashier. In some stores, such as delicatessens, counter service provides the bulk of the store's income. As for their percent of profits on sales, convenience stores usually do better than most other stores with similar product assortments.

For the consumer, convenience does have a price. Convenience stores usually charge more than their competitors because customers are willing to pay a little more rather than spend the extra time traveling or waiting at a checkout counter.

Convenience stores are usually either mom-and-pop or franchise operations. The largest single operator of convenience stores is Southland Corporation's 7-Eleven Stores.

# Flea Markets

*Flea markets are derived from fairs*

Strictly speaking, flea markets are fairs. As you have read, fairs have existed in one form or another since early European times. These fairs were sometimes associated with religious festivals. Today vestiges of them remain in the form of church bazaars. Most European fairs were regulated, but from time to time unregulated fairs sprang up in various districts. Goods sold at these fairs were of lesser quality and sometimes second-hand.

In addition to their low-quality goods, unregulated fairs were also known for dishonest merchants, beggars, pickpockets, and unsavory practices. One such fair, in Paris, was dubbed Marché aux Puces, or "market of fleas"; hence the term *flea market*.

In America, flea markets are enjoying a revival. While many flea market vendors are part-time merchants and on the fringes of retailing, some people have carved out careers in flea marketing, and flea markets are attracting conventional retailers.

Until recently, virtually all flea market merchandise was secondhand. Though this situation still prevails in some markets, there has been a decided trend toward selling new merchandise. As vendors have tested the market, it has become obvious that increasing numbers of consumers are willing to shop for new goods at flea markets instead of at conventional retail outlets.

*Characteristics of flea markets*

The most distinctive characteristic of a flea market is that it is composed of a collection of independent retailers who sell different lines of goods and are arranged haphazardly without regard to merchandise. The number of types of used merchandise found in flea markets is almost unlimited. Shoppers can locate anything from kitchen gadgets to cars, from clothing to books, and from craftware to stereo equipment. Many flea markets also have food and beverage stands.

Flea markets may be open permanently, for limited periods, or only on weekends. The market itself may be indoors (e.g., in an arena) or outdoors (e.g., in a drive-in theatre or a parking lot), or both. Space is rented to independent retailers, who set up stalls, tables, or other open displays.

The popularity of flea markets has risen to the point where many conventional retail stores rent space in them. For some, it is a way of attracting customers to their main store. For others, it is an inexpensive way of opening a small outlet for the sale of selected items from their main store.

Many flea market merchants purchase their goods from wholesalers. In fact, there are now wholesalers that specialize in selling merchandise to flea market operators.

# Barn Stores

Throughout retailing history certain kinds of merchandise have been considered unsuitable for selling in conventional retail outlets and have often created problems for manufacturers and merchants alike. The chart in Figure 7-1 describes these goods and indicates why they create problems for conventional stores.

| Type of Merchandise | Description | Problems for Conventional Stores |
|---|---|---|
| Factory seconds | Imperfect merchandise with manufacturing flaws | • Detracts from other merchandise<br>• Lowers image of the store |
| Distressed goods | Items that have been damaged or soiled in shipping or handling | • Detracts from other merchandise<br>• Lowers image of the store |
| Salvage goods | Shipments of goods that have been damaged in transit or storage | • Detracts from other merchandise<br>• Lowers the image of the store |
| Closeouts | Discontinued merchandise or inventories of stores that have closed or gone into bankruptcy | • Limited selections<br>• No reorders |
| Manufacturers' overruns | Quantities of custom-made articles in excess of retailers' orders | • Limited selections<br>• Specialized items<br>• No reorders |
| Abandoned goods | Unclaimed merchandise at post offices, customs offices, shippers' storehouses, etc., sometimes sold in sealed shipping cartons | • Quantities and types of goods unknown when sold in unopened containers<br>• Limited selections<br>• Specialized goods<br>• Difficult to inventory<br>• No reorders |

**FIGURE 7-1**
Barn store merchandise.

In the past, **factory seconds, distressed and salvage goods, closeouts, overruns, and abandoned goods** were customarily destroyed, discarded, sold for scrap, or given to charity. Fearful of tarnishing their image, many manufacturers and retailers preferred to destroy imperfect goods rather than allow them onto the market. Later, cost-conscious manufacturers and retailers tried to find satisfactory ways of selling these goods without damaging the reputation of the business. Some factories maintained small company stores in which they sold seconds to employees and local townspeople. Retailers experimented with basement stores in which merchandise was racked, binned, and priced for clearance. The **barn store,** also called a **bargain store,** which specializes in salvaging job lots (end-of-season manufacturer leftover merchandise) has proven a successful answer to this retailing problem. It provides an outlet for otherwise nonmarketable goods, and enables consumers to purchase goods at very low prices.

The inventory carried by barn stores is unpredictable, and there are no reorders. Barn stores buy almost anything they think they can resell. The merchandise ranges from canned goods and apparel to home furnishings and small appliances. The quality of the merchandise is usually low, but there is an occasional high-quality "find." The stores pay so little for their merchandise that they can take a high profit and still sell at a price that most consumers consider cheap. Since everything is sold as is, there are no exchanges or returns.

*Barn stores are also known as bargain stores*

## General Stores

Since this type of retail organization was discussed in the history of retailing, it will not be discussed further here. It should be recalled, however, that general stores still persist, particularly in the southwestern part of the country.

## New Types of General-Merchandise Stores

*Large, self-service stores*

The most recent types of general-merchandise stores to emerge on the retail scene are the following.

1   Box stores
    Warehouse stores
    Limited-item stores
2   Combination stores (combostores)
3   Superstores
4   Hypermarkets
5   Warehouse outlets

All of them are large and generally carry both food and nonfood products. *Box stores* include both warehouse and limited-item stores. *Warehouse stores* stock several thousand items, including limited lines of perishables and meat. They are inexpensively constructed and show high unit sales. Merchandise is displayed in cartons, and customers bag their own purchases. **Limited-item stores** carry fewer than 1000 products, with few

The exterior of a Grand Union warehouse store known as Basics.

perishables and a limited number of brands. There is no item pricing on goods, and customers bag their own purchases. **Combination stores,** sometimes called **combo-stores,** offer more services than box stores and carry full lines of food products, including perishables. In addition, they maintain substantial quantities of health, cosmetic, and drug items. These stores attempt to create one-stop shopping for customers. **Superstores** are similar to combination stores, but their inventory includes a greater proportion of food products than the combination stores. Both combination and superstores feature wide displays of general merchandise. **Hypermarkets** originated in France and Germany during the 1960s as extremely large self-service retail outlets. Forgoing fancy furnishings and fixtures, they create a warehouse setting, with 10- to 15-foot-high racks and hundreds of wire containers loaded with goods. The merchandise consists of food and nonfood items, including furniture.

The new general-merchandise stores operate on a mass sales basis. Safeway Stores, Inc., the nation's largest supermarket chain, has converted a number of its stores into no-frills discount warehouses known as Food Barns. These outlets contain the following features: Customers *bring bags and bag their own purchases* (there is a small charge for the store's bags!); cigarettes are sold by the carton only; produce comes unpackaged, and customers are charged for check cashing. The Pathmark "Super Center" in Wood-bridge, New Jersey, is one of some twenty that the chain's owner, Supermarkets General Corporation, has opened. Meijer, Inc., operates a gigantic hypermarket in Grand Rapids, Michigan, with almost seventy cashier stations. Chicago, Detroit, and several other cities contain large stores covering acres of land. Though most of these outlets now carry essentially staple products (goods for which demand is constant), in the future they may branch into higher-priced merchandise like furniture.

Some warehouse outlets specialize in a particular line of nonfood merchandise

Another type of general merchandise store is a **warehouse outlet.** It specializes in a particular line of nonfood merchandise, such as furniture, toys, or sporting goods. A typical outlet contains large quantities of merchandise (some still in cartons) ready for immediate sale. Projecting a low-price image, such no-frills operations are usually located in low-rent districts. Even though warehouses are sometimes in out-of-the-way places, consumers are attracted by the prospects of savings and immediate delivery.

Warehouses offer delivery services, but customers can avoid delivery charges and delays by taking the merchandise with them. These retailers usually do business on a cash-and-carry basis, which further lowers costs to the customer. Although minimal services provide savings to customers, some find the lack of service unsatisfactory. Also, because many items are in cartons, they are difficult to inspect, may be damaged, and may have to be returned.

The Levitz Furniture Corporation is a well-known retailer that has been successful with warehouse centers, possibly because it has showrooms connected to its warehouses. After browsing through attractive displays arranged in home settings (living rooms, bedrooms, etc.), shoppers can take immediate possession of the merchandise they purchase because it is stored on the premises.

# LIMITED-LINE STORES (SPECIALTY STORES)

Limited-line stores adopt a different strategy than general-merchandise stores. They attract customers by specializing in a particular line of merchandise (specialty goods), such as sporting goods or women's apparel, and offer extensive selections within that line.

These stores cater to a specific market and have a distinct image. They make no effort to offer one-stop shopping as general-merchandise stores do. They seek, however, to meet the special needs of customers, who often require personal service.

The outstanding characteristics of specialty stores are

1 Personalized service
2 Wide assortment of specific categories of merchandise
3 Product expertise

## Personalized Service

Understanding their markets, specialty store buyers often purchase with particular lifestyles in mind and select merchandise to meet specific customer needs and demands. Salespeople often develop one-to-one relationships with shoppers, getting to know steady customers by name.

## Wide Assortment of Specific Categories of Merchandise

Specialty stores carry limited lines of merchandise in wide assortments for a specific target market. Because they deal in fewer categories of goods, they stock these items in great depth. In fact, customers travel to these shops because they expect to find better selections. For example, a shopper looking for a particular toy or game has a much better chance of finding it at a Toys-R-Us store than in the toy department of a general-merchandise store. A golfer looking for a new set of clubs has a wide selection from which to choose at a pro shop or a sporting goods store.

# Product Expertise

Shoppers expect more from the sales help and staff in specialty stores than from employees in most general-merchandise stores. They feel that these people know more about the merchandise they sell and instill greater confidence as advisers. For example, in a shop that specializes in photography equipment and supplies, it is not uncommon for the entire staff to be well versed in the operation of the equipment. Even though shoppers expect more product knowledge from specialty store personnel, some general-merchandise stores provide similar expertise.

*Specialty stores: independents and chains*

The major competition in specialty store retailing pits independents against chain specialty stores. Chain specialty retailers have the advantage of strength through numbers. Since they are large operations, they purchase merchandise, store fixtures, and equipment in large quantities and thereby receive better prices. They also have the advantage of benefiting from wide area advertising that ranges from newspaper ads to television commercials. On a per-store basis, even the advertising is cheaper because to advertise one store is to advertise many in the chain.

# Supermarkets

*Supermarkets are limited-line, departmentalized food stores*

Although supermarkets are known largely for food products, they are classified as limited-line stores with departmentalized sections of food—dairy and meat products, produce, groceries—and many nonfood products. Even though supermarkets stock more food items than anything else, they have added so many nonfood items that they often appear to be combination food and variety stores. The nonfood merchandise commonly sold by supermarkets includes books, magazines, greeting cards, hardware, housewares, clothing and accessories, plants, and toiletries. Some of these products are provided by **rack jobbers,** wholesalers that the store allows to install and maintain displays. Rack jobbers are paid only for what is sold. The jobbers, not the store, are responsible for selecting assortments, stocking and replenishing displays, and removing outdated merchandise. Books, housewares, and toys are examples of the types of goods that rack jobbers place in stores.

Some retailers have extended their food–nonfood mix to form somewhat different types of retail outlets. Pathmark, for example, operates both supermarkets and discount drugstores. In some locations it combines the two operations and increases the number of nonfood items carried by its supermarkets.

*Supermarket sales strategy: self-service, low prices*

Supermarkets appeal to consumers on the basis of low prices. This appeal is enhanced by a wide variety of merchandise that allows one-stop shopping for *basic* household items. Self-service display is another important supermarket feature from which the consumer and the store benefit: the consumer, through faster selection of goods and lower prices; the store manager, through a reduced sales force and lower costs.

Supermarkets helped pioneer self-service retailing. Early experiments with self-service displays showed that customers were inclined to buy more if they did not have to ask for items or be advised about what to buy. Other types of retailers started to adopt self-service on the basis of supermarket's success with product displays and reduced labor costs. Unfortunately, one of the problems with self-service displays is an increase in shoplifting.

Supermarkets have also contributed to retailing in another way. They were among the first retailers to study the importance of merchandise location and the customer's movements through a store. Since then other retailers have conducted sophisticated studies in order to increase the profitability of their selling space.

While some independents have succumbed to supermarket competition, many specialty food stores, including delicatessens, bakeries, cheese stores, gourmet shops, and health food stores, have not been affected significantly. This is because their products require special handling, customized service, or a wider assortment than supermarkets can provide. Certain of these stores are even able to carry on their business next door to supermarkets. Some, however, have been co-opted into leasing departments *within* supermarkets.

**NEW TERMS**

| | |
|---|---|
| abandoned goods | general merchandise |
| bantam store | hypermarket |
| bargain store | limited-item store |
| barn store | limited-line merchandise |
| branch store | overrun |
| catalog showroom | rack jobber |
| closeout | salvage goods |
| combination store | scrambled merchandising |
| combostore | seasonal merchandise |
| convenience goods | shopping goods |
| convenience store | specialty goods |
| discount department store | staple goods |
| distressed goods | superstore |
| factory seconds | twig |
| fashion goods | warehouse outlet |

# CHAPTER HIGHLIGHTS

1 A widening of the number of types of goods carried by a store is known as scrambled merchandising.

2 Merchandise is classified as follows: general or limited line; staple or fashion; seasonal; and convenience, shopping, or specialty.

3 General-merchandise stores include department stores, discount department stores, variety stores, catalog showrooms, convenience stores, flea markets, barn stores, general stores, box stores, combination stores, superstores, and hypermarkets.

4 Many department stores have extended their operations to suburban areas by opening smaller stores called branches and twigs. Branches are scaled-down versions of the main store, while twigs stock only one kind of merchandise or several related lines.

5 Though similar in some respects to department stores, discount department stores differ from the latter in the quality and price of their merchandise as well as in the services they offer customers.

6 Variety stores sell a wide assortment of goods in the low-to-popular price range. Some also carry higher-priced merchandise.

7 Catalog showrooms are stores in which customers shop and order through catalogs. They stock nonclothing, nonfood products.

8 Convenience stores carry merchandise that is inexpensive, consumed daily or frequently, purchased frequently, and easy to sell. The merchandise includes food, health and beauty aids, tobacco products, and small housewares.

9 Flea markets consist of independent retailers who rent space indoors or outdoors in which to sell a great variety of used and new merchandise. Though most flea market merchants operate on a part-time basis, some also own conventional retail outlets.

10 Barn stores, also known as bargain stores, sell factory seconds, distressed and salvage goods, closeouts, manufacturers' overruns, and abandoned goods at low prices.

11 Large self-service retail outlets that sell food and nonfood products include box stores, combination stores, superstores, hypermarkets, and warehouse outlets.

12 Limited-line (specialty) stores specialize in a particular line of merchandise. They compete with general-merchandise stores by offering wide assortments within their product line, rendering personal services to their customers, and maintaining product expertise.

13 Supermarkets use self-service techniques to sell food and nonfood products at low cost. Despite encroachment by supermarkets, independent specialty food stores continue to thrive.

# QUESTIONS

1 How do shopping goods differ from convenience goods?

2 What was the main reason for the development of department store branches and twigs?

3 How are today's discount department stores different from the original discount stores of the 1940s and 1950s?

4 Why do combination stores qualify as general-merchandise stores?

5 How did variety stores respond to changing consumer buying patterns?

6 How does the use of catalogs as a primary selling device benefit catalog showroom retailers?

7 What methods do convenience stores use to remain competitive?

8 Why do conventional retailers sometimes expand their operations by renting space in flea markets?

9 Why are barn stores also known as bargain stores?

10 What is the basic difference between a limited-line store and a general-merchandise store?

11 In what ways have supermarkets pioneered new retailing practices?

# FIELD PROJECTS

1 Your community probably contains one or more of each of the following types of retail outlets.
   department store
   discount department store
   variety store
   supermarket
   box store (warehouse or limited-item)
   convenience store
   Visit three of these types of stores and compare the following.
   a The prices of the following products:
      100-watt lightbulb
      7-ounce tube of toothpaste
      14-ounce can of baby powder
   b The types of personal services they offer—for example, credit cards, delivery service, and so on.

2 The number of flea markets in this country has risen dramatically in the past few years. In addition, flea market vendors sell a greater variety of merchandise than in previous years. In fact, consumers who are first-time visitors to flea markets are usually surprised by the extent of their product mix. Visit a flea market and compile a list of the types of merchandise sold there (e.g., men's sportswear, hardware, furniture).

# CASES

1 For the consumer, the opportunity to save money is the chief motivation for shopping in no-frills stores, such as box stores. The customer is willing to forgo services (e.g., no bagging and limited variety) in order to keep prices to a minimum. As a result, the no-frills stores are making a dent in the traditional supermarket business.

   This situation has caused supermarket executives to examine innovative ways to meet the competition. Recognizing the impact of the "wheel of retailing," they are anxious to develop retailing strategies to retain and expand their customer base.

   a If you were a traditional supermarket owner, how would you attempt to retain a competitive advantage over these innovative stores?
   b What disadvantages do no-frills retailers face? How do these owners maintain a competitive advantage?

**2**   The Lorna Corporation is a large convenience store chain with hundreds of stores and self-service gasoline stations, largely in the Northeast and Southwest. In an effort to widen its customer base, the company is considering starting a fast-food service selling chicken parts and chicken-related foods. At present the stores do not sell chicken products.

Though Lorna has had no experience in the fast-food field, its management is confident that it can organize a successful operation. Much of this confidence is based on the recent offering of similar services by other convenience store chains. Prior to starting the new service, however, the company intends to study the situation.

    **a**   What possible problems should Lorna's management consider in its study?

    **b**   How might the introduction of chicken products affect the store's present merchandise selection?

**3**   Eddie Bauer, Inc., one of the country's largest retailers of quality outdoor clothing and gear, is part of the specialty retail division of General Mills, Inc. Second in sales only to L. L. Bean, a mail order firm that sells similar items, Bauer developed its reputation as a limited-line outlet with one store and a mail order business. So desirable were its products that the U.S. Army Air Corps outfitted much of its personnel in Bauer clothing during World War II.

When General Mills bought the Bauer company in 1971, it broadened the firm's product line to include summer sportswear to accompany its long-established camping and related clothing assortments. Contrary to expectations, such specialty items as tennis and golf garments sold poorly and were eventually discontinued. However, the firm continued to sell summer clothing of an all-around nature.

Most of Bauer's customers are well-to-do people who have continued their families' custom of purchasing Bauer products. Though they have responded favorably to General Mills' broadening of Bauer's outdoor-product lines, they have been less than enthusiastic about the firm's extension to specialty summer wear.

    **a**   What may have accounted for the failure of Bauer's attempt to establish a specialty summer line?

    **b**   Why has Bauer's been successful in widening its traditional outdoor-merchandise lines?

# REFERENCES

Bergmann, J., "See How They Grow: Expansion Plans," *Stores,* 63 (August 1981), pp. 9–11.

Brand, E. A., *Modern Supermarket Operation* (New York: Fairchild, 1963).

Brownstone, D. L., *How to Run a Specialty Food Store* (New York: Wiley, 1978).

Bucklin, L. P., "Technological Change and Store Operations: The Supermarket Case," *Journal of Retailing,* 56 (Spring 1980), pp. 3–15.

"Catalog Showrooms: Strange Bedfellows," *Retail Directions,* 127 (April-May 1973), pp. 32–33.

"Discounters: Holding Their Own," *Retailweek,* November 1, 1979, pp. 14–16.

Gill, P., "How Stores Are Seeking to Enter New Businesses," *Stores,* 63 (July 1981), pp. 40, 41, 43.

Hirschman, E. C., "Intratype Competition Among Department Stores," *Journal of Retailing,* 55 (Winter 1979), pp. 20–34.

King, C. W., and L. J. Ring, "Market Positioning Across Retail Fashion Institutions: A Comparative Analysis of Store Types," *Journal of Retailing,* 56 (Spring 1980), pp. 37–55.

Korgaonkar, P. K., "Shopping Orientations of Catalog Showroom Patrons," *Journal of Retailing,* 57 (Spring 1981), pp. 78–90.

Le Bernardi, J. M., *The Catalog Showroom Formula* (New York: Chain Store Age Books, 1974).

*Merchandising Problems in Opening the New Branch Store* (New York: National Retail Merchants Association, Merchandising Division, 1969).

Moldafsky, A., *The Good Buy Book* (Chicago: Rand McNally, 1980).

Stanton, E. M., *Branch Stores: A Complete Branch Store Operating Guide* (New York: National Retail Dry Goods Association, 1955).

# chapter 8
# RETAIL INSTITUTIONS, BY NONSTORE SELLING METHODS

After completing this chapter, you should be able to:

**1** Explain nonstore selling methods: door-to-door retailing, party plans, vending machines, mail order retailing, catalog retailing, telephone selling, and electronic retailing.

**2** Identify services sold by retailers.

# NONSTORE
# SELLING METHODS

In Chapters 6 and 7 we identified retail institutions by ownership and types of merchandise sold. We saw that in both categories selling takes place in stores or in physical settings that are closely related to stores. However, retailing includes methods of selling that do not require stores; hence the description "nonstore" selling. These methods include door-to-door retailing, party plans, vending machines, mail order retailing, catalog retailing, telephone selling, and electronic retailing.

## Door-to-Door Retailing

*Door-to-door selling is also called direct sales*

As a method of retailing, **door-to-door selling,** also called **direct sales,** can be traced back to the itinerant peddler. In analyzing this form of retailing, it is interesting to note its major, though perhaps obvious, underlying assumption: that there is a large consumer population that is, by choice or circumstance, at home most of the time. At one time this population consisted mostly of mothers, homemakers, disabled people, and retirees. But affluence, technology, the large-scale entry of women into the labor force, and the development of alternate lifestyles have led to greater mobility for each of these groups and for the population at large. Consequently, with fewer people at home at predictable times, these person-to-person salespeople have had to adjust their selling schedules.

Though products sold door-to-door have been oriented more toward women, today's changing lifestyles have directed merchandise to both sexes. Typical products are cosmetics, vacuum cleaners, small housewares, encyclopedias, dairy products, newspapers, and clothing.

*Canvassing, route selling, and consultive appointments are types of door-to-door retailing*

In door-to-door retailing there are three principal methods of selling: canvassing, route selling, and consultive appointments. **Canvassing** is the method most people think of when they hear the term door-to-door selling. Canvassing is usually a one-time effort by a salesperson to cover an entire area. Vacuum cleaners, encyclopedias, and other infrequently purchased specialty items are usually sold by this method. In this kind of selling, the salesperson commonly makes what is known as a cold call. That is, the salesperson arrives unannounced at each home and makes a "sales pitch"—a planned speech emphasizing product benefits. In one way or another the salesperson must earn the right to continue until the customer accepts the offer. The salesperson may then attempt to expand the sale to cover additional items or close the sale and take the order.

In a variation of this type of selling, the retailer or salesperson screens customers by telephone to qualify them as prospects. This is a useful technique for two reasons. First, it eliminates cold-call resistance. Though some cold calls may interrupt consumers at inconvenient times, others are receptive to visits from salespeople. Screening allows the salesperson to arrange sales calls at times that are convenient to prospects. Since rising crime rates have made people wary of unknown visitors, screening serves to introduce the salesperson and prepare the consumer for the visit.

Second, screening reduces the high costs of travel and increases the productivity of door-to-door selling by identifying people who may be receptive to a call and eliminating those who will not be receptive at all. For those who are interested, a convenient

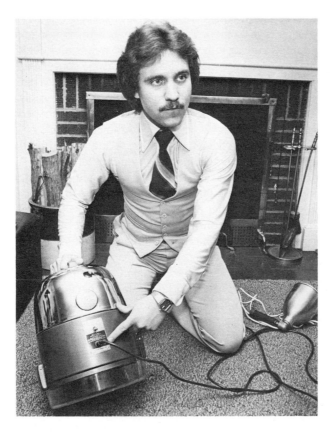

Through canvassing, this salesman is able to demonstrate his product in a home.

time can be arranged; in addition, the salesperson can manage his or her time more effectively by scheduling several calls in the same area on the same day.

Many reputable businesses, such as World Book, Inc. (World Book Encyclopedias) and Consolidated Foods (Electrolux vacuum cleaners), continue to do business in this way. However, some disreputable individuals and firms have created problems for these companies by misrepresenting products or payment terms. This has led to legal restrictions on door-to-door retailing in some areas and a low image of some products.

**Route selling** is a method of door-to-door selling that is used by retailers who sell frequently purchased convenience items like newspapers, cosmetics, and food products. In the past, route selling was the accepted means of selling certain products. As late as the 1950s many people still had standing orders with milkmen who represented dairy firms and delivered daily. Some small produce retailers also used trucks or horse-drawn wagons to sell to customers along regular routes. Jewel Tea Company, a food and home products company, once sold its products in this way. So did Dugan's, a baker retailer. Newspapers are another item that is still sold on a route.

Route salespeople are generally order takers. Their products are presold because of local custom or reputation. Owing to the availability of other retail outlets, however, route selling is on the decline.

**Consultive appointments** involve consultive selling. This is not just a door-to-door selling technique. It is a method of selling in which the salesperson consults with the consumer to identify the consumer's problems or needs and determine what products and services will satisfy those needs. For this reason, consultive selling is sometimes called the needs-satisfaction approach. It differs from the "sales pitch," which the salesperson delivers regardless of the consumer's response. Consultive selling is a dialog between buyer and seller, and the direction of the dialog is shaped by the salesperson, who modifies his or her approach according to the consumer's response.

Among door-to-door retailers, consultive selling is used by decorator consultants who work for home furnishing businesses or department stores. Although these salespeople usually operate out of a store, their operations are still considered a type of door-to-door retailing. And though they sell in the consumer's home, the interaction is almost always initiated by the consumer and a home visit arranged *at the consumer's request.* Decorator consultants usually consult about and sell upholstery, drapes, floor coverings, and other custom work that requires measurement, estimates, and selection of materials. Although these decorator consultants may appear to be order takers or service personnel, they are in fact order getters because part of their job is to be sensitive to the customer's surroundings and to expand the sale whenever possible.

Ethical door-to-door retailing benefits consumers by providing convenient, personalized service and complete demonstrations in a relaxed atmosphere that is familiar to the consumer. Psychologists and researchers also point out that in this situation the consumer is in a position of greater power than in many store environments. However, the salesperson still controls the direction of the interaction.

*Career opportunities in door-to-door selling*

Though door-to-door selling is distasteful to many would-be salespeople, it does offer a challenge and an opportunity for people with outgoing personalities. The selling can be done full or part time; attractive incentives are offered by direct-sales companies; and management opportunities are available to successful salespeople. Managers receive commissions on their own sales plus additional commissions on sales by representatives whom they have recruited.

## Party Plans

*How party plan selling works*

Cold-call resistance, greater consumer mobility, and low sales force productivity caused some traditional door-to-door retailers to update their selling methods. Their response to these difficulties was the **party plan,** a direct-sales method of retailing in which a salesperson enlists the aid of one consumer in selling to others within a community. Party plans usually work something like this. A community resident becomes a sales representative or dealer for a party plan retailer. He or she then invites friends to their home for refreshments and a presentation or demonstration of the products.

At the party the dealer delivers a planned talk (lecture–demonstration) about the product or products. After the presentation the dealer takes orders and approaches interested guests about hosting parties for other friends. In exchange for giving a party, the dealer offers the hostess-to-be a collection of selected items from the line, plus assistance with party preparations. Dealers and the distributors who supervise them receive commissions on party plan sales, but the consumer–host(esses) receive merchandise. In addition to commissions, some companies offer bonuses to dealers who reach sales goals.

The problem with party plan retailing is high turnover in the sales force. Unless dealers receive adequate training and are committed to selling as an occupation, they often quit after selling to their immediate circle of friends. Local markets are quickly saturated, and dealers have to travel longer and longer distances to reach new customers. Also, the further a dealer travels from her community, the more resistance she is likely to meet because she is not well known.

Mary Kay Cosmetics and Vanda sell cosmetics and beauty aids through party plans. Tupperware, a division of Dart Industries, uses party plan retailing to sell household plastic goods. Stanley Home Products distributes household products in this way.

Career opportunities in party plan retailing

Party plan selling accounts for something under 20 percent of direct sales. Started by Stanley Home Products a half-century ago, it provides hundreds of thousands of ambitious people with an opportunity to supplement their incomes on a full- or part-time basis. As with door-to-door retailing, successful party plan dealers are eligible for attractive management positions in their firms.

In order to serve the public interest and promote the direct selling method of retailing, leading firms involved in marketing through independent salespeople conduct activities (e.g., consumer advocacy, legislation) via the Direct Selling Association. The salespeople involved use party plans and other person-to-person methods to reach consumers.

# Vending Machines

As retailers added impulse and convenience items to their lines, they found that they spent the same amount of time collecting money, making change, and recording transactions for low- as for higher-priced items. In many cases this caused difficulties because of the cost and effort involved. The invention of **vending machines** helped retailers minimize this problem.

The history of vending machines

Early automated vending machines dispensed small quantities of a single item, such as candy, gum, or nuts, that sold for a penny. The machines were placed near cashiers so that customers who needed change could get it. For the cashier, the occasional service of making change involved less time than a full sales transaction, and customers could still be served quickly.

Some retailers found that they already had dispensing machines that could be automated. Nickelodeons were early hand-cranked "movie theater" machines that dispensed entertainment in the form of rapidly changing cards. Operators of nickelodeons charged a general admission fee (five cents—hence the name *nickelodeon*), and customers were free to wander about and view a different show in each machine. The development of coin-operated machines allowed these retailers to increase sales by charging each time a show was viewed. As the popularity of the machines increased, nickelodeon owners added other amusement devices, such as music boxes and fortune-telling machines. Eventually the wider assortments and one-cent machine prices gave rise to the name *penny arcade.*

In tourist areas other enterprising retailers took advantage of the developing technology and installed pay telescopes and binoculars. Telephone companies began selling their services through pay telephones. Advances in refrigeration led to the development of machines that dispensed cold soft drinks in bottles.

As the technology expanded, so did the lines of products sold in vending machines. Retailers installed machines in transportation and entertainment centers, stores, and other service establishments, and eventually in factories, business offices, hospitals, and schools. Today there are vending machines that sell goods like handkerchiefs, combs, paperbacks, aspirin, toiletries, newspapers, snacks, and other food products. Other vending machines sell such services as shoeshines, photocopying, and rides for children.

Some stores have installed vending machines in areas that are accessible to shoppers after the store has closed. Retailers in Europe, primarily Germany, Austria, and Switzerland, have installed large machines that sell hundreds of items. In Sweden retailers have even experimented with fully automated stores.

For retailers, the advantages of vending machines are as follows.

*Advantages and disadvantages of vending machine retailing*

1 They eliminate the need for salespeople and cashiers.
2 They are always open for business.
3 They may be located indoors or outdoors.
4 They can be installed where other types of selling would be disruptive or prohibitive.

Although vending-machine retailing has merit, it also has disadvantages. First of all, vending machines require maintenance. Even when they are well maintained, breakdowns are inevitable. Unless machines are checked regularly, broken ones can sit idle—and unprofitable—for long periods. Second, most vending machines in the past were stocked with low-cost, low-quality convenience items. This gave vending-machine merchandise a poor image. Third, machines require correct change, and while some machines give change, many do not. Finally, the inability to inspect or exchange goods has caused many customers to resist buying items from a vending machine.

The future of vending machines is uncertain and will depend on developing technologies and new retailing techniques. However, the sales statistics for this form of retailing are impressive. In 1980 vending-machine sales amounted to about $14 billion. Soft drinks and tobacco products accounted for about 60 percent of this total.

## Mail Order Retailing

**Mail order retailing** developed as a means of selling to customers over a wide geographic area without the use of stores or a field sales force. Using this retailing method, mail order merchants were able to minimize the overhead costs arising from store operations and sales salaries. Selling was oriented toward consumers in isolated areas whose needs could not be satisfied by distant stores.

Mail order retailers provided customers with catalogs from which they could select merchandise. Customers placed their orders by mail, and the merchandise was usually delivered in the same way. There have been many changes in mail order retailing since its early days, but the following characteristics still allow it to qualify as a special category of retailing.

1 Customers use published materials or direct-mail offerings to shop or preshop for merchandise.

2   Customers place orders with the mail order retailer.

3   The retailer arranges for delivery of the goods to the consumer.

Early mail order retailing relied almost exclusively on catalogs. Today mail order retailers inform customers about merchandise and solicit orders in several ways. In addition to catalogs, they utilize magazines, newspapers, direct mail, clubs-of-the-month, and television. Although the use of these media has increased mail order sales, catalogs are still responsible for the majority of those sales.

Mail order retailers handle very narrow to very wide assortments of merchandise. General mail order houses are the mail order equivalent of general-merchandise stores. They carry assortments of merchandise as wide as those at some department stores. In fact, three of the four top mail order companies—Sears, J. C. Penney, and Montgomery Ward (Speigel is the fourth)—also operate department store chains. Special-line mail order houses, on the other hand, correspond to specialty stores.

By the 1920s automobiles and better roads had reduced the need and demand for mail order retailing, and many companies failed. Others like Sears, Roebuck and Montgomery Ward, had stronger market positions and survived by changing their lines to appeal to more urban markets. At the same time that they established this new image, these companies also opened catalog stores and department store chains and branches. J. C. Penney, on the other hand, was originally a department store. It developed plans for mail order retailing in the early 1960s, partly to expand its services and partly to enable it to broaden its assortment of merchandise. In 1966 it bought a small mail order business and put desks in its stores to take catalog orders. Unlike Sears and Montgomery Ward, Penney did not open catalog stores. It simply found a good way to expand in-store lines without enlarging its stores, buying real estate, or otherwise increasing in-store overhead. Penney's experiment proved successful.

Unlike the top three mail order retailers, Speigel maintains catalog stores and some small variety stores, but does not at present have a department store chain. Together, the four leading mail order companies account for 75 percent of all mail order sales.

The quality of general mail order house merchandise is good. It ranges from inexpensive items like handkerchiefs to hard goods and artworks that cost thousands of dollars. Special-line mail order houses are smaller than general houses and specialize in limited lines of goods like apparel, home furnishings, gift items, craft materials, novelties, food items, records, and books. Some of the better known of these houses are Horchow Mail Order, Inc., Sunset House, and Publishers Central Bureau. Like Penney's, some specialty stores, such as Lane Bryant, have set up mail order operations.

Mail order retailing is not limited to goods. Certain kinds of services lend themselves to mail order retailing, too. Insurance companies, photographic film developers, printers, and even astrologists sell services by mail.

Although increased consumer mobility caused a decline in retail mail order sales in rural areas, it had the opposite effect in urban areas. Increased mobility led to traffic congestion in downtown shopping areas. Fuel costs, parking problems, and new lifestyles led urban consumers to seek more flexible and convenient ways of shopping. Mail order retailing provided them.

## Advantages of Mail Order Retailing for Consumers

Mail order retailing offers the following benefits to consumers.

The covers of the Horchow and L. L. Bean catalogs. These firms are well-known specialty mail order retailers.

Advantages and disadvantages of mail order retailing

1   It saves the consumer time.

2   Catalogs usually offer a wider selection of merchandise than can be found in most stores.

3   Mail order houses guarantee customer satisfaction.

### Disadvantages of Mail Order Retailing for Consumers

From the customer's point of view, the disadvantages of mail order retailing are as follows.

1   Consumers cannot inspect goods prior to purchasing them.

2   Consumers must fill out forms and compute charges.

3   Consumers must arrange for deliveries and returns.

### Advantages of Mail Order Retailing for Retailers

Retailers derive the following advantages from mail order retailing.

1   The business is operated out of inexpensive warehouses.

2   It allows retailers to reach wider geographic areas.

3   It enables stores with mail order features to reach additional consumers.

4   Salespeople are replaced by lower-paid clerks.

5   Special seasonal catalogs stimulate sales. The Christmas catalogs of Neiman-Marcus and FAO Schwarz (toys and games) are widely admired.

### Disadvantages of Mail Order Retailing for Retailers
The disadvantages of mail order retailing for retailers include the following.

1 Catalogs are expensive to produce.
2 Catalogs become outdated and cause problems for both consumers and retailers.
3 Increased mailing costs have resulted in higher catalog prices.

Mail order businesses have sometimes been used as a means of defrauding consumers. This has created a bad reputation, which legitimate mail order businesses have had to fight to overcome. It has also led to strict government regulations about the use of the mails to do business.

# Catalog Retailing

Although selling through catalogs is a long-standing practice, it has expanded recently because of an increase in the number of working women, the impact of gasoline price hikes, and the growing popularity of nonstore retailing. As evidenced at the National Retail Merchants Association's 71st Annual Convention and the Retailers Business & Equipment Exposition in January 1982, retailers are studying new techniques in order to reach more people with catalogs.

After receiving a catalog from a firm, the consumer studies its contents and orders merchandise according to the retailer's instructions for purchasing. Catalogs may contain general, specialty, or seasonal merchandise assortments. For example, Sears publishes a general catalog of more than 1000 pages as well as specialty catalogs of a few hundred pages.

J. C. Penney and Sears publish general catalogs, left, and reach additional customers through seasonal specialty catalogs, right.

While a retailer's costs and selling prices are lower with **catalog retailing,** the firm must contend with more frequent merchandise returns as well as different notification techniques for announcing price changes.

Although still in the experimental stage, we can look forward to a modified catalog retailing system in which merchandise specifications are contained on video discs. The consumer will select items by using a hookup between the discs and the home TV set.

## Telephone Selling

In the early 1900s many small retailers accepted telephone orders and delivered merchandise to customers. However, **telephone selling** was not widely used until the 1930s. Today many mail order houses have toll-free long-distance numbers that customers may use to place orders.

*Department stores use telephone selling methods*

Many department stores that are closed on Sundays keep their switchboards and order departments open to handle responses to ads on special catalog and newspaper offerings. Other stores list special numbers and have orders taken by a service. Still other stores, such as Simpson-Sears in Canada, have made arrangements through which owners of touch-tone phones can call in orders and communicate directly with the store's computer.

When retailers take the initiative in reaching customers by telephone, solicitations must be handled carefully. Otherwise the salesperson may encounter cold-call problems and resistance. To avoid this, some stores have salespeople initiate calls by offering to extend credit to the potential customer in the form of a store card or by calling customers to revive inactive credit accounts. Consumers sometimes resist telephone solicitations because unethical companies and overly aggressive salespeople have abused this method of selling.

## Electronic Retailing

Technological advances like two-way cable television, videophones, and personal computers will undoubtedly affect retailing in drastic ways. Experiments with these communication media are being conducted today, but the costs involved and the limited amount of equipment in consumers' homes make **electronic retailing** impractical at present.

However, someday customers will be able to view merchandise and demonstrations on command by calling up tapes or files to be displayed on television monitors in their homes. When ready to place an order, the customer will communicate directly with a store's computer, which will record the sale and process the order. Touch-sensitive panels on television screens may even eliminate the need for customers to do anything but check the items they want.

## SERVICES SOLD BY RETAILERS

We identify retailers that sell services rather than goods by the types of services they offer. The major classifications of services are

Categories of services sold by retailers

1 Rentals.

2 Repairs, maintenance, and custom work.

3 Personal services.

Figure 8-1 lists examples of each type of service. The examples shown for rentals are only a small part of what consumers can actually rent. The cost of rentals ranges from low prices for power tools to much higher ones for automobiles. The examples for the remaining two categories can be expanded considerably, too.

Though some retailers sell only services, others sell goods *and* services. For example, department stores frequently maintain hair styling salons in addition to their merchandise departments. Many car dealers lease vehicles as well as sell them. Movie theatres sell candy and other items to augment their income from films. And so on.

Well-known service retailers include H & R Block, the "income tax people," Arthur Murray Studios, a school for dance instruction; Century 21, a real estate firm; and Jack LaLanne Health Spas. An interesting retailing service that developed in the 1950s involves home and building inspections. Started by Arthur Tauscher, a professional engineer in Rockville Centre, New York, this type of business has mushroomed in both numbers and popularity. In fact, Tauscher now has more than thirty franchises across the country. Other firms in this field include Nationwide Real Estate Inspection Service, Inc., and Accurate Building Inspectors. A more detailed treatment of service retailing is contained in Chapter 26.

| Category | Examples |
| --- | --- |
| Rentals | Apartments |
| | Automobiles |
| | Costumes |
| | Formal attire |
| | Furniture |
| | Hotels |
| | Power tools |
| Repairs, maintenance, and custom work | Dry cleaning |
| | Interior decorating |
| | Lawn care |
| | Plumbing |
| | Shoe repair |
| | Television repair |
| | Upholstering |
| Personal services | Accounting |
| | Child care |
| | Hair styling |
| | Medical care |
| | Restaurants |
| | Teaching |
| | Theatres |

**FIGURE 8-1**
Retail services.

Arthur Tauscher, founder of a franchised home and building inspection service, examining a building for a client.

**NEW TERMS**

canvassing

catalog retailing

consultive appointment

direct sales

door-to-door selling

electronic retailing

mail order retailing

party plan

route selling

telephone selling

vending machine

# CHAPTER HIGHLIGHTS

1   Nonstore selling methods include door-to-door and party plan retailing, vending machines, mail order techniques, catalog retailing, telephone selling, and electronic retailing.

2   Door-to-door retailing includes three principal methods of selling: canvassing, route selling, and consultive appointments.

3   In party plan selling, a community resident becomes a sales representative for a party plan retailer. Selling to friends takes place at the representative's home, and further parties are arranged through friends who indicate interest.

4  A vending machine is an automated piece of equipment that dispenses a wide variety of goods and services. Soft drinks and tobacco products account for most vending-machine sales.

5  Mail order retailing is carried on by general mail order firms like Sears, Roebuck and Montgomery Ward and by special-line mail order houses like Horchow Mail Order, Inc., and Sunset House.

6  Mail order retailing involves the sale of services as well as goods.

7  Catalog retailing has expanded, and plans are being made to conduct it through video discs.

8  Telephone selling is a feature of both mail order and store retailing.

9  Electronic retailing, though in its infancy, contains promise for the sale of goods and services through store–home communications. It will probably involve computers and video equipment.

10  Services sold by retailers include rentals (e.g., hotel rooms and automobiles), repairs (e.g., television sets), maintenance work (e.g., lawn care), custom work (e.g., upholstering), and personal services (e.g., accounting and hair styling).

## QUESTIONS

1  What is the major assumption underlying the attractiveness of door-to-door selling as a retail method?

2  Of what value is screening in door-to-door selling?

3  Why is consultive selling described as "a dialog between buyer and seller"?

4  With regard to maintaining a sales force, what is the main problem of party plan selling?

5  What advantages do vending-machine operators have over other types of retailers?

6  What do you foresee as the future of vending-machine retailing? Why?

7  Why did J.C. Penney enter the mail order business? Why did it prove successful?

8  How has consumer mobility affected mail order retailing in urban areas?

9  Do you think electronic retailing will be accepted by consumers in this country? Why?

10  Identify the three categories of services sold by retailers and give an example of each.

## FIELD PROJECTS

1  The purpose of this project is to enable you to learn about party plan selling at first hand. Ask your parents, relatives, or friends if they know someone who is or has been a party plan representative. Try to arrange an interview with the representative to determine the following.

   a  How the representative became involved in party plan selling.

   b   What happened at the first sales party.
   c   The basis on which the representative receives compensation.

2  As you have read in this chapter, vending machines account for about $14 billion in annual retail sales. They can be seen in every community of our nation. Check your school to determine
   a   The types of merchandise sold from the school's vending machines.
   b   The number of vending machines in the school.

# CASES

1  One of the problems facing direct-sales retailers is the large turnover of sales representatives. It has been estimated that of the 4 million people who sell from door to door or at parties each year, only half of them are active salespeople at any one time during the year. Though many of the inactive representatives assume active roles from time to time, the instability of the work force requires direct-sales companies to maintain costly recruitment programs.

The Brooke Walde Company, a direct-sales jewelry retailer whose representatives either canvass or conduct house parties, is anxious to reduce its high rate of labor attrition. The firm has decided to engage an outside consultant for advice.

   a   What information about the company's target market should the consultant seek?
   b   What additional data regarding direct-sales retailing of jewelry might the company provide?
   c   How might the consultant determine the reasons for the company's labor attrition?

2  Vending-machine sales show a direct correlation with the state of the economy. When times are good, sales are up; when there is a downturn, sales decrease. The vending-machine areas that are affected most severely by a faltering economy are those that contain large concentrations of industrial workers. On the other hand, the effects are much less severe in suburban and rural areas and those with large numbers of office workers.

The Ven-Mac Company, which is located in a large midwestern industrial area, dispenses food and variety items from 2000 machines located in factories, schools, and theatres. Having been hurt during the last recession, the firm wants to minimize the damage from future economic downturns.

   a   Might a change in its merchandise mix help the company's sales during periods when economic conditions are poor? How?
   b   Should the company consider the adoption of service-type vending machines to augment its present equipment? Why?

3  Telecommunications, combined with other advanced technologies, can transform retailing from stores to nonstore systems. The rapid growth of nonstore retailing is beginning to take a large share of sales away from the traditional stores. In fact, according

to Davidson and Rodgers, nonstore sales have expanded much faster than sales by traditional stores.[1]

Reasons for the growth of nonstore selling include

- Exclusive offering through TV of many products, such as hardware specialties, records, and the like.
- Increased use of catalog shopping.
- Increase in mail shopping using credit cards.
- Large volume of telephone and mail-order retailing done by traditional stores.
- Experimental use of cable TV to order merchandise.

Advanced technology has made it possible for customers to shop at home for a variety of products. The use of the computer and an in-home video catalog will make it possible for consumers to order goods and services. Retailers equipped to do business via telecommunication merchandising systems will be ready to deliver merchandise without seeing the customer.

Warner Communications has invested approximately $14 million in its Qube division, which offers goods and services to the consumer via cable TV. Qube is an experiment in this type of retailing. It is being used in approximately 30,000 households in the Columbus, Ohio, area, with expansion to other areas in sight. All socioeconomic groups are represented in the Qube population, which parallels the nation's demographic composition.

The consumer pays $11 per month for the service. Retailers who have advertised and participated in this system include Lazarus department stores and American Express. A growing number of consumers appear to be interested in the system for a variety of reasons.

- It is a time-saving convenience.
- Television clearly illustrates the product in action.
- It saves the cost of car use and gasoline.
- Consumers can avoid crowded shopping areas and the carrying of products from stores to home.

Furthermore, in-home use of several catalogs is an ideal way to comparison shop.

In conclusion, if cable TV systems offer consumers the possibility of ordering at home, having the product delivered, and paying through financial transfer systems, all that is needed to produce a retail revolution is large-scale acceptance of nonstore shopping by consumers.

a  What will be the effect on traditional retailing of the emergence of two-way cable TV retailing systems?

b  What effect will the system have on small, independent stores that sell convenience products?

c  How might the physical structure of communities and cities change if stores are no longer needed?

[1]William R. Davidson and Alice Rodgers, "Non-Store Retailing: Its Importance to and Impact on Merchandise Suppliers," in *The Growth of Non-Store Retailing* (New York: New York University, Institute of Retail Management, 1979).

    **d** As consumers place more value on their time, which types of stores might be endangered most?

    **e** Can this system really replace personal shopping? Consider that many people view shopping as a social activity as well as a necessity. Explain fully.

# REFERENCES

"Avon's Part in the Beauty Business," *Stores,* 63 (September 1981), p. 63.

Berkowitz, E. N., J. R. Walton, and O. C. Walker, Jr., "In-Home Shoppers: The Market for Innovative Distribution Systems," *Journal of Retailing,* 55 (Summer 1979), pp. 15–33.

Davis, D. L., J. P. Guiltinan, and W. H. Jones, "Service Characteristics, Consumer Research, and the Classification of Retail Services," *Journal of Retailing,* 55 (Fall 1979), pp. 3–23.

Gillett, P. L., "A Profile of Urban In-Home Shoppers," *Journal of Marketing,* 34 (July 1970), pp. 40–45.

Greenberg, J., M. T. Topol, E. Sherman, and K. Cooperman, "The Itinerant Street Vendor: A Form of Non-Store Selling," *Journal of Retailing,* 56 (Summer 1980), pp. 66–80.

James, D. L., B. J. Walker, and M. J. Etzel, *Retailing Today* (New York: Harcourt Brace Jovanovich, 1981), chap. 20.

Marks, N. E., *Vending Machines: Introduction and Innovation* (Austin: University of Texas at Austin, Bureau of Business Research, 1969).

"1976 Mail Order Sales Rose 13.8 Per Cent to $19.2 Billion, Sroge Reports," *Marketing News,* 11 (November 1977), p. 3.

Scott, W., *How to Make Big Profits in Service Businesses* (Englewood Cliffs, N.J.: Parker, 1977).

Spalding, L. A., "B(uy) the Book!," *Stores,* 62 (May 1980), pp. 11–16.

"Teleshopping: The Future Is Now!," *Stores,* 62 (September 1980), pp. 71–72.

Weil, G. L., *Sears, Roebuck, U.S.A.* (New York: Stein and Day, 1977).

# chapter 9
# ORGANIZING THE STORE

After completing this chapter, you should be able to:

1 Differentiate between line and line-and-staff organizations.
2 Explain store organizations for small retailers, department stores, branch stores, and chain stores.
3 Distinguish between centralization and decentralization of store management.
4 Identify informal and formal methods of communication.

A retailer's prime objective

It is safe to say that the primary objective of any firm is to be successful. It is difficult to imagine a merchant beginning an operation with any other intent. But what does "successful" mean to a retailer? If retailing involves the selling of goods and services to the ultimate consumer, it follows that successful retailers satisfy the wants and needs of their customers and thereby earn a fair profit.

For retailers to achieve their primary objective, an organizational structure must be developed. Answers to the following questions must be secured: Who will actually do the work? Who has the overall responsibility? In what order are things to be done? To whom does each worker report?

As a retail store expands, organization is vital

Some organizational structures develop as companies grow. For example, the owner of a small retail shop is generally in charge of all facets of the business. (e.g., buying, selling, and financing). As the store grows, more employees are hired, larger quantities of merchandise are purchased, and greater sums of money are involved. When it becomes too difficult for one person to handle all these functions, division of responsibility and authority becomes necessary. In very small firms no formal organization is needed, since each person's job is easily understood. However, when many people are involved, a more formal organization is required in order to separate the functions and responsibilities.

# ORGANIZATION CHARTS

Organization charts pinpoint responsibility

Diagrams that clearly indicate lines of authority and responsibility are known as **organization charts.** They pinpoint the people who will do the actual work and those who are responsible for getting the job done. Charts indicate the flow of communications by establishing a hierarchy of authority. Organization charts are custom made to meet the specific needs of retail institutions. Therefore, they differ for small stores, department stores, branches, and chains.

Organization charts are developed according to the number of employees, the specific activities to be carried out, and the departments in which those activities are to take place. Depending on the size of the firm, they can be simple in design or greatly detailed.

The types of organization charts most commonly used today are (1) line and (2) line and staff.

## A Line Organization Chart

Line organization: direct communication

A **line organization chart** (Figure 9-1) shows each worker's position with relation to his or her immediate superior or supervisor. In terms of the flow of communications and delegated authority, the structure eliminates many questions regarding responsibilities. The salesperson reports to the assistant buyer, who reports to the buyer, and so forth. The advantages of this form of organization are that (1) it is easily understood, (2) communications are direct, and (3) supervision is obvious. The disadvantages are that

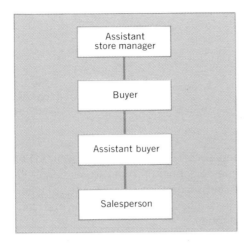

**FIGURE 9-1**
Line organization.

(1) there can be too much responsibility and authority at the top, (2) coordination can be difficult without crossing lines, and (3) each supervisor needs to be a specialist in several areas of management.

# A Line-and-Staff Organization Chart

*Specialists perform staff functions*

A **line-and-staff organization chart** (Figure 9-2) combines the lines of delegated authority (Figure 9-1) with specialists (staff) who provide expertise. Staff activities include all work performed by non-line employees. This type of organization makes it possible for specialists to aid and advise line people who are not equipped with certain skills. Staff people do not make decisions; their role is to advise and recommend. The advantages of a line and staff organization are that it (1) allows for specialists to consult with and advise line people, and (2) maintains the ease of direct communication (each em-

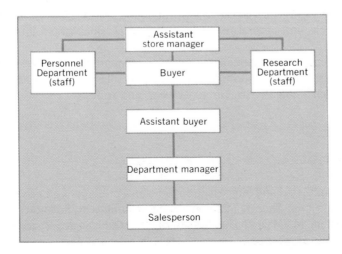

**FIGURE 9-2**
Line-and-staff organization.

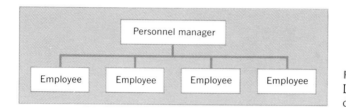

**FIGURE 9-3**
Lines of authority in a staff department.

Staff aid line personnel

ployee reporting to one supervisor). The disadvantages occur (1) when staff employees try to exert authority over line personnel (in order to have their ideas carried out), (2) when line employees follow staff suggestions that fail, and (3) when there is jealousy or friction between line and staff members. Nevertheless, line and staff is the organizational form that is most often used today.

It should be noted that in a staff department there are also lines of authority. For example, in a personnel department the personnel manager supervises other employees within the department (Figure 9-3).

There are more complex charts than those discussed here, which show every position or department in a firm. These charts help employees understand their jobs in relation to other positions. In addition, they help people in authority assign duties and responsibilities.

It is important to keep charts up to date. Since the charts contain the names of employees, they must be revised whenever personnel changes take place. In firms with a high rate of employee turnover, this is considered a disadvantage.

# ORGANIZATION FOR THE SMALL RETAILER

The structure of small independent retailers is simple, even though they perform the same functions as large retailers. Because a small store has fewer employees (approximately six to eight), little specialization, and many tasks to be performed, each employee is responsible for several functions. A typical small-store structure is shown in Figure 9-4.

As a small store expands, there is more opportunity for specialization and departmentalization. When departments are created, salespeople are assigned to particular sections, such as menswear, women's wear, and so forth.

# ORGANIZATION FOR DEPARTMENT STORES

Mazur plan: organization by four functions

Many medium-sized and large department stores are organized according to the various retailing functions. The original concept of "planning by functions" was developed in 1927 by Paul M. Mazur. The **Mazur plan** divided all retail store activities into the following four major areas.

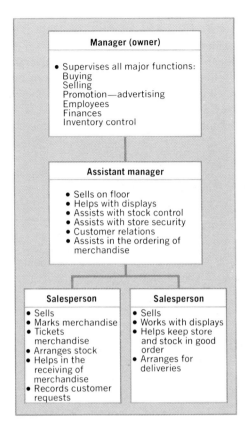

**FIGURE 9-4**
Organization of a small store.

1  Merchandising
2  Publicity
3  Store management
4  Control

## Merchandising

This is considered the most important function of all and includes responsibility for all the activities involved in buying and selling merchandise. This area is headed by the general merchandise manager, who supervises all the merchandising activities in the main store and other locations. The major activities in this area are as follows.

Buying

Selling

Planning merchandise promotions

Merchandise inventory management and control

## Publicity

This operation is concerned with all nonpersonal selling activities (e.g., sales promotions, advertising, and public relations). The publicity manager (or advertising manager) heads this area and works with all other areas. The major activities of this operation are the following.

Planning promotions for the entire store (adviser to the merchandise department)
Advertising
Public relations
Displays (interiors and window)

## Store Management

This area is concerned with all activities in the store except buying, selling, promotion, and finance. The store manager is in charge of this operation. The major activities are as follows.

Personnel
    staffing the store
    training
    compensation
Store maintenance
Purchasing of supplies and equipment to operate the store
Operations
    receiving, marking, checking
    warehouse distribution
    shipping
Customer services
Store security

## Control

This division is responsible for protecting the firm's financial status. The use of computers and data processing has increased the need for specialists to run this division. The controller, sometimes called the treasurer, heads this operation. Its major activities are as follows.

Accounting and record keeping
Credit and collections
Budgeting
Inventory control

# Application of the Mazur Plan

Use of the Mazur plan allows for greater specialization and utilization of staff talent. The organization chart in Figure 9-5 indicates how the Mazur plan divides the four areas of responsibility in a department store. Under this arrangement the four area managers provide staff functions for each other. For example, the merchandise manager, who is responsible for planning promotional events related to merchandise, such as clearance sales, consults with the publicity manager, the person who is responsible for executing store promotions. The two managers plan merchandise promotions together.

It should be emphasized that although no single plan meets the needs of all retail organizations, the basic Mazur plan, with adjustments, can be adapted to most department and specialty store needs. For example, the complex changes in personnel activities brought about by such considerations as labor laws and unions have led to the treatment

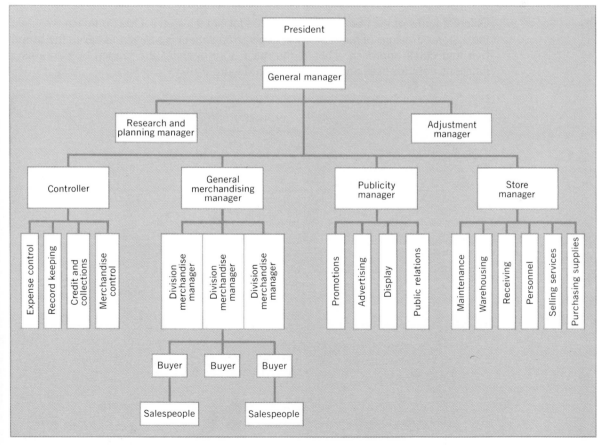

**FIGURE 9-5**
The Mazur plan for department stores.

of personnel as a separate function. In fact, a five-function organizational plan is the most commonly used structure in department and large specialty stores.

Department stores that use the Mazur plan combine the responsibilities for buying and selling. With the growth of branch stores, however, the tendency has been to separate the buying and selling activities. This is similar to the structure developed by chain store organizations. In fact, a major criticism of the Mazur plan has to do with the responsibility for selling.

Critics of the Mazur plan claim that selling, the most important function in retailing, should be concentrated in one area. Instead, two areas besides the merchandise division are involved in the selling activity. For example, the publicity division becomes involved when a sales promotion is planned. On the other hand, the management division, through its personnel department, is responsible for the training of salespeople.

# ORGANIZATION FOR BRANCH STORES

Different forms of the Mazur plan are utilized for branch stores. One approach is to treat these stores as wings of the main store. This arrangement is sometimes called the **brood hen and chick** approach. That is, the main store operates the branch by performing functions both for itself and for the branch (Figure 9-6).

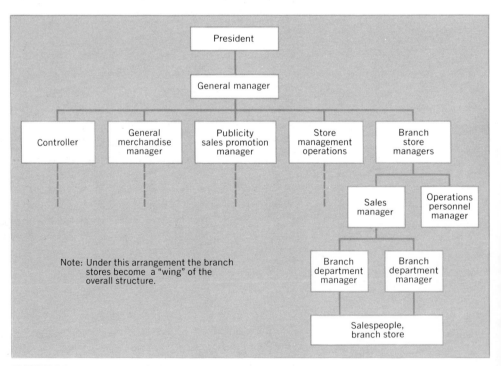

**FIGURE 9-6**
The "brood hen and chick" concept of branch store organization.

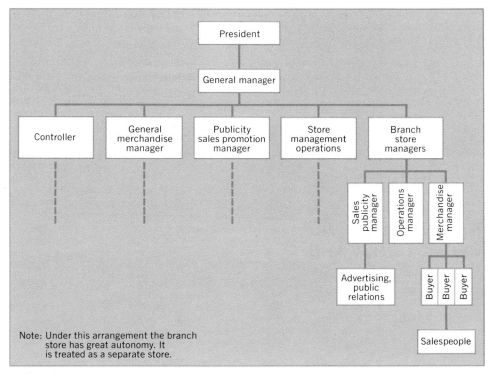

**FIGURE 9-7**
The separate-unit concept of branch store organization.

Another approach (Figure 9-7) is to have the branch operate as a separate unit with a great deal of autonomy. Under this arrangement each branch is responsible for its own buying and selling functions. This structure is found when the number of branches increase to the point where main-store buyers cannot carry out these functions effectively. Under an autonomous arrangement, however, the company risks the loss of a consistent image.

Another variation (Figure 9-8) is known as the **equal store,** in which the buying and selling activities are separated. The buying is done through a central or regional office, with central buyers responsible for the branch stores' merchandise needs. The branches are responsible for the remaining activities of sales and promotion.

# ORGANIZATION FOR CHAIN STORES

Chain stores perform many of the same functions as department stores. However, they differ somewhat in organizational structure becauuse of the products handled, the size of the outlets, the number of units, and geographic spread. Most chain store organizational patterns have the following characteristics (Figure 9-9).

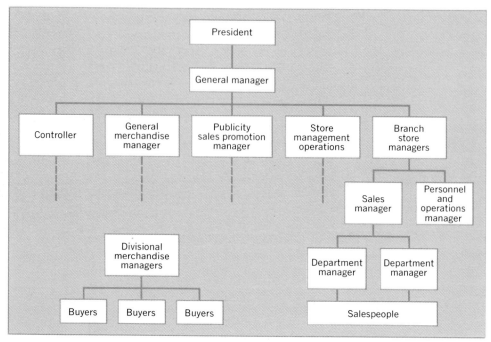

**FIGURE 9-8**
The equal-store concept of branch store organization.

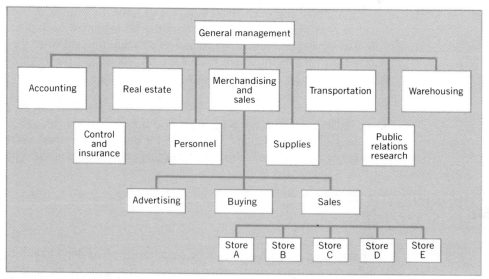

**FIGURE 9-9**
Chain organization.

Centralization and control of operating functions administered in chain's home office

1 **Centralization** of the major store functions (buying, personnel, promotion, control, etc.), which are controlled through a regional or home office. **Decentralization** of the selling and sales promotion activities is the main departure from the chain store's commitment to centralization.

2 A larger number of divisions than department stores, including real estate, warehousing, personnel, and transportation.

3 Trained specialists in the home office, who assume a great deal of the individual store manager's burdens.

4 Highly centralized, autocratic lines of authority and responsibility, which coordinate the total operation.

5 Control of individual stores through the filing of up-to-date reports with the home office.

6 Standardized operations regarding merchandise, prices, credit, services, store layouts, and fixtures.

# CENTRALIZATION AND DECENTRALIZATION

Centralization and control of the major retailing operations have made chain store organization one of the most efficient and economical forms of retailing. The advantages of centralized buying, standardized operations, and control have made it possible for chains to benefit from major savings, large profits, and expansion.

Despite their successes, however, chains have found it necessary to change their methods of delegating authority between individual stores and the central office. In fact, some chains have become more decentralized, giving store managers greater autonomy in making decisions about merchandising and operating policies.

The rationale for decentralizing the buying function is to make the buyer of the goods responsible for the sale of the merchandise, too. Those who favor this position argue that under centralization the buyers are removed from the customers and stores. Consequently, they are not in the best position to recognize local needs and problems.

J. C. Penney is an example of a firm that promotes more management flexibility at the store level. It has granted store managers more decision-making responsibility with regard to local merchandising, advertising, and promotion. In addition, there is evidence of decentralization among other retailers, including Montgomery Ward, Kroger, Sears, and A&P.

Another retailer that has great flexibility at the store level is Nordstrom, Inc., the third-largest specialty retailer in the country. Its organizational structure follows merchandising and management techniques that most retailers gave up long ago. While its competitors became more centralized as they grew, Nordstrom split up responsibility. Consequently, each individual store has its own staff of buyers who also spend three to four hours a day waiting on customers. Furthermore, store managers, not division heads, are responsible for cost control.

Regional decentralization

Competition among supermarket chains has led to some decentralization of merchandising decisions regarding price and promotion policies, allowing individual units to respond to local competition more effectively.

Despite these trends, some chains with a wide geographic spread continue to move toward centralization because it allows for greater control. This is especially so because of improved computer equipment that transmits information at ever-increasing speeds to the central office.

In another vein, the increase of department store branches has stimulated centralized buying for some large department stores. By considering all their branches as similar units, these retailers find that centralized buying is efficient.

Regional decentralization attempts to achieve a balance between centralization and decentralization. At K mart, for example, the buying is done through central headquarters, but the individual store manager can specify merchandise for his or her store, hire and train employees, and maintain control in conjunction with the home office. At Sears, management has devised a regional arrangement whereby individual stores develop merchandising plans in conjunction with regional headquarters. Senior management at Sears' Chicago base then makes final decisions about merchandising structure and strategy.

Because chains differ in products sold, size, and geography, it is difficult to construct an ideal form of organization for chain management. Nevertheless, retailers continue to search for a structure to blend the efficiency and economic advantages of centralization with some degree of decentralization.

# ORGANIZATION FOR COMMUNICATION

Retailers also utilize organizational structures for communicating with their employees. Organization for effective interaction between employees and management is essential for successful retail management.

Effective communication helps employees understand store objectives, policies, and employee opportunities. On the other hand, communication gives management a means for recognizing the wants and needs of its employees and customers.

*Communication channels are vertical and horizontal*

Commonly used channels of communication are downward vertical, upward vertical, and horizontal. Most organizations depend on the line of command for communications, such as managers sending messages to subordinates (downward vertical). When messages originate with employees and progress to management levels, the channel is known as upward vertical. Horizontal communication is passed along on the same level (e.g., managers to managers, salespeople to salespeople, etc.).

# Informal and Formal Communication

*Communication methods are informal and formal*

The methods used to communicate through the channels are either informal or formal. **Informal communication** is the use of vertical and horizontal lines for verbal communication. This system has its limitations because messages may be misunderstood or deliberately distorted.

## FILENE'S ECHO

# 5

FILENE'S FIVE

1. **GREET** the customer
2. **DETERMINE** the customer's needs
3. **SELL** merchandise features and benefits
4. **SUGGEST** multiple/alternative sales
5. **CLOSE** the sale nicely

Filene's helps employees understand store objectives by using written communications.

An unofficial communication network is referred to as a **grapevine.** (See Figure 9-10.) Grapevines interweave throughout the firm and are speedy. Not surprisingly, messages usually travel faster through them than through official channels. Sometimes the grapevine is used deliberately to convey messages that management prefers to keep unofficial.

Unfortunately, some messages are distorted by the time they reach the end of the line. Also, grapevines often spread rumors, some of which are harmful to employee morale.

It is essential for management to kill rumors before they get out of hand. Management must keep the upward and downward channels open so that employee reactions to policy and change are known and understood.

*Formal communication*

**Formal communication** involves the use of employee handbooks, suggestion systems, house organs, bulletins, and meetings.

Handbooks are distributed to new employees by most large retailers. They generally contain information about the company's history, wages and hours of work, employee benefits and services, company policies and rules, and the union contract (if there is one).

A suggestion system is a formal way to encourage communication upward through the firm. Using this method, employees have an opportunity to suggest ways to improve or change conditions. This type of communication develops loyalty and helps build employee morale. Some firms go further by rewarding employees for useful suggestions. Suggestion systems should give prompt feedback to all employees who submit suggestions.

**FIGURE 9-10**

The grapevine is an informal means of communication.

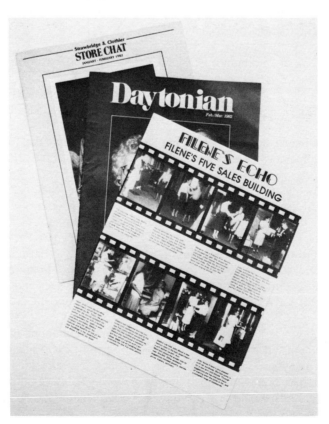

The house organs of Dayton's, Filene's, and Strawbridge & Clothier.

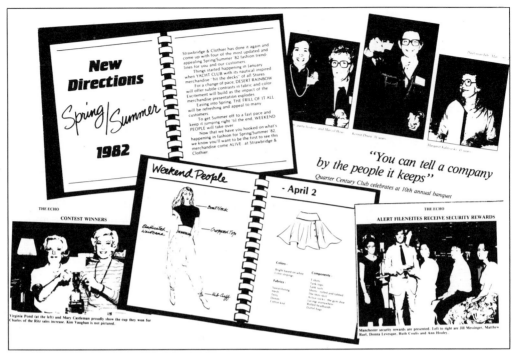

House organs, magazines, and bulletins keep employees informed of store happenings.

A house organ may take the form of a newspaper, magazine, or store newsletter. It generally contains news about the store, its operations, and employees and their families. It provides information about employee promotions and retirements, and often includes letters written by employees. The publication serves as a vehicle for good internal relations and keeps employees abreast of store news.

Bulletins are issued when important information needs to be announced quickly. They are a fast way of informing employees of some activity or change.

General meetings are effective for face-to-face communication. In most large retail firms, however, it is difficult to find a time when all employees are available.

*General meetings are effective face-to-face communication*

### NEW TERMS

| | |
|---|---|
| brood hen and chick | informal communication |
| centralization | line-and-staff organization chart |
| decentralization | line organization chart |
| equal store | Mazur plan |
| formal communication | organization chart |
| grapevine | |

## CHAPTER HIGHLIGHTS

1 The prime objective of every retailer is to be successful. Successful retailers satisfy the wants and needs of their customers.

2 Organizational structures develop as companies grow. In small firms with few employees, no formal structure is needed. When many workers are involved, a more formal organization is required.

3 Diagrams that indicate lines of authority and responsibility are known as organization charts. The most commonly used charts are (a) line and (b) line and staff. Line charts show each worker's position with relation to his or her immediate superior. Line-and-staff charts combine the lines of delegated authority with specialists (staff) who act as consultants.

4 Depending on the size of the firm, charts can be simple or complex. The organization chart for small independent retailers is simple. Employers carry out many functions in small firms.

5 Many department stores are organized according to the functions their employees perform. The Mazur plan divides all retail store activities into four major areas: merchandising, publicity, store management, and control. With adjustment and tailoring, the basic Mazur plan can be applied to most department and individual stores.

6 Basically, there are three approaches to branch store organization. They are the "brood hen and chick" approach, the separate unit, and the equal-store concept.

7 In chains, centralization and control of the major functions is performed through a home office. There are more divisions in chain organizations than in department stores. The additional divisions include real estate, warehousing, transportation, and personnel. The chain organization is one of the most efficient, economical retailing systems yet devised.

8 Trends indicate an increase in decentralization among some large retail chains, while others have become more centralized. Regional decentralization is a combination of both centralization and decentralization.

9 Retailers utilize organizational structures to help them communicate with their employees. Effective communication helps employees understand store objectives, policies, and employee opportunities.

10 Channels of communication are vertical (upward and downward) and horizontal. The methods used to communicate through channels may be formal or informal. An unofficial communication network is referred to as a grapevine. Sometimes grapevines are used to convey messages that management prefers to keep unofficial.

11 Formal communications involve the use of handbooks, suggestion systems, house organs, bulletins, and meetings.

## QUESTIONS

1 What are the differences between line and line-and-staff organizations?
2 What are the disadvantages of line-and-staff organization?
3 Why is it important for retail firms to develop organization charts?

4 Explain the four functions associated with the Mazur plan.

5 What is the role of staff people in a retail organization?

6 What are the major differences between centralization and decentralization?

7 What are the three types of branch store management?

8 How can effective communication help retailers carry out their objectives?

9 List three examples of a horizontal channel of communication in a department store.

10 How are grapevines used effectively? Destructively?

# FIELD PROJECTS

1 Interview three students who hold part-time jobs in a retail store and prepare a report based on the following questions.
   a Do you know your immediate supervisor?
   b Do you know his or her supervisor?
   c Were you ever given an organizational chart or any literature about your firm?
   d What kind of training did you receive after you were hired?
   e Are the salespeople in your store unionized?

2 A small independent retailer has decided to departmentalize her children's wear specialty shop. She has added shoes and outerwear to her regular merchandise. There are three salespeople, one deliveryman, and the owner, who also serves as manager. Prepare an organizational chart for the store.

# CASES

1 In the last few years several large department stores have suffered losses because of the competitive onslaught of discount firms and specialty stores. In an attempt to improve its competitive position, Montgomery Ward and Company reorganized its management.

A new chief operating officer was brought in from the outside, and he decided to put together his own management team. A dramatic "voluntary separation" program was instituted so that a new group could be hired. Ward asked more than 600 senior executives, each with more than ten years of experience, to consider leaving the company in return for cash payments ranging from 50 percent to 150 percent of a year's pay. Those who refused the offer could take their chances on remaining with the company.

The plan was not aimed at early retirement, since it was offered to executives of all ages.

   a How do you think the senior executives reacted when faced with the separation program?
   b What are some of the positive aspects of a management shakeup for a company? Negative aspects?

2 The 1980s, according to some retailing experts, will witness the disappearance or

takeover of many small retail firms and domination of the specialty store field by large chains. Rona's Fashion Stores is one such organization, having acquired an upper-level income chain, the Dream Specialty Stores, and incorporated it into its existing business.

In constructing an organization chart for the merged businesses, the senior executives developed the following merchandising and operations relationships.

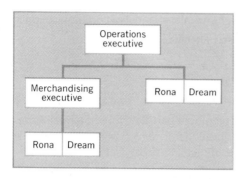

Though the executive in charge of the merchandising function is responsible for both the Rona and Dream stores, he must report to the executive in charge of operations. The latter is also responsible for the operation of the Rona and Dream outlets.

**a** What conflicts do you see in the organizational structure shown?
**b** How might the structure be reorganized for smoother functioning?

3 In 1980–1981 Sears, Roebuck, the nation's largest retailer in terms of sales volume, undertook a dramatic change in its management structure. The move was attributed to a loss of customers and reduced profits caused by an unwieldy structure.

Prior to the change, the president of Sears had been responsible for its three major divisions: insurance (Allstate), real estate, and merchandising (stores and catalogs). The merchandising division suffered from lack of coordination between the president (at the company's headquarters in Chicago) and the heads of individual stores. This situation was attributed to an oversized management group that resulted in inefficient decision making.

A major consequence of the previous management arrangement was the blurred direction of merchandising policies; that is, the company lacked a cohesive image owing to the independence of individual stores and the absence of strong central control. This resulted in merchandise shortages at critical times, unattractive store areas, and reduced display effectiveness.

The new Sears management structure provides active interaction between headquarters executives and regional and store managers. Planning has become a two-way process, with central management suggesting targets and strategy. Regional offices as well as individual stores follow up with their own plans, after which final, coordinated, binding decisions are made. In fact, Sears has reduced the number of its field administrative territories from five to four in order to keep costs down and gain better control.

During the reorganization, more than 1200 Sears executives retired voluntarily in response to an attractive money offer by the company. It was expected that their departure would streamline the management organization.

a  How do you think the new organizational structure affected the morale of Sears' veteran executives? Explain.
b  In what way might greater central control improve Sears' merchandise image?

# REFERENCES

Berman, B., and J. R. Evans, *Retail Management: A Strategic Approach* (New York: Macmillan, 1979), chap. 9.

Bolen, W. H., *Contemporary Retailing* (Englewood Cliffs, N.J.: Prentice-Hall, 1978), chap. 7.

James, D. L., B. J. Walker, and M. J. Etzel, *Retailing Today* (New York: Harcourt Brace Jovanovich, 1981).

Judelle, B., *The Branch Manager's Manual* (New York: National Retail Merchants Association, Operations Division, 1968).

Mazur, P. M., *Principles of Organization Applied to Modern Retailing* (New York: Harper & Row, 1927).

National Retail Merchants Association, Personnel Group, *Communications Downward and Upward* (New York, 1967).

National Retail Merchants Association, Personnel Group, *Retail Employee Discounts* (New York, 1965).

Posner, J., "Marketing Manager: The Missing Link," *Retail Directions*, 127 (February-March 1973), pp. 56–57.

Robinson, O. P., J. G. Robinson, and M. P. Matthews, *Store Organization and Operation*, 2nd ed. (Englewood Cliffs, N.J.: Prentice-Hall, 1957).

Roe, R. G., *Retail Management* (Hinsdale, Ill.: Dryden Press, 1979).

Silver, G. A., *Introduction to Management* (St. Paul, Minn.: West, 1981).

"Upgrading the Human Side," *Retail Directions*, 128 (September 1974), pp. 13–14.

# chapter 10
# HUMAN RESOURCE MANAGEMENT

After completing this chapter, you should be able to:

1 List the methods used by retailers to recruit and hire new employees.

2 Identify the techniques used to train and retrain new employees.

3 Explain the responsibilities of a store's personnel department with regard to the transfer, promotion, and discharge of employees.

4 Explain wage and compensation scales used in retailing.

5 Identify fringe benefits administered by personnel departments.

6 Explain the responsibilities of personnel departments in dealing with organized labor.

Having examined the organization of a store, we turn our attention to the people who work there. To a large extent, the success or failure of a retail firm is dependent on its employees.

This chapter examines the staffing of a store and the responsibilities of its personnel department. It considers the hiring and training of new employees as well as policies concerning existing staff. It also identifies wage and compensation scales and fringe benefits, and discusses personnel departments in their relation to labor organizations.

# THE PERSONNEL DEPARTMENT

A vital aspect of operating a successful retail store is managing the company's human resources, that is, its employees. As businesses become larger and more complex, the personnel department has more responsibility for maintaining an adequate labor force. Modern personnel management, then, is concerned with hiring, training, motivating, and understanding the needs of employees in order to develop a productive work force.

In large companies the personnel division is concerned with

*Personnel functions*

1 Recruiting and hiring new employees.
2 Training and retraining employees.
3 Working with personnel transfers, promotions, and discharges.
4 Establishing wage and compensation scales.
5 Establishing and managing employee fringe benefits.

# Recruiting and Hiring New Employees

The retail employment environment has special characteristics. Among them are a very high employee turnover, the existence of many part-time jobs, and the need for extra hiring at peak periods (e.g., Christmas and Easter).

The types of jobs and the qualifications for them must be determined prior to recruitment. To accomplish these ends, job analyses and job descriptions are developed. A **job analysis** is a detailed study of the duties and abilities needed to perform a job efficiently. The information from a job analysis is written up to create a **job description.** A **job specification** sets forth the qualifications required by the job. Using these tools, personnel managers who recruit for new employees can determine exactly the types of people and qualifications needed for specific jobs.

*Sources of personnel*

Sources from which new employees can be selected are found within as well as outside the firm.

## In-Store Sources
Within the firm, sources of new employees include the following.

1 Employees who are interested in changing jobs (by transfering to other areas).

2 Present employees' recommendations.

3 Promotion from within—filling jobs with present employees.

## Outside Sources

The personnel department can recruit new employees from outside the firm through the following means.

1 Advertising in newspapers, trade papers, radio, and the store window.

2 Employment agencies (public and private).

3 Schools, colleges, and universities.

4 Transient applications (large, prestigious firms attract unsolicited requests for employment).

The most common means of advertising for new employees is to use the classified advertising sections of newspapers. Two types of advertisements are generally used: the **open ad** and the **blind ad.** An open ad supplies all the information about the job, as well as the name, address, and telephone number of the store. A blind ad does not identify the store and provides only a post office box number. There are advantages and disadvantages to both types. An open ad (Figure 10-1) encourages a great many applicants to write and call. This often requires additional personnel to handle the responses and screen applicants for interviews. On the other hand, a blind ad eliminates hours of work because the mail can be reviewed before applicants are told when or where to apply. Though this is somewhat of an advantage, it should be noted that many employed people who are looking for a job change hesitate to answer blind ads for fear of writing to their own employer.

## The Process of Hiring New Employees

In small stores the hiring procedure is informal, with the owner or manager interviewing the potential employee and recording the necessary information. In large firms the procedures are more formal. Prospects may have to go through an initial screening known as the **rail interview.** This is a brief interview before a prospective applicant is asked to fill out an **application form.** This technique is used to eliminate candidates who are clearly unqualified. For example, if a particular job specification includes certain educational requirements and the interviewee does not possess the appropriate background, there is no need to continue the recruitment procedure. When a rail interview is successful, the prospect is asked to fill out an application form similar to the one in Figure 10-2.

Dayton's application for employment adheres to the Federal Civil Rights Act of 1964, which makes it illegal and discriminatory to request information about race, creed, religion, and so forth. It is illegal to hire or favor one applicant over another solely on the basis of race or sex. However, the application form does ask for necessary information so that a proper determination can be made as to the prospect's qualifications and background. Educational background, past work experience, and references are required. References are people or past employers who can be contacted regarding the character and ability of the person applying for the job.

The initial screening is known as the rail interview

*Lord & Taylor*

*We are interviewing now for entry-level Operations and Merchandising Executives*

Are you an aggressive, growth-oriented individual eager to join an Executive Development Program? Our programs give you the opportunity to manage the profitability of a multi-million dollar business within three years. We invite you to apply for these programs which are scheduled to start soon. Not everyone will qualify. If you think you do, please send your resume in confidence to: Director of Recruitment

Lord & Taylor
424 Fifth Avenue
New York, New York 10018

An Equal Opportunity Employer, M/F

**FIGURE 10-1**
An open ad for recruitment of executives.

Checking references is one of the procedures that is required in the employment process. Background checks are made to gain additional data and to verify information given by the applicant on the application form. Reference checks are made by phone or mail, and many retailers use simple forms that are mailed to the applicant's references. Some firms will not hire employees until their references have responded favorably.

Another method of checking job seekers' honesty is the use of **polygraph instruments**, commonly known as **lie detectors**. By checking a person's pulse, blood pressure,

## DAYTON·S ⟫⟫ Application for Employment

### EQUAL OPPORTUNITY EMPLOYER

| NAME - PLEASE PRINT - LAST, FIRST, MIDDLE | DATE APPLIED |
|---|---|

CURRENT ADDRESS - ADDRESS, CITY, STATE, ZIP

PRIOR ADDRESS - ADDRESS, CITY, STATE, ZIP

| HOME TELEPHONE NUMBER | SOCIAL SECURITY NUMBER | IF NOT U.S. CITIZEN PROVIDE VISA NUMBER |
|---|---|---|

| | | | IF YES TO ANY OF THE FOUR QUESTIONS, PLEASE EXPLAIN: |
|---|---|---|---|
| HAVE YOU BEEN REFUSED BOND? | NO ☐ | YES ☐ | |
| HAVE YOU BEEN CONVICTED OF A FELONY OR MISDEMEANOR? | NO ☐ | YES ☐ | |
| HAVE YOUR WAGES EVER BEEN GARNISHED WITHIN THE LAST 7 YEARS? | NO ☐ | YES ☐ | |
| HAVE YOU FILED BANKRUPTCY IN THE LAST 7 YEARS? | NO ☐ | YES ☐ | |

| NAME OF HIGH SCHOOL | ADDRESS | GRADE COMPLETED | DATE COMPLETED |
|---|---|---|---|

| ADVANCED EDUCATION | ADDRESS | YEAR COMPLETED | DATE |
|---|---|---|---|

| POSITION(S) DESIRED | ☐ FULL TIME ☐ PERMANENT  ☐ PART TIME ☐ TEMPORARY |
|---|---|
| DAYS AND HOURS AVAILABLE | WAGE DESIRED: |

995 (5/79)

---

### PREVIOUS EMPLOYMENT RECORD (List most recent employer first, if none list reference other than relatives.)

| EMPLOYER | DATES | POSITION(S) | WAGE | WHY LEFT |
|---|---|---|---|---|
| 1. CO. NAME | FROM | START | START | |
| CO. ADDRESS | TO | FINAL | FINAL | |
| CO. PHONE NUMBER | SUPERVISOR(S) | | | |
| 2. CO. NAME | FROM | START | START | |
| CO. ADDRESS | TO | FINAL | FINAL | |
| CO. PHONE NUMBER | SUPERVISOR(S) | | | |
| 3. CO. NAME | FROM | START | START | |
| CO. ADDRESS | TO | FINAL | FINAL | |
| CO. PHONE NUMBER | SUPERVISOR(S) | | | |

| HAVE YOU EVER BEEN EMPLOYED BY DAYTON'S? | FROM TO | WHAT STORE? | WHAT DEPT.? |
|---|---|---|---|

LIST ALL FRIENDS AND RELATIVES EMPLOYED AT DAYTON'S. (Specify Store Location)

IF CURRENTLY EMPLOYED ☐ Yes ☐ No    MAY BE CONTACT YOUR PRESENT EMPLOYER ☐ Yes ☐ No

HOW WERE YOU REFERRED TO DAYTON'S?

| **IMPORTANT: READ BEFORE SIGNING!** | I understand and agree that; (a) any false statement on this application will be cause for dismissal, (b) I will abide by the policies of Dayton's as a condition of my employment, (c) I will be bonded, (d) reference investigations may be made regarding my credit status, character and work record as it relates to my employment. |
|---|---|
| SIGNATURE | |

**FIGURE 10-2**

A typical department store application form. (Reproduced by permission of Dayton's.)

This prospect is undergoing a rail interview prior to receiving an application form.

and breathing, and with proper interpretation, these devices indicate whether the answers to questions are lies or the truth. This method is growing in popularity and has been accepted by hundreds of department stores, fast-food chains, drugstores, and other retailers. Despite adverse criticism by the Civil Liberties Union, use of the polygraph test is becoming widespread.

Security companies maintain that the polygraph can be more than 95 percent accurate. However, this depends on the expertise of the person who interprets the graph it produces. Retail firms that use polygraph instruments include Gimbel's, Fortunoff's, Crazy Eddie, Wrangler Jeans, Chemical Bank, and Duane Reade drugstores.

## Testing

Testing is another step in the employment process. It includes data on aptitude, skills, personality, and the like. Personnel must be careful to avoid any type of discrimination so as not to break the law. Although the Civil Rights Act of 1964 permits testing, the tests must be the same for all applicants. Large firms generally administer and evaluate these tests themselves. Smaller firms may use private testing bureaus. Some firms evaluate academic records, courses, and grades, while others use school **internship programs** as a means of "testing" future employees. This is a form of on-the-job evaluation. If a prospect is successful during a prescribed period, he or she is offered the job. In some instances companies require physical examinations as well.

### Interviews

Interviews are another important aspect of the employment process. Further information concerning the applicant's aptitude, verbal ability, and reasons for wanting the job are revealed during an interview session. Additional information concerning different experiences can be advantageous to the applicant. The personal interview also gives the prospect an opportunity to ask questions about the job, the store, and opportunities for promotion.

# Training and Retraining

### Training

Training for new employees

Another major responsibility of the personnel department is to plan and implement the training of new employees. Small and large firms have some form of instruction in order to supply employees with the skills and knowledge to do an effective job.

**Orientation training** covers such topics as the history of the firm, procedures and policies, and rules and regulations regarding payroll, promotions, fringe benefits, and so forth.

With small firms, **on-the-job training** is very common. The inexperienced employee is assigned to a more experienced person, frequently the owner or manager, until he or she has gained enough experience.

In larger firms, trainees are assigned after some formal training has taken place. While lectures and seminars are used for large-group instruction, tapes and audio-visual

This applicant is undergoing a lie detector test as part of a store's screening process.

equipment are other commonly employed techniques. When employees are trained prior to assignment, the stores use their own classrooms. This type of instruction is sometimes referred to as **vestibule training.** For example, retail stores train employees in the use of the cash register before they are assigned to the selling floor.

## Retraining

Older employees may require additional training for various reasons, such as new technology, transfers, upgrading, and promotions. Employees who need to be retrained are instructed by the personnel department or consultants, or take special courses in schools.

Some firms institute management training or executive training as part of their in-service training or for promotions. This type of training utilizes seminars and job rotation. **Job rotation** moves the employee from one area to another and gives the worker an opportunity to view the total business operation prior to permanent assignment.

Many stores use outside consultants or educational programs for employees who need skill in handling delicate problems. Although sensitivity training, as it is called, is still considered experimental, it is often used in an attempt to improve human relations within a firm by helping the employees develop insight and greater understanding. The employees participate in groups, classes, simulations, or games in which they learn about themselves. Within this group setting, they observe and discuss human behavior. They ask such questions as

- What they dislike about a certain manager.
- What causes them to be nonproductive at certain times.
- What happens outside the job that interferes with their concentration on the job.

The "insight" training also deals with such topics as feeling stronger about yourself and handling anger.

Employees may be asked to look at the ways in which they are unconsciously or unintentionally counterproductive to the firm. Some personnel consultants consider it useful in a work situation for people to be able to talk about their feelings. However, in order for them to make positive behavioral changes, they must be in an atmosphere

*Sensitivity training needed to handle people problems*

Dayton's is one of many stores that uses classroom training for newly hired employees.

Job rotation allows new retail employees to view different aspects of a store's operations.

that does not pose a threat because of what they say. They must also be motivated to change.

In many cases programs like these help supervisors improve their sensitivity to people with whom they work, thus reducing employee turnover.

# Transfer, Promotion, and Discharge

Transfer, promotion, and discharge are other responsibilities of the personnel department. Assigning an experienced worker to another job within the store or to a branch store is known as a **job transfer.** Employees are transferred either because their skills are needed elsewhere or because they are unhappy with co-workers or the job situation.

When an employee is moved to another position that carries greater responsibility and an increase in salary, it is defined as a **promotion.** A promotion generally advances the worker to a job that requires greater skill and ability.

Many corporations are adopting promotion-from-within policies. That is, they attempt to upgrade employees from within the organization and to promote from among their own staffs. Sears, Roebuck & Company is known to use this method. This policy minimizes hiring from outside the company and makes internal training more important because employees must be trained to do upper-level jobs when necessary. Firms that promote from within usually have employees with good morale and motivation.

*Discharged* and *fired* are synonymous

When employees are **discharged,** they are permanently separated from the company. The word *discharged* is synonymous with the better-known term *fired.* Reasons for being fired range from incompetence and dishonesty to not getting along or "fitting in" with other store personnel.

When an employee is temporarily or permanently terminated owing to an economic slowdown or problems within the firm, it is known as a **layoff.** For example, when Korvette's, a large discount department store chain, closed its stores in 1980, it terminated all of its employees permanently.

In order to carry out the responsibilities of transfers, promotions, and discharges effectively, personnel managers use a variety of evaluation methods.

## Evaluation

Evaluation is a personnel tool that measures employee performance and the effectiveness of training. In most retail firms the methods used to rate employees involve observation and written reports.

**Observation** Immediate supervisors, such as department managers, assistant buyers, and buyers, observe the salespeople and stock clerks in their departments. They take note of their appearance, their attitudes toward customers and staff, and how well they comply with store regulations and procedures. To a large degree, well-kept stockrooms and healthy sales are measures of productivity. In small stores the supervisor is generally the owner or assistant manager.

Sometimes salespeople are evaluated by professionals who pose as customers. They rate the salesperson's selling performance, compliance with rules and regulations, personal behavior, attitude, and grooming. This is known as a **shopper's report.**

**Written Reports** Reviews and ratings are less complicated for first-level jobs (sales help, part-timers, stock). These reports are usually completed by the employee's immediate supervisor.

Printed forms are used by most large retailers to rate management trainees. Figure 10-3 is an example of an individual trainee evaluation form used by Dayton's. This form has three sections to be completed, one each for the buyer, the department manager, and the divisional manager.

The buyer determines the training objectives for the trainee two weeks after the latter has joined the department. Four months later the trainee is reviewed by the buyer, the department manager, and the divisional manager.

The buyer rates the individual, explains the rating, and makes recommendations as to the type of improvement program needed. The department manager rates the trainee's overall progress as a management trainee, while the divisional manager comments about the trainee's potential and possible advancement.

After trainees are advanced in the program, other forms are used to evaluate performance. Figure 10-4 is an evaluation form that measures the trainee's ability and leadership characteristics in the following manner.

**Part I: Management Traits** The supervisor rates the trainee's behavior, initiative, planning, leadership, tolerance for stress, and so forth by selecting appropriate descriptive phrases.

**Parts II, III, IV, V, VI** The supervisor rates the trainee's performance, skills, and personality using a numerical rating scale. The specific areas measured are selling, management, operations, personnel, and personality.

Trainees, too, have an opportunity to give management their opinions and ratings regarding their training experience. As noted in Figure 10-5, trainees must complete a written report regarding their experiences.

(*Text continued on page 199.*)

---

Sidenotes (left margin):

Evaluation measures employee performance and training

Trainees are evaluated by the buyer, the department manager, and the divisional manager

Trainees rate branch store training

# INDIVIDUAL TRAINEE EVALUATION

TRAINEE NAME:_____

DEPARTMENT NAME/NUMBER:_____

DATE STARTED IN DEPARTMENT:_____

DATE OBJECTIVES SET:_____
  (*Within two weeks after joining department*)

BUYER:_____    EXT:  _____

REVIEW DATE:_____
  (*Four months after joining department*)

QUESTIONS ON SETTING OBJECTIVES OR EVALUATING THE TRAINEE SHOULD BE DIRECTED TO STEVE CLARK, EXTENSION 3055.

cc: (Cover sheet & objectives)

    Divisional Merchandise Manager
    Manager, Manpower Planning

cc: (Completed review)

    Manager, Manpower Planning

| | Points Assigned | Points Earned |
|---|---|---|
| **SECTION I** | | |
| **A. Objective: Communications** | | |
| 1 Relate counts on basic, non-basic and clearance merchandise to stores monthly. | _____ | _____ |
| 2 Maintain a product description book, reviewed monthly. | _____ | _____ |
| 3 Inform seven days in advance of all upcoming events, promotions, due dates for merchandise counts, product mix and pricing changes. Establish a monthly calendar of events. | _____ | _____ |
| 4 Visit all branch stores in metro area twice per month and remote stores as designated by DMM or Buyer. Write a branch store visit report on each visit. | _____ | _____ |
| 5 Keep Buyer informed of all major developments in areas of his responsibility. | _____ | _____ |
| Explain rating:_____ | Total | Total |

State improvement program if needed:_____
_____
_____

**FIGURE 10-3**

An individual trainee evaluation form used by Dayton's. (Reproduced by permission of Dayton's.)

*(Figure 10-3, cont'd.)*

| | Points Assigned | Points Earned |
|---|---|---|
| **B.  Objective: Stock Control** | | |
| **1** Maintain count control books, determine rate of sale, and place reorders on a regular basis for all items stocked based on rate of sales. | _____ | _____ |
| **2** Update control books once per season and review with sales managers. | _____ | _____ |
| **3** Maintain stock levels within plan for each class and always be in stock on basic merchandise. | _____ | _____ |
| **4** Maintain never out list, review seasonally with salesmanagers and place reorders regularly to maintain a 95% in stock level on never out items. | _____ | _____ |
| **5** Maintain flow of discontinued and damaged merchandise into the Outlet Store, Warehouse Sales, and OFBD. | _____ | _____ |
| **6** Supervise chargebacks to manufacturer. | _____ | _____ |
| Explain rating:_____ | _____ | _____ |
| | Total | Total |

State improvement program if needed: _____

| | Points Assigned | Points Earned |
|---|---|---|
| **C.  Objective: Accounting** | | |
| **1** Review the purchase journal weekly and make necessary corrections. | _____ | _____ |
| **2** Review the over-45-day-old file in Pre-Retailing monthly along with the trouble folder. | _____ | _____ |
| **3** Gain a full understanding and working knowledge of departmental plans, records and statements. | _____ | _____ |
| Explain rating:_____ | _____ | _____ |
| | Total | Total |

State improvement program if needed:_____

| | Points Assigned | Points Earned |
|---|---|---|
| **D.  Objective: Advertising** | | |
| **1** Maintain the departmental ad book, including copies of all ads with first week and total sales results. | _____ | _____ |
| **2** Make sure all advertised merchandise is ordered, received in stores and signed for each event. | _____ | _____ |
| **3** Assist in formulating departmental advertising plan at least three months in advance of event. | _____ | _____ |
| **4** Review competitors' ads monthly with buyer and in conjunction with competitive store visit reports from | | |

*(Figure 10-3, cont'd.)* visiting each major competitor at least once each season.

Explain rating:_____

_____ ‖ ═══════ ═══════
                                           Total       Total

_____

State improvement program if needed:_____

| **E.  Objective: Vendor Analysis and Relationships** | **Points Assigned** | **Points Earned** |
|---|---|---|
| **1** Review each vendor seasonally to determine their importance to Dayton's, recommending to buyer further action (add lines, delete, drop resource, etc.) | _____ | _____ |
| **2** Utilize representatives to improve product knowledge by holding vendor meetings with sales personnel once each season to introduce new items and review current lines. | _____ | _____ |

Explain rating:_____

                                           Total       Total

State improvement program if needed:_____

| **F.  Objective: Personnel Management and Supervision** | **Points Assigned** | **Points Earned** |
|---|---|---|
| **1** Maintain a high level of knowledge and skills among clericals, heads of stock, stock personnel and sales people by holding regular meetings to discuss new procedures and review existing ones. | _____ | _____ |

Explain rating:_____

                                           Total       Total

State improvement program if needed:_____

-------------------------------------------------------------------

**Rating Scale:**     45–50   Excellent
                        40–45   Above Average
                        30–40   Average
                          0–30   Below Average

**Total Section I**         _____         _____
                                   Total points assigned        Total points earned
                                                            (0–50)

**SECTION II** *(To be filled in by department manager after four months)*

How do you rate the trainee's overall progress as a Management Trainee? *(Score your evaluation according to this scale for each item.)*

| | | | |
|---|---|---|---|
| *(Figure 10-3, cont'd.)* | Unsatisfactory . . . . . . . . . . . . . . . . . . . . . . . .0–5 | High. . . . . . . . . . . . . . . . . . . . . . . . . . . . . . . .8–9 |
| | Satisfactory. . . . . . . . . . . . . . . . . . . . . . . .6–7 | Excellent . . . . . . . . . . . . . . . . . . . . . . . . . . .10 |

**Points Earned**

### A. Planning

Keep in mind the opportunities you have given the trainee to plan. Did he/she draw on the knowledge of the people around in planning? Did he/she come reasonably close to reaching the established objectives, or were they unrealistic?

Explain rating:_____

_____

_____

_____

### B. Organizing

How well does the trainee organize to get the job done? Does he/she communicate the plan and the organization to your people so that they understand what is expected of them?

Explain rating:_____

_____

_____

_____

### C. Relationships

Keep in mind the responsibility and authority you have given the trainee. Is he/she able to sell a program to people at all levels? Do people feel free to come to him/her on all problems? Are relationships with others such that he/she receives and gives cooperation on all problems?

Explain rating:_____

_____

_____

_____

### D. Follow Through

Does he/she follow through to the task's completion?

Explain rating:_____

_____

_____

_____

### E. General Comments on Managerial Effectiveness

_____

_____

_____

_____

_____

_____

_____

*(Figure 10-3, cont'd.)*  **Rating Scale:**    90–100    Excellent          *Date:*_____
                                            80– 89    Above Average
                                            60– 79    Average
                                            0– 59    Below Average

Reviewed by:_____

Trainee's signature:_____

Total point evaluation
Section I (0–50)                    _____

Total point evaluation
Section II (0–50)                   _____

Total point evaluation
Sections I and II (0–100)           _____

**SECTION III** (*To be filled in by divisional manager after four months*)

**A.  Comments**

_____
_____
_____
_____
_____
_____
_____
_____

**B.  Potential**

What is the next step ahead for this individual and does he/she have further potential beyond
the next step? If so, outline:

_____
_____
_____
_____
_____

**C.  Recommended Action**

_____
_____
_____
_____
_____
_____

Reviewed by:_____

Date:_____

Trainee's signature:_____

_____

---

# DAYTON'S
# MANAGEMENT TRAINEE EVALUATION

---

NAME _____

TRAINEE'S NAME _____

STORE _____ DEPT. _____

EVALUATION PERIOD: FROM _____ TO _____

## PART I:  MANAGEMENT TRAITS

Rate the following factors by circling the letter which indicates the most accurate appraisal of the trainee's behavior:

### 1  Initiative

**a**  Constantly searches for improved methods; suggests new concepts and procedures.

**b**  Resourceful; usually alert to opportunities for improvement.

**c**  Makes occasional suggestions for improvement. Usually does the same thing every day.

**d**  Not an independent thinker. Rarely initiates innovative ideas.

### 2  Planning

**a**  Plans work to avoid difficulties. Establishes excellent priorities.

**b**  Sets good priorities. Usually plans well enough to prevent major problems.

**c**  Cannot always distinguish important from unimportant. Difficulties sometimes arise through lack of planning.

**d**  Firefighter; no predetermined plan or program to accomplish tasks effectively.

### 3  Leadership

**a**  Excellent ability to delegate responsibility, administer and control operation. Would inspire teamwork.

**b**  Can delegate responsibility with some degree of success. Usually motivates others.

**c**  Occasionally has difficulty delegating responsibility and following through on details. Minimal ability to motivate others.

**d**  Does not work well with others; unable to inspire teamwork. Exhibits little ability to delegate responsibility.

### 4  Tolerance for Stress

**a**  Remains calm, rational and analytical despite heavy workloads, many problems, pressures of time.

**b**  Generally retains composure in high pressure situations. Occasionally distracted by stressful situations.

**c**  Sometimes overwhelmed by heavy workloads, problems, pressures, or time. Finds stress disturbing.

**d**  Easily excitable; gets flustered when pressured by demands of time, workloads, etc. Emotional.

FIGURE 10-4

Dayton's management trainee evaluation form. (Reproduced by permission of Dayton's.)

*(Figure 10-4 cont'd.)*

**5 Communication Skills**

   **a** Excellent ability to communicate effectively orally with customers, superiors and co-workers.

   **b** Usually maintains effective oral communication with customers, superiors and co-workers.

   **c** Has difficulty communicating orally with customers, superiors or co-workers.

**6 Analytical Ability**

   **a** Always makes critical, rational, logical analyses of situations. Quickly digests relevant factors and reaches sound conclusions.

   **b** Usually demonstrates logical approach to problem solving. Generally arrives at sound decisions.

   **c** Has difficulty digesting relevant information. Sometimes approaches problems emotionally rather than analytically.

   **d** Does not approach problems logically, rationally or critically. Unable to use relevant information to reach sound conclusions.

**DIRECTIONS**
**PARTS II, III, IV, V, VI**

Indicate your judgment of the trainee's performance by checking the appropriate box for each item. Please use this scale:

     4 = Excellent, reflects superior performance.

     3 = Very good, reflects highly competent performance.

     2 = Good, reflects average performance.

     1 = Adequate, reflects minimally acceptable performance.

     0 = Unsatisfactory, reflects substandard performance.

**PART II:   SELLING SKILLS**

| | 4 | 3 | 2 | 1 | 0 |
|---|---|---|---|---|---|
| **1** Completes sales documents accurately and legibly. | | | | | |
| **2** Greets customers promptly and positively. | | | | | |
| **3** Seeks understanding of customer wants. | | | | | |
| **4** Directs customer interest toward appropriate merchandise. | | | | | |
| **5** Avoids negatives in selling process. | | | | | |
| **6** Creates positive value of merchandise to customers. | | | | | |
| **7** Presents merchandise with pride. | | | | | |
| **8** Anticipates and overcomes customer objections. | | | | | |
| **9** Seeks ways to be of service to customers. | | | | | |
| **10** Follows through on customer requests. | | | | | |
| **11** Demonstrates initiative and/or interest in increasing sales. | | | | | |
| **12** Demonstrates initiative and/or interest in acquiring product knowledge. | | | | | |
| **13** Transfers product knowledge to selling situations. | | | | | |
| **14** Demonstrates ability to train others. | | | | | |

*(Figure 10-4 cont'd.)* **15** Uses training aids provided by company to obtain sales goals.

4 | 3 | 2 | 1 | 0

**16** Measures weekly sales results as compared to goal.

**17** Exhibits creative concern when sales goals are not met.

**18** Conducts product information and sales training meetings with sales staff.

**19** Exhibits ability to motivate others.

## PART III:   MANAGEMENT SKILLS

**1** Accepts and carries out responsibility as well as authority.

**2** Demonstrates willingness to delegate authority as well as responsibility.

**3** Follows through on all tasks previously mastered with minimum supervision.

**4** Demonstrates willingness to arrive early, stay late and to be absent seldom.

**5** Offers criticism constructively.

**6** Handles complaints and other customer service matters promptly, tactfully and intelligently.

**7** Demonstrates understanding and adherence to company policies and procedures.

## PART IV:   OPERATIONAL SKILLS

**1** Learned location of merchandise, by department, throughout store.

**2** Exhibits understanding and acceptance of merchandise trend concepts.

**3** Demonstrates dedication to profitable operation.

**4** Exhibits expense control awareness.

**5** Demonstrates knowledge of merchandise receiving procedure.

**6** Demonstrates understanding of these documents and their relevance:
   purchase journal
   operating statement

**7** Demonstrates concern for store security.

**8** Demonstrates knowledge of security procedures.

**9** Participates in store housekeeping duties.

**10** Demonstrates concern for orderly merchandise.

**11** Acts promptly on all your requests.

**12** Promptly investigates and rectifies customer complaints.

**13** Observes company policy with respect to employee discounts and accounts.

**14** Demonstrates ability to use merchandise systems.

**15** Reviews all merchandise categories and makes recommendations to improve the sales of each.

**16** Follows up promptly on special orders.

| | 4 | 3 | 2 | 1 | 0 |
|---|---|---|---|---|---|

*(Figure 10-4 cont'd.)*

**17** Exhibits awareness of advertising in planning and selling around ad schedules.

**18** Demonstrates ability to create attractive displays.

## PART V:  PERSONNEL SKILLS

**1** Demonstrates ability to train and supervise all personnel in the store.

**2** Eager to know aspects of the job of each employee.

**3** Demonstrates ability to plan effective work schedules.

## PART VI:  PERSONALITY

**1** Demonstrates a pleasant, businesslike attitude toward both customers and co-workers.

**2** Exhibits respect and courtesy toward others.

**3** Exercises patience in dealing with customers and co-workers.

**4** Seeks and respects the opinions of others.

**5** Avoids debates and arguments with others—especially customers.

**6** Exhibits justified self-confidence while retaining personal modesty.

**7** Demonstrates enthusiastic initiative in acquiring new skills.

**8** Presents a professional personal image—impeccable grooming.

**9** Reacts calmly in critical situations.

**10** Retains objectivity in emotional situations.

**11** Accepts criticism constructively.

**12** Produces a high volume of work, enthusiastically and consistently.

**13** Demonstrates willingness to work evenings, weekends and holidays.

**14** Exhibits positive optimism.

**15** Exhibits sound judgment in making decisions.

**16** Smiles more often than not.

**17** Demonstrates dependability.

Employees need assurance that they are doing a good job. Consequently, evaluations can either serve as a morale booster or decrease employee motivation. Skill in handling ratings is very delicate and important. Because of their potential impact on job performance, evaluations and ratings are usually discussed with employees and trainees. In some instances the employee must sign a review.

Ratings and evaluations are used as a basis for raises. Many large retailers review employees twice a year, at which times raises may be recommended. Ratings are also used to decide on promotions, discharges, and transfers.

# Establishing Wage and Compensation Scales

Establishing wages for employees is another very important aspect of the personnel function. Compensation plans are developed according to several factors: the nature of

# MANAGEMENT TRAINING PROGRAM EVALUATION

NAME _____

Please complete the attached evaluation of your branch store training in detail. Rate each question according to the following guidelines and explain your answer fully and completely.

1 = UNSATISFCTORY
2 = MARGINAL
3 = AVERAGE
4 = VERY GOOD
5 = SUPERIOR

*(To be completed by the trainee.)*

Evaluate your branch store experience:

**1** Consider: quality and quantity of time spent with you; willingness to teach; clarity of instruction; thoroughness of instruction.

**2** Consider: follow-up and discussions of your required activities; constructive suggestions and help given to enable you to accomplish all your activities; constructive criticism given.

**3** Consider: observed strengths and weaknesses of your Sales Manager; quality and quantity of work produced; organizational skills; competence in human relations; effect of the above factors on you and your performance.

**4** Consider: exposure received to various duties and responsibilities; exposure to other managers; Store Manager, Group Manager, other departments.

**5** Additional comments.

**FIGURE 10-5**

A form used by trainees to evaluate the store's management training program. (Reproduced by permission of Dayton's.)

Developing wage
and compensation
plans is a
personnel function

the job, prevailing wages within the industry, competition for qualified employees, and availability of capital.

The various forms of compensation include the following.

Guaranteed annual wage

Straight salary

Hourly wage

Straight salary plus commission

Salary plus bonus

Straight commission

Quota bonus

## Guaranteed Annual Wage

Workers are paid *every* week despite business conditions.

## Straight Salary

A fixed amount of wages is paid by the week, by the month, or on some similar basis.

## Hourly Wage

Workers are paid according to hours worked. The prevailing minimum wages for the retail industry are generally used as a guideline. Sunday and holiday store hours usually call for higher hourly wages.

## Straight Salary Plus Commission

This method is used in many retail stores for different jobs. Cosmetics, shoes, and furniture are generally sold with commission as an added employee incentive. This form of compensation usually motivates the worker to try harder for sales.

## Salary Plus Bonus

This form of compensation includes a special addition to salary. It is generally given to executives when business is good or to regular employees at certain times of the year, such as Christmas.

## Straight Commission

In this case salespeople are paid a percentage of their total sales. This arrangement is common in the sale of high-ticket items like furniture, furs, and jewelry. The amount of commission varies according to the product and the store. This type of compensation arrangement provides the greatest incentive for salespeople. That is, the more they sell, the more they earn.

Straight
commission
subjects workers
to pressure

However, commission workers are subjected to pressure because earnings are reduced during low-sales periods. As a result, employees may have difficulty budgeting for their living expenses. For this reason, many salespeople are on a **drawing account.** They ''draw'' or take a set amount each payday regardless of their sales. This ''draw'' is subtracted from the total commission earned. If the amount is below what the salesperson should receive, that person receives the difference. When salespeople overdraw (take more than they earn), the excess amount is deducted the next month.

At Nordstrom Inc., nearly 90 percent of the clerks work on commission and the pressure to produce is high. Interestingly, many members of the owner's family also work on the selling floor. They compete with each other and expect other employees to do the same. Computers clock each clerk's sales per hour. The incentives to work hard are obvious, and commissions plus additional prizes are awarded to the highest producers.

### Quota Bonus

Salespeople must meet quota set by management

In this system salespeople are paid according to quotas set by management, and each salesperson is expected to meet a certain quota. A predetermined percentage (bonus) is paid on all sales above the established quota. For example, if the sales quota is set at $6000 and the salesperson has made sales totaling $8000, he or she will be entitled to a bonus based on $2000.

### Additional Compensation Plans

In order to motivate workers and reduce turnover, many firms have adopted plans known as **profit sharing, stock options,** and **salary supplements.** Whereas some companies offer these incentives only to management, others include all workers who are employed beyond a probationary period.

**Profit Sharing** In this plan the employee is given an opportunity to share in the success (profits) of the firm. A certain percentage of the profits is distributed to employees according to their salary levels. Some large retailers, such as Sears, Roebuck and Company, offer profit sharing to their employees. This plan is said to keep labor turnover to a minimum. Indeed, as a result of profit-sharing accumulations over long periods of employment, many of Sears' employees have retired with large sums of money.

**Stock Option Plans** Some firms allow employees to buy company stock at inside prices, that is, prices that are lower than the market value of the stock. These investments have generally been lucrative and have served to motivate workers.

**Salary Supplements** In order to increase the sales of a particular type of merchandise, salespeople are sometimes offered additional money or prizes. The terms **spiffs** and **PMs** (premium, prize, or **push money**) are used to identify this practice. The extra commissions are sometimes paid for by manufacturers. Prizes may consist of vacations or high-ticket merchandise.

# Establishing and Managing Fringe Benefits

Fringe benefits add to job attractiveness

The personnel department is also responsible for the management of fringe benefits, or employee services. Fringe benefits involve the indirect payments that workers receive, such as health insurance, paid vacations, sick leave, retirement plans, employee discounts, credit unions, and the like. These benefits add to the attraction of the job and help maintain good employee morale.

## Insurance Plans

Some form of dental, medical, and/or hospital plan is offered to all full-time employees. Some retailers pay the entire cost of these plans, while others share the costs with the employee. Some retailers allow medical coverage to be offered to part-time regulars.

## Credit Unions

Credit unions operate as banks and give employees an opportunity to save or borrow money at lower interest rates.

## Retirement Plans

Retirement benefits (pension plans) are also available as a fringe benefit. Pension plans are benefits that help develop company loyalty, motivate the worker, and reduce personnel turnover. A variety of pension plans are offered by large retailers. Some are paid entirely by the company and others are funded jointly by the firm and its employees. Some are transferable, while others terminate when employees leave the firm. A good plan has a tendency to "lock" the employee into staying with the company, thereby reducing labor turnover.

# LABOR AND THE LAW

*Unions—another responsibility of the personnel department*

Another responsibility of the personnel department is dealing with organized labor. The growth of unions in the retail industry has been slow. Until recently only a small percentage of salespeople were organized. Union membership was confined essentially to nonselling personnel, such as warehouse workers, truck drivers, and maintenance employees.

To some extent, sales personnel have been reluctant to join unions because they are not anxious to have their wages reduced by union dues, while part-time workers do not view their jobs as careers. Furthermore, salespeople do not view themselves as blue-collar workers; they tend to identify themselves as white-collar workers aspiring to management positions. However, the current trend is toward unions.

At present, most large supermarkets are unionized, most often with the Retail Clerks International Association. Macy's and Gimbel's are additional examples of large retail organizations that are unionized.

The efforts of unions in the retailing industry are similar to those in other industries. They strive for better working conditions, more fringe benefits, job security, more objective criteria for promotion and salary increases, and the like. The personnel department is involved with union negotiations, employee grievances, and the monitoring of rules and union contract guidelines.

### NEW TERMS

| | |
|---|---|
| application form | internship program |
| blind ad | job analysis |
| discharged | job description |
| drawing account | job rotation |

| | |
|---|---|
| job specification | profit sharing |
| job transfer | promotion |
| layoff | push money |
| lie detector | rail interview |
| on-the-job training | salary supplement |
| open ad | shopper's report |
| orientation training | spiff |
| PM | stock option |
| polygraph instrument | vestibule training |

# CHAPTER HIGHLIGHTS

1 Personnel management is composed of the following activities: recruitment and hiring, training and retraining, transfers, promotion and discharge, wage and compensation scales, and fringe benefits.

2 Recruitment involves solicitation of job applicants. Sources of new personnel exist both within the firm (employee recommendations, transfers, promotions) and outside it (employment agencies, schools, advertisements).

3 The selection process includes job analyses, job descriptions, application blanks, interviews, and testing. After selection, employees often undergo training.

4 Compensation plans include a guaranteed annual wage, straight salary, hourly wage, straight salary plus commission, salary plus bonus, straight commission, and quota bonus.

5 In order to reduce labor turnover and motivate workers, many firms adopt profit sharing, stock option plans, and salary supplements.

6 Until recently retail sales personnel were reluctant to join unions. The efforts of retail unions are similar to those in other industries, involving better working conditions, increased fringe benefits, and job security. As a result, the personnel department must sometimes deal with unions.

# QUESTIONS

1 What are the main activities of the personnel department?

2 How does the law affect the hiring process in the retail industry?

3 How does an application blank help screen employees?

4 How does the training of new, inexperienced employees differ from the retraining of older, experienced workers?

5 How can effective employee evaluation help both employees and management?

6 Which methods of compensation are most motivating for the salesperson? Explain.

7 What is the rationale for retailers offering fringe benefits that are not required by law?

8 How will the growth of unionization affect communication between store managers and employees?

9 Why are many employed people reluctant to answer blind ads for retail jobs?

10 Why does the use of polygraph instruments in the hiring process cause controversy?

11 How does job rotation improve an employee's understanding of his or her store's operations?

# FIELD PROJECTS

1 Compare the approaches used in the recruitment of retail employees through the classified sections of
A daily newspaper
A trade paper like *Chain Store Age* or *Women's Wear Daily*
A professional magazine like *Stores*
   a How do the ads differ?
   b How do the types of jobs listed in the ads differ?

2 Visit the personnel office of two large retailers, one that is unionized and one that is not. Compare the two stores in terms of the following fringe benefits.
Health insurance
Paid vacations
Sick leave
Retirement plans
Employee discounts

# CASES

1 Rodeo Drive in Beverly Hills, California, is a famous street filled with exclusive shops. Among them is Bijan, a men's store that is considered one of the world's most expensive stores. For example, the lowest-priced item is a $65 tie. The people who shop there routinely spend $150,000 in an afternoon. According to the owner, Bijan Palizad, customers are requested to make an appointment to shop. Only one client is served at a time, and those who make appointments have the entire staff available to them.

The owner considers himself a "clothing doctor" who prescribes an image for his clients. He merchandises for the richest of the rich, keeping a file on each customer in order to avoid errors as to customer preferences, habits, and background. He will not disclose the names of his customers, but they include royalty, heads of state, and many other famous people.

   a Assume that Mr. Palizad has called your employment office for qualified people to fill three sales positions. How will you screen applicants for these positions?
   b If Mr. Palizad were considering a new training program, how would you advise him?

**2** When thousands of dollars' worth of jewelry disappeared from the store, a large jewelry retailer hired a firm to administer lie detector tests to its employees rather than dismiss them summarily. This was done because the rate of internal thefts had reached alarming proportions.

The merchant undertook this action without consulting with the employees. He felt that the use of a polygraph instrument was the prerogative of the employer, and took a negative view of employees who might refuse to take the test.

When the employees were asked to take the test, they were also asked to sign a release form that would make the results available to other retailers.

    **a**  What are your opinions regarding the use of the test in this case?
    **b**  How do you feel about the release form?
    **c**  Do you agree with the merchant's view of employees who refuse to take lie detector tests?

**3** A large variety store chain has found that there are many problems associated with its plan to transfer promising executives to another branch in a different geographic location. To a large extent, this is due to the increased number of women in the work force. The fact is that people who are happy in their own jobs are not interested in their spouse's relocating without some assurance of a good job for themselves as well.

In the case of one particularly talented executive who is willing to transfer, his wife's job status has also become pertinent. Not only is her job important to her, but the couple recognizes that the second income is vital to the family's budget.

At first the personnel director tried to deal with the problem by providing lists of employment agencies at the new location, tips on handling job interviews, and the like. The couple did not consider these suggestions adequate and requested a position for the wife within the chain organization at the new location.

Unfortunately, the personnel director cannot offer a job to the wife because of the chain's rule against nepotism, that is, a restriction on husbands, wives, or other family members working for the firm at the same time. However, the couple in this case has asked that the rule be waived so that the transfer can be achieved.

    **a**  If you were the personnel director, what action would you take?
    **b**  What type of program might be developed to help with problems like this one in the future? List and explain some of the details.

# REFERENCES

Berman, B., and J. R. Evans, *Retail Management: A Strategic Approach* (New York: Macmillan, 1979), chap. 9.

Broadwell, M. M., *The Supervisor and On-the-Job Training* (Reading, Mass.: Addison-Wesley, 1975).

Churchill, G. A., R. H. Collins, and W. A. Strang, "Should Retail Salespersons Be Similar to Their Customers?" *Journal of Retailing*, 51 (Fall 1975), pp. 29–42.

Connellan, T. K., *How to Improve Human Performance* (New York: Harper & Row, 1978).

Hartzler, F., *The Retail Salesperson,* 2nd ed. (New York: McGraw-Hill, 1979).

Hollon, C. J., and M. Gable, "Information Sources in Retail Employment Decision-Making Process," *Journal of Retailing,* 55 (Fall 1979), pp. 58–74.

Johnson, R. G., *The Appraisal Interview Guide* (New York: AMACOM, 1979).

Muczyk, J. P., T. H. Mattheiss, and M. Gable, "Predicting Success of Store Managers," *Journal of Retailing,* 50 (Summer 1974), pp. 43–49, 104.

Rotondi, A. M., "Nonfinancial Compensation: A Productive Motivator," *Supervision,* September 1978, pp. 9–10.

Spivey, W. A., J. M. Munson, and W. B. Locander, "Meeting Retail Staffing Needs Via Improved Selection," *Journal of Retailing,* 55 (Winter 1979), pp. 3–19.

Stidger, R. W., *The Competence Game* (New York: Van Nostrand Reinhold, Thomond Press, 1980).

Still, R. R., E. W. Cundiff, and N. A. P. Gouvine, *Sales Management* (Englewood Cliffs, N.J.: Prentice-Hall, 1981).

Strauss, G., and L. R. Sayles, *Personnel: The Human Problems of Management* (Englewood Cliffs, N.J.: Prentice-Hall, 1980).

Williams, J. R., "President's Letter," *Stores,* 62 (August 1980), p. 56.

# chapter 11
# STORE LOCATION

**After completing this chapter, you should be able to:**

1   Identify the reasons why store location is important.
2   List the factors that determine the location of a store.
3   List the six categories of retail locations.
4   Identify the factors that retailers consider when choosing a site.
5   Discuss the advantages and disadvantages of buying or renting a retail outlet.
6   Identify trends in store location.

In the previous chapter you learned about the ways in which retail stores are organized and staffed. You saw that planning is essential to the development of sound business procedures, and that lines of organization depend on the type of retail outlet under consideration. It was pointed out, however, that no organizational plan is effective without the involvement of trained personnel.

*Stores usually locate according to carefully developed plans*

In this chapter we turn our attention to the location of retail stores. Have you ever wondered why supermarkets are usually surrounded by a variety of small stores? Or why several department stores frequently occupy space close to one another? There are logical reasons for these patterns, and they emerge from carefully developed plans. In fact, for large stores these plans are so elaborate that computers are often used to analyze information and make decisions. In this chapter we will examine the various aspects of store location.

# THE IMPORTANCE OF STORE LOCATION

## Return on Investment

Since the opening of a store requires a substantial initial investment, the retailer seeks a location that will return that investment within a reasonable time. Even starting a small store can cost many thousands of dollars, while department stores and other large retail organizations entail investments of hundreds of thousands of dollars—and more. Since investment funds are either borrowed or accumulated, or both, it is crucial that a store's location provide the new owner with a good chance of recouping that money.

## The Need for Profits

Needless to say, retail businesses, like any other type of business, must show profits. In the case of retailing, however, the extent of those profits depends in large measure on the store's location. From this point of view, for example, opening a store to sell maternity clothes in a fast-growing community with many young couples makes good business sense, while starting a similar enterprise in a stable, older area does not.

You have already learned that management efficiency and effective merchandising policies contribute to a store's success. Despite these characteristics, however, a poor location will almost certainly result in the store's failure.

## Convenience to Consumers

Since consumers require a variety of products, they need convenient access to stores that satisfy those requirements. In addition, the locations of these stores should meet their particular shopping needs. For example, establishments like food, drug, and dry cleaning stores that sell convenience items and services should be within easy reach of the shopper. This is so because people make frequent trips to such stores and expect them to be close to their home or place of business. On the other hand, consumers are willing to travel longer distances for less frequently purchased items (shopping goods), such as clothing, appliances, and furniture. As a result, department, specialty, and discount stores that sell such merchandise are often located farther away. Frequently, too, several department stores are located close to each other in order to attract more customers.

# DECISION FACTORS IN STORE LOCATION

*Definition of a trading area*

Before discussing the factors that determine the location of a store, we must identify the types of areas in which stores are located. The term that is most frequently used to describe a store's customer potential is **trading area.** Basically, a trading area is a geographic section from which a store draws the bulk of its customers. For stores that sell convenience items, the area might encompass a few city streets; in a suburban setting, it might include several distinct residential developments; in a rural district, it could encompass several square miles. On the other hand, the trading area for larger stores is usually much greater. For example, Filene's department store in Boston attracts customers from the entire Boston metropolitan area as well as from outside of the state. The Metrocenter in Phoenix, a well-known shopping center, caters to consumers from the newly developed suburban areas surrounding Phoenix as well as from the sunbelt city itself. It follows, then, that retailers that are planning new stores must select locations with a clear understanding of the extent of their trading area. Once this is understood, the retailer is ready to consider the factors that determine the store's location.

Filene's trading area includes Boston residents as well as consumers from outlying areas.

# The Population of the Trading Area

### Current Population Figures

Obviously, the trading area should contain a sufficient number of potential customers to satisfy the new store's planned sales. Population counts can be secured from municipalities, chambers of commerce, and trade associations. The federal government takes a population census every ten years (the latest one was done in 1980), and those figures are valuable for planning purposes. Of course, supplemental local and regional data should be used when a community's census information is no longer reliable.

### Income Levels and Occupations in the Trading Area

*A close look at the people in the trading area*

Every effort should be made to determine the income levels and occupational clusters in the trading area. Opening a specialty store selling high-priced jewelry in an essentially working-class district would be unwise. Similar situations can be imagined with regard to low-priced merchandise. Information about income levels and occupations can be secured from census reports and local banks.

### Seasonal Changes, Trading Area Business, and Industry

Most retail firms depend on year-round sales to sustain their revenues. Consequently, they must avoid locating in areas that cater mostly to tourists and vacationers. On the other hand, quite a few retailers sustain themselves on revenues that come in during short periods of each year. These firms generally operate in resort areas that attract skiers, boat enthusiasts, sightseers, and the like. These retailers might close their doors during off-peak months, or reduce their stock accordingly.

*The importance of business and industry in a trading area*

Another important consideration is the business and industrial composition of the trading area. A community that depends on one industry for its sustenance is subject to that industry's problems. So are the retailers who serve that area. A case in point is the New England textile industry, which suffered terrible reverses in the 1950s. As a result of high unemployment resulting from bankruptcies of textile firms, local retailers suffered greatly. That experience has been duplicated elsewhere and has caused new retail businesses to seek more industrially diversified trading areas.

A more recent example of the adverse impact of industrial reverses on retailers occurred in 1980. As a result of severely reduced demand for automobiles, car manufacturers laid off large numbers of workers and even closed plants. This had the "ripple effect" of closing many retail car dealerships and damaging a variety of stores that depended on car workers' patronage.

### Age Groups—Sexual Composition of the Trading Area

*Singles, young marrieds, senior citizens, etc.*

To a large extent, success in a trading area is tied to the number of consumers in particular age groups. Thus, it is important that the new retailer consider such age-related statistics as the numbers of singles, young marrieds, families whose children no longer live at home, senior citizens, and teenagers living in the trading area. The types of merchandise carried and the selling strategies employed are obviously tied to the needs and lifestyles of these groups.

The retailer who intends to sell primarily or exclusively to members of one sex must know the approximate proportion of that population in the trading area. In addition, a breakdown of the data by age within each sex category helps the retailer gauge the potential market. These data can be secured from census reports.

## Ethnic, Religious, and Special Consumer Groups

Since our society contains many distinct ethnic and religious groups, retailers must know whether consumers in those groups have special needs that reflect their cultures and religious practices. For example, the dress requirements of the Pennsylvania Amish differ radically from those of California's Chicanos. In the same vein, the food preferences of Chinese Americans are quite unlike those of other ethnic groups in our country.

*Special consumer groups*

Special consumer groups, such as college youth, gays, and the handicapped, are also found in communities. To a large extent, these groups have particular buying needs that can be turned into profitable sales by sensitive and perceptive retailers.

## Apartments Versus Homes

Some trading areas consist largely of homes, others of apartments, and still others of a combination of the two. Since the needs of homeowners differ to some extent from those of apartment dwellers, retail location planning should consider the mix of dwellings in the trading area.

## Population Dynamics

*Growth, decline, and constancy of trading area populations*

Having considered the basic population characteristics of a trading area, the retailer must determine whether the population is expected to grow, decline, or remain constant. This is important for two reasons: (1) because it enables the merchant to estimate short-range sales (perhaps 1 to 3 years), and (2) because it is a predictor of long-range business possibilities. Obviously, a trading area with a growing population presents a radically different profit potential than a stable or declining one.

The consumers of this modern Grand Union supermarket are primarily apartment house dwellers.

# Socioeconomic Conditions in the Trading Area

### Employment and Unemployment

As indicated earlier, the extent of business and industry in a trading area is an important consideration in locating a retail outlet. Associated with this factor is the normal level of employment provided by firms in the area. Needless to say, retailing flourishes best where employment is steady. The new retailer, then, should examine the employment history of the area, using census data, state labor department reports, and chamber of commerce statistics.

### The Vitality of the Trading Area

Some communities are active places, while others are not. Some areas boast fine schools, socially conscious trade associations, frequent community events, and even tourist attractions. Other areas show few signs of vitality and poor interrelationships among community groups. It should be obvious that the retailer with a choice of location will opt for the more dynamic community, expecting (correctly) that that community will provide a more favorable setting for retail businesses.

### Laws That Affect Retailers

The retailer seeking a new location should check local and state laws that affect retail enterprises. These laws generally refer to taxes: income, sales, property, occupancy, and so forth; credit regulations, such as maximum interest rates that may be charged on customers' past-due accounts; license requirements; and store business hours. When the trading area encompasses communities in more than one state, these items must be checked carefully for their impact on sales, expenses, and profits.

### Traffic Considerations

You have already learned that some types of retail outlets, such as convenience stores, are located close to their potential customers. On the other hand, consumers are willing to travel to other types of retail stores, such as warehouse outlets and combination stores. Nevertheless, whether they are shopping on foot, by car, by bus, or by rail, consumers should be able to reach their destination without great inconvenience. When cars are involved, highways and access roads should service customers without frequent bumper-to-bumper tie-ups.

A retail store should also be located a reasonable distance from its suppliers. This allows the store to restock items quickly for the convenience of customers.

### Miscellaneous Socioeconomic Considerations

Several other factors affect the location of a retail store. Among them are the following.

1  Local attractions like museums and parks often bring people from outside the trading area to the area's retail outlets.

2  Parking space should be adequate. Nothing so turns off a potential customer as driving through a packed parking lot.

3   The trading area or its vicinity should contain banks that welcome retail businesses. Since retailers borrow funds from time to time, they need bankers with an appreciation of retailers' needs.

4   In view of current crime rates, a trading area should provide satisfactory police and fire protection. In some cases private guards and even guard dogs must be employed to augment local police forces. In such instances the cost of the additional protection is an added expense for the retailer.

5   Since many retailers advertise on a regular basis, the community and surrounding communities should contain adequate advertising outlets. These media might include local and regional newspapers, radio, television, public vehicles (buses and trains), and local magazines.

## Competition

*Assessing the competition*

The final factor to consider in locating a store is the nature and extent of competing outlets. The following matters should be studied.

1   The number and types of competing stores. If the trading area already contains a sufficient number of such stores, it would probably be unwise to open a new one.

2   The extent of chain ownership among competitors. This is important to know because of the drawing power and financial strength of chains.

3   The existence of shopping facilities in the trading area that attract large segments of the trading area's population. If the new retail outlet cannot be located in those facilities, it must be prepared to do business with smaller groups of people.

4   The possibility that existing stores may try to destroy the new store's chances of success by underselling and developing irresistible sales promotions. Existing stores are sometimes willing to spend substantial sums to stifle new competition.

# TYPES OF SHOPPING AREAS

From your reading in previous chapters you have already learned that retail outlets are diverse in their purposes, appeal, and selling strategies. Tied to this diversity is the community area or facility in which they locate. Let's examine the types of shopping locations found in our country.

*Six categories of retail locations*

Basically, there are six categories of retail locations. They are

1   Central (downtown) shopping districts
2   Secondary shopping areas
3   Neighborhood shopping districts
4   Shopping centers
5   Highway outlets, including freestanding stores
6   Specialty shopping areas

Each of these categories contains retail outlets whose appeal is reflected by their location. Let's take a closer look at these shopping areas.

## Central (Downtown) Shopping Districts

Every city and town has at least one **central shopping district,** also called a **downtown shopping district,** that contains a variety of stores. These range from department stores to chain and independent specialty shops. Customers in such areas consist of local residents, workers in area businesses, and shoppers from outlying communities. As a result of this high concentration of consumers, retail space in a central district is generally valuable and expensive.

The typical cluster of stores selling shopping goods in a downtown area allows the consumer to comparison shop for best values and selections with a minimum of travel and inconvenience. It is no accident that so many of the best-known stores are located so close to each other. Contrary to what many beginning students of retailing believe, the stores actually benefit from each other's attempts to attract customers to their stores.

A number of convenience stores are usually found alongside the shopping goods establishments. Capitalizing on the presence of out-of-area consumers, stores that sell food, drug, and variety items augment their anticipated revenues. The mix of shopping goods and convenience stores, coupled with the high population density of the downtown area, provides a picture of bustling activity. This, in turn, creates a psychological appeal to consumers to shop "where the action is."

## Secondary Shopping Areas

In addition to central districts, cities contain other shopping areas that are similar to, but smaller than, the downtown district. Known as **secondary shopping areas,** they also

Located in Seattle's central shopping district, this was J. C. Penney's first city store.

Secondary shopping areas are smaller than central districts

contain a mix of shopping goods establishments and convenience stores. These areas attract local consumers as well as those from nearby communities who are unwilling to travel to the central district.

Compared to central districts, secondary shopping areas provide consumers with a limited selection of merchandise. Nevertheless, the proximity of these areas to consumers' homes, the availability of public transit, and the adequacy of parking attract sufficient numbers of shoppers to make secondary shopping areas desirable retail locations.

# Neighborhood
# Shopping Districts

Neighborhood shopping districts contain convenience stores

Undoubtedly, the neighborhood in which you live contains convenience stores that provide you and members of your family with the food and nonfood items you require daily. These stores, plus an occasional specialty store, comprise what is known as a **neighborhood shopping district.** A typical district has a selection of the following types of stores: bakery, hardware store, drugstore, meat market, grocery and produce stores, florist, laundromat, and variety store. Among specialty outlets, the most common types are those that carry ready-to-wear merchandise.

In an effort to rehabilitate run-down areas, some localities have constructed neighborhood malls that contain both convenience and specialty stores. Though they are modest in design, these malls enable consumers to shop in pleasant surroundings and encourage retailers to maintain attractive stores.

# Shopping Centers

To understand the development of shopping centers, you should know that before World War II the United States was made up of urban and rural areas, with few suburbs. With the return of veterans and the start of many new families, however, the intense need for housing impelled builders to construct suburban communities. This fact, plus the mobility provided by automobiles, led to the development of suburban shopping centers.

Shopping centers are regional, community, or neighborhood

These centers are of three types: regional, community, and neighborhood. A **regional shopping center** serves consumers from a number of communities, with the trading area containing about 150,000 people. It is built either by a developer who rents the stores to retailers or by a large retailer, such as May Department Stores, that operates a main (anchor) store in the center and rents the remaining stores to other retailers. The center usually has one or more large department store branches plus an assortment of limited-line, convenience, and variety stores. Chains invariably have outlets in these centers.

The activities permitted to retailers in regional shopping centers are usually specified in their leases (rental contracts). Thus, the number and types of competitive outlets are controlled; business hours are regulated; and sharing of advertising and promotion costs is generally required. In return for compliance with these controls, however, the center provides convenient parking, pleasant surroundings, easy access, and in many cases, enclosed malls.

At first, regional shopping centers met with little resistance from cities and towns. Recently, however, the picture has changed considerably. As a result of pressure by municipalities and environmental groups, the federal government has issued a policy called community conservation guidance. In effect, it gives a community the right to object to projects undertaken by another community if it feels that such projects will damage its interests. In the case of planned shopping centers, it requires federal agencies to study and report on community opposition to the centers. If the report agrees with a community's position, the shopping center's developers can be prevented from proceeding with their plans. Though some of the protest against new shopping centers is based on energy and environmental considerations, much of it stems from the commercial conflict between urban retail centers and suburban developers. The U.S. Department of Housing and Urban Development has indicated that many municipalities have filed protests. Among those involved were New Brunswick, New Jersey; Burlington, Vermont; and Duluth, Minnesota.

Sometimes community and commercial pressure cause shopping center developers to change their plans. Such was the case with Hartz Mountain Industries, which halted plans for a regional shopping center in the New Jersey Meadowlands in 1980 because of opposition from community organizations, retailers in the district, and community planners.

A **community shopping center** is smaller than a regional one, and has as its largest tenant either a scaled-down department store or a specialty store. Its trading area consists of 40,000 to 150,000 people, and it has much in common with secondary shopping areas. Owners of community shopping centers provide adequate parking, planned competition, and easy access. The centers also contain a variety of convenience stores.

A **neighborhood shopping center,** sometimes called a **strip center,** is a relatively small group of stores alongside each other. Its largest tenant is usually a supermarket,

This strip center is located on a well-traveled road.

Changes in strip
centers

a variety store, or a drugstore, and its trading area population runs between 7,000 and 40,000. Convenience stores comprise the remaining tenants, and the "strip" is generally constructed on main neighborhood roads that carry substantial traffic.

Some retail analysts detect a movement away from regional shopping centers and toward strip centers. However, the newer centers are different from conventional ones in that they combine retail stores with office and residential construction. To some extent, this change to more modest shopping centers is due to the energy and environmental crises.

In an attempt to attract consumers, strip centers are being built with unusual architectural designs. Some are constructed in wooded areas; others use beautiful landscaping, atriums, and canopies to create an atmosphere of gracious living. Still others develop their buildings and stores around special themes to strike a note of originality and individuality.

Despite careful planning and expert advice, however, even large stores are sometimes located poorly. An example of an unfortunate location for a suburban store is provided by Bergdorf Goodman, the prestigious Fifth Avenue (New York City) women's specialty shop. Bergdorf opened its first branch store in White Plains, a suburb of New York City, in 1974. However, management found that it was unable to transfer its moneyed image to a suburban setting and closed its doors early in 1980. Despite this experience, the New York City location continues to operate successfully.

As part of their urban renewal programs, some communities have constructed new shopping centers in their central districts. Contrary to fears expressed by other merchants in those areas, the new centers have attracted additional shoppers to the downtown areas, thereby aiding the merchants already there.

# Highway Outlets, Including Freestanding Stores

Anyone who has traveled on major or secondary highways has seen stores of all kinds along the way. You may come across a large furniture outlet with attractive window

Highway outlets provide comfortable parking for shoppers.

Highway outlets
are either strings
of stores or
freestanding

displays; or you may pass a shoe discount store with imposing posters announcing low prices; you will probably also find a well-known discount department store.

In recent years **highway outlets** have become more popular with shoppers. This is due to the ease of reaching them, the excellent parking they provide, the low prices they offer, and the extensive advertising done by the stores. Unlike shopping centers, in which stores benefit from each other's ability to attract customers, highway stores rely on their own efforts to bring in customers.

A highway outlet may stand by itself (**freestanding**) or be one of a number of stores. For example, it may be a lone discount center or a chain operation surrounded by fast-food and convenience stores. In some cases the arrangement of stores is planned, and in others it results from unplanned and uncoordinated decisions by retailers.

# Specialty Shopping Areas

Specialty
shopping areas
contain limited-
line stores that sell
similar
merchandise

Most cities contain shopping areas containing a number of stores that sell the same kind of limited-line goods. Known as **specialty shopping areas,** they cater to consumers who are willing to travel in order to have a choice among wide selections of merchandise and prices. The following illustration indicates the attraction these areas hold for shoppers. Suppose a woman wants to buy a particular type of ring. She might go to a central or secondary shopping area or perhaps to a shopping center for her purchase. She will probably find a good selection of rings at those locations. However, a shopping area that specializes in the sale of jewelry would undoubtedly widen the choices available to her. With a minimum of inconvenience, she could walk from one specialty shop to another and examine hundreds of rings.

In addition to areas that specialize in jewelry, there are specialty shopping areas devoted to home furnishings, trimmings, art galleries, automobiles, boats, and many other types of merchandise. It is conceivable that this type of location will grow in popularity as cities become more attractive places in which to shop.

One other aspect of retail store locations is worthy of comment. The preliminary census count for 1980 indicated a shift of population clusters from urban and suburban areas to more distant suburbs, small municipalities, and rural districts. As a result, we can expect new retail locations to reflect these changes.

# CHOOSING A SITE

Factors in
selecting a store
location

Having examined the decision factors used in locating a retail outlet, and having discussed the various types of shopping areas, we turn our attention to the selection of a specific store location. There are a number of matters that the new retailer should consider if the enterprise is to get off to a good start. They are

1 Closeness to competitors
2 Correct blend of stores
3 Potential sales

4 Traffic patterns
5 Visibility of the store
6 Parking
7 Zoning laws

# Closeness to Competitors

Competition can work for or against new retailers

Curious as it may sound, competition may work for or against new retailers. As you have seen, department stores are often grouped in the same shopping area. Since each store brings different consumers into the area, there can be benefits for all. The same situation prevails in specialty store areas.

On the other hand, competition can sometimes be damaging to a new store. For example, an enterprising young man with little retailing experience decided to open a hardware store in a secondary shopping area. Neglecting to check the trading area carefully, he missed the fact that it already contained another hardware store, an auto supply store that carried hardware items, and a discount center that also sold hardware. Unfortunately for the young man, his store failed in its first year because the trading area's population was insufficient to support an additional hardware outlet.

# Correct Blend of Stores

A new retailer must be careful to locate where the store will be compatible with other stores nearby. That is, neighboring stores should attract consumers who may also be willing to shop in the new store. For example, opening a children's clothing store close to women's-wear stores makes sense. On the other hand, the same store surrounded by bars and grills, office equipment outlets, or auto repair shops makes little sense. The merchant, then, should survey the immediate and surrounding areas carefully in order to make a correct assessment of the planned store's compatibility with other stores.

# Potential Sales

You have already learned that a trading area should be studied for population size and composition, income levels, occupations, and so forth. This information helps the new retailer judge the number of potential customers for the planned store. However, more precise figures are needed to estimate the new store's sales. These may be determined from

Techniques for estimating potential sales

1 A count of people who pass by the location of the store.
2 A check of how well competitors appear to be doing. This can be accomplished by visiting these outlets and counting the number of customers, employees, departments, and so on.
3 Interviews with manufacturers, jobbers, and wholesalers.
4 Discussions with chamber of commerce members, bank executives, and municipal officials.

## Traffic Patterns

A new retailer who will depend on travel convenience as a means of attracting customers should examine several traffic factors. In the case of suburban shopping centers and highway outlets, consideration should be given to road conditions and the number of cars passing by or close to the store. If the store is to be located in an urban setting, attention should be paid to the availability of mass transit facilities (buses, trains, etc.) and, where automobiles are involved, the condition of roads and access streets.

## Visibility of the Store

The more visible a store, the higher its potential sales

You have probably visited shopping areas where traffic is heavier on one side of a street than on the other. You may also have noticed that corner stores usually have more window space than other stores. Of course, the more visible a store is to passing pedestrians and cars, the more valuable the location. Since rents are usually higher in such locations, the new retailer must judge whether it is worth paying the additional cost. This decision can best be made by estimating the number of potential customers—and, hence, sales—that may be derived from the favorable location of the store.

## Parking

Though suburban shopping centers almost always provide parking for customers, the parking area must be large enough to accommodate shoppers adequately. In the case of urban stores, parking should be available to customers who drive to the shopping area. Consideration must also be given to the cost of parking in municipal and private parking facilities.

## Zoning Laws

Communities enact laws governing building projects

The recent emphasis on environmental problems has caused municipalities to strengthen their **zoning laws,** also known as **zoning codes.** These regulations generally restrict the types of building that are permitted in a community. The new retailer should check zoning laws carefully for their possible impact on both short- and long-term business prospects. At times it is necessary to secure the services of an attorney for careful consideration of the regulations.

# BUYING OR RENTING A RETAIL OUTLET

One final matter must be considered by the new retailer. This is the question of whether to purchase or rent the store. Let's examine both possibilities.

## Purchasing a Retail Outlet

Though ownership of a store (and possibly the site) may be expensive, it has its advantages. These include the following.

1 The ability to make physical changes in the store without interference. (Zoning laws must be checked, however.)

2 The possibility of renting store space to other retailers, thereby increasing income.

3 The possibility that the store may increase in value over time.

4 The profit that accrues to the owner if the property is sold at a price that is higher than the purchase price.

On the other hand, the new owner must also contend with the following disadvantages.

1 Maintenance costs.

2 Potential tax increases.

3 The possibility of a decrease in the value of the location.

4 Losses due to fire, flood, or natural disasters.

## Renting a Retail Outlet

When renting a store, a retailer signs a *lease,* (i.e., a contract) with a landlord. Leases are often renewable for non-shopping-center stores, and the retailer (tenant) is usually required to pay a fixed sum each month for a number of years. In some leases the sum increases after a certain period. In both cases, the rent remains fixed regardless of the amount of business the retailer does.

Shopping center leases are generally tied to the retailer's sales volume. A typical lease guarantees the landlord a certain minimum amount plus a percentage of sales. Thus, if the retailer's guarantee is $2,500 a year plus 5 percent of sales, the landlord will receive a total of $7,500 for a year when sales amount to $100,000 [$2,500 + (.05 × $100,000)]. In addition to the payment of rent, shopping center leases often require tenants to contribute to the center's advertising and maintenance costs.

A retail tenant is usually expected to bear the finishing costs of the store. These include carpentry and plumbing work, fixtures, shelving, flooring, and the like.

The advantages of leasing a store are as follows.

1 No initial investment for a building and/or land.

2 The opportunity to move elsewhere at the expiration of the lease.

3 The ability to concentrate on merchandising instead of on real estate problems.

The main disadvantage of leasing involves the restrictions imposed on the retailer by the lease. These may involve business hours, store alterations, types of merchandise carried, and limitations on displays.

A typical lease for a retailer is shown in the appendix at the end of this chapter.

# TRENDS IN
# STORE LOCATION

Though retailing is a volatile field in which any prediction is fraught with danger, the following trends appear to be emerging.

Retailing is an
ever-changing
field

1 A revitalization of downtown retail stores. Aided in many cases by federal funds, decaying cities and towns show signs of renewed vigor. St. Louis and Detroit are two examples of this trend.

2 Strong challenges to the construction of regional shopping centers by communities, planners, and environmental groups.

3 Subleasing by retailers of part or all of their leased store buildings. This allows the retailers (prime tenants) to cut costs.

4 A move toward strip rather than regional shopping centers.

5 A preference for enclosed malls rather than open areas.

6 The inclusion of tax escalation provisions in shopping center leases. With this addition, tenants, not landlords, pay tax increases.

7 A tendency for owners of real estate in urban areas not to renew the leases of large-area tenants like supermarkets. Instead, the vacated space is divided into smaller spaces for specialty stores and convenience stores, thereby earning the landlord higher rents.

8 Larger shopping centers combine retail outlets with recreational and amusement facilities. Families make shopping a "day out," with activities provided for children while the adults shop.

9 A reluctance on the part of retailers to rent space in high-rise buildings where rents are costly. More planning and care characterize merchants' searches for new city locations.

This enclosed multi-level shopping center in Richmond, California, attracts consumers with its many stores and recreational conveniences.

10 A move toward fewer and smaller supermarkets in cities because of spiraling rents and soaring energy costs.

**NEW TERMS**

| | |
|---|---|
| central shopping district | regional shopping center |
| community shopping center | secondary shopping area |
| downtown shopping district | specialty shopping area |
| freestanding store | strip center |
| highway outlet | trading area |
| neighborhood shopping center | zoning code |
| neighborhood shopping district | zoning law |

# CHAPTER HIGHLIGHTS

1 Retailers seek store locations that will provide an adequate return on investment within a reasonable time.

2 Despite efficient management and wise merchandising policies, a store can fail because of poor location.

3 While consumers are willing to travel some distance for shopping goods, they expect convenience stores to be located near their home or place of business.

4 A trading area is a geographic section from which a store draws the bulk of its customers.

5 In describing the population of a trading area, a retailer is interested in current population; income and occupation; seasonal changes; the character of the trading area's business and industry; age groups; sex composition; ethnic, religious, and special groups; apartments and homes; and the dynamics of the population.

6 The following socioeconomic conditions of a trading area should be studied for their retail potential: employment and unemployment, laws that affect retailers, traffic considerations, local attractions, parking, the attitude of banks toward retailers, police and fire protection, and advertising outlets.

7 When analyzing the nature and extent of competing stores in a trading area, a new retailer should consider the number and types of competing outlets, the extent of chain ownership among competitors, the existence of large shopping facilities, and the possibility that existing stores may try to destroy the new store's chances of success by means of underselling and special sales promotions.

8 The categories of retail location are as follows: central or downtown districts, secondary shopping areas, neighborhood shopping districts, shopping centers, highway outlets (including freestanding stores), and specialty shopping areas.

9 In selecting a specific store location, a new retailer should consider the following matters: closeness to competitors, blend of stores, potential sales, traffic patterns, visibility of the store, parking, and zoning laws.

10 A new retailer must consider whether to buy or rent a store. While a store owner

has more freedom in the use of the property, he or she must contend with maintenance costs and taxes. Renting a store involves paying either a fixed amount for the duration of the lease or a minimum amount plus a percentage of sales.

11   Trends in store location range from revitalization of downtown shopping districts to the increased popularity of strip shopping centers.

## QUESTIONS

1   How can a poor location hurt a store that is managed efficiently and maintains effective merchandising policies?

2   Why are there several types of trading areas?

3   Where can a new retailer secure a population count for a particular trading area?

4   Why should a retailer be interested in the incomes and occupations of a trading area's population?

5   How are seasonal changes related to the retail sales potential of a trading area?

6   Name several special consumer groups in addition to those mentioned in this chapter. How do retailers benefit from understanding the needs of these special groups?

7   Why is it important to know whether a trading area's population is constant, growing, or declining?

8   Do you agree with state laws that limit the maximum rate of interest that retailers may charge on customers' past-due accounts? Why?

9   In what ways might an existing shopping center attempt to undercut a new competitor? In your opinion, is this practice ethical? Why?

10   What do you think will happen to downtown shopping districts during the next 10 years?

11   Do you agree with federal intervention in cases of community opposition to regional shopping centers? Why?

12   What are some of the characteristics of highway outlets that make them attractive to shoppers?

13   If you were opening a women's shoe store, what types of stores would you *not* want nearby? (List at least five types.)

14   In what ways might zoning laws affect retail outlets?

15   If you had the option of buying or renting a freestanding store, which would you prefer? Why? (Assume that you have the funds to start the store.)

## FIELD PROJECTS

1   Visit a shopping area in your community or a nearby one. Find out the following information.

    a   The type of trading area it is.

    b   The categories of retail outlets in the trading area (department stores, specialty stores, etc.) and the number in each category.

2 Visit an independent store owner in your community and secure answers to the following questions.

    a  Is the store owned or leased?

    b  What are the advantages of the store's location?

    c  Are there problems with the store's location?

    d  Does the store advertise? If so, in what media?

# CASES

1 In 1980 a well-known discount department store locked its side entrance doors during business hours to reduce the security problems brought about by a reduction in staff. As a result, smaller stores in the shopping strip lost sales because customers had previously used the side entrance to walk through to get to the smaller stores. Many shoppers apparently were unwilling to walk around the discount store to get to the smaller stores.

Prompted by the complaints of the small retailers, the shopping center's landlord reminded the discounter that its lease required it to pay a rental based on a percentage of gross sales. The landlord also stressed that by closing its side entrance doors it had broken its implied obligation to produce the highest possible volume of gross sales. However, the landlord indicated that the store would not be breaching its lease if it could show that it had not lost sales by closing the side doors.

    a  Do you think the discounter had the right to close its side doors? Why?

    b  How do you feel about the smaller retailers' complaint?

    c  If the discounter's sales did decrease, do you think the landlord would take further action? What do you think would be the outcome?

2 After studying a secondary shopping area, Tim Darcy was on the verge of negotiating a lease for a retail paint store, to be open six days a week from 9 A.M. to 6 P.M. However, he felt that several aspects of the situation required additional study.

- Parking for the store was limited.
- A movie theatre with inadequate parking was situated next to the planned store. The theatre opened at 5 P.M. on weekdays and at 2 P.M. on weekends.
- Two banks with their own restricted parking lots were located on the same street.
- The municipal parking area, two streets away, was open twenty-four hours a day and charged a modest fee.

Darcy liked the socioeconomic conditions of the trading area but was concerned about the parking conditions.

    a  What dangers might the parking situation pose for the new store?

    b  What advice would you give to Darcy?

3 Sakowitz, a family-held group of specialty stores in the Southwest, carries fashion merchandise and caters to the same types of shoppers as I. Magnin, Bergdorf Goodman, and Neiman-Marcus. Its flagship store is located in the Post Oak–Galleria area outside of Houston, Texas. There are six Sakowitz stores in Houston, and others in Amarillo and Dallas (Texas) and Scottsdale (Arizona). In 1981 plans were laid to open additional

stores in Midland (Texas) and Tulsa (Oklahoma). For some years it has generally been acknowledged that Sakowitz is the predominant high-fashion retailer in Houston while Neiman-Marcus occupies a similar position in Dallas.

In 1981 Sakowitz opened a new store in Dallas with the obvious intention of challenging Neiman-Marcus on its home turf. Located in the Prestonwood shopping center, the store is situated adjacent to its competitor and, perhaps by design, is somewhat taller, too. Some observers have even suggested that this superiority in height is symbolic of Sakowitz' plans to surpass its competitor in sales.

Neiman-Marcus has indicated its intention to maintain its first-place position in the Dallas market. With Sakowitz already showing surprisingly good sales volumes, Neiman's expects other prestigious department stores, such as Marshall Field, to locate in the Prestonwood shopping center as well. With its reputation for effective store promotions, Neiman's can be expected to develop additional innovative practices to retain and enlarge its customer base.

Dallas is a large metropolis with an expanding population. Along with other cities in the Southwest, it attracts people who are seeking new careers as well as northerners seeking a warmer climate. The city's demographic mix continues to contain a good number of shoppers who are interested in fashion merchandise. In fact, Sakowitz believes that about one-third of the population is fashion oriented.

**a** What may have prompted Sakowitz to open a store in the Prestonwood center so close to Neiman-Marcus?

**b** Why might other fashion specialty stores locate in the Prestonwood center?

# REFERENCES

"In Fort Lauderdale: Galleria," *Stores,* 63 (May 1981), pp. 24–26.

Meyers, P., *The Planning of Branch Stores: Choosing a Store Site* (New York: National Retail Merchants Association, 1960).

National Retail Merchants Association, Merchandising Division, *The Shopping Center—What Makes It Click* (New York, 1960).

Phillips, P., "For Stores on the Move," *Stores,* 62 (April 1980), pp. 40–41.

Prichard, R. E., and T. J. Hindelang, *The Lease/Buy Decision* (New York: AMACOM, 1980).

"Searching for New Places to Grow," *Stores,* 63 (June 1981), pp. 41, 44.

Simmons, J., *The Changing Pattern of Retail Location* (Chicago: University of Chicago Press, 1964).

Spalding, L. A., "Amsterdam, N.Y.," *Stores,* 63 (August 1981), pp. 28–29, 33, 55.

———, "Beating the Bushes for New Store Locations," *Stores,* 62 (October 1980), pp. 30–35.

———, "What to Look for in Analyzing a Lease," *Stores,* 63 (June 1981), pp. 45–48.

Stark, M. S., "Downtown: Tide Turning?," *Stores,* 62 (March 1980), pp. 20–22.

———, "Mixed Use and 'Theme' Centers," *Stores,* 62 (April 1980), pp. 50–52.

# APPENDIX

# A Store Lease*

A 35—Lease, Business Premises.
Loft, Office or Store. 2-85

JULIUS BLUMBERG, INC., LAW BLANK PUBLISHERS

**This Lease** made the                  day of                  19       between

hereinafter referred to as LANDLORD, and

hereinafter jointly, severally and collectively referred to as TENANT.

**Witnesseth,** that the Landlord hereby leases to the Tenant, and the Tenant hereby hires and takes

from the Landlord

in the building known as

to be used and occupied by the Tenant

and for no other purpose, for a term to commence on                                    19     , and to end

on                            19     , unless sooner terminated as hereinafter provided, at the ANNUAL RENT of

all payable in equal monthly instalments in advance on the first day of each and every calendar month during said term,

except the first instalment, which shall be paid upon the execution hereof.

THE TENANT JOINTLY AND SEVERALLY COVENANTS:

FIRST.—That the Tenant will pay the rent as above provided.

**REPAIRS**

SECOND.—That, throughout said term the Tenant will take good care of the demised premises, fixtures and appurtenances, and all alterations, additions and improvements to either; make all repairs in and about the same necessary to preserve them in good order and condition, which repairs shall be, in quality and class, equal to the original work; promptly pay the expense of such repairs; suffer no waste or injury; give prompt notice to the Landlord of any fire that may occur; execute and comply with all laws, rules, orders, ordinances and regulations at any time issued or in force (except those requiring structural alterations), applicable to the demised premises or to the Tenant's occupation thereof, of the Federal, State and Local Governments, and of each and every department, bureau and official thereof, and of the New York Board of Fire Underwriters; permit at all times during usual business hours, the Landlord and representatives of the Landlord to enter the demised premises for the purpose of inspection, and to exhibit them for purposes of sale or rental; suffer the Landlord to make repairs and improvements to all parts of the building, and to comply with all orders and requirements of governmental authority applicable to said building or to any occupation thereof; suffer the Landlord to erect, use, maintain, repair and replace pipes and conduits in the demised premises and to the floors above and below; forever indemnify and save harmless the Landlord for and against any and all liability, penalties, damages, expenses and judgments arising from injury during said term to person or property of any nature, occasioned wholly or in part by any act or acts, omission or omissions of the Tenant, or of the employees, guests, agents, assigns or undertenants of the Tenant and also for any matter or thing growing out of the occupation of the demised premises or of the streets, sidewalks or vaults adjacent thereto; permit, during the six months next prior to the expiration of the term the usual notice "To Let" to be placed and to remain unmolested in a conspicuous place upon the exterior of the demised premises; repair, at or before the end of the term, all injury done by the installation or removal of furniture and property; and at the end of the term, to quit and surrender the demised premises with all alterations, additions and improvements in good order and condition.

**ORDINANCES AND VIOLATIONS**

**ENTRY**

**INDEMNIFY LANDLORD**

**MOVING INJURY SURRENDER**

THIRD.—That the Tenant will not disfigure or deface any part of the building, or suffer the same to be done, except so far as may be necessary to affix such trade fixtures as are herein consented to by the Tenant; the Tenant will not obstruct, or permit the obstruction of the street or the sidewalk adjacent thereto; will not do anything, or suffer anything to be done upon the demised premises which will increase the rate of fire insurance upon the building or any of its contents, or be liable to cause structural injury to said building; will not permit the accumulation of waste or refuse matter, and will not, without the written consent of the Landlord first obtained in each case, either sell, assign, mortgage or transfer this lease, underlet the demised premises or any part thereof, permit the same or any part thereof to be occupied by anybody other than the Tenant and the Tenant's employees, make any alterations in the demised premises, use the demised premises or any part thereof for any purpose other than the one first above stipulated, or for any purpose deemed extra hazardous on account of fire risk, nor in violation of any law or ordinance. That the Tenant will not obstruct or permit the obstruction of the light, halls, stairway or entrances to the building, and will not erect or inscribe any sign, signals or advertisements unless and until the style and location thereof have been approved by the Landlord; and if any be erected or inscribed without such approval, the Landlord may remove the same. No water cooler, air conditioning unit or system or other apparatus shall be installed or used without the prior written consent of Landlord.

**NEGATIVE COVENANTS**

**OBSTRUCTION SIGNS**

**AIR CONDITIONING**

IT IS MUTUALLY COVENANTED AND AGREED, THAT

**FIRE CLAUSE**

FOURTH.—If the demised premises shall be partially damaged by fire or other cause without the fault or neglect of Tenant, Tenant's servants, employees, agents, visitors or licensees, the damages shall be repaired by and at the expense of Landlord and the rent until such repairs shall be made shall be apportioned according to the part of the demised premises which is usable by Tenant. But if such partial damage is due to the fault or neglect of Tenant, Tenant's servants, employees, agents, visitors or licensees, without prejudice to any other rights and remedies of Landlord and without prejudice to the rights of subrogation of Landlord's insurer, the damages shall be repaired by Landlord but there shall be no apportionment of rent. No penalty shall accrue for reasonable delay which may arise by reason of adjustment of insurance on the part of Landlord and/or Tenant, and for reasonable delay on account of "labor troubles", or any other cause beyond Landlord's control. If the demised premises are totally damaged or are rendered wholly untenantable by fire or other cause, and if Landlord shall decide not to restore or not to rebuild the same, or if the building shall be so damaged that Landlord shall decide to demolish it or to rebuild it, then or in any of such events Landlord may, within ninety (90) days after such fire or other cause, give Tenant a notice in writing of such decision, which notice shall be given as in Paragraph Twelve hereof provided, and thereupon the term of this lease shall expire by lapse of time upon the third day after such notice is given, and Tenant shall vacate the demised premises and surrender the same to Landlord. If Tenant shall not be in default under this lease then, upon the termination of this lease under the conditions provided for in the sentence immediately preceding, Tenant's liability for rent shall cease as of the day following the casualty. Tenant hereby expressly waives the provisions of Section 227 of the Real Property Law and agrees that the foregoing provisions of this Article shall govern and control in lieu thereof. If the damage or destruction be due to the fault or neglect of Tenant the debris shall be removed by, and at the expense of, Tenant.

**EMINENT DOMAIN**

FIFTH.—If the whole or any part of the premises hereby demised shall be taken or condemned by any competent authority for any public use or purpose then the term hereby granted shall cease from the time when possession of the part so taken shall be required for such public use or purpose and without apportionment of award, the Tenant hereby assigning to the Landlord all right and claim to any such award, the current rent, however, in such case to be apportioned.

**LEASE NOT IN EFFECT**

SIXTH.—If, before the commencement of the term, the Tenant be adjudicated a bankrupt, or make a "general assignment," or take the benefit of any insolvent act, or if a Receiver or Trustee be appointed for the Tenant's property, or if this lease or the estate of the Tenant hereunder be transferred or pass to or devolve upon any other person or corporation, or if the Tenant shall default in the performance of any agreement by the Tenant contained in any other lease to the Tenant by the Landlord or by any corporation of which an officer of the Landlord is a Director, this lease shall thereby, at the option of the Landlord, be terminated and in that case, neither the Tenant nor anybody claiming under the Tenant shall be entitled to go into possession of the demised premises. If after the commencement of the term, any of the events mentioned above in this sub-division shall occur, or if Tenant shall make default in fulfilling any of the covenants of this lease, other than the covenants for the payment of rent or "additional rent" or if the demised premises become vacant or deserted, the Landlord may give to the Tenant ten days' notice of intention to end the term of this lease, and thereupon at the expiration of said ten days' (if said condition which was the basis of said notice shall continue to exist) the term under this lease shall expire as fully and completely as if that day were the date herein definitely fixed for the expiration of the term and the Tenant will then quit and surrender the demised premises to the Landlord, but the Tenant shall remain liable as hereinafter provided.

**DEFAULTS**

**TEN DAY NOTICE**

**RE-POSSESSION BY LANDLORD**
**RE-LETTING**
**WAIVER BY TENANT**

If the Tenant shall make default in the payment of the rent reserved hereunder, or any item of "additional rent" herein mentioned, or any part of either or in making any other payment herein provided for, or if the notice last above provided for shall have been given and if the condition which was the basis of said notice shall exist at the expiration of said ten days' period, the Landlord may immediately, or at any time thereafter, re-enter the demised premises and remove all persons and all or any property therefrom, either by summary dispossess proceedings, or by any suitable action or proceeding at law, or by force or otherwise, without being liable to indictment, prosecution or damages therefor, and re-possess and enjoy said premises together with all additions, alterations and improvements. In any such case or in the event that this lease be "terminated" before the commencement of the term, as above provided, the Landlord may either re-let the demised premises or any part or parts thereof for the Landlord's own account, or may, at the Landlord's option, re-let the demised premises or any part or parts thereof as the agent of the Tenant, and receive the rents therefor, applying the same first to the payment of such expenses as the Landlord may have incurred, and then to the fulfillment of the covenants of the Tenant herein, and the balance, if any, at the expiration of the term first above provided for, shall be paid to the Tenant. Landlord may rent the premises for a term extending beyond the term hereby granted without releasing Tenant from any liability. In the event that the term of this lease shall expire as above in this subdivision "Sixth" provided, or terminate by summary proceedings or otherwise, and if the Landlord shall not re-let the demised premises for the Landlord's own account, then, whether or not the premises be re-let, the Tenant shall remain liable for, and the Tenant hereby agrees to pay to the Landlord, until the time when this lease would have expired but for such termination or expiration, the equivalent of the amount of all of the rent and "additional rent" reserved herein, less the avails of reletting, if any, and the same shall be due and payable by the Tenant to the Landlord on the several rent days above specified, that is, upon each of such rent days the Tenant shall pay to the Landlord the amount of deficiency then existing. The Tenant hereby expressly waives any and all right of redemption in case the Tenant shall be dispossessed by judgment or warrant of any court or judge, and the Tenant waives and will waive all right to trial by jury in any summary proceedings hereafter instituted by the Landlord against the Tenant in respect to the demised premises. The words "re-enter" and "re-entry" as used in this lease are not restricted to their technical legal meaning.

**REMEDIES ARE CUMULATIVE**

In the event of a breach or threatened breach by the Tenant of any of the covenants or provisions hereof, the Landlord shall have the right of injunction and the right to invoke any remedy allowed at law or in equity, as if re-entry, summary proceedings and other remedies were not herein provided for.

**LANDLORD MAY PERFORM**
**ADDITIONAL RENT**

SEVENTH.—If the Tenant shall make default in the performance of any covenant herein contained, the Landlord may immediately, or at any time thereafter, without notice, perform the same for the account of the Tenant. If a notice of mechanic's lien be filed against the demised premises or against premises of which the demised premises are part, for, or purporting to be for, labor or material alleged to have been furnished, or to be furnished to or for the Tenant at the demised premises, and if the Tenant shall fail to take such action as shall cause such lien to be discharged within fifteen days after the filing of such notice, the Landlord may pay the amount of such lien or discharge the same by deposit or by bonding proceedings, and in the event of such deposit or bonding proceedings, the Landlord may require the lienor to prosecute an appropriate action to enforce the lienor's claim. In such case, the Landlord may pay any judgment recovered on such claim. Any amount paid or expense incurred by the Landlord as in this subdivision of this lease provided, and any amount as to which the Tenant shall at any time be in default for or in respect to the use of water, electric current or sprinkler supervisory service, and any expense incurred or sum of money paid by the Landlord by reason of the failure of the Tenant to comply with any provision hereof, or in defending any such action, shall be deemed to be "additional rent" for the demised premises, and shall be due and payable by the Tenant to the Landlord on the first day of the next following month, or, at the option of the Landlord, on the first day of any succeeding month. The receipt by the Landlord of any instalment of the regular stipulated rent hereunder or any of said "additional rent" shall not be a waiver of any other "additional rent" then due.

**AS TO WAIVERS**

EIGHTH.—The failure of the Landlord to insist, in any one or more instances upon a strict performance of any of the covenants of this lease, or to exercise any option herein contained, shall not be construed as a waiver or a relinquishment for the future of such covenant or option, but the same shall continue and remain in full force and effect. The receipt by the Landlord of rent, with knowledge of the breach of any covenant hereof, shall not be deemed a waiver of such breach and no waiver by the Landlord of any provision hereof shall be deemed to have been made unless expressed in writing and signed by the Landlord. Even though the Landlord shall consent to an assignment hereof no further assignment shall be made without express consent in writing by the Landlord.

**COLLECTION OF RENT FROM OTHERS**

NINTH.—If this lease be assigned, or if the demised premises or any part thereof be underlet or occupied by anybody other than the Tenant the Landlord may collect rent from the assignee, under-tenant or occupant, and apply the net amount collected to the rent herein reserved, and no such collection shall be deemed a waiver of the covenant herein against assignment and underletting, or the acceptance of the assignee, under-tenant or occupant as tenant, or a release of the Tenant from the further performance by the Tenant of the covenants herein contained on the part of the Tenant.

**MORTGAGES**

TENTH.—This lease shall be subject and subordinate at all times, to the lien of the mortgages now on the demised premises, and to all advances made or hereafter to be made upon the security thereof, and subject and subordinate to the lien of any mortgage or mortgages which at any time may be made a lien upon the premises. The Tenant will execute and deliver such further instrument or instruments subordinating this lease to the lien of any such mortgage or mortgages as shall be desired by any mortgagee or proposed mortgagee. The Tenant hereby appoints the Landlord the attorney-in-fact of the Tenant, irrevocable, to execute and deliver any such instrument or instruments for the Tenant.

**IMPROVEMENTS**

ELEVENTH.—All improvements made by the Tenant to or upon the demised premises, except said trade fixtures, shall when made, at once be deemed to be attached to the freehold, and become the property of the Landlord, and at the end or other expiration of the term, shall be surrendered to the Landlord in as good order and condition as they were when installed, reasonable wear and damages by the elements excepted.

**NOTICES**

TWELFTH.—Any notice or demand which under the terms of this lease or under any statute must or may be given or made by the parties hereto shall be in writing and shall be given or made by mailing the same by certified or registered mail addressed to the respective parties at the addresses set forth in this lease.

**NO LIABILITY**

THIRTEENTH.—The Landlord shall not be liable for any failure of water supply or electrical current, sprinkler damage, or failure of sprinkler service, nor for injury or damage to person or property caused by the elements or by other tenants or persons in said building, or resulting from steam, gas, electricity, water, rain or snow, which may leak or flow from any part of said buildings, or from the pipes, appliances or plumbing works of the same, or from the street or sub-surface, or from any other place, nor for interference with light or other incorporeal hereditaments by anybody other than the Landlord, or caused by operations by or for a governmental authority in construction of any public or quasi-public work, neither shall the Landlord be liable for any latent defect in the building.

**NO ABATEMENT**

FOURTEENTH.—No diminution or abatement of rent, or other compensation shall be claimed or allowed for inconvenience or discomfort arising from the making of repairs or improvements to the building or to its appliances, nor for any space taken to comply with any law, ordinance or order of a governmental authority. In respect to the various "services," if any, herein expressly or impliedly agreed to be furnished by the Landlord to the Tenant, it is agreed that there shall be no diminution or abatement of the rent, or any other compensation, for interruption or curtailment of such "service" when such interruption or curtailment shall be due to accident, alterations or repairs desirable or necessary to be made or to inability or difficulty in securing supplies or labor for the maintenance of such "service" or to some other cause, not gross negligence on the part of the Landlord. No such interruption or curtailment of any such "service" shall be deemed a constructive eviction. The Landlord shall not be required to furnish, and the Tenant shall not be entitled to receive, any of such "services" during any period wherein the Tenant shall be in default in respect to the payment of rent. Neither shall there be any abatement or diminution of rent because of making of repairs, improvements or decorations to the demised premises after the date above fixed for the commencement of the term, it being understood that rent shall, in any event, commence to run at such date so above fixed.

**RULES, ETC.**

FIFTEENTH.—The Landlord may prescribe and regulate the placing of safes, machinery, quantities of merchandise and other things. The Landlord may also prescribe and regulate which elevator and entrances shall be used by the Tenant's employees, and for the Tenant's shipping. The Landlord may make such other and further rules and regulations as, in the Landlord's judgment, may from time to time be needful for the safety, care or cleanliness of the building, and for the preservation of good order therein. The Tenant and the employees and agents of the Tenant will observe and conform to all such rules and regulations.

**SHORING OF WALLS**

SIXTEENTH.—In the event that an excavation shall be made for building or other purposes upon land adjacent to the demised premises or shall be contemplated to be made, the Tenant shall afford to the person or persons causing or to cause such excavation, license to enter upon the demised premises for the purpose of doing such work as said person or persons shall deem to be necessary to preserve the wall or walls, structure or structures upon the demised premises from injury and to support the same by proper foundations.

**VAULT SPACE**

SEVENTEENTH.—No vaults or space not within the property line of the building are leased hereunder. Landlord makes no representation as to the location of the property line of the building. Such vaults or space as Tenant may be permitted to use or occupy are to be used or occupied under a revocable license and if such license be revoked by the Landlord as to the use of part or all of the vaults or space Landlord shall not be subject to any liability; Tenant shall not be entitled to any compensation or reduction in rent nor shall this be deemed constructive or actual eviction. Any tax, fee or charge of municipal or other authorities for such vaults or space shall be paid by the Tenant for the period of the Tenant's use or occupancy thereof.

**ENTRY**

EIGHTEENTH.—That during seven months prior to the expiration of the term hereby granted, applicants shall be admitted at all reasonable hours of the day to view the premises until rented; and the Landlord and the Landlord's agents shall be permitted at any time during the term to visit and examine them at any reasonable hour of the day, and workmen may enter at any time, when authorized by the Landlord or the Landlord's agents, to make or facilitate repairs in any part of the building; and if the said Tenant shall not be personally present to open and permit an entry into said premises, at any time, when for any reason an entry therein shall be necessary or permissible hereunder, the Landlord or the Landlord's agents may forcibly enter the same without rendering the Landlord or such agents liable to any claim or cause of action for damages by reason thereof (if during such entry the Landlord shall accord reasonable care to the Tenant's property) and without in any manner affecting the obligations and covenants of this lease; it is, however, expressly understood that the right and authority hereby reserved, does not impose, nor does the Landlord assume, by reason thereof, any responsibility or liability whatsoever for the care or supervision of said premises, or any of the pipes, fixtures, appliances or appurtenances therein contained or therewith in any manner connected.

**NO REPRESENTATIONS**

NINETEENTH.—The Landlord has made no representations or promises in respect to said building or to the demised premises except those contained herein, and those, if any, contained in some written communication to the Tenant, signed by the Landlord. This instrument may not be changed, modified, discharged or terminated orally.

**ATTORNEY'S FEES**

TWENTIETH.—If the Tenant shall at any time be in default hereunder, and if the Landlord shall institute an action or summary proceeding against the Tenant based upon such default, then the Tenant will reimburse the Landlord for the expense of attorneys' fees and disbursements thereby incurred by the Landlord, so far as the same are reasonable in amount. Also so long as the Tenant shall be a tenant hereunder the amount of such expenses shall be deemed to be "additional rent" hereunder and shall be due from the Tenant to the Landlord on the first day of the month following the incurring of such respective expenses.

**POSSESSION**

TWENTY-FIRST.—Landlord shall not be liable for failure to give possession of the premises upon commencement date by reason of the fact that premises are not ready for occupancy, or due to a prior Tenant wrongfully holding over or any other person wrongfully in possession or for any other reason: in such event the rent shall not commence until possession is given or is available, but the term herein shall not be extended.

THE TENANT FURTHER COVENANTS:

**IF A FIRST FLOOR**

TWENTY-SECOND —If the demised premises or any part thereof consist of a store, or of a first floor, or of any part thereof, the Tenant will keep the sidewalk and curb in front thereof clean at all times and free from snow and ice, and will keep insured in favor of the Landlord, all plate glass therein and furnish the Landlord with policies of insurance covering the same.

**INCREASED FIRE INSURANCE RATE**

TWENTY-THIRD.—If by reason of the conduct upon the demised premises of a business not herein permitted, or if by reason of the improper or careless conduct of any business upon or use of the demised premises, the fire insurance rate shall at any time be higher than it otherwise would be, then the Tenant will reimburse the Landlord, as additional rent hereunder, for that part of all fire insurance premiums hereafter paid out by the Landlord which shall have been charged because of the conduct of such business so permitted, or because of the improper or careless conduct of any business upon or use of the demised premises, and will make such reimbursement upon the first day of the month following such outlay by the Landlord; but this covenant shall not apply to a premium for any period beyond the expiration date of this lease, first above specified. In any action or proceeding wherein the Landlord and Tenant are parties, a schedule or "make up" of rate for the building on the demised premises, purporting to have been issued by New York Fire Insurance Exchange, or other body making fire insurance rates for the demised premises, shall be prima facie evidence of the facts therein stated and of the several items and charges included in the fire insurance rate then applicable to the demised premises.

**WATER RENT**

**SEWER**

TWENTY-FOURTH.—If a separate water meter be installed for the demised premises, or any part thereof, the Tenant will keep the same in repair and pay the charges made by the municipality or water supply company for or in respect to the consumption of water, as and when bills therefor are rendered. If the demised premises, or any part thereof, be supplied with water through a meter which supplies other premises, the Tenant will pay to the Landlord, as and when bills are rendered therefor, the Tenant's proportionate part of all charges which the municipality or water supply company shall make for all water consumed through said meter, as indicated by said meter. Such proportionate part shall be fixed by apportioning the respective charge according to floor area against all of the rentable floor area in the building (exclusive of the basement) which shall have been occupied during the period of the respective charges, taking into account the period that each part of such area was occupied. Tenant agrees to pay as additional rent the Tenant's proportionate part, determined as aforesaid, of the sewer rent or charge imposed or assessed upon the building of which the premises are a part.

**ELECTRIC CURRENT**

TWENTY-FIFTH.—That the Tenant will purchase from the Landlord, if the Landlord shall so desire, all electric current that the Tenant requires at the demised premises, and will pay the Landlord for the same, as the amount of consumption shall be indicated by the meter furnished therefor. The price for said current shall be the same as that charged for consumption similar to that of the Tenant by the company supplying electricity in the same community. Payments shall be due as and when bills shall be rendered. The Tenant shall comply with like rules, regulations and contract provisions as those prescribed by said company for a consumption similar to that of the Tenant.

**SPRINKLER SYSTEM**

TWENTY-SIXTH.—If there now is or shall be installed in said building a "sprinkler system" the Tenant agrees to keep the appliances thereto in the demised premises in repair and good working condition, and if the New York Board of Fire Underwriters or the New York Fire Insurance Exchange or any bureau, department or official of the State or local government requires or recommends that any changes, modifications, alterations or additional sprinkler heads or other equipment be made or supplied by reason of the Tenant's business, or the location of partitions, trade fixtures, or other contents of the demised premises, or if such changes, modifications, alterations, additional sprinkler heads or other equipment in the demised premises are necessary to prevent the imposition of a penalty or charge against the full allowance for a sprinkler system in the fire insurance rate as fixed by said Exchange, or by any Fire Insurance Company, the Tenant will at the Tenant's own expense, promptly make and supply such changes, modifications, alterations, additional sprinkler heads or other equipment. As additional rent hereunder the Tenant will pay to the Landlord, annually in advance, throughout the term $.......................... toward the contract price for sprinkler supervisory service.

**SECURITY**

TWENTY-SEVENTH.—The sum of................................................................................Dollars is deposited by the Tenant herein with the Landlord as security for the faithful performance of all the covenants and conditions of the lease by the said Tenant. If the Tenant faithfully performs all the covenants and conditions on his part to be performed, then the sum deposited shall be returned to said Tenant.

**NUISANCE**

TWENTY-EIGHTH.—This lease is granted and accepted on the especially understood and agreed condition that the Tenant will conduct his business in such a manner, both as regards noise and kindred nuisances, as will in no wise interfere with, annoy, or disturb any other tenants, in the conduct of their several businesses, or the landlord in the management of the building; under penalty of forfeiture of this lease and consequential damages.

**BROKERS COMMISSIONS**

TWENTY-NINTH.—The Landlord hereby recognizes                                   as the broker who negotiated and consummated this lease with the Tenant herein, and agrees that if, as, and when the Tenant exercises the option, if any, contained herein to renew this lease, or fails to exercise the option, if any, contained therein to cancel this lease, the Landlord will pay to said broker a further commission in accordance with the rules and commission rates of the Real Estate Board in the community. A sale, transfer, or other disposition of the Landlord's interest in said lease shall not operate to defeat the Landlord's obligation to pay the said commission to the said broker. The Tenant herein hereby represents to the Landlord that the said broker is the sole and only broker who negotiated and consummated this lease with the Tenant.

**WINDOW CLEANING**

THIRTIETH.—The Tenant agrees that it will not require, permit, suffer, nor allow the cleaning of any window, or windows, in the demised premises from the outside (within the meaning of Section 202 of the Labor Law) unless the equipment and safety devices required by law, ordinance, regulation or rule, including, without limitation, Section 202 of the New York Labor Law, are provided and used, and unless the rules, or any supplemental rules of the Industrial Board of the State of New York are fully complied with; and the Tenant hereby agrees to indemnify the Landlord, Owner, Agent, Manager and/or Superintendent, as a result of the Tenant's requiring, permitting, suffering, or allowing any window, or windows in the demised premises to be cleaned from the outside in violation of the requirements of the aforesaid laws, ordinances, regulations and/or rules.

**VALIDITY**

THIRTY-FIRST.—The invalidity or unenforceability of any provision of this lease shall in no way affect the validity or enforceability of any other provision hereof.

**EXECUTION & DELIVERY OF LEASE**

THIRTY-SECOND.—In order to avoid delay, this lease has been prepared and submitted to the Tenant for signature with the understanding that it shall not bind the Landlord unless and until it is executed and delivered by the Landlord.

**EXTERIOR OF PREMISES**

THIRTY-THIRD.—The Tenant will keep clean and polished all metal, trim, marble and stonework which are a part of the exterior of the premises, using such materials and methods as the Landlord may direct, and if the Tenant shall fail to comply with the provisions of this paragraph, the Landlord may cause such work to be done at the expense of the Tenant.

**PLATE GLASS**

THIRTY-FOURTH.—The Landlord shall replace at the expense of the Tenant any and all broken glass in the skylights, doors and walls in and about the demised premises. The Landlord may insure and keep insured all plate glass in the skylights, doors and walls in the demised premises, for and in the name of the Landlord and bills for the premiums therefor shall be rendered by the Landlord to the Tenant at such times as the Landlord may elect, and shall be due from and payable by the Tenant when rendered, and the amount thereof shall be deemed to be, and shall be paid as, additional rent.

**WAR EMERGENCY**

THIRTY-FIFTH.—This lease and the obligation of Tenant to pay rent hereunder and perform all of the other covenants and agreements hereunder on part of Tenant to be performed shall in nowise be affected, impaired or excused because Landlord is unable to supply or is delayed in supplying any service expressly or impliedly to be supplied or is unable to make, or is delayed in making any repairs, additions, alterations or decorations or is unable to supply or is delayed in supplying any equipment or fixtures if Landlord is prevented or delayed from so doing by reason of governmental preemption in connection with a National Emergency declared by the President of the United States or in connection with any rule, order or regulation of any department or subdivision thereof of any government agency or by reason of the conditions of supply and demand which have been or are affected by war or other emergency.

THE LANDLORD COVENANTS

**QUIET POSSESSION**

FIRST.—That if and so long as the Tenant pays the rent and "additional rent" reserved hereby, and performs and observes the covenants and provisions hereof, the Tenant shall quietly enjoy the demised premises, subject, however, to the terms of this lease, and to the mortgages above mentioned, provided however, that this covenant shall be conditioned upon the retention of title to the premises by Landlord.

**ELEVATOR**

**HEAT**

SECOND.—Subject to the provisions of Paragraph "Fourteenth" above the Landlord will furnish the following respective services: (a) Elevator service, if the building shall contain an elevator or elevators, on all days except Sundays and holidays, from            A.M. to            P.M. and on Saturdays from            A.M. to            P.M.; (b) Heat, during the same hours on the same days in the cold season in each year.

And it is mutually understood and agreed that the covenants and agreements contained in the within lease shall be binding upon the parties hereto and their respective successors, heirs, executors and administrators.

**In Witness Whereof,** the Landlord and Tenant have respectively signed and sealed these presents the day and year first above written.

...............................................................[L. S.]
*Landlord*

In presence of:

...............................................................[L. S.]
*Tenant*

State of New York, County of                                        ss:

On the            day of                        19        , before me personally came
                                        , to me known, who, being by me duly sworn, did depose and say that he resides at
                                        ; that he is                                        of
                                        , the corporation described in and which executed the within
instrument; that he knows the seal of said corporation; that the seal affixed to said instrument is such corporate seal; that
it was so affixed by order of the Board of Directors of said corporation, and that he signed his name thereto by like order.

State of New York, County of                                        ss:

On the            day of                        19        , before me personally came
                                        , to me known, who, being by me duly sworn, did depose and say that he resides at
                                        ; that he is                                        of
                                        , the corporation described in and which executed the within
instrument; that he knows the seal of said corporation; that the seal affixed to said instrument is such corporate seal; that
it was so affixed by order of the Board of Directors of said corporation, and that he signed his name thereto by like order.

State of New York, County of                                        ss:

On the            day of                        19  '     , before me personally came
to me known and known to me to be the individual described in and who executed the foregoing instrument, and duly
acknowledged that he executed the same.

State of New York, County of                                        ss:

On the            day of                        19        , before me personally came
                                        , subscribing witness to the foregoing instrument, with whom I am personally acquainted,
who, being by me duly sworn, did depose and say, that he resided, at the time of the execution of said instrument, and
still resides, in                                        that he is and then was acquainted with
                                        , and knew                        to be                        the
individual described in and who executed the foregoing instrument; and that he, said subscribing witness, was present and
saw                                        execute the same; and that he, said witness, thereupon at the same time subscribed his name
as witness thereto.

*Landlord*                        *Tenant*

*to*

# LEASE

BUILDING.......................

**Premises**.......................

## GUARANTY

In consideration of the letting of the premises within mentioned to the Tenant within named, and of the sum of One
Dollar, to the undersigned in hand paid by the Landlord within named, the undersigned hereby guarantees to the Landlord
and to the heirs, successors and/or assigns of the Landlord, the payment by the Tenant of the rent, within provided for,
and the performance by the Tenant of all of the provisions of the within lease. Notice of all defaults is waived, and consent
is hereby given to all extensions of time that any Landlord may grant.

Dated,                        19

........................................................................................L. S.

STATE OF                        COUNTY OF                        ss:

On this            day of                        , 19        , before me personally appeared

to me known and known to me to be the individual described in and who executed the foregoing instrument, and duly acknowledged to me that he executed the same.

# chapter 12
## THE STORE

After completing this chapter, you should be able to:

**1** Identify the important aspects of a store's exterior.

**2** Identify the important aspects of a store's interior.

**3** Explain store modernization in terms of the growth of an enterprise.

**4** Explain store layout in terms of objectives, space, merchandise and department placement, and type of store.

**5** Discuss the following aspects of store interiors: air conditioning, transportation within the store, customer services, customer safety and conveniences, store security, and storage.

You have already learned that the proper location of a retail outlet is essential to its financial success. Having secured a favorable location, the new retailer turns to the store itself. It cannot be emphasized too strongly that, in addition to the site, the nature of the store's image is crucial to its continued acceptance by customers.

Among the aspects of store image to be studied in this chapter are the exterior and interior designs of the store, the importance of modernization, layout and design factors, the impact of displays, the movement of merchandise and customers, customer safety, store services, store security, and storage.

# THE EXTERIOR OF THE STORE

*A store's image distinguishes it from its competitors*

A store must present a distinct image that distinguishes it from its competition. This image, which is projected through the store's exterior and interior design, layout, displays, and services, gives it an identity that shapes customers' objective and subjective perceptions of the store. These perceptions define the store for the customer and position it relative to other stores with regard to its merchandise, staff, policies, services, and convenience. Called **impression management,** it is a major consideration in planning a store. Stores must provide a pleasant environment in which to shop. On the other hand, the store must be functional and meet the operating needs of the business in terms of providing adequate facilities for sales, storage, administration, maintenance, customer traffic, and the like.

## Preparing the Store for Occupancy

Once a retailer has chosen a site for a new store, it becomes necessary to prepare the physical plant for occupancy. Depending on the real estate involved, this may require

The old Lazarus building reflected the store's image, just as the new one does in a modern vein.

constructing a new building or renovating an old one. In either case, the retailer must consider four major areas in terms of utility and image when planning the store: (1) building size, height, and exterior design; (2) interior layout and design; (3) interior decoration; and (4) displays and arrangement of products and services within departments. Exteriors draw customers into stores; interiors keep customers' attention, and influence them to stay and buy.

*Using consultants to design a store*

Store design and planning require extraordinary amounts of technical knowledge in many areas. Retailers do not have all this expertise. They retain designers and architects as consultants to develop property in a way that best suits their needs. The retailer must, however, clearly define the needs of the business in terms of store policy, long-range plans, current and projected sales, services, selling techniques, merchandise, support activities, and flexibility. In developing a store plan, retail managers may also consult with suppliers to learn about the most up-to-date equipment and fixtures available. Large and small stores may resort to outside consultants. Large stores are better able to afford the expenses of such consultation and also avail themselves of professional discounts on equipment and supplies that they might not be able to get without the aid of the consultant. Even when larger stores have their own planning staff, they may occasionally retain independent consultants to provide a fresh point of view. Although smaller retailers sometimes use independent consultants, their budgets often require that they determine their needs as best they can and then work directly with contractors to have store plans implemented. In the long run this may prove more costly than hiring a consultant because the retailer lacks the requisite knowledge and experience.

## Physical Structure

*A store's physical structure can be a selling device*

The physical structure of the store is a major component of the store's image and is itself a selling device. Large, tall buildings can either intimidate customers or give them an impression of permanence, solidity, and success. While the height of a building can be disguised by the construction of floors below street level, it is often difficult to disguise the size of a building. Still, architects and retailers have worked together to find creative structural and cosmetic solutions to this problem.

## Visibility

The storefront and any show windows should be visible to both pedestrians and vehicular traffic. Some shopping centers, however, are constructed in such a way that not all of the stores are visible from the highway. In such cases stores often make use of billboards to make their presence known.

It is important that the architecture of a store be in keeping with that of the buildings that surround it. It should also to some degree be in keeping with the lifestyles of the residents of the neighborhoods it serves. Unusual architectural devices and design help give a store a distinctive identity in the minds of customers. The costs of constructing such features can be quite high, however.

*Show windows and store image*

Show windows often emphasize the presence of a store and project its image. Stores that feature low prices often have price tags on the items that they display. On the other hand, stores like Tiffany's, an expensive specialty store, which have an image

This storefront is easily seen by passers-by.

of exclusivity and prestige, often do not display prices. Tiffany's windows sometimes feature one-of-a-kind items that are so integrated into the display that they are not readily visible. The window design, not the merchandise, is what stands out. By displaying very expensive merchandise in this seemingly offhand way, Tiffany's image projects a concern for aesthetics that goes beyond considerations of price. Tiffany's assumes that the customer can afford the merchandise no matter how expensive it is. It is selling taste and service.

Retailers also use seasonal or holiday themes that feature specific merchandise. Sometimes they devote show windows to displays that have nothing to do with merchandise. During the Christmas season, for example, many stores feature animated window displays that portray traditional or fantasy scenes that represent the holiday season.

Some stores have windows that are not used to display merchandise. Without anything immediate to focus on, the customer looks into the interior of the store and observes the sweep of merchandise, decor, and activities. Other stores—for example, some supermarkets—have their interiors completly shut off from outside view. In these cases the owners have decided that visibility of the store's interior from the outside is unimportant.

## Entrances

The number and location of entrances is influenced by such factors as shoplifting, security, customer mobility, and safety. Entrances should be wide to provide easy access to the store. One of the more popular types of entrances is the air curtain, which keeps out dust and dirt. It maintains the internal temperature of the store, yet allows customers to move freely into and out of the store without bothering with doors.

# Parking

Inadequate
parking is
sometimes ·
unavoidable

Parking facilities and their distance from the store are other important considerations. You read in the last chapter that retailers try to provide customers with convenient parking. However, this is not always possible, especially during major holiday seasons or prior to special occasions like Mother's Day. At such times, even though parking for many stores is inadequate, customers tend to understand the situation and show more patience than at other times.

One of the reasons for the resurgence of downtown shopping is the construction of attractive and convenient parking areas close to the main stores. Virtually every city has developed such areas as part of its master plan for the revitalization of decaying urban centers.

# Construction Costs

Cost-effective
construction is
related to better
planning

Inflation and the rising costs of materials and labor have led retailers to seek more efficient and cost-effective construction through better planning. Retailers have also sought to minimize construction costs by using less costly materials and fixtures. In some cases they have used prefabricated structures that are manufactured in parts and assembled on site. Chain stores have avoided some cost increases by adopting a uniform design for each new construction. This saves on architectural fees and allows the chain to negotiate a quantity discount with contractors and suppliers when there are several construction sites and installations in a given area.

# Exteriors of Supermarkets

Because supermarkets are a significant and distinct segment of retailing, certain aspects of their exterior design warrant comment. First of all, most supermarkets are similar in basic construction. That is, they are rectangular or square one-level stores that are distinguished from one another by architectural variations in their roofs or fronts. Surprisingly, the reason for this basic design appears to be the public's expectation that supermarkets will be constructed in this manner. Second, though they take on some general characteristics of other neighborhood stores, supermarkets are designed to look different from their competitors. Finally, supermarket fronts show a surprising variety of appearances. Some storefronts are almost entirely glass, revealing much of the interior. Others are made completely of brick or some other opaque material, precluding any interior visibility. Still others are composed of glass and opaque materials, providing some interior visibility as well as interior display or storage space.

# THE INTERIOR OF THE STORE

Interiors must be appealing and make a favorable impression on customers. Spacious aisles, appropriate lighting, and imaginative, well-thought-out displays are far more inviting than narrow, crowded aisles, stark fluorescent lighting, and a hodge-podge of unrelated displays provided by manufacturers. Decorative floor, wall, and ceiling treatments also make shopping more pleasant and merchandise more attractive, as do well-planned placements of elevators, escalators, and other store fixtures and equipment.

# Lighting

Store lighting serves many purposes

Lighting has both practical and dramatic applications. It is used to call attention to the store; to illuminate the store's interior so customers can examine merchandise and see price tags; to create atmosphere; to draw attention to specific areas, displays, or merchandise; and to illuminate nonselling areas. Color, position, and type of lamp and fixture all work together to produce the desired effect. Lighting design is a specialty. Lighting a store can be as intricate as lighting a play in a theatre. It is no wonder that many department stores hire professional consultants to assist with or create the store's lighting design. The need for these consultants has been heightened by the energy crisis, which has caused stores to try to cut energy costs wherever possible.

## Lighting Levels

Stores have the same lighting needs as always; however, the energy crisis is causing them to reevaluate their lighting designs in terms of costs and local and state government regulations. So far, the most noticeable effect has been that retailers have reduced the general level of lighting in their stores. This has allowed store owners to lower the levels of spotlights used to accent merchandise or special areas. Generally speaking, lighting designers feel that it is preferable to have many low-wattage spotlights than just a few high-wattage ones.

Reductions in the intensity of background lighting have been achieved in many ways. One of the simplest ways of reducing the general level of lighting is to use fewer lamps in fluorescent fixtures. Many stores have cut energy costs by using only half the lamps that their lighting fixtures were designed to hold. Gimbel's and Abraham and Straus have eliminated lights over the aisles between departments. The results have

This department in a Neiman-Marcus store demonstrates the dramatic effects of well-planned lighting.

been effective in terms of both reducing costs and creating more subtle contrasts between departments. These stores have also found that lower lighting levels produce a more intimate look and that customers are drawn into the more brightly lit areas. Manufacturers are also responding to the energy crisis by producing energy-saving lamps in both their fluorescent and their incandescent lines.

## Types of Lighting

Incandescent, fluorescent, and metallic-vapor lights

Incandescent lights like those found in the average home are generally used for accent lights because they provide a full spectrum of color. It is easier to determine the true color of merchandise under incandescent lights than under fluorescent or metallic-vapor lights. Fluorescent and metallic-vapor lights, although less expensive to operate, give off a blue light that gives colors an unnatural blue cast; therefore, they are generally used for background lighting. Some stores, particularly specialty stores like Garfinckel's, a department store, which traditionally used only incandescent lighting, are experimenting successfully with improved fluorescent lights for general lighting purposes. Some of the improved fluorescents have coatings that compensate for the blue light and therefore simulate daylight, thereby providing a warmer, broader-spectrum light than the cold, blue fluorescents. In their furniture departments many stores have substituted portable table and floor lamps for most of their overhead lighting, particularly in model rooms. This has the added benefit of displaying additional merchandise in a "lifestyle" setting.

Newer stores and shopping centers have been designed to make better use of daylight in such areas as entrances and courtyards. However, there are limits on the use stores can make of daylight. Two of the main reasons that stores cannot use more natural light are that (1) it is inconstant because of changes in weather and (2) prolonged exposure to sunlight bleaches, discolors, and otherwise damages goods and fixtures. Besides, fewer windows in a store mean fewer distractions and give a store greater ability to direct customers' attention toward merchandise.

Reductions in lighting levels affect other areas of store design. Light colors reflect light and dark colors absorb it; likewise, glossy finishes reflect and matte finishes do not. It is not surprising then that many stores are using lighter-colored, higher-gloss finishes on walls, ceilings, floors, and fixtures. Metallic and mirrored surfaces are also popular ways of creating more light in an area. Mirrors in particular are useful because they create the illusion of more space and provide a means for customers to see how they look in the items they try on. Care must be taken to make sure highly reflective surfaces do not produce glare, which is distracting and uncomfortable for both customers and staff. Mirrors must be used judiciously to avoid creating a confusing, fun house atmosphere.

Commercial lighting fixtures range from lights inside closed cases to overhead strip lighting, from subtle indirect lighting to dramatic spotlights and chandeliers. As with all store fixtures, lighting fixtures must be evaluated not only in terms of the effects they produce but also in terms of their flexibility, ease of maintenance, and cost of operation. Care must also be taken in constructing the store to provide adequate wiring for permanent and temporary lighting needs.

Supermarket lighting ranges from conventional fluorescent fixtures that give aisles and merchandise a clean, crisp appearance and fancy fixtures that highlight displays and appointments. The type of lighting used depends on two management decisions: the store image desired and the amount budgeted for lighting.

# Exterior Lighting

The importance of exterior lighting

Store planners must also consider exterior lighting needs. First and foremost, customers must be able to find a store after dark. Electric or illuminated signs and dramatically lit storefronts not only draw and guide customers to a store but also keep the presence of the store in the customer's mind. Even if the store is closed, its lighted sign and facade serve as an advertisement and reminder to passers-by. Parking lots, too, require illumination for convenience and safety.

# Modernization

Store growth is the ultimate purpose of modernization

Remodeling or renovating a store will not solve problems arising from poor management decisions, untrained personnel, or poor store location. It can, however, maintain or improve a store's image, increase efficiency and productivity, make shopping more pleasant, and improve employee morale. In time, all buildings, fixtures, and equipment deteriorate or become obsolete. Outdated, run-down exteriors and interiors detract from a store's image.

Actually, the term *modernization* as it applies to retailing implies growth. Perceptive owners recognize that modernization is done for two reasons: (1) to maintain and increase the store's appeal to customers through new appointments and fixtures, and (2) to reduce expenses through the installation of labor-saving devices and more efficient merchandising techniques.

Experience has shown that retailers who are the first to institute intelligent modernization programs reap the benefits of their efforts to a greater extent than their imitators. For example, a change from conventional exteriors to more exciting façades has weaned consumers away from their customary shopping centers to the modernized ones. Even when competitors followed suit, many of their former customers continued to patronize the new centers.

Modernization programs, of course, require money, and substantial sums are usually involved. The larger retailers have little difficulty securing the necessary financing and expertise. Smaller stores, however, are often unable to modernize for lack of funds, or can do so only in limited ways. In some instances they secure advice from suppliers, manufacturers, and trade associations.

# Layout

Store layout: making the most productive use of space

In terms of store design, layout refers to the planned arrangement of selling and administrative areas, fixtures, equipment, and merchandise. When store planners decide on the layout of a store, they must consider the size and shape of the building and how many floors it has, the kinds of merchandise sold and the fixtures and equipment involved in handling it, the need for service areas, the shopping patterns of customers, and the competition. The chief goal in planning a layout is to make the most productive use of space by apportioning it according to the profitability of the various departments and then determining the optimum arrangement of merchandise, fixtures, and equipment within individual and common areas.

## Layout Objectives
In planning a store's layout, the objectives are as follows.

Good customer traffic flow results from carefully planned store layouts.

1  To provide aisles that are wide enough to avoid crowding customers, allow customers to move quickly from one department to another, and allow for the movement of equipment used to deliver merchandise to the selling floors.

2  To provide unobstructed views of the selling floors. This encourages customers to visit other departments and allows closer surveillance of customers by the security force.

3  To group related merchandise together in order to encourage purchases of related items.

4  To reduce resistance to shopping by creating a familiar arrangement of departments. This involves studying and paralleling the layouts of competitors.

5  To provide a means of moving customers quickly through or past departments in which they may feel uncomfortable. For example, women are generally more willing than men to shop for personal garments for members of the opposite sex. This is due partly to the traditional roles of men and women, in which women were often expected to make these purchases for their husbands and sons. Although some men now make similar purchases for their wives, many still feel uncomfortable in a lingerie department.

6  To combine merchandise according to ensembles and lifestyles. This may cause problems by duplicating merchandise sold in other departments (making it difficult to determine who is responsible for buying and managing the merchandise) and requiring salespeople who have experience and expertise in selling several kinds of merchandise.

## Allotting Space

The amount of space that is allotted to a particular department is determined by the retailer's judgment of how much space is required to display a proper assortment of the merchandise. The location of departments and of merchandise within departments is decided primarily on the basis of their contribution to profits, which is usually figured on the basis of profits per square foot of floor space. The departments and merchandise that have the highest profit margins are given the best locations in the store. The process of determining these locations is called **mapping.**

The most valuable space is near entrances on the main floor

Research on customers' traffic and shopping patterns has shown that the most valuable space in a store is near the entrances on the main floor. Merchandise in these locations receives the most exposure because customers see it upon entering and leaving the store. Perfumes, cosmetics, handbags, shirts, neckties, and umbrellas are among the items that retailers most frequently place on the main floor. The least valuable space is on the topmost floor at the greatest distance from the elevators and escalators. Restaurants, furniture departments, and floor covering departments are customarily located on upper floors. These two locations—main and upper floors—represent the extremes of space value within a store.

## Merchandise Placement

Convenience goods are located differently than shopping goods

Convenience, impulse, and other inexpensive items that sell quickly are located in high-traffic areas next to entrances, elevators, and escalators. Shopping goods, which are more expensive items and are purchased infrequently, are placed on the upper floors. In order to draw attention to merchandise on upper levels, retailers sometimes split departments. That is, they set up areas on the main floor that contain representative samples of merchandise from departments on upper floors. For example, men's apparel as well as women's may occupy one or more floors and offer a complete assortment of clothing ranging from socks and underwear to topcoats and from blue jeans to formal wear. On the one hand, this provides a convenience to shoppers who have very general ideas about the merchandise that will fill their needs. It allows them to survey the full range of available goods, define their needs and preferences, and select items that are coordinated with and complement their wardrobes.

However, many customers undoubtedly purchase socks and underwear on a routine basis and do not want to make their way through several departments in order to make such small purchases. Therefore, stores may feature trimmed-down versions of their full departments on the main floor. In the case of men's clothing, these main floor departments usually stock socks, underwear, shirts, ties, toiletries, and accessories like belts, cuff links, tie pins, cologne, and lotions. There may even be a limited selection of ready-to-wear slacks. The idea is to provide convenience shopping and a sample of goods to be found in the full department.

Other considerations in planning a store's layout are the location of departments in relation to inventories stored off the selling floor, and the location of departments in relation to one another.

## Supermarket and Specialty Stores

Supermarket layouts are also planned on the basis of selling, storage, and administrative requirements. Though not generally considered as such, supermarkets are highly departmentalized. There are distinct areas for groceries, produce, meat, and so forth. In deciding the amount of space needed for each department, planners consider such matters as display equipment (e.g., freezers), the store's concentration on special merchandise categories, space for rack jobbers, and departmental profit expectations. The latter means simply that more space will be allotted to the departments that give the store its largest profits. The size of storage and administrative areas is kept to a minimum consistent with the smooth flow of merchandise, employees, and customers.

Merchandise placement in specialty stores has changed

At one time specialty stores tended to minimize the amount of merchandise on the selling floors. This policy was consistent with their emphasis on service and consultive selling. Today, however, the reverse is true, with only the most exclusive stores clinging to the earlier practice. The fact is that the soaring costs of space compel most specialty stores to maximize the size of their selling areas and to display as much merchandise as possible.

## Small-Store Considerations

When deciding on layout, proprietors of small stores should plan for aisles that allow customers easy movement and afford them an opportunity to view and handle merchandise in comfort. Space for goods that will be on sale, or for slow-moving merchandise, should be located in areas of highest customer concentration. The guidelines used for departmentalizing large stores also apply to smaller ones.

## Securing Help with Layouts

Retailers can obtain information about layouts from trade magazines like *Retailweek* and *Stores;* trade associations like the National Retail Merchants Association, the Institute for Store Planners, and the National Retail Hardware Association; and the U.S. Department of Commerce.

# Displays

Large-store displays involve decisions by several experts

Decisions regarding construction, interior design, interior decoration, and store layout are made by store owners or top management. Depending on the size of the store and its staff and policies, decisions about interior displays may be made by a display department, an experienced salesperson, or a team of designers, merchandise managers, and salespeople. Merchandise managers and salespeople contribute information as to what merchandise the displays should contain and the customers they are trying to reach. Designers contribute their expertise in color, texture, arrangement, and general visual impact. The people involved in display decisions are also determined by the scope and complexity of the display. In large department stores display departments are generally responsible for designing, coordinating, and implementing storewide theme displays like those for holiday seasons. Like show windows, these displays may or may not involve merchandise. Display departments may also be responsible for designing and overseeing the construction of boutiques organized around special groupings of merchandise especially purchased for the boutique or collected from other departments and placed in an ensemble or a lifestyle display.

It is important to distinguish between displays and arrangements of merchandise on the selling floor, although in practice this is not always easy to do. Displays require many decisions regarding the message and implementation of the display. Some of the primary considerations are the following.

1   What and how much merchandise should be displayed? Department stores often have large assortments of merchandise. Displays incorporating every item the store carries would take up too much space on the selling floor, overwhelm the customer by the sheer number of items, and be meaningless because each item would detract from others in the display.

2   What kind of fixtures does the merchandise require for display? Expensive jewelry should be kept in well-lit closed cases, open to customers' view. Fresh meat and dairy products require refrigerated cases. Suits, dresses, and coats require racks.

Individual products are arranged according to size, color, brand, and the amount of personal selling and service they require.

Displays have much to do with the volume of a store's sales. In fact, some retailers estimate that more than one-fourth of their sales are generated through displays. To prepare a display properly, one must understand the effects of combining merchandise with color, lights, and tasteful props.

The knowledgeable use of glass, metal, plastic, cloth, and wood results in displays that interest customers. The idea is to create a mood that induces the shopper to buy. This is true for displays in supermarkets as well as for those in department stores and styled specialty shops.

A good display often suggests merchandise that may not even be an intrinsic part of the display. For example, a scene showing a backyard on a summer day emphasizing lawn furniture may contain a few nicely designed dishes and silverware as well. If the display is done artfully, these related items will cause some shoppers to look for the merchandise.

An additional treatment of displays as they contribute to store promotions is contained in Chapter 18.

Attractive fixtures contribute to the effectiveness of displays.

# Air Conditioning

Stores today are designed with central air conditioning, and enclosed shopping malls have total climate control. Air conditioning provides a clean, comfortable environment in which to shop and work. Customers expect to find adequate climate control in stores, and most retail outlets, particularly large department stores, must provide it to maintain a competitive position. Some small independent stores have not installed air conditioning because of space or financial limitations.

# Transportation Within the Store

Elevators and escalators

Stairs are generally adequate for two- or three-level stores, but elevators or escalators are needed in taller structures. Escalators eliminate the waiting required by elevators, and reduce congestion. Also, escalators take up less space than a bank of elevators and give customers a bird's-eye view of one floor as they ascend to the next. Large stores still provide elevators to move customers quickly between departments that are several floors apart. Elevators are also provided as an accommodation for the aged and the handicapped.

Customer traffic flow is manipulated in many stores by placing such items as impulse merchandise and food products within sight of escalators. In some cases up and down escalators are widely separated so that shoppers must move through large sections of the store to get from one to the other. While this arrangement exposes customers to more merchandise, its inconvenience sometimes causes them to shop elsewhere.

A major consideration in the design of in-store transportation is the desire to pull or push customer traffic to areas with the highest profit potential. Little wonder, then, that architects and engineers pay great attention to a retailer's instructions in the development of a store's physical plans.

# Customer Services

Customer services are often tied to store image

In planning a store, consideration must be given to the types of services offered to customers. With some stores, the development of an image depends greatly on the extent and quality of such services. With others, such as no-frills operations, customers expect and receive little in the way of services, looking for low prices instead.

To the extent that customer services require store space—either exterior or interior—planners must include proper facilities for them. Listed here are examples of the kinds of services found in retail establishments. By no stretch of the imagination is this list complete; in fact, in their quest for additional customers, innovative retailers seem constantly to invent new services.

## Phone and Mail Orders

In Chapter 8 you learned that some retail outlets, especially department stores (mail order houses do all their business by mail), depend on phone and mail orders for a modest percentage of their sales. To conduct these operations, adequate space and modern facilities must be provided.

### Gift Wrapping

Customers expect this service in department and certain specialty stores. Consequently, an area that is convenient to shoppers must be set aside for it.

### Gift Certificates

This service enables customers to purchase gifts without having to shop for specific merchandise. The shopper receives a certificate in exchange for cash or a credit charge. The holder may redeem the certificate in the store's merchandise. Proper space for the sale of gift certificates must be planned.

### Delivery

Delivery service is not restricted to large stores. Historically, even the smallest retail outlets have delivered merchandise to customers. Today, however, the existence or extent of delivery service depends on the nature of the business. As a general rule, the more personalized the operation, the greater the commitment to delivery.

To provide delivery service, adequate packing and vehicular space must be planned. Though generally out of sight to shoppers, these areas are integral parts of a store's physical arrangement.

### Eating Facilities

*In-store food service keeps customers in shopping areas longer*

Many specialty stores, department stores, and shopping centers feature restaurants, snack bars, or luncheonettes. Their main purpose is to keep shoppers in the stores longer, thereby increasing the possibility of sales. Until recently, in-store eating places were money losers but were maintained for the convenience of customers. Having learned some basics about food services, however, many stores are realizing profits from their eating facilities. In addition, employees often welcome the opportunity to have meals without leaving the store.

Since eating quarters require substantial investments in space, equipment, furniture, and appointments, retailers make careful judgments before committing themselves to food services.

The alteration of garments is an important service provided by many ready-to-wear retailers.

### Alterations

Stores that sell ready-to-wear men's and/or women's clothing frequently provide alteration services for customers, with or without an added cost. The trend today is toward charging fees for altering women's garments, but none for simple modifications of men's clothing, such as putting cuffs on trousers.

Obviously, space is required to do alterations properly. This includes working space for tailors and fitters, equipment, and storage. This space is normally located near the selling areas.

### Other Customer Services

In addition to those already discussed, customer services include prepackaging of certain types of merchandise, information booths, merchandise returns, baby-sitting, extended store hours, bridal registry, gift mailing, **lay-away** plans (in which the customer gives the store a deposit on merchandise, which is held until a later date), check cashing, and credit. This last service will be discussed fully in Chapter 23.

# Customer Safety and Conveniences

Fire procedures and controls are essential

Though it may be unnecessary, a word should be said about providing for the safety of customers. With so many shoppers passing through most stores, it is absolutely essential that management provide for fire emergencies. This involves installing fire extinguishers, developing and posting procedures to be followed in the event of a fire, and, at least in the case of large stores, installing automatic sprinkler systems. In addition, the many recent tragedies in which people in public places have been unable to reach exits during a fire have made us more conscious of the need for adequate and identifiable exits. All communities have building codes with specific fire safety regulations, and most retailers have conformed to them.

Store owners and managers must also insist on aisles that are free from debris, exit signs that are properly lit, and safe parking areas. They should be certain that electrical and plumbing fixtures are in proper working condition, and that electric wires and outlets are checked periodically. Elevators and escalators are subject to municipal inspection and must be repaired quickly.

Needless to say, many stores provide at least minimal toilet facilities for customers. Larger ones offer other conveniences, such as attractive lounges, selling area seating, first aid, and doormen. Some firms supply customers with coffee or other refreshments, and others pipe tasteful music into their selling departments.

# Store Security

Shoplifting is costly to consumers

At the first national Shoplifting Prevention Conference, held in Atlanta, Georgia, in August 1980, it was estimated that shoplifting was costing retailers (and, hence, consumers) $16 billion a year. Stated another way, Americans were paying 5 percent of every dollar they spent in stores on shoplifting. Other estimates placed losses due to shoplifting—retailers call it **shrinkage**—at $3 billion to $4 billion a year in general-merchandise stores alone. To make matters worse, theft in stores was on the increase, showing few signs of reversing itself.

This is not to say that shoplifting is the only type of crime committed in stores. Far from it! Others include burglary, robbery, pilferage by employees, arson, and vandalism. How does a store defend itself against these criminal acts? The following are some features of store security that tend to minimize the damage caused by retail crime.

1 Clerk and cashier stations are positioned to bring most or all of the selling areas under surveillance.

2 As far as possible, in some stores exits are accessible only after the customer has passed through a checkout counter. This is particularly true in self-service stores.

3 Closed-circuit television systems and carefully placed cameras discourage potential shoplifters. Though some shoppers complain about the threatening nature of the equipment, on the whole this technique is accepted by most consumers. It is certainly one of the most effective methods in use.

4 Electric alarm systems are used at entrances and around windows. When an illegal entry occurs, an alarm sounds in specific locations.

5 Mirrors are placed at strategic locations to reveal customer activities that would otherwise be hidden.

6 Warning signs are located in certain areas to caution against shoplifting. The effectiveness of this technique is still being debated in the retail industry.

7 Safes are used to store particularly valuable merchandise, such as jewelry and furs.

8 Although they present no serious problem to professional burglars, locks and barred windows are used with some success.

9 The persistence of burglary has caused many retailers in crime-ridden areas to fasten their storefronts with accordion steel gates upon closing. Though it is unsightly, a well-constructed metal "fence" acts as a fairly good deterrent to burglars.

10 Camouflaged blinds are installed in certain selling areas, allowing store personnel to view customer activity without being seen themselves.

11 Some stores use electronic systems that transmit high- or low-frequency radio beams that pick up signals from tags attached to merchandise. If someone leaves the store with an item to which a tag is still attached, the system alerts security forces in the store.

12 In-store private detectives and security guards are additional deterrents.

The preceding list obviously could be expanded, particularly since new techniques are being perfected constantly. Nevertheless, the list should give you some idea of the efforts retailers have made to reduce store crime. Additional security measures centering on the protection of merchandise will be identified in Chapter 16.

## Storage

In many retail stores (e.g., supermarkets and catalog showrooms) an important non-selling area is the area where merchandise is stored. The nature of the store's physical handling of goods determines the size and location of the storage area. Consequently, careful planning must be done to ensure an efficient flow of merchandise from the time it is received to the time it is placed in storage and finally in the selling area. Even a minor mistake in routing goods can be costly in terms of employee time, space needs, and energy consumption.

A more detailed treatment of storing goods is contained in Chapter 16, "Handling and Protecting Merchandise."

**NEW TERMS**

| | |
|---|---|
| impression management | mapping |
| lay-away plan | shrinkage |

# CHAPTER HIGHLIGHTS

1  Large stores use consultants to prepare a store for occupancy. Small stores generally lack this capability; they work directly with contractors.

2  A store's physical structure is an important part of its image.

3  A store's architecture should blend with that of surrounding stores and neighborhoods.

4  The number and location of store entrances are related to concerns of shoplifting, security, and safety.

5  Though adequate at most times, parking space may be insufficient during busy holiday seasons or special-occasion shopping days like Mother's Day.

6  Increases in construction costs cause retailers to plan more carefully.

7  Most supermarkets are built as one-level rectangular or square stores with special exterior features that distinguish them from their competitors.

8  Store lighting has both practical and dramatic applications. Exterior lighting is important for reasons of safety, convenience, and appearance. Management is conscious of energy consumption, making every effort to maintain a good appearance at a lower cost. Incandescent, fluorescent, and metallic-vapor lights are used for particular effects.

9  The ultimate purpose of store modernization, which involves remodeling or renovating, is the growth of an enterprise. Stores are modernized to increase their appeal and reduce expenses.

10  Store layout involves identifying objectives, allotting space, and arranging merchandise and departments. Today, contrary to past practice, most specialty stores maximize the size of their selling areas and display as much merchandise as possible.

11  Displays of merchandise contribute significantly to a store's sales. Good displays motivate shoppers to buy.

12  Transportation for customers in large stores includes elevators and escalators.

13  Customer services include phone and mail orders, gift wrapping, gift certificates, delivery, eating facilities, alterations, prepackaging, information booths, merchan-

dise returns, baby-sitting, extended store hours, bridal registry, gift mailing, lay-away plans, check cashing, and credit.

14 Customer safety calls for fire protection, aisles that are free from debris, well-lit exit signs, and safe parking. Customer conveniences include rest rooms, lounges, selling area seating, first aid treatment, doormen, refreshments, and music.

15 Store security is needed to control shoplifting, burglary, robbery, pilferage by employees, arson, and vandalism. Techniques to control store crime run from the strategic positioning of sales stations to sophisticated electronic systems.

# QUESTIONS

1 In order to use a consultant properly, what needs must a retailer identify when planning a new store?

2 Can a store's image be judged from its show window displays? Explain.

3 How have chain stores minimized the rising costs of store construction?

4 What are some of the distinguishing exterior characteristics of supermarkets?

5 How is interior store lighting related to a store's image?

6 What are the two basic reasons for store modernization, and what is its ultimate purpose?

7 If you were opening a store to sell men's clothing and accessories, what merchandise items would you place near the entrance? Explain.

8 What are some objectives to consider in the development of an in-store display?

9 Of the customer services listed in this chapter, which might be available in a small independent food store?

10 How might piped-in music add to a store's image? Can you think of any objections to such music? Explain.

11 Of the security measures to control shoplifting mentioned in this chapter, which do you think are most effective? Why?

12 Why would the storage of merchandise present a different problem for a supermarket than for a specialty store selling middle-priced menswear?

# FIELD PROJECTS

1 Visit two stores in your community for the purpose of viewing their displays. In one store, examine an interior display; in the other check a show window. For each display, answer the following questions.
   a What is the main theme?
   b How does it reflect the store's image?
   c What particular effect (lights, colors, props) are used to establish a shopping mood?

2   All department stores provide for the safety and comfort of their customers. Visit a department store near you and determine the following.
   a   The safety measures the store has taken to protect customers.
   b   The conveniences the stores has provided for customers.

# CASES

1   The Mardee Department Store uses an electronic system to detect shoplifting. During one busy afternoon the system signaled a theft by a well-groomed man in his 50s. When confronted, the accused individual denied his guilt indignantly and threatened to sue the store.

   a   What should the store's policy be in such a case?
   b   Should the store's policy depend on the store's image? Why?

2   Dawn Lee and Sharon Strong are partners in a middle-priced ready-to-wear women's clothing store. The store is located in a neighborhood shopping district. Though the business has made satisfactory profits, Strong feels that it needs to be modernized in order to attract new customers. Lee, on the other hand, doesn't want to make the substantial investment required and is content to continue the business the way it is.

   a   With whose position do you agree, Strong's or Lee's? Explain.
   b   What factors should the partners consider in making a decision?

3   A typical supermarket in the South covers an area of 20,000 square feet. In addition to groceries, produce, and other food products, it sells a variety of nonfood items, including hardware, kitchen gadgets, and health and cosmetic merchandise. Its windows are usually covered with advertisements, without any planned attempt to create an attractive exterior.
      The stores are divided into merchandise areas, with each section identified by the type of products stocked. Advertised specials are located either near the checkout counters or in the appropriate merchandise areas. Lighting is uniform throughout the store and consists mostly of fluorescent fixtures. Customer traffic is aided by wide aisles.
      Though some of the stores feature gourmet food sections, they depart little from traditional supermarket offerings and displays. Emphasis is placed on a suffused consumer mix, with little attention paid to specific ethnic or social needs. However, the stores do offer such personal services as check cashing and assistance with packages.
      With this situation in mind, Len Rolson has been thinking about opening two supermarkets in the same city—using a radically different concept. Banking on the expectation that many consumers will respond positively to innovative supermarket designs, offerings, and practices, he is considering the following.

   •   12,000-square-foot stores, resulting in lower rents.
   •   Ethnic food sections catering to the needs and desires of the majority of ethnic groups in the trading areas.
   •   Elaborate gourmet areas with international displays and special lighting effects.

- A reduced emphasis on nonfood items and a corresponding broadening of food selections, with each food area entered through decorated archways.
- Tastefully lit signs announcing the day's specials in each section of the store.
- An information desk at the entrance to the store that is staffed full time and stocked with advertising materials.

While Rolson recognizes that his costs will be higher than those of other supermarkets, he feels that shoppers will pay more for selected items because of his stores' uniqueness. He hopes that visits to his stores will be "shopping experiences."

a What is your opinion of Rolson's planned innovations?

b Do you think shoppers will pay higher prices for some items, as Rolson hopes? Why?

# REFERENCES

"A Pictorial Report on Store Interiors," *Stores of the Year* (New York: Retail Reporting Bureau, 1979–1980).

Brand, E. A., *Modern Supermarket Operation* (New York: Fairchild, 1963).

Crabtree, J. C., "Energy and Display," *Stores*, 61 (June 1979), p. 36.

Guffey, H. J., J. R. Harris, and J. F. Laumer, Jr., "Shopper Attitudes Toward Shoplifting and Shoplifting Preventive Devices," *Journal of Retailing*, 55 (Fall 1979), pp. 75–89.

"The Intimate Details About Macy's Private Lives," *Stores*, 62 (December 1980), pp. 34–35.

Israel, L. J., "Store Design," *Stores*, 62 (December 1980), pp. 31–33.

National Retail Merchants Association, Store Management Group, *Customer Services Provided by Department and Specialty Stores* (New York: National Retail Merchants Association, 1964).

Novak, A., and J. Tolman, *Store Planning and Design* (New York: Lebhar-Friedman Books, 1977).

Pessemier, E. A., "Store Image and Positioning," *Journal of Retailing*, 56 (Spring 1980), pp. 94–106.

"Renovation for Faster ROI," *Stores*, 63 (May 1981), pp. 42–44.

Spalding, L. A., "How They Are Shedding New Light!," *Stores*, 62 (December 1980), pp. 26–28, 49.

———, "How They're Striving to Be Unique," *Stores*, 63 (March 1981), pp. 30–31.

Spalding, L. A., "When and Why They Update and Re-Do," *Stores*, 62 (August 1980), pp. 32–34.

# part three
# MERCHANDISING

**P**art Three is concerned with merchandise policies and procedures: how the buying of goods is organized and planned, how products are priced, and how merchandise is handled and protected.

Chapter 13 analyzes the buying function by detailing the manner in which it is organized and implemented. We study the services rendered by resident buying offices and examine the major merchandise sources available to retail buyers. We also see how retailers manage their buying operations through the utilization of retailing cooperatives and store-owned merchandise resources.

In its treatment of merchandise planning, Chapter 14 deals with the determination of *what* and *how much* a store should buy. On the basis of a compiliation of consumer and trade information, we see how buyers are able to make informed decisions on the types of goods to buy. We then deal with desired levels of purchasing by studying open-to-buy techniques and assortment plans. The chapter ends with a discussion of vendor relations, including terms of purchase, sales and profit experience, and negotiations.

The pricing of merchandise follows its purchase, and Chapter 15 outlines the ways in which retailers determine prices. We analyze the customer, competition, costs, and laws as elements in pricing decisions. Then we look at the variety of price policies used by retailers. Next we study the arithmetic of pricing by calculating markups, and we complete the chapter with an examination of markdowns.

Part Three ends with a discussion of how stores handle and protect merchandise. In Chapter 16 we follow the path taken by merchandise as it is received, checked, marked, stored, and distributed. We also indicate how retailers are coping with the crucial problem of employee and shopper theft.

# chapter 13
# THE BUYING FUNCTION: ORGANIZATION FOR BUYING

After completing this chapter, you should be able to:

1  List the personal qualifications of buyers.
2  Identify the buying elements that are basic to all types of stores.
3  Identify the approaches used in organizing the buying activities of different retail organizations.
4  Compare the chain store buyer's responsibilities and authority under central buying and central distribution.
5  List the services performed for retailers by resident buying offices.
6  Identify the reasons for selecting a resident buying office.
7  List the major merchandise sources available to retail store buyers.

In the last chapter you read about the importance of merchandise placement and space allocation for the variety of goods that a store carries. In Chapters 13 and 14 we turn our attention to the methods of buying the merchandise that a store stocks and sells.

"Goods well bought are half sold"

It is commonly stated in retail circles that "goods well bought are half sold." The best window displays, location, and sales help are of little use if goods are not available when a customer wants them. Although a store may be well financed, it may suffer losses or even business failure for lack of good buying sense—knowledge of when and what to buy and at what price.

The buyer is responsible for this aspect of retailing, that is, for stocking the store with the proper merchandise assortment at a price that customers are willing to pay and at a time when the goods are needed. If merchants were able to achieve this, they would reach the ideal state of merchandising, in which all goods are on hand and are sold without any need for price reductions. This is no small task, and a good buyer must be intelligent, well trained, and able to make appropriate decisions.

# PERSONAL QUALIFICATIONS OF BUYERS

## Managerial and Planning Skills

A good buyer is a good manager and planner. Timing of merchandise purchases is all-important: Goods must be available to the consumer when they are needed.

Buyers must plan for delivery of merchandise at the proper time. For example, purchases of dresses are made ten to twelve weeks in advance, while basic lines like underwear, lamps, and housewares require three to five months.

## Skill in Analyzing the Market

A good buyer is a good market analyst. Buyers must be able to look ahead and sense what customers will want and the prices they will be willing to pay. In order to interpret consumer demand, they must be skilled in gathering information from such sources as consumer surveys, past sales records, trade publications, manufacturers, other merchants, and store personnel.

Buying is complicated because the basic question is seldom what consumers want today but, rather, what they want tomorrow. In fact, some merchants feel that buyers need a sixth sense. In spite of all the sophisticated tools for forecasting demand, buyers still need the ability to make good decisions unswayed by personal preferences.

## Understanding of Finance

A good buyer must be interested in the financial status of suppliers and the quality of the merchandise they carry. The vendor's financial position, work force, and production

A buyer's activities include managerial as well as merchandising activities.

capabilities generally affect the delivery and quality of merchandise. Consequently, the buyer must investigate these aspects prior to selecing merchandise.

# Understanding of the Consumer

Qualifications of a good buyer

A good buyer should be a consumer advocate in the sense that he or she conveys consumer wants and needs to vendors. The buyer should be sensitive to potential consumer satisfaction with new products, materials, and product changes. Buyers also serve as advisers to manufacturers—they supply them with market information and investigate product quality and value.

# Skill in Public Relations

Good buyers represent their stores. As such, they have a responsibility to vendors, store personnel, the retail industry, and the community for which they buy. They therefore should project a positive image and abide by all aspects of the law.

## Skill in Communicating

In addition to the qualities just noted, buyers must have the ability to motivate sales personnel. Whether written or verbal, information to promote sales is necessary, and buyers must take the lead in providing the facts.

# THE ELEMENTS OF BUYING

Intelligent buying procedures contain certain elements that are basic in all types of retail establishments, large or small. Buying involves the following steps.

1 Determining the demand for a particular product.
2 Evaluating merchandise in stock.
3 Planning for the type, brand, and quantity of merchandise needed.
4 Selecting the sources of merchandise (suppliers, resources).
5 Negotiating for the purchase of goods and placing the orders.
6 Receiving and inspecting the merchandise, placing the goods in stock, and pricing.
7 Checking the selling pace or movement of the merchandise. Systems for keeping track of merchandise are discussed later in this chapter (see Figure 13-1).
8 Reordering merchandise that remains in demand (see Figure 13-2).

All of these steps should lead to intelligent buying, which in turn should make for ready sales. A major goal of the buyer, then, is to purchase a steady flow of profitable merchandise for resale. But first it is necessary to develop a system that gets the job done.

| DATE RECEIVED IN OFFICE | | OVERSTOCK LIST AND TRANSFER SHEET | | | Vendor | | Date | |
|---|---|---|---|---|---|---|---|---|
| | | | | | Store # | | Mgr. | |
| | | | | | For office use only | | | |
| Comm. # | Description | Reg. retail | Current retail | Overstock qty. | Transfer to | Qty. | Date/comments | |
| | | | | | | | | |
| | | | | | | | | |
| | | | | | | | | |
| | | | | | | | | |
| | | | | | | | | |
| | | | | | | | | |
| | | | | | | | | |

FIGURE 13-1

Keeping track of merchandise. This form indicates overstocked and transfered merchandise.

*Speedy Order List*

VENDOR ______________ Pg. ____ Of ____

DATE ______________ MANAGER ______________

STORE NAME ______________ STORE NO. ______

| STYLE NUMBER | QTY. | UNIT RETAIL | STYLE NUMBER | QTY. | UNIT RETAIL | STYLE NUMBER | QTY. | UNIT RETAIL | STYLE NUMBER | QTY. | UNIT RETAIL |
|---|---|---|---|---|---|---|---|---|---|---|---|
| | | | | | | | | | | | |
| | | | | | | | | | | | |
| | | | | | | | | | | | |
| | | | | | | | | | | | |
| | | | | | | | | | | | |
| | | | | | | | | | | | |
| | | | | | | | | | | | |
| | | | | | | | | | | | |
| | | | | | | | | | | | |

**FIGURE 13-2**
An order form used by a small or medium-sized store.

Several approaches are used in organizing the buying function

Even though the buying activities are the same for all retailing institutions, several approaches are used in organizing the buying function because stores vary in size and type.

# ORGANIZATION FOR BUYING

## The Small Independent Stores

In small independent stores, buying is not treated separately from other functions. In fact, as stated in Chapter 9, the owner or manager of a small retail shop is generally in charge of all facets of the business, including buying.

Because the sales volume of a small store is lower than that of large retailers and there are fewer employees, the buying task is not as clearly defined as it would be in a more formal structure. In fact, because the buyer–owner makes the decisions, there is greater flexibility with much lower operational costs. Often the smaller retailer becomes affiliated with independent buying offices. As indicated later in this chapter, these resident buying offices advise retailers on the best sources of merchandise and work with them on merchandise selection.

Many small store buyers rely on help from manufacturers' sales representatives, who come to the store with samples of new items and up-to-date merchandise information. In stores that carry fast-moving products like food and drugs, it is not uncommon for sales representatives to make daily or weekly visits. In the apparel industry, visits are scheduled much less frequently, generally for the major market seasons (see Figures 13-3 and 13-4). These are times when manufacturers show their products to buyers.

## Large Stores

Larger stores treat the buying function as a separate activity. Experienced people are assigned to a specific department to carry out the task of buying. The size of this de-

# 1980 Dallas Market Center
# 1980 Dallas Market Center
# 1980 Dallas Market Center
# 1980 Dallas Market Center

## Market Dates by Categories

**Apparel**

Women's & Children's
Midsummer Apparel Market **(A)** — Jan. 19-23
SWMBAC Fall Clothing &
Summer Sportswear Market **(A)** — Feb. 3-6
Southwestern Shoe Travelers Fall
Shoe Show **(A)** — Mar. 9-11
SWMBAC Fall & Back-to-School
Market **(A)** — Mar. 16-19
Women's & Children's Early Fall
Apparel Market **(A)** — Mar. 22-27
Women's & Children's Fall
Apparel Market **(A)** — May 24-28
SWMBAC Spring & Holiday
Market **(A)** — Aug. 10-13
Southwestern Shoe Travelers
Spring Shoe Show **(A)** — Aug. 17-19
Women's & Children's Midwinter
Apparel Market **(A)** — Aug. 23-27

SWMBAC Spring/Summer
Clothing & Early Spring
Sportswear Market **(A)** — Oct. 5-8
Women's & Children's Spring
Apparel Market **(A)** — Oct. 25-30
**Bath, Bed & Linen**
Bath, Bed & Linen Show **(T/W)** — April 25-28
**Cosmetics**
The Cosmetic Show **(A)** — Aug. 23-27
**Furniture/Floorcovering**
Winter Homefurnishings Market
**(H/W/T/D/M)** — Jan. 13-18
CONDES 80-Dallas Contract/
Design Show **(W/T/D/H)** — Jan. 16-18
Spring Market Days **(H/T/W/D)** — April 27-28
Summer Homefurnishings Market
**(H/W/T/D/M)** — July 6-11
National Market for Casual Living
**(T/W/D/H)** — Sept. 14-18

Fall Market Days **(H/T/W/D)** — Nov. 2-3
**Gifts**
Spring Gift & Jewelry
Show **(T/W/M)** — Feb. 17-22
Spring Market Days **(H/T/W/D)** — April 27-28
Christmas Gift & Jewelry
Show **(T/W/M)** — June 28-July 4
Fall Gift & Jewelry Show **(T/W/M)** — Aug. 31- Sept. 5
Fall Market Days **(H/T/W/D)** — Nov. 2-3
**Gourmet/Housewares**
Dallas Gourmet Show **(T/W)** — April 9-12 (noon)
Southwest Housewares
Show **(T/W)** — April 9-12 (noon)
**Tennis**
Tennis & Active Sportswear **(A)** — May 17-19
Tennis & Active Sportswear **(A)** — Nov. 1-3
**Toy**
Dallas Toy Show **(T/W)** — Mar. 23-27
Dallas Toy Show **(T/W)** — Sept. 24-26

**(A)** — Apparel Mart    **(D)** — Decorative Center    **(H)** — Homefurnishings Mart    **(T)** — Trade Mart    **(W)** — World Trade Center    **(M)** — Market Hall

For Hotel Reservations or Buyer Pass Information Call Toll-Free: 1-800-527-9065 or 1-800-442-7111 (In Texas)

## JAN

| S | M | T | W | T | F | S |
|---|---|---|---|---|---|---|
|   |   | 1 | 2 | 3 | 4 | 5 |
| 6 | 7 | 8 | 9 | 10 | 11 | 12 |
| 13 | 14 | 15 | 16 | 17 | 18 | 19 |
| 20 | 21 | 22 | 23 | 24 | 25 | 26 |
| 27 | 28 | 29 | 30 | 31 |   |   |

| Jan. 13-18 | Winter Homefurnishings Market |
| Jan. 16-18 | CONDES 80-Dallas Contract/Design Show |
| Jan. 19-23 | Women's & Children's Midsummer Apparel Market |

## FEB

| S | M | T | W | T | F | S |
|---|---|---|---|---|---|---|
|   |   |   |   |   | 1 | 2 |
| 3 | 4 | 5 | 6 | 7 | 8 | 9 |
| 10 | 11 | 12 | 13 | 14 | 15 | 16 |
| 17 | 18 | 19 | 20 | 21 | 22 | 23 |
| 24 | 25 | 26 | 27 | 28 | 29 |   |

| Feb. 3-6 | SWMBAC Fall Clothing & Summer Sportswear Market |
| Feb. 17-22 | Spring Gift & Jewelry Show |
| 17-21 (noon) 17-19 (6 pm) | Market Hall Hotel Anatole |

## MAR

| S | M | T | W | T | F | S |
|---|---|---|---|---|---|---|
|   |   |   |   |   |   | 1 |
| 2 | 3 | 4 | 5 | 6 | 7 | 8 |
| 9 | 10 | 11 | 12 | 13 | 14 | 15 |
| 16 | 17 | 18 | 19 | 20 | 21 | 22 |
| 23 | 24 | 25 | 26 | 27 | 28 | 29 |
| 30 | 31 |   |   |   |   |   |

| Mar. 9-11 | Southwestern Shoe Travelers Fall Shoe Show |
| Mar. 16-19 | SWMBAC Fall & Back-to-School Market |
| Mar. 22-27 | Women's & Children's Early Fall Apparel Market |
| Mar. 23-27 | Dallas Toy Show |

## APR

| S | M | T | W | T | F | S |
|---|---|---|---|---|---|---|
|   |   | 1 | 2 | 3 | 4 | 5 |
| 6 | 7 | 8 | 9 | 10 | 11 | 12 |
| 13 | 14 | 15 | 16 | 17 | 18 | 19 |
| 20 | 21 | 22 | 23 | 24 | 25 | 26 |
| 27 | 28 | 29 | 30 |   |   |   |

| April 9-12 (noon) | Dallas Gourmet Show |
| April 9-12 (noon) | Southwest Housewares Show |
| April 25-28 | Bath, Bed & Linen Show |
| April 27-28 | Homefurnishings, Floorcovering, Contract, Gifts & Accessories Market Days |

**FIGURE 13-3**

A calendar of market dates for the Dallas Regional Market Center. (Reproduced by permission of Dallas Market Center.)

*Buyers may specialize in one product category*

partment depends on the store and its merchandise needs. Some stores have buyers who specialize in only one product category, for example, coats, lingerie, or shoes. This arrangement requires a larger staff, with correspondingly higher costs. The advantage of specialized buying is the in-depth knowledge that the buyers develop as a result.

## Stores with Branches

Buyers in department stores with branches are responsible for buying for the branches as well as the main store. Their offices are generally in the main store. The number of

**California Showcase**

at the

Women's and Children's
Midsummer Apparel Market

January 18-23, 1980

4th Floor Balcony
West Atrium
Adjacent to Group III

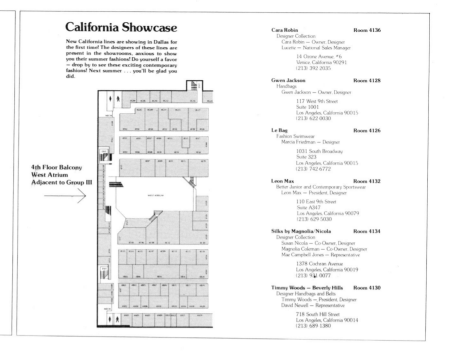

**California Showcase**

New California lines are showing in Dallas for the first time! The designers of these lines are present in the showrooms, anxious to show you their summer fashions! Do yourself a favor – drop by to see these exciting contemporary fashions! Next summer . . . you'll be glad you did.

**4th Floor Balcony
West Atrium
Adjacent to Group III**

**Cara Robin**   Room 4136
   Designer Collection
      Cara Robin — Owner, Designer
      Lucette — National Sales Manager
         14 Ozone Avenue, #6
         Venice, California 90291
         (213) 392-2035

**Gwen Jackson**   Room 4128
   Handbags
      Gwen Jackson — Owner, Designer
         117 West 9th Street
         Suite 1001
         Los Angeles, California 90015
         (213) 622-0030

**Le Bag**   Room 4126
   Fashion Swimwear
      Marcia Friedman — Designer
         1031 South Broadway
         Suite 323
         Los Angeles, California 90015
         (213) 742-6772

**Leon Max**   Room 4132
   Better Junior and Contemporary Sportswear
      Leon Max — President, Designer
         110 East 9th Street
         Suite A347
         Los Angeles, California 90079
         (213) 629-5030

**Silks by Magnolia/Nicola**   Room 4134
   Designer Collection
      Susan Nicola — Co-Owner, Designer
      Magnolia Coleman — Co-Owner, Designer
      Mae Campbell Jones — Representative
         1378 Cochran Avenue
         Los Angeles, California 90019
         (213) 931-0077

**Timmy Woods — Beverly Hills**   Room 4130
   Designer Handbags and Belts
      Timmy Woods — President, Designer
      David Newell — Representative
         718 South Hill Street
         Los Angeles, California 90014
         (213) 689-1380

**FIGURE 13-4**

An example of how buyers are invited and directed to a market. (Reproduced by permission of Dallas Market Center.)

lines for which each buyer is responsible depends on the size of the department and the sales volume of each line. Some stores have several buyers in one merchandise area, each buying a separate line. For example, in the children's department, infants' wear might be handled by one buyer while children's wear is purchased by another buyer.

Buying for branches can present complications when the branch store's customers have different needs from those of the main store's customers. In these cases, some stores have separate buyers at the branch. In other cases, **associate buyers** work with the main store buyer. While the main store buyer carries the responsibility for running a profitable department in the main store as well as in the branches, the associate buyer's major responsibility consists of ordering merchandise for branch store customers.

When branch store involvement becomes too great a burden for a main store buyer, the buyer's responsibilities may be changed. For example, it is not uncommon to see store buyers actually selling during peak hours. This is done because contact with customers gives the buyer firsthand information regarding their needs and wants. However, because of their branch store responsibilities, many buyers are relieved of selling functions and rely on reports from associate buyers and their assistants. **Assistant buyers** help buyers and associate buyers perform their duties.

Specifically, associate and assistant buyers aid main store buyers with reorders and follow-up orders. At times they accompany buyers on visits to suppliers. A good buyer uses the input from assistants who maintain consumer contact through floor selling.

Some of the very large retailers maintain offices for their buyers away from the stores. This is similar to the central buying arrangement used by chain stores (Chapter 9), in which buying and selling activities are separated. In these cases the branches are responsible for all merchandise activities other than buying.

# Chain Stores

*Chain store buyers generally are trained specialists*

In most chain organizations control of the buying function is exercised by trained specialists through a regional or home office. The practice of employing buying specialists for each kind of merchandise is demonstrated by chain stores like J. C. Penney and Sears, which may have a buyer who purchases only, say, carpets. This buyer is responsible for researching the market for carpets, comparing the quality and prices of competing goods, and buying the product at the best price.

Chain store buyers' responsibilities and authority differ from one chain to another because the buying structures may be different. The method used depends on the kinds of merchandise and the amount of autonomy delegated to store managers.

## Centralized Buying

Some chains use a **central buying** system in which the buyers make all the decisions regarding selection, quantities, and distribution to stores. This system is most commonly used for fashion goods because it allows for speedy action. The central buyer has full authority to order and plan each store's inventory.

## Central Distribution

Other chains use a **central distribution plan** (central warehousing). Under this plan buyers make all the purchasing decisions. However, the individual store managers have control over the depth of their stock because they order what they need from a distribution center. This method is most often used in food and drug chains because it works best with items that are in steady demand. Since the store managers are provided with checklists from which to order, they are responsible for maintaining sufficient stock of items that are in demand.

## Price List Agreements

In still other arrangements the central buyer develops merchandise catalogs or lists that are distributed to the different store managers for selection. Under these **listing plans,** also known as **price list agreements,** the central buyer shops for the merchandise and arranges price agreements with vendors. The store managers may order directly from these sources, and they have greater say regarding the merchandise stocked in their units. The catalogs and lists are prepared often so that a continuous flow of new merchandise is available to the stores. Variety chains generally use price list agreements for staple and semistaple merchandise.

## Specification Buying

*Specification buying gives the retailer unique merchandise*

Concentration of buying power in one place contributes to lower costs because of volume discounts, and allows for savings and quality control through **specification buying.** In this method buyers develop product specifications for their purchases rather than selecting from what is available in the market.

Specification buying allows the merchant to design unusual goods that are not in direct competition with branded merchandise. Manufacturers are willing to produce such products when the orders are large enough. The obvious advantage to the retailer is a product that is exclusive. Generally, only large retailers can take advantage of specification buying because small retailers cannot order in sufficient quantities to make it worthwhile for a manufacturer to produce the desired item.

J. C. Penney is notable for its use of this practice. Since Penney does not manufacture the merchandise it sells, it must buy from others. Eighty-five percent of Penney's domestic merchandise is purchased by specification buying, which involves negotiations by buyers for the development of J. C. Penney items of predetermined quality and design. The specifications are issued in writing and usually are highly detailed. The Penney specifications for a dress shirt, for example, run to eight typewritten pages.

## Private Labels

**Private labels (store brands),** like specification buying, require a fairly high degree of purchasing power. Large stores or groups that buy together use private labels to give the stores some individuality and freedom from direct price competition.

This system of centralized buying has made it possible for chains to amass great savings and profits. In fact, in 1912 F. W. Woolworth wrote, ''The success of our organization may be attributed to great buying power and the ability to take advantage of all cash discounts combined with economy of distribution.'' This could equally well describe the policy of most chains today.

## Buying and New Technology

*Computers are the key to efficiency and lower costs*

Because chain organizations are much larger than independent stores, they have the means to operate more efficiently at lower costs and to save their customers money. Today buyers for chains with hundreds of units can keep track of merchandise through the use of computers. Applying new technology to buying makes it easier, as buyers say, to ''have the right merchandise in the right place at the right time in the right colors, sizes, and styles and at the right price.'' Computerized cash registers, for example, compile information on the movement of merchandise and other data needed by management.

A **semiautomatic stock control system (SASC)** replenishes stocks of nonseasonal merchandise quickly and almost automatically. At J. C. Penney the SASC uses punched tickets that are mailed from the store to the nearest Penney data center. The information is transmitted overnight to the data center in New York, where the SASC system processes the information and then issues orders to the many thousands of Penney vendors.

A **buyer's commitment system (BUYCOM)** is connected directly to the company's corporate information data base. This system provides the buyer with the facts required to respond immediately to the merchandise needs of the stores.

A **retail merchandise management system (RMM)** tracks the performance of merchandise, reordering hot items (''checkouts'') and identifying the cold ones (''dogs''), which are then reduced in price. The information generated for point-of-sale transactions enables store buyers to make timely decisions about reorders, price reductions, item promotions, and cost control.

Retailers often use a **stockkeeping unit (SKU)** as the basis for a merchandise management system. An SKU represents one item of inventory that has distinct characteristics. For example, if a store has 18 identical ceramic jars in stock (same shape, glaze, size, etc.) it recognizes them as one SKU. If at the same time the store also has 15 units of the same type of jar in stock (but with a different glaze), it has two SKUs. In other words, the store is carrying 33 jars—but 2 SKUs. By using SKUs, computers can be programmed to keep track of quantities and types of merchandise, thus aiding the buyer in making inventory decisions.

Independents buy cooperatively to get lower prices

New technology has also resulted in an increase in central buying for others, such as voluntary groups of independents. These small retailers pool their orders and buy cooperatively, thereby obtaining lower prices. This practice enables them to compete more effectively with the large chains.

# RESIDENT BUYING OFFICES

Buying can be performed internally or by outside consultants

Retailers must decide whether buying is to be performed by staff, consultants, or a buying organization. When merchants utilize store personnel to perform the buying task, they bear the cost of staff buyers. To save these operating costs, small merchants often do the purchasing themselves, while others use outside sources to assist them.

**FIGURE 13-5**

A bulletin from a resident buying office notifying clients about import resource information and how to place an import order. (Reprinted by permission of Felix Lilienthal & Co., Inc., New York.)

Trips to the market are time-consuming and costly. In order to have up-to-the-minute merchandise information and complete market coverage, both large and small retailers utilize the services of **resident buying offices.** These are service organizations that help retailers buy merchandise. Small stores that are located far from manufacturers' showrooms find it vital to engage the services of resident buying offices in order to have complete market coverage, good prices, and help in promoting sales.

Resident buying offices are situated in the major market centers. The largest concentration of buying offices is in New York City; however, substantial offices exist in Dallas, Los Angeles, Chicago, St. Louis, and Miami.

Resident buying offices employ personnel to scan the market for new merchandise and supplier resources. They also provide **trending services** (information bulletins on current fashion trends) and act as buying agents for stores. Some offices render aid in private labeling and import merchandising. Furthermore, they offer merchants the use of office space and services when they travel to the markets. (See Figures 13-5 and 13-6.)

Resident buying offices can be independent, store-owned (private), cooperative (associated), or corporate (syndicated).

**FIGURE 13-6**

A sample bulletin that a resident buying office sends to its clients about new merchandise and fashion trends. (Reprinted by permission of Felix Lilienthal & Co., Inc., New York.)

# Independent

An **independent resident buying office** serves both large and small noncompeting retailers. The office charges fees that are generally based on the types of services performed and the volume of merchandise purchased. Fee arrangements differ and are spelled out in one- to two-year contracts. Two of the well-known independent buying offices are Felix Lilienthal & Company, Inc., and Independent Retailers Syndicate (IRS). This type of office sets its own policies.

# Store-Owned or Private Office

A **store-owned** or **private resident buying office** is owned by the firm it serves. For example, the Montgomery Ward resident office buys exclusively for stores in that organization. In fact, Ward's maintains resident buying offices in several of the major market centers, including New York, Los Angeles, Dallas, and Chicago.

Store-owned offices are very costly operations and are generally limited to the giant chains, department stores, and large specialty stores. However, some of the large retailers do not maintain their own offices. They reason that the exchange of market information in a store-owned office is too limited because it is confined to their own noncompeting stores. Because of this, many very large firms use other types of resident offices.

# Cooperative (Associated) Office

When a group of stores own and manage a buying office cooperatively, it is known as a **cooperative** or **associated resident buying office.** The stores share the operating expenses according to the size of each store and the services it requires. Although this type is more expensive than an independent office, it more than compensates by offering its members a high degree of information exchange and mutual assistance. Even though they exchange a great deal of confidential information, the member stores do not feel threatened because they do not compete in the same areas.

One of the better-known associated offices is the Associated Merchandising Corporation. Its member stores include Federated Stores, which operates Bullock's, Bloomingdale's, and Abraham and Straus. Other members are Strawbridge & Clothier and Hutzler Bros.

# Corporate (Syndicated) Buying Office

A **corporate resident buying office** is owned and operated by a parent company for its own stores. The office is a division of a large corporation that owns a number of retail chains. Though the chains may not be alike, the corporate buying office meets the needs of each by maintaining a well-staffed group of specialists.

Because a corporate office buys and distributes merchandise for all its stores, it has a great deal of buying power. Examples of this type of office are the Allied Stores Marketing Corporation and Macy's Corporate Buying Office.

# SELECTION OF A BUYING OFFICE

In selecting a buying office to represent them, many small retailers are limited to an independent office or a cooperative arrangement because they are too small to absorb the costs of separate offices.

*Selecting an office that meets the store's service needs*

It is important to select an office that provides all the services a merchant requires. The following are a few of the services that a resident office may provide to its members.

1   Market and resource information.

2   Appropriate mix of store members to allow for meaningful data exchange.

3   Proper merchandise specialists (buyers).

4   Access to imported merchandise.

5   A good private-label program—development of private brands (mostly in accessories and apparel).

6   A good communication system so that information is accurate, timely, and meaningful (see Figure 13-7).

---

## PROMPT SERVICE REPLY

TO _____

_____ DATE _____ 19 ____

_____ DEPT. NO. _____

WITH REFERENCE TO YOUR COMMUNICATION
PLEASE BE ADVISED THAT:

| Order No. | Dated | Resource | Shipped Via | Date |
|-----------|-------|----------|-------------|------|
|           |       |          |             |      |

Per _____

**FIGURE 13-7**
A form used by a resident buying office to communicate with its clients. This form is frequently sent to the store when goods have not been received, the store wants to cancel, or the merchant wants to return goods. A copy is retained by the buyer. (Reproduced by permission of Felix Lilienthal & Co., Inc., New York.)

In addition, a resident office usually does the following.

1 Places orders for store buyers (see Figure 13-8).

2 Sends bulletins on fashion trends and current prices (see Figure 13-6).

3 Arranges for vendor showings.

4 Makes arrangements for and accompanies store buyers on visits to vendors.

5 Arranges for fashion shows for new merchandise.

6 Keeps track of deliveries and cancellations (see Figure 13-9).

7 Organizes and assists with promotions and advertising.

8 Is available for advice.

Merchants view their need for a buying office in various ways, and make their selections accordingly. When interviewed regarding the role of a buying office, store executives made comments like these: "We need fashion strength as well as promotional buying from our resident office"; "The office is a good bird dog"; "Cross-pollenization of information is another reason for joining a buying office"; "Private labels and import programs are important for many stores in budget areas."

**Special areas important to the merchant**

A buying office provides merchandise to fill the need for goods in special areas (e.g., private labels for small stores, promotional items, and imports). Since many stores

## NOTICE OF PLACEMENT OF YOUR ORDERS

DATE _____

STORE _____ DEPT. _____

CITY _____ STATE _____

Orders listed below have been checked and placed.
Any changes noted below.

| Store Order # | Manu- fac- turer | Deliv- ery Date | Style Nos. | Remarks on Changes | Amount of Order |
|---|---|---|---|---|---|
| | | | | | |
| | | | | | |
| | | | | | |
| | | | | | |
| | | | | | |
| | | | | | |

FIGURE 13-8

A notice of placement of orders used by a resident buying office. Buyers send this form to stores when orders have been placed with vendors, and retain a copy. (Reproduced by permission of Felix Lilienthal & Co., Inc., New York.)

## IMMEDIATE ACTION NECESSARY

DATE___

TO: _____     RE: STORE_____
    _____     DEPT. #_____
    _____     ADDRESS _____
    _____     ORDER #_____
                      DATED _____

Gentlemen:
Will you kindly *CANCEL* any unshipped balance against the order you have on hand for the above account immediately upon receipt of this letter.

Please acknowledge receipt of these instructions to the writer's attention, by return mail, and send a duplicate copy to the store. Thank you.

Very truly yours.

**FIGURE 13-9**
A resident buying office's cancelation form. This form is sent by the buyer to the vendor and the store as notification of a stopped shipment. A copy is retained for the buyer's files. (Reproduced by permission of Felix Lilienthal & Co., Inc., New York.)

require a unique image, they rely on the services of a resident office for private labels, imports, and special promotions to establish that identity.

# MAJOR MERCHANDISE SOURCES FOR RETAIL BUYERS

**Buyer links merchandise resource, store, and customer**

You have seen that the buyer is a key figure in the success of a retail store. Every time a customer purchases a suit, he or she is exercising "demand." To meet that demand, the retail buyer must, in turn, have purchased the suit from some resource. The buyer, therefore, links the merchandise resource, the store, and the customer.

The sources of merchandise include wholesalers, manufacturers, retailing cooperatives, resident buying offices, store-owned suppliers, and foreign sources.

## Wholesalers

Traditionally, wholesalers have been a major source of supply for retailing. They are middlemen who buy from manufacturers in large quantities and sell to retailers in substantially smaller quantities. The wholesaler carries a stock of merchandise, sometimes

The Regional Market in Dallas conducts fashion shows that enable buyers to preview manufacturers' lines.

makes deliveries, extends credit, and provides sales help to retailers. To a large degree, wholesalers act as buying agents for their retailer customers in the same manner that retailers act as "purchasing agents" for store customers.

## Full-Service Wholesalers

*Wholesalers are middlemen*

**Full-service wholesalers** are particularly valuable to small retailers because of the services they perform. For example, they research the market in order to stock merchandise for resale to the retailer. In addition, they provide storage, prompt delivery, credit, valuable market information, and help with displays and advertising. These services are particularly valuable to small and medium-sized retailers, who use this source of supply most frequently. A large retailer, such as Sears or A&P, often takes over many of the functions of a wholesaler. However, even large retailers utilize wholesalers when it is more economical for them to do so.

## Limited-Function Wholesalers

Though **limited-function wholesalers** do not provide many services, they render a warehouse service and stock fast-moving items that are available to retailers in small quantities. Because they eliminate sales help, credit, and delivery service, they are able to offer lower prices to retailers, an important factor for small merchants.

*Rack jobbers maintain stock, replace slow items with fast-moving goods*

Rack jobbers, as discussed in Chapter 7, stock and maintain assortments of goods on special display racks. They select the goods, arrange the displays, price the merchandise, and provide materials for selling assistance. In addition, they guarantee a specified profit to the retailer. Thus, the retailer is relieved of all risks other than providing selling space. Rack jobbers generally check merchandise on a weekly basis and charge the retailer only for the goods sold.

Although rack jobbers work with a variety of retail outlets, they are credited with the growth of scrambled merchandising in supermarkets, a departure from the traditional food merchandising policy. Rack jobbers introduced nonfood items like hardware, toiletries, cosmetics, books, and toys. L'eggs is a well-known product handled by rack jobbers.

This rack jobber is checking a store display.

# Manufacturers

Many retailers buy their goods directly from manufacturers. When this happens, the services that are usually performed by wholesalers are assumed by the manufacturers or the stores themselves.

Direct buying is common among large chains like Montgomery Ward because they can purchase merchandise at lower prices. In addition to obtaining a volume discount, large retailers can purchase goods made to their own specifications, and they may have their own labels (private labels) attached to merchandise.

In the fashion field, direct buying enables the retailer to get merchandise into the store faster than would be the case if a wholesaler (middleman) were involved. Since customers' tastes in fashion goods change rapidly, time is an important consideration. It is too risky for both the retailer and the manufacturer to chance storing large inventories of fashion goods that may become obsolete.

In the case of physically perishable items, not only is it important to buy directly from the producer, it is necessary to purchase more often.

Retailers have the opportunity to examine a manufacturer's line of merchandise at the showroom of a manufacturer's representative. (Courtesy Telisman Sales, Dallas Mart.)

Other benefits of direct buying include lower prices, market information, help in training salespeople, and assistance with advertising and displays.

# Retailing Cooperatives and Resident Buying Offices

Voluntary groups are an important source for small retailers

As noted previously, independent retailers have formed groups to secure greater strength in buying. For example, voluntary chains have been organized by wholesalers, which assume the burden of supply to enable small retailers to compete with the chains. The retailers buy all needed goods from the wholesaler and benefit from lower prices through volume purchases. The Independent Grocers' Alliance and Western Auto Stores are examples of voluntary chains. A recent trend toward cooperative buying exists in the hardware line, with such participating companies as Tru-Val Hardware and American Hardware Co.

We also noted earlier that resident buying offices are also vital to retailers' access to major merchandise markets. Because they exist to link the two, resident buyers are important for both retailers and the manufacturer.

# Store-Owned Merchandise Resources

Store-owned resources require high investment

Several chains, franchised retailers, and mail order houses own their own factories and produce the merchandise that their stores request. This arrangement is found in the apparel and household drug industry. It makes it easier to coordinate customer demands with production. However, depending solely on one's own facility involves more risk and higher investment, and restricts assortments. Some companies that do their own manufacturing also purchase a portion of their goods from others. For example, Sears, Roebuck and Company has arrangements with manufacturers to produce a portion of the merchandise it sells. On the other hand, Thom McAn Shoe Company produces all its own shoes.

# Foreign Sources

Stores use foreign merchandise for several reasons: The items are more exclusive, more difficult to comparison shop, may be less expensive to purchase, and are not available from American sources. On the other hand, delivery is slower; contacting foreign sources is complicated; travel is expensive; and shopping and import duties are costly. In addition, currency changes are difficult to anticipate, so that goods can cost more than originally expected.

Some American buying offices have representatives in foreign markets. If a store requires foreign goods, it is advisable to use such a buying office because it assists with all purchases.

Foreign goods

Foreign buying offices located abroad are known as **commissionaires.** Like American resident houses, they charge a fee or percentage.

**Importers** are located in this country, but they research merchandise and buy in foreign markets. They are like other wholesalers that buy in large quantities and sell to retailers in smaller quantities.

In the next chapter we will see how buyers actually select resources from among manufacturers, middlemen, and other intermediaries.

---

## Geraldine Stutz
## A SPECIALTY STORE FASHION WHIZ

A woman as president of one of America's major fashion specialty stores? Not only a president, but a very successful one at that! Selected in 1957 to lead Henri Bendel, a sophisticated high-fashion shop, Geraldine Stutz converted a losing retail venture into a profitable one within five years—and proceeded to increase the profits in succeeding years. And her appointment took place at a time when female executives were rarely found in top retail management positions.

Stutz tried a number of fields before entering retailing—acting, journalism, and modeling among them. She served as fashion editor for several movie publications, and then assumed editorial responsibilities for *Glamour* magazine. Her experience with shoe fashions led to an appointment with I. Miller Company, a prestigious shoe retailer that she eventually headed.

Ultimately Stutz was selected by Genesco, an apparel conglomerate and Bendel's parent company, to reverse Bendel's fortunes. She accomplished her task through a shrewd combination of store image, merchandise selection, and chic ambience. Her construction of Bendel's well-known Street of Shops within the Bendel store catapulted its reputation to new heights. A sufficient number of affluent shoppers responded enthusiastically to the store's clearly defined merchandise offerings to form a loyal following. A variety of clothing, accessories, cosmetics, handbags, and housewares were stocked to satisfy the tastes of these customers.

Stutz's plans for Henri Bendel, a New York store, included expansion to other major American cities. With her success already highly acclaimed, Geraldine Stutz seems likely to remain an active figure in retailing.

---

## NEW TERMS

assistant buyer

associate buyer

associated resident buying office

buyer's commitment system (BUYCOM)

central buying

central distribution plan

commissionaire

cooperative resident buying office

corporate resident buying office

full-service wholesaler

importer

independent resident buying office

limited-function wholesaler

listing plan

price list agreement

private resident buying office

private label

resident buying office

retail merchandise management system (RMM)

semiautomatic stock control system (SASC)

specification buying

stockkeeping unit (SKU)

store brand

store-owned resident buying office

trending service

# CHAPTER HIGHLIGHTS

1 The personal qualifications of buyers include the following skills: managerial and planning skills, ability to analyze the market, understanding finance, understanding of the consumer, skill in public relations, and communications skills.

2 The buying procedure contains eight basic elements for both large and small retailers.

3 Since stores vary in size and type, several approaches are used in organizing the buying function.

4 In contrast to larger retailers, small stores do not treat buying as a separate function.

5 Some stores have buyers who specialize in only one product category.

6 In department stores with branches, the main store buyer has the added responsiblity of stocking the branches.

7 When main store buyers have too many responsibilities, they are relieved of selling functions and rely on assistants for feedback.

8 A good buyer uses feedback from assistants and associate buyers who maintain customer contacts.

9 Chain stores hire specialists to buy for all their units. They perform the buying function in a regional or home office away from the stores.

10 Central buying gives the buyer the responsibility for ordering merchandise and controlling inventory in all stores.

11 A central distribution plan is basically a warehousing setup. This plan gives store managers an opportunity to select merchandise for their units.

12 Under price list agreements store managers have a greater say regarding the merchandise stocked in their stores.

13 Specification buying and private labeling help the retailer cut down on product competition, but they require a large amount of purchasing power.

14 Centralized buying has made it possible for chains to obtain great savings and profits.

15 The new technology (computers) has made it easier to "have the right merchandise at the right place at the right time."

16 Resident buying offices are situated in the major market centers. They can be independent, store-owned, cooperative, or corporate.

17 Buying offices provide a host of services to their members, including market information, access to import merchandise, private labels, and trending services. In addition, they usually perform such activities as placing orders and arranging for store buyers' visits.

18 Sources of merchandise for the retail buyer are wholesalers, manufacturers, retailing cooperatives, resident buying offices, and company-owned suppliers.

19 Foreign buying sources include American buying offices in foreign countries, commissionaires, and importers.

# QUESTIONS

1 Buying functions are the same for large and small retailing organizations. Explain how a buyer's job differs in a small independent store, a department store, and a larger store with branches.

2 How has the increasing number of branch stores complicated the department store buyer's job?

3 Why do chain stores maintain central buying organizations?

4 In chain organizations, a buyer's responsibilities depend on the amount of control they share with store managers. Explain.

5 Explain why chain stores have been able to amass great profits through centralized buying.

6 Price list agreements or listing plans comprise a form of central buying that affords the store manager greater autonomy. What are the advantages of such plans?

7 What are the main reasons for small stores using outside buying consultants and resident buying offices?

8 List the different types of resident buying offices and the types of services they provide for their members.

9 Why do corporate buying offices carry such great buying power?

10 Why do many retailers maintain their own market representatives in a resident buying office in addition to their store-based buying operations?

11 What criteria should be used by a retailer in selecting a resident buying office?

12 What are the advantages of specification buying? Why is this method of buying best suited to large retailers?

13 How can small retailers compete with the buying power of large chains? Be specific.

14 The major merchandise resources for retail buyers are either direct or indirect. Explain.

15 What are the advantages of using wholesalers as a source of merchandise?

16 Why is it important to buy directly from the manufacturer in the case of fashion goods?

# FIELD PROJECTS

1 Many buyers follow advertisements in the consumer and dealer press. They also read direct mail pieces in their search for new resources.

Assume that you are the buyer for a specialty chain.

- Select a product classification in which you are interested, such as cosmetics, men's toiletries, or stationery.
- Visit your local library and check several magazines and newspapers for advertisements of products that you would buy for your stores. Prepare a list of these products (names and descriptions), together with the names and addresses of the manufacturers or wholesalers that sell them.

a How can a buyer use this list in preparation for buying new merchandise?

b What kind of product information did you read about?

c How many different price ranges are there for your product?

2 Visit your local supermarket and delicatessen to determine the items that are supplied by rack jobbers. (Ask the store manager or owner for help.)

a How many different classifications of merchandise (e.g., toys, hardware, etc.) did you find? Observe the customer activity around these items.

b Without asking the store manager, how might you determine whether they are profitable for the merchant–retailer?

c Ask the merchant how often the rack jobber comes to restock the rack display.

# CASES

1 The 69 Cents Shop, a discount chain, is trading up after twenty years. Because of rising prices and the increase in the cost of doing business, the chain will change its name to the 88 Cents Shop.

The stores will raise all their prices to 88 cents and alter the mix of their 3500 items. The owners claim that the reasons for these changes are rising prices and inability to obtain suitable goods to be sold in volume. The owners are quoted as saying, "Now we feel we can buy merchandise that has been priced out of range until this point."

The stores sell a broad array of branded and unbranded housewares, hardware, and health and beauty aids. In 1979 the company had $4 million in sales.

The 69 Cents Shop has made a niche in the discount field for certain products. It is recognized by a segment of customers as reliable and well stocked with certain types of merchandise, all of which was sold at 69 cents.

a If you were the owner of a successful chain like the 69 Cents Shop, would you make the proposed changes? Explain.

b What are some alternatives? How would you handle the problems of improving the merchandise selection?

c How do you think the old customers will perceive the changes?

d What are the opportunities for developing a new clientele?

2 J. C. Penney and Earl C. Sams, both executives of J. C. Penney Company, tried to open a central buying office in Salt Lake City in 1905. The project flopped mainly

because their store managers resented it and wouldn't support the idea. They were accustomed to buying for their own stores and wanted to continue the practice.

Penney and Sams recognized that store managers were in direct contact with customers and were acutely aware of their changing preferences. Nevertheless, in 1913 the Penney Company opened a buying office in New York City. Although its specific location has changed several times, the New York office still exists. In addition, Penney has fashion and specialized buying offices in Dallas, Miami, Los Angeles, Hong Kong, Tokyo, and Milan.

    a  Do you think today's Penney store managers would react the same way the managers did in 1905 regarding a central buying office? Explain.

    b  Do you believe that central buying offices can provide individual stores with profitable merchandise without input from the store managers? Explain.

**3**  Store expansion and the development of additional units sometimes cause conflicts for buying offices. For example, when an independent buying office services a store, it generally does not service the store's immediate competitors. As stores expand into additional units, however, they meet other accounts of the same office, which can cause problems if they are not handled carefully. For example, many stores want to keep certain lines and styles out of competitors' inventories to distinguish them from the latters' offerings.

An example of territorial conflict existed between B. Altman & Company, based in New York City, and Wanamaker's, based in Philadelphia. Each moved into the other's territory, Wanamaker's with a branch in Westchester County, a suburb of New York City, and Altman's with a large store in Philadelphia. Since both stores cater to a similar customer base, it is difficult for them to find merchandise that is truly distinctive from the other's offerings.

Territorial conflicts with the store-owned Associated Merchandising Corporation are also occurring. For example, Federated Stores (part of AMC) has been expanding many of its divisions into areas where other AMC stores are located. As a result, Federated's move of Bloomingdale's to Philadelphia posed a threat to Philadelphia-based Strawbridge & Clothier. Both of these stores are heavy advertisers and promote unusual special events. They are both recognized as having an impact on fashion.

    a  How can these stores maintain their own identity and develop store patronage?

    b  What are the problems faced by the resident office with so many stores preparing for expansion?

# REFERENCES

Belden, D. L., *The Role of the Buyer in Mass Merchandising* (New York: Chain Store Age Books, 1971).

Berman, B., and J. R. Evans, *Retail Management: A Strategic Approach* (New York: Macmillan, 1979), chap. 10.

Bolen, W. H., *Contemporary Retailing* (Englewood Cliffs, N.J.: Prentice-Hall, 1978), chap. 10.

Cash, R. P., *The Buyers Manual* (New York: National Retail Merchants Association, 1979).

Dickenson, R. A., *Buyer Decision Making* (Los Angeles: University of California, Los Angeles, Institute of Business and Economic Research, 1967).

Gillespie, K. R., and J. C. Hecht, *Retail Business Management* (New York: McGraw-Hill, 1977), chap. 11.

Johnston, J. W., *The Department Store Buyer* (Austin: University of Texas at Austin, Bureau of Business Research, 1969).

Martin, C. R., Jr., "The Contribution of the Professional Buyer to a Store's Success or Failure," *Journal of Retailing*, 49 (Summer 1973), pp. 69–80.

McCreevy, R., "Survival for the Independent," *Retail Directions*, 127 (January 1973), p. 25.

Miller, K. E., and K. L. Granzin, "Simultaneous Loyalty and Benefit Segmentation of Retail Store Customers," *Journal of Retailing*, 55 (Spring 1979), pp. 47–60.

Wingate, J. and J. Friedlander, *The Management of Retail Buying* (Englewood Cliffs, N.J.: Prentice-Hall, 1978).

# chapter 14
# MERCHANDISE PLANNING

After completing this chapter, you should be able to:

**1** List the ways in which buyers determine what merchandise to buy, how much to buy, from whom to buy, and when to buy.

**2** Compute open-to-buy.

**3** Identify common discount and dating terms.

**4** List the major aspects of vendor–retailer negotiations.

Retailers often survey consumers to determine their merchandise needs and preferences.

What, when, how much to buy

As stated in Chapter 13, the elements of buying are similar for small and large stores. In this chapter we will deal with the planning aspect of buying merchandise.

A major consideration that confronts buyers is the ability to stock their stores with merchandise that can be sold profitably. In order to do this, it is necessary to plan for the "right merchandise to be at the right place, at the right time, in the right quantities, and at the right price."[1] In other words, the buyer is faced with the decisions of *what* to buy, *how* much to buy, from *whom* to buy, and *when* to buy.

# WHAT TO BUY— CONSUMER DEMAND

Since a store's image depends a great deal on the type and price of merchandise it sells, the desired image determines the goods that must be purchased. Uppermost in the buyer's mind, therefore, must be the needs and desires of the customers that the store wishes to attract. For example, Henri Bendel, an exclusive shop in New York City, caters to customers in a small size range. According to the president, Geraldine Stutz, "We picked a customer to concentrate on—we try to have everything for a size 2 to 10." The merchandise that this store sells is expensive, trendy, and sophisticated. Bendel's does not extend the welcome mat to oversized people in its ready-to-wear areas. The Lane Bryant chain, on the other hand, caters to "the big woman." Both stores have decided on a target customer and buy accordingly.

Predicting *what* the consumer will want is not easy. Because buyers must avoid

[1]Committee on Definitions, *Marketing: A Glossary of Marketing Terms*, (Chicago, American Marketing Association, 1960).

stocking inappropriate goods, they seek information to use in interpreting consumer demand. Sources of reliable information include the consumer, the trade, and store records.

# Consumer Information

*Anticipating consumer demand is not easy*

It is important for merchants and buyers to "listen" to their customers. After all, it is the consumer who decides what and where to buy. The retailer is able to study the consumer by keeping track of buying habits. For example, merchants can assess customers' "taste" requirements by tracking fast-selling items (Figure 14-1). They can also observe the most popular shopping hours and how purchases are paid for.

Through the use of telephones and in-store interviews, merchants use surveys to determine merchandise preferences. They also mail printed questionnaires, which are sent to charge customers to obtain feedback on store brands, merchandise performance, and the like. Some retailers conduct consumer panels for direct contact regarding customers' purchase plans as well as their likes and dislikes. Other research techniques utilized by retailers are discussed in depth in Chapter 24.

# Trade Information

## Suppliers

Manufacturers, wholesalers, and other intermediaries do their own research in analyzing the market. Since vendors must also study consumer demand, they can provide the retailer with facts and figures that might be helpful in making merchandise decisions (Figure 14-2).

*Information can come from suppliers, competitors, or others*

## Competition

It is important to observe how the competition analyzes consumer demand. Retailers can comparison shop at other stores and study the stock they carry. They can also investigate displays and analyze competitive promotions and advertising.

**BEST-SELLERS**
Include the top five selling items in each department for the November/December period.

| Dept. # | Style # | Vendor Name | Description of Item | Class | Price | Units Sold | Comments |
|---------|---------|-------------|---------------------|-------|-------|------------|----------|
|  |  |  |  |  |  |  |  |
|  |  |  |  |  |  |  |  |
|  |  |  |  |  |  |  |  |
|  |  |  |  |  |  |  |  |
|  |  |  |  |  |  |  |  |
|  |  |  |  |  |  |  |  |
|  |  |  |  |  |  |  |  |

**FIGURE 14-1**
A department store form used to determine best-selling merchandise.

## 25 - 12 OZ. BLENDED DENIM
64% COTTON 36% POLYESTER      SPC-12

| DESCRIPTION | | COLORS | UVM COLOR | TELE- CODE | TOTAL CODE | DELIVERY DATE | SIZE SCALE | | | | | | |
|---|---|---|---|---|---|---|---|---|---|---|---|---|---|
| | **25400-25** **YOKE EMBROIDERED JEAN** Clean front jean with back yoke and embroidered asymmetric back pockets. 18'' leg opening. $16.00 | (16) Indigo | 48 | 700 | | | 8 | 10 | 12 | 14 | 16 | 18 | |
| | UVM: R 18840     P 27340025 | | | | | | 108 | 110 | 112 | 114 | 116 | 118 | |
| | **25414-25** **5 POCKET JEAN** Classic five-pocket jean straight leg. 17'' leg opening. $15.75 | (16) Indigo | 48 | 701 | | | 8 | 10 | 12 | 14 | 16 | 18 | 20 |
| | UVM: R 18840     P 27341425 | | | | | | 108 | 110 | 112 | 114 | 116 | 118 | 120 |
| | **25488-25** **EMBROIDERED JEAN** Clean front jean with embroidered spade back pockets. 18'' leg opening. $16.00 | (16) Indigo | 48 | 702 | | | 8 | 10 | 12 | 14 | 16 | 18 | |
| | UVM: R 18840     P 27348825 | | | | | | 108 | 110 | 112 | 114 | 116 | 118 | |

**FIGURE 14-2**

3

A page of a manufacturer's catalog for the placement of seasonal orders by buyers. (Reproduced by permission of Levi Strauss & Co.)

## Noncompeting Stores

Retailers in different markets often exchange predictions regarding merchandise, trends, and special promotions. For example, a Chicago merchant who sells giftware will share information about successful items with another giftware retailer in Michigan.

## Publications, Trade Shows, and Market Weeks

There are many publications that contain excellent information for buyers. They include *Women's Wear Daily, Chain Store Age, Daily News Record, Stores* magazine, and *Home Furnishings Daily.* These trade papers report on new products, business statistics, demand trends, and important items for the specialty retailer.

Manufacturers often present their new merchandise at trade shows (Figure 14-3), which are generally organized by trade associations. Vendors usually have representatives at these shows to explain their products and provide current product information and market trends. For example, the Gift Show has suppliers who deal in items that are usually sold in specialty or department stores. As a result, buyers have a firsthand opportunity to see new products that vendors feel will be in demand during the coming season.

---

Right now, designers and manufacturers all over the country are getting ready for our Women's and Children's Midsummer Apparel Market. In all, there'll be some 10,000 lines at our show. As well as sneak previews, trend-setting fashion shows and enlightening seminars. (You'll find 86 acres of free parking, too. Along with free transportation to downtown and area hotels.) If you're ready for it, call toll free for hotel reservations and more information. 800-527-9065. (In Texas, call 800-442-7111.)

**New California designers and manufacturers will be showing in Dallas for the first time during the Women's & Children's Midsummer Apparel Market. Visit the West Atrium, 4th floor balcony area, adjacent to Group III.**

**Special reminder:**
**The 5th Annual Flying Colors Fashion Awards program begins at the Midsummer Market. Ballots will be available at registration desks during market so you can vote in all 10 categories.**

# Special Events

## Friday, January 18
### SAMA's Midsummer Dream
Sponsored by the Southwest Apparel Manufacturers Association
6:00 p.m., Great Hall
Fashion Show/Cocktails
All Buyers Invited

## Saturday, January 19
### Summer Childrenswear Show
7:30 a.m., Fashion Theatre, Third Floor
Fashion Show/Continental Breakfast
All Childrenswear Buyers Invited

### Fashion Shows? How, When, Where and Why
Speakers: Kim Dawson, Fashion Director, Dallas Apparel Mart and Fashion Staff
12:00 Noon, Fashion Theatre, Third Floor
Seminar/Luncheon
Admission by Ticket Only*
Tickets: $6.00 in advance
$7.00 on Saturday

---

**FIGURE 14-3**

An announcement to the retail apparel trade about market week in Dallas. (Reproduced by permission of Dallas Market Center.)

In some lines, such as toys, a large percentage of the purchasing is often done at the annual trade show. Other well-known shows are the National Boutique Show and the International Fur Show.

Several months prior to the start of a new season, retailers are able to view new merchandise during "Market Weeks." The major regional markets (New York City, Dallas, Los Angeles, etc.) sponsor new showings of merchandise for a specific line of goods.

### The Resident Buying Office

Another valuable source of information that helps store buyers make intelligent merchandise decisions is the resident buying office. Since resident buyers are in the market every day, they see new products almost immediately and maintain reliable lists of suppliers.

## Store Records and Personnel

*Information about the consumer*

Some retailers maintain a "want slip" system for consumer requests about out-of-stock or unstocked goods. These records are definite indications of consumer demand. Records produced by computers provide buyers with up-to-the-moment information about customer merchandise selection and fast- and slow-moving lines (Figure 14-4). Sales personnel can also provide valuable feedback because they are in direct contact with customers and can observe their buying habits. Information regarding prices, desired styles, and merchandise lines are passed along to the buyer (Figure 14-5).

A store's position regarding fashion leadership is another factor in considering the potential demand for certain product lines. The buyer needs a clear picture of how the store's clientele fits into the fashion adoption process. As discussed in Chapter 3, the buyer must determine whether the store's customers are the avant-garde, who buy in the early stages of style development, or the latecomers, who wait for the style to become established.

In some lines, a large percentage of buying by retailers is done at trade shows.

X DEPT 513 CLASSIFICATION SUMMARY REPORT

LEVEL 2 - ALL STORES

NOV WK 1 1980

UNITS AND DOLLARS — PERCENTAGE DISTRIBUTION

WEEKLY CLASSIFICATION REPORT LEVEL 1A & 2

| DESCRIPTION | SALES TREND NOV TY | NOV LY | PTD | NOV WK 1 TY | NOV WK 1 LY | | CURRENT LIABILITY OH | OO | OTB | LAST YEAR 4 FUTURE WEEKS SALES NOV WK 2 | NOV WK 3 | NOV WK 4 | DEC WK 1 | LAST YEAR 3 FUTURE MOS. SALES NOV | DEC | JAN | SALES NOV PTD TY | NOV PTD LY | THIS WEEK TY | THIS WEEK LY | CURRENT LIABILITY OH | OO | L.Y. FUTURE PERIOD SALES NEXT 4 WKS | 3 FUTURE MONTHS NOV | DEC | JAN |
|---|---|---|---|---|---|---|---|---|---|---|---|---|---|---|---|---|---|---|---|---|---|---|---|---|---|---|
| 57 | | UNITS | | | ***** | | | | | **** | | | | | | | | | | | | | | | | |
| B | | 13 | | | 13 | | | | | 9 | 1 | 3 | 6 | 26 | 51 | | | 5 | | 5 | | | | | | |
| J | | 2 | | | 2 | | | | | -1 | | 2 | 1 | 3 | | 1 | | 1 | | 1 | | | | | | |
| H | | | | | | | | | | 1 | 1 | | 3 | 2 | 37 | 1 | | | | | | | | | | |
| N | | 8 | | | 8 | | | | | 9 | 9 | 6 | 3 | 32 | 21 | | | 4 | | 4 | | | 1 | 1 | | |
| U | | 6 | | | 6 | | | | | 3 | 1 | 7 | 13 | 17 | 99 | -3 | | 6 | | 6 | | | 1 | 1 | 1 | |
| R | | 1 | | | 1 | | | | | 1 | 1 | 2 | 4 | 5 | 13 | | | 1 | | 1 | | | | | | |
| W | | | | | | | | | | | 3 | 1 | 2 | 4 | 1 | | | | | | | | | | | |
| A | | 3 | | | 3 | | | | | 4 | 2 | 11 | 14 | 20 | 54 | 2 | | 1 | | 1 | | | | | | |
| M | | 3 | | | 3 | | | | | 4 | 3 | 5 | 2 | 15 | 19 | 2 | | 3 | | 3 | | | | 1 | | |
| MKDN UNITS | | | | | | | | | | | | | | | | | | | | | | | | | | |
| REG UNITS | | 36 | | | 36 | | | | | 30 | 21 | 37 | 48 | 124 | 295 | 3 | | 2 | | 2 | | | | | | |
| TOT UNITS | | 36 | | | 36 | | | | | 30 | 21 | 37 | 48 | 124 | 295 | 3 | | 2 | | 2 | | | | | | |
| 57 | | DOLLARS | | | ***** | | | | | **** | | | | | | | | | | | | | | | | |
| B | | .2 | | | .2 | | | | | .1 | | | .2 | .4 | 1.2 | | | 5 | | 5 | | | | 1 | | |
| J | | | | | | | | | | | | | | | | | | | | | | | | | | |
| H | | | | | | | | | | | | | | | .6 | | | | | | | | | | | |
| N | | .1 | | | .1 | | | | | .2 | .1 | .1 | .1 | .5 | .3 | | | 4 | | 4 | | | 1 | 2 | | |
| U | | .1 | | | .1 | | | | | | | .1 | .1 | .2 | .4 | | | 6 | | 6 | | | | 1 | | |
| R | | | | | | | | | | | | | .1 | .1 | .2 | | | 1 | | 1 | | | | | | |
| W | | | | | | | | | | | | | | | | | | | | | | | | | | |
| A | | .1 | | | .1 | | | | | .1 | | .1 | .2 | .3 | .8 | | | 1 | | 1 | | | | | | |
| M | | | | | | | | | | .1 | | .1 | | .2 | .2 | .1 | | 3 | | 3 | | | | 1 | | |
| MKDN DOLL | | | | | | | | | | | | | | | | | | | | | | | | | | |
| REG DOLL | | .5 | | | .5 | | | | | .5 | .3 | .5 | .7 | 1.8 | 3.7 | .1 | | 2 | | 2 | | | | | | |
| TOT DOLL | | .5 | | | .5 | | | | | .5 | .3 | .5 | .7 | 1.8 | 3.7 | .1 | | 2 | | 2 | | | | | | |
| 5 | | TOT UNITS | | | *****JEWELRY | | | | | **** | | | | | | | | | | | | | | | | |
| B | | 13 | | | 13 | | | | | 9 | 1 | 3 | 6 | 26 | 51 | | | 5 | | 5 | | | | | | |
| J | | 2 | | | 2 | | | | | -1 | | 2 | 1 | 3 | | 1 | | 1 | | 1 | | | | | | |
| H | | | | | | | | | | 1 | 1 | | 3 | 2 | 37 | 1 | | | | | | | | | | |
| N | | 8 | | | 8 | | | | | 9 | 9 | 6 | 3 | 32 | 21 | | | 4 | | 4 | | | 1 | 1 | | |
| U | | 6 | | | 6 | | | | | 3 | 1 | 7 | 13 | 17 | 99 | -3 | | 6 | | 6 | | | 1 | 1 | 1 | |
| R | | 1 | | | 1 | | | | | 1 | 1 | 2 | 4 | 5 | 13 | | | 1 | | 1 | | | | | | |
| W | | | | | | | | | | | 3 | 1 | 2 | 4 | 1 | | | | | | | | | | | |
| A | | 3 | | | 3 | | | | | 4 | 2 | 11 | 14 | 20 | 54 | 2 | | 1 | | 1 | | | | | | |
| M | | 3 | | | 3 | | | | | 4 | 3 | 5 | 2 | 15 | 19 | 2 | | 3 | | 3 | | | | 1 | | |
| MKDN UNITS | | | | | | | | | | | | | | | | | | | | | | | | | | |
| REG UNITS | | 36 | | | 36 | | | | | 30 | 21 | 37 | 48 | 124 | 295 | 3 | | 2 | | 2 | | | | | | |
| TOT UNITS | | 36 | | | 36 | | | | | 30 | 21 | 37 | 48 | 124 | 295 | 3 | | 2 | | 2 | | | | | | |
| 5 | | TOT DOLLARS | | | *****JEWELRY | | | | | **** | | | | | | | | | | | | | | | | |
| B | | .2 | | | .2 | | | | | .1 | | | .2 | .4 | 1.2 | | | 5 | | 5 | | | | 1 | | |
| J | | | | | | | | | | | | | | | | | | | | | | | | | | |
| H | | | | | | | | | | | | | | | .6 | | | | | | | | | | | |
| N | | .1 | | | .1 | | | | | .2 | .1 | .1 | .1 | .5 | .3 | | | 4 | | 4 | | | 1 | 2 | | |
| U | | .1 | | | .1 | | | | | | | .1 | .1 | .2 | .4 | | | 6 | | 6 | | | | 1 | | |
| R | | | | | | | | | | | | | .1 | .1 | .2 | | | 1 | | 1 | | | | | | |
| W | | | | | | | | | | | | | | | | | | | | | | | | | | |
| A | | .1 | | | .1 | | | | | .1 | | .1 | .2 | .3 | .8 | | | 1 | | 1 | | | | | | |
| M | | | | | | | | | | .1 | | .1 | | .2 | .2 | .1 | | 3 | | 3 | | | | 1 | | |
| MKDN DOLL | | | | | | | | | | | | | | | | | | | | | | | | | | |
| REG DOLL | | .5 | | | .5 | | | | | .5 | .3 | .5 | .7 | 1.8 | 3.7 | .1 | | 2 | | 2 | | | | | | |
| TOT DOLL | | .5 | | | .5 | | | | | .5 | .3 | .5 | .7 | 1.8 | 3.7 | .1 | | 2 | | 2 | | | | | | |

X10355

RUN DATE 11/09/80 LEVEL 2 - ALL STORES MEDIA DATE W/E 11/08/80 RUN PAGE 2759 MI06R01

DEPT 513 DEPT-PG 6 NOV WK 1 1980 HNTGTN #1

Y 1 DEPT 20 CLSS SEQUENCE REPORT THRU 12-06

| STYLE DESCRIPTION: CLASS CODES / LAST ACTION & DATE | VEND. | STYLE | STYLE NAME | COST / INT. MU% | CURR. RETAIL / 1ST RETAIL | ALL STORES COMBINED: LIFE HISTORY | RECENT SALES & STOCK HISTORY: 4 WEEKS AGO | 3 WEEKS AGO | 2 WEEKS AGO | 1 WEEK AGO | | ALL STORES |
|---|---|---|---|---|---|---|---|---|---|---|---|---|
| | 117 | 924 | CREW HEATHER | | | SLS 260 | | 23 | 65 | 32 | CURR SLS | 65 |
| 62 00 | | | | .01 | 16.99 | RCPTS 378 | 302 | 279 | 215 | 183 | ON HAND | 118 |
| RECPT 11-22 | | | | 100.0 % | 20.00 | RETURNS 17 | LAST RCPT | 2 WKS AGO | | | PRV 1WKS | 32 |
| | | | | | | | FIRST RCPT | 14 WKS AGO | | | LIFE | 260 |
| | 117 | 925 | V HEATHER | | | SLS 339 | 9 | 40 | 54 | 48 | CURR SLS | 74 |
| 62 00 | | | | .01 | 16.99 | RCPTS | -.1 | -.2 | -.2 | -.3 | ON HAND | -.3 |
| TRANF 11-26 | | | | 100.0 % | 20.00 | RETURNS 21 | LAST RCPT ** | WKS AGO | ORD | 1 | PRV 1WKS | 48 |
| | | | | | | | FIRST RCPT ** | WKS AGO | | | LIFE | 339 |
| | 117 | 860 | PROMO LAMBSWOOL | | | SLS 3.5 | 123 | 153 | 215 | 240 | CURR SLS | 584 |
| 62 00 | | | | .01 | 20.00 | RCPTS 5.1 | 2.8 | 2.6 | 2.4 | 2.2 | ON HAND | 1.6 |
| RECPT 12-03 *CUM MD $ 7205.00 | | | | 100.0 % | 22.50 | RETURNS 197 | LAST RCPT | WKS AGO | | | PRV 1WKS | 240 |
| MD#1 11-08 2882 PCS. | | | | | | | FIRST RCPT | 10 WKS AGO | | | LIFE | 3.5 |
| | 851 | 13102 | | | | SLS | | | | | CURR SLS | |
| 62 00 | | | | .01 | 20.00 | RCPTS 78 | | | 78 | 78 | ON HAND | 78 |
| RECPT 11-19 | | | | 100.0 % | | RETURNS | LAST RCPT | 2 WKS AGO | | | PRV 1WKS | |
| | | | | | | | FIRST RCPT | 2 WKS AGO | | | LIFE | |
| | 851 | 102 | BLEND V NECK | | | SLS 4.8 | 170 | 253 | 430 | 340 | CURR SLS | 2.4 |
| 62 00 | | | | 2.17 | 21.00 | RCPTS 9.2 | 2.2 | 2.8 | 3.7 | 5.2 | ON HAND | 4.4 |
| RECPT 12-06 | | | | 90.0 % | | RETURNS 220 | LAST RCPT | WKS AGO | | | PRV 1WKS | 340 |
| | | | | | | | FIRST RCPT | 21 WKS AGO | | | LIFE | 4.8 |

**FIGURE 14-4**

Computer-generated data sheets showing customer merchandise selection and the movement of merchandise lines.

**SALES RESULTS**

| Dept. # & Name | Week Ending | | Week Ending | | Week Ending | | Week Ending | | Week Ending | | Week Ending | | |
|---|---|---|---|---|---|---|---|---|---|---|---|---|---|
| | TY 11/22 | LY 11/24 | TY 11/29 | LY 12/1 | TY 12/6 | LY 12/8 | TY 12/13 | LY 12/15 | TY 12/20 | LY 12/22 | TY 12/27 | LY 12/29 | |
| | | | | | | | | | | | | | |
| | | | | | | | | | | | | | |
| | | | | | | | | | | | | | |
| | | | | | | | | | | | | | |
| | | | | | | | | | | | | | |
| | | | | | | | | | | | | | |

**FIGURE 14-5**

A comparative sales results form.

Six-Month Merchandising Plan

| **Fall 1983** | | Aug. | Sep. | Oct. | Nov. | Dec. | Jan. | Total |
|---|---|---|---|---|---|---|---|---|
| Sales | Last year | | | | | | | |
| | Plan (this year) | | | | | | | |
| | Revision | | | | | | | |
| | Actual | | | | | | | |
| Inventory (beginning of month) | Last year | | | | | | | (Inventory |
| | Plan (this year) | | | | | | | Jan. 31) |
| | Revision | | | | | | | |
| | Actual | | | | | | | |
| Reductions (markdowns + shortages + discounts) | Last year | | | | | | | |
| | Plan (this year) | | | | | | | |
| | Revision | | | | | | | |
| | Actual | | | | | | | |
| Purchases | Last year | | | | | | | |
| | Plan (this year) | | | | | | | |
| | Revision | | | | | | | |
| | Actual | | | | | | | |

**FIGURE 14-6**

This is a typical form used by retailers for developing their merchandise plans in advance of the period to which they refer. Plans should always be completed before actual buying for the season begins.

# ASSORTMENT— HOW MUCH TO BUY

After determining what to buy, the buyer must choose the assortment and quantity of stock to carry. Merchants must buy in large enough quantities to avoid running out of stock and thereby lose sales. On the other hand, they should not overbuy and wind up with too much inventory. In order to buy in proper amounts, buyers should make carefully developed plans and check current details. One way the buyer begins to accomplish this task is through the six-month seasonal merchandise plan (see Figure 4-6). Plans used by retailers before buying include **open-to-buy (OTB)**, which sets the dollar amount of merchandise that a buyer can order for a particular period, and assortment plans, which ensure a proper variety of stock for a particular period.

## Open-to-Buy

*Open-to-buy
helps buyers plan
purchases*

Open-to-buy is the difference between planned purchases and stock already ordered (commitments). The OTB, therefore, is the amount of money a buyer has left for ordering merchandise at any time during a certain period.

OTB is computed by the following formula.

Suppose a furniture merchant plans to sell $120,000 worth of goods during the month of October. The planned inventory is $80,000 for October 1 and $70,000 for October 31. Planned reductions (discounts, shortages, markdowns) for the month are $9,000. Stock on order is $25,000. (All amounts are at retail prices.)

| | | |
|---|---:|---:|
| Merchandise needed | | |
| Planned sales | $120,000 | |
| Planned end-of-month inventory | 70,000 | |
| Planned reductions | 9,000 | |
| | | $199,000 |
| Merchandise available | | |
| Planned opening inventory | $ 80,000 | |
| Stock on order | 25,000 | |
| | | $105,000 |

Open-to-buy = $199,000 − 105,000 = $94,000

The buyer's open-to-buy for the remainder of the period is $94,000.

The OTB concept is important for several reasons. First of all, it gives the buyer some flexibility in replacing goods that are sold. Second, it avoids an improper balance between inventory and sales. Thus, it is easier for the buyer to maintain planned inventories without overbuying or underbuying. Third, it indicates how the retailer can adjust purchases at any time during the buying period. Finally, it gives the buyer an opportunity to purchase additional "hot items" (fast-moving products) or order something new.

There are times when buyers need to know the open-to-buy figure before the end of the planned period. For example, a buyer may have good reason to expect that sales will be better than expected or that business conditions may warrant quick steps to reduce the stock on hand. In either event, by simply adjusting the example to include the sales actually recorded and the actual reductions, the open-to-buy can be computed for any date (October 13 in our illustration).

| | | |
|---|---:|---:|
| Merchandise needed, October 13–31 | | |
|     Planned sales, October 1–31 | $120,000 | |
|     Actual sales, October 1–12 | −70,000 | |
|     Balance of planned sales | | $ 50,000 |
|     Planned EOM inventory | | 70,000 |
|     Planned reductions, October 1–31 | 9,000 | |
|     Actual reductions, October 1–12 | −2,000 | |
|     Balance of planned reductions | | 7,000 |
|       Total merchandise needed | | $127,000 |
| Merchandise available, October 13–31 | | |
|     Planned opening inventory | $ 80,000 | |
|     Merchandise received, October 1–12 | +14,000 | |
|     Total merchandise handled, October 1–12 | $ 94,000 | |
|     Actual sales, October 1–12 | −70,000 | |
|     Merchandise on hand, October 12 | $24,000 | |
|     Merchandise on order, October 13 | +21,000 | |
|     Total merchandise available | | $ 45,000 |
|     Open-to-buy, October 13 | | $ 82,000 |

## Merchandise Turnover

An important measure for determining how quickly merchandise has been sold is called **merchandise turnover** or **stock turnover.** It enables retailers to plan their purchases more accurately, and reduces the possibility of over- and understocking their inventory. The computation of merchandise turnover is discussed in Chapter 21.

## Assortment Plans

**Assortment plans** help the buyer achieve merchandise balance. A stock of merchandise is properly assorted when it is composed of lines of goods that are suited to the demands of customers. One drugstore, for example, may have a proper assortment when it carries prescription and nonprescription items, cosmetics, and toiletries, but another drugstore

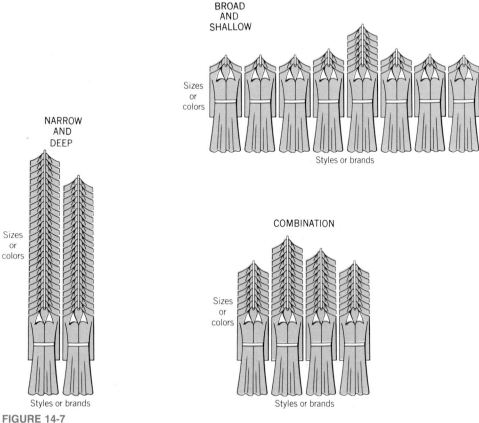

**FIGURE 14-7**
Types of breadth and depth assortment plans.

might have a proper assortment when it carries prescription and nonprescription items, cosmetics, giftware, small games, and stationery. In other words, the merchandise lines carried bear a direct relationship to consumer demand.

Retailers must decide whether their inventory composition should have breadth or depth. **Breadth,** or **width,** refers to the number of product classifications that a merchant stocks. **Depth** refers to the number of styles or brands within a product classification. There are three types of relationships between breadth and depth (Figure 14-7).

1  *Narrow and deep.* Only a few selections are offered, but they are stocked in depth (e.g., two styles of jeans, but in all sizes and colors).

2  *Broad and shallow.* The merchant carries a little of many styles in a product class (e.g., a large variety of designer jeans, with limited size selection).

3  *Combination.* A combination of (1) and (2) (e.g., four styles of jeans, in several colors and sizes).

# FROM WHOM TO BUY

In Chapter 13 we discussed the major merchandise sources for retail buyers. We will now see how buyers actually select among those resources.

Merchants always look for goods that can be sold in their own stores. Although improvements in production, distribution, and communications aid retailers in their search for merchandise, their buying depends on their ability to ferret out good sources of supply (Figure 14-8).

## Vendor Relations

In selecting resources, buyers must find vendors who can supply merchandise reliably and consistently. To determine the value of a resource, the retailer should consider the following factors.

- Quality of merchandise
- Vendor's reputation
- Location of vendor
- Resale aid
- Vendor's brand policy
- Terms of purchase
- Sales and profit experience

### Quality of Merchandise

The quality of goods must meet the needs of the store's clientele

The vendor's merchandise must be suitable for the retailer's clientele. The market to which the retailer caters may prefer low-, medium-, or high-priced lines. The preference may be avant-garde (advanced) or conservative styles. It may also be either staples or specialty goods that cannot be substituted for or found elsewhere. Whatever the preferences of customers, the retailer must consider them when selecting vendors. Those

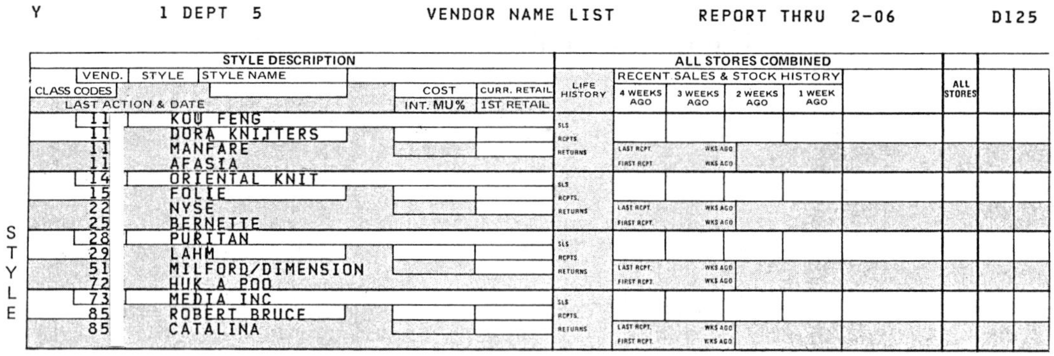
Y 1 DEPT 5 VENDOR NAME LIST REPORT THRU 2-06 D125

STYLE DESCRIPTION | ALL STORES COMBINED

VEND. STYLE STYLE NAME | CLASS CODES | COST | CURR. RETAIL | INT. MU% | 1ST RETAIL | LAST ACTION & DATE | LIFE HISTORY | RECENT SALES & STOCK HISTORY: 4 WEEKS AGO, 3 WEEKS AGO, 2 WEEKS AGO, 1 WEEK AGO | ALL STORES

11 KOU FENG
11 DORA KNITTERS
11 MANFARE
11 AFASIA
14 ORIENTAL KNIT
15 FOLIE
22 NYSE
25 BERNETTE
28 PURITAN
29 LAHM
51 MILFORD/DIMENSION
72 HUK A POO
73 MEDIA INC
85 ROBERT BRUCE
85 CATALINA

STYLE

FIGURE 14-8

An example of a vendor name list stored by a computer that helps buyers determine good sources of supply.

who do not carry the quality of goods required are not good sources of supply. No matter how attractive their prices or how desirable they are to deal with, the buyer cannot consider them as suppliers.

## Vendor's Reputation

A vendor's reputation is indicated by the guarantee that it places behind its merchandise. Ethics are also an important standard by which to choose. Perhaps the size of the vendor's business or how long it has been in business are good indications of its reliability.

An unethical vendor is not likely to remain in business long. Sometimes buyers secure information about suppliers through mercantile agencies that issue confidential reports. Inquiries from noncompeting retailers are another way of learning about vendors.

Large retailers investigate vendors in an attempt to judge their ability to deliver quality goods. In addition, they check on their reputations for honesty. Unfortunately, errors regarding quantities, prices, and the like are not always innocent. Also, since a weak supplier may go out of business and thereby interrupt the supply of merchandise, retailers are interested in the financial strength of their vendors.

Some financially weak vendors are good sources but lack capital. In some cases large retailers that are interested in these vendors' merchandise advance funds against future orders.

## Location of Vendor

Transportation costs may be a deterrent

Obtaining merchandise from distant vendors generally entails higher transportation costs than obtaining merchandise locally. Higher costs, of course, can be a deterrent to handling such merchandise. On the other hand, if transportation costs are not a significant factor, and especially if the supplier is dependable, it may be advisable to use such a vendor.

When goods are sold, the buyer and seller must agree on which of them will pay the cost of transportation. There are two terms used to indicate responsibility: **FOB shipping point** and **FOB destination.** FOB stands for "free on board."

Retailers check merchandise to evaluate the performance and reliability of their vendors.

If the terms are FOB shipping point, the seller delivers the merchandise to the starting point of shipment. From that point on, the buyer pays transportation costs, has title (ownership) to the goods, and suffers any loss if the merchandise is damaged during shipment. When the terms are FOB destination, the seller pays the costs of transportation to the buyer's location, retains title to the goods while they are in transit, and suffers any loss if the merchandise is damaged during shipment.

It goes without saying that vendors that are reliable are preferred over those that renege on delivery promises. Buyers therefore should keep records regarding delivery performance so that vendors can be evaluated fairly.

### Resale Aid

Some vendors are well aware of how important it is for the retailer to move goods into the hands of the consumer. Such vendors help the retailer sell the goods by providing assistance with displays, advertising, and sales promotion. This type of help is very important to small retailers.

### Vendor's Brand Policy

*Some retailers need vendors for both branded and unbranded goods*

A vendor's brand policy is another standard for selection. Some retailers prefer to handle only nationally advertised goods. Others prefer to develop and promote their own brands. The very large retailers find it worthwhile to develop and promote their own brands and, at the same time, handle some nationally advertised merchandise. In these instances vendors of both branded and unbranded merchandise must be selected.

### Terms of Purchase

An important standard by which vendors should be selected are the credit terms they offer. Although there is a good deal of standardization of terms, individual vendors often differ. Credit terms also vary with market conditions. Specific terms are treated later in this chapter.

### Sales and Profit Experience

*Careful records should be kept on vendor performance*

Retailers should keep careful records of vendor performance. Comparisons can be made over time on the basis of customer returns, extent of markdowns, competition, markups, and the total sales picture. Obviously, the larger the sales volume, the more valuable the vendor.

## Negotiations

Some vendors have set terms that are the same for all retailers. These terms vary from one resource to another and change as business conditions change. In a seller's market, the terms are not so liberal for the retailer. In a buyer's market, however, retailers can sometimes insist on their own terms.

Terms of purchase also vary according to the trade. In the food trade, for example, the terms of purchase are not as liberal as in the apparel trade. As a rule, the faster the merchandise is sold, the shorter the terms and the smaller the discount. Discounts alone, however, should not lure a buyer into a purchase that is not suitable for the store's clientele.

# Discounts and Dating

## Discounts

The most common terms of purchase are **cash discounts.** The discounts are listed in percentages of total purchase price and are offered in return for prompt payment. A cash discount has three elements: a percentage figure, a discount period consisting of a certain number of days, and a net period.

The date of the invoice usually determines when the discount and net periods expire. If the retailer does not take advantage of the cash discount by paying early, the full amount must be paid within the net period computed from the date of the invoice.

Suppose the terms of an invoice are 2/10, net/30 and the invoice date is May 1. The retailer may deduct 2 percent of the bill if it is paid within ten days (May 11), but must pay the full price if it is paid after May 11. In any case, the bill must be paid no later than May 31 (30 days from the invoice date). Since discounts mean additional capital for retailers, they make every effort to pay bills early.

**Anticipation** is an extra discount that retailers ask for if they pay their bills before the expiration of the cash discount period. The rationale for this additional discount is that the vendor has the use of the retailer's money and any interest it might earn. As interest rates have risen, retailers are demanding higher anticipation discounts. It is not uncommon for stores to request rates as high as 1 percent monthly or 12 percent a year. When anticipation is granted by the vendor, it is deducted from the invoice price.

## Dating

**Dating** refers to the period allowed by vendors to buyers for the payment of bills. It includes both the discount period and the net period. These periods vary and may include any of the following.

**ROG (Receipt of Goods)** The cash discount period begins with the receipt of the merchandise rather than the actual date of the invoice. If goods are bought under terms of 2/10, net 60 ROG, the 2 percent discount may be taken if the bill is paid within ten days after the receipt of the goods. This is generally used when the invoice date and the date of arrival of merchandise are not the same because of long distances between retailer and vendor.

**DOI (Date of Invoice)** This is called ordinary or regular dating; payment starts with the invoice date.

**EOM (End of Month)** The discount period starts at the end of the month in which the invoice is dated. For example, if an invoice date is April 8 and the terms are 2/10 EOM, net/60, the retailer can deduct a 2 percent discount if the bill is paid by May 10.

**Extra Dating** Sometimes a retailer requests additional time in which to take advantage of a cash discount. When the discount period is extended, it is known as **extra dating** and is denoted by a capital $X$ or the term *extra*. For example, "2/10 – 30X" or "2/10 – 30 extra" on an invoice extends the regular discount period from 10 to 40 days (10 + 30) from the date of the invoice.

**Postdating** Similar to extra dating, **postdating** is a common practice in the apparel industry. It extends the cash discount period for an additional month when the invoice is dated on or after the twenty-fifth of the month and end-of-month terms are given. For example, if an invoice is dated September 26 with terms of 6/10 EOM, the retailer has until October 10 in which to take the discount. With postdating, the retailer has until November 10 to qualify for the discount.

Advance dating is a help to retailers with seasonal products

**Advance Dating**  When ordering goods during a slow period, the merchant may sometimes arrange to pay for the merchandise after it has been sold. The merchant arranges to have the credit date based on a date later than the invoice date. Toys and Christmas items are often ordered in this way. Because retailers are motivated to purchase early, manufacturers benefit by not having to store the merchandise. Thus, an invoice for a shipment of toys could be dated July 1, effective November 10. If a cash discount of 2/10 were in order, the 2 percent discount could be deducted through November 20.

## Trade Discounts

Trade discounts are given by vendors according to the type of customer. That is, they are given according to the quantities purchased and the functions performed by the purchaser. In most cases wholesalers receive larger discounts than retailers. This is due either to the volume of purchases made by wholesalers or to the many marketing functions they assume, functions that ordinarily are handled by the manufacturers. In the latter case the manufacturers pass along their reduced costs in the form of trade discounts. Since large chains and department stores buy much larger quantities than some wholesalers, they are able to secure trade discounts, too.

## Other Aspects of Negotiations

Sometimes there are other concessions that make a buyer select a particular vendor. The following are among those that are considered most often.

Other factors in selecting a vendor

**Market Exclusivity**  For some goods, limits on the type or number of competitors may be required if a store is to make a reasonable profit. For example, a ladies' handbag line that is discounted within a particular trading area might not be a wise purchase for a traditional department store in that area.

**Lower Costs**  Lower costs are always of interest to buyers, especially for merchandise categories in which competition is severe.

**Advertising**  Vendors may offer financial assistance to support retail advertisements. (Retail advertising and cooperative arrangements are discussed in Chapter 19.)

**Guaranteed Sales**  Under a system of **guaranteed sales,** before an order is received from a retailer, the vendor agrees to take back merchandise that the retailer cannot sell within a specified time (see Figure 14-9). For example, a dress manufacturer could make such an agreement to move end-of-season stock. The buyer benefits from the arrangement because no OTB dollars have to be committed for the stock and no markdown dollars will have to be spent if the dresses do not sell.

**Consignment Buying**  In **consignment buying,** the vendor permits the retailer to pay only for goods that are sold. In this arrangement the seller retains ownership of the goods and more or less dictates the terms of sale. It is used with high-priced specialty goods that a store might want to "try."

# Womenswear Returned Goods Policy

Requests to return all first quality and worn defective Womenswear merchandise must be made through your Sales Representative within a 30-day period from the date of shipment. Please include in your request for the return the number and date of the invoice relating to the merchandise. Upon approval of your request, we will send you an addressed shipping label which will serve as your authorization to return the merchandise. This authorization label will direct your return to the proper location and will contain coded information enabling us to credit your account promptly.

We strive to answer all requests for returns within 25 working days of receipt. If you have not been contacted within this time period, please contact the Womenswear Regional Office.

In the case of damaged or worn merchandise (consumer returns), your request need not be made within the aforementioned 30-day period, nor is it necessary to refer to any invoices.

In the case of new defective merchandise returns, address correspondence to:

LEVI STRAUSS & CO.
Quality Assurance
10901 Airport Blvd.
Amarillo, Texas 79111

ABSOLUTELY NO RETURNS FOR WORN OR NEW MERCHANDISE CAN BE ACCEPTED BY OUR DISTRIBUTION CENTER WITHOUT AN AUTHORIZATION LABEL.

All Womenswear styles shipped F.O.B. Amarillo, Texas.

Prices in this Levi's® catalog apply only to shipments within the continental United States including Alaska, Hawaii, and Puerto Rico, and are subject to change without notice.

The words "LEVI'S®", "STA-PREST®", "BEND OVER®", AND THE POCKET TAB are registered trademarks of Levi Strauss & Co.

QUALITY NEVER GOES OUT OF STYLE.®

## CREDIT TERMS
## 8/10 - EOM

LEVI STRAUSS & CO. • WOMENSWEAR DIVISION • 1155 BATTERY STREET • SAN FRANCISCO, CA 94106

FIGURE 14-9

An example of a vendor's returned-goods policy. (Reproduced by permission of Levi Strauss & Co.)

**Service** Some vendors offer additional services that attract purchasers. For example, vendors take stock counts (in the store) of merchandise that they supply, offer sales assistance in the store, and help train salespeople.

Another valuable vendor service is **premarking,** also known as **source marking.** Premarked merchandise arrives in the store completely marked (i.e., ticketed) by the vendor according to the merchant's specifications (price, style, size, etc.). The advantages to the retailer are reduced store marking costs, more accurate ticketing, and the ability to get the merchandise onto the selling floor earlier. (Premarking is covered in greater detail in Chapter 16.)

**Backup Stock** Backup stock is merchandise that a vendor will reserve without the store's having any obligation to purchase it. This arrangement allows the merchant to buy in smaller quantities and still "have" stock.

**Special Features** Some manufacturers are willing to add a distinctive merchandise feature to a regular item for some stores. This can give added value by creating a degree of exclusivity.

# ETHICS

Legal and ethical constraints on negotiations

Buyers have the obligation to negotiate the best possible terms of sale for the goods they purchase. The negotiations, however, are subject to certain legal and ethical constraints. A handy tool for buyers is *The Buyer's Manual,*[2] which lists unethical buyer–seller practices. The following list contains common abuses, some of which can be attributed to retailers, some to manufacturers, and some to both.

- Attempts to evade contractual obligations
- Excessive demands for service
- Unjust price concessions
- Abnormal credit extensions
- Discrimination based on the superior bargaining power of large groups
- Lack of sound business methods
- Unjust cancelations

Many difficulties arise in buying and negotiating for merchandise. Ethical practices are necessary for a store's public relations. For example, when the buyers of three well-known retail firms arranged with vendors to raise, fix, and maintain the retail prices charged for women's clothing, their carefully developed public image was tarnished.

### NEW TERMS

| | |
|---|---|
| advance dating | breadth |
| anticipation | cash discount |
| assortment plan | consignment buying |
| backup stock | date of invoice (DOI) |

[2]Moeser, David E., *The Buyers' Manual* (New York: National Retail Merchants Association, 1965).

| | |
|---|---|
| dating | open-to-buy (OTB) |
| depth | postdating |
| end of month (EOM) | premarking |
| extra dating | receipt of goods (ROG) |
| FOB destination | source marking |
| FOB shipping point | stock turnover |
| guaranteed sales | trade discount |
| merchandise turnover | width |

## CHAPTER HIGHLIGHTS

1 Buyers must stock the store with merchandise that can be sold profitably.

2 Buyers are faced with the decisions of what to buy, how much to buy, from whom to buy, and when to buy.

3 A store's image and the clientele it attracts depend to a large extent on the type of merchandise it sells.

4 Purchasing the right merchandise involves interpretation of consumer demand. Retailers seek information from their consumers, the trade, and company records.

5 A "want slip" system is a definite indication of consumer merchandise requests at a given time. These systems are helpful to buyers.

6 It is important for the buyer to understand the store's fashion position and how its clientele fits into the fashion adoption process.

7 The open-to-buy (OTB) concept is important for two reasons: It provides the buyer with flexibility and results in a proper balance between inventory and sales.

8 Assortment plans help the buyer achieve merchandise balance.

9 The success of retailers depends on their ability to ferret out good sources of merchandise. Several factors should be considered in selecting a vendor: quality of merchandise, vendor's reputation, location of vendor, resale aid, vendor's brand policy, terms of purchase, and sales and profit experience.

10 Negotiations involve terms of purchase, exclusive arrangements, and special vendor considerations and services.

11 Terms of purchase vary from one trade to another and involve a variety of credit terms.

12 Buyers have the obligation to negotiate the best possible terms of sale within certain legal and ethical constraints.

## QUESTIONS

1 What are the major decisions that a buyer has to make with regard to stocking a store?

2 Why does merchandise play an important role in creating a store's image?

3  How can the retailer assess consumer demand? How are consumers helpful in the interpretation of consumer demand?

4  Why are "want slip" systems important for the buyer? For the store in general?

5  What is the relationship between a store's fashion position and the merchandise it purchases?

6  Why is open-to-buy a valuable tool for the buyer? For the store?

7  What is meant by planned sales, planned inventory, and planned commitments?

8  Why is it important to have assortment plans?

9  What are the factors to be considered in selecting a vendor?

10  Why would a buyer check on the reputation of a vendor?

11  Why would a buyer be concerned about the financial strength of a vendor?

12  What kinds of records should be kept by a store once a vendor has been used as a source of supply?

13  How might a charge of unethical buying practices affect a store's image?

14  Why is it crucial for buyers to abide by the law in their dealings with vendors?

## FIELD PROJECTS

1  Visit your school or local library and select any three items from among the following: consumer magazines (e.g., *McCall's, Seventeen, Esquire*), newspapers, and trade publications (if available). Assume that you are a buyer of men's or women's jewelry. Compile a list of manufacturers that advertise jewelry. Select those from which you would consider buying for your small specialty shop in a suburban town.
   a  How many resources did you find?
   b  Why did you select the names on your list?
   c  Where are they located in relation to your store?

2  Visit the sporting goods department in a department store or at your local sporting goods specialty store.
   a  Compile a list of items that are sold there but are not directly related to sporting goods.
   b  What type of assistance do you think the buyer needed to purchase these items?
   c  Did you see any foreign goods? If so, do you think the size of the assortment is large enough to have been bought directly from manufacturers? Explain.

## CASES

1  J. C. Penney maintains its own testing laboratories, which are known as mechanical testing centers. The centers perform some 100,000 tests each year on actual and potential Penney merchandise. One of the centers tests power mowers, chain saws, and paint. It even has a lake for testing boats, outboard motors, and fishing equipment.

The concept of quality control begins with the buyer's initial evaluation of the supplier's product. Another check on quality takes place during production, when field specialists visit the suppliers' factories.

    a  How does this operation serve as a check on both buyer and vendor?

    b  With all these testing facilities, is it still necessary for the Penney buyer to consider the reliability of the vendor? Why?

2   Gloria Shops are located in two small suburban towns near a major city. They specialize in high-priced giftware such as china, glassware, and other items for the home. A large shopping center that recently opened nearby includes a large giftware chain. This chain discounts many of the items carried by the Gloria Shops. Consequently, Gloria's buyer is faced with the problem of meeting the new competition. Until the shopping center opened, the Gloria Shops enjoyed a fine clientele that shopped there often. Their customers were well satisfied with their selection of wares.

    The new center became very popular and attracted many Gloria Shop customers to its apparel stores. Once they were at the center, they noticed the lower prices at the newly opened giftware store. Since many of the items carried there were the same as those sold at Gloria Shops, the latter began to lose customers. The buyer for the Gloria Shops decided that the stores needed new, noncompetitive lines of merchandise.

    a  What do you think of the buyer's decision?

    b  How should the buyer go about implementing that decision?

    c  What are the consequences of adding new lines?

    d  What other alternatives are there?

3   Recently two executives made a presentation to the president of a large retail firm regarding a new way to plan purchases. Basically, it was an integrated system for programming merchandise with the retailer's key vendors. The plan consisted of the following.

- The merchant's chief executives and the top-level personnel of several key vendors would jointly develop a merchandise plan.
- The plan would take into consideration several factors.

    Merchandise, including basic stock, fashion assortments, and profit structures.

    Sales training by vendor specialists.

    An advertising and promotional program to include displays, feature promotions, and printed advertising.

    A detailed organization chart designating the responsibilities and directions for carrying out the plan.

    When the plan was presented, the following arguments for adoption were made.

- The store would become a "known" quantity and would benefit as a preferred customer.
- The key vendors would concentrate on providing the store with better service, premarked merchandise, and better shipping arrangements.

- Vendors would work directly with the store's inventory and reordering schedules.
- The relationship between the store and key sources would be closer, with fewer problems and simpler procedures for solving misunderstandings.
- Because decision making would involve only top-level executives, it would be easier to make necessary changes.

After listening to the presentation, the president indicated that he would consider the proposal and make a decision within a week.

    **a** If you were the president of the retail firm, would you adopt this plan? State your reasons for acceptance or refusal.

    **b** What types of stores might benefit from a programmed merchandising system? What types of stores might be handicapped by this arrangement?

# REFERENCES

Berens, J. S., "A Decision Matrix Approach to Supplier Selection," *Journal of Retailing*, 47 (Winter 1971–1972), pp. 47–53.

Bergmann, J., "Let's Not Make These the 'Embattled 80's!' " *Stores*, 62 (March 1980), p. 14.

Bolen, W. H., *Contemporary Retailing* (Englewood Cliffs, N.J.: Prentice-Hall, 1978), chap. 11.

Cash, R. P., *The Buyers Manual* (New York: National Retail Merchants Association, 1979).

Diamond, J., and G. Pintel, *Retail Buying* (Englewood Cliffs, N.J.: Prentice-Hall, 1976).

"Disco: More than Music," *Retailweek*, April 15, 1979, pp. 39–40.

Gillespie, K. R., and J. C. Hecht, *Retail Business Management* (New York: McGraw-Hill, 1977), chap. 12.

Goldenthal, I., *How to Plan Stocks, Sales, and Open-to-Buy* (Radnor, Pa.: Chilton, 1958–1959).

Lillis, C. M., and D. F. Hawkins, "Retail Expenditure Flows in Contiguous Trade Areas," *Journal of Retailing*, 50 (Summer 1974), pp. 30–42, 101.

Packard, S., *The Buying Game* (New York: Fairchild, 1979).

Williams, J. R., "President's Letter," *Stores*, 62 (April 1980), p. 59.

Wingate, J., and J. S. Friedlander, *The Management of Retail Buying*, 2nd ed. (Englewood Cliffs, N.J.: Prentice-Hall, 1978).

# chapter 15
# PRICING

After completing this chapter, you should be able to:

1  Discuss the four elements in pricing decisions: the customer, the competition, the cost of doing business, and the laws.

2  Identify common price policies followed by retailers.

3  Identify markup terms and compute markups.

4  List the reasons for markdowns and calculate markdown percentages.

In Chapter 13 we discussed the factors that retailers consider when buying merchandise. Buying methods and the buyer's role were explored, and sources of merchandise were examined. Chapter 14 dealt with the planning aspect of merchandise: its objectives, stock strategy, and buying levels.

*Retail pricing is a complex process*

Having decided on a general approach to the purchase of goods, the retailer must consider the prices at which to sell the merchandise. Contrary to what many people think, retail pricing is a complex process involving a variety of factors. In addition, pricing is a key element in the eventual success or failure of an enterprise. That being so, it is essential to study this critical aspect of retailing.

# THE IMPORTANCE OF CORRECT PRICING POLICIES

The pricing policies established by a retail enterprise must appeal to its customers. This holds true for high-priced fashion shops as well as for low-priced convenience stores. The essential point is that the store's overall price levels must match the image it projects. Without this blend of price and image, customers become confused and frequently turn elsewhere for their needs.

*A retail price includes the cost of the goods, overhead, and profit*

Correct pricing policies are essential to the profitability of a business. This is so because the price of an item must cover the cost of the product, the **overhead** (e.g., rent, salaries, and advertising) of the business, and the profit the retailer wants to make. For example, if a retailer buys an item for $6, estimates overhead at $4, and desires a profit of $2, the item must be sold for $12 (Figure 15-1). Though many other factors enter into the determination of price, the retailer's ultimate consideration must be the maintenance of a satisfactory profit level.

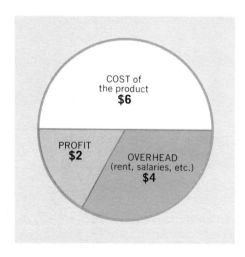

**FIGURE 15-1**
Price components of a product that sells for $12.

# ELEMENTS IN PRICING DECISIONS

## The Customer

As indicated previously, the customer is one of the retailer's main concerns in the development of a price structure. An analysis of this concern takes into consideration the following aspects of the customer's status.

1 Income levels
2 Customer motivation
3 Psychological aspects
4 Store image concepts
5 Value concepts

### Income Levels

In discussing the population of a trading area in Chapter 11, we stressed the importance of knowing the economic status of the area's consumers. Without this information, a retailer could hardly plan an appropriate merchandise line or establish realistic prices. With a good understanding of the public's buying capabilities, however, it is possible to draw some simple, yet valuable, conclusions about price levels. For example, a trading area that consists primarily of low-income people could not be expected to support a variety of high-priced stores. On the other hand, stores that carry products with prices keyed to the area's ability to pay might do quite well.

*Retailers must watch for changes in consumers' income levels*

Retailers must be alert to changes in consumers' income levels because even subtle shifts in neighborhood populations can have a serious effect on sales. For example, the closing of an auto factory can change the character of a community and, with it, the public's purchasing potential. Therefore, price policies need to be reviewed periodically in the light of possible changes in a population of a trading area.

### Customer Motivation

Despite the importance of income levels in the determination of consumer spending, other factors often influence shoppers when they buy. These include personal services offered by retailers, the availability of discounts, and the assortment of merchandise carried by stores. In addition, a consumer's purchases may be affected by his or her age, education, ethnic group, personality, and occupation. Though prices cannot take all of these influences into account, retailers should consider those that appear to have the greatest impact on their sales.

### Psychological Aspects

*Odd pricing is still used, but its effectiveness is declining*

Have you ever wondered why stores sometimes sell merchandise at such odd prices as 59¢, $8.95, and $16.99? After all, amounts of 60¢, $9.00, and $17.00 are much simpler for both retailers and customers to use. The most commonly accepted reason appears to be the customer's feeling that **odd prices** (prices just below even amounts) result in real savings. Though this psychological approach to pricing may have been effective in

Supermarkets sometimes use posters to provide shoppers with price information. This supermarket poster provides the shopper with price and product information.

the past, it has lost some of its appeal in today's market. Many consumers have become too sophisticated to be taken in by such price arrangements, and pay little attention to them. However, because of tradition or custom, a significant though declining number of retailers still cling to the practice. When these stores' sales volume is large, the loss of pennies on each sale can reduce their profits appeciably. There is considerable doubt, moreover, that odd prices motivate their customers to purchase.

## Store Image Concepts

*Store image can be molded by price*

Not all consumers buy on the basis of price. For some shoppers, a store's image is the main reason that they shop there. This is particularly true for prestigious stores like Neiman-Marcus and Marshall Field. Such factors as display, decor, atmosphere, and store reputation appeal more to these consumers than low prices. The stores maintain their reputations—and their customers—by cultivating a clearly defined affluent image.

Of course, store image can be molded by price, too. For example, consumers generally think of discount operations in terms of money-saving merchandise. Whether shoppers actually pay lower prices at such stores depends on the specific products purchased, the competition, the store itself, and similar factors. What draws them to these stores is the images the stores project through years of advertising, word of mouth, and personal contact with shoppers.

## Value Concepts

People have general ideas about how much they expect to pay for most products. For example, they know that designer jeans cost more because of the status of a well-known name, that fruits and vegetables fall into specific price categories, and that well-made furniture runs into hundreds or thousands of dollars. With these understandings in mind, shoppers expect to pay prices at or close to their perceptions. When this is not the case, sales resistance develops. Let's look at two typical examples.

Kate Lee intended to shop for a coffee maker. After checking with friends about quality and price, she expected to pay about $40.00 for good quality. She located a store that carried small appliances, and to her surprise it was selling coffee makers at $14 to $18, considerably below what her friends had suggested she would have to pay. Fearing substandard quality or defects in the products, Kate hesitated to make a purchase.

For some time Phil Marron had been reading newspaper advertisements about stereo cassette players. The model he wanted sold for approximately $325. Visiting a catalog showroom where he had shopped previously, he fully intended to purchase the player there. However, the store had priced the product at $337.50, an amount that Phil felt was exorbitant for a catalog showroom. Expressing annoyance to one of the clerks, he left without buying the player.

*The danger of jarring customers' price expectations*

Both of these situations illustrate the danger retailers face in pricing merchandise contrary to customers' expectations. When consumers' value judgments are jarred by unexpected prices, not only are sales lost, but particular customers may be lost for good.

# Competition

Having considered the factors that influence consumer buying habits, the retailer must analyze the competition. This involves asking such questions as "Am I competitive?" "Should I offer some additional service to my customers?" "Should I sell some products close to cost to attract additional customers?" and "Can I change prices without affecting the level of my sales?"

*All retailers use pricing techniques to remain competitive*

Obviously, large retailers have more options for meeting competition than small ones. Nevertheless, an astute small retailer can use a number of pricing techniques to remain competitive. To deal with competing stores, both large and small retailers usually consider the following.

1  Competitors' prices and services
2  Pricing to meet the competition
3  Private brands

## Competitors' Prices and Services

Without knowing their competitors' prices, most retailers would be hard pressed to establish realistic prices. For example, how could a new women's-wear store specializing in **misses merchandise lines** (clothing for mature women) specify prices without checking prices in competing department and specialty stores? Ignorance of those prices could have disastrous consequences for the new retailer.

In addition to being aware of competitors' prices, some types of stores must also know the nature of the customer services offered by competitors. Gift wrapping, free delivery, alterations—these are often the factors that help shoppers decide which stores to patronize. The addition of even one new service can sometimes attract new customers or retain old ones.

Comparison
shoppers check
competitors' prices
and services

In order to maintain current information about rival stores, larger retailers employ **comparison shoppers.** Their job is to check the merchandise sold by competitors for price, assortment, and the like. They also note the services offered by competitors. At times they purchase selected items in competing stores for purposes of analysis and planning by their own buyers. Since smaller retailers cannot afford the luxury of comparison shoppers, they carry out this function themselves or send out employees to do so.

## Pricing to Meet the Competition

A retailer's control
over prices
depends on the
nature of the
business

The nature of a retail establishment has much to do with its degree of freedom in setting prices. With some types of businesses, such as gas stations and newspaper/magazine stores, there is little leeway to depart from prevailing prices. This is so because there are so many stores in each category, all of which compete directly with each other and sell the same kinds of products. Even a one-cent reduction in the price of gas, for example, can cause drivers to switch from one gas station to another. Unless a station offers unusual services or is located away from competition, it must maintain competitive prices in order to survive.

On the other hand, other types of retailers can sometimes exercise considerable control over prices. For example, specialty stores often carry a wide assortment of merchandise that customers find appealing. Department stores may offer services that are not available elsewhere. Convenience stores are located close to where people live or work. Whatever the reason, such stores attract shoppers who are more interested in assortment, services, or convenience than in price. Consequently, these stores can maintain higher prices and still be competitive.

Having succeeded in attracting and retaining customers, these retailers have additional options open to them. For example, they can stock brands that other retailers

Pricing to meet the competition. Notice the odd pricing.

cannot afford to carry. They can also be more selective about pricing individual items; that is, they can lower prices in direct competition with other stores, or raise them when they see little danger in doing so.

Retailers who set prices below competitive levels (discounters) are usually restricted in the variety of goods they can carry. Relying on low prices to bring in customers, they give up the luxury of more costly and attractive merchandising policies. Because of their low profit-per-unit goal, they must sell goods quickly in order to avoid the expense of keeping merchandise on their shelves.

*Price wars are harmful to most retailers*

From time to time retailers that sell similar types of merchandise engage in ruthless competition, slashing prices on specific items in an attempt to steal customers from each other. These **price wars** may involve clothing, gas, food, or liquor products. Until the retailers themselves, or their suppliers, put a stop to the "war," consumers have a field day while the retailers usually suffer financial losses. These price struggles illustrate the often harmful consequences of fierce competition.

## Private Brands

*Private brands give some retailers a competitive edge*

One of the ways in which retailers sometimes gain a competitive edge is through the sale of private brands. As you recall, these are products that carry the retailer's or middleman's label instead of a manufacturer's national brand. Since national brands usually cost more than private brands because of the extensive advertising and other marketing expenses borne by manufacturers, retailers can sell private-label goods for less. As a result, the savings can be passed along to consumers in the form of lower prices, with the retailer still making the desired profit.

In order to give customers a choice, many retailers stock both private and national brands of particular products. For example, Waldbaum, Inc., a supermarket chain, sells cans of chunk pineapple under its own label as well as under the label "Dole," a national brand distributed by Castle & Cooke Foods of San Francisco. Since the Waldbaum pineapple is sold for less than the Dole pineapple, shoppers have the opportunity to either save money or purchase a better-known product with a national name. It should be noted that the ingredients and size of the products are similar.

Some stores that cater to affluent shoppers sell some of their own brands at higher prices than manufacturer-labeled goods. This occurs when the retailer's reputation is more important to customers than the manufacturer's name. For example, a man's suit sold at Saks Fifth Avenue and carrying that famous store's label is more attractive to many of Saks' customers than even well-known manufacturers' brands. Thus, the Saks name enhances its prospects for success against competitors.

Because of their reputations and advertising power, some chains have developed their private-brand merchandise into products with national recognition. A&P's Ann Page line and Sears, Roebuck's Kenmore selection are examples of this achievement. In these cases the chains have great flexibility in developing their product assortments and prices.

*Competitors can be helpful or harmful*

In concluding this discussion of retail competition, it should be understood that most competitive practices are legal and widespread. In a capitalistic society like ours, this is as it should be. Retailers expect and even thrive on competition, while consumers reap its benefits. Nevertheless, store rivalry occasionally reaches emotional levels, with competing retailers engaging in illegal and dangerous acts. A case in point arose in 1980

This Grand Union store carries both private and national brands.

and involved two fast-food restaurants in a suburban area. Each accused the other of infringing on its area in distributing advertisements, and one of the owners reportedly hired two men to set fire to the rival store. In the fire, five other stores were destroyed along with the competitor's, while seven stores sustained smoke and water damage. Needless to say, this type of "competition" is unworthy of the name. Fortunately, however, occurrences of this kind are not common.

## The Cost of Doing Business

The cost of doing business is the cost of merchandise plus overhead

Another important element in decisions about prices is the cost of doing business. This involves two factors: the cost of merchandise and the overhead. Regardless of the type of merchandise sold or the nature of the store, retailers want to get the best product they can buy at the most favorable price. To accomplish this goal, they need the latest information about product availability, product quality, prices, and sources of supply. With experience, retailers get to know which suppliers are most reliable. However, they are almost always open to contacts with new manufacturers and distributors who can help them increase their profit margins, attract customers, and be counted on to deliver on time. Though the cost of merchandise is central to making purchasing decisions, retailers sometimes sacrifice price in exchange for valuable services rendered by suppliers, such as advertising.

As you learned earlier, overhead consists of the expenses of running a business. It goes without saying that the lower the overhead, the lower the price at which a retailer can sell a product. This translates into a possible advantage over competitors. For this reason, astute retailers keep a constant watch on expenses, going so far as to reward employees for cost-saving suggestions.

# Laws and the Setting of Prices

Small retailers require legal protection against price discrimination

In some instances any consideration of customers, competition, and costs is superseded by laws—local, state, and federal—that affect retail prices. At one time competitive practices were so blatant and discriminatory that state and federal legislation was necessary to restrict them. By and large, this was essential for the protection of small retailers, which were hurt by the greater purchasing power of larger firms.

For example, the Sherman Antitrust Act of 1890 was passed to prevent **horizontal price fixing** in any type of business. Acting within a general prohibition of restraint of trade, this federal law makes it illegal for retailers, wholesalers, or manufacturers to fix prices. Thus, a group of retailers act illegally if they conspire to set specific prices. The obvious purpose of such an agreement would be to stifle competition, a situation that in the past hurt small retailers most.

A number of states have passed unfair trade practices laws, sometimes called **minimum price laws,** which require retailers to charge a minimum price for goods based on the cost of the merchandise plus a percentage for overhead. These acts, too, protect small retailers that might otherwise be undercut by larger stores.

The Robinson-Patman Act imposes restrictions on both manufacturers and retailers in the setting and receipt of prices that discriminate against other retailers. For example, manufacturer A and retailers B and C are guilty under this federal act if they agree on the price of an item that is not offered to other retailers in the same trading area at the same price. However, the act allows manufacturers to establish price differentials based on cost differences in selling to retailers if they can prove that specific price agreements do not hinder competition. Like the Sherman Antitrust Act and minimum price laws, the Robinson-Patman Act protects small retailers from adverse effects of price favoritism.

# PRICE POLICIES

Price policies are designed to fit a retailer's needs

By now you have probably guessed that a store may establish a number of different price policies to fit its needs. For example, it might set only high or low prices for all its products. Or it might vary its price levels, charging high prices for some classes of merchandise and lower ones for others. The determination of prices involves considerations of customers, competition, and other factors. Although many price policies are found in the retailing industry today, we will examine only the more common ones.

1 One price versus variable prices
2 Multiple pricing
3 Unit pricing
4 Price lining
5 Manufacturers' prepriced labels
6 Matching competitors' prices
7 Leader pricing and loss leaders

8 Single pricing

9 Discounting for employees and other groups

10 Automatic price reductions

# One Price Versus Variable Prices

One-price policy: all customers pay the same price

A **one-price policy** means that all customers pay the same price for the same product. To retailers, the advantages of such a policy are as follows.

1 It reduces the time needed for selling merchandise. Since no bargaining is involved, fewer salespeople are required to conduct transactions.

2 It permits self-service retail operations. Customers select their goods with full knowledge of the nonnegotiable prices.

3 Since it speeds sales transactions, mass merchandising operations are possible. Supermarkets and discount stores are able to sell large quantities of goods quickly.

4 It facilitates catalog and vending-machine retailing. Imagine trying to operate a catalog showroom with indefinite prices listed in the catalog!

Customers benefit from a one-price policy by the assurance that all shoppers in the store pay the same price. Thus, they have no fear that they will be "cheated." This sense of security develops consumer confidence and ultimately benefits the retailer as well. Since the turn of the century, a one-price policy has been the rule among most retailers in this country.

A variable-price policy encourages bargaining

A **variable-price policy,** also called **flexible pricing,** enables customers to bargain over prices. Contrary to most consumers, who prefer a set price, some shoppers enjoy the challenge of haggling with retailers. Because sales transactions involving bargaining require time and attention, retailers must pay for additional salespeople. Consequently, variable pricing is generally restricted to high-ticket merchandise, such as furniture, cars, and appliances. This type of retailing also involves fewer customers and less frequent purchasing by shoppers.

A variable-price policy gives retailers flexibility in dealing with customers. For example, they can take trade-ins from shoppers or offer services in order to secure the desired price. However, self-service retailing is out of the question, and retailers also run the risk of reduced customer confidence.

# Multiple Pricing

Stores that follow a **multiple-price policy** offer two or more of the same item at a unit price that is lower than the unit price if only one item is bought. For example, six boxes of Jell-O gelatin dessert might be sold for $1.02, making the unit price 17¢, while a box purchased individually might sell for 18¢. Thus, the customer must choose between a larger quantity at a lower price and a smaller quantity at a higher price. Though the retailer's profit per unit is reduced, sales volume is probably increased. The result is usually an increase in overall profits on sales.

Multiple pricing
acts as a
"psychological
pull" on shoppers

The psychological pull of multiple pricing works with many shoppers, but not with all. Nevertheless, it is a regular policy at supermarkets and variety stores. Paint stores frequently advertise "two for one" sales. Customers expect to find such "bargains," and retailers continue to offer them.

## Unit Pricing

Over the years supermarket shoppers have complained about the difficulty of comparing prices of similar products that are packaged in different quantities. For example, they are unable to judge whether a 16-ounce can of Del Monte peas and carrots selling for 49¢ is a more sensible buy than an 8½-ounce can selling for 33¢. The only way they can decide which can costs less per ounce is by dividing the cost of each can by the number of ounces in it. Needless to say, many consumers either cannot or will not perform the necessary arithmetic.

Unit pricing helps
consumers make
shopping
decisions

As a result of consumer annoyance and protest, many supermarkets have adopted **unit pricing** to aid customers in making shopping decisions. In effect, the stores do the computations for their customers. Since the merchandise is marked with the regular prices, this requires additional labels containing unit prices (Figure 15-2). This is a considerable printing and clerical chore for the retailer.

Some states and many localities have mandated unit pricing, while stores in other areas have voluntarily adopted such a policy. Under unit pricing, a can containing 5 ounces might show a regular total price of 50¢ and a unit price of 10¢ an ounce; a box containing 15 ounces might show a regular total price of 75¢ and a unit price of 5¢ an ounce. Labels containing unit prices are often attached to the shelf on which the merchandise is displayed.

As you saw in an earlier chapter, many stores use optical scanning of the universal product code at checkout counters. Prices stored in a computer are processed through detection of the UPC on the merchandise.

**FIGURE 15-2**
Supermarket unit pricing labels.

# Price Lining

A progressive retailer makes shopping as easy and pleasant as possible for customers. One way to accomplish this objective is to establish a **price lining** policy. The retailer sells several lines of a given product, each with a different price, and carries an adequate assortment of goods at each price. For example, sweaters may be sold for $17, $21, and $25. Customers then have a choice between low and high prices for the item, as well as a price in the middle range. Contrast this policy with one that offers sweaters at $17, $18, $20, $21, $23, and $25. With this expanded price range, a customer would probably be confused about the differences in quality among products with such closely related prices. The result may be annoyance and frustration.

Price lines are planned on the basis of past sales, competitive prices, and suppliers' suggested prices. Though a particular price line may contain as many as six different prices, most lines contain three prices.

*Advantages of price lining*

The advantages of price lining are as follows.

1   Reduced confusion among customers about merchandise selection.
2   A wider assortment of goods within each price range.
3   A possible reduction in the total inventory carried by a retailer.
4   Less need for salespeople to remember prices; fewer customer questions about merchandise quality.
5   Easier buying for the retailer.

*Disadvantages of price lining*

The disadvantages of price lining are as follows.

1   The necessity of changing price ranges during inflationary periods. Without such action, profitability is endangered.
2   The difficulty of maintaining a price line in the face of lower prices offered by competing stores.
3   A restriction in the variety of goods available to a store's buyer, since purchasing must be done within certain price ranges.
4   The danger of selecting a price range that does not appeal to shoppers.

Price lining is common in furniture, apparel, and department stores where shopping goods are prevalent. It is not popular in supermarkets and other stores that sell staple merchandise.

# Manufacturers' Prepriced Labels

Many types of merchandise have the price printed on the outside of the container or box. Retailers may, and often do, sell the goods for less than the manufacturer's suggested price. Shoppers often feel that this policy allows them to compare merchandise on the basis of both price and quality.

# Matching Competitors' Prices

You have probably seen store advertisements announcing, "We will not be undersold!" or "We'll meet any competitive price!" This policy acts as an inducement to a store's customers to buy at the store even when a competitor's prices are lower. Assuming that the store continues to provide the customer with the services to which he or she has become accustomed, matching the competition reinforces the customer's loyalty to the store. However, the store is obligated to employ comparison shoppers to verify competitors' prices.

# Leader Pricing and Loss Leaders

The highly competitive nature of retailing, as you have seen, impels retailers to devise ways of attracting shoppers. In one of the methods used, called **leader pricing,** the retailer sells one or more products at lower-than-usual prices, with reduced profits. The idea is to induce customers to shop for the "leader" merchandise in the hope that they will purchase other, regularly priced goods as well. In the final analysis, the objective is to increase total sales volume *and* profits.

Leader items are found in many types of stores and consist of merchandise that shoppers generally need. The goods are neither high priced, attracting a limited number of consumers, nor so low priced that customers can't perceive a bargain. In order to avoid customer resentment, retailers must carry sufficient leader merchandise to satisfy demand. To do otherwise is to invite charges of trickery. In fact, some states require retailers to give "rain checks" to customers when they run out of advertised leader merchandise.

In the past some retailers sold items at or below cost. Called **loss leaders,** sales of this type hurt small retailers badly. Today loss leader selling is found infrequently, is disdained by reputable retailers as unfair competition, and is prohibited in some states by minimum price laws.

Another practice that is frowned upon, in this instance because of outright deception, is **bait-and-switch pricing.** Suppose a retailer advertises a three-piece livingroom set for $280. Never intending to sell such low-priced merchandise, the salesperson steers the unsuspecting customer toward a higher-priced set. Sometimes the lower-priced set is conveniently "out of stock." The store, of course, sets the "bait" and attempts to "switch" the customer to more profitable goods. Bait-and-switch pricing is particularly harmful to low-income consumers, who are also less sophisticated about retail buying than more affluent consumers.

# Single Pricing

With a **single-price** policy, all the merchandise is sold at one price, as, for example, in a tie shop that prices all of its ties at $3. Banking on favorable consumer response to the appeal of a single price, the store can select goods only within a limited range. Many consumers enjoy the ease and novelty of single-price shopping.

Small variety and clothing stores have had success with single pricing, but the restriction on merchandise selection precludes expansion. In an effort to widen their product assortments, single-price stores pay various prices for their merchandise. The average cost, however, must allow the stores to make a reasonable profit from the single retail price.

## Discounting for Employees and Other Groups

*Employees can buy at the store for less*

Many retailers offer their employees reductions from regular store prices. The usual discounts run from 10 percent to 30 percent of the selling price and are supposed to act as incentives for better employee performance. For example, a salesperson who saves $12 on a $60 dress (20% discount) might perform her job more enthusiastically because of the discount. Since discounting for employees is so prevalent, however, it is difficult to judge its long-term effect on employee morale.

Some stores offer discounts to special groups, usually civic, religious, or charitable organizations. By means of these price accommodations the stores develop community good will and often secure new patronage from members of the organizations to which the discounts are granted.

## Automatic Price Reductions

In order to sell off merchandise that is not moving as quickly as the store would like it to move, some retailers follow a policy of planned **markdowns,** that is, reductions in selling price. As customers become aware of this policy, the thriftier ones wait for the markdowns, thereby making room for new stock. Some retailers, such as Filene's in Boston and New York, and Syms of New Jersey and New York, reduce prices whenever goods remain unsold for a specified period.

## THE ARITHMETIC OF PRICING

Having considered the elements that go into price decisions as well as several specific pricing policies, we turn our attention to the computation of retail prices. Without going into the more advanced mathematics used by large stores, we will examine the basic arithmetic concepts that all retailers should know. We will also identify some arithmetic terms used in the retail trade.

## Calculating Markups

### Initial and Maintained Markups

Suppose the Reddy Wear Store purchases dresses costing $18 each and sells them for $30 each. The difference between the two unit prices, $12, is called the **markup.** In other words, markup is the difference between the selling price (retail) and the cost. It may be stated as follows.

$$\begin{aligned} \text{Markup} &= \text{retail} - \text{cost} \\ \$12 &= \$30 - \$18 \end{aligned}$$

The relationships may also be shown as follows.

$$\begin{aligned} \text{Cost} + \text{markup} &= \text{retail} \\ \$18 + \$12 &= \$30 \end{aligned}$$

Though Reddy Wear intends to sell the dress for $30, it may find it difficult to do so. Let's assume that the dress can be sold for $24. In that case the markup is lowered to $6 [$24 (new retail) − $18 (cost)]. The first markup, $12, is called the **initial** or **original markup,** while the second one, $6, is known as the **maintained markup** or **gross margin.**

## Determining the Cost of Merchandise

*Transportation charges and cash discounts alter the cost of merchandise*

In the preceding example the cost of the dress ($18) included only the invoice cost of the merchandise. Sometimes, however, this cost is increased or decreased by other factors. Suppose, for example, that the store had to pay an additional $2 for transportation, for a total cost of $20. Also assume that Reddy Wear took advantage of the supplier's offer to reduce the invoice cost by 3 percent by taking a **cash discount.** As a result, the actual cost to the store was $19.46.

| | |
|---|---|
| Invoice cost | $18.00 |
| Less: 3% cash discount | 0.54 (0.03 × $18) |
| | $17.46 |
| Plus: transportation | 2.00 |
| Actual cost | $19.46 |

At the original selling price of $30, the initial markup would have been $10.54 ($30.00 − $19.46) and the maintained markup would have been $4.54 ($24.00 − $19.46). Note that the cash discount is deducted from the invoice cost, with the transportation charge added later.

## Markups Expressed in Dollars and as Percentages

In the Reddy Wear illustration the markups were stated in dollars and cents. Though many retailers feel comfortable with this way of expressing markups, most stores—especially large ones—prefer to use percentages. This permits more direct comparison of markups with those of previous periods, even though prices may have changed. It also enables a store to compare its markups with those of competitors.

Though some retailers compute markups as percentages based on cost prices, most merchants use selling prices as the base. A major reason for doing this is the common practice of reporting such expenses as advertising and salaries as percentages based on selling prices. In this way a store's markups can more easily be compared with its expenses.

*Computing a markup percentage*

Let's see how a markup percentage based on selling price (retail) is computed. Assume the following.

$$\begin{aligned} \text{Cost} + \text{markup} &= \text{retail} \\ \$12 + \$4 &= \$16 \end{aligned}$$

Solution: Divide the markup by the retail price.

$$\frac{\text{Markup}}{\text{Retail}} = \frac{\$4}{\$16} = \frac{1}{4} = 25\% \text{ markup percentage}$$

As indicated previously, the 25 percent markup can be used for comparative purposes. Using the same illustration, the markup percentage based on cost is

$$\frac{\text{Markup}}{\text{Cost}} = \frac{\$4}{\$12} = \frac{1}{3} = 33\frac{1}{3}\%$$

Notice that the markup based on retail results in a lower percentage than that based on cost. This is so because the retail price (*denominator*) is higher than the cost (*denominator*), and the fraction is therefore smaller.

Figure 15-3 contains some equivalent markup percentages based on cost and retail prices. For example, a 10 percent markup based on retail is equivalent to an 11.1 percent markup based on cost. Here is an illustration.

Equivalent markup percentages

$$\begin{array}{ccc} \text{Cost} + \text{markup} = \text{retail} \\ \$90 + \$10 = \$100 \end{array}$$

Markup based on retail:

$$\frac{\$10}{\$100} = \frac{1}{10} = 10\%$$

Markup based on cost:

$$\frac{\$10}{\$90} = \frac{1}{9} = 11.1\%$$

Additional markup equivalents can, of course, be computed in similar fashion.

| Markup Percent Based on Retail | Markup Percent Based on Cost |
| --- | --- |
| 4.0 | 4.2 |
| 6.0 | 6.4 |
| 8.0 | 8.7 |
| 10.0 | 11.1 |
| 10.7 | 12.0 |
| 12.5 | 14.3 |
| 13.0 | 15.0 |
| 18.0 | 22.0 |
| 23.1 | 30.0 |
| 30.0 | 42.9 |
| 40.0 | 66.7 |
| 50.0 | 100.0 |
| 60.0 | 150.0 (see example) |

**FIGURE 15-3**
Equivalent markup percentages based on cost and retail prices.

As you can see, markups based on cost can be greater than 100 percent. For example,

$$\text{Cost} + \text{markup} = \text{retail}$$
$$\$80 + \$120 = \$200$$

Therefore,

$$\frac{\text{Markup}}{\text{Retail}} = \frac{\$120}{\$200} = \frac{3}{5} = 60\%$$

and

$$\frac{\text{Markup}}{\text{Cost}} = \frac{\$120}{\$80} = \frac{3}{2} = 150\%$$

Markups based on retail can approach but never equal 100 percent.

## Composition of the Markup

*Markup consists of overhead and profit*

Since markup is the difference between retail and cost, it consists of two items: the store's overhead and the desired profit. For example, a $10 markup might include $6 to cover expenses (rent, salaries, etc.) and a $4 profit. Therefore,

$$\text{Cost} + \text{markup (overhead} + \text{profit)} = \text{retail}$$
$$\$10 \quad (\$6 + \$4)$$

## Markups by Category

*A markup can be set for each category of merchandise*

Sometimes a retailer uses a separate markup for each merchandise category. The individual markups reflect such considerations as the ease with which the merchandise can be sold and the nature of the products themselves. Higher-priced goods, for example, might carry higher markups than more frequently sold convenience items. Regardless of how the individual markups are constructed, the dollar total of the markups is designed to equal the total planned markup for the store.

Let's examine a specific example. Suppose a toy store sets a 20 percent markup on its inexpensive toys and a 40 percent markup on the more costly ones. It plans total sales of $60,000, with an overall store markup of 33⅓ percent. Assume the following additional information.

| | |
|---|---|
| Planned sales of inexpensive toys | $20,000 |
| Planned sales of more costly toys | $40,000 |
| Total sales | $60,000 |

Therefore,

| | Markup Percent | Planned Sales | Dollar Markup |
|---|---|---|---|
| Inexpensive toys: | 20% | × $20,000 = | $ 4,000 |
| More costly toys: | 40% | × $40,000 = | $16,000 |
| | | Total | $20,000 |
| Overall store markup: | 33⅓% | × $60,000 = | $20,000 |

# MARKDOWNS

## Reasons for Markdowns

There is an old saying that "what goes up must come down." This is often true in retail pricing because the final selling price of an article is usually less than the original price. As you have seen, a reduction in price is known as a **markdown.**

Markdowns may occur for any of the following reasons:

1　Judgments by store buyers
2　Mistakes in setting prices
3　Mistakes in selling techniques
4　Unpredictable factors

### Judgments by Store Buyers

Despite the most careful planning, a buyer may purchase too much of a particular item, resulting in leftover inventory. In order to stimulate sales, the merchandise is sold at a marked-down price. Sometimes an item has lukewarm appeal to customers, perhaps owing to design, color, or changes in consumer taste. In this case a price reduction may overcome purchase resistance. Merchandise bought too late in a selling season is usually marked down to attract customers.

### Mistakes in Setting Prices

When the price of an article is set too high, a markdown is inevitable in order to move the merchandise. It should be understood, however, that pricing is based on judgments made by people. As such, prices that prove to be incorrect must be changed.

### Mistakes in Selling Techniques

In Chapter 12 you learned that poor displays and layouts affect sales volume adversely. When this happens markdowns are necessary to spur sales. Merchandise may also move slowly because of improper actions by salespeople. For example, an employee who sells a particular line of blouses aggressively, but ignores a less popular line, may cause an early markdown on the latter line. In the case of the first line of blouses, overselling may cause customer dissatisfaction and merchandise returns. Sometimes this merchandise is returned soiled or damaged, so that markdowns are necessary.

### Unpredictable Factors

Poor economic conditions, sudden changes in weather, slow-moving merchandise, and the appearance of new, competing merchandise all affect sales. Appropriate markdowns must then be taken to move merchandise and maintain a competitive edge.

## When Markdowns Are Taken

Markdowns are a strategic part of selling

Contrary to popular impressions, retailers view markdowns as a strategic part of selling. Some stores apply markdowns early in order to generate more cash for further purchases of stock.

In some prestige stores markdowns are not noted on price tickets. Instead, the merchandise is shifted to an area devoted to a lower price line. Other prestige stores delay taking markdowns in order to discourage bargain hunting. The timing of markdowns often depends on the type of merchandise involved. For example, fashion goods that are unlikely to be salable next year call for markdowns at times that will ensure sales. On the other hand, staple goods like stationery are often marked down when they become shopworn. Regardless of the product, retailers must be alert to establish markdowns at the most favorable times because unsold merchandise represents an investment that is not producing earnings.

## How Large a Markdown?

The size of a markdown is important

Markdowns must be sufficiently large for customers to respond favorably. For example, a chair that is marked down from $54.99 to $47.99 will probably sell, whereas a reduction to $53.99 might not. Through experience retailers learn how large a markdown is required to attract customers.

## Calculating Markdown Percentages

Retailers express markdowns as percentages of actual (new) selling prices

Since a markdown is a reduction in selling price, the resulting or new price is the actual price for which an item is sold. For example, a $30 jacket marked down $5 has a new selling price of $25. To compute the markdown percent, do the following.

$$\frac{\text{Markdown}}{\text{New selling price}} = \text{markdown percentage}$$

$$\frac{\$5}{\$25} = 20\%$$

Though retailers express markdowns as percentages of new selling prices, customers see them as percentages of the old selling prices. Thus, in our illustration a customer would calculate the markdown percent as follows.

$$\frac{\text{Markdown}}{\text{Old selling price}} = \frac{\$5}{\$30} = 16\frac{2}{3}\%$$

Some retailers express markdowns in dollars only and rarely refer to markdown percents. At the end of a given period they compute total markdown dollars.

**NEW TERMS**

| | |
|---|---|
| bait-and-switch pricing | leader pricing |
| cash discount | loss leader |
| comparison shopper | maintained markup |
| flexible pricing | markdown |
| gross margin | markup |
| horizontal price fixing | minimum price law |
| initial markup | misses merchandise line |

| | |
|---|---|
| multiple-price policy | price lining |
| odd prices | price war |
| one-price policy | single-price policy |
| original markup | unit pricing |
| overhead | variable-price policy |

## CHAPTER HIGHLIGHTS

1 The price of an item must cover the cost of the product, the overhead, and the profit.

2 An analysis of the customer as an element in pricing decisions includes consideration of income, motivation, psychological aspects, store image, and value concepts.

3 Odd pricing (59¢, $16.99) is used as a psychological pricing technique by a significant but declining number of retailers.

4 Some shoppers buy on the basis of price. Others are influenced by a store's image.

5 People have general ideas about the prices they expect to pay. Purchase resistance develops when their expectations prove wrong.

6 In order to deal effectively with competing stores, retailers consider competitors' prices and services, pricing to meet the competition, and private brands.

7 Larger retailers employ comparison shoppers to check competitors' prices and services.

8 The nature of a retail business has much to do with its freedom in setting prices. When retailers that sell similar merchandise engage in ruthless competition, they sometimes stage price wars.

9 Private brands carry a retailer's or middleman's label instead of a manufacturer's national brand. The use of private brands often gives retailers a competitive edge.

10 Manufacturers sometimes sell to one retailer in a trading area, preventing consumers from checking competing prices.

11 A retailer's costs include the cost of merchandise and overhead. The lower these are, the lower the price that can be charged.

12 There are local, state, and federal laws regulating retail price practices. The Sherman Antitrust Act prevents horizontal price fixing, that is, conspiracies to arrange prices for the purpose of stifling competition. State unfair trade practices laws (minimum price laws) require retailers to charge a minimum price for goods based on the cost of the merchandise plus a percentage for overhead. The Robinson-Patman Act prohibits manufacturers and retailers from engaging in discriminatory price practices.

13 Among the price policies in use today are the following.
   a *One price versus variable prices.* Under a one-price policy all customers pay the same price. A variable-price policy allows customers to bargain.
   b *Multiple pricing.* Under this policy a customer can buy two or more of an item at a unit price that is less than the unit price if only one item is bought.
   c *Unit pricing.* Merchandise is labeled with the unit price as well as the total price.

d *Price lining.* Several lines of a given product are carried, each with a different price.

e *Manufacturers' prepriced labels.* These selling prices, printed on the outside of containers and boxes, are sometimes lowered by retailers, allowing consumers to compare merchandise on the basis of price and quality.

f *Matching competitors' prices.* A retailer knows the competitors' prices.

g *Leader pricing and loss leaders.* Leader pricing involves the sale of merchandise below the usual selling price in order to attract customers. A loss leader is an item that is sold below cost. In some states loss leaders are prohibited by minimum price laws.

h *Single pricing.* All goods in a store are sold for the same price.

i *Discounting for employees and other groups.* Store employees and local groups are given discounts from regular prices.

14 Markup is the difference between the retail price and the cost of goods. Initial markup (original markup) is the first markup, while maintained markup (gross margin) is the final markup.

15 Transportation charges increase, and cash discounts decrease, the cost of merchandise.

16 Markups may be expressed as dollars or percentages. Retailers usually base markups on retail prices. A markup consists of overhead and profit, and may be computed for each category of merchandise.

17 A reduction in a retail price is called a markdown. Markdowns are due to judgments by store buyers, mistakes in setting prices, mistakes in selling techniques, and unpredictable factors. The timing of markdowns is dictated by the nature of the store and its selling strategy. Part of this strategy involves the size of a markdown. Retailers express markdowns as percentages of actual selling prices.

# QUESTIONS

1 Why is it important for retailers to review their price policies?

2 Why has odd pricing lost some of its traditional effectiveness?

3 Why is low price not a major consideration for customers who shop at prestigious stores?

4 Why must a retailer consider shoppers' value concepts in the setting of prices?

5 How does comparison shopping help a store remain competitive?

6 Under what circumstances might a store charge higher prices than its competitors and still attract customers?

7 Considering similar merchandise, are there stores that sometimes sell private brands for more than manufacturers' national brands? Explain.

8 Why might a retailer pay a supplier a higher price than might be secured from a different supplier?

9 If competition is the lifeblood of free enterprise, why are there laws that regulate competition? How do you feel about them?

10 Why do some retailers maintain a variable-price policy?

11 How does unit pricing aid shoppers?

12 Why is price lining feasible in stores that sell shopping goods?

13 What are the objectives of leader pricing?

14 Why do some stores offer discounts to special groups?

15 If an invoice price is $42, transportation charges $2, and the cash discount 2 percent, what is the cost of the merchandise if the retailer pays the bill within the cash discount period?

16 If an article costs $9 and is marked up $3, what is the markup percentage based on retail? On cost?

17 Why do retailers consider markdowns a strategic part of selling?

18 If a skirt selling for $40 is marked down $10, how would a retailer express the markdown as a percentage?

# FIELD PROJECTS

1 Visit a supermarket (or other type of store that carries food products) that specifies unit prices. Prepare a list of regular and unit prices for five different food items. Determine whether the unit price is on a shelf label, on the packaging itself, or both.

2 For each of the following pricing policies, identify a store in your community that follows that policy:
   Variable pricing
   Price lining
   Multiple pricing

# CASES

1 In September 1980 a New York State appeals court ruled that a state regulation setting minimum prices on retail wine sales was unconstitutional. This resulted in a wine price war. A similar decision was reached by a California court in March 1980. The contested New York law required liquor stores to sell wine at a price at least 50 percent above the wholesale price.

Owners of smaller stores opposed the decision, contending that they would be forced out of business by high-volume stores that could cut prices drastically. Larger stores maintained that lower prices would attract more customers.

a Do you agree with the views of the small stores or with those of the large stores? Why?

b Do you feel that minimum retail prices are justified in some instances? Explain.

**2** Dara Lopez, the owner of a ladies'-wear store, had cultivated customer loyalty for twenty-five years. She found that she was losing some customers to a newly opened discount rival. In an attempt to recapture their patronage, Lopez offered to match her competitor's prices. This tactic had some success, but not enough to satisfy her. She needed advice regarding how to approach her former customers.

    **a** Do you think Lopez should lower prices below her competitor's? Why?
    **b** Might a price leader produce favorable results for Lopez? Why?

**3** The Dali Fashion Center is a ladies'-wear shop located in a strip shopping center in a suburban community. It carries low- to middle-priced merchandise and maintains three price lines. The store has been at the same location for twenty-six years and caters to women of all ages. Its customers are basically middle-income consumers who have demonstrated consistent loyalty to the store over the years.

A popular feature of Dali's is an alcove containing specially discounted merchandise. Started fifteen years ago by the owner in an attempt to sell slow-moving merchandise, the innovation became an instant hit with Dali's steady customers. Interestingly enough, the discount alcove had little effect on the sale of other goods.

From the outset, prices were set at even dollar or half-dollar amounts. For example, a particular style of sweater might be price-lined at $28, $32, and $35, or at $16.50, $19.50, and $23.50. The owner's negative attitude toward odd pricing is based on the feeling that most consumers are not influenced by this "psychological" approach to pricing.

Because Dali's is located some distance from another strip center and even farther from the nearest regional shopping center, it has had little serious competition. The store has, however, lost some business to shops in those centers because of its decision to remain closed on Sundays, Sunday opening being permitted under a two-year-old law.

Several months ago Dali's owner learned about the construction of a competitive freestanding store within its trading area. The newcomer is to occupy three times the space of Dali's store, and has advertised itself as a "quality discount fashion shop." As near as Dali's can determine, the new store will stock merchandise in direct competition with its own. In addition, the new shop will be open on Sundays.

    **a** How might Dali's alter its price policies to counter the competition?
    **b** Should Dali's change its Sunday closing policy? Why?

# REFERENCES

Harris, B. F., and M. K. Mills, "The Impact of Item Price Removal on Grocery Shopping Behavior," *Journal of Retailing,* 56 (Winter 1980), pp. 73–93.

Jolson, M. A., "Markup Calculations—Still a Fuzzy Area?" *Journal of Retailing,* 49 (Fall 1973), pp. 77–80.

Kneider, A. P., *Mathematics of Merchandising* (Englewood Cliffs, N.J.: Prentice-Hall, 1974).

Lambert, Z. V., "Perceived Prices as Related to Odd and Even Price Endings," *Journal of Retailing,* 51 (Fall 1975), pp. 13–22.

McElroy, B. F., and D. A. Aaker, "Unit Pricing Six Years After Introduction," *Journal of Retailing,* 55 (Fall 1979), pp. 44–57.

Monroe, K. B., "Buyers' Subjective Perceptions of Price," *Journal of Marketing Research,* 10 (February 1973), pp. 70–80.

————, *Pricing: Making Profitable Decisions* (New York: McGraw-Hill, 1979), pp. 37–48.

National Retail Merchants Association, Merchandising Division, *Markdowns: Their Causes, Their Prevention, Their Correction* (New York, 1957).

————, *198 Ways of Controlling Markdowns* (New York, 1963).

Oxenfeldt, A. R., "Multi-Stage Approach to Pricing," *Harvard Business Review,* 38 (July–August 1960), pp. 125–133.

Shapiro, B. P., "Price Reliance: Existence and Sources," *Journal of Marketing Research,* 10 (August 1973), pp. 286–294.

U.S. Department of Commerce, Small Business Administration, *Boost Profits by Cutting Markdowns,* Bulletin 78 (Washington, D.C.).

Widrick, S. M., "Quantity Surcharge: A Pricing Practice Among Grocery Store Items—Validation and Extension," *Journal of Retailing,* 55 (Summer 1979), pp. 47–58.

# chapter 16
# HANDLING AND PROTECTING MERCHANDISE

After completing this chapter, you should be able to:

1   Identify and describe receiving area facilities and records found in stores.
2   Describe checking and marking procedures used in stores.
3   Identify procedures used by retailers for the storage and distribution of merchandise.
4   List security measures taken by retailers to control the theft of merchandise by employees and outsiders.

Having established merchandise pricing policies, a retailer must consider the physical handling of the goods. Without a smooth flow of inventory from the receiving area to the selling areas, a store can lose customer good will and actual sales. In addition, merchandise must be checked for quantity and quality, marked with prices, and stored carefully for ready movement to appropriate departments. Finally, attention must be paid to the security of goods in receiving and storage areas and on the selling floor. This chapter explores each of these concerns.

# HANDLING THE MERCHANDISE

Receiving merchandise from suppliers

As shoppers, our exposure to store merchandise is usually limited to what we see on shelves, in displays, and so forth. The retailer, however, must carry out a number of functions before goods reach the selling areas. Of these, the first involves procedures for receiving merchandise from suppliers. This is true for both large and small stores, with the former requiring rather elaborate arrangements. Small retailers, on the other hand, establish simple routines for the receipt of merchandise, with the owner or employee handling the shipments personally. In this chapter we will deal mainly with the physical handling of goods in large retail organizations.

Figure 16-1 outlines the usual steps in the handling of merchandise. Each step will be discussed as it relates to eventually getting the goods into selling areas for display and sale.

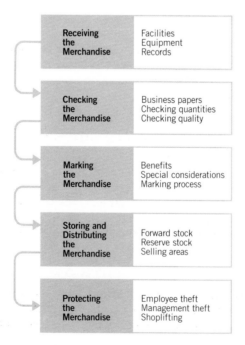

FIGURE 16-1
Steps in the handling of merchandise.

The size and composition of a receiving area depend on the type and volume of merchandise carried.

# RECEIVING THE MERCHANDISE

## Receiving Facilities

The need for a receiving area

Since the receipt of goods is an important activity in all retail organizations, it is essential that proper facilities exist for accepting deliveries. When you consider the tremendous volume and variety of merchandise reaching a large store each day, you can appreciate the need for adequate receiving areas.

### Loading Platforms

Sometimes called a **loading dock** or a **receiving dock,** a **loading platform** accommodates trucks or other vehicles for the unloading of merchandise. The area must be large enough to service the oversized trucks in use today. In most cases the platform is located either in the back or on the side of the store.

Delivery of merchandise to small stores usually takes place on a sidewalk or at the rear. Since the quantity of goods is limited, no special unloading facility is required. Instead, goods are carried directly into the store by the most convenient or accessible entrance.

### Warehouses

Large stores that sell major appliances and furniture generally maintain warehouses for storage of these goods until delivery to the customer. In instances in which a store also carries other types of goods, the receiving function may take place at the warehouse for the large-ticket items and at the store for the remaining merchandise. In busy urban areas warehouses are sometimes used to carry out the main receiving functions.

## Receiving Areas in the Store

When goods are brought into the store, they should be placed in an area that is large enough to accommodate checking and marking functions and close enough to stockroom and selling areas for quick transfer. Precious time that can be translated into lost sales is wasted when the facilities are far apart. An exception exists in stores that utilize electrical and mechanical equipment for speedy movement of merchandise.

*Receiving areas are not conducive to selling*

Store planners recognize that selling space is extremely valuable. Consequently, receiving sections are located in areas that are not conducive to selling. Upper floors, with adequate freight elevator service, are usually used in stores that contain several levels, while one-story structures utilize back-room space. Though selling space is crucial to the profitability of a business, the receiving area must be large enough to allow for the smooth handling and flow of goods. Any other arrangement results in delays before merchandise reaches the selling areas, in possible loss or damage of goods, and in inefficient use of employee time.

Adequate planning considers seasonal and special-occasion receiving requirements. For example, receiving and stockroom areas that are just large enough for normal business activities may be inadequate during intense selling periods like Christmas and Mother's Day. Unless the store can rearrange space to accommodate heavy shipments during these periods, it must plan the size of its receiving areas accordingly.

## Receiving Area Equipment

*Using elevators, conveyors, and chutes for merchandise*

There are a number of ways in which merchandise may be transported from a loading platform to a receiving room within the store. Mechanical equipment is widely used to minimize the need for human labor and to maximize operating efficiency. The type of equipment employed depends on the physical characteristics of the store. For example, a multistory building might be serviced by elevators or by conveyors that connect with receiving rooms. A one-story edifice might utilize a horizontal beltlike conveyor that carries goods directly to checking areas. When a basement serves as a receiving room, merchandise is slid down chutes to checking stations. Of course, there are other types of equipment, for example, electric trucks.

*Tables, conveyor mechanisms, and bins are used to prepare goods for selling*

Within the store, equipment and furniture must be available to prepare the merchandise for delivery to selling areas. A basic arrangement utilizes **stationary tables** for receiving goods after they have been unpacked. In some instances, merchandise is separated by department, with tables assigned to particular departments. In other cases, tables are designated for each type of merchandise. Checking and marking are done on the tables, after which the goods are taken either to a stockroom for future use or directly to a selling area.

A variation of this arrangement involves the use of **portable (movable) tables**. In this design, merchandise is put on tables that can be wheeled to other areas. This allows the checking of goods to be done in one area and the marking in another without the merchandise itself having to be moved. The division of functions ensures better control over the merchandise, since quantity checking is completed before goods are marked. After the merchandise has been checked, it is wheeled, still on the same tables, to separate marking areas.

A more elaborate system used in many large stores involves **conveyor mechanisms** that carry goods from receiving areas to stockrooms or selling spaces. On the way to their destination, the goods are checked and marked. Clothing is generally moved by overhead conveyor rollers, while most other merchandise is transported on belt systems. Goods on roller equipment or belts may be removed at specified points for inspection. However, care must be taken to prevent anxious buyers and selling personnel from removing merchandise before it has been fully processed.

One further checking–marking arrangement is worth mentioning. Some stores use **bins** as receptacles for incoming merchandise. After merchandise has been unpacked and checked in one section of the receiving area, it is placed in bins for movement to the marking area. Since checking is done at a separate location, unauthorized personnel can be kept away more easily.

## Receiving-Department Records

The constant burden of incoming merchandise requires that stores maintain accurate receiving records. Large stores, of course, have more elaborate records than small ones, but no store can ignore the need for sensible records without suffering losses.

After checking the accuracy of a shipment against either a **delivery receipt** supplied by the **carrier** (shipper) or the **invoice** (bill) itself, the receiving clerk notes any discrepancies on the receipt or invoice (Figure 16-2). If packages are missing or damaged, the details are written on the document so that the store can justify any adjustments made when paying bills.

Standard receiving practice involves recording incoming goods in some kind of **receiving book** or on a form (Figure 16-3). The information recorded usually includes quantity of packages, date and time of receipt, weight of packages (if appropriate), type of transportation, name of carrier, shipping costs, damaged containers, and name of vendor or intercompany store. (Figure 16-3 is a receiving record for interstore transfers.) In addition, the supplier's invoice number and the invoice amount are recorded when they are available, which they usually are since invoices generally arrive before merchandise is received.

*Receiving records and computers*

For companies that use computers to process information, receiving records are tied into the overall record-keeping system. Since purchasing data are stored in the computer, information supplied by receiving clerks is compared electronically with the stored data for immediate verification.

Small stores usually confine their receiving records to the maintenance of delivery receipt files. Since the owner either handles or supervises deliveries, all that is required is a simple system for tying merchandise received to timely payment of bills.

| Function | Record |
|---|---|
| Checking accuracy of shipment | • Delivery receipt<br>• Invoice |
| Recording incoming goods | • Receiving book |

**FIGURE 16-2**
Receiving department functions and records.

| Week Ending _____ | | | | Store No. _____ Location _____ | |
|---|---|---|---|---|---|
| Date Received | Interstore Transfer Control No. | Received from | | Received Via (Freight Co., UPS, etc.) | No. of Cartons Received |
| | | Store No. | Store Name | | |
| | | | | | |
| | | | | | |
| | | | | | |
| | | | | | |
| | | | | | |
| | | | | | |
| | | | | | |

FIGURE 16-3
A receiving record.

# CHECKING THE MERCHANDISE

The next step in the handling of merchandise involves procedures for determining the specific goods received. The basic reason for checking merchandise is to be certain that payment is made only for goods that have actually been delivered. Shortages and damage in deliveries might go undetected without a sound system for checking incoming shipments.

## Business Papers Used in Purchasing Goods

*Purchase orders and invoices*

Before discussing the procedures for checking merchandise, we need to examine two common business documents that are used in purchasing. One is called a **purchase order;** the other is the **invoice.**

As shown in Figure 16-4, a purchase order is prepared by the purchaser (the retailer), in this case the Ted Lane Co., and is made out to the supplier, Vicki Spar, Inc. In addition to information concerning dates, shipping instructions, and terms, the document indicates what the store wants to buy and how much it has agreed to pay. A copy of the purchase order is often sent to the receiving department. Upon receiving the original of the purchase order, the supplier prepares and sends an invoice to the store and ships the goods. Figure 16-5 shows that the invoice contains information similar to the purchase order. If the supplier does not fill the entire order, however, the invoice omits the missing items. Notice that the customer's order number on the invoice, 1553, matches the number on the purchase order. This cross-referencing is useful to the store when checking incoming merchandise.

When a purchase order is prepared, many buyers insert a cancelation date on which the order is automatically canceled if the merchandise has not arrived. Receiving departments have to be told about such cancelation dates so that they will not take in merchandise that the store may no longer want or need. This is of particular importance for seasonal goods.

**Purchase Order**

**Purchase Order**

Ted Lane Co.
143 W. Chase Street
Chicago, IL 60626

No. 1453
Date 6/1/82 Date Required 6/26/82
Ship Via Truck
F.O.B. Shipping Point
Terms 2/10, n/30
Ship to Ted Lane Co.
143 W. Chase Street
Chicago, IL 60626

To Vicki Spar, Inc.
121 Pauling Avenue
Southfield, MI 48076

| Quantity | ✓ | Stock Number/Description | Price | Per | |
|---|---|---|---|---|---|
| 10 | | 3691 Plaid skirts | 16 00 | 1 | $160 00 |
| 20 | | 4833 Pleated dresses | 20 00 | 1 | 400 00 |
| 10 | | 3720 Slacks--jean-cut | 22 00 | 1 | 220 00 |
| | | Total | | | $780 00 |

**Important**
Our Order Number must appear on Invoices
Packages and Correspondence.
Acknowledge if unable to deliver by date required.

By__________

WilsonJones
© 1976 • PRINTED IN U.S.A.

Original /Purchase Order
479

FIGURE 16-4
A purchase order. (Product of Wilson Jones Company.)

**Invoice** 44-404

**Invoice**

Vicki Spar, Inc.
121 Pauling Avenue
Southfield, MI 48076

No. 3125
Date 6/24/82

Sold To Ted Lane Co.
143 W. Chase Street
Chicago, IL 60626

Shipped to Ted Lane Co.
143 W. Chase Street
Chicago, IL 60626

| Your Order No. | Our Order No. | Salesman | |
|---|---|---|---|
| 1453 | | Burke | |
| **Date Shipped** | **Shipped Via** | **F.O.B.** | **Terms** |
| 6/24 | Truck | Shipping Point | 2/10, n/30 |

| Quantity Ordered | Quantity Shipped | Stock Number/Description | Price | Per | Amount |
|---|---|---|---|---|---|
| 10 | 10 | 3691 Plaid skirts | 16 00 | 1 | $160 00 |
| 20 | 20 | 4833 Pleated dresses | 20 00 | 1 | 400 00 |
| 10 | 10 | 3720 Slacks--jean-cut | 22 00 | 1 | 220 00 |
| | | Total | | | $780 00 |

WilsonJones
© 1976 • PRINTED IN U.S.A.
977

Original /Invoice

FIGURE 16-5
An invoice. (Product of Wilson Jones Company.)

# Procedures for Checking Goods

## Checking Quantities

Though there are a variety of methods for checking quantities, most stores employ one or a combination of the following procedures.

1 Direct checking
2 Indirect checking (blind checking)
3 Semi-indirect checking (semiblind checking)
4 Spot checking
5 Bulk checking

**Direct Checking** In **direct checking,** as containers are unpacked, the items are checked against the invoice for accuracy. This allows the checker to indicate any shortages or damage on the invoice. If the checker is a reliable employee, the store is assured that payment will be made only for merchandise received. On the other hand, a careless checker may not count the shipment accurately, simply assuming that the items received are exactly the ones listed on the invoice. It is obvious, therefore, that direct checking is effective only when it is done by careful employees. This type of checking is quick and relatively inexpensive.

In cases in which an invoice has not arrived, the store must make a decision: either to count and list the merchandise and send it on for marking, or to leave the containers unopened until the invoice is received. In the first instance, merchandise reaches the stockroom or selling areas quickly, but rechecking the goods is difficult or impossible. In the second instance, shortages may occur in selling areas owing to delayed processing, but accurate checking can be done. Despite the risks in checking without the benefit of an invoice, many stores adopt this policy in the desire to get merchandise to selling areas as quickly as possible. Because retailers are anxious to have invoices for checking purposes, however, suppliers sometimes enclose them with the shipments.

**Indirect Checking** When a store does not want a checker to rely on invoices, **indirect** or **blind checking** may be used. As goods are unpacked, the checker lists them on special forms. Not having an invoice to work from, the checker is compelled to conduct a more thorough check. When the count has been completed, the forms are compared with the invoices. While indirect checking usually results in a more accurate count of goods, the time required to list the contents of packages makes it more expensive than direct checking. However, it has the advantage of eliminating delays in sending merchandise to selling areas.

**Semi-indirect Checking** Suppose you were a checker using an invoice with the quantities deliberately omitted by the store. Wouldn't you have to count the packages received, knowing that your figures would be compared with the missing invoice quantities? On the other hand, wouldn't you save considerable time by not having to write the names of the items received? Using this procedure, called **semi-indirect checking** or **semiblind checking,** gives the store better information about merchandise received while reducing the time spent by the checker.

**Spot Checking** Unwilling to spend much time or effort on checking and assuming that most shipments are correct, some retailers **spot check** large deliveries. That is, the checker counts the number of containers and the contents of particular ones. If they coincide with the invoice or purchase order quantities, the merchandise is sent on for marking. If not, the remaining items are checked and shortages are noted. This method is far less accurate than other procedures.

**Bulk Checking** In **bulk checking,** when goods are packed in specific bulk quantities by number or weight (e.g., 100-dozen packages or 50-pound containers), they sometimes are not opened. Instead, the supplier's quantities, as listed on the cartons or other containers, are compared with the invoice figures.

### Follow-Up of Shortages or Damaged Goods

*Notification of damaged goods and shortages upon arrival*

A shortage of merchandise or damage of various kinds may be caused by either the supplier or the shipping company (the carrier). Whichever appears to be responsible for the problem, the store must protect itself. In all cases, the supplier or carrier must be notified immediately. Sometimes damaged goods are returned and replaced with new merchandise; at other times, financial adjustments are made with the supplier or carrier. In some instances shortages are made up by subsequent deliveries. However, if a new delivery will arrive too late, the store deducts the amount of the missing goods from the invoice total and refuses additional shipments.

### Checking Quality

Though checkers can make superficial judgments about the quality of incoming merchandise, they are unqualified to make reliable decisions. Checking the quality of goods, therefore, is left to those who specialize in merchandising: buyers, store managers, and the like. To make certain that the merchandise conforms to specifications, many large retailers compare incoming items with samples that are secured at the time of purchase. Whether a store is large or small, displaying or selling inferior merchandise damages its reputation.

# MARKING THE MERCHANDISE

Customers entering a store, whether it is a clothing shop, a supermarket, or some other type of store, expect to find prices identified clearly. The exception may be a high-fashion store whose image calls for discreet discussion of prices. Since most stores therefore require precise indication of prices, they develop systems for achieving that objective. **Marking** is the recording of a retail price on an item of merchandise.

# The Benefits of Marking

*Marking goods helps customers, salespeople, and the store*

Since stores commit significant amounts of time and money to the marking of goods, they expect their efforts to produce positive benefits. For example,

1   Customers derive immediate satisfaction from the quick identification of prices.

Marking is the recording of a retail price on an item of merchandise before it reaches the selling floor.

2 Because salespeople need not check prices with other personnel, they can devote their time to making sales.

3 Customers generally feel secure in the knowledge that they pay the same prices as others.

4 Listing on the price tag the date on which the merchandise was placed on the selling floor helps the store decide on markdowns and clearances.

5 Marking enables retailers to maintain self-service features. As a matter of fact, supermarkets and other stores with self-service features could not function without proper marking of prices.

6 With additional accounting information placed on price tags, such as size, style, and department name, stores can compute total costs, sales, and profits more easily. This can be done for each department or merchandise category.

## Special Marking Considerations

There are several special concerns related to marking that should be noted before we discuss marking procedures.

## Expediting Marking with Preretailing

*Preretailing speeds up the marking process*

In order to speed up the marking process, some retailers follow a procedure called **preretailing.** It requires the buyer to list retail prices on purchase orders. Subsequently, copies of purchase orders are sent to receiving locations and are used for marking purposes as soon as merchandise has been checked. Though preretailing works well with goods whose prices remain stable, it is not suitable for merchandise with fluctuating prices.

## Computerized Marking

*UPC marking*

In Chapter 3 we discussed the use of computerized operations at checkout stations through the stamping of universal product code symbols on packages. Since UPC marking is generally done by manufacturers, retailers are relieved of the need for marking merchandise with detailed cost and related information. Of course, stores must still indicate retail prices on packages, shelves, or bins.

## Saving Time by Premarking

*Premarking saves time for retailers*

In some instances, as you read in Chapter 14, suppliers or manufacturers mark prices on merchandise in actual figures. Called premarking or source marking, this involves stamping prices on packages or attaching price tags to the merchandise itself. For example, items like magazines often have prices preprinted on them. Though premarking saves retailers time, the expenses involved are passed along to the stores as part of the cost of the goods.

# The Marking Process

The next time you go into a supermarket or a small neighborhood store, see if someone is either stamping a price on merchandise or attaching a price tag or ticket to it. If you see this being done, you will be watching a marking process. Since retailers use a wide variety of marking procedures, we need to examine the more common ones.

## Price Tags and Price Tickets

The information on tags and tickets can be printed, stamped, or punched by equipment or by hand (Figure 16-6). Tags are usually attached to goods with string, while tickets may be stapled, held fast by buttons, or looped around items like bracelets.

*The use of cost codes*

Some stores put cost codes, which indicate the cost of an item, on tags or tickets. This is valuable in instances in which bargaining over price is store policy and the retailer wants the cost known to salespeople but not to customers. Knowing the cost enables the salesperson to determine the range of possible retail prices of an item.

Using a ten-letter code, any cost can be listed on a tag or label. For example, using the following scheme, a $16.50 cost would be coded as PTIE.

$$P \; R \; O \; F \; I \; T \qquad L \; A \; N \; E$$
$$1 \; 2 \; 3 \; 4 \; 5 \; 6 \qquad 7 \; 8 \; 9 \; 0$$

## Gummed Labels

After information has been listed on labels, the labels are attached to products by means of a gummed substance. This type of marking is commonly used on hard surfaces like boxes, glass, and plastic.

(a)

*Your Logo*

| DEPT. | CENTS |
|---|---|
| C05 | $12.00 |

DP  CL  VEN  STYLE  CTL CODE

0569644062263439

00 1300

COL  SIZE

13

U053778095

DEPT.  SKU NO.

JUNIOR

22°⁰  $12⁰⁰

(b)

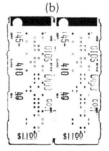

(c)

FURNITURE
CLEARANCE
CENTER

89  49

SALE
PRICE

49

ALL SALES FINAL – CASH & CARRY

(d)

C18 4632 4

U7156 5012

>$37.75

C18 4632 4

U7156 5012

>$37.75

No. RO 7432 (2⅞ x 1¼)
SKU, Department and
Price with duplicate stub
for batch reading

(d)

C32130012

P39149336  14½

M30210 $125.00

No. RO 4845 (1⅞ x 1¾)
Full SKU, Department and
Price (plus non-OCR size)

**FIGURE 16-6**

Types of price tags, tickets, and labels.
(a) and (b) Kimball tickets, (c) ordinary
tag, (d) tags containing SKUs, and (e)
Kimball labels containing SKUs.

(e)

C614 78421

U54364 538

>$44.50

No. RP 3530 (1⅜ x 1³⁄₁₆)
SKU, Department and
Price

C192 42207

U618 49214

>$29.95

No. RP 3837 (1½ x 1⁷⁄₁₆)
SKU, Department and
Price

This electronic imprinting system coordinates tag and label information with management methods of record-keeping.

### Stamping

Instead of using gummed labels, many stores apply prices with rubber stamps. This saves time and is a popular method with convenience stores and supermarkets. Other hand-operated marking devices include the band stamp, which contains rotating number columns, and the label gun, which affixes price labels to merchandise. Marking machines may be hand operated or electrically powered.

### Marking by Hand

Many small stores continue to mark by hand, using grease pencils and multicolored pens. While it is relatively slow, this method serves the modest needs of cost-conscious retailers.

### Nonmarking

In an effort to save time and money, some retailers do not mark merchandise. Instead, prices are listed on shelves, posters, bins, showcases, and so forth. For example, stores that sell record albums generally categorize the albums by type (e.g., rock, jazz, classical). Using a letter or color code, the customer checks prices on posters located at strategic points in the store. An added benefit of **nonmarking** is the ease of changing prices on posters as contrasted with doing so on the merchandise itself.

### Remarking Merchandise

Remarking is used to show markdowns or markups

To avoid preparing new price tags or tickets when markdowns or additional markups occur, some stores simply cross out the old price and write in or stamp the new price. This is called **re-marking,** and is sometimes done when merchandise is returned by customers, when it is damaged, or when it remains unsold after a certain period. To maintain control over remarked merchandise, buyers in large stores authorize price changes via special forms.

Store policy dictates whether markdowns are shown on the original tag or a new tag is prepared. The policy depends on the store's perception of customers' feelings: Do customers think they are getting a bargain, or do they conclude that the merchandise was overpriced originally? Obviously, the nature of a store's clientele determines which course the store will follow.

## UVM and OCR-A

In Chapter 3, we indicated that optical scanning is being used more and more by retailers in conjunction with UPC. It was noted that a scanner transmits UPC product information to a computer where it is processed for customer and accounting purposes.

A relatively new system for marking and controlling inventory, approved by the National Retail Merchants Association, is known as **Universal Vendor Marking (UVM).** Similar in purpose to UPC, UVM involves the premarking of merchandise by manufacturers and includes manufacturer identification, size, color, and style. Unlike the markings on UPC that can be read only by machines, UVM uses numbers and letters that can be read by both people and equipment.

The classification system used in UVM is called **Optical Character Recognition— Font A (OCR-A).** Font A refers to the type of print used with OCR. UVM is used in department and specialty stores, while UPC is found more often in the food industry.

Retailers that use UVM add a department code, price, and additional information to their price tickets by imprinting a label and attaching it to the vendor's ticket. There is growing evidence that a retailer's marking costs are substantially lower with UVM than the present estimated cost of all marking functions.

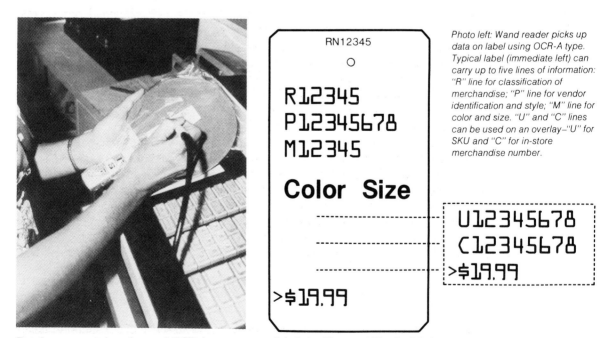

*Photo left: Wand reader picks up data on label using OCR-A type. Typical label (immediate left) can carry up to five lines of information: "R" line for classification of merchandise; "P" line for vendor identification and style; "M" line for color and size. "U" and "C" lines can be used on an overlay–"U" for SKU and "C" for in-store merchandise number.*

Retailers use wand readers and OCR-A type on price labels for Universal Vendor Marking (UVM).

# STORING AND DISTRIBUTING THE MERCHANDISE

*Efficient storage provides for forward and reserve stock*

In Chapter 12 we stressed the importance of providing adequate space for storage of merchandise that is not displayed in selling areas immediately after marking. Sometimes merchandise is stored in drawers or bins, or on racks in or close to a selling area. This is called **forward stock.** At other times it goes to a central stockroom within the store or to the individual stockroom adjoining each department. This is known as **reserve stock.** However, some large stores do not maintain reserve stock. Instead, all merchandise on hand is displayed. When goods are needed, they are requisitioned from a strategically located distribution center.

When a store consists of more than one unit, the goods may be sent from one store, in which receiving, checking, and marking are done, to one or more of the other stores.

Though small stores have limited storage space, they too must make merchandise readily available to customers. Owners, managers, and salespeople in these stores follow established routines for maintaining stockrooms and forwarding goods to selling areas.

# PROTECTING THE MERCHANDISE

*The high cost of merchandise crime*

While the handling of merchandise generally follows carefully designed procedures, retailers continue to sustain substantial losses of goods due to theft by both employees and outsiders. This is a pervasive problem for most stores. In 1981 losses due to inventory shortages amounted to a greater percentage of sales than after-tax profits did. Retailers have expressed great concern about these losses. Organizations like the National Retail Merchants Association publish data about the high costs of shoplifting, while groups of retailers and individual stores ponder long-range solutions. It is important, therefore, to understand both the depth of the problem and its treatment.

In Chapter 12 we took a preliminary look at the problem of merchandise theft and identified a number of security techniques used by stores today. It was pointed out that different types of crimes are involved in the pilferage of merchandise and that stores must be organized to deal with them. Here we take a closer look at the situation.

It must be understood that inventory shortages have a variety of causes, not all of which involve crimes. For example, a broken jar in a supermarket reduces inventory, as does an honest mistake by a salesperson in packing goods for a customer. In the remainder of this chapter, however, we will be concerned only with shortages caused by crimes, both internal and external.

## Thefts by Employees

Surprising as it may seem, many retailers believe that the amount of merchandise stolen by store personnel is greater than the amount stolen by outsiders. Whether this is due to the ease with which merchandise can be stolen by employees, to job dissatisfaction, to the low pay received by some workers, or to some other reason, the fact remains that internal theft is a serious problem. Thefts by employees generally occur in the following store areas.

## The Receiving Area

As you saw earlier in this chapter, the receiving area is a hub of activity where store personnel mingle with truck drivers, delivery people, and others. With virtually all merchandise moving through the receiving, checking, and marking functions, it is here that potential thieves have their best opportunity to steal goods. Working by themselves or in collusion with other employees or outsiders, the thieves develop a variety of techniques.

**Controlling Receiving-Area Theft** Security personnel may be assigned to receiving areas, allowing only authorized people into or out of specific sections. Cartons, trash containers, and bags are inspected for hidden goods. Some stores require employees to leave by certain exits. Owners and managers of small stores try to maintain control of back and side doors, using signs, warnings, and door mechanisms to prevent unauthorized people from using them.

## The Front Area(s)

Retailers have always known that checkout areas are places where dishonest employees plan thefts. Operating by themselves or in collusion with "customers," they develop ingenious ways to pilfer merchandise. For example, they put more goods into bags or boxes than the collaborating "customer" pays for; or, where there is no security guard, they deliberately overlook a "customer" leaving the store with unpaid merchandise.

Accounting control systems minimize theft

**Controlling Front-Area Theft** Large stores have accounting control systems for tying receipts (cash, checks, and credit cards) to merchandise purchased. For example, accounting department personnel might check total receipts against price tags or tickets removed from sold merchandise. Many stores post security guards at exits to make sure that packages containing goods purchased at the store have sales receipts attached to them. Some stores use cameras to survey activities in checkout areas.

## Thefts by Management Personnel

Though not so common as thefts by other employees, there are instances of managerial personnel stealing goods. Since managers supervise and control store operations, their merchandise crimes are more difficult to uncover.

**Controlling Theft by Management Personnel** The most effective way to control thefts by managers is to encourage and develop store loyalty. This is usually accomplished through opportunities for promotion, satisfactory pay levels, incentive programs, and recognition of effort.

## General Approaches to Reducing Employee Theft

While the techniques mentioned previously for controlling the theft of merchandise by employees have some effect, store owners and managers recognize that basic employee

Basic employee honesty is a store's best protection against employee theft

honesty is by far the store's best protection. Consequently, strong efforts are usually made to hire people of integrity. Employment procedures generally include the completion of application forms and the screening of job applicants.

**Application Forms** All large and most moderate-sized retail organizations require prospective employees to complete application forms. As shown in Chapter 10 (Figure 10-1), the form generally contains the following: an identification of personal characteristics and educational achievement, a listing of prior employment, and an indication of the position applied for. Some applications also call for a listing of references. Others include a release to be signed by the applicant, giving the store the right to investigate him or her. Generally excluded from this release is the employer's right to check references or previous employment, which may be done without the applicant's permission.

When fully completed, an application form should reveal the applicant's entire employment history. Unexplained gaps should be investigated for possible involvement by the applicant in an illegal act or an unpleasant employment incident. Anything that bears on the applicant's honesty and reliability should be investigated.

**Screening Applicants** In Chapter 10 we discussed the rail interview, an initial screening of job seekers prior to the completion of an application form. The purpose of the interview is to eliminate unqualified candidates from further consideration.

Screening is a continuous process

However, screening of employees is a continuous process, necessitated by the possibility that current workers may be susceptible and even involved in merchandise crimes. Only a naive person would assume that financial and home problems, career frustration, and difficulties with supervisors or other workers might not cause some employees to steal. Therefore, managers must be sensitive to changes in employee behavior and their living standards, using discreet screening techniques to detect possible malfeasance. If there is any suspicion of an employee's honesty—even if his or her record has been satisfactory—the situation should be investigated immediately.

# Theft by Shoppers

Shoplifters run the gamut of society

People who enter stores with the intention of stealing merchandise may act alone or in collusion with others. Surprisingly, they include representatives of all levels of society: well-to-do and poor, young and old, educated and uneducated, and so forth. With so varied a potential security population, retailers must devise systems for minimizing (elimination is probably impossible) the amount of merchandise theft.

In addition to the security techniques discussed in Chapter 12, a recently developed innovation involves the use of electronic beams to alert security forces to possible thefts of merchandise. A leading manufacturer of electronic merchandise security systems, the Sensormatic Electronics Corporation, produces sophisticated equipment and supplies for most types of retailers. Other major manufacturers include Knogo Corporation, Checkpoint Systems, Inc., and Minnesota Mining & Manufacturing, which produces a system for libraries and bookstores.

Reusable tags sensitive to electronic beams can prevent shoplifting

A commonly found design is the Sensormatic system. It employs reusable tags that contain semiconductor materials. A tag is attached to every merchandise item that requires protection, and when a sale is made, the tag is removed by an employee. Scan-

Reusable tags are sensitive to electronic beams that are located at store exits to alert a store's security personnel.

ning pedestals or overhead units are located at the store's exits; these broadcast an electronic signal that can detect tags entering the scanning field. If shoplifting is attempted, the tag activates an alarm when it is near an exit. The alarm, which may be either audible or visual, is located near the exit or monitored in a remote security room.

Sensormatic's analysis of the shoplifting menace and its involvement in **electronic article surveillance (EAS)** display the increasing concern of retailers and security equipment manufacturers in the protection of merchandise. The Appendix at the end of this chapter contains an interview with George M. Harbin, Jr., Senior Vice President of Sensormatic, and gives us his views on shoplifting and EAS.

*Retailers using EAS*

Sophisticated EAS systems are being used by many retailers, for example department stores like Lord & Taylor, Jordan Marsh, Rich's, and Sears, Roebuck & Co.; specialty stores like Lerner Shops, Elizabeth Arden, Dallas Carriage Shops, and Peaches Records & Tapes; and discounters and hypermarchés like Ayr-Way Stores, Fed-Mart, Woolco-Woolworth, and Zayres.

## POS and Store Security

One of the most recent contributions to store security is the spin-off benefits of POS (point-of-sale) terminals. With appropriate programming, the equipment can do the following.

- Enable salespeople to alert store security personnel to a problem by entering a code into POS terminals.
- Permit store personnel to detect shoplifting trouble spots quickly by matching POS sales and inventory data against actual merchandise counts.
- Alert the security department automatically for a cash pickup when a cash register contains more than a certain amount of money.

**NEW TERMS**

bin
blind checking
bulk checking
carrier
conveyor mechanism
delivery receipt
direct checking
electronic article surveillance (EAS)
forward stock
indirect checking
invoice
loading dock
loading platform
marking
movable table

nonmarking
Optical Character Recognition—Font A (OCR-A)
portable table
preretailing
purchase order
receiving book
receiving dock
remarking
reserve stock
semiblind checking
semi-indirect checking
spot checking
stationary table
Universal Vendor Marking (UVM)

# CHAPTER HIGHLIGHTS

1   Large stores that sell major appliances and furniture maintain warehouses for the storage of these goods until delivery to the customer.

2   Since selling space is valuable, receiving sections are located in areas that are not conducive to selling.

3   Receiving equipment within a store may consist of elevators, conveyors, and chutes.

4   The preparation of merchandise for delivery to selling areas is facilitated by the use of stationary tables, portable tables, conveyor mechanisms, and bins.

5   Information about incoming goods is entered in a receiving book and includes quantities, date and time of receipt, weight, type of transportation, name of carrier, shipping costs, damaged containers, and vendor's name.

6   A purchase order prepared by a retailer specifies the goods ordered. Upon receipt of the purchase order, the supplier sends the retailer an invoice.

7   In the receiving process, quantities may be checked by a variety of procedures: direct checking, indirect checking or blind checking, semi-indirect checking or semi-blind checking, spot checking, and bulk checking.

8   Notification must be given by retailers to suppliers or carriers in the event of shortages or damaged goods.

9   Merchandise quality is checked by buyers and/or store managers, not by checkers.

10   The marking of prices on goods benefits customers, salespeople, and the store.

11   Preretailing is a procedure that requires a buyer to list retail prices on purchase orders.

12  Computerized marking is done by manufacturers through use of the universal product code.

13  Premarking or source marking takes place when suppliers or manufacturers mark merchandise for retailers.

14  The marking process may involve the use of price tags, price tickets, gummed labels, stamping, or hand marking.

15  Remarking prices on goods may be used when goods are returned by customers, when they are damaged, or when they remain unsold after a certain period.

16  Forward stock is stored in or close to selling areas. Reserve stock goes to a central stockroom or to an individual stockroom adjoining each department.

17  Thefts of merchandise by store personnel occur in both receiving and front areas. Stores must institute procedures to control theft. Since the basic honesty of store employees is the store's best protection against employee theft, large and moderate-sized stores have applicants complete application forms and undergo screening. Because employees may be tempted to steal, screening should be a continuous process.

18  Many well-known department and specialty stores, discounters, and hypermarchés use electronic article surveillance (EAS) to control shoplifting.

## QUESTIONS

1  How do some stores overcome the difficulties caused by the wide separation of their receiving sections from their stockroom and selling areas?

2  Why is it important to restrict access to checking and marking areas by buyers and selling personnel?

3  What is the purpose of comparing information supplied by receiving clerks with purchasing data that is stored in the computer?

4  What is one of the items found on both a purchase order and an invoice that is used for cross-referencing? What is its purpose?

5  How does direct checking of merchandise differ from indirect checking? What are the advantages of each?

6  Why is spot checking sometimes used for large deliveries?

7  How do large retailers sometimes check the quality of incoming goods?

8  In what ways does the marking of goods benefit customers, salespeople, and the store?

9  How does computerized marking and premarking help the retailer?

10  How does a store decide whether remarking is to be done on the original price tag or on a new one?

11  How do forward and reserve stock differ?

12 What are some techniques used by stores to control the theft of merchandise by employees in receiving and front areas?

13 Why is it important to check a job applicant's history?

14 Why should the screening of employees be a continuous process?

15 In discussing shoplifting, what does George M. Harbin of the Sensormatic Electronics Corporation mean by the "mental triangle"?

# FIELD PROJECTS

1 The purpose of this project is to determine how observant you are regarding a store's security arrangements. Visit a local department, specialty, or discount store—or even a supermarket. As you walk through the store, check for any type of security device or system that may have been installed. Also, see if security guards are posted.

   a Compile a list of the security measures the store has taken.
   b Does the store appear to have a strong, fair, or weak security program? Explain.
   c Does the store use EAS tags or related devices?

2 The purpose of this project is to give you an opportunity to observe the marking techniques used by retailers. Go into some stores and ask permission to identify the specific marking methods they employ. Check for price tags, price tickets, gummed labels, stamping, and hand marking. You might try different types of stores.

   a For each marking technique, list the type of merchandise involved and the stores in which you find it.
   b Did you find evidence of re-marking? If so, on what types of goods?

# CASES

1 The Brighton Falls Department Store maintains a warehouse for storage of its major appliance and furniture goods. The store contains displays of the items, but merchandise is shipped to customers directly from the warehouse.

In an effort to enlarge its selling area, the store's management is considering warehousing additional, smaller types of merchandise. If this were done, some stockroom space could be converted into selling space. The managers have not yet analyzed the consequences of the projected change.

   a What might be the impact of the proposed change on customer satisfaction?
   b Other than the proposed change, what options should management consider for enlarging the selling area?

2 The Kilbee Auto Center sells automobile parts, including tires. It also installs and balances tires and does wheel alignments.

The company's arrangement for receiving, checking, and marking incoming goods is shown in the following diagram.

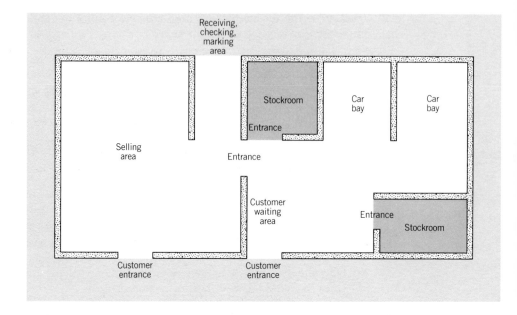

a What problems might the company have with regard to the control of merchandise?

b What changes would you suggest to give the company better control over the handling of merchandise? How would those changes improve the store's layout?

3 The J. T. Mandy Company, a discount department store with annual sales of over $40 million, is plagued by merchandise theft. Its inventory shortage rate was 1.9 percent of sales in 1970, but had risen to 2.5 percent by 1981. Despite the installation of such equipment as hidden closed-circuit television cameras and receivers, theft remains a serious problem.

Mandy's executives know that the firm's largest volume of thefts occurs in its leather goods department, followed closely by the costume jewelry and sporting goods departments. Consequently, it recently stationed uniformed security personnel in those areas to maintain constant observation of shoppers.

The head of Mandy's security department has suggested that the store develop an employee incentive program in an effort to reduce theft. He recommends that employees who notify security personnel about dishonest employees and on-the-spot shoplifting be awarded cash sums for their help; the reward could be either a flat amount or one based on the value of the goods involved. He also feels that cooperating employees should be considered for promotion.

Another of his suggestions is that many part-time workers be dismissed and replaced with full-time personnel. He reasons that full-timers are more reliable, honest, and loyal than part-timers. While recognizing the payroll savings that accrue from staffing the store with substantial numbers of part-time people, he contends that these savings would be more than offset by reduced inventory shortages.

Though top management is anxious to control the theft problem, it does not want to create other problems by adopting new procedures. Since its members are concerned about employee morale and customer comfort, management intends to proceed carefully and prudently.

  a  What arguments would you advance for and against the employee incentive program?
  b  What is your opinion about the suggestion regarding part- and full-time personnel?
  c  Should new security procedures be applied storewide, or should they be tested in the leather goods, costume jewelry, and sporting goods departments?

# REFERENCES

Blood, J., "Break-In, Break-Out," *Stores*, 63 (June 1981), pp. 53–55.

Hughes, M. M., *Successful Retail Security: An Anthology* (Los Angeles: Security World, 1978).

Jaspan, N., *Mind Your Own Business* (Englewood Cliffs, N.J.: Prentice-Hall, 1974).

Leininger, S., *Internal Theft: An Anthology* (Los Angeles: Security World, 1975).

Lipton, J. M., "New Data," *Stores*, 63 (July 1981), pp. 46–48.

Mongeon, F. M., and E. Hally, *Receiving Department Operations Manual* (New York: National Retail Merchants Association, Traffic Group, 1960).

"Moving Merchandise at Mervyn's," *Stores*, 62 (September 1980), pp. 83–84.

Rothman, M. B., "EAS for All?," *Stores*, 62 (June 1980), pp. 31–32.

———, "Reducing Freight Costs," *Stores*, 62 (April 1980), pp. 37–38.

Spalding, L. A., "Computer-Controlled Distribution at Dylex," *Stores*, 63 (May 1981), pp. 20–21.

———, "Off the Wall!," *Stores*, 62 (December 1980), pp. 45–48.

———, "Transportation as a Profit Center? A New Role," *Stores*, 63 (September 1981), pp. 30–34.

Williams, J. R., "President's Letter," *Stores*, 62 (February 1980), p. 74.

———, "President's Letter," *Stores*, 62 (July 1980), pp. 63–64.

# APPENDIX

## An Interview with George M. Harbin, Jr., Senior Vice President of Sensormatic Electronics Corporation*

Q  *What are the costs of shoplifting to retailers and ultimately to consumers?*

A  Nationwide inventory losses due to shoplifting are now estimated to be in excess of $8.5 billion annually and rising. This means that the theft of merchandise is reaching

*George M. Harbin, Jr., in Sensormatic Electronics Corporation, *Annual Report 1979*, pp. 5–8.

the astronomical figure of $23 million per day. Shoplifting now costs the average family about $265 a year. Various industry studies show that if shoplifting losses and the related security costs were eliminated, retail prices conceivably could be reduced by as much as 15 percent.

**Q**  *What kind of people become shoplifters and what influences them to shoplift?*

**A**  Through our studies, we have concluded that anyone can be a potential shoplifter. Shoplifting is not a teenage or minority problem. Retailers with a preconceived notion that shoplifters are young or members of a minority group have a tendency to look out for these individuals, resulting in those shoplifters fitting that description being most often caught in the act. But our studies show that the profile of the average shoplifter in most stores will match the profile of their average customer.

The easiest way to explain what influences a person to shoplift is through a theory expounded by many psychologists as the "mental triangle." If all three sides of this mental triangle come into place at the same time, an individual will take something that does not belong to him or her.

One side of the triangle is frustration. Think of the average shopper today. The great American middle class is being squeezed by the energy crisis and by inflation in general. With the cost of labor rising and fewer sales clerks on the floor, it is harder to get waited on and prices continue to climb. What we once considered necessities are now becoming unaffordable. Frustration clearly exists.

Side two of the triangle is opportunity. With fewer people on the sales floor to watch for shoplifting and merchandise being openly displayed for self-selection and self-service, opportunity is greater than ever.

Side three is the low risk of getting caught. The rising cost of labor means not only fewer sales employees but also reductions in security personnel. There just isn't any way the retailer can hire enough people to change the low risk side.

Awareness that merchandise is protected by the Sensormatic System removes the low risk side of the triangle. Low risk becomes a high risk of getting caught. Shoplifters will go to an unprotected store instead or will not commit the act.

**Q**  *In last year's annual report, you stressed the inevitability of electronic article surveillance. I thought the only things certain in life were death and taxes.*

**A**  In today's world you can add inflation to that list. It is because of inflation that the use of article surveillance has become inevitable and will accelerate.

The biggest problems facing retailers today are based on inflation. Labor costs are constantly increasing. In 1977, the minimum wage was raised to $2.65 an hour and in 1981, retailers will be paying minimum wage employees $3.35 per hour, with supervisory and security personnel receiving equivalent raises in salary. This estimated 26.4 percent increase in direct payroll cost alone will result in continued reductions in personnel on the selling floor. With fewer people on the selling floor, merchandise is more exposed to theft. The only constant we have seen over the past ten years regarding shoplifting is that it increases in proportion to the reductions in personnel on the sales floor.

Coupled with the problem of labor costs is the escalating cost of space. In order to meet the ever rising overhead expenses and to produce a profit, the retailer must display and sell more merchandise per square foot of floor space. Double and triple racking is becoming a practice in discount stores and will soon become commonplace in department stores. With fewer people on the selling floor, and higher displays of merchandise protecting the shoplifter from observation, shoplifting will increase while profits decrease.

I know of no other product the retailer can buy for his store that will allow him to come to grips with the retailer's three inflation-rooted problem areas: employee productivity, productivity of floor space, and decreasing profit margins. The inevitable solution to the retailer's inflationary problems is the Sensormatic System. By automating the surveillance process with our System, employee productivity is increased without increasing costs. Sales personnel, currently trained also to watch customers, can now devote all their efforts to sales.

With Sensormatic tag protection, more merchandise can be openly displayed per square foot. More merchandise on the selling floor means more sales, resulting in a more profitable store. Therefore Sensormatic is not just a product to eliminate shortage; it is a product that increases productivity of people and space, as well as reducing shortages by up to 85 percent.

**Q** *How effective is the Sensormatic System in cutting shortages and increasing retail profits?*

**A** It is important to realize that the retailer's profits nationwide average 2 percent to 2J percent of sales while shortages average between 2J percent and 3 percent of sales, and sometimes run as high as 7 percent to 8 percent of sales.

There are really three elements that make up retail shortages. They are paperwork, internal theft, and shoplifting. Retailers have worked on the paperwork side of the business for a number of years, harnessing the power of the computer to come to grips with the veritable blizzard of numbers that occur in retailing. By and large this area of the retail business is in good shape.

In addition, retailers have spent a great deal of time and money in personnel training, selection, and follow through. These efforts have produced significant results in the control of internal theft.

However, the retailer is still left with the problem of shoplifting. We believe this accounts for the major portion of shortage today. (Many retailers disagree!) When merchandise is protected by the Sensormatic System, retailers can experience shortage reductions as high as 85 percent, thus greatly improving their profitability.

**Q** *Is the Sensormatic System affordable?*

**A** Yes, obviously, the thousands of retailers worldwide utilizing and expanding their use of Sensormatic products have proven they dramatically reduce shoplifting losses and thus increase their profits after taking into account the costs of using Sensormatic products. Experience has shown that a typical payback period to the retailer for his investment in Sensormatic equipment is between 12 and 18 months. Additional personnel, the alternative to electronic article surveillance, is more expensive as well as less effective. A typical Sensormatic system costs less than the addition of one part-time clerk. Sensormatic is not only affordable, retailers facing shrinking profit margins can hardly afford not to use it.

**Q** *Who is your toughest competitor?*

**A** Our toughest competitor is the retailer's traditional way of attempting to handle the problem of shortage. The traditional approach has been "eyeball to eyeball" security, that is, people watching people to apprehend shoplifters, which even with the aid of cameras and two-way mirrors is generally ineffective. Moreover, apprehensions are not good for business, the store's image, or productivity. Retailers are interested not in the number of apprehensions, but in the reduction of bottom line shortage. What is required is a deterrence to shoplifting.

Retailers have also traditionally tried to cut shortages by locking up merchandise. But this deters shoplifting at the expense of sales. When shoppers can touch and examine merchandise, impulse buying is encouraged and sales increase dramatically. Electronic article surveillance allows the retailer to openly display his merchandise and protect it at the same time.

Our main job is to reach each prospective customer and fairly present the concept of article surveillance and explain its power as a much more productive tool than traditional methods.

**part four**

# PROMOTION: COMMUNICATING WITH THE CUSTOMER

**P**reparing goods for sale is of little value unless customers know they are available. Part Four covers the ways in which retailers communicate with consumers. Chapter 17 is devoted to personal selling, and we note the differences between order taking and creative selling. We then explore the principles of effective retail selling, with an explanation of the selling process. Finally we examine the major aspects of sales training programs.

Chapter 18 continues our coverage of the retailer–customer communication process with an examination of visual merchandising techniques. First we see how window displays convey information to shoppers. Then we study interior displays in two categories: merchandise and point-of-purchase. The chapter ends with a discussion of responsibility for displays and a list of guidelines for interior arrangement and display.

In Chapter 19 we see how advertising acts as a communication medium for retailers. After examining the different kinds of advertising that merchants use, we study the development of an advertising plan. Our discussion includes a plan's objectives, the media available for communicating with customers, the formulation of an advertising budget, and evaluation of the plan.

Chapter 20 takes us through the communication areas of sales promotion and public relations. We identify the types of promotions that retailers use, such as trading stamps and contests, and learn how responsibility for their implementation is shared. We also study public relations and publicity activities, ranging from community services and fashion shows to the use of free space and time in various media.

# chapter 17
# PERSONAL SELLING

After completing this chapter, you should be able to:

1 Identify and define the types of personal selling found in retailing.
2 Explain the stimulus–response, problem-solving, and step theories of retail selling.
3 Explain substitute selling, trading up, and TO.
4 Explain the rationale for out-of-store selling.
5 List the elements of a good sales training program.

Of all the retailing activities designed to generate sales and serve customers, the most important may be the selling that takes place when a customer and a salesperson interact. **Personal selling** differs from other means of communicating with consumers in its face-to-face nature. It can best be explained as the methods used in helping customers solve their buying problems.

Interaction of salesperson and customer

Although many stores have turned to self-service in an effort to cut selling costs, certain types of merchandise can be sold only by salespeople. It would be most difficult, for example, to buy such items as food processors, stereos, cars, or sewing machines without the help of a salesperson.

It is difficult to develop a good sales force

Merchants often suffer lost sales because the quality of their sales effort is poor. Store image is also affected by the impressions customers receive from their contact with salespeople. Despite attractive decor, merchandise, and prices, a poor sales team can lose many sales. Though retailers are aware of this, the development of a good sales force is no easy task. Retail selling attracts few top-caliber applicants because the wages are somewhat lower than in other fields. In addition, many people feel that a salesperson's job has low status.

## TYPES OF RETAIL SELLING

The two basic types of retail selling are **order taking** and **creative selling.**

Personal selling is as important today as it was in this 1925 Sears store.

# Order Taking

Routine selling

Order taking, or clerking, takes place when the clerk in a store does little more than fill a request, make change, or wrap items. Order takers generally work in a highly structured environment, such as McDonald's, Consumers Distributors, and Pizza Hut, or in stores with a strong mix of self-services. This form of selling may require a combination of skills, including the ability to operate quickly and to handle several customers at the same time. Order takers may also function as checkout clerks and cashiers.

# Creative Selling

Creative selling

Creative selling requires more product knowledge than order taking. It also calls for the ability to persuade and an appreciation of customers' needs. For example, salespeople at Streets & Co., a store that caters to the up-scale professional woman, uses unusual sales approaches. The staff is trained to sell a whole wardrobe concept to consumers. First the customer fills out a card to determine the "gaps" in her wardrobe. In consultation with a salesperson, she then completes her wardrobe. Since single-customer sales run as high as $2,500 and more, this type of selling requires customers to have great confidence in the staff. Employees who do creative selling are sometimes called sales consultants. This type of selling is commonly found in departments that sell "big-ticket" items like furniture and appliances.

Employees affect store image

A salesperson's personality traits and communication skills are very important because the impression a salesperson conveys often influences a customer's buying decisions. In fact, a store's image is directly associated with the type of employees it has. Retailers who are anxious to build a favorable image, therefore, are advised to consider the personality of any employee who comes into contact with customers.

Personal qualities such as appearance, speech, tact, friendliness, resourcefulness, and initiative are additional traits that help build good customer–salesperson relationships. Studies indicate that the quality of store employees is the most frequently mentioned reason for patronizing a particular store.

Even in shops that rely predominantly on self-service, employees are an important consideration. This is so because they may be called upon to answer questions about the quality of particular products, the location of certain items, and so forth. Consequently, they, too, affect the general atmosphere of the store. Their friendliness and helpfulness become part of the store's "personality" (Figure 17-1).

# PRINCIPLES OF EFFECTIVE RETAIL SELLING

Effective selling matches merchandise with customer needs

Salespeople are hired to sell. In order to do so effectively, they must learn all they can about the merchandise, find out what their customers require, and use appropriate selling techniques to satisfy them. Salespeople are obliged to help customers make the best buying decisions with regard to their needs and economic resources. Personal selling in retailing, then, is essentially the process of matching the store's merchandise and services with the customer's needs.

**FIGURE 17-1**
Dimensions of retail selling.

The most commonly cited theories of retail selling are

1 The **stimulus–response theory**
2 The **problem-solving theory**
3 The **step theory**

## The Stimulus–Response Theory

As indicated in Chapter 4, this theory is based on the experiments conducted by the Russian scientist Pavlov, who conditioned dogs to respond to specific and repeated stimuli. In a selling situation, the salesperson attempts to provide the "right" stimulus so that the customer responds positively. This requires the salesperson to recognize the behavior patterns of different types of customers.

## The Problem-Solving Theory

According to this theory, the salesperson must uncover and fully understand the customer's buying problem, and attempt to solve it by presenting the appropriate merchandise. For this, the salesperson's ability to select the *correct* merchandise is the key. A salesperson who understands merchandise features and benefits can relate them to the customer's needs.

## The Step Theory

AIDA = *attention, interest, desire,* and *action*

In the step theory, which is also known as formula selling, the customer's decision making follows a pattern of easily identifiable steps that lead to a decision to buy or not to buy. When a salesperson understands the theory, he or she is frequently able to lead the customer to the successful close of a sale. The steps in the process are commonly referred to as AIDA: attention, interest, desire, and action. This theory is based on the assumption that the customer's *attention* must be gained before a sale can be made. This can be accomplished by an advertisement, a display, or the salesperson's approach. *Interest* is basically prolonged attention. It is aroused when the salesperson recognizes the customer's wants and presents the correct merchandise to meet his or her buying needs. *Desire* to possess the goods can be stimulated by demonstrating how the product will satisfy those needs. For example, a customer who is looking at a tennis racket or golf club should be encouraged to grasp the handle and simulate a swing. Customers who are interested in clothing should be persuaded to try on a suit or dress. In other words, the psychological effect of touching or trying an item increases the desire to own the product. Theoretically, when the customer is convinced that the product is right, the last step, *action*, takes place. During this phase the customer orders or takes the goods.

The application of AIDA usually involves the following steps.

1 Approaching the customer
2 Determining customer needs

3  Presenting the merchandise

4  Meeting or answering objections

5  Closing the sale

6  Suggesting additional merchandise

## Approaching the Customer

When approaching the customer, the salesperson should try to gain the person's attention, create interest, and then proceed with the sale. There are three commonly used approaches.

1  A simple greeting

2  A service approach

3  A merchandise approach

A *simple greeting* like "Good afternoon, Mrs. Jones," or "Good morning" is informal, friendly, and welcoming. *Service approaches* like "Would you care for some help?," "Is there something you would like to see?," and "How may I help you?" are not always effective with a browsing customer. However, they are particularly useful when a customer needs someone to explain how a product works, or when the customer appears to have made a selection. *Merchandise approaches* are comments by a salesperson about articles that a customer has stopped to examine. For example, an effective opening might be, "These shirts are new and come in the latest fashion colors."

## Determining Customer Needs

The salesperson must ask good questions and be a good listener in order to understand what the customer is searching for. For example, "How will you use the product?," "When do you need it?," and "What size do you need?" are acceptable questions. By asking appropriate questions about the need that the customer is seeking to fill, the salesperson will gain a better idea of what goods to present or demonstrate.

## Presenting the Merchandise

Even though much merchandise is tagged and labeled, there are many items that require the assistance of a salesperson's demonstration or explanation. Examples are typewriters, cameras, stereos, and appliances. Technical equipment should be operated so that the buyer is convinced that it is easy to use, for example, by test-driving a car. Special features or selling points should be emphasized.

## Meeting or Answering Objections

Questions and objections by the customer are strong signs of interest. A salesperson with good product knowledge can often turn objections into reasons to buy. For example, when a customer says, "This quilt seems too light to be warm," the salesperson might say, "Because it is made of 100 percent down, it has warmth without much weight. It is very comfortable to use."

Some objections to a product are really excuses not to buy. By means of careful questioning, the salesperson can separate price or quality objections from excuses. Thus, by asking, "What exactly don't you like about the product?" or "What would you care

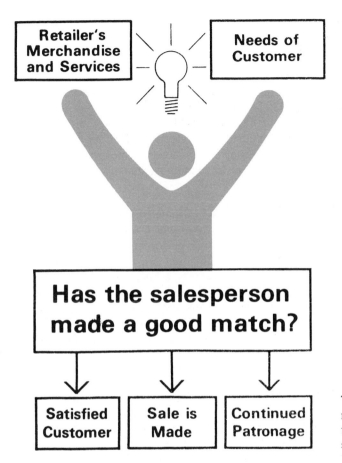

The salesperson attempts to match a customer's needs with the retailer's merchandise and services.

to spend for a product of this kind?," the salesperson can gain a better understanding of the customer. Salespeople should learn to treat objections as unanswered questions.

## Closing the Sale

As the objections are answered, the salesperson should attempt to close the sale. Up to this point the entire process has involved getting the customer to make a buying decision. Some decisions are made quickly, as in the case of a customer who knows exactly what he or she wants. At other times, however, a more creative close is required. This is especially so when the salesperson must assist a customer who has difficulty making decisions or does not have the confidence to express his or her decisions. There are several effective closing techniques that may be used in such cases.

Closing
techniques

1 Asking pointed questions such as "Will this be cash or charge?," "Shall we send it gift wrapped?," or "When would you like this delivered?"

2 Watching and listening for signals from the customer. For example, questions like "Can this be returned?" or "How long will it take to be delivered?" are signals. Facial expressions may also indicate that a buying decision is close.

3 Offering inducements or special services (when appropriate). These are typical comments: "The sale price is available today only"; "Free alterations are available today"; "We will not charge you for delivery." Customers are tempted to say yes under these conditions, and generally are pleased with the salesperson's suggestions.

4 Recognizing that the customer might need the approval of another member of the family when dealing with expensive items. In this case the salesperson should try to arrange another meeting. A resourceful salesperson tries to guarantee the customer's return by taking the customer's telephone number and other information. It is important to remember that even if a sale is not made, the customer is a potential future buyer. In other words, spending a little more time with the customer promotes good will.

### Suggesting Additional Merchandise

**Suggestion selling** is another way in which a retail salesperson can add to sales and profits. After a sale has been made, a customer is usually receptive to further discussion, and it may be wise to suggest additional items that relate to the original purchase. For example, the salesperson might suggest a beach hat to complement a bathing suit, a tie for a shirt, a belt for a dress, and so forth.

Suggesting a special offer that may or may not be related to the item already purchased is sometimes effective. In addition, the rapport between a salesperson and customer may allow the former to suggest a special department or store promotion.

## Special Retail Situations

In cases in which a customer asks for a specific brand that the store does not carry, the salesperson may offer an alternative item to satisfy the customer's needs. This is known as **substitute selling.** Without this additional effort, the sale is usually lost.

When a salesperson persuades the customer to buy a more expensive item or a larger quantity than originally intended, it is known as **trading up.** Trading up increases sales and profits but must be used with care to avoid pressuring customers.

Another important selling practice is the use of a **TO,** or **turnover.** This involves turning over a customer to someone else when it appears that a sale will not be closed. Depending on the store, the turnover person is generally someone in authority or someone with particular expertise. This may be the manager, the assistant manager, a buyer, or a senior salesperson.

A TO is used only when the salesperson realizes that he or she will not be successful in making the sale. The main reasons for the TO are

1 To save the sale

2 To serve customers by doing what is necessary to solve their buying problems

3 To change salespeople when a personality clash has occurred

When a TO is used, the salesperson introduces the designated individual to the customer by name. The introduction might go as follows: "Madam, this is Mr. Worth, our department buyer. I know he will be able to find what you want." In this case the salesperson has given the customer the impression that the TO person will be able to do more than he or she did. There must be a valid reason for effecting a TO if the customer is to accept the new "salesperson" with confidence. Two commonly accepted reasons are the following.

1 A person with greater authority should be able to do a better job than the salesperson.
2 The new person has a special ability or expertise that may be used to solve the customer's immediate problem.

A TO is called for when, at a particular point in the sale, the customer is too confused or discouraged to buy. The move is made to prevent the customer from giving up. The introduction of a new person can make a customer think, "Ah, this person knows more about my problem and will be able to help."

# Personal Selling Outside the Store

*Product specialist*

Interior designers and decorators are employed by many department stores to sell outside the store. These salespeople visit the customer's home equipped with various samples and illustrations of fabrics, wallpaper, carpets, and other home furnishings. They attempt to help the customer solve his or her decorating problems by selecting appropriate merchandise. Retailers that sell air conditioning, kitchen and bathroom fixtures, and remodeling often send salespeople to the customer's home to help design the layout of the room.

Out-of-store, house-to-house sales forces are gaining in popularity with customers because of the convenient services they offer, as well as the help they render in making buying decisions. For customers who lack shopping time, an out-of-store seller often provides the service at times that differ from regular store hours.

*Better opportunity to demonstrate the product*

In situations in which the customer requires more product information, the out-of-store seller gets a chance to demonstrate the product where it will be used—in the home. For example, customers who are interested in slipcovering their livingroom furniture have an opportunity of seeing various fabric samples on their furniture in the correct setting. These customers need not worry about the appropriateness of their selections.

To be successful, the out-of-store seller must develop strong sales skills in addition to becoming a product specialist. In a brief visit, the salesperson must gain acceptance, win the confidence of the customer, develop an interest in the product, create a desire to buy, and close the sale. Even if the sale is not closed, enough interest and motivation may be developed to produce future sales.

# TRAINING THE RETAIL SALESPERSON

In recent years the quality of retail selling has been criticized, suggesting that there is a need for change. For example, in stores where customers expect service, they are sometimes disappointed because of insufficient numbers of salespeople. And if one is lucky enough to secure a salesperson, they lack merchandise information. Furthermore, in outlets where customers need directions or simple answers, the sales help is often misinformed, lacking proper information and less than sufficiently attentive.

In the last several decades the trend toward self-service and the marketing strategy of preselling merchandise have diminished the role of retail selling. As a result, the importance of the retail salesperson has declined.

The importance of personal selling varies with different types of stores, their desired images, and the products they carry. Basically, personal selling is most important in department and specialty shops that offer a wide range of services. It plays a lesser role and is sometimes almost totally missing in self-service stores such as discount operations, supermarkets, and the like. Personal selling influences a customer's decisions and perceptions, and requires adequate training.

Training can increase employee productivity, lead to better morale, reduce job turnover, and motivate employees to foster good customer relations.

A good training program stresses

1   Sales techniques and customer service
2   Product information
3   Standards and evaluation

# Sales Techniques and Customer Service

A program aimed at improving salespeople's skills should do the following.

1   Train salespeople to recognize and handle different types of customers and special problems.
2   Train salespeople to sell from the viewpoint of customers by understanding their buying motives.
3   Instruct sales personnel as to the steps needed for effective selling.
4   Instruct salespeople in providing customer service.

## Handling Different Types of Customers

Certain types of customers are frequently encountered by salespeople. The manner in which the salesperson pays attention to them can mean the difference between closing or losing a sale. Customers may be of either sex, and any age, race, or nationality. The more common types are the following.

> **The argumentative customer** who disagrees with many statements and tends to disbelieve what he or she is told. The salesperson should avoid trying to win an argument, since the sale may ultimately be lost. Instead, the salesperson needs to overcome objections with facts and strong emphasis on merchandise benefits.

> **The procrastinator** lacks confidence in his or her own judgment, but will listen to the salesperson. This customer likes to postpone buying decisions with state-

ments like "I'll wait till next week." The salesperson must help this customer decide by reinforcing his or her judgments. The astute salesperson narrows the selection by putting away the merchandise in which the customer seems disinterested. In other words, the salesperson must help this person decide.

**The looker** may be a customer who is "shopping around," making comparisons, or on the way to another department. When greeted by the salesperson, this customer frequently replies, "I'm just looking." The salesperson might answer, "That's all right, we're glad to have you. I'll be over there if you need assistance." By offering help and making the customer feel welcome, the salesperson lays a foundation for future sales.

**The silent customer** talks little, but pays attention. The salesperson must ask direct questions that require more than a yes-or-no answer.

**The decided customer** knows what he or she wants and is confident about making decisions. Though not generally interested in other opinions, this customer respects quality, service, and so forth.

**The angry customer,** recognizable by his or her "chip on the shoulder" attitude, is obviously in a bad mood and is easily provoked. The salesperson should stick to facts and avoid arguments.

Training sessions that illustrate various types of customers and how to handle them can be very helpful to inexperienced salespeople. Some stores use role playing to dramatize selling situations with difficult customers. Role playing consists of acting out the customer–salesperson relationship. One person plays the part of the customer and the other that of the salesperson. This method enables salespeople to see various sales situations from the customer's point of view. The skill of "sizing up" a customer (learning to recognize his or her needs) can be cultivated through role playing.

## Handling Special Problems in Retail Selling

There are certain situations that all salespeople encounter, such as the need to handle two or more customers at once, the parent with a child, and the group shopper. Each of these situations presents a special problem that requires special handling.

**Handling More Than One Customer at a Time** All customers want attention and service, and sometimes salespeople find that they must handle several customers at once. This is not an easy task, even for the most experienced salesperson. Nevertheless, some salespeople are adept at doing this without antagonizing customers, and are able to increase sales thereby.

When waiting on one customer, it is wise to acknowledge the others by some greeting or comment, such as "I'll be with you as soon as I can." While one customer is looking at merchandise, the salesperson might excuse himself or herself and attempt to serve another customer. People are usually considerate when they see that a salesperson is trying to help them. Nevertheless, dealing with two or more customers requires tact and patience.

**Parent and Child** Many customers shop with their children. This situation can be difficult if the salesperson is not aware of the potential problems. In order to go through the selling process quickly and efficiently, the salesperson needs the customer's undivided attention. If the shopper is distracted by efforts to keep the child out of mischief, the situation becomes difficult and the customer may say, "I'll come back later *alone.*" The salesperson's best technique is to befriend the child. This generally flatters and pleases the parent, who will probably attempt to keep the child quiet. By paying attention to the child, the salesperson enlists the cooperation of both parties.

**The Group Shopper** When friends or family accompany the customer, they do so to provide advice about the purchase. This situation presents a real problem to the salesperson unless diplomacy and tact are used. The salesperson must avoid the slightest disparagement of the views of any member of the group.

The salesperson should determine which member of the group has the greatest influence on the customer. With the aid of that person, the sale may be closed quickly. The strategy is to include the person in the sales talk. For example, as a product is presented to the customer, the salesperson should direct one or two comments to the other member as well. By doing this, the salesperson indicates that his or her opinion is valued, and an ally is gained. More selling is needed when two or more people are involved, but care must be taken to direct enough remarks to the friend to win his or her support while not seeming to exert pressure.

## The Customer's Viewpoint

Effective salespeople develop the ability to sell from the consumer's point of view by putting themselves in the customer's shoes. They can better understand the shopper's needs because they become the buyers rather than the sellers. When this happens, the salesperson develops awareness of the customer's motives for buying.

*All merchandise satisfies some consumer need*

Customers buy because they are motivated by certain emotional or rational motives, such as pride, beauty, convenience, or romance (Chapter 4). For example, when a person desires recognition as a leader, the pride motive may stimulate the purchase of a large boat or car. On the other hand, if time is a factor, the convenience motive may prompt the purchase of a microwave oven.

When salespeople become familiar with the individual drives that cause people to buy, they are in a better position to match the qualities and benefits of a product with the consumer's motive for buying.

## Training for Effective Selling

*Instructional methods used in training*

Salespeople must be knowledgeable about the steps that are required in order to make a sale. Training for effective selling involves the teaching of techniques for opening a sale, presenting merchandise, answering objections, closing a sale, and selling additional merchandise. Role playing, video cassettes, sales meetings, and seminars are effective training methods.

**Role Playing** As you have seen, this involves acting out a scene between a customer and a salesperson.

**Video Tapes and Cassettes** Many large firms have taped instructions for their employees. This form of teaching is becoming popular because employees can watch and listen at their convenience. Some tapes demonstrate the sales presentation from start to finish. Sometimes they indicate right and wrong ways to approach a customer, meet objections, and close a sale. Instructional tapes can be developed by the store or pur-

Store training involves customer-salesperson simulation (Courtesy of Dayton's.)

chased from professional organizations. Some tapes are developed by manufacturers to aid in the selling of their products. These are very specific regarding the selling qualities and benefits of the merchandise.

**Sales Meetings and Seminars** These methods are generally helpful because they afford managers an opportunity to discuss the features of new products, changes in store policies, new merchandise strategies, or other matters related to the store's merchandise and services. Sessions conducted regularly prompt the interchange of ideas because salespeople enjoy sharing their "tales of sales."

## Training for Customer Service

In addition to selling, the salesperson is often faced with nonselling activities that involve customer contact. These include following up on orders, wrapping packages, accepting returns, and answering complaints.

**Checking and Calling Customers** Following up customer orders may be part of the job when one is selling major items like appliances and furniture. Checking to see that customers are satisfied develops good will and customer loyalty. Salespeople may also call a list of regular customers when the store runs sales or when new merchandise is expected.

**Wrapping Packages** Some salespeople are responsible for wrapping packages for their customers. When they do so with speed and care, they have an opportunity to add to the customer's satisfaction. Customers generally like this arrangement because one individual is able to complete the entire transaction.

In some stores the salesperson is responsible for goods that are to be mailed, or for carrying merchandise to a delivery vehicle. Even though a sale has been made, the follow-through to avoid errors is important for the development of customer good will.

**Handling Returns and Complaints** Handling complaints properly can change a discontented customer into a happy patron. For example, in many stores merchandise is returned directly to the selling departments. If the salespeople show concern and are helpful in resolving return problems, customers are generally satisfied. Since refunds and credit policies are keys to the level of store service, most stores are willing to accept merchandise returns in order to maintain customer good will.

Complaints are a tangible way in which customers inform the store of their dissatisfaction. Though there are many reasons for complaints, in this chapter we are concerned with those that arise from poor salesmanship, incorrectly filled orders, damaged merchandise owing to negligent packing, and unwanted purchases made through excessive sales pressure.

### Learning About the Store

It is important for salespeople to be cordial and helpful even when they are called upon to answer questions that are not related to their area. In order to have salespeople build customer good will, training should also include information about the store and its policies. In this way salespeople are able to provide the customer with correct information concerning the locations of departments, services, and special events.

## Product Information

Salespeople should have a thorough knowledge of the merchandise they are selling because

- It develops selling confidence.
- It makes for a better sales demonstration.
- It helps match the selling qualities of the product with the customer's needs.
- It provides a basis for successfully overcoming objections.
- It makes for a smoother transaction.

If salespeople are to have the necessary product information, they should become familiar with sources of product information. Most merchants, managers, and buyers have access to trade materials that provide information about the products they handle. Manufacturers and wholesalers provide them with excellent product information (literature, periodic sales meetings, etc.), which serves as resource material for salespeople.

### Buyers

Buyers are very concerned about how merchandise sells in their departments. Resourceful buyers hold instructional programs or seminars about their merchandise, identifying particular selling features and explaining what the merchandise can do for the customer. For example, when selling an expensive hand cream one should stress its importance to soft, smooth skin or its function as protection against cold weather. In other words, a salesperson should sell product benefits.

### Vendors

Salespeople must be confident about the merchandise they sell in order to instill confidence in their customers. Consequently, when products are technical or require special demonstrations, vendors prepare information for their merchandise and sometimes conduct sales lectures at the store.

## Labels

Merchandise tags and labels offer information regarding fiber content, instructions for care, quantities, and so forth. The purpose of an informative label is to enable the consumer to buy wisely and to minimize the likelihood of returns and customer dissatisfaction. The salesperson can use labels to point out specific benefits to customers. The following list contains information found on labels.

* Manufacturer (name and address—how to contact)
* Performance (color, permanence, strength, resistance to water and perspiration, light, etc.)
* Content (kind of fiber, metal, leather, plastic, etc.)
* Construction (how the product is made, size, weight, finish, hand or machine made, etc.)
* Care and uses (most suitable uses, instructions for washing, cleaning, storage, etc.)

Figure 17-2 contains some product care instructions.

## Catalog Descriptions

Many mail order companies send catalogs filled with product information and descriptions. These can be helpful to the salesperson because they are easy to understand and explain product quality in specific terms.

## Government Standards

Another excellent resource for salespeople consists of government publications that contain standards and regulations for many products. They are available through agencies like the Department of Commerce and the Office of Consumer Affairs.

## Private Agencies and Testing Laboratories

There are agencies that operate testing laboratories for the guidance and protection of consumers. In these cases, labels or seals are used to show that the articles have met

---

Warm Wash–Tumble Dry–Color May Transfer When New–Wash Alone Before Wearing (Prewashed).

Warm Wash–Tumble Dry–Remove Promptly–Do Not Bleach–Fabric Will Snag–Avoid Rough Surfaces.

Machine Wash–Warm **Separately**–Tumble Dry–Low Heat.

No Soak–No Hand Wash–Hot Wash With Detergent–Color Transfer When New–Wash Alone Before Wearing–Shrinks About 3%.

Machine Washable–Warm Setting–Tumble Dry–Low Heat.

Machine Washable–Warm Setting–Tumble Dry–Low Heat–Color May Transfer Or Bleed–Wash Alone Before Wearing.

---

FIGURE 17-2

Salespeople can learn about the care of products by reading labels. This list contains typical care instructions that are included with many products. (Reproduced by permission of Levi Strauss & Co.)

certain standards. *Consumer Reports, Good Housekeeping,* and *Parents* magazine are examples of publications that perform tests on products and make the public aware of the results. Large retailers like J. C. Penney operate their own testing facilities to check the quality of the products they sell.

### Publications and Professional Organizations

Trade publications like *Women's Wear Daily, Daily News Record,* and *Chain Store Age* are just a few of the publications that keep salespeople up to date. Trade organizations like the National Retail Merchants Association also publish a great deal of material.

## Standards and Evaluation of Sales Performance

All training programs should include guidelines or standards so that employees know what is expected of them and how they are evaluated. Employee evaluation and training were discussed fully in Chapter 10. In this chapter we are concerned primarily with the personal selling process and evaluation of the salesperson's performance.

Sales records provide specific information that can be used to measure the effectiveness of the individual salesperson. Though some people are more productive than others, the number of transactions by an employee and sales volume are important measures of sales performance.

It is important to compare salespeople in similar departments with similar responsibilities because salespeople are often involved in related activities such as stock work, maintaining merchandise and work areas, arranging displays, handling returns, and awaiting customer arrivals. Studies indicate that sales personnel may spend only 50 percent of their time actually selling. Consequently, another consideration should be the value of the salesperson's performance in nonselling activities. Regardless of the standards set for evaluating sales performance, it is essential that they are understood clearly by the salesperson so that they are easy to measure and calculate.

### NEW TERMS

| | |
|---|---|
| creative selling | stimulus–response theory |
| order taking | substitute selling |
| personal selling | suggestion selling |
| problem-solving theory | TO (turnover) |
| step theory | trading up |

## CHAPTER HIGHLIGHTS

1  Personal selling can best be explained as the methods used to help customers with their buying problems. The face-to-face nature of the activity distinguishes it from other forms of communication with the consumer.

## Charles Tiffany
## A RETAIL TREND SETTER

Of all the well-known glassware, jewelry, and silver retail firms in this country, Tiffany & Co. is probably the most famous. Catering to the wealthy as well as the middle class, the store, located on Fifth Avenue in New York City, is a major attraction for tourists as well as shoppers.

Started in 1837 by Charles Tiffany and John P. Young, the store originally sold stationery and variety goods. Like so many other retail ventures, this one would have failed but for the determination and energy of its two young owners.

In addition to an uncanny knack for selecting salable merchandise, Tiffany dared to try out new ideas. For example, he marked every piece of merchandise with its selling price—a radical departure from the prevailing practice. He also disproved the contention that women of the time lacked taste by successfully selling a line of Parisian jewelry. This feat convinced Tiffany to discontinue the sale of costume jewelry and carry only genuine goods.

Tiffany's recognition of the importance of publicity involved him with such celebrities as Jenny Lind, the famous Swedish singer; P. T. Barnum, the American showman; and Cyrus W. Field, the American financier who built the first transatlantic telegraph cable. These publicity stunts promoted Tiffany's name worldwide and added enormously to its success.

One of Charles Tiffany's unsuccessful ventures was his attempt to manufacture watches in a factory in Geneva, Switzerland. Because Swiss craftsmen would or could not adapt to assembly line production methods, the factory closed. Nevertheless, Tiffany continued to purchase and sell Swiss watches with great success.

Tiffany's is known for many other exciting possessions and designs, among them the Tiffany diamond (a 128.51-carat gem), the magnificent Mackay silver service, and the famous Tiffany lamps. Today Tiffany's is a far cry from the knickknack store opened in 1837, and Charles Tiffany's genius as a merchant endures in its preeminent position in American retailing.

2  The two basic categories of selling are order taking and creative selling. In general, order taking has little to do with helping customers make buying decisions, whereas creative selling involves the use of selling techniques to help solve customers' problems.

3  The quality of a store's employees affects the extent to which customers patronize the store. Personality factors and appearance influence salesperson–customer relations. Effective salespeople match a customer's needs with the store's merchandise and services.

4  The most commonly cited theories underlying retail selling are the stimulus–response theory, the problem-solving theory, and the step theory.

5 Although different selling techniques are used in retailing, they all involve approaching and greeting the customer, determining needs, showing merchandise, meeting or answering objections, closing the sale, and suggesting additional purchases.

6 Special retail situations may call for substitute selling, trading up, or TO (turning over a customer to another salesperson).

7 Because some situations require more product information, many department stores employ interior designers and decorators to sell outside the store. They visit customers' homes and demonstrate products where they are most likely to be used.

8 Out-of-store, house-to-house sales forces are gaining in popularity because they are convenient and help customers with their buying decisions.

9 Because the quality of retail selling has been criticized, greater attention to training is suggested. Training can increase employee productivity, lead to better morale, reduce employee turnover, and motivate employees to foster good customer relations.

10 The manner in which a salesperson deals with different types of customers can mean the difference between closing or losing a sale.

11 Retail selling entails handling special problems, such as dealing with more than one customer at a time, the parent and child, and the group shopper.

12 Retail training methods include role playing, video cassettes, sales meetings, and seminars.

13 Training for customer service involves checking and calling customers, wrapping packages, handling returns and complaints, and learning about the store.

14 Sources of product information for salespeople include buyers, vendors, labels, catalog descriptions, government standards, private agencies and testing laboratories, and publications and professional organizations.

15 Training programs should include guidelines or standards so that employees know what is expected of them.

## QUESTIONS

1 How can merchants attract high-caliber applicants for retail sales positions?

2 Identify the types of personal selling found in fast-food operations, discount houses, department stores, and exclusive specialty shops.

3 Explain how face-to-face communication affects a store's image. How can the salesperson's personality influence the customer?

4 List and describe the major steps in a retail sale.

5 Part of a salesperson's job is to approach customers promptly in a friendly manner. Cite an example of each of the common types of approaches. When should they be used for maximum effectiveness?

6 How can a salesperson present the following merchandise dramatically: washing machine, fur coat, ski jacket, camera?

7  Explain the usual technique for closing a sale.

8  In addition to increasing a store's sales, how does suggestion selling help the customer?

9  What are some of the dangers of trading up?

10  How can salespeople become product specialists? What information is available to them?

11  How can training increase employee productivity?

12  What are the elements of a good training program?

13  What factors should be considered when evaluating the performance of a salesperson?

# FIELD PROJECTS

1  Take a survey of students in your class who are employed in retail stores as sales help. List the responsibilities they have and indicate what proportion of their time is devoted to stock work, setting up displays, marking, and selling. Develop a chart showing how their time is apportioned among the various aspects of their job and indicate the kinds of stores in which they work. Is there a pattern of greater selling time at stores with more services? Do the employees in the self-service or discount stores in the survey devote any time to selling?

2  Visit one department store, one discount operation, and one supermarket. Try to determine what type of training is used for new employees and for those already on staff. Prepare a checksheet listing the various training methods used, such as role playing, video cassettes, classes, meetings, and so forth. Compare the extent of training in the stores to the level of services offered.

# CASES

1  When the William F. Gable department store, a ninety-six-year-old institution in Altoona, Pennsylvania, was scheduled to go out of business, the city's residents rallied in an attempt to keep the store open.

The store, located in the heart of the downtown shopping district, was closed as part of the bankruptcy proceedings ordered by a federal judge. After the store applied for a going-out-of-business license, many of Altoona's 60,000 residents made it clear that they would fight the decision to close the store.

The executives at the store, as well as city officials, received hundreds of calls from customers complaining about the closing. A number of customers visited the store to pay off their charge account balances early. Multitudes of shoppers, as many as 15,000 a day, poured into the store for the final sale, not only to buy but to complain about the closing.

These actions by Gable's customers created such a stir that the bankruptcy proceedings were reconsidered.

    a  How do you explain the actions of Gable's customers?

    b  What types of selling services do you think Gable's offered? Can you see this happening where you live? Why?

**2**  Push money is commonly used by major stores in the selling of cosmetics. Large manufacturers offer specific dollar amounts to salespeople who sell their product lines aggressively.

Retailers sometimes use push money programs as an added bonus to motivate salespeople to sell slow-moving merchandise. Though many retailers feel that this type of program is effective in encouraging greater merchandise turnover, they sometimes ignore potential problems. Other merchants hesitate to become involved with push money programs because of the problems involved. For example, manufacturers who pay for a program sometimes want a greater say in how the product is sold, displayed, and so on. In addition, salespeople are sometimes pressured into selling one product line at the expense of others.

    a  If you were a retailer, would you use a push money program? Why?

    b  Do you feel that this is an effective way of increasing sales? Explain.

**3**  Retailers at the National Retail Merchants Association session on consumer attitudes were enlightened regarding the sensitivity of the consumer in the 1980s. Lawrence Light, an advertising executive, pointed out that each consumer has several personalities with different buying needs. "Feelings are becoming fashionable again—people want the benefit of old-fashioned values in a new-fashioned world." According to Light, a great passion for *pride* exists among American consumers, and they are willing to pay a premium for things or services that enhance this feeling.

If merchants are to sell effectively, they will have to emphasize pride as well as price; in other words, they must stress value, performance, and quality. Light further suggests that the American consumer seems to be faced with a choice between price and performance, or between convenience and quality. The question is, Why must they choose? The way retailers treat their customers will determine whether or not they will be successful.

Merchants will have to concentrate on respecting customers' feelings in order to enhance their feeling of pride—the commodity the consumer is looking for.

    a  How would you train salespeople to appreciate consumers' feelings?

    b  Do you believe people will pay more for things that give them a feeling of pride? Cite some products or services as examples.

# REFERENCES

Berman, B., and J. R. Evans, *Retail Management: A Strategic Approach* (New York: Macmillan, 1979).

Gillespie, K. R., and J. C. Hecht, *Retail Business Management* (New York: McGraw-Hill, 1977), chap. 27.

Glueck, W. F., *Foundations of Personnel* (Dallas: Business Publications, 1979).

Harrington, M., *The Retail Clerks* (New York: Wiley, 1962).

Hartzler, F. E., *The Retail Salesperson* (New York: McGraw-Hill, 1979).

James, D. L., B. J. Walker, and M. J. Etzel, *Retailing Today* (New York: Harcourt Brace Jovanovich, 1981), chap. 13.

Schnake, M. E., "Performance Evaluation as a Motivating Tool," *Supervisory Management,* July 1978, pp. 29–32.

Shockey, R., "Selling Is a Science!," *Department Store Economist,* 29 (January 1966), p. 40.

Williams, J. R., "President's Letter," *Stores,* 63 (April 1981), p. 64.

Zimmer, A. E., *The Strategy of Successful Retail Salesmanship* (New York: McGraw-Hill, 1966).

# chapter 18
# DISPLAY—VISUAL MERCHANDISING

After completing this chapter, you should be able to:

1. Identify and describe the two main types of display, window and interior.
2. Define and illustrate the differences between promotional and institutional displays.
3. List the basic principles of display and the ways in which they affect sales.
4. Identify the requirements of effective displays.

Display is still one of the most important communication devices available to retail management, and is one type of promotion that no store can do without. From the earliest days of retailing, merchants displayed their wares at fairs, in the marketplace, and even along highways so that passers-by would stop, look, and buy. Merchants, of course, still display their wares, and while more sophisticated display techniques are used today, the objective is still stop, look, and buy.

*A nonpersonal form of selling*

**Displays** are a nonpersonal approach to the selling process. Through the use of windows, signs, and fixtures, the merchant tries to attract attention, create interest and desire, and prompt the shopper to inquire and buy.

As a promotional device, display involves two major categories: window display and interior display. In this chapter we present an overview and some basic principles of display.

# WINDOW DISPLAYS

**Window displays** create the prospective customer's first impression of the store. Since this is so, shops make certain that their displays reflect their merchandise policies and store image. Effective window displays indicate the quality of merchandise handled, price lines, and whether the store is up to date. They add to the prestige of the store by including unusual creations, and generate business in the same way that advertising does. For example, department stores in large cities often design windows that become tourist attractions during holiday seasons, especially the Christmas season.

*Windows are "street theater"*

Henri Bendel, one of New York City's trendier stores, is famous for its inventive windows. When Geraldine Stutz became president of the store, she bought exclusive designs and presented the merchandise as though the store were a stage. Bendel's window displays were hailed as "street theater." One spring, during the Paris showings of fall styles, pictures of the parading models were flashed in disco style on a screen in a window. At another time Bendel promoted lingerie by means of a boudoir murder scene and generated a great deal of publicity. Stutz was quoted as saying, "The store is my theater and my show, and I am the producer and director."

*Windows are traffic builders*

As a selling device, window displays attempt to draw people into a store and can become a round-the-clock sales force. In fact, many retailers consider window display space more valuable than advertising because they are nearer to the point of purchase. In addition, the actual merchandise can be displayed more dramatically through the use of mannequins, lighting, animation, and color. When used properly, window displays help tie in other advertising and promotional efforts. For some small stores, show windows are the chief means of creating traffic.

In recent years the value of store windows has been questioned by some retailers. These merchants consider modern glass fronts, through which passers-by look directly into a store's interior, more valuable than street windows. In these cases the whole store interior becomes part of the "window display." The interaction of customers, merchandise, and salespeople produces a lively setting with lots of movement by day and, if lighted properly, an attention-getting scene at night.

Other positive features of glass fronts are the following.

1  They give the store more selling space.

This glass front allows passers-by and shoppers to view the store's interior.

2 They are easier and less expensive to maintain because they eliminate frequent display changes.

Decline in use of show windows

New approaches to construction in shopping centers have almost eliminated street windows. In these cases the store windows are built to face the inside of a mall or passageway. The store's exterior faces the parking lot and looks more like a warehouse than a store. Despite the waning interest in glass fronts, window shopping is still a popular activity in large cities where streets are known for their collections of unusual stores. These include Fifth Avenue in New York, Michigan Avenue in Chicago, Rodeo Drive in Beverly Hills, and Melrose Avenue in Los Angeles.

Window displays, like advertising, help draw people into the store. The window display should harmonize with the store's merchandising policies so that the store's image is clear in the consumer's mind. The window's selling message should reach passers-by on sight. For example, discounters display a sample of most of their items, with the implied message: "We have what you want at low prices." Supermarkets cover their windows with posters announcing specials—"Come in for bargains." Exclusive stores have windows that contain few items, the message being "This is expensive and unique."

# What Should Be Displayed

The merchandise displayed depends on the purpose of the display

If the purpose of a show window is to get people to stop and look, the window must attract attention to the displayed merchandise. Although an unlimited variety of arrangements are possible, they fall into two main categories: promotional and institutional. **Promotional displays** attempt to sell merchandise directly and dramatically by displaying

1 Products carried by the store, such as store or national brands.
2 Merchandise that requires great effort to be sold within a reasonable time.
3 New lines of merchandise.
4 Fast-selling lines.

A store's image is reflected in its window displays.

5   Special items related to holidays, seasons, and the like.

Windows that sell the store

**Institutional displays** attempt to "sell" the store by building good will. Merchants often permit charities, schools, famous figures, or the arts to become the central themes of their windows. Customers react favorably to retail outlets that show community interest through their involvement in such activities as charity collections. When Lord & Taylor, for example, renovated its Manhattan flagship store, it removed all goods from the display windows and replaced them with large signs reading, "New York, We Love You." As a consequence, the mayor declared a Lord & Taylor's Day in 1976.

# How Much Should Be Displayed

Image quality versus quantity

A major display objective is to be consistent with the store's merchandising policy. For example, too much merchandise in the window creates an impression of low quality; too little creates an air of distinctiveness and high prices. If a store intends to emphasize bargains and appeals to a price-conscious customer, a considerable amount of merchandise may be shown in the window. This creates the impression that the store has almost everything the shopper may want at low prices. As noted previously, discounters display a little of almost all their merchandise, indicating that the goods are available and cheap. On the other hand, if the store's merchandise policy is to appeal to shoppers who are interested in quality, the quantity of merchandise displayed in windows will not be great. Prestige stores have smaller windows and display relatively few items, indicating that they carry expensive merchandise. For a department store with thousands of items and many departments, window treatments generally highlight merchandise in a fashionable way.

*Displaying the merchandise at the right time*

Displays should contain timely, coordinated merchandise that has been advertised in newspapers. Today's displays show related items and take advantage of seasonal events, utilizing thematic presentations such as "Easter Parade," "Back-to-School," and "Mother's Day." In addition, these displays "teach" customers how to put together the "look" of the season. Unusual effects are created through imaginative use of appropriate merchandise, fixtures, and mannequins. Good taste in executing and designing displays adds to the total store image.

This Saks Fifth Avenue institutional display shown in 1981 depicts the charm of a bygone Christmas on New York City's Fifth Avenue.

# Changing Window Displays

It is important for retailers to consider the frequency with which window displays should be changed. Windows can present a negative image if they are changed infrequently or appear outdated. Windows that become stale suggest an inefficient, stagnant business.

*Responsibility for window changes*

Because window dressing is an art, most large stores assign regular staff members to this important aspect of retailing. Sometimes consultants are engaged to provide plans and materials for special occasions. Large stores plan their changes well in advance so that appropriate merchandise can be selected from the various departments. Usually each department is represented in window promotion at one time or another.

In some chain organizations display specialists are based at the central office. They plan and set up window displays, which are photographed for the various stores. The individual outlets reproduce the displays according to detailed instructions.

Small stores often engage the services of freelance display specialists, who come to the store either on a scheduled basis or when called.

J. C. Penney's instructions for a promotional window are clearly spelled out so that the display can be easily duplicated (see below). As you can see, the theme, "Fur You," is developed with a snowstorm window effect, using snowy netting and snow floor covering as props.

*Guidelines for changing windows*

There are guidelines which retailers can use to determine how often they should change their windows.

Good fakes and the genuine article keep out the cold in the poshest possible way, and have a special gift appeal at Christmas. Jackets and full length coats are available in a variety of styles, from sporty to glamourous. Many have this year's wrap belt treatments.

**window**

Create the snow storm window with supplementals #628 (snowy netting) and #634 (snow floor covering). Add mannequin cards and sign theme with white slant back letters.

For interior mannequin presentation, show one jacket style along with one full coat style. Highlight display with the poinsettia supplemental.
**lot numbers: 3907, 3906**

J. C. Penney's instructions make it easy to duplicate promotional windows throughout the chain.

1 **The location and size of the store.** When the same people pass the store frequently, it is wise to change the windows often so that passers-by see a variety of merchandise and paying attention to the window becomes a habit.

2 **The pedestrian traffic.** Stores located in large cities are generally exposed to a variety of pedestrians. In these instances a display has a longer "life." Many large stores located in cities change their windows as often as twice a week. Others change them once a week. The value of window displays to the retailer is realized by frequent changes. Small stores should change their displays more often than stores in regional shopping centers because they probably experience the same pedestrian traffic repeatedly. Though changing merchandise displays at least once every two weeks is wise, too many small merchants neglect to do so. Streets & Co., for example, finds that windows need to be changed completely every other week.

3 **The types of goods sold.** Fashion merchandise is considered "perishable," and displays of such goods should be changed often. Because fashion-conscious customers are interested in new and different items, styles that are displayed too long become "stale" and lose their appeal. Furniture and hardware displays, on the other hand, are changed less frequently.

# Planning Window Displays

Planning allows the retailer to coordinate window displays with other promotional activities. For example, if it is determined that merchandise that is featured in advertising should also be displayed in the window, advance planning is vital. The main considerations for such planning are as follows.

1 Determine policy regarding the relationship between newspaper advertising and the merchandise to be displayed.

2 Determine policy regarding price tags and printed messages in the window.

3 Determine policy with regard to the use of manufacturer displays. While vendor-supplied materials can be helpful to small merchants, they should be selected to tie in with store image.

4 Determine the frequency of window changes so that displays that should remain longer will have the proper time allotted to them.

Planning should consider departments' needs

5 Schedule window displays in larger stores to give the various departments proper representation.

6 Determine policy with regard to informing salespeople about displayed merchandise. Too often salespeople are not aware of what is "advertised" in the store's windows.

In addition to the considerations just noted, Figure 18-1 lists the guidelines for window displays suggested by the U.S. Small Business Administration.

### I. MERCHANDISE SELECTED

1 Is the merchandise timely?

2 Is it representative of the stock assortment?

3 Are the articles harmonious—in type, color, texture, and use?

4 Are the price lines of the merchandise suited to the interests of passers-by?

5 Is the quantity on display suitable (that is, neither overcrowded nor sparse)?

### II. SETTING

1 Are glass, floor, props, and merchandise clean?

2 Is the lighting adequate (so that reflection from the street is avoided)?

3 Are spotlights used to highlight certain parts of the display?

4 Is every piece of merchandise carefully draped, pinned, or arranged?

5 Is the background suitable, enhancing the merchandise?

6 Are the props well suited to the merchandise?

7 Are window cards used, and are they neat and well placed?

8 Is the entire composition balanced?

9 Does the composition suggest rhythm and movement?

### III. SELLING POWER

1 Does the window present a readily recognized central theme?

2 Does the window exhibit have power to stop passers-by through the dramatic use of light, color, size, motion, composition, and/or item selection?

3 Does the window arouse a desire to buy (as measured by shoppers entering the store)?

**FIGURE 18-1**

Guidelines for a window display. (U.S. Small Business Administration, *Small Store Planning for Growth*, 2nd ed., Small Business Management Series, no. 33, Washington, D.C., U.S. Government Printing Office, 1977, p. 77.)

# INTERIOR DISPLAYS

When customers enter a store, they expect the displays and departments to reflect the store's image. In addition to the decor and furnishings, the general tone or atmosphere of the store is set by the merchandise arrangements, displays, and fixtures. While **interior displays** can take a variety of forms, depending on the merchandise carried and the store's image, the entire interior should be considered from the point of view of promoting sales.

*Self-service increases the importance of interior displays*

Though the value of window displays has been questioned by some retailers, interior displays have become more important with the growth of self-service. In stores where self-service is the key factor in sales, it is the interior display that has to "sell" the merchandise. Good displays are very effective in creating product awareness and stim-

Then and now, interior displays set the tone for the promotion of sales.

ulating unplanned purchases (impulse buying). In these cases interior displays rely on the use of descriptive signs and informative labels to encourage customers to try a product. The arrangement of merchandise requires the display of related product lines in settings that interest the customer. For maximum success, supermarkets, variety stores, drugstores, and hardware stores generally coordinate their displays with their advertising.

Interior displays can be classified in two main categories: **merchandise displays** and vendor or store **point-of-purchase (p-o-p) displays.**

## Merchandise Displays

Merchandise displays are of several types.

- **Open displays** are shown on tables, carts, and baskets. These displays are designed to make the merchandise accessible to the customer by allowing handling

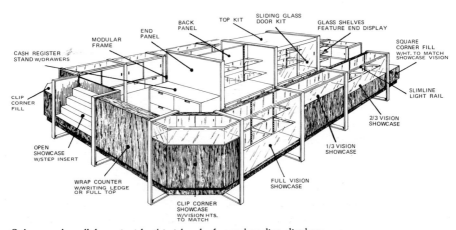

Salespeople sell from inside this island of merchandise displays.

of the products. Sometimes the merchandise is heaped in a pile without any real order (**dump display**). The psychological effect is that the items are available at bargain prices.

- **Closed displays** contain more valuable items like jewelry, cameras, silver, and antiques. The products are behind glass and may be handled only by a salesperson.
- **End-aisle displays** are placed in vacant areas at the ends of aisles in supermarkets, variety stores, and the like, and generally carry advertised specials.
- **Related-merchandise displays,** found in such stores as supermarkets and drugstores, contain arrangements with matching products (e.g., cheese and crackers, pasta and sauces).
- **Area displays** are set up for special lifestyle merchandising or long-term displays such as model rooms in a furniture department or sports equipment (with related clothing) on a seasonal basis. The latter may include ski equipment and clothes for winter, tennis accessories and clothes for spring and summer, and so forth.
- **Special-event displays** are used by department stores and mass merchandisers for thematic storewide promotions. For example, a department store promotion of items imported from China might feature Chinese wares throughout the store, from clothing to gift items, while a supermarket might carry "health foods" in every department.

Related-merchandise displays are effective with sports equipment.

In this theme display, the natural straw products create a mood for shopping

- **Checkout counter displays** are the last opportunity to communicate with shoppers. These up-front displays always feature "impulse items" close to the cashier and usually contain things like magazines, candy, and cigarettes.
- **Assortment displays** show a complete line of merchandise in depth, including colors, sizes, styles, and prices. The advantages of assortment displays are that they enable customers to help themselves and to make selections quickly.
- **Theme displays** are designed around an idea, such as "Back to School" and "Hunting Season On." The theme should stimulate the interest of consumers.
- **Ensemble displays** are those in which the item to be promoted is combined with related merchandise for a complete effect. For example, swimsuits shown in an ensemble display can be combined with robes, slippers, beach hats, and the like.

# Point-of-Purchase Displays

P-O-P displays are sponsored by vendors

In-store displays are planned to stimulate customers to buy or to inquire about a product. They encourage unplanned purchases and are largely decorative. Many of these displays are supplied by manufacturers and are a key element of sales promotion.

Point-of-purchase (P-O-P) displays are structures or devices that are used in, on, or adjacent to any point of sale. They are usually planned by manufacturers to increase sales of their products at the store. The following are examples of the most commonly used P-O-P displays.

- **On-the-shelf displays** utilize shelf space as the basis for displaying merchandise. Included in this group are "shelf talkers," dividers, and extenders. Shelf talkers provide an on-the-spot communication utilizing signs like SPECIAL, LOW PRICE, or TODAY ONLY. Dividers are constructed so that when they are placed on a shelf the products are displayed at a favorable angle. Extenders are secured at the ends of shelves to create more space.

- **Mobiles** are displays hung from beams on the ceiling. As the name implies, they move and attract attention.
- **Cut-case displays** are packing boxes that are really self-contained displays. By means of cutting and folding, these cases are easily converted into display units. Retailers appreciate them because they can be displayed immediately, do not require shelf space, and provide a colorful display of the product.
- **Catchall displays** are large containers, such as barrels, baskets, and carts, that hold large quantities of one kind of merchandise. The careless manner in which the merchandise is "dumped" into the container implies that it is a bargain. These units are generally displayed in food, drug, and discount houses.
- **Display stands** are a more permanent kind of self-service display that carry such items as paperback books. They come in various heights and are often made so that they can be rotated by the customer. Retailers like these displays because they are attractive, store a great deal of merchandise, and occupy little space. Furthermore, they often help the retailer convert unused space into a profitable merchandising area.
- **Counter displays** are used in areas where it is easy to sell related merchandise. The more elaborate ones are used in department stores and specialty shops to "suggest" additional items, for example, on counters where costume jewelry is sold. In other areas a counter display may be a simple poster at a checkout counter where impulse items are sold.

P-O-P displays are tied to store image

P-O-P materials are used a good deal with other sales aids, such as coupons, to generate excitement about a product. Because such materials have been so successful, merchants should find out what P-O-P material is available from their suppliers. Manufacturers are more than eager to supply these displays because they mean more sales. Nevertheless, it is important for the merchant to evaluate the use of these displays in terms of store image. Other considerations are the amount of selling space they occupy relative to sales and the cost in terms of lighting needs.

The P-O-P counter display reminds customers of products they might need or want.

# Responsibility for Display

In small stores, the responsibility for displays generally lies with the owner or an assistant. In department stores, the responsibility may rest with the display manager, who, in turn, is supervised by the sales promotion director. In some cases stores have resident window display directors as well as interior display directors. Display personnel, also known as dressers or trimmers, have workshops in the store in which they plan and construct in-store displays. They generally have a stock of fixtures and mannequins as well as appropriate background props. In addition, there are many kinds of shelving, brackets, and display holders that can be used. A creative display artist looks for unique items like an old ship's wheel, a Chinese screen, or a fisherman's net.

Many of the large retail chains distribute detailed display information to their individual branches or stores. Displays are planned, photographed, and diagramed for the

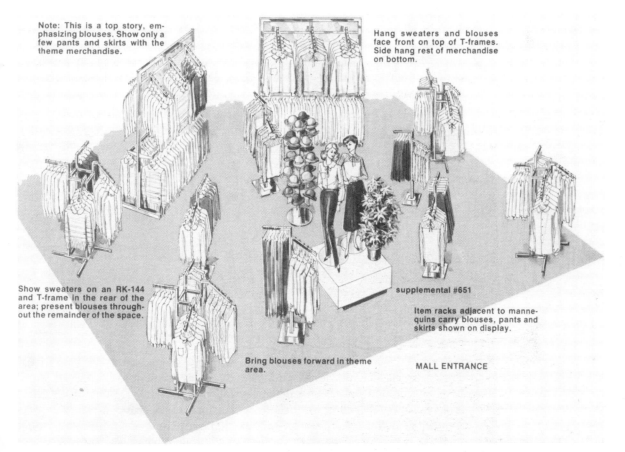

Note: This is a top story, emphasizing blouses. Show only a few pants and skirts with the theme merchandise.

Hang sweaters and blouses face front on top of T-frames. Side hang rest of merchandise on bottom.

Show sweaters on an RK-144 and T-frame in the rear of the area; present blouses throughout the remainder of the space.

supplemental #651

Item racks adjacent to mannequins carry blouses, pants and skirts shown on display.

Bring blouses forward in theme area.

MALL ENTRANCE

**FIGURE 18-2**
Instructions for a store entrance in a mall, illustrating display racks, mannequins, and merchandise. (Reproduced by permission of J. C. Penney.)

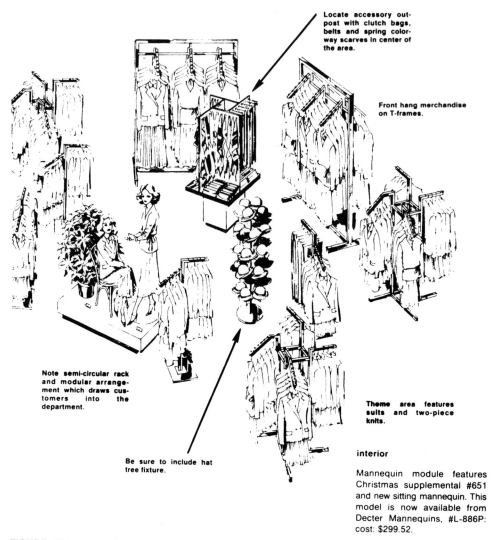

Locate accessory out-post with clutch bags, belts and spring color-way scarves in center of the area.

Front hang merchandise on T-frames.

Note semi-circular rack and modular arrange-ment which draws cus-tomers into the department.

Be sure to include hat tree fixture.

Theme area features suits and two-piece knits.

interior

Mannequin module features Christmas supplemental #651 and new sitting mannequin. This model is now available from Decter Mannequins, #L-886P: cost: $299.52.

**FIGURE 18-3**

Instructions for the layout of a store interior. (Reproduced by permission of J. C. Penney.)

individual stores. This reduces the cost of large display staffs and saves time in the execution of displays. Complete instructions and layouts are sent to the general mer-chandise manager, the buyer, and the presentation supervisor. Figures 18-2, 18-3, 18-4, and 18-5 show diagrams, instructions, and fixtures for effective displays.

Some chain stores have crews of window trimmers who travel from one location to another. In these cases the central office usually coordinates all the materials in advance so as to provide directions to the various outlets. Some large chains hire outside consultants and agencies.

Very often supermarket chains give store managers detailed plans showing exactly where each product belongs on the shelf. The most profitable and fastest-moving items

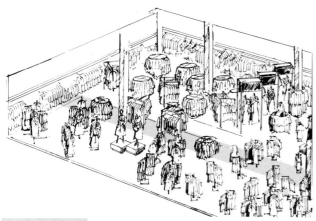

## interior aisles

Interior aisles play an important role in outerwear, as in all other fashion departments:

- department store image
- easy for the customer to shop
- make a clear passage for rolling racks, as well as customers

**Interior aisles** are particularly important for **deep departments, breaking up** the **wide** expanse of **carpet** and **allowing more merchandise exposure.**

| OUTERWEAR | DRESSES | LARGE SIZES | MISSES SPORTSWEAR |
|---|---|---|---|
| | | | |

MAIN AISLE

### the aisle story

**create departments in the children's area**

- Using aisles in the children's area provides maximum customer exposure for all age groups.
- Utilize fashion racks (4-way, item, tri-circle) in the forward section of each area, creating "windows-on-the-aisles."
- Highlight each department with a coordinated mannequin display.

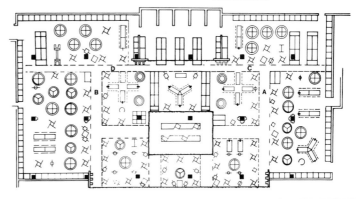

aisle leading to boys' pre-school area          aisle leading to girls' pre-school area

**FIGURE 18-4**

Instructions for arranging interior aisles; creating departments by using aisles, racks, and mannequins; and using fixtures and racks to group outerwear. (Reproduced by permission of J. C. Penney.)

## fixtures

R-967A

RK-137

DC-241

DC-274

metro stores/issued march '80   outerwear   page 7

## avoid

• merchandising both half and petite sizes on one rack, as it can be misleading and very difficult for the customer to shop.

**FIGURE 18-5**

How to display merchandise and what arrangements to avoid. The correct fixtures to use are indicated clearly. (Reproduced by permission of J. C. Penney Company.)

are placed at eye level to make them easy for shoppers to reach. Studies indicate that more products are picked up from eye-level shelves than from any other type of shelf. It is not by chance, then, that the most popular brands of soap and expensive cheeses are usually displayed at eye level.

Figure 18-6 contains guidelines for interior arrangement and display.

---

### I.  LAYOUT

**1** Are your fixtures low enough and signs so placed that the customer can get a bird's-eye view of the store and tell in what direction to go for wanted goods?

**2** Do your aisle and counter arrangements tend to stimulate a circular traffic flow through the store?

**3** Do your fixtures (and their arrangement), signs, lettering, and colors all create a coordinated and unified effect?

**4** Before any supplier's fixtures are accepted, do you make sure they conform in color and design to what you already have?

**5** Do you limit the use of hanging signs to special sale events?

**6** Are your counters and aisle tables *not* overcrowded with merchandise?

**7** Are your ledges and cashier/wrapping stations kept free of boxes, unneeded wrapping materials, personal effects, and odds and ends?

**8** Do you keep trash bins out of sight?

## II. MERCHANDISE EMPHASIS

1 Do your signs referring to specific goods tell the customer something significant about them, rather than simply naming the products and their prices?

2 For your advertised goods, do you have prominent signs, including tear sheets at the entrances, to inform and guide customers to their exact location in the store?

3 Do you prominently display both advertised and nonadvertised specials at the ends of counters as well as at the point of sale?

4 Are both your national and private brands highlighted in your arrangement and window display?

5 Wherever feasible, do you give the more colorful merchandise in your stock preference in display?

6 In the case of apparel and home furnishings, do the items that reflect your store's fashion sense or fashion leadership get special display attention at all times?

7 In locating merchandise in your store, do you always consider the productivity of space—vertical as well as horizontal?

8 Is your self-service merchandise arranged so as to attract the customer and assist in selection by the means indicated below?

   **a** Is each category grouped under a separate sign?

   **b** Is the merchandise in each category arranged according to its most significant characteristic—whether color, style, size, or price?

   **c** In apparel categories, is the merchandise arranged by price lines or zones to assist the customer to make a selection quickly?

   **d** Is horizontal space usually devoted to different items and styles within a category (vertical space being used for different sizes—smallest at the top, largest at the bottom)?

   **e** Are impulse items interspersed with demand items and *not* placed across the aisle from them, where many customers will not see them?

9 Do you plan your windows and displays in advance?

10 Do you meet with your sales force after windows are trimmed to discuss the items displayed?

11 Do you use seasonal, monthly, and weekly plans for interior and window displays, determining the fixtures to be used and merchandise to be displayed?

12 Do your displays reflect the image of your store?

13 Do you budget the dollars you will set aside for fixtures and props to be used in your displays, as well as the expense of setting them up and maintaining them?

14 Do you keep your fixtures and windows clean and dust free?

15 Do you replace burned-out light bulbs immediately?

16 Do you take safety precautions in setting up your fixtures?

17 Do garments fit properly on mannequins and fixtures?

FIGURE 18-6

Guidelines for interior arrangement and display. (U.S. Small Business Administration, *Small Store Planning for Growth*, 2nd ed., Small Business Management Series, no. 33, Washington, D.C., U.S. Government Printing Office, 1977, pp. 101–102.)

**NEW TERMS**

area display
assortment display
catchall display
checkout counter display
closed display
counter display
cut-case display
display
display stand
dump display
end aisle display
ensemble display

institutional display
interior display
merchandise display
mobile
on-the-shelf display
open display
point-of-purchase (P-O-P) display
promotional display
related-merchandise display
special-event display
theme display
window display

# CHAPTER HIGHLIGHTS

1 Display is a nonpersonal approach to the selling process. Through the use of windows, signs, and fixtures, the retailer attempts to attract attention, create interest, stimulate desire, and prompt the shopper to buy.

2 As a promotional device, display involves two major categories: window display and interior display.

3 Window displays are a reflection of the store, including its merchandise, policies, and image. They are generally planned to promote specific merchandise or the store itself.

4 As a selling device, window displays draw people into a store and are considered by some retailers to be more valuable than advertising.

5 In recent years many retailers have switched from street windows to modern glass fronts. These retailers feel that it is valuable for potential customers to see movement inside the store.

6 Because window dressing is an art, most large stores have regular staff assigned to plan and execute their displays.

7 Displays should be attractive, imaginative, and timely, and should be changed frequently.

8 Manufacturers frequently supply retailers with display materials. Retailers must select those that tie in with the merchandise and services offered by the store.

9 Some vendor displays, such as shelf talkers, dividers, and extenders, help retailers get the most mileage out of their shelf space. In addition, display stands enable retailers to convert unused floor space into profitable merchandising areas.

10 The responsibility for display varies with different types of retailers. Some stores have resident display staffs and in-house workshops, while others use consultants. Some chains have floating crews that travel from one unit to another, while others plan and design displays in the central office. Under these conditions detailed layouts and photographs are distributed to the individual stores for execution.

# QUESTIONS

1 Where can one still see merchants displaying their wares as they did in the early days of retailing?

2 Why is display considered to be nonpersonal?

3 How does window display affect store image? How do retailers communicate whether theirs are low- or high-price stores?

4 Explain the statement, "Window displays play a similar role to advertising." Why do some retailers consider window displays more valuable than advertising?

5 How can retailers use displays to communicate the types of merchandise and services they offer?

6 In light of the increase in self-service shopping, what type of display would be effective for a new line of cosmetics targeted to the 18–25 age range?

7 What are the basic considerations for creating an effective display?

8 How have stores changed their merchandise presentations and layouts to allow customers to help themselves?

9 What factors should the retailer consider before using vendor displays?

10 How do P-O-P displays help the retailer?

11 Explain how centralized planning for displays is carried out in a chain's local units.

# FIELD PROJECTS

1 Evaluating a store window
Select any retail store with which you are familiar and describe the store, its location, the type of merchandise carried, and its clientele.
   a Is the window display in keeping with the store image?
   b Describe or sketch the window display and list the types of merchandise used.
   c Evaluate the display and its contents in terms of stopping power, holding power, and selling power by answering the following questions.

|  |  |  | Yes | No |
|---|---|---|---|---|
| Stopping power | (Attention) | Would you stop and look at this window? | | |
| | | Did it attract your attention? | | |
| Holding power | (Interest) | Does it hold your attention and stimulate interest in reading the signs or descriptive material? | | |
| | | Are you tempted to investigate further? | | |
| Selling power | (Desire) (Action) | Is the display exciting enough so that you imagine owning any of the merchandise? | | |

> Are you prompted to further examine the merchandise?
>
> Would you consider going into the store to see, touch, or try on any of the products?

Do you feel that this display could be improved? Explain.

2 Compare a discount operation with a department store and evaluate the different interior displays listed here. (Select displays showing the same kind of merchandise.)

floor displays
aisle displays
counter displays
wall displays

# CASES

1 Manufacturers often approach small stores, particularly in the food and drug lines, with offers of display assistance. The display service supplied by a manufacturer may be the entire window display or material to be used as part of a display. When complete windows are offered, they generally feature only the manufacturer's merchandise.

The ABC Drug Store has been offered the services of a manufacturer's display specialist plus a complete window trim utilizing the manufacturer's product line. Mr. Morgan, the senior partner, is sold on the product and likes the idea of promoting it. In addition, he sees it as an easy way of getting a free window display. The younger partner, Mr. Strong, does not want to go along with the display because the product is not a major line in the store. Furthermore, he feels that such a promotional effort and display space are not justified for a product that has not been a major profit producer.

a Do you agree with Morgan or Strong? Why?
b What are the possible advantages to the manufacturer if ABC Drug Store goes ahead with the display?
c In the event that the store decides against this plan, what are some of the alternatives that might be suggested to the manufacturer?

2 A change in strategy for merchandise presentation was suggested at the 1981 meeting of the National Retail Merchants Association. A shift away from "lifestyle" merchandising and back to classification presentation, resulting in the separation of merchandise by price line categories (e.g., budget, moderate, and better), was recommended.

According to Lasker Meyer, chairman of Abraham & Straus, there has been an overemphasis on lifestyle merchandising and a tendency to separate departments by vendor. Often four or five departments carry similar merchandise. Meyer recommends pulling these items together in order to eliminate duplicate merchandise as well as help customers locate goods more easily. He maintains that contemporary or lifestyle departments have invariably shown lower profits than classification departments. Also since there has been a noticeable decline in the number of salespeople in major stores, store layouts and merchandise displays require adjustments to allow customers to help themselves.

    **a** Lifestyle merchandising separates departments because it is intended to present merchandise as it relates to the customer's lifestyle. Displays are developed with merchandise brought together from all areas of the store. The range of merchandise thus is narrowed for one particular lifestyle and the merchandise is grouped and displayed as the customer would buy it. Meyer suggests a change back to a traditional way of grouping goods. How do you think his suggestion might affect the display of merchandise?

    **b** What types of displays would you suggest that stores use to present merchandise in depth and for greater self-service?

**3**   Supermarkets are experimenting with the positioning of products to maximize purchases by shoppers of both sexes. The most profitable and fastest-moving products are placed at eye level to make them easy for shoppers to reach. Studies indicate that more items are picked from eye-level shelves than from any others. Because of this, supermarkets and food stores generally display popular brands of detergents, expensive gourmet foods, and imported cheeses at eye level.

Supermarket professionals have some difficulty deciding what should be considered eye-level shelving. The eye-level shelf has traditionally been slightly under five feet from the floor, which is the right height for the average female shopper (5'4"). However, supermarket studies indicate that more men are shopping than ever before. In one recent study, men did the family food shopping in almost 30 percent of the households. This is not surprising, considering that more than half of the adult women in the United States work all or part of each day.

Since the average male shopper is about 5 feet 10 inches tall, to accommodate males an eye-level shelf would need to be higher than the former standard. The shift in shopping practices has caused planners of supermarket chains to reconsider display positions for many products. One supermarket professional said, "This problem is driving us mad. We have changed the position of Best crackers five times this month, and we still can't figure out where to put them."

Even though the majority of shoppers are women, men almost make up for the difference by making a greater number of impulse purchases. Generally speaking, when a woman goes to a supermarket for a few items, she usually ends up buying eight or ten. On the other hand, a man usually walks out of the store with twice as many impulse purchases. This may be so because men use shopping lists less than half as often as women.

It is easy to see why supermarket planners are anxious to display popular foods on the shelves that will catch the eyes of "impulsive male shoppers." At the same time, however, they do not want to place those products out of reach of female shoppers.

    **a** What suggestions do you have for eye-level displays in supermarkets?

    **b** Should displays be geared to men and women separately? What types of displays do you recommend?

# REFERENCES

Curhan, R. C., "The Relationship Between Shelf Space and Unit Sales in Supermarkets," *Journal of Marketing Research,* 9 (November 1972), pp. 406–412.

Fuda, G. E., and E. L. Nelson, *The Display Specialist* (New York: McGraw-Hill, 1976).

Hayett, W., *Display and Exhibit Handbook* (New York: Reinhold, 1967).

"How to Make Displays More Sales Productive," *Progressive Grocer,* 50 (February 1971), p. 38.

Jacobs, L. W., "The Continuity Factor in Retail Store Display," *Journal of the Academy of Marketing Science,* 2 (Spring 1974), pp. 340–350.

Joel, S., *Fairchild's Book of Window Display* (New York: Fairchild, 1973).

Kennedy, J. R., "The Effect of Display Location on the Sales and Pilferage of Cigarettes," *Journal of Marketing Research,* 70 (May 1970), pp. 210–215.

"Let It All Hang Out," *Retail Directions,* 129 (January-February 1975), p. 29.

Mickel, L., and K. Kaspar, *International Window Display* (New York: Praeger, 1966).

"Window Shoppers," *Retail Directions,* 127 (January 1973), pp. 30–31.

# chapter 19
# ADVERTISING

After completing this chapter, you should be able to:

1 Define advertising and identify the types of advertising used by retailers.
2 Discuss the importance of the advertising plan and the setting of objectives.
3 Discuss the importance of the advertising budget and how it is used.
4 List and explain the advantages and disadvantages to the retailer of the following media: newspapers, magazines, radio, television, direct mail, outdoor, transit.
5 Explain how retailers evaluate the impact and value of their advertising efforts.

Advertising was used as a sales message

Throughout history retailers have advertised in order to increase sales and store traffic. After the Civil War, merchants concentrated on the use of advertising to bring in the local trade. By the 1880s and 1890s, both local and national media were experiencing tremendous growth because of retail advertising.

Marshall Field's approach was expressed by the slogans, "Give the lady what she wants" and "The customer is always right." The Wanamaker company advertised that it consistently followed "the golden rule of business," and John Wanamaker became identified with business virtues more than other merchants. When the Wanamaker's men's and boy's shop opened in Philadelphia, practically all of the first day's sales receipts ($24.67) were invested in advertising; a mere 67 cents was left in the cash drawer for change. From then on, the ads never stopped. In 1865 John Wanamaker became the first retailer to run a full-page newspaper spread announcing a money-back guarantee—writing most of the copy himself. In 1875 he advertised the opening of the Wanamaker Grand Depot so extensively that 70,000 people swarmed into the store on the first day.

A large part of Macy's success is credited to aggressive pricing policies that became well known because of advertising. The store's first single-price ad appeared in 1851.

Another term for low prices

Huntington Hartford and George Gilman, the founders of A&P, advertised their imported tea at "**cargo prices.**"[1] They had these ads printed in circulars and then through newspapers and the mail. They, too, offered money-back guarantees and became known for low prices. Advertised "cargo prices" became synonymous with discounting or lower prices.

## ADVERTISING DEFINED

In today's market merchants are still trying to increase their customer base and to attract as many people as possible. They attempt to do this through daily use of **advertising.** The primary function of retail advertising is to draw consumers into the store. The American Marketing Association defines advertising as "any paid form of nonpersonal presentation and promotion of ideas, goods, or services by an identified sponsor." The important terms are

- **Paid form** The retailer pays for the message so that it will be read in newspapers, magazines, etc.; viewed on television, movie screens, etc.; or listened to on the radio and other broadcast devices. The advertiser–retailer controls the placement and content of the message.
- **Nonpersonal** There is no face-to-face communication as in a salesperson–customer transaction. The selling message is communicated through newspapers, radio, television, and other media.
- **Identified sponsor** The name and location of the business or person paying for the advertisement are included.

[1]The genesis of the A&P chain was the buying of clipper ship cargoes of tea and reselling them at low or cargo prices.

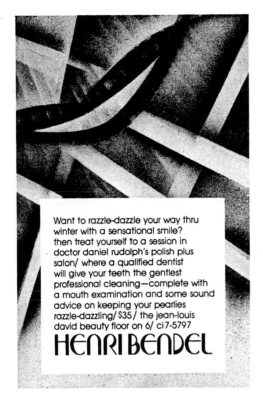

Want to razzle-dazzle your way thru winter with a sensational smile? then treat yourself to a session in doctor daniel rudolph's polish plus salon/ where a qualified dentist will give your teeth the gentlest professional cleaning—complete with a mouth examination and some sound advice on keeping your pearlies razzle-dazzling/ $35/ the jean-louis david beauty floor on 6/ ci 7-5797

## HENRI BENDEL

This unusual ad is an attempt to broaden the store's customer base.

# KINDS OF RETAIL ADVERTISING

*The primary function of advertising is to bring customers to a store*

Retailers use different kinds of advertising to attract attention to their store, services, and merchandise. These include institutional, promotional, combination, and cooperative advertising.

## Institutional Advertising

**Institutional advertising** attempts to convey an idea about the store. Basically, it is designed to "sell" the entire concept of the store and its image rather than a particular type of merchandise. In fact, some marketers refer to it as image advertising.

*Some ads sell the store*

When retailers advertise "institutionally" they aim for long-range sales results as opposed to direct sales action. These advertisements concentrate on building the reputation of the store, focusing on unique qualities and services. They help create customer confidence in the store. While some advertisements attempt to build an image of fashion leadership, others stress unique services. In either case, marketing the total store is as important as advertising certain items. For example, during the Bicentennial celebration

The year was 1930
and we came to Ardmore

With the kind of insight...some said daring...that has been our style
since 1868, we built a superb art deco building and created our own
kind of department store shopping on the Main Line.
This first branch store survived the depression, thrived mightily,
became an Ardmore institution. And the Strawbridge & Clothier
experience prevailed. Shopping in our family-managed, independent
department store remains and will remain an unique pleasure, one
rarely enjoyed in this world of conglomerates and takeovers.

The year is 1980
and the future is exciting

The Ardmore store will be refurbished in keeping with the new
vitality of Suburban Square. We will be placing our merchandise
emphasis on classic Main Line shopping preferences, relating
even more closely to the way you are, the way you live.
One thing will not change. The personal commitment of our
store family to the people of the Main Line is as old-fashioned
as it ever was. In celebrating our first 50 years, we embrace
with high excitement the promise of the next fifty.

Strawbridge & Clothier      Strawbridge & Clothier

This Strawbridge & Clothier institutional ad strengthens the store's image with customers in Philadelphia and the surrounding communities.

Dayton's paid tribute to famous Americans in a series of institutional ads. These personalities were quoted in messages that were relevant to life in the United States. A patriotic gesture like this creates good will toward the store.

## Promotional Advertising

Day-to-day advertising

**Promotional advertising** is routine advertising that attempts to sell specific items or services and is designed to bring customers to a store for immediate action. It is the type of advertisement that retailers depend on for their day-to-day traffic and sales.

The bulk of retail advertising is promotional in nature. This category includes advertisements for specific items, special sales, special events, and new items and services.

## Combination Advertising

As the name implies, **combination advertising** combines the functions of promotional and institutional advertising. It advertises a specific item or service for immediate results and builds a favorable image of the store as well. For example, one hardware store advertised air conditioners and fans. The same ad included a list of hints about saving energy and staying cool.

Filene's developed a series of combination ads that were most effective. For a set of apparel ads it used a format highlighting important fashion stories. At the top of the advertisement was a human-interest story about why Filene's is considered progressive and innovative. As an illustration, one ad indicated that Filene's was "the first store to have a zoo on the roof." (At the top was a picture of the Filene zoo, and part of the ad showed children's fashions.) Another read, "In 1913 Filene's opened Boston's first commercial wireless station." These ads demonstrate how combination advertising can sell specific merchandise and the store simultaneously. Combined promotional and institutional advertising has become very popular and appears to be on the rise.

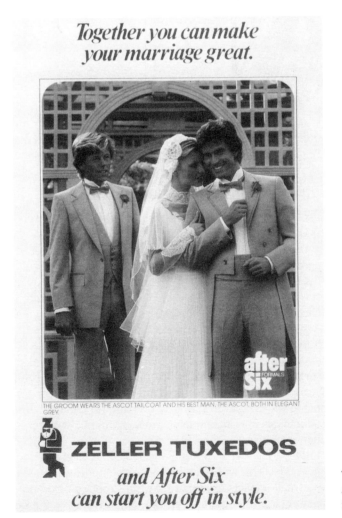

*Together you can make your marriage great.*

THE GROOM WEARS THE ASCOT TAILCOAT AND HIS BEST MAN, THE ASCOT, BOTH IN ELEGANT GREY.

**ZELLER TUXEDOS**
*and After Six can start you off in style.*

This promotional ad is an example of cooperative advertising.

This combination ad is selling apparel by using a human interest story.

## Cooperative Advertising

Shared costs of advertising

When retailers share the costs of advertising with manufacturers, suppliers, or other merchants, it is known as **cooperative advertising** (see Figure 19-1 and Appendix). Such ads can be arranged either vertically or horizontally. Under a vertical cooperative-advertising agreement, manufacturers or suppliers pay part of the costs for featuring specified items or brands. Retailers are reimbursed after the ads have been printed or aired. Invoices or documents from the media, such as **tear sheets** (advertising cutouts), are required to substantiate the publication of the advertisements. In some cases the manufacturer supplies a variety of aids to the retailer, such as completed art work and advertising copy containing open space for the retailer's name.

Horizontal arrangements increase traffic and product demand

In a horizontal cooperative-advertising agreement, several retailers sponsor and pay for the costs of advertising to increase traffic to an area or increase the demand for a product. Groups of merchants in shopping centers often sponsor ads jointly in order to draw people to the center. To stimulate demand for certain items, merchants carrying the same product lines in noncompeting areas frequently sponsor ads jointly in order to spread product awareness.

Robinson-Patman Act treats small buyers in the same way as large buyers

It is estimated that over $4 billion is available to retailers for cooperative advertising, and that another $1 billion of available cooperative funds goes unused. This is so mainly because many small retailers are unaware of this money or do not know how to apply for it. Manufacturers push large retailers into joint advertising but do not do so for small merchants, partly because it is more costly to administer cooperative advertising pro-

Cooperative advertising is intended to help promote the sale of ABC merchandise. It is available to all ABC dealers. ABC will pay 50 percent of dealer advertising provided that the ads meet the following qualifications:

1. The only approved media are newspapers, including school and college papers, and radio.
2. Newspaper advertisements must be at least 400 agate lines.
3. The ABC name, and in printed matter the ABC logo, must be featured.
4. Advertisements must not include competitive merchandise.
5. Only first-quality merchandise is to be advertised. No closeouts or irregulars.
6. All claims must be submitted within 60 days of the ad date. Payment will be made by check upon submission of claim with full newspaper tear page and necessary rate data, or in the case of radio with rate data and copy of text along with copy of station invoice to:

> ABC Co-Op
> The Advertising Checking Bureau
> P.O. Box 000
> Memphis, Tennessee

DO NOT DEDUCT AD CHARGES FROM REMITTANCES FOR MERCHANDISE.

7. Any advertisement or series of advertisements that results in an advertising expense substantially higher than a normal percentage of advertising cost to sales volume is inconsistent with the intent of this plan. ABC shall be the sole judge as to whether any advertising cost is excessive and may at its discretion reject such ad(s). ABC reserves the right to withdraw this plan without notice.

FIGURE 19-1

An example of a cooperative-advertising agreement.

grams when many small merchants are involved. However, the Robinson-Patman Act requires sellers to give the same allowance for promotion to all buyers on a "proportionately equal basis." Therefore, if a seller gives a large department store chain a 5 percent advertising allowance, all other buyers (large and small) are entitled to the same arrangement.

It is predicted that cooperative advertising in local media will increase for several reasons. First, the cost of advertising can probably be reduced for small retailers. Second, many newspapers and radio stations have added staff members to coordinate cooperative-advertising funds. In this way small retailers will have help in finding and using money for advertising.

Retailers must look at the total picture before they join a cooperative-advertising venture. Listed here are some of the important advantages and disadvantages of such ventures.

### Advantages

* Cooperative advertising reduces costs.
* It provides small retailers with professional ads.
* It helps small stores build a prestige image.

- It increases bargaining power with media because of greater quantity.
- It communicates store message to a greater number of prospects.
- It promotes a positive relationship between suppliers and merchants.

### Disadvantages

*Cooperative advertising is not feasible for all retailers*

- There is less control and flexibility.
- Ads prepared for national coverage may not fit local situations.
- Ads may not fit a store's image.
- Reimbursement is not immediate; the retailer must submit media invoices to suppliers.
- The program may require additional investment in merchandise.

# THE ADVERTISING PLAN

Retailers that conduct advertising programs must consider what they want to accomplish, how much money they have to work with, and how to reach the widest possible market. In other words, merchants must determine the overall objectives, the budget, and the types of media to use. These make up the **advertising plan.**

## Objectives

*Develop a profile of the store and its customers*

The desired objectives are the results that merchants want to achieve through an advertising program. These include increasing sales and profits, maintaining loyal customers, and attracting additional customers with appropriate offerings. In order to do so, merchants need answers to such questions as

- What is the store's main business?
- What kind of image does the store project?
- What kind of image do we want to project?
- What quality of merchandise does the store carry?
- How does the store compare with its competition?
- What customer services does the store offer?
- Who are the store's steady customers?
- What are the customers' tastes and income levels?
- Why do its customers buy from this store?
- Who are the store's potential customers?
- What are potential customers' tastes and income levels?
- What might attract potential customers to the store?

The answers to these questions help in constructing profiles of the merchant and the customers so that the store's message can be directed to loyal customers, those who already buy from the store, and the potential market.

In addition, an examination of customers' taste and income levels will give the merchant insight into *what* to advertise. The most appropriate offerings will vary according to the type of store, economic conditions, the season, and the local competition. Nevertheless, a good rule would be to feature a product that is wanted, timely, stocked in depth, and typical of the store.

In large stores decisions about an advertising plan and the setting of objectives are made jointly by upper-level executives, merchandising personnel such as buyers and merchandise managers, and advertising executives. These decisions include the planned cost of the advertising and the amounts needed to help sales grow.

# Establishing a Budget

Advertising is a
controllable
expense

**Advertising budgets** are tools for controlling and allocating advertising dollars. The budget establishes guidelines for assessing the amount of advertising as well as its timing.

Several methods are used in establishing advertising budgets, each with its own benefits and problems. These include the **percentage-of-sales method**, the **objective-and-task method**, and the **unit-of-sales method**.

## The Percentage-of-Sales Method

The easiest and most commonly used way to prepare a budget is to base it on a percentage of a sales figure such as past sales, anticipated sales, or a combination of the two.

- **Past sales** The sales figures of the last year or an average for several years are used as the basis for calculating the budget.
- **Anticipated sales** Estimated future sales volume is used as the basis for calculating the budget. There is a risk of optimistically assuming that the business and business conditions will be good, however.
- **Past sales and estimated future sales** This is considered the middle ground between a too optimistic and a too conservative approach. Consequently, this method is a little more realistic during periods of changing economic conditions because it allows for a study of trends and business in general.

By simply multiplying past or future sales figures by a percentage, one can calculate the advertising budget for the next fiscal or calendar year. However, the merchant must first decide what percentage will be allocated to advertising.

Percentages vary according to the following factors.

- The condition of the business
- The size of the store
- The extent of the trading area
- The local competition
- The age of the store
- The nature of the merchandise carried
- Merchandising practices
- Media costs
- Store objectives
- Past practices and advertising results

Trade journals, the Census, and Internal Revenue Service reports offer comparative percentage statistics on an industry-wide basis. The merchant can choose a percentage-of-sales figure on the basis of what other businesses in the same line are doing. Stores should not, however, base their advertising budgets only on the activities of competitors.

The percentage-of-sales method is generally sound for stable merchants and established businesses, but it has limitations for new merchants. The need to attract attention to a new business requires advertising expenditures in excess of what its immediate sales volume would justify. New merchants therefore are generally advised to use the objective-and-task method.

## The Objective-and-Task Method

The most accurate of all methods of preparing advertising budgets is the objective-and-task method, but it is also the most difficult. Basically, it relates the advertising budget to sales objectives for the coming year. To establish the budget by this method, the merchant must look at the total marketing program and consider store image, location, size, and so forth. For example, certain product offerings, such as women's luxury apparel, require a more aggressive advertising strategy, resulting in a larger budget.

The task method sets down what the merchant must accomplish and what must be done to meet objectives. Although it is difficult to judge the level of advertising needed to achieve specific tasks, expenditures are directly related to the specific task. For example, if the objective is to sell a new product and service to professional women, the merchant must determine what media will best reach this market and estimate how much it will cost to do the job. The tasks and costs are then calculated to achieve this objective.

An Objective-and-Task Method Breakdown

| Objective | Task | Cost |
|---|---|---|
| Create awareness of the target market—professional women | Use Sunday supplements in local newspapers; full pages; 3 times | $6,000 |
| Gain awareness of professional women | Use professional journals; ½ page; 4 times | $3,000 |
| Gain awareness of professional women | Use radio commercials; 5 times; prime time | $ 200 |
| | | $9,200 |

The process is repeated for each of the objectives. When the total has been determined, the projected budget is finished. Since merchants may find that they cannot afford to advertise exactly the way they would like to, it is important to rank priorities and to change them if necessary. The major weakness of this method is the difficulty of setting specific tasks and objectives and then determining the expenditure needed to reach the objectives.

## The Unit-of-Sales Method

This budget is based on the unit (number) of sales rather than on dollar amounts, with a fixed sum set aside for each unit the merchant expects to sell. For example, if it takes 5 cents' worth of advertising to sell a turkey and the supermarket plans to sell 15,000 turkeys, the store must plan to spend 15,000 × 5¢, or $750, on advertising for that product. Past experience is the key to unit-of-sales planning because it is important to know how much advertising it takes to sell a particular unit. This method is most useful for retailers of specialty goods like appliances, china, and cars. It is difficult to use when the merchant deals in many different kinds of products, and it is not dependable in sporadic, irregular markets or for style merchandise.

# Allocating the Budget

Once the advertising budget is prepared, the merchant must decide how to allocate the money. This is accomplished by determining the type of advertising (institutional or promotional), the merchandise lines to be promoted (departments), the timing of the advertising (calendar periods), and media selection.

## Departmental Budgets

This common method allocates dollars by percent of sales. The departments with the largest sales volumes receive the largest share of the budget.

Allocating the budget by departments also allows for the promotion of goods that require advertising to stimulate sales.

## Timing

The budget must be divided into specific periods. Retailers plan their advertising on a seasonal basis, dividing each season into months, weeks, and days. The percentage-of-sales method is useful in determining the amount of money to allocate according to time periods.

It is convenient for retailers to base their advertising on planned monthly sales. For example, if April contributes 7 percent of the year's sales, they plan to spend 7 percent of the advertising budget during that month. If February accounts for 5 percent of sales, then 5 percent is allocated to that month. Of course, the budget usually requires flexibility. For example, though Christmas might contribute as much as 30 percent of annual sales volume, it would probably be unwise to spend that much of the total budget in that period.

Flexibility can be built into budgets when the planning also includes a six-month block. This allows for spending Christmas advertising dollars in October and November in preparation for Christmas. As you might imagine, there is no set pattern, and the budget should allow for changes to meet immediate needs.

## Media Selection

The amount of advertising placed in each medium (radio, newspapers, direct mail, etc.) should be based on past experience, competition, and advice from specialists.

As you have seen, media are the "vehicles" by which the advertiser's selling message is carried to the consumer. If a retailer intends to make an impact with advertising, it is vital for the store's message to reach the correct target market. Media selection is the key to having the right audience read, see, or hear the store's communications. There are three major categories of media that retailers use: print, broadcast, and out-door/transit. (The merits and limitations of the major retail advertising media are summarized in Figure 19-3.)

## Print Media

Print media include newspapers, magazines, direct mail, telephone directories, and flyers.

*Flexibility and wide circulation*

**Newspapers**  Newspapers are the backbone of retail advertising. Day in and day out the newspaper is the merchant's best medium because it offers flexibility and a short lead time, and lends itself to very wide circulation. A major limitation can be the cost of waste circulation. The kinds of newspapers found in large metropolitan areas are as follows.

- **Daily**
  **Morning editions**  These are excellent for merchants who are looking for an immediate reaction to the ad. The paper is out early enough to allow readers to act on advertisements the same day.
  **Evening editions**  These papers have smaller circulations than morning editions, but the papers are kept longer and read more thoroughly. They are used a good deal by department stores.
- **Weekly**  These are generally published in rural communities and are considered hometown papers. They have a longer life than other papers, and readers are very receptive to retail advertising.

*Printed primarily for the advertising*

- **Weekly shoppers**  These are published primarily for advertising and offer little in the way of news items. They are generally distributed free of charge. Simplified printing methods have made it possible for this type of publication to grow and prosper. Most are tabloids that are either mailed to "occupant" or distributed by hand. In metropolitan areas they are stacked near mailboxes, in lobbies, or on counters in local stores. It is estimated that they are received by more than 75 percent of people over 18 years of age.
- **Sunday newspapers**  These are usually divided into special-interest sections, which attract ads that are suited to those sections. For example, apparel and ready-to-wear ads could be placed in the family, magazine, or home section. These sections are also excellent for "big-ticket" items for which the whole family takes part in the decision-making process.

*Inserts are popular*

- **Inserts**  These are not part of the newspaper run but are distributed by the local newspaper. They are known as supplements, special sections, freestanding inserts, stuffers, free-falls, and tabloids. This category has grown to over $400 million in advertising billings (over 12 billion pieces) and is expected to increase. At one time inserts were found only in Sunday papers, but now many dailies allow them to "ride along" inside the paper on "best buys" day editions. "Best buy" days or "best food" days are usually Wednesdays, when most supermarkets and national advertisers run their ads. Next to the news, inserts have the highest readership, which explains their great popularity with department stores, chains, discounters, and local retailers. Because they are preprinted, they are of much better quality than ads reproduced in newspaper runs.

**The Sensual Silk Blouse**
Our Fall Collection of blouses combines the ease of 100%
silk crepe de chine with sophisticated styling. Choose from
the largest assortment ever available at Bolton's. In the
most tempting colors of the season in both solid and yarn
dyed stripes and plaids. As sold in other fine stores for
$55-$68. Our price $29.99.

**$29.99 ea.**

*Bolton's* **Manhattan's largest designer discount store**

| | | | | |
|---|---|---|---|---|
| 225 E. 57th St. | 27 W. 57th St. | 2251 Broadway | 1180 Madison | 53 W. 23rd St. |
| 43 E. 8th St. | 59 Liberty St. | Paramus | White Plains | New Rochelle | Cedarhurst* |

open Sundays 12-5

An example of a high-quality discounter advertising in a daily newspaper.

Local merchants place ads in regional editions of national magazines

**Magazines** In the past, magazine advertising was limited to retail giants like Sears and Penney. The well-known consumer magazines were too expensive for local merchants to use because they had to pay for waste circulation. However, in recent years many national magazines have introduced regional and even local editions in an attempt to receive a greater share of the local retailer's advertising dollar. This practice is known as offering a **split run,** a method whereby the publisher divides the national circulation into smaller sections. In this case merchants pay only for the geographic areas that feature their ads. Among the magazines that offer regional flexibility are

Better Homes & Gardens
TV Guide

This catalog retailer's ad was found in the magazine section of a newspaper.

Time

Family Circle

Seventeen

Newsweek

Ladies Home Journal

Magazines offer the retailer an opportunity to reach specific audiences (Figure 19-2) and feature long ad life and fine-quality color. The limitations include added costs for retailers because ads must be ready for printing and most magazines do not offer free or low-cost services. In addition, the lead time for publication is generally long (two to three months), a fact that limits the effectiveness of this medium for retailers.

Magazines offer retailers well-defined audiences because they are separated into many categories depending on readers' interests, sex, age, and ethnic background.

**Automotive, Mechanics, Science**

*Car & Driver*
*Hot Rod*
*Motor Trend*
*Road & Track*
*Popular Mechanics*
*Popular Science*

**Sports**

*Golf*
*Sport*

**Business, Finance, News**

*Barron's*
*Business Week*
*Forbes*
*Fortune*
*Newsweek*
*New York*
*Time*
*U.S. News & World Report*

**Movies**

*Modern Romance*
*Modern Screen*
*True Story*

**Youth**

*American Girl*
*Boy's Life*
*Co-ed*
*Seventeen*
*Teen Beat*

**Men's**

*Argosy*
*Esquire*
*Penthouse*
*Playboy*
*True*

**Fashion**

*Glamour*
*Harper's Bazaar*
*Vogue*
*Mademoiselle*

**Homes**

*American Home*
*Better Homes & Gardens*
*House Beautiful*

**Sophisticated Editorial**

*Harper's Atlantic*
*Psychology Today*
*New Yorker*

**General Editorial**

*People*
*Reader's Digest*
*TV Guide*

**Ethnic**

*Ebony*
*Essence*
*Black Sports*
*Temas*
*Pimienta*
*Revista Rotaria*
*Reader's Digest (Spanish edition)*

**Women's**

*Cosmopolitan*
*Family Circle*
*Good Housekeeping*
*Parents'*
*Woman's Day*
*Ladies Home Journal*

FIGURE 19-2
Magazines offer retailers an opportunity to reach specific audiences.

The most direct medium

**Direct Mail  Direct mail** is the medium that retailers use to send catalogs and brochures to customers. Also in this category are the **stuffers** that accompany billing statements. The main benefits are the advertiser's control over the mailing, the audience it goes to, and the ability to tailor it to a specific promotion or event. In addition, it is highly flexible

| Medium | Benefits | Limitations |
|---|---|---|
| **Newspaper** | Universal circulation (reaches everybody at relatively low cost) <br> Most people generally see a daily newspaper <br> Products can be illustrated <br> Frequent publication <br> Flexible—booked with minimum advance notice <br> Ads can be in various sizes <br> Routinely used as a shopping guide <br> Offer services to retailers for ad preparation (either free or for low fees) | Waste circulation when target audience does not match paper's circulation <br> Appearance of ad may be unattractive due to poor reproduction of illustrations or poor color <br> Short life for ad |
| **Magazines** | Repeated exposure (long life because people save magazines) <br> Ads can be produced in high-quality color reproduction <br> Retailer's image enhanced because of expense factor | Sometimes difficult to reach target market with circulation <br> Higher production costs |
| **Direct mail** | Controlled circulation (reaches select market—goes directly to prospect) <br> Flexibility in terms of timing, message, artwork, color <br> Can be low cost (mailing lists can be maintained and kept current) <br> Personalized | Junk mail image—sometimes never opened (waste factor) <br> High cost for large mailings <br> Difficult and expensive to compile good lists |
| **Telephone directories** | Widespread customer usage and long life, usually one year | Limited to people searching for the product or service <br> Long lead time—cannot change ad easily |
| **Flyers** | Inexpensive <br> Easy to prepare, can be produced immediately | Heavy waste—high nonreadership <br> Expensive to distribute |
| **Radio** | Can stimulate excitement (sound more persuasive than print) <br> Blanket coverage (everyone has a radio at home, at work, in the car) <br> Short lead time allows for last-minute changes <br> Personalized by use of voice | Excess market coverage <br> Nonvisual <br> No tangible attributes (nothing to hold onto); handicap if price or location of advertiser needed <br> Difficult to know who heard message <br> Poor message may annoy listeners |

| Medium | Benefits | Limitations |
|---|---|---|
| | Can be selective (programs have different appeal to various groups)<br>Relatively inexpensive<br>Good for stores appealing to teens, commuters, etc. | Short life for message<br>Needs to be played often for impact |
| Television | Product can be demonstrated more effectively because of sound, motion, color<br>Wide market coverage | Production costs are high<br>Expensive for small or middle-sized retailer<br>Message short lived (no tangible attributes)<br>Excess market coverage<br>May not reach target market<br>Complicated to produce |
| Outdoor advertising | Long life<br>Costs low per person reached<br>Good backup medium<br>Geographically selective<br>Dramatic because of size | Copy limitations<br>Expensive<br>Difficult for good selling message |
| Transit | Low cost per person reached<br>Good repeat value<br>Well read<br>Good for commuters | Not suitable to direct selling<br>Evaluation difficult<br>Limited audience |

FIGURE 19-3

Benefits and limitations of major retail advertising.

in that it can be produced in any size or color. The disadvantages include its high cost compared with other media, its negative "junk mail" image, its high throwaway rate, and the risk of outdated mailing lists. Nevertheless, direct mail is widely used by retailers.

**Telephone Directories and Yellow Pages** The Yellow Pages are a great help to merchants because they list types of businesses. Potential customers who are searching for a product or service find these directories most helpful. A well-planned advertisement can lead to a great deal of business and has a life as long as one year. Its limitation is that it is not easy to change. However, the costs are relatively low.

The Yellow Pages are invaluable for businesses in specific product or service categories, (e.g., restaurants, limousine services), but are much less effective for department stores and similar institutions.

The regular telephone directories are listed alphabetically and information in them is easy to find. Every telephone user is entitled to one free listing.

**Flyers** Flyers are another means by which retailers reach their target audience. They are particularly useful for the small neighborhood retailer and offer great flexibility. They can be produced very quickly and inexpensively.

A stuffer that accompanied the store's billing statement.

## Broadcast Media

This category includes radio and TV advertising. Radio is characterized by immediacy in scheduling, lower rates compared with other media, and popularity with retailers. The main benefits are its short lead time, wide reach (home, car, almost anywhere), and ability to reach specific audiences. For example, certain groups tend to listen to particular shows, music, and news.

Television is also utilized by many retailers, and since the stations sell local ad times, more retailers are taking advantage of this medium. It has the greatest impact because it allows for dramatic demonstrations. Its main strengths are the ability to combine motion, sound, color, music, and drama, and the ability to reach specific target groups. Its main limitations are high costs and limited time slots. At present, only large retailers like K mart, Wards', and Sears use national TV to any degree. The use of local TV is growing not only with these large merchants but also with service institutions and local retailers.

## Outdoor Advertising

This category includes outdoor billboards and signs. They are generally located along highways and in strategic metro areas leading to the store. They are designed to appeal to general audiences and are of a more permanent nature. Some billboards remain unchanged for many years. In fact, they often become well-known landmarks. They are limited in the amount of copy they can hold, and are not flexible. Prime locations are difficult to obtain and are expensive. In addition, environmentalists sometimes object to this type of advertising.

## Transit

This medium is viewed in and around bus and train stations and comprises the cards and posters seen in trains, buses, taxis, and platforms. It exploits the commuter's boredom to gain readership. Car cards need a lead time of two to three months and have a limited audience.

## Evaluation of Media

Selecting the most effective medium is vital to getting the most from a store's advertising dollar. The retailer must determine whether to use a single medium or a media mix. Many merchants have found that a media mix works best for them. For example, some department stores no longer depend solely on newspaper coverage because the in-

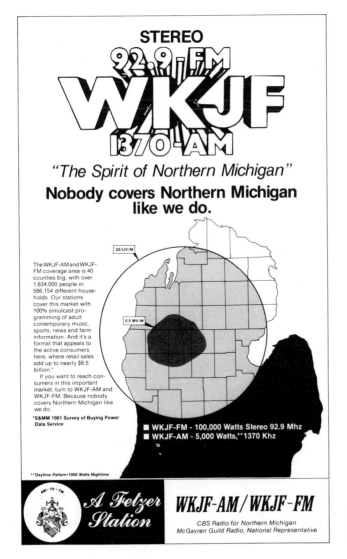

**FIGURE 19-4**

A radio station's ad to attract retail advertisers.

FIGURE 19-5
Magazines often advertise to attract retail advertisers.

creased importance of branch stores has forced them to reevaluate their trading areas. In one case a sales promotion director in a leading department store chain found that in order to reach all its branches it would have to advertise in five newspapers. As a result, the store relies instead on radio and direct mail. Nonetheless, many stores in similar situations claim that newspaper advertising remains their number one vehicle.

Although media use differs according to users' needs, the process for choosing a specific channel is similar. The first step should be a careful review of the benefits and limitations of newspapers, magazines, television, radio, direct mail, and other media. (The various media advertise to attract advertisers; see Figures 19-4 and 19-5.) The next step would consist of examining the effectiveness of the media by checking costs, reach, and frequency.

**Costs** CPM (cost per thousand) is the most commonly used formula for assessing a medium's impact. CPM refers to the cost of reaching 1,000 people in a desired audience (viewers, listeners, or readers). Originally, radio and TV buyers used this formula to learn how much it would cost to put an advertising message before one potential customer. This handy formula has also been adopted by print buyers. The cost is measured by dividing the cost of an advertisement by the number of people reached. The formula is

$$CPM = \frac{total\ cost}{circulation\ or\ audience\ in\ thousands}$$

**Reach, Frequency, and Continuity** Reach refers to the number of people in a target audience, in other words, the range of people who will view, listen to, or read the advertising message. Frequency refers to the number of times the target audience will view, listen to, or read the advertised message. Continuity refers to the length of time an advertising message runs in a given media schedule.

## Evaluation of Advertising

Measuring the effectiveness of the total advertising program involves various research methods that will be discussed in Chapter 24. However, it should be noted that it is important to check the results of advertising expenditures. Every advertisement should be followed up to determine whether or not it fulfilled its objective. In many cases this can be done during the period of the ad. For example, many stores rely on the departmental results on the day of or a few days immediately following the appearance of the ad. They compare their current figures with those for the previous year, when presumably the same ad was not run. Other retailers measure the effectiveness by the mail and phone orders generated, and still others consider the traffic in the store.

### NEW TERMS

| | |
|---|---|
| advertising | institutional advertising |
| advertising budget | objective-and-task method |
| advertising plan | percentage-of-sales method |
| "cargo prices" | promotional advertising |
| combination advertising | split run |
| cooperative advertising | tear sheet |
| CPM | unit-of-sales method |
| direct mail | |

# CHAPTER HIGHLIGHTS

1   After the Civil War, merchants employed advertising to bring in the local trade.

2   Early retailing giants like Marshall Field, John Wanamaker, R. H. Macy, and Huntington Hartford all advertised heavily.

3   The main function of retail advertising is to attract customers to the store. Advertising is a nonpersonal, paid-for sales message using mass media such as newspapers, television, radio, and magazines.

4   Retailers use different kinds of advertising to attract customers, including institutional, promotional, combination, and cooperative advertising. While these methods

are directed to the same groups of customers and potential markets, each conveys its message in a different way.

5   Institutional advertising attempts to "sell" the store; promotional advertising is routine advertising designed to sell specific items; combination advertising combines these elements in the same ad.

6   When retailers share the cost of advertising with manufacturers, suppliers, or other retailers, it is known as cooperative advertising. It is predicted that this form of advertising will grow because it offers many benefits to retailers.

7   An advertising plan must reflect the store's objectives, the budget, and the type of media to be used.

8   In determining advertising objectives, it is wise to develop a profile of the store and its customers so that the store's message will be directed to the correct market.

9   Advertising costs are a controllable expense. The advertising budget is the means of determining and controlling this expense and dividing it wisely among departments, merchandise lines, and services.

10   Various methods are used in establishing an advertising budget. These include the percentage-of-sales method, the objective-and-task method, and the unit-of-sales method.

11   The percentage-of-sales method is the easiest and most commonly used way to prepare a budget, while the objective-and-task method is the most difficult and the most accurate. The unit-of-sales approach to a budget is more limited than either of the others.

12   Allocating a budget consists of breaking down the total budget by departments, time, and media.

13   *Media* are the channels by which the advertiser's selling message is carried to the consumer. There are three major categories of media: print, broadcast, and outdoor/transit.

14   Newspapers are the backbone of retail advertising because they offer retailers great flexibility, wide circulation, relatively low cost, and a short lead time.

15   In the past, magazine advertising has seldom been used by retailers, except for large ones. There is greater flexibility today, however, because many national magazines offer regional and local editions.

16   The evaluation of media includes a consideration of costs, reach, and frequency. Advertising is evaluated by specific research methods.

17   Direct mail is the medium that retailers use to send catalogs and brochures to customers. The advertiser controls the mailing so that it reaches the desired market.

18   Broadcast media include radio and TV advertising. Radio is characterized by immediacy in scheduling, lower rates, and popularity with retailers.

## QUESTIONS

1   Who were the early retailers who pioneered institutional advertising?

2   What is the primary function of local advertising?

3 Explain these key terms in the definition of advertising: *nonpersonal, paid form, identified sponsor.*

4 How does promotional advertising differ from institutional advertising?

5 Distinguish between horizontal and vertical cooperative-advertising agreements.

6 What effect does the Robinson-Patman Act have on cooperative advertising? How does this affect small retailers?

7 Why does a significant part of the money set aside for cooperative advertising often remain unused?

8 Why is it wise to develop a profile of the store and its customers in determining advertising objectives?

9 What is meant by ''advertising is a controllable expense''?

10 List and explain the various methods for preparing an advertising budget. What are the advantages and disadvantages of each?

11 How are advertising budgets allocated?

12 What are the major categories of retail advertising media?

13 Why has newspaper advertising been the backbone of retail advertising?

14 What is the best method for making an effective evaluation of the advertising effort?

# FIELD PROJECTS

1 Advertisers are aware that the use of a combination of media will probably do more to promote goods and services than the use of just one source. Moreover, because certain products require different approaches, it is wise to be informed about all the advertising media available. Assume that you are a small retailer in your town and that you are about to advertise a special offer of repair service with each new TV purchased.

    a Investigate what advertising media are available in your community. Visit the local library or chamber of commerce, or check the Yellow Pages.

    b Visit one of the sources and try to obtain the following information.

        rates
        rules for submitting ads
        services available
        lead time

2 The successful retailer plans an advertising budget for the effective promotion of sales. In this project you are to plan two advertising budgets, one based on last year's sales and the other based on anticipated sales. Use a six-month period.

## Budget Based on Last Year's Sales

The Morgan Store uses an advertising budget based on 3 percent of last year's sales.

| Month | Last Year's Sales | Next Year's Budget |
|---|---|---|
| January | $10,000 | _____ |
| February | 14,000 | _____ |

| | | |
|---|---|---|
| March | 16,000 | _____ |
| April | 17,000 | _____ |
| May | 19,000 | _____ |
| June | 24,000 | _____ |

**a** How much will be budgeted for the first six months during the next year?
**b** What are the advantages of developing a budget based on last year's sales?

### Budget Based on Anticipated Sales

The Morgan Store is able to calculate an advertising budget using the anticipated-sales approach (using 3 percent of anticipated sales).

| Month | Anticipated Sales | Next Year's Budget |
|---|---|---|
| January | $12,000 | _____ |
| February | 16,000 | _____ |
| March | 17,000 | _____ |
| April | 17,000 | _____ |
| May | 23,000 | _____ |
| June | 27,000 | _____ |

**c** What is the difference (in dollars) between the two budgets?
**d** What are the advantages of developing a budget based on the anticipated-sales approach?

## CASES

**1** As more people have started to use cents-off coupons, co-op couponing has become a popular area of sales promotion. A recent entry into this field is a weekday "best foods day" free-fall coupon insert that is a monthly feature in newspapers. Wednesday is usually selected as "best foods day" because most supermarkets and national advertisers run their ads on that day.

In 1981 a new firm called Ad-Serts promised advertisers a circulation of more than 29 million home-delivered once-a-month Wednesday inserts in 150 newspapers in 138 markets. Competition in the newspaper insert business consists primarily of insert advertising in Sunday papers. The owner of Ad-Serts, Carl Turnblom, claimed that 29 million best foods day Ad-Serts equaled 35 million Sunday inserts.

**a** How do you think the Ad-Sert idea might affect local food stores?
**b** Do you agree that inserts will be more effective than ordinary newspaper promotional ads? Why?

**2** A local specialty store retailer advertised biweekly for six months in an attempt to increase his sales and improve his store's image. One of the products featured in his ads could have qualified for the manufacturer's cooperative advertising funds. The media representative informed the merchant of this possibility and suggested that he apply for reimbursement.

After reading the manufacturer's strict guidelines, the merchant decided not to apply. His reasons were that national advertising did not ring his cash register, but local advertising did. He was convinced that his advertising copy was more effective for his target population than the manufacturer's. In effect, he concluded, retailers know their store and their customers.

  a  What do you think of this retailer's analysis?
  b  What would you do if you were the retailer?

3  A new advertising medium was introduced in 1980. Known as on-line media (OMI system), it is basically a nationwide commercial-only television network shown on closed-circuit, 19-inch color monitors set above checkout counters. (They can also be seen from all parts of the store.) The commercials are silent to avoid disturbing customers and cashiers.

More than twenty-five advertisers in the prototype contracted to pay upwards of $60,000 every two weeks for a 10-second spot. Stores using on-line media received $6 for every 1,000 paying customers in the checkout line. OMI handles the cost of installation, supply, and maintenance. Advertisers purchase spots of 3, 5, or 11 seconds on a 6-minute continuous loop at a guaranteed cost-per-thousand-viewer rate of $0.60, $1.10, and $1.75, respectively.

Advertisers have some doubts about the OMI system. Is it as effective for shelf items as for products sold at the checkout counter? Can a silent ad measure up to expectations? Will the novelty of television monitors in supermarkets wear off? The innovators of the system feel that the system can work for any ad that can be displayed on a billboard because it is really reminder advertising.

  a  Do you think this type of advertising might replace network or print media?
  b  How can you see this system working for special promotions, new-product introduction, and nongrocery products?
  c  How might retailers use this medium?
  d  Is the cost of this new method worth the potential results? Explain.

# REFERENCES

Berg, J., "More Creative Ways to Use Co-op," *Stores,* 63 (June 1981), pp. 58–60.

Clymer, F., *Early Advertising Art* (New York: Bonanza, 1955).

Cook, H. R., *Selecting Advertising Media,* Small Business Management Series no. 34 (Washington, D.C.: Small Business Administration, 1969).

Crimmins, E. C., *A Management Guide to Cooperative Advertising* (New York: Association of National Advertisers, 1970).

De Lozier, W. M., *The Marketing Communications Process* (New York: McGraw-Hill, 1976).

Gentile, R. J., *Retail Advertising* (Chain Store Publishing, 1976).

"More Stretch for Ad Dollars," *Stores,* 62 (September 1980), pp. 37–40.

Norris, J. S., *Advertising* (Reston, Va.: Reston Publishing, 1980).

Ocko, J. Y., *Retail Advertising Copy: The How, the What, the Why* (New York: National Retail Merchants Association, 1971).

Shea, S., "When It Comes to Cooperative Advertising, Retailers, Too, Have Ground Rules," *Sales and Marketing Management,* July 9, 1979, pp. 50–58.

Teel, J. E., and Bearden, W. O., "A Media Planning Algorithm for Retail Advertisers," *Journal of Retailing,* 56 (Winter 1980), pp. 23–40.

# APPENDIX

## Levi's Cooperative Advertising*

.

*Reproduced by permission of Levi Strauss & Co.

**LEVI'S WOMENSWEAR**

QUALITY NEVER GOES OUT OF STYLE.®

# FALL 1981
# LEVI'S® JUNIORS SPORTSWEAR
## Cooperative Advertising Plan
**Qualifying ad dates: 8/2/81-9/13/81 and 11/22/81-12/27/81**

## Qualifying Garments

All first quality Levi's® Juniors Sportswear merchandise qualifies for co-op advertising under the terms of this program.

## Qualifying Media and Percentages of Reimbursement

| Medium | Reimbursement Rate for Fully Qualifying Ads* |
|---|---|
| Newspaper | 50% documented net space costs |
| | 50% documented color premium charges |
| **Radio | 50% documented net time costs |
| **Television | 50% documented net time costs |
| **Catalog | 50% documented printing/mailing costs |
| Pre-print Insert | 50% documented printing/insertion costs |

*No production or programming charges will be reimbursed

Total reimbursement is subject to your 2% maximum allowance. Advertising in any other medium will not qualify for Levi's® Juniors Sportswear co-op.

**Prior approval is required for advertising in this medium.

## Maximum Reimbursement: 2% of Shipments

For qualifying advertising run under this program, your Levi's® Juniors Sportswear allowance will be 2% of your first quality Juniors shipments made during the period June-November 1980 or 1981, whichever is greater. Please contact the Womenswear Advertising Department to obtain your allowance.

## Trademark Rules

1. The word Levi's® must always be followed by a noun specifying the division, merchandise group, or item it identifies.
2. The word Levi's® must always be written and, in broadcast advertising, pronounced with an apostrophe s ('s). The word "Levi" should be used only as part of the corporate name Levi Strauss & Co. The letter L in Levi's® must always be capitalized.
3. The ® and ™ must be used when referring to trademarks owned by Levi Strauss & Co. Please note their use in each co-op plan or price list.
4. Any design marks or trademarks such as the pocket tab must be illustrated as shown on the garments.

## General Information

1. Qualified claims submitted within the 60 day deadline will be reimbursed by check. Do not deduct an advertising claim from a merchandise invoice. Deductions are illegal and will result in the suspension of Levi Strauss & Co. shipments.
2. Only first quality merchandise qualifies for co-op advertising reimbursement. Advertisement of irregulars does not qualify.
3. Manufacturer's close-outs (items purchased from Levi Strauss & Co. at less than the regular wholesale price) and seconds do not generate an advertising allowance but may be cooperatively advertised with dollars accumulated from regularly priced goods. Rate of reimbursement remains the same
4. Only one store name may appear in any qualifying ad, however where two stores are part of the same legal entity, both store names may be used. In such cases, prior approval must be obtained. Stores which are part of separate subsidiaries of the same parent company do not qualify.
5. To qualify for reimbursement, ads must be in good taste.
6. Media that has been purchased through trade or exchange (barter) does not qualify.
7. If it is not practical to use any of the qualifying media listed in this plan, please contact the Womenswear Advertising Department regarding the cost of special point-of-purchase display materials.
8. This plan is subject to change with 15 days written notice.
9. This plan serves as our co-op advertising contract. Retail contracts for Levi's® co-op advertisements will not be signed. If you have any questions regarding this plan, please contact the Womenswear Advertising Department, c/o Levi Strauss & Co., Two Embarcadero Center, San Francisco, CA 94106, or call (415) 544-7836.

---

## Pre-Print Insert Advertising

1. Qualifying pre-print inserts must:
   A. Be inserted into a qualifying newspaper.
   B. Carry the name of the paper/date on the cover of the insert.
2. Ad content requirements:
   A. Featured Levi's® Juniors Sportswear merchandise must be illustrated.
   B. Size ranges of featured merchandise must be included
   C. Headline requirements for standard size newspaper pages are outlined under the heading "Newspaper Advertising". In tabloid size (or smaller) pre-print inserts, the name Levi's® Womenswear or the Levi's® Womenswear logo must appear in the minimum size shown below:

   | AD SIZE | LEVI'S® WOMENSWEAR TYPE SIZE |
   |---|---|
   | less than 1/2 page | 3/16'' high |
   | 1/2 page to full page | 1/4'' high |

   D. Competitive merchandise (branded or unbranded) may not be featured by the same retailer within an ad, on the same page, or on the opposite page of a double truck ad. Competitive merchandise means any bottoms, (skirts, jeans, slacks, shorts, etc.) or tops (shirts, knit tops, tee shirts, jackets, vests, sweaters, etc.) other than Levi's® branded merchandise.
   E. Please refer to TRADEMARK RULES/GENERAL INFORMATION sections
3. Claim documentation requirements:
   A. Send invoices (printer's invoice, newspaper insertion invoices) and copies of the insert (one for each newspaper into which it was inserted) to Womenswear Advertising, c/o Advertising Checking Bureau, P.O. Box 3834, Rincon Annex, San Francisco, CA 94119.
   B. Claims must be submitted within 60 days after the end of each month during which the advertising ran. Qualified claims will be reimbursed by check.

### IMPORTANT

COMPLETE CATALOG DETAILS MUST BE SUBMITTED FOR REVIEW PRIOR TO PRODUCTION.

PLEASE COMPLETE THE REVERSE AND SEND TO: Womenswear Advertising Department
Levi Strauss & Co.
Two Embarcadero Center
San Francisco, California 94106

---

### IMPORTANT

RADIO:
COMPLETE RADIO SCRIPTS AND SCHEDULE DETAILS MUST BE SUBMITTED IN ADVANCE OF AIR DATE.

TELEVISION:
AN AUDIO/VIDEO STORYBOARD AND SCHEDULE DETAILS MUST BE SUBMITTED IN ADVANCE OF AIR DATE.

PLEASE COMPLETE THE REVERSE AND SEND TO: Womenswear Advertising Department
Levi Strauss & Co.
Two Embarcadero Center
San Francisco, California 94106

# Catalog Advertising

1. Qualifying catalogs must:
   A. Be devoted to one retailer.
   B. Be printed on glossy or cover stock (newsprint does not qualify).
   C. Be distributed by a mailing devoted exclusively to the catalog to specific names and addresses or be inserted into a qualifying newspaper.
   D. Have at least a portion of their mailing take place, OR the prices quoted therein must be in effect anytime between 8/2/81-9/13/81 or 11/22/81-12/27/81.
2. Ad content requirements:
   A. Featured Levi's® Juniors Sportswear merchandise must be illustrated.
   B. Size ranges of featured merchandise must be included.
   C. The name Levi's® Juniors Sportswear or the Levi's® Womenswear logo must appear prominently. Minimum prominence requirement: bold lead-in to body copy.
   D. Competitive merchandise may be featured on the same page with Levi's® Womenswear merchandise, however they may not be featured on the same figure or model.
   E. Please refer to TRADEMARK RULES/GENERAL INFORMATION sections.
3. Prior approval procedure:
   Your catalog ad plans must be submitted in advance. Please submit a completed Catalog Approval form to receive your advance approval and estimated reimbursement. Reimbursement will be based on a national rate schedule for catalogs.
4. Claim documentation requirements:
   A. Send invoices (printer's invoice, post office receipts) with a catalog copy to Womenswear Advertising, c/o Advertising Checking Bureau, P.O. Box 3834, Rincon Annex, San Francisco, CA 94119.
   B. Claims must be submitted within 60 days following the end of each month during which the advertising ran. Qualified claims will be reimbursed by check.

---

## WOMENSWEAR DIVISION     Catalog Approval Coupon

Note: Catalog qualify only if:
1) A portion of the mailing takes place between 8/2/81 through 9/13/81 or 11/22/81 through 12/27/81 OR
2) Prices quoted therein are in effect anytime between 9/13/81 or 11/22/81 through 12/27/81.
We plan to run catalog advertising as outlined below.

Store Name _____     Store Address _____

Buyer _____     Advertising Manager _____     Telephone # _____
1. Paper stock                                                                6. If less than a full page is devoted to LEVI'S®, Womenswear, other items to be featured

| | (Glossy) | (Cover) | |
|---|---|---|---|
| 2. Size of catalog | | (Size of Page) | |
| | (# of Pages) | (Size) | # of Copies) 7. Circulation |
| 3. LEVI'S® Womenswear ad | | | Mailing |
| | # of Copies) | | |
| 4. Garments to be featured | | (# of Copies) | Inserting |
| | | | (Date of Mailing) |
| | | | (Newspaper) |

Note: The amount approved will be based on our established national average of catalog printing cost plus distribution costs.

5. Expected 50% Reimbursement _____

Juniors Sportswear

---

## WOMENSWEAR DIVISION     Radio/Television Approval Coupon

Qualifying Ad Dates: 8/2/81-9/13/81
11/22/81-12/27/81

☐ We plan to run the radio schedule outlined below (All scripts to broadcast are attached).
☐ We plan to run the television schedule outlined below (A copy of our commercial and script are attached).

Store Name _____     Your Name _____

Store Address _____     City, State _____     Zip Code _____     Telephone # _____

Station _____     Start Date _____     End Date _____     Total Spots _____     LEVI'S® Cost 50%

Send schedule & copy to: Attn: Womenswear Advertising, Levi Strauss & Co. Two Embarcadero Center, San Francisco, CA 94106

Juniors Sportswear

---

# Newspaper Advertising

1. The following types of newspapers qualify:
   A. Local daily papers.
   B. Weekly papers with at least 50% paid circulation.
   C. "Community" weeklies with a minimum of 25% news or editorial content, controlled audited circulation, and circulation and net advertising rates which can be verified by independent audit.
   D. Magazine and other editorial supplements to above qualifying papers.
   E. Official school newspapers.
2. Ad content requirements:
   A. The name Levi's® Womenswear or the Levi's® Womenswear logo must appear in the minimum size shown below.

   | AD SIZE | LEVI'S® WOMENSWEAR TYPE SIZE |
   |---|---|
   | 1/4 page or smaller | 1/8'' high |
   | over 1/4 page to 1/2 page | 3/16'' high |
   | over 1/2 page to 3/4 page | 1/4'' high |
   | over 3/4 page to full page | 3/8'' high |

   (A slick of Womenswear logos is available upon request.)
   For Levi's® Week product subhead requirements, please contact the Womenswear Advertising Department.
   B. Featured Levi's® Juniors Sportswear products must be illustrated. (Slicks of Juniors items are available upon request.)
   C. Size ranges of featured merchandise must be included.
   D. Competitive merchandise (branded or unbranded) may not be advertised by the same retailer within an ad, on same page, or on the opposite page of a double-truck ad. Competitive merchandise means any bottoms (skirts, jeans, slacks, shorts, etc.) or tops (shirts, knit tops, tee shirts, jackets, vests, sweaters, etc.) other than Levi's® branded merchandise.
   E. Please refer to TRADEMARK RULES/GENERAL INFORMATION sections.
3. Claim documentation requirements:
   A. Please submit a tearsheet and all applicable invoices to: Womenswear Advertising, c/o Advertising Checking Bureau, P.O. Box 3834, Rincon Annex, San Francisco, CA 94119. If corresponding newspaper invoices are not provided, reimbursement will be based on your paper's low contract rate.
   B. Claims must be submitted within 60 days after the end of each month during which the advertising ran. Qualified claims will be reimbursed by check.

---

# Radio/Television Advertising

1. The following types of broadcast qualify:
   A. 30 and 60 second radio spots broadcast on FCC licensed radio stations.
   B. 30 and 60 second television spots broadcast on FCC licensed television stations.
2. Ad content requirements:
   A. Spots must be devoted exclusively to promoting your store and Levi's® Juniors Sportswear merchandise (50/50). No other items may be mentioned. (Suggested radio scripts are available upon request.)
   B. Mention must be made of the garments' features, i.e. fit, styling, quality, variety of colors.
   C. The words "Levi's® Womenswear" must be mentioned at least once in all commercials. Copy must also make reference to the product line or sizes offered.
   D. Television spots must show the featured Juniors merchandise.
   E. Television spots must include a visual of the Womenswear division housemark (logo) in either blue or black.
   F. Please refer to TRADEMARK RULES/GENERAL INFORMATION sections.
3. Prior approval procedures:
   A. Complete radio scripts (including jingles and tags) and complete TV storyboards must be submitted with all schedule details in advance of airing. To submit, please use the radio or TV approval form provided and allow 10 working days for the processing of your request.
   B. If your commercials and schedule meet the requirements of this plan, you will receive an approval letter assigning an identification number for your eventual claim.
4. Claim documentation requirements:
   A. The approved Association of National Advertisers, Inc./Radio Advertising Bureau (ANA/RAB) or Television Advertising Bureau (ANA/TVB) documentation format is required without exception.
      1. Station invoice showing the dates and times run, cost per spot, total cost, and product advertised.
      2. Copy of each commercial broadcast (radio script, TV tape) bearing the ANA certification must be attached to the invoice.
   B. In the case of television advertising, a videocassette of the actual spot must be submitted for review.
   C. Please submit above to: Womenswear Advertising, c/o Advertising Checking Bureau, P.O. Box 3834, Rincon Annex, San Francisco, CA 94119.
   D. Claims must be submitted within 60 days after the end of each month during which the advertising ran. If you cannot provide complete broadcast documentation within 60 days, notify the Womenswear Advertising Department in advance of the deadline for an extension. Qualified claims will be reimbursed by check.

# chapter 20
# SALES PROMOTION AND PUBLIC RELATIONS

After completing this chapter, you should be able to:

1 Define sales promotion and indicate its primary objectives.
2 Identify sales promotion activities conducted by retailers.
3 Describe the advantages and disadvantages of sales promotion activities.
4 Identify retail personnel who are responsible for sales promotion.
5 Identify the ways in which retailers develop good will through public relations.

Advertising, display, personal selling, and sales promotion are the means by which a retailer conveys to the customer messages about the store, its merchandise, and its services. Basically, it is how the retailer communicates to the customer in order to sell more merchandise and create good will. As noted earlier, advertising and display help attract customers to the store, while personal selling attempts to get them to buy. Sales promotion, on the other hand, supplements the store's advertising, display, and personal-selling activities by attracting additional customers.

# SALES PROMOTION

**Sales promotion** includes all the activities through which a merchant attempts to generate immediate sales, attract customers to the store, build customer loyalty, and promote good will. These activities include trading stamps, contests, games, premium offers, samples, coupons, price promotions, and special events such as demonstrations and shows.

## Reasons for Using Sales Promotions

Retailers use promotions for the following reasons.

Objectives of sales promotion

- To attract new customers
- To introduce a new service or product
- To offset seasonal declines
- To offset competitive promotions

### Attracting New Customers

The aim of some promotions is to gain new customers. Because shoppers are creatures of habit, the offerings should be substantial enough to wean potential customers from their usual retail outlets. For example, if a customer sees a reduction of $20 on a $600 item, it may not be viewed as significant. On the other hand, a reduction of $100 may be significant enough to cause a change in shopping habits.

### Introducing a New Service or Product

Some promotions are used to encourage customers to try a product or service for the first time. New services enhance the store's image, attract new customers, and motivate regular customers to participate.

### Offsetting Seasonal Declines

The aim of these promotions is to encourage shoppers to buy off-season merchandise (e.g., to buy Christmas cards and decorations in January) or to stock up on a product before they need it. Successful promotions of this nature brighten the sales picture during slow times. In fact, if the promotional incentives are attractive enough, they encourage the purchaser to buy just to take advantage of the offer.

### Offsetting Competitive Promotions

Sometimes merchants must develop promotions to avoid losing business to other retailers who are using sales incentives.

# Types of Sales Promotions

Care must be taken in selecting a promotion

Merchants must decide what they expect their promotions to accomplish before selecting a particular incentive. The costs must also be evaluated against expectations. It should be noted that good promotions cannot overcome poor product performance or replace sound merchandising strategies. Consequently, merchants should plan and research their offerings carefully.

### Trading Stamps, Contests, and Games

The purpose of these incentives is to develop customer loyalty and repeat business. The lure of stamps and the opportunity to win prizes make shopping more exciting for some customers and bring them back to the store again and again.

Historically, the principal users of stamps, contests, and games have been supermarkets, service stations, and small retailers. The customers have the feeling of getting something for nothing, and are given an opportunity to acquire products that they would not normally buy.

**Trading Stamps** **Trading stamps** are given to shoppers who spend a specific dollar amount. The stamps or coupons are accumulated and can be traded in for merchandise at redemption centers or through a mail order center.

Stamps traded for a variety of merchandise

Redemption centers display products and prizes that are available for designated amounts of stamps. The stamps are "traded" for merchandise that runs the gamut of household products, appliances, and sporting goods. The centers are owned and operated by the companies that issue the stamps. Among the largest of these is the Sperry & Hutchinson Company (S&H Green Stamps).

Shoppers who are interested in trading in their stamps by mail have an opportunity to do so. The S&H National Mail Order Center offers a prompt, prepaid shipment service. Customers know what to order because they are issued an attractive catalog, *The Ideabook*.

Stamps are costly to retailers

Retailers must carefully consider the pros and cons of stamps before offering this form of promotion. Because stamp companies charge retailers anywhere from 1½ to 3 percent of sales, stamp promotions can be more costly than advertising. Also, many of the more sophisticated consumers are well aware that stamps are not free and shop at stores that offer lower prices. Furthermore, once a retailer begins a stamp promotion, it is dangerous to stop it abruptly because of customer objections.

Contests and games must adhere to legal regulations

**Contests and Games** These promotions give the customer an opportunity to compete for prizes. Some are based on skills, such as completing a puzzle, while others resemble a sweepstakes in which prizes or money are awarded on the basis of lucky numbers and the like. Purchases are not necessary, and all the shopper need do is fill out a card or entry blank in the store. Sweepstakes create a great deal of interest and can be an

A distribution of colorful pictures, cards, and gifts helped bring traffic to the early A & P stores.

inexpensive form of promotion. It is important for retailers that are interested in contests and games to seek legal advice because such promotions must adhere to legal regulations, and these vary from one state to another.

Trading stamps and contests saturated the market in the 1950s and 1960s. Because so many merchants offered them, they began to lose their competitive advantage and practically disappeared in the 1970s. However, the 1980s are witnessing renewed interest in stamps and contests on the part of supermarket chains.

## Premium Offers and Samples

**Premiums** are articles of merchandise that are offered to the shopper as incentives to buy. They are either given away free after the customer has bought or tried a product or service, or sold at cost. In either case, premiums leave the consumer with a direct, tangible benefit.

A **direct premium** is the basic type of premium. It is an item that is offered *free* with a purchase and is received by the customer at the time of purchase. This "something extra" philosophy is really the key to all premium techniques. In supermarkets premiums are often physically tied to the product by a special package or container, or banded together. This type of direct premium is generally packaged at the factory and is known as a "factory pack." Its advantages are as follows.

- It is visible at the point of sale.
- It attracts attention on the store shelf.
- It frequently moves more products without destroying a price pattern.

*A self-liquidator pays for itself*

A **self-liquidator premium,** on the other hand, is *sold* (usually at cost) to the shopper after he or she has bought some item or tried a new service. The principle of the self-liquidator is simple: The retailer buys the merchandise at the best possible price, adds handling costs, and arrives at a total that becomes (approximately) the offering

Contests are used by retailers to stimulate customer interest.

price to the shopper. The idea is to make the item very attractive to the customer by offering it at a price that is much lower than the normal retail value of the merchandise.

Traffic builders over longer periods

Some premiums are designed to build traffic over a longer period. One such type is the **purchase privilege offer.** This type of promotion is offered on a limited basis (6 to 10 weeks is common). For example, with a specified minimum purchase—say, $5 or $10 worth of groceries—the customer is entitled to buy the premium at a self-liquidating price. The sale of encyclopedias on a volume-a-week basis is a common program of this type. Kitchen tools, glassware, dinnerware, and flatware are also used in this type of promotion.

Premiums may also be offered as a one-time promotion. Banks use this concept in offering gifts to new depositors. **Referral premiums** are gifts that are awarded to customers who send in the names of potential customers. They are popular with direct sellers such as party plan operators, insurance salespeople, and various service companies.

Whether a premium is used as a direct tie-in with a purchase, a new-customer referral, or a traffic builder, the success of the promotion depends on the premium selected. Retailers therefore must decide on the markets they want to reach in order to provide the right incentives.

Sampling can create customer awareness

When a retailer offers a **sample** as a premium, it is usually provided by the manufacturer as an inducement to shoppers to try a product. Usually, trial or sample sizes of a product are handed out in the store. Cosmetics and cigarette companies do a great deal of "sample" promotion. The theory behind sampling is that shoppers need to be convinced by trying a product before buying it.

Bakeries, specialty food stores, and cheese shops often offer free samples in order to get customers to buy or try new items. Sampling is not difficult to arrange and can be relatively inexpensive. It is most suitable for products whose benefits cannot easily be communicated through advertising.

## Coupons

This form of promotion allows a specific reduction in the price of an item. **Coupons** for national brands are offered by manufacturers (through newspapers and magazines) and are redeemable at stores that carry the brand. Manufacturers pay for the cost of redemption plus the retailer's handling cost. Even though they are one of the oldest forms of incentive merchandising, with beginnings well before the start of this century, coupon incentive programs have become a separate industry. Newsletters about coupons are distributed; they are discussed on TV and radio shows; and groups have been formed to trade them. The word *couponing* is a recognized term for this industry, which is expected to grow 10 to 15 percent a year. Its increasing popularity is attributed partially to spiraling inflation and to the fact that customers appear to like coupon incentives. According to statistics from A. C. Nielsen & Co., in 1980 over 80 billion coupons were issued by 1,000 companies, representing savings of $610 million to the nation's shoppers.

Advantages and disadvantages of coupons

Coupons build brand loyalty for manufacturers and retailers, reduce the costs of products to consumers, and encourage consumers to try new products. Some of the disadvantages are that they can be misused and redeemed fraudulently, with the additional costs passed on to the consumer. Also, retailers are sometimes pressured by customers to redeem coupons even when the product in question is not purchased. This

More than 80 percent of food shoppers use coupons.

may occur when no proof of purchase is required. The paper work and record keeping involved can also be bothersome to retailers. Furthermore, retailers have little control over this form of sales promotion, since it is initiated by the manufacturer.

In addition to manufacturers' coupons, some retailers offer coupons that are redeemable only at their stores. This is usually part of a price promotion strategy (see Figure 20-1).

## Price Promotions

*Sales affect store image*

Storewide sales or special sales are common retailer promotions. The purpose is to generate immediate sales, attract customers to the store, and increase profits through higher sales volume. Stores differ in their approaches to sales because of their varied merchandising policies and store images (see Figure 20-2). While some merchants never hold sales because of their negative impact on store image, other stores are known for their once-a-year clearance sales. Supermarkets generally have sales at least once a week, whereas other stores sell at "reduced" prices all year long. Still other retailers conduct recognized sales events on special occasions—back-to-school, Washington's Birthday, January clearance, and so forth.

**This Gift Certificate at some of the best New York City outlets IS YOURS with our compliments, whether or not you hook up to Manhattan Cable TV.**

**Just tear off and use!**

**FIGURE 20-1**
A premium used as an inducement to investigate cable TV.

Storewide sales are a major type of promotion that includes displays, advertising, and long-range planning. As stated previously, the price reductions must be significant if the promotion is to be effective.

The most common arguments against the use of special price promotions are the following.

- Some customers who expect a sale postpone purchasing until sale time.
- An excess of price promotions results in a loss of effectiveness.
- Complaints from customers increase when promotions end.
- Special sales sometimes increase expenses with no corresponding increase in profits.

## Special Events

In this section we will note some of the special activities that attract trade to the store because the offerings are excitement, showmanship, or information, rather than lower prices. These events add to the atmosphere and image of the store in addition to stimulating sales (Figure 20-3).

*Some products lend themselves to demonstrations*

**Demonstrations and Shows** Demonstrations can be very effective in promoting such products as cosmetics, cooking utensils, and electronic devices. Because a good demonstration requires someone who is trained in the use of the product, many manufacturers supply professional demonstrators to help promote their products. For example, in order to promote a new pan for making crepes, one manufacturer hired several chefs to demonstrate and instruct customers in the proper use of the product. Demonstrations

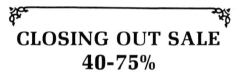

# CLOSING OUT SALE
## 40-75%

**Sheepskins † Shearlings † Leathers † Suedes**
**Coats † Jackets † Raincoats**

*2 Full Floors of Mens and Ladies Sportswear*

MENS 3 pc 100% WORSTED WOOL SUITS
$125.00 (Reg. $250.00)

**\*\*\*\* BALLY SHOES - 1/2 PRICE \*\*\*\***

**JEANS —** Jordache   Calvin Klein   Sergio Valente
Clouds   Cacharel   HIS   Tale Lords   Zena
Sasson   Oscar De La Renta   Faded Glory and many more

*(Even the Flea Market Can't Beat Our Prices)*
WED TO FRI. 10-9 TUES. & SAT. 10-6 MON. 11-5 SUN. 1-5

**FIGURE 20-2**
A retailer's special price promotion.

were held in the housewares departments of a select group of stores, and customers were invited to stop by for the demonstration and a "crepe treat." The chefs prepared various crepes with such ease that some customers ascribed "magical qualities" to the pan. The free food samples attracted large crowds, boosted sales, and enhanced the store atmosphere.

*Demonstrations add excitement to a store's image*

In-store demonstrations are used by Carson Pirie Scott in Chicago to generate excitement about luggage. Luggage and packing seminars are held two to three times a year to increase sales as well as enhance the luggage department's image. Most of the major manufacturers get involved by sending their representatives to help. They teach

Some products lend themselves to demonstrations.

**FIGURE 20-3**

Examples of exciting store promotions. (Reproduced by permission of Strawbridge & Clothier.)

This customer is learning how to tie a scarf Western style through use of the store's video cassette.

customers luggage-packing techniques and emphasize major features of the merchandise. The store uses signs in the store to attract walk-through traffic. Bloomingdale's in New York also uses demonstrations to help build traffic and sales of luggage. However, the store usually confines these events to December pre-Christmas promotions. Manufacturers' representatives demonstrate the unique benefits of their companies' products.

Video cassettes and tapes are also used in demonstrations to attract customers. In these cases the demonstrations are taped and can be played at any time. More and more manufacturers are using this method because trained demonstrators are expensive and can be in only one place at a time. Since many stores make video players available, manufacturers supply the tapes or the entire package.

According to an executive at Leonard's, a Phoenix-based regional chain, video cassette machines are effective in generating customer interest. By demonstating how products are made and cared for, continuous-play tapes have helped increase the chain's sales.

Fashion shows are used widely in most department stores and some specialty shops to display the latest fashions. The main objectives are to sell merchandise and to communicate the store's fashion stance.

A show requires a great deal of advance preparation, organization, and planning. Usually the store's fashion director is responsible for selecting the merchandise and the overall theme, preparing the commentary, and working with the models. Large retail firms generally use professional models.

Designers frequently sponsor shows at selected stores. Of course, the stores must have the right customers for the designer's clothes.

Some shows are produced by stores themselves, with staff members serving as models. This is especially true of informal showings in a store's restaurant. Lunch hour fashion shows are popular and attract a great deal of attention. For one thing, the audience is captive and the models can get very close to the tables. Customers are often able to touch the fabrics and ask questions.

Fashion shows are particularly popular in the sale of furs. In fact, some stores are noted for their fur shows. Neiman-Marcus offers refreshments and tries to make the show more of a social event than a sale. According to the store's fur buyer, this technique attracts many male customers.

**Theme Promotions**   The important aspect of a theme promotion is the selection of an idea that will stimulate the interest of consumers and attract them to the store. A theme need not be elaborate, but it should develop an idea in a dramatic way. The following examples illustrate a range of thematic promotions.

*Themes can involve many store areas*

Britain's prestigious department store, Harrods, held a week-long salute to Italy, "Buongiorno Italia." One of the largest storewide promotions ever undertaken by the store, it brought together Italian foods, fashions, furniture, and craftspeople. The Italian theme developed because Harrods found in Italy a wonderful source of exciting, high-quality merchandise. In keeping with the theme, the central exhibition hall was transformed into an Italian villa and courtyard. Over 60 different window displays set the background for fashion, home furnishings, and food displays. In addition, top Italian craftspeople demonstrated decorative wood and cameo carving, illustrated sixteenth-century ceramic reproductions, constructed mosaic pictures with semiprecious stones, and lectured on the art of hand printing on paper. Youngsters were entertained in the toy department by giant Sicilian puppets.

During the opening week customers sipped complimentary glasses of Italian wine and Harrods' restaurant offered specialty dishes from well-known trattoria. Two of Italy's best-known restaurant owners discussed the essentials of Tuscan food and wines with interested customers.

A special aspect of the promotion was the great number of Italian artists and craftspeople who demonstrated their skills throughout the store. Harrods also received considerable assistance from the Italian Ministry for Foreign Trade, the Italian Institute for Foreign Trade, and the Italian State Tourist Office, which cosponsored the promotion.

*Bridal themes can be his and hers*

Bridal themes are another popular type of promotion, with many stores putting together programs of equal interest to brides and grooms. For example, tie-in presentations include travel planning information, a his-and-hers trousseau fashion show, and the like. Merchandising the honeymoon has such potential that hotels and travel agencies often supply free champagne, travel cases, and similar items.

A well-known star or comic figure can be the inspiration for a theme. Here are some examples.

- Stores around the country have cashed in on promotions featuring Popeye, Olive Oyl, and Superman.
- The movie "Star Wars" was such a great promotional success that it spawned a successfully licensed toy line.
- When Bloomingdale's ran a party for Disney's animated film "The Fox and the Hound," the store was overrun with people dressed as Disney characters, who generated great excitement.

- Inspired by Prince Charles' first appearance in New York, many merchants held promotions featuring products made in England.

## Public Service

Community events build good will

Themes that concentrate on public-service events attempt mainly to build good will. When Lord & Taylor opened it first Florida store in Palm Beach, for example, a great deal of planning went into promoting the opening. Three days of civic and philanthropic festivities took place, topped by a dinner dance for the benefit of a local hospital. As a gracious gesture, long-stemmed roses, the chain's trademark, were distributed to each woman at the dance. There are many other examples of civic and charitable events giving companies a dimension of community responsibility and helping them establish stores in new markets.

Dayton's, located in Minneapolis, is well known for its innovative ideas and community involvement. It sponsors many exciting programs and public-service events, which are presented in a 12,000-square-foot auditorium. Benefit shows, fashion shows, art exhibits, concerts, and lectures are held there. More than 200,000 visitors attend the store's annual Christmas event and its spring flower show, both of which have become traditions in the Midwest.

Another illustration of public service is the store that caters to professional women through information seminars (e.g., "Putting Together a Business Wardrobe"). The sessions are held in the store and at other locations, including colleges and graduate schools. At the seminars, which last about 1½ hours, models and slides augment oral presentations and allow for questions and answers. Informative sessions like these are viewed as a true public service, especially by women who are entering the business world for the first time.

## Group Promotions

Group promotions help small retailers

Shopping center associations may sponsor events that involve all or most of their merchant members. In these cases small shops can take advantage of promotions that they cannot normally conduct by themselves. For example, many regional shopping centers or malls conduct auto shows, art shows, auctions, and flower shows. Music, entertainment, banners, and a great deal of advance advertising and publicity accompany these promotions. Merchants generally share the expenses in proportion to the size of their stores. Because of the scope of the event, many people are usually drawn to the center, and while the merchant is not assured of increased sales, increased traffic is generated.

Cooperative promotions may also take the form of tie-ins with other companies, manufacturers, or institutions. For example, several of the daytime soap operas tie in with local merchants. The TV show offers exposure of the store's name in exchange for clothing or props used on the show. Such exposure adds a measure of prestige to the shop. Similarly, a travel agency may display luggage and travel accessories for a local merchant. In exchange, the merchant may display brochures regarding the agency. There are unlimited ways in which creative merchants can sponsor or cosponsor events. However, the retailer must always consider the objectives of the promotion, its cost, and the nature of the store. Following are some guidelines for staging promotions of this type.

1 Stay on your own "turf"—know your market and aim your promotions toward its interests.

2 Make your events frequent enough to develop the impression that something *interesting* is *always* happening at your store.

3 Planning for special events must be very thorough—allow for possible foul-ups. A foul-up can often be turned into an advantage.

4 When it is practical, work with vendors or other merchants for their support.

5 Advise newspapers and other media contacts well in advance; follow up several times so that some media coverage is possible.

6 Stick to your sales promotion aim.

# Responsibility for Promotion

Who should be responsible for the promotion function? In small firms, the owner or manager generally makes the decisions as to what, how, where, and when to promote. In large retail organizations, the work is generally divided among specialists such as sales promotion directors, artists, illustrators, copywriters, production managers, and display artists. Figure 20-4 is an example of an organizational structure used for carrying out the sales promotion function in a large store. Of course, smaller firms have fewer people on staff to do the work. In these cases one individual may be responsible for several activities.

Sales promotion planning is essential to timely decisions about the types of promotions needed to meet the competition, reach the store's sales goals, and create the right atmosphere for increased customers. Major store promotions are generally planned six months in advance so that all the necessary elements of the promotion are brought

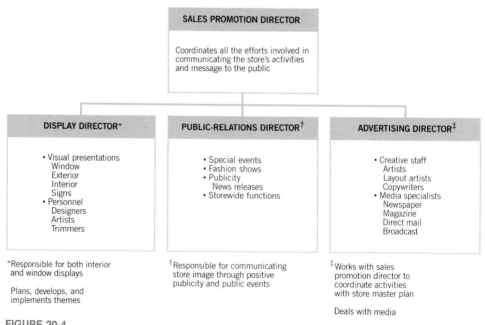

**FIGURE 20-4**

An organizational chart for use in planning advertising, display, and public relations activities.

together at the right time. For example, the merchandise needed for the promotion must be ordered months ahead; the materials needed for display must be prepared; the printing and publicity arrangements must be completed; and the hiring of necessary personnel must take place. Because of these details, large stores also hold periodic reviews as the promotion date approaches.

Stores use various tools to keep on top of their promotion activities. A **promotion calendar** is used to pinpoint special events, local and national events, holiday promotions, advertising, and the like. This calendar expands the special days noted on a normal calendar by indicating the dates of retail sales promotions (Figure 20-5).

## PROMOTION CALENDAR—PERIOD IV—1980

**May**

| Date | | Events Last Year—1979 | Date | | Events This Year—1980 |
|---|---|---|---|---|---|
| S | 6 | Air Conditioner Sale | S | 4 | |
| M | 7 | Lauren PWP, Lauder PWP | M | 5 | |
| T | 8 | CLOVER DAY | T | 6 | |
| W | 9 | CLOVER DAY | W | 7 | |
| T | 10 | | T | 8 | |
| F | 11 | | F | 9 | |
| S | 12 | Bedding Sale | S | 10 | Bedding Bonanza, Lees Semi-Annual Sale Ends |
| S | 13 | MOTHER'S DAY, Almay PWP | S | 11 | MOTHER'S DAY |
| M | 14 | | M | 12 | |
| T | 15 | | T | 13 | CLOVER DAY |
| W | 16 | | W | 14 | CLOVER DAY |
| T | 17 | | T | 15 | |
| F | 18 | Anniversary Sale CD | F | 16 | |
| S | 19 | Anniversary Sale CD | S | 17 | Chair Sale |
| S | 20 | Anniversary Sale CD | S | 18 | |
| M | 21 | Anniversary Sale CD Monteil PWP, Revlon PWP, Polo GWP | M | 19 | |
| T | 22 | Anniversary Sale Begins | T | 20 | |
| W | 23 | | W | 21 | Anniversary Sale Mailer Mails |
| T | 24 | | T | 22 | |
| F | 25 | | F | 23 | |
| S | 26 | | S | 24 | Bedding Sale |
| S | 27 | Lauder PWP | S | 25 | Lauder Promotion Begins |
| M | 28 | MEMORIAL DAY | M | 26 | MEMORIAL DAY |
| T | 29 | | T | 27 | |
| W | 30 | Anniversary Sale Ends | W | 28 | |
| T | 31 | | T | 29 | |
| F | 1 | | F | 30 | Anniversary Sale CD |
| S | 2 | | S | 31 | Anniversary Sale CD |

*Note:* Anniversary Sale begins Sunday, June 1 and ends Sunday, June 8.

**FIGURE 20-5**

A promotion calendar. (Reproduced by permission of Strawbridge & Clothier.)

Planning for promotion costs requires the development of a promotion budget. Each activity involves manpower, media expenses, supplies, printing, and so forth. Preparation for a budget includes the following considerations: the type and size of the store, its location and clientele, the type of merchandise carried, the local competition and business conditions, and the cost of local media.

# PUBLIC RELATIONS
# AND PUBLICITY

Publicity is free
coverage by the
media

Many special events, such as educational seminars, shows, and charitable functions, are unusual enough to receive special attention from the media. **Publicity** is free space and time provided by newspapers, magazines, radio, and TV for newsworthy events. For example, the famous annual Macy's Thanksgiving Day parade is covered extensively by the media. Stories abound about the celebrities involved, the beautiful floats, the giant balloons, and the parade watchers. This free media coverage is distinguished from

Macy's annual Thanksgiving Day parade generates excitement and extensive media coverage.

This Lazarus public relations advertisement was designed to generate excitement for its new store opening.

advertising because of its nonpaid feature. It should be noted, however, that whereas retailers do not pay for publicity, they cannot always control the time, coverage, or content of the communication.

Publicity also takes the form of reporting a store's newsworthy activities of special seminars, shows, visits by celebrities, and personnel visits to schools and other institutions. For example, many personnel directors visit colleges and high schools to discuss career opportunities in retailing. These activities usually receive recognition from school and local papers, as well as from local radio stations. In addition, retailers support the activities of the Distributive Education Clubs of America, a national organization composed of students of retailing.

Publicity is one of the tools of a total **public-relations** program, a continuing management function whose goal is to encourage positive public attitudes. Favorable public relations are another means of promoting a store, its services, and its image. A public-relations program is designed to influence the opinions and attitudes of the store's various publics. These include customer publics, community publics (e.g., Boy Scouts and Little League), employee publics, and suppliers.

A good public-relations program includes a store's internal public, meaning the people employed by the store. Happy employees serve the store's customers pleasantly and with dedication. Company publications containing news about store personnel are other important public-relations tools.

When handled correctly, customer services such as credit, alterations, and returns are another avenue toward favorable public relations.

**Press releases** are formal statements prepared by a firm and submitted to the media for publication. The message may be about a product, a special event, a store opening, or some change in store management. For example, when Bonwit Teller reopened its flagship store in New York, the press was sent announcements regarding the new director and store manager. Because it was newsworthy, the media printed the message at no cost to the store.

The major activities involved in carrying out the public-relations function are preparation of press releases, planning of community events, and development of good channels of communication with the media and the community. The mechanics of securing and reporting the appropriate information involves communication skills like writing ability.

*Press releases are prepared for the media*

### NEW TERMS

| | |
|---|---|
| coupon | purchase privilege offer |
| direct premium | referral premium |
| premium | sales promotion |
| press release | sample (offered as a premium) |
| promotion calendar | self-liquidator premium |
| public relations | trading stamps |
| publicity | |

# CHAPTER HIGHLIGHTS

1 Retailers communicate to customers through advertising, display, personal selling, and sales promotion.

2 Sales promotion attracts additional customers through specific activities such as trading stamps, contests, games, premium offers, samples, coupons, price promotions, and special events.

3 Retailers also use promotions to introduce new services and products and to offset slow periods and competition.

4 Trading stamps, contests, and games help develop customer loyalty and repeat business. The principal users of these types of promotion are supermarkets, service stations, and small retailers.

5 Retailers must consider the use of stamps carefully before they adopt such promotions because they are expensive and difficult to terminate because of negative customer reactions.

6 Contests and games are exciting for customers and can be successful for retailers. However, they must adhere to legal regulations.

7 Premiums are items that are offered as incentives to shoppers. They include direct premiums, self-liquidators, purchase privilege offers, referral gifts, and samples.

8 Coupon incentive programs offer specific reductions in the prices of certain items. They build brand loyalty and reduce the costs of products. Some of the disadvantages are their occasional misuse and fraudulent redemption.

9 Price promotions by way of storewide sales increase customer traffic and generate higher sales volume. Some stores conduct sales on a regular basis, while others never hold sales because they believe sales would hurt their image.

10 Special events utilize excitement, showmanship, or information rather than price inducements. They include demonstrations and shows, theme promotions, and public-service events.

11 In large firms, specialists perform the sales promotion function. In small ones, the owner or manager is responsible for decisions about what, how, and when to promote.

12 Major store promotions and promotion budgets are generally planned months in advance.

13 Preparing a promotion budget depends on the size of the store, its location, its clientele, the type of merchandise carried, the local competition, local business conditions, and the cost of local media.

14 A promotion calendar is used for planning special events over time.

15 Publicity is free space and time that is given by newspapers, magazines, radio, and television for newsworthy events like seminars, shows, and visits by celebrities.

16 The public-relations program is a continuing management function whose purpose is to create a positive public attitude toward the retailer.

17   The publicity and public-relations department is concerned with communicating the store's program to the various publics. These include customer publics, community publics, employee publics, and suppliers.

# QUESTIONS

1   What are the main reasons for a retailer's use of sales promotions?

2   Explain how trading stamps and contests can build customer loyalty. What are some of the drawbacks of trading stamps?

3   What are the reasons for the popularity of coupons?

4   How are premiums used most effectively?

5   Why do some merchants feel that price promotions will have a negative effect on their store's image?

6   What types of special events are suitable for each of the following: department stores, supermarkets, small retailers, shopping centers?

7   How are bridal themes changing today? Why?

8   Why are coupon promotions becoming controversial?

9   Why is it important for a retailer to be first with an idea or theme?

10   Why are major store promotions planned so far in advance? Why is the promotion budget so important?

11   How does publicity differ from advertising? In what ways can a store create favorable publicity?

12   Why is it important for a store to communicate with its various publics?

# FIELD PROJECTS

1   Visit a local shopping center and prepare a list of the various types of store promotions that are being used.
   a   How do these promotions fit in with the image of the stores?
   b   Are there any promotions that would be considered cooperative or group promotions?

2   Most shopping centers have promotion directors who are in charge of developing and implementing promotions for the center. They generally plan events to coincide with such times as Easter and Christmas. Assume that you are the promotion director for a regional shopping center. Plan a six-month calendar of special events to attract customers to the center. (Select January through June or July through December.) Remember that both small and large merchants are involved.

# CASES

1   A local supermarket chain sent the following letter to new residents in a community:

Dear Mrs. _____:

Welcome to our neighborhood. We hope your move was not a trying experience and that ABC Supermarkets can be of service to you. We believe that we are part of the community of each of our stores, and are proud of the quality of our meats, fruits, vegetables, and dairy products. We offer our customers the fullest line of products available, including a full line of national brand items.

To better serve you, we have enclosed an application for an ABC check cashing card. Please complete the form and bring it to your store manager. Feel free to ask for help at any time.

Sincerely,

This promotion was not very successful.

    **a**  Why do you think this promotion was ineffective?

    **b**  What might the chain have done to improve the promotion?

**2**  Five KFC franchise units in the Yakima, Washington, area conducted a unique promotion. They attempted to capitalize on the eruption of Mt. St. Helens in 1980 by utilizing volcanic ash removed from their roofs and parking lots. It cost each franchisee $4,800 to have the ash picked up. Not being sure where to dump it, they offered free samples of volcanic ash to customers who were making purchases, selling them for 50 cents to those who did not make a purchase.

Other KFC franchisees in northern California and Utah joined in the promotion, and almost 250,000 four-ounce vials of the ash were distributed to these stores during a two-week period. Banners advertising the ash were prominently displayed in the store windows. This approach helped the units recoup some of the $4,800 fee for ash removal, and also boosted sales. It was a thrill to schoolchildren, who took the ash to school for "show and tell," and to curious adults, who displayed it at home.

Although the sponsoring franchisees are recognized for successful offbeat promotions, this one subsequently backfired. The promotion antagonized some customers, who thought the retailers had gone too far in promoting an event that had caused the death of some ninety people. Several even questioned whether the ashes of any of the victims were in the samples given away or sold by KFC units. Customers called the franchisor and complained that the promotion was in questionable taste. One customer protested that the promotion of these ashes was as horrifying as the Holocaust of World War II. Although the comparison was exaggerated, it did indicate the depth of emotional feelings about the issue.

    **a**  What do you think the franchise units should have decided to do when the complaints came in?

    **b**  The KFC Company, the franchisor, remained neutral and took no stand on the issue. Do you think the clout of the corporation should have been brought to bear on the situation before it got out of hand?

    **c**  Do you think the franchisees' image was tarnished? If so, how might they have remedied the situation?

3   Coupons have generated controversy as well as sales. In 1979 American consumers received about $610 million from manufacturers for redeemed coupons. Retailers earned $170 million from manufacturers in coupon fees, and according to figures from the U.S. Department of Agriculture, coupons add approximately three-tenths of one percent to the nation's grocery bill.

It has been estimated, also by the Department of Agriculture, that 80 percent of American food shoppers use coupons in an attempt to cut their food bills. The average family redeems about 70 coupons annually, at an approximate average value of 18 cents each. Shoppers clip and use coupons from daily newspapers, magazines, and mail brochures, and from the products themselves.

Esther Peterson, formerly special assistant to the President for consumer affairs, has commented that coupon promotions should be ended, provided that consumers receive the savings. She feels that coupons are used largely for what some nutritionists describe as "gimmick foods." Nevertheless, she believes that at least some portion of the promotion money spent by food companies has filtered down to the consumer.

The Community Nutrition Institute of Washington also has mixed feelings about coupons. Although it is opposed to coupons, it has not taken any formal position because of the possibility of savings for low-income families. Although lower-income people have been increasing their use of coupons, the highest rate of coupon redemption is still found among middle- and upper-income families.

According to Josephine Swanson, a consumer education instructor and food shopping consultant for Cornell University's Cooperative Extension in Ithaca, New York, coupons can "trap" shoppers, costing them more money in the long run. This is so because shoppers benefit from using coupons only if they use them to buy products that they normally purchase. However, the "trap" occurs when consumers are enticed by coupons into buying something that they wouldn't ordinarily purchase. This is especially so in the case of the double and triple couponing offered by several supermarket chains. This type of promotion actually doubles or triples the value of each coupon redeemed, thereby increasing the incentive to spend money on items that are not considered to be "durable household items." Such spending is a source of concern regarding the use of coupons by lower-income people.

Supermarket professionals support both arguments. Some feel that coupons improve consumer awareness and encourage shoppers to switch brands, thereby broadening the consumer's choices. Other defenders maintain that coupon promotions have not raised prices, but that higher prices are due to increased charges by wholesalers. On the other hand, Giant Food, Inc., a chain of 122 stores based in Virginia, Maryland, and Washington, contends that it might be wise for manufacturers to eliminate coupons because the costs to supermarkets and other retailers are very high, with the savings to consumers insignificant.

Still another area of concern is coupon fraud. It is estimated that almost 20 percent of redeemed coupons are redeemed fraudulently by trade and store personnel. Consequently, the money value of these coupons is not paid to consumers. According to a Procter & Gamble executive, the costs of fraud eventually are reflected in consumer prices. To help curb this problem, the United States Postal Service and the Federal Bureau of Investigation probe possible cases of coupon fraud.

a   What do you think will be the outcome of the coupon controversy?
b   Do you agree that ending the use of coupons will save the consumer money? Explain.
c   Since basic foods like fruit, vegetables, milk, and meat are rarely couponed, do you feel that couponed items can be eliminated without affecting the average family's food budget? Explain.
d   Do you believe the costs of fraudulently redeemed coupons are reflected in consumer prices? Why?

# REFERENCES

Beyea, A., "How to Create Action Fever!," *Stores,* 62 (July 1980), p. 43.

"Carson's Looks Beyond the Future," *Stores,* 62 (November 1980), pp. 50–52.

Darrow, R. W., and D. J. Forrestal, *The Dartnell Public Relations Handbook,* 2nd ed. (Chicago: Dartnell Corp., 1979).

De Lozier, W. M., *The Marketing Communications Process* (New York: McGraw-Hill, 1976).

Fulop, C. *The Role of Trading Stamps in Retail Competition* (London: Institute of Economic Affairs, 1973).

Fulweiler, J. H., *How to Promote Your Shopping Center,* (New York: Chain Store Publishing, 1973).

Golden, H., and K. Hanson, *How to Plan, Produce and Publicize Special Events* (Dobbs Ferry, N.Y.: Oceana Publications, 1960).

Lesly, P., *Lesly's Public Relations Handbook,* 2nd ed. (Englewood Cliffs, N.J.: Prentice-Hall, 1978).

Marston, J. E., *Modern Public Relations* (New York: McGraw-Hill, 1979).

"More Than Words," *Stores,* 63 (March 1981), p. 45.

Phillips, P., "On Stage!," *Stores,* 62 (March 1980), pp. 47–53.

"Sales Promotion: A Three-Ring Circus," *Retailweek,* November 1, 1979, pp. 36–40.

Samtur, S. J., and T. Tuleja, *Cashing in at the Checkout* (New York: Stonesong Press, 1979).

Silbey, P., "See How They Play," *Stores,* 62 (December 1980), pp. 38–41.

———, "What Developers Are Doing for Christmas," *Stores,* 63 (April 1981), pp. 40–46.

Spalding, L. A., "Getting More From Sales Promo $," *Stores,* 63 (January 1981), pp. 56–59.

# part five
# CONTROLS

N o retail business can remain successful for long without a system for managing money, records, inventory, and credit. So complex have commercial activities become that even small retailers are conscious of the need for controls. Chapter 21 introduces us to the meaning of accounting and the reasons for its importance. We study basic accounting procedures and delve into the meaning of financial reports. In connection with the reports, we learn about the usefulness of certain balance sheet and income statement measurements. We also discuss the significance and development of budgets, as well as the operation of accounting systems.

Chapter 22 is concerned with inventory control. After identifying the three merchandise categories used to describe inventory levels, we study the causes of and remedies for inadequate and excessive inventories. We then examine the factors that shape a store's inventory control system and show how perpetual and periodic inventory methods are used in dollar and unit control systems. We also learn how to estimate an inventory by the retail method. In order to determine a firm's profitability, we see how ending inventories are computed on a cost basis using different methods. We also examine the effects on profitability of over- or underestimating ending inventory.

In Chapter 23 we look at the role that credit plays in retail operations. After studying the different types of credit plans available to consumers, we look at the customer as a credit risk and list criteria for granting credit. Then we analyze the billing and collection techniques used by retailers. Finally, we examine the major federal laws regulating the extension of credit.

# chapter 21
# ACCOUNTING AND CONTROL SYSTEMS

After completing this chapter, you should be able to:

1  Identify external and internal users of accounting information.
2  Explain the recording, classifying, reporting, and interpreting functions of accounting.
3  Explain the sections and terms of a balance sheet and an income statement.
4  Compute current ratio, quick ratio, merchandise turnover, average collection period, and return on investment (ROI).
5  Compute increases and decreases in operating expenses and explain how retailers evaluate expenses.
6  Explain expense, cash, advertising, and merchandise budgets and indicate their relationship to accounting data.
7  List resources for the development of sales forecasts.
8  Explain how accounting records are maintained by large and small retailers.

We have seen how retailers plan and execute a variety of strategies toward two ends: to satisfy customers and to make a profit. With the correct mix of staff, location, physical facilities, and merchandise, successful retailers develop a store image that sustains customer loyalty. Through effective promotions and advertising, they maintain contact with consumers and seek to enlarge their customer base.

The next matter of concern for a store is the system by which it controls the financial aspects of the business. Without carefully designed procedures for ensuring accuracy and completeness in the maintenance of records, management could not make the myriad decisions required of it each day. Nor would it have the necessary information for a correct analysis of operations. In this chapter we examine some important features of financial records.

# THE MEANING OF ACCOUNTING

*Accounting for control, analysis, and decision making*

Accounting is the compilation of financial data for purposes of control, analysis, and decision making. This definition applies to all types of businesses, including retailing. Though retailers need not know accounting techniques to understand financial reports, they should be familiar with some basic terms and concepts found in those reports. Without this knowledge, they will be handicapped in efforts to interpret the results of business activities.

# WHY ACCOUNTING RECORDS ARE IMPORTANT

Businesses maintain accounting records for a number of reasons. Owners and managers require information in order to make daily and long-range decisions. Knowing the level of expenditures for such items as salaries and advertising helps management control overall costs. Some accounting information (e.g., payroll and sales taxes) is required by law. Finally, a company's financial records may be of interest to private individuals and groups. Let's take a closer look at those who depend on accounting information to meet their needs.

## Users of Accounting Information

*External and internal users of accounting*

Users of accounting data may be classified as external and internal. External users include

1  Stockholders in retail corporations, who share in its profits and losses but do not participate in its operations.

2  Creditors who sell merchandise to retailers.

3  Creditors who lend money to retailers.

4 Government agencies, which require retailers to file income, sales, excise, and payroll tax reports.

5 Retail trade groups, which publish articles and reports.

6 Financial analysts, such as stock brokerage companies.

Internal users of accounting records are the individuals within a retail business who make operational decisions. For example, a buyer needs to know the volume of current sales in order to plan markdowns or additional purchases. A store manager requires information about departmental sales in order to capitalize on strong sales areas and correct the difficulties in weak ones. An advertising manager needs sales data to judge the effectiveness of the store's advertising efforts. In short, few planning and control decisions can be made without adequate accounting systems.

# Accounting and Data-Processing Systems

Reference to retail data-processing systems was made earlier in this book. It was pointed out that the use of computers to provide accurate and speedy accounting information for retail managers is taken for granted. Even smaller stores recognize the value of data processing and are resorting to computers or computer service companies to meet some of their accounting needs. In the future we can expect retailers to rely even more heavily on computer-generated data as business operations increase in complexity and competition for the consumer's dollar intensifies.

# Retail Budgets

A budget is a plan that estimates future sales, expenses, or some other financial aspect of a company. The use of budgets to plan, evaluate, and control retail operations is common to well-run stores. Whether it is a simple budget prepared by the owner of a small store or a departmentalized budget designed for a large retailer, accounting information is essential for its preparation. More will be said later about the relationship of accounting data to retail budgets.

# ACCOUNTING PROCEDURES

Recording, classifying, reporting, and interpreting accounting information

In order to provide useful information to merchants, accounting procedures are broken down into the following functions.

1 Recording financial information

2 Classifying the information

3 Reporting the information

4 Interpreting the information

# Recording Financial Information

This includes keeping records of purchases, sales, inventory, expenses, payroll, and other financial items. Some retailers use computers to maintain records, while others employ mechanical equipment or hand methods.

# Classifying the Information

So that retail owners and executives can understand accounting records more easily, the data are arranged in clearly designated categories. For example, sales may be classified by cash or credit. Salaries are classified as selling, office, or maintenance expenses.

# Reporting the Information

From time to time the information is summarized and arranged in financial reports, also called financial statements. These reports enable merchants and others to study the results of operations.

# Interpreting the Information

Information contained in financial reports is analyzed to determine a firm's status and progress. The analysis involves many financial aspects of a company's operation, including sales trends, inventory costs, overhead changes, and profitability.

# UNDERSTANDING FINANCIAL REPORTS

The two most commonly used financial reports are the **balance sheet,** or statement of financial position, and the **income statement.**

## The Balance Sheet

*The balance sheet: assets, liabilities, owner's equity*

This report contains information about the **assets** (the things a business owns) and **liabilities** (debts) of a business as of a particular date. Subtracting the liabilities from the assets results in the **owner's equity,** or **net worth.** For example, a retailer whose assets and liabilities are $40,000 and $30,000, respectively, has an owner's equity of $10,000. The amounts may be expressed as follows.

| | |
|---|---:|
| Assets | $40,000 |
| Less: liabilities | 30,000 |
| Owner's equity | $10,000 |

Stated another way, assets equal liabilities plus owner's equity. Corporations often call their net worth **stockholders' equity.**

For comparative purposes, many retailers list the previous year's figures as well as current ones. This allows them to detect significant changes from one period to the next. Figure 21-1 shows the balance sheet of a retail corporation. The sections of the statement are analyzed in the following paragraphs. (The appendix for this chapter contains a balance sheet for the J. C. Penney Company.)

## FOUR-STAR STORES CORPORATION
## BALANCE SHEET
## DECEMBER 31

### ASSETS

| Current Assets | 1981 | 1980 |
|---|---|---|
| Cash | $150,000 | $120,000 |
| Accounts receivable | 280,000 | 250,000 |
| Merchandise inventory | 200,000 | 220,000 |
| Supplies | 40,000 | 18,000 |
| Total current assets | $670,000 | $608,000 |

| Plant and Equipment Assets | | |
|---|---|---|
| Delivery equipment (after depreciation) | $ 58,000 | $ 62,000 |
| Furniture and fixtures (after depreciation) | 85,000 | 82,000 |
| Office equipment (after depreciation) | 22,000 | 26,000 |
| Total plant and equipment assets | $165,000 | $170,000 |
| Total assets | $835,000 | $778,000 |

### LIABILITIES

| Current Liabilities | | |
|---|---|---|
| Accounts payable | $282,000 | $236,000 |
| Notes payable | 50,000 | 20,000 |
| Salaries payable | 3,000 | 5,000 |
| Total current liabilities | $335,000 | $261,000 |

| Long-Term Liabilities | | |
|---|---|---|
| Notes payable (due 1983) | 40,000 | 40,000 |
| Total liabilities | $375,000 | $301,000 |

| Stockholders' Equity | | |
|---|---|---|
| Capital stock | $300,000 | $300,000 |
| Retained earnings | 160,000 | 177,000 |
| Total stockholders' equity | $460,000 | $477,000 |
| Total liabilities and stockholders' equity | $835,000 | $778,000 |

FIGURE 21-1

The balance sheet of a retail corporation.

### Current Assets

These assets consist of cash and assets that are expected to be either converted into cash or expended within a year. Accounts receivable, for example, represent money owed by customers and usually are collected within a year. Merchandise inventory, or stock, is assumed to be sold within a year. Supplies, including store and office supplies, are generally used within a year of purchase.

### Plant and Equipment Assets

These are long-lived assets that are periodically reduced in value (depreciated) because of wear and tear, obsolescence, or inadequacy.

### Current Liabilities

This category consists of debts that will probably be repaid within one year of their assumption. For example, *accounts payable,* which consist of debts owed to *creditors* (those to whom the retailer owes money) for purchases, are customarily paid in less than one year (e.g., 30 days or 60 days). *Notes payable* that are included in current liabilities are short-term loans (e.g., 60 or 90 days), which are scheduled for repayment in less than a year. *Salaries payable* are moneys that are due to employees at the balance sheet date.

### Long-Term Liabilities

These are debts that run for more than a year. For example, the *notes payable* due in 1983 may have arisen from the purchase of furniture and fixtures on a long-term basis, with the retailer not liable for part of the payment until 1983. Of course, interest will be paid along with the amount of the note.

### Stockholders' Equity

This section of the balance sheet contains the net worth of the business. Capital stock refers to the investment by stockholders (owners) in the corporation, while retained earnings are profits made by the company that have not yet been distributed to the stockholders. Distributed profits of a corporation are called **dividends.**

## Useful Balance Sheet Measurements

Retailers frequently use balance sheets to determine the relationships among their assets, liabilities, and owner's equity. Through the application of simple mathematical procedures, they can judge the status of a particular aspect of the business. As you will see, they often compare their results with retail industry averages. (For convenience, all financial-statement measurements discussed in this chapter are summarized later.)

### Current Ratio (CR)

Current and quick ratios

By matching current assets (CA) against current liabilities (CL), the retailer learns how well the business is positioned to pay its current debts. Here's how it's done.

Current assets ÷ current liabilities = **current ratio**

Using the 1981 amounts in Figure 21-1, we find

$$\frac{CA}{(\$670,000)} \div \frac{CL}{(\$335,000)} = \frac{CR}{(2:1)}$$

The ratio is usually expressed as 2 to 1, meaning that there are $2 of current assets available to pay every $1 of current liabilities.

A current ratio of 2 to 1 or a bit higher is usually considered satisfactory. When the CR is significantly lower, the retailer may have difficulty paying current debts. When it is too high, the retailer may have excessive cash or merchandise on hand, assets that are not earning money for the business.

## Quick Ratio

Though the current ratio is often of value, it is sometimes a deceptive indication of a retailer's ability to pay current debts. This happens, for example, when the merchandise inventory is a very large part of the current assets. Since it is not easy to turn a large inventory into cash quickly, a business with such an inventory may have insufficient funds for the payment of current liabilities. (Supplies are also omitted from the computations because they are usually small in amount.) A more realistic test in this instance would be the **quick ratio,** sometimes called the acid test. Here's how this measure is computed.

(Cash + receivables) ÷ current liabilities = quick ratio

Returning to the 1981 amounts in Figure 21-1, we get

($150,000 + $280,000) ÷ $335,000 = 1.3:1

In other words, the quick ratio is 1.3 to 1, which means that there is $1.30 of current assets (not including inventory and supplies) available to pay each $1.00 of current liabilities. Since banks and other lending institutions usually require a quick ratio of approximately 1 to 1, the Four-Star Stores Corporation may be in a favorable position for securing loans.

Though the current and quick ratios serve useful analytical purposes, they are generally considered along with other important factors. For example, retailers often compare ratios against ratios for previous accounting periods or those of competitive stores. In other words, an informed retailer rarely relies on only one factor in making decisions.

# The Income Statement

*The income statement: sales, cost of goods sold, operating expenses*

An income statement, also known as a profit and loss statement or an operating statement, indicates whether a company has made a profit or sustained a loss over a specific period. It includes information about sales, merchandise costs, and operating expenses. It is particularly valuable when compared to a report for a prior, similar period. For example, it might be helpful to compare operating figures for two successive Christmas seasons in making plans for the next one.

Figure 21-2 contains the three sections of an income statement. The first, "Revenue from Sales," shows that after returns and allowances by customers are deducted, net sales increased from $910,000 in 1980 to $970,000 in 1981. The second section,

## FOUR-STAR STORES CORPORATION
## INCOME STATEMENT
## JANUARY 1–DECEMBER 31

| Revenue from Sales | 1981 | | 1980 | |
|---|---|---|---|---|
| Sales | $990,000 | | $920,000 | |
| Less: returns and allowances | 20,000 | | 10,000 | |
| Net sales | | $970,000 | | $910,000 |
| **Cost of Goods Sold** | | | | |
| Merchandise inventory, Jan. 1 | $220,000 | | $190,000 | |
| Add: purchases | 480,000 | | 430,000 | |
| Cost of goods available for sale | $700,000 | | $620,000 | |
| Less: merchandise inventory, Dec. 31 | 200,000 | | 220,000 | |
| Cost of goods sold | | 500,000 | | 400,000 |
| Gross margin (gross profit) | | $470,000 | | $510,000 |
| **Operating Expenses** | | | | |
| Salaries | $110,000 | | $105,000 | |
| Rent | 90,000 | | 90,000 | |
| Advertising | 70,000 | | 80,000 | |
| Utilities | 50,000 | | 45,000 | |
| Insurance | 20,000 | | 20,000 | |
| Supplies and postage | 24,000 | | 18,000 | |
| Depreciation | 16,000 | | 12,000 | |
| Total expenses | | 380,000 | | 370,000 |
| Net income | | $ 90,000 | | $140,000 |

**FIGURE 21-2**
The income statement of a retail corporation.

"Cost of Goods Sold," reveals an increase from $400,000 in 1980 to $500,000 in 1981. The amounts in the second section are computed by

1 Adding the merchandise inventory on hand at the beginning of the year to the purchases for the year. The result is the *cost of goods available for sale.*

2 Subtracting the merchandise on hand at the end of the year from the cost of goods available for sale. The result is *the cost of goods sold.*

This section also shows that the *gross margin* (profit before deducting expenses) decreased from $510,000 to $470,000. The third section, "Operating Expenses," lists an increase in expenses (overhead) from $370,000 in 1980 to $380,000 in 1981. Finally, the statement shows that the net income (net profit) decreased from $140,000 to $90,000. (The appendix for this chapter contains an income statement for the J. C. Penney Company.)

# Useful Income Statement Measurements

Additional
valuable retail
ratios

Retailers use a combination of income statement and balance sheet amounts to construct additional ratios and business indicators. As with balance sheet ratios, these measurements enable merchants to assess the effectiveness of business operations and to make important decisions. (The balance sheet and income statement measurements covered in this chapter are summarized in Figure 21-3.)

## Merchandise Turnover

This measure, sometimes called stock turnover, indicates how quickly merchandise has been sold. It is important to have this information because unsold goods occupy valuable shelf space and also represent a costly monetary investment. To compute the merchandise turnover, use the following formula.

$$\text{Net sales} \div \frac{\text{average inventory}}{\text{at retail}} = \text{merchandise turnover}$$

| Name of Measurement | Financial Statement From Which Information is Taken | Formula | Purpose |
|---|---|---|---|
| **Current ratio** | Balance sheet | Current assets ÷ current liabilities | Enables retailer to determine how well the business is able to pay current debts |
| **Quick ratio** | Balance sheet | (Cash + receivables) ÷ current liabilities | Used instead of the current ratio when merchandise inventory is a very large part of current assets |
| **Merchandise turnover** | Balance sheet and income statement | Net sales ÷ average inventory at retail | Indicates how quickly merchandise has been sold |
| **Average collection period** | Balance sheet and income statement | Year-end receivables ÷ average sales per day | Tells retailer the approximate time it has taken to collect the store's debts |
| **Return on investment (ROI)** | Balance sheet and income statement | Net income ÷ stockholders' equity (owner's equity) | Indicates the percent earned on investment in the business |

FIGURE 21-3
Financial statement measurements.

The net sales are taken from the first section of the income statement. For the purposes of the following illustration, the average inventory at *retail* is an average of the inventory at *retail* prices at the beginning and end of the year. Assuming the following inventories at *retail* price for the Four-Star Stores Corporation in 1980,

| | |
|---|---|
| January 1 | $280,000 |
| December 31 | 300,000 |

the average inventory was $290,000.

$$($280,000 + $300,000) \div 2 = $290,000$$

Computing the 1980 merchandise turnover, we get

$$$910,000 \div $290,000 = 3.1$$

Assuming the following inventories at *retail* price for 1981,

| | |
|---|---|
| January 1 | $300,000 |
| December 31 | 290,000 |

the average inventory was $295,000 and the merchandise turnover was 3.3, computed as follows.

$$$970,000 \div $295,000 = 3.3$$

Now, what do turnovers of 3.1 and 3.3 mean? These figures indicate that the average amount of merchandise on hand was turned over (sold) 3.1 times in 1980 and 3.3 times in 1981. These numbers are significant *only* when they are related to the type of retail business involved. For example, stores, such as jewelry shops, that carry high-priced merchandise generally show low turnover rates, while gasoline stations and many food stores have high rates. Merchants compare their turnover rate to rates for previous periods to detect the relative frequency of sales activity. A significant change in a rate may call for an analysis of sales and inventory operations. Some retailers also compare their turnovers to rates reported by other merchants in similar businesses.

In the preceding illustration the average inventory was the average of the inventories at the beginning and end of the year. Since inventories are usually low at these times, however, this average may not be representative of the amount of stock that a retailer usually maintains. To reduce the chances of distortion, most retailers include several monthly inventories in their computations. Some, in fact, use the inventory on hand at the beginning of each month (12 months) in addition to the inventory at the end of the year (1 month), thereby obtaining thirteen separate inventory amounts for averaging.

## Average Turnover Days

Having computed the merchandise turnover, some retailers go one step further and convert the turnover rate into **average turnover days.** This is accomplished by dividing the number of days in the accounting period by the turnover rate. For 1981 the Four-Star Store Corporation shows

$$365 \text{ days} \div 3.3 \text{ turnover rate} = 111 \text{ average number of}$$
days for each
merchandise turnover

In other words, it took approximately 111 days to sell the inventory once. Of course, the shorter the turnover time, the less chance there is for merchandise to become obsolete, soiled, or damaged. Retailers match turnover days against those for previous periods as an additional check on the movement of stock.

## Average Collection Period

This measure tells the retailer the approximate time it has taken to collect the store's debts. It is computed as follows.

$$\text{Year-end receivables} \div \frac{\text{average sales}}{\text{per day}} = \frac{\textbf{average}}{\textbf{collection}}$$
$$\textbf{period}$$

The average sales per day are derived by dividing the net sales (found on the income statement) by the number of days in the year. For Four-Star Stores at the end of 1981, we get

$$\$970,000 \div 365 \text{ days} = \$2658 \text{ average sales per day}$$

Next we substitute both the $2658 and the year-end accounts receivables, $280,000, taken from the 1981 balance sheet, to find the average collection period.

$$\$280,000 \div \$2658 = 105 \text{ days}$$

In other words, it took an average of 105 days for the company to collect from a customer. The length of a collection period depends on the time a retailer allows customers to pay bills and the extent to which it enforces collections. The more delinquent customers are, of course, the longer the average collection period. To remain operational, therefore, retailers must attempt to extend credit only to reliable consumers and must institute workable collection procedures. (Credit and collections are discussed further in Chapter 23.)

## Return on Investment

How does a retailer or an investor in a retail company determine whether the monetary investment is a sound one? A method that is often used to answer the question is to compute a measure called **return on investment,** or ROI. Here's how it's done.

$$\text{Net income} \div \frac{\text{stockholders' equity}}{\text{(owner's equity)}} = \text{return on investment}$$

The net income is taken from the income statement, while the stockholders' equity comes from the balance sheet. The stockholders' equity used is the average of the equities at the beginning and end of the year. Using Four-Star Stores' 1981 figures, the average equity is

$$(\$477,000 + \$460,000) \div 2 = \$468,500$$

The return on investment for 1981, then, is

$$\$90,000 \div \$468,500 = .192, \text{ or } 19.2\% \text{ ROI}$$

This means that Four-Star Stores earned 19.2 percent on its investment in 1981. Should an investor be content with this return? The answer depends on a number of factors,

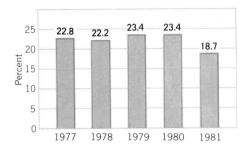

FIGURE 21-4
Shareholders' return on average equity.

such as the possibility of the investor's earning a higher return from some other venture or investment, the financial outlook for Four-Star Stores, the state of the economy, and so forth.

Figure 21-4 shows how a retail firm might chart its ROI for a number of years.

# Measuring Operating Expenses

It is obvious that the lower a retailer's expenses, the higher its possible net income. In order to control operating expenses, the merchant needs to determine the extent to which individual expenses increase or decrease over time. An analysis of this information often makes it possible to reduce particular overhead items.

It is much easier to judge the significance of increases and decreases by using percents rather than dollars. To understand why this is so, look at Table 21-1. Company A's advertising expenses increased by $10,000, or 5 percent, from 1980 to 1981. Company B's advertising expenses also increased by $10,000, but its *percent* increase was 20 percent, four times as much! Though the dollar increases were identical, the percent increases showed the true relative changes. This is why retailers frequently use percentages to compare progress in one period with progress in another, or to compare their statistics with those of competitors.

Table 21-2 shows how a retailer might analyze expenses in terms of its own operations. Utilities expenses increased by $1000, or 50 percent from 1979 to 1980. It increased by an even larger amount, $1200, from 1980 to 1981, yet the *percent* increase was only 40 percent. The insurance expenses decreased by $1200, or 25 percent, from 1979 to 1980. It decreased by a lesser amount, $1080, from 1980 to 1981, yet the *percent* decrease was 30 percent. In both cases the percents were a more realistic indicator of change than the dollars.

**TABLE 21-1**   Using Dollars and Percents for Comparisons

| Company | Advertising Expenses | | Increase | |
| | 1980 | 1981 | Dollars | Percent |
|---|---|---|---|---|
| A | $200,000 | $210,000 | $10,000 | 5 |
| B | 50,000 | 60,000 | 10,000 | 20 |

**TABLE 21-2**   An Illustration of Increases (Decreases) in Expenses

| Expense | 1979 Actual Expense | Actual Expense | 1980 Increase (Decrease) from 1979 | | Actual Expense | 1981 Increase (Decrease) from 1980 | |
|---|---|---|---|---|---|---|---|
| | | | Dollars | Percent | | Dollars | Percent |
| Utilities | $2000 | $3000 | $1000 | 50 | $4200 | $1200 | 40 |
| Insurance | 4800 | 3600 | (1200) | (25) | 2520 | (1080) | (30) |

We turn our attention once more to the Four-Star Stores income statement. Table 21-3 contains the dollar and percentage changes from 1980 to 1981 for net sales and for selected expense categories. On the basis of the changes, management might ask the following questions.

Management questions about expenses

To what extent was the 4.8 percent increase in salaries responsible for the 6.6 percent increase in net sales? Would hiring additional salespeople result in an even better sales performance?

Why was there an increase in net sales despite a 12½ percent decrease in advertising expenses? Are advertising expense dollars being used most effectively?

Was the 33⅓ percent increase in supplies and postage due largely to inflation and higher mailing costs? Might these expenses be reduced with better management controls?

# Evaluating Operating Expenses

Many retailers evaluate each operating expense as it relates to net sales. The assumptions underlying this method are as follows.

1   Sales can be produced only through the outlay of operating expenses.
2   Funds for operating expenses should be used where they are most likely to increase sales.

**TABLE 21-3**   Four-Star Stores Corporation—Analysis of Income Statement Changes, 1980 to 1981

| Income Statement Item | 1980 | 1981 | Increase (Decrease) | |
|---|---|---|---|---|
| | | | Dollars | Percent |
| Net sales | $910,000 | $970,000 | $60,000 | 6.6 |
| Salaries expense | 105,000 | 110,000 | 5,000 | 4.8 |
| Advertising expense | 80,000 | 70,000 | (10,000) | (12½) |
| Supplies and postage expense | 18,000 | 24,000 | 6,000 | 33⅓ |

3 A reduction in expenses does not necessarily result in a decrease in sales.

4 Unnecessary expenditures do not increase sales and should be eliminated.

Table 21-4 shows the relationship of each of Four-Star Stores' operating expenses to net sales for the years 1980 and 1981. On the basis of the statistics, the owners or managers might ask questions like the following.

| | |
|---|---|
| **Salaries** | What were the reasons for the decrease from 11.5 percent to 11.3 percent despite a $5,000 increase in actual salaries? What accounted for the $5,000 increase in salaries? Employee raises or benefits? Additional personnel? |
| **Rent** | How much longer does the store's lease have to run? How would a substantial increase in rent affect the relationship between rent expense and projected sales? |
| **Advertising** | Why did net sales increase despite a reduction of $10,000 in advertising expenses? Might advertising expenditures be reduced further without hurting sales? |
| **Utilities** | Is the increase from 4.9 percent to 5.2 percent reasonable in the light of escalating costs of energy? Are there alternate forms of store lighting that should be explored? |
| **Insurance** | Does the slight decrease from 2.2 percent to 2.1 percent have implications for the adequacy of the store's insurance coverage? When can the company expect an increase in insurance rates? To what extent? |
| **Supplies and Postage** | What accounted for the increase from 2.0 percent to 2.5 percent? Prices of supplies and/or increased postal rates? Can outgoing mail be reduced without damaging sales? |
| **Depreciation** | Depreciation is the decrease in the value of an asset owing to wear and tear and other physical causes. It is considered an expense of operating a business. Is the increase from 1.3 percent to 1.6 percent a reflection of a wise investment in physical assets? Are additional equipment, furniture, and fixtures needed? |

# BUDGETS

Budgets and accounting data

Earlier in this chapter we stressed the need for accounting information in the development of retail budgets. Now we'll identify specific budgets and indicate their relationship to accounting data.

## Expense Budget

We have already indicated the importance of controlling operating expenses. In order to do this, many retailers prepare **expense budgets,** which consist of estimated expense outlays over a specific period—six months, one month, one week, and so on. These

**TABLE 21-4**   Four-Star Stores Corporation—Relationship of Operating Expenses to Net Sales, 1980 and 1981[a]

| Operating Expense | 1981 | | 1980 | |
| --- | --- | --- | --- | --- |
| | Dollars | Percent of Net Sales | Dollars | Percent of Net Sales |
| Salaries | $110,000 | 11.3 | $105,000 | 11.5 |
| Rent | 90,000 | 9.3 | 90,000 | 9.9 |
| Advertising | 70,000 | 7.2 | 80,000 | 8.8 |
| Utilities | 50,000 | 5.2 | 45,000 | 4.9 |
| Insurance | 20,000 | 2.1 | 20,000 | 2.2 |
| Supplies and postage | 24,000 | 2.5 | 18,000 | 2.0 |
| Depreciation | 16,000 | 1.6 | 12,000 | 1.3 |

[a]Net sales: 1980, $910,000; 1981, $970,000.

estimates are based on past experience and future plans. Actual expenses are then compared with the estimates to determine how well specific areas or departments are staying within the estimates.

Budgets must be flexible to accommodate sudden changes in operations. For example, a newspaper strike may affect sales so severely that a store may require additional funds for alternative advertising outlets.

A budget pinpoints responsibility for the expenditure of funds. Consequently, specific store personnel can be held accountable for expense overruns or rewarded for reducing expenses. Ideally, those who are responsible for incurring expenses should be involved in the development of the budget estimates.

Accounting records allow for the listing of specific expenses. In this way the retailer has day-to-day information on expenditures and uses the expense budget to make decisions.

## Cash Budget

As you have seen, one of the most crucial financial considerations facing retailers is the need to have sufficient current assets to pay bills as they come due. Of all the current assets, the most essential one is cash. This is so because only cash can satisfy the payment demands of creditors and employees. It should be noted, however, that an excess of cash is wasteful, since idle money does not earn anything for business. The excess might be used more productively for the purchase of additional stock or for investment.

In order to plan cash activities prudently, retailers develop a **cash budget.** This budget is an estimate of cash receipts and payments for a given period. Receipts are determined from forecasts of cash sales, accounts receivable collections, and miscellaneous income. Payments are based on anticipated expenditures for merchandise, expenses, miscellaneous items, and income taxes. As with expense budgets, actual intakes and outlays of cash are periodically matched against cash budget estimates to evaluate the company's cash position and take whatever action is necessary. Retailers often refer to their cash status as their cash flow position. A sample cash budget is shown in Figure 21-5.

## Advertising Budget

In Chapter 19 you saw that advertising is an extremely important function in a retail organization. In order to use advertising dollars effectively, many retailers develop advertising budgets. Estimates are usually based on the following factors: an evaluation of consumer demand, a selection of appropriate advertising media, a clear understanding of the retailer's objectives, and an appreciation of past practices and results. Up-to-date accounting information is essential if one is to determine how well the budget is serving as a useful guide to expenditures.

Despite the availability of useful advertising budget techniques, too many retailers base their estimates on a single consideration, such as competitors' practices, a tie-in to estimated sales volume, or an arbitrary determination of available funds. Retailers who fail to identify specific goals in the construction of advertising budgets frequently waste precious funds. For example, a store whose image is unclear might do well to commit some advertising dollars to strengthening its image rather than spending it all on conventional campaigns aimed at increasing sales.

## Merchandise Budget

A **merchandise budget** contains estimates of the factors that affect merchandise activities. It guides the retailer in the development of buying and selling plans. In this sense

## LOREL'S TOY ROOM— CASH BUDGET FOR QUARTER ENDED JUNE 30, 1982

|  | April | May | June |
|---|---|---|---|
| Cash balance, 1st day of month | $22,000 | $24,000 | $25,000 |
| Cash receipts |  |  |  |
| Cash sales | 12,000 | 11,000 | 14,000 |
| Accounts receivable collections | 15,000 | 17,000 | 18,000 |
| Rent from leased departments | 1,000 | 1,000 | 1,000 |
|  | $50,000 | $53,000 | $58,000 |
| Cash payments |  |  |  |
| Purchase of merchandise | $38,000 | $34,000 | $31,000 |
| Operating expenses | 11,000 | 10,000 | 8,000 |
| Installment on notes payable |  | 2,000 | 2,000 |
| Income taxes | 5,000 | 5,000 | 5,000 |
|  | $54,000 | $51,000 | $46,000 |
| Cash balance, last day of month | ($ 4,000) | $ 2,000 | $12,000 |

FIGURE 21-5
A cash budget.

it is also a mechanism for the control and evaluation of employees who are involved in merchandise functions.

The budget considers the following items: projected sales, inventory levels, open-to-buy, and gross margin. It provides for

1   An analysis of changes in the trading area
2   An examination of short- and long-range selling facilities
3   A consideration of additional merchandise categories
4   An identification of competitive practices

It plans for inventory shifts on the basis of opening stock levels, planned purchases, markdowns, discounts, and shortages.

A carefully developed merchandise budget provides a framework for sound business practices. It should be specific yet flexible, and must be attentive to past practices yet open to new ideas. Detailed performance statistics maintained in usable accounting form are essential to its success.

# SALES FORECASTING

*Sales forecasting: a key element in budgeting*

Our discussion of merchandise budgets indicated that one of the key items in such a budget is a projection of sales. This is true because a material over- or underestimation of sales has a serious effect on merchandising decisions. Consequently, it is essential that the retailer project future sales with a good degree of accuracy. As stated in Chapter 3, this predictive feature is often referred to as sales forecasting.

A small merchant develops forecasts on the basis of

1   Experience
2   Knowledge of the field
3   Contacts with suppliers
4   Opinions of salespeople
5   Input from professionals (e.g., accountants)

Minicomputers are being used by small retailers with increasing frequency in the development of sales forecasts.

Large retail companies

1   Gather information from their own executives and buyers
2   Secure data from consulting firms
3   Study journals of retail opinion, such as *Women's Wear Daily*
4   Use computers to identify trends and problems

All retailers rely on consumer attitudes and behavior to chart future actions.

# OPERATING AN ACCOUNTING SYSTEM

Large retailers utilize computers for most of their accounting functions. This enables them to secure daily reports on a variety of activities: sales, accounts receivables, inventory, and so forth. Input to computers is accomplished through the use of magnetic tapes, magnetic disks, or cash register tie-lines. In many instances source documents such as sales slips, checks, and credit slips are written by hand and then transfered to an input medium for computer processing. In addition to maintaining their own staffs for handling accounting functions, large retailers retain independent accounting firms to audit their records, prepare tax reports, and advise management.

Small retailers rely on independent accountants to design their accounting systems. Records are maintained by hand, by electromechanical equipment such as billing machines, or by outside computer service companies. Depending on the size of the store, daily records are kept by the owner or by bookkeepers and clerks. The accounting firm makes periodic visits to summarize and analyze the data. It is also responsible for the preparation of tax reports, and usually provides advice to the retailer.

**NEW TERMS**

| | |
|---|---|
| average collection period | liabilities |
| average turnover days | merchandise budget |
| balance sheet | net worth |
| cash budget | owner's equity |
| current ratio | quick ratio |
| dividend | return on investment (ROI) |
| expense budget | stockholders' equity |
| income statement | |

# CHAPTER HIGHLIGHTS

1 Accounting is the compilation of financial data for purposes of control, analysis, and decision making. Accounting records are important to owners, managers, government agencies, and private individuals and groups.

2 Individuals who make use of accounting data are classified as external users (outside the business) and internal users (within the business).

3 Accounting procedures include the functions of recording, classifying, reporting, and interpreting financial information.

4 The most commonly used financial reports are the balance sheet and the income statement.

5 A balance sheet contains a list of assets and liabilities, as well as owner's equity. Assets are categorized as current or long-lived, depending on how long they are expected to be available, while liabilities are listed as current or long term, depending on when they are scheduled for repayment.

## George Huntington Hartford
## THE A&P EMPIRE

Born in Augusta, Maine, in 1833, George Huntington Hartford worked in a dry-goods store in Boston to learn the basics of business. From there he went west to seek his fortune in the meat and hide center of St. Louis. However, the politics and hardships of frontier life convinced him that his merchant mind was better suited to the commerce of the East.

Hartford was hired by Benjamin F. Gilman, a successful businessman, to work in his leather firm and his newly developed tea-importing business. Within a short time the two men had expanded the tea enterprise into a retail and mail order tea business, undercutting competitors by means of a shrewd sales strategy. Thus was born the Great American Tea Company.

In 1869 Gilman and Hartford started a new company called Great Atlantic & Pacific Tea Company. Soon everyone was referring to it simply as A&P. By 1876 there were more than twenty stores extending as far west as St. Paul, Minnesota, and shortly thereafter there were a total of fifty-two outlets.

In 1878 Hartford secured control and management of A&P and could boast a sales volume of over $1 million. He introduced premium coupons, horse-drawn A&P wagons, and city directory advertising. Meanwhile the number of outlets had increased to over 200. By this time Hartford's sons were actively involved in the business.

After several terms as mayor of Orange, New Jersey, Hartford became active in turning A&P from a partnership into a corporation. In addition, the company changed its operations from credit-based stores to cash-and-carry stores, with startling decreases in costs and prices. By 1914 there were hundreds of A&P stores across the country.

George Huntington Hartford died in 1917, by which time he owned more than 4000 stores. By then A&P had become a household name, with the physical similarities of all A&P outlets embedded in the public mind. The concept of mass merchandising in the grocery field had come of age through A&P, paving the way for the emergence of the supermarket.

6 Several measurements based on balance sheet figures are useful to retailers. Among them are the current ratio (matching current assets against current liabilities) and the quick ratio (matching cash and receivables against current liabilities).

7 An income statement contains three sections: revenue from sales, cost of goods sold, and operating expenses. The final amount on the statement indicates net income (profit) or net loss.

8 A combination of balance sheet and income statement amounts provides retailers with the following measurements: merchandise turnover, which indicates how quickly merchandise has been sold; average collection period, which tells a retailer the

approximate time it has taken to collect from customers; and return on investment (ROI), which indicates the rate of return on a financial investment in a business.

9  Retailers often analyze expenses in terms of their increases or decreases from one period to another. Percents are a more realistic indication of such changes than dollars.

10  Operating expenses may be evaluated as a percent of net sales. This procedure allows retailers to judge the effect of overhead expenditures on sales volume.

11  Budgets are important for planning purposes and are also used to judge current operations. The following budgets are among those used by retailers: expense, cash, advertising, and merchandise.

12  Sales forecasting involves projecting sales. Both small and large retailers rely on internal and external resources to help them develop forecasts.

13  Large retailers use computers for most of their accounting functions, while small ones rely on hand methods, electromechanical equipment, or outside computer service companies.

# QUESTIONS

1  Prepare a list of users of retail accounting information and indicate how the data are used by each.

2  Why are the reporting and interpreting aspects of accounting procedures important to retailers?

3  How do current assets differ from plant and equipment assets? Why does a balance sheet contain both categories?

4  If a retailer's balance sheet shows current assets of $180,000 and current liabilities of $80,000, what is the current ratio? Is the ratio a favorable one?

5  Why is the quick ratio sometimes a better indicator of a retailer's ability to pay current debts than the current ratio?

6  If a retailer's income statement shows net sales of $230,000, cost of goods sold of $140,000, and operating expenses of $40,000, is the result a net income or net loss? In what amount?

7  Indicate whether each of the following retail operations should normally anticipate a *high* or a *low* merchandise turnover. State reasons for your answers.

A Marshall Field furniture department
A Burger King franchise
A Sears, Roebuck stereo department

8  A store's net sales for the year total $1,095,000 and its year-end accounts receivable amount to $45,000. What was its average collection period? Of what significance is this measurement?

9  A retailer's salary payments increased from $40,000 in October to $50,000 in November. What was the percent increase?

10 The following information is taken from the first-quarter operations of Lindy's Specialty Store for 1980 and 1981. On the basis of the data, answer the following questions.
   a What may have accounted for the percent decrease of delivery expenses in 1981 from the 1980 figure?
   b What questions should be asked about the change in advertising expenses?

Lindy's Specialty Store—First Quarter, 1980 and 1981

| | 1981 | | 1980 | |
|---|---|---|---|---|
| **Operating Expense** | **Dollars** | **Percent of Net Sales** | **Dollars** | **Percent of Net Sales** |
| Delivery | $ 3,000 | 5 | $ 4,000 | 8 |
| Advertising | 12,000 | 20 | 10,000 | 20 |

Net sales: 1980, $50,000; 1981, $60,000.

11 Explain why cash and merchandise budgets are of value to retailers.

12 Why is sales forecasting essential to the development of a merchandise budget?

# FIELD PROJECTS

1 Visit a local merchant to learn about his or her accounting system. Ask the following questions.
   a Who maintains the records?
   b Are the records kept in books or on machines, or is some other method used?
   c How often does the accountant visit the merchant?
   d What does the retailer discuss with the accountant during a visit?

2 Accounting textbooks contain balance sheets and income statements for wholesale and retail firms. Visit your school or local library and locate each of these financial statements in one of the textbooks. Compute the following measurements.
   a Current ratio
   b Quick ratio
   c Merchandise turnover

# CASES

1 Cyd Lesser and Randy Dee decided to open a retail bookstore as a partnership. While they were knowledgeable about the book business, they knew little about record-keeping requirements or accounting procedures. Friends had cautioned them about the need for accurate records as well as the importance of using accounting information for decision making.

The partners agreed to hire an accountant to design their accounting system. They were also anxious to utilize the accountant on a regular basis to evaluate the financial aspects of the business.

a  With regard to the development of an accounting system, what are some appropriate questions that the partners might ask of the accountant?

b  Might it be necessary for the accountant to prepare a balance sheet and income statement each month for the first year of operations? Why?

2  The following items were taken from the year-end financial statements and other records of a small specialty store.

| | |
|---|---|
| Total current assets | $20,000 |
| Cash | 4,000 |
| Receivables | 8,000 |
| Total current liabilities | 10,000 |
| Net sales | 72,000 |
| Beginning-of-year inventory at retail | 15,000 |
| End-of-year inventory at retail | 20,000 |

a  What were the current and quick ratios?

b  What was the rate of merchandise turnover?

c  From the turnover rate, would you judge that the store sells high- or low-priced goods? Why?

3  Three partners operate the Orleans Department Store. They have been in business for five years, registering a higher net income in each year. Though he is satisfied with the increasing profits, one of the partners feels that the store has been operating very much in the dark with regard to expense and cash items. He believes that the company should at least prepare expense and cash budgets as well as expense analyses. He argues that the store might do even better with a detailed understanding of its financial operations.

The other partners contend that a knowledge of merchandising is sufficient for business success. They point to the company's profit picture as proof of their position. Their feeling is that increased sales, generated through more advertising, will enable the store to continue its progress. They also claim that the financial aspects of the business should be left to the accountants and that retailers should concentrate on merchandising.

Because he is outnumbered, the first partner recognizes the need to support his position with hard facts. He also understands that the accounting records and financial statements for the past five years may not substantiate his position. Yet he is determined to make his case as strong as possible.

a  If you were the first partner, what information would you ask the accountant to prepare? Would you require data for all five years? Why?

    **b**  Do you agree with the two other partners that increased sales would guarantee continued profits? Why?

    **c**  With whose position do you agree? Why?

# REFERENCES

Bintinger, T. P., "Accounting and Financial Reporting Issues: An Update," *Retail Control,* 48 (April-May 1980), pp. 35–43.

Dubbs, E. S., "National Retail Merchants Association's Annual Merchandising and Operating Results: 1976 Analyzed," *Stores,* 59 (September 1977), pp. 36–37.

National Retail Merchants Association, Controllers' Congress, *Retail Accounting Manual* (New York, 1962).

———, Financial Executives Division, *Retail Accounting Manual,* rev. (New York, 1976), p. XI-1.

———, Merchandising Division, *Turnover: The Many Ways to Improve It* (New York, 1965).

———, Store Management Group, *Reducing Expense Ratios* (New York, 1966).

Needles, B. E., Jr., H. R. Anderson, and J. C. Caldwell, *Principles of Accounting,* (Boston: Houghton Mifflin 1981).

Reynolds, I. N., A. Slavin, and A. B. Sanders, *Elementary Accounting* (Hinsdale, Ill.: Dryden Press, 1981).

Scher, J., "Financial and Operating Results of Department and Specialty Stores of 1977," (New York: National Retail Merchants Assoc., 1978), p. 26.

# J. C. Penney's Statement of Income and Balance Sheet*

## Statement of Income
## Statement of Reinvested Earnings
(In millions except per share data)

| Statement of Income | 52 weeks ended January 26, 1980 | 52 weeks ended January 27, 1979 |
|---|---|---|
| Sales | $11,274 | $10,845 |
| **Costs and expenses** | | |
| Cost of goods sold, occupancy, buying, and warehousing costs | 8,005 | 7,650 |
| Selling, general, and administrative expenses | 2,632 | 2,522 |
| Interest, after deduction of income before income taxes of J.C. Penney Financial Corporation | 254 | 208 |
| Total costs and expenses | 10,891 | 10,380 |
| Income before income taxes and other unconsolidated subsidiaries | 383 | 465 |
| Income taxes | 166 | 212 |
| Income before other unconsolidated subsidiaries | 217 | 253 |
| Net income of other unconsolidated subsidiaries | 27 | 23 |
| Net income | $ 244 | $ 276 |
| Net income per share | $ 3.52 | $ 4.12 |

| Statement of Reinvested Earnings | | |
|---|---|---|
| Reinvested earnings at beginning of year | $ 1,613 | $ 1,456 |
| Net income for the year | 244 | 276 |
| Changes in unrealized decline in value of equity securities | 2 | (1) |
| Dividends | (122) | (118) |
| Reinvested earnings at end of year | $ 1,737 | $ 1,613 |

*Reproduced by permission of the J. C. Penney Company.

# Balance Sheet

(In millions)

| Assets | January 26, 1980 | January 27, 1979 |
|---|---:|---:|
| **Current assets** | | |
| Cash and short term investments | $ 99 | $ 78 |
| Receivables, net | 665 | 467 |
| Merchandise inventories | 1,749 | 2,046 |
| Prepaid expenses | 118 | 101 |
| **Total current assets** | 2,631 | 2,692 |
| **Investment in and advances to unconsolidated subsidiaries** | 579 | 498 |
| **Properties and property rights, net of accumulated depreciation and amortization of $641 and $569** | 1,823 | 1,609 |
| **Other assets** | 44 | 34 |
| | $5,077 | $4,833 |

| Liabilities and Stockholders' Equity | | |
|---|---:|---:|
| **Current liabilities** | | |
| Accounts payable and accrued liabilities | $1,084 | $1,077 |
| Dividend payable | 31 | 30 |
| Income taxes | 41 | 45 |
| Deferred credits, principally tax effects applicable to installment sales | 466 | 404 |
| **Total current liabilities** | 1,622 | 1,556 |
| **Long term debt and commitments under capital leases** | 836 | 841 |
| **Deferred credits,** principally tax effects applicable to depreciation and capital leases, net | 99 | 79 |
| **Stockholders' equity** | | |
| Preferred stock, without par value: Authorized, 5 million shares— issued, none | | |
| Common stock, par value 50¢: Authorized, 100 million shares— issued, 69.7 million shares | 783 | 744 |
| Reinvested earnings | 1,737 | 1,613 |
| **Total stockholders' equity** | 2,520 | 2,357 |
| | $5,077 | $4,833 |

# chapter 22
# INVENTORY CONTROL

## After completing this chapter, you should be able to:

1 Define inventory control and explain why it is important to retailers.

2 Identify the three merchandise categories used to describe inventory levels.

3 Identify the causes of inadequate and excessive inventories and suggest remedies for them.

4 List the factors that shape a store's inventory control system.

5 Describe the use of perpetual and periodic inventory methods in dollar control and unit control systems.

6 Estimate ending inventory using the retail method, and list the method's advantages and disadvantages.

7 Compute ending inventory by the FIFO (first in, first out) and LIFO (last in, first out) methods and explain their effect on income statements during inflationary and deflationary periods.

8 Explain the significance of the "lower of cost or market" rule when using the FIFO, LIFO, weighted-average, and specific-identification methods of computing ending inventory.

9 Explain how an over- or understatement of ending inventory on an income statement affects gross margin and net income.

In the last chapter you saw that merchandise inventory is an essential element of both the balance sheet and the income statement. The inventory value on the balance sheet tells the retailer the available stock on the last day of the accounting period, while the beginning and ending inventory values on the income statement are used to determine the cost of goods sold and gross margin for the period. Since inventory is so large a part of a store's assets and because it figures so prominently in the determination of profit or loss, it is important that retailers understand its effect on various phases of store operation.

# THE NEED FOR INVENTORY CONTROL

It has already been pointed out that, ideally, a store should contain sufficient merchandise at all times to satisfy customers. Reaching the ideal is not a simple matter, however. It calls for planning, alertness, and, in the case of larger stores, sophisticated record keeping.

## Types of Inventory

For purposes of identifying inventory levels, merchandise may be categorized as follows.

1  Basic inventory
2  Assortments
3  New inventory

**Basic inventory** consists of items that a store always stocks. For example, one would certainly expect to find hammers, pliers, and screwdrivers in a hardware store or in the hardware department of a department store. For the store to be out of any of these items would be most disturbing to a customer looking for them. To avoid customer annoyance, then, the store must be careful in keeping track of its basic stock.

*Assortments develop customer loyalty*

**Assortments** refer to varieties within basic inventories. In the case of hammers, for example, a store might carry nail, sledge, and ball peen hammers as basic inventory. To accommodate special customers, it might also sell riveting and bricklayer hammers. The variety and quantity of assortments depend largely on customer demand, but resourceful retailers plan and maintain assortments in such a way as to develop and sustain customer loyalty.

**New inventory** consists of items introduced by the store for the first time. Such items may be newly designed products or products not formerly carried by the store. For example, a food store that carries a hosiery line for the first time is experimenting with a new product. On the basis of its experience, it may eventually widen its offerings of new inventory. If it does, it may then be obligated to maintain stock levels that are sufficient to satisfy customer demand.

# The Adequacy of Inventory Levels

Regardless of the type of inventory, care must be taken to assure adequate stock on hand. This involves constant awareness of the following factors.

1   The quantity of goods in selling areas, stockrooms, and warehouses.
2   The frequency of sales of each inventory item.
3   The type and quantity of stock on order.

With this information, the retailer can make timely decisions on whether to increase the supply of quick-selling products or mark down slow-selling items for speedier sale. For example, a T-shirt with specific appeal to young boys that had been expected to sell only moderately, suddenly "takes off." With proper controls, the store can detect the trend and prepare to replenish the stock in time to tap the shirt's popularity.

Inadequate inventory may result from

1   Improper anticipation of sales.
2   Late deliveries by suppliers.
3   Insufficient funds for purchases.
4   Unexpected customer demand.

Strategies for avoiding inadequate inventory

Though it is not always possible to avoid these problems, the retailer can plan a course of action to avoid at least the first three of the above items. For example, information obtained from manufacturers, distributors, or trade publications is an aid in predicting sales volume. Awareness of a supplier's past delivery record or well-placed pressure on

This ad emphasizes the importance of computers in making decisions about inventories.

the supplier may minimize late deliveries. Finally, alternate sources of funds (e.g., short- and long-term notes at banks) may bring in the money required for purchases.

The consequences of an inadequate inventory are, of course, reduced sales and disappointed shoppers. While lost revenue may be recaptured through additional promotions and advertising, it is not always possible to entice unhappy customers back to the store.

While insufficient inventory should be avoided, so should excessive quantities of stock. Too much merchandise on hand arises from

1 Poor sales performance.
2 Overordering.
3 Ordering incorrect items.

As in the case of inadequate levels, the keys to preventing inventory overages are obtaining reliable information from suppliers and pinpointing consumer demand.

Excessive stock, as you have seen, ties up funds and space needlessly. Particularly during periods of high interest rates, when it is expensive to borrow money to buy merchandise, retailers must make every effort to maintain sensible stock levels. Otherwise, they may watch their profits dwindle as unnecessary merchandise remains unsold.

# INVENTORY CONTROL SYSTEMS

Since it is important to keep inventory at satisfactory levels, a store requires a workable plan to carry out this goal. Whatever system is adopted must provide usable information for decision making and not be too costly to maintain. The system used by any given retailer depends on the following factors.

## The Size of the Inventory

*Factors that shape inventory control systems*

Some owners of small stores attempt to assess the size of inventories by means of observation of merchandise on shelves and in stockrooms. Unfortunately, this approach is fraught with the danger of over- or underestimating inventory levels, and indicates lack of managerial know-how. A more objective approach requires written records. Inventories in large stores, of course, require considerably more attention than those in smaller ones because of the sheer quantity and variety of items for sale. Figure 22-1 shows a tie-in between a price ticket and an inventory sheet.

## The Assortments Within the Inventory

Stores that have relatively few categories of merchandise can keep tabs on inventory levels fairly easily. However, those with great product diversification are faced with more serious information problems.

## The Information Needed by Top and Middle Management

Top management is concerned primarily with overall store performance: sales, cost of purchases, gross margin, net income, and so forth. Middle management, on the other

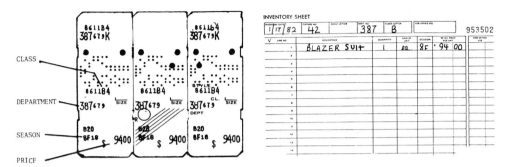

**FIGURE 22-1**
Recording information from a price ticket (Kimball ticket) to an inventory sheet.

hand, needs more detailed inventory statistics: sizes, styles, colors, and the like. Both levels of management require data about departments and sections within departments.

Two widely used systems for gathering information about inventory are **dollar control** and **unit control**. The former indicates the dollar value of merchandise, while the latter treats merchandise in terms of quantity. Let's look at each system in detail.

# Dollar Control

In this system retail dollar values are used for all calculations. Therefore, when one is computing an inventory at any particular time, the inventory is stated at its retail value. As you will see later in this chapter, however, the retail value can easily be converted into the cost price of the inventory.

Dollar control reveals the performance of broad segments of a store; that is, it shows the sales, purchases, markdowns, and ending inventories for the entire store or for some segment of the store, such as a department or a merchandise category. Dollar control does not, however, deal with inventory quantities. There are two methods for maintaining dollar control of inventories. One is called perpetual inventory and the other periodic inventory.

## Perpetual Inventory in Dollar Control

The word *perpetual* signifies the continual occurrence of an event. A **perpetual inventory** is defined as a method for knowing the value of an inventory at any given time. This requires an understanding of the flow of merchandise in a business as well as an appreciation of the necessary records.

Basically, inventory in a retail store moves as follows: First it is received and stored or put out for sale; next it is sold; finally, whatever remains unsold is listed as ending inventory. Now examine Figure 22-2. You are looking at a perpetual inventory record for a particular style of jeans. It indicates that there was a jeans inventory of $3000 at the beginning of July. The sales of $700 on July 2 left a balance of $2300. On July 3 the $1000 worth of merchandise received raised the balance to $3300. The sales for July 5 and 6 ($600 and $800) reduced the inventory on hand to $2700 and $1900, respectively.

As you can see, the inventory on hand is known each time merchandise is received or sold—provided that the inventory control card is kept up to date or a computer is

## INVENTORY CONTROL
## JEANS—STYLE NO. 104L

| Date | Received | Sales | Inventory on Hand |
|------|----------|-------|-------------------|
| July 1 | | | $3000 |
| 2 | | $700 | 2300 |
| 3 | $1000 | | 3300 |
| 5 | | 600 | 2700 |
| 6 | | 800 | 1900 |

**FIGURE 22-2**
An inventory control card for a perpetual-inventory system—dollar control.

used. The inventory record is valuable for making daily decisions about how merchandise is moving, which items require restocking, which items should be marked down, and so forth. However, the data on the card are only an *estimate* of the inventory on hand each day, since shortages (pilferage, etc.) or customer returns may have reduced or increased the stock.

Notice, too, that each different inventory item requires a separate control card. Depending on the size of the store and its financial capacity, the information may be recorded by computers, by mechanical equipment, or by hand.

Since shortages are inevitable in retail businesses, it is necessary to take a periodic physical count of the merchandise to check the accuracy of the inventory control cards. Any discrepancies between the *estimated* amounts on the cards and the *actual* amounts from the physical count are corrected on the cards. Since an inventory count is a time-consuming and expensive procedure, it is usually done only once or twice a year.

Because record keeping can be costly, the perpetual-inventory method is better suited to high-ticket items like cars and appliances than to low-priced products like food and notions. This is apparent when one considers the smaller number of types of inventory carried by a car dealer as compared with a variety store. Nevertheless, a perpetual-inventory record can be maintained by any retailer whose cash register or credit system is tied to a computer. In fact, increasing numbers of stores are installing cash registers with special sensing devices and "tear-off" price tags to record sales and, thus, inventory changes.

*Perpetual inventory records are checked by periodic physical counts*

### Periodic Inventory in Dollar Control

Unlike the perpetual-inventory method, the **periodic-inventory** method involves finding the value of merchandise at a particular time *only* by taking a physical count of the stock. It is used by retailers who do not require constant knowledge of inventory levels or find the cost of maintaining perpetual-inventory records prohibitive.

Some retailers take physical counts several times a year. However, the cost of such counts restricts most merchants to one or two counts a year, usually during January–February and July–August. In effect, then, the difference between a store that uses a perpetual-inventory record with one or two physical counts a year and a store that uses a periodic method with the same counts is that the former has a continuous stream of information for decision making. The latter, instead, must rely largely on observation of inventory on shelves and in stockrooms for merchandise information, or on some type of written record.

*Taking inventory* means making a physical count of merchandise. The specific time when inventory is taken, however, depends on a store's needs. Some large stores take counts based on specific inventory categories (e.g., sportswear). Others stagger their counts, with each department being inventoried during a different month.

To ensure a realistic count, a specific inventory-taking date is set. All transactions that affect the inventory balance on that date are taken into account: receipts of goods, sales, returns, and so on. While some stores check inventory while business is in progress, most retailers do so when their stores are closed (i.e., on holidays or after hours). The actual counting is done by employees or by an outside contractor whose staff is trained to take inventories. Records are maintained by hand on specially designed columnar sheets or with the aid of electronic devices that detect sensed markings (codes) on shelves or packages.

# Unit Control

As indicated previously, unit control involves quantities rather than dollars. Depending on the store's needs, it provides the retailer with a number of vital facts.

1   The number of items on hand, arranged by size, color, style, or other merchandise classifications.
2   Products that are selling at fast or slow rates.
3   An indication of how well each vendor's merchandise is moving.
4   Detection of stock shortages.
5   The points at which stock should be reordered, and the quantities needed.

Taking inventory electronically involves bar code scanning and reduces clerical time.

As with dollar control, unit control can be maintained through the use of perpetual or periodic inventory methods. Let's examine each of these possibilities.

## Perpetual Inventory in Unit Control

Figure 22-3 shows an inventory control card for a particular model and color of gas range. On August 1 there were 6 ranges in stock. On August 2 three additional ranges were received, resulting in a new inventory on hand of 9 units. The sales on August 5, 8, and 10 reduced the on-hand inventories to 7, 4, and 3, respectively. The heading of the form indicates a reorder point of 4 units. This tells the retailer that when the inventory on hand drops to 4, additional ranges should be ordered to avoid running out of merchandise. Notice that the reorder point was reached on August 8. Obviously, the retailer requires a procedure for employees to follow in order to obtain the needed merchandise in the correct style, color, and quantity. Computers meet this need admirably.

As you can see, in the perpetual-inventory method the arithmetic procedures are similar for both dollar and unit control. In fact, the most effective use of the method combines both controls; this approach is used by many retailers. Shortages can easily be checked with unit control by matching inventory control card figures with actual counts.

Unit control through perpetual inventory is used primarily by retailers that sell merchandise at high prices or in distinctive units such as fashion apparel and footwear. It is costly and cumbersome with quick-selling items like drugs and food products. As mentioned previously, however, improvements in data processing equipment and techniques allow merchants to maintain perpetual-inventory unit control through the use of electronic cash registers and charge account procedures.

*Perpetual inventory with dollar and unit control*

## Periodic Inventory in Unit Control

Here, as in dollar control, inventory on hand—or ending inventory, as it is usually called—is determined by physical count. Inventory not on hand is presumed to be sold or lost as a result of shortages.

When an ending inventory figure has been determined, financial statements are

### INVENTORY CONTROL
### GAS RANGE — MODEL NO. L254 — COLOR: RED
### REORDER POINT: 4

| Date | Units Received | Units Sold | Units on Hand |
|---|---|---|---|
| August 1 | | | 6 |
| 2 | 3 | | 9 |
| 5 | | 2 | 7 |
| 8 | | 3 | 4* |
| 10 | | 1 | 3 |

*Reorder point.

**FIGURE 22-3**
An inventory control card for perpetual-inventory system—unit control.

prepared. From these reports the merchant obtains key results such as gross margin and net income.

Individual items offered by a merchant often undergo a stock count periodically on a rotating basis to determine whether they are running low or not selling.

# ESTIMATING AN INVENTORY

Though formal financial statements are generally prepared once a year, many retailers require balance sheets and especially income statements more frequently. In such cases accountants usually submit monthly or interim statements (as opposed to formal statements). With data on the cost of goods sold, gross margin, operating expenses, and net income (or loss), merchants can make decisions based on timely information.

A problem arises with regard to the development of the income statement when the periodic-inventory method is used. You will recall that an ending inventory is required in order to compute the cost of goods sold as well as the gross margin. Furthermore, for income statement purposes the ending inventory must be the *cost,* not the retail, figure. A review of a section of an income statement may be helpful before we proceed (see Figure 22-4).

Since retailers generally maintain inventory records at retail prices, some way is needed to estimate the ending inventory at retail and then convert that figure to its cost equivalent. A very popular method, especially among large and medium-sized stores, is the retail method.

## The Retail Method for Estimating Inventory

The **retail method** for estimating an inventory at cost is used by many retailers and is accepted by the federal government for tax purposes. In order to use it, the retailer must have available both the cost and the retail prices of beginning inventories and purchases. You will see shortly why this is so.

### INCOME STATEMENT

| | | |
|---|---:|---:|
| Net sales | | $50,000 |
| **Cost of goods sold** | | |
| Beginning inventory (at cost) | $18,000 | |
| Add: purchases (at cost) | 22,000 | |
| Cost of goods available for sale (at cost) | 40,000 | |
| Less: ending inventory (at cost) | 25,000 | |
| Cost of goods sold | | 15,000 |
| Gross margin | | $35,000 |

**FIGURE 22-4**
An abbreviated income statement.

Suppose Carol Rich, the owner of Carol's Handmade Pottery, wants to estimate her inventory at cost price on February 28 in order to prepare an income statement for the month. Her records reveal the following.

| | |
|---|---|
| Inventory, February 1, at cost | $10,000 |
| Inventory, February 1, at retail | 20,000 |
| Purchases for February, at cost | 15,000 |
| Purchases for February, at retail | 30,000 |

Steps in estimating ending inventory by the retail method

Rich takes the following steps to estimate her ending inventory.

1 She determines the goods available for sale at both cost and retail prices.

| | Cost | Retail |
|---|---|---|
| Inventory, February 1 | $10,000 | $20,000 |
| Add: February purchases | 15,000 | 30,000 |
| Goods available for sale during February | $25,000 | $50,000 |

2 She computes the relationship between the goods available for sale at cost and at retail. This is called the *cost ratio*.

Goods available for sale:

$$\text{At cost } \frac{\$25,000}{\$50,000} = \frac{1}{2} = 50\% \text{ cost ratio}$$

In other words, for the month of February the total cost of the merchandise available for sale was 50 percent of its retail price.

3 From her accounting records she determines the sales for February to be $39,000, markdowns $700, and stock shrinkage $300. The total reduction in inventory of $40,000 is subtracted from the goods available for sale at retail ($50,000, from step 1) to find the February 28 inventory (ending inventory) at retail.

| | | |
|---|---|---|
| February sales | $39,000 | |
| February markdowns | 700 | |
| February shrinkage | 300 | |
| Total reduction in inventory | $40,000 | |
| Goods available for sale (retail) | | $50,000 |
| Total reduction in inventory | | 40,000 |
| February 28 inventory (retail) | | $10,000 |

4 Finally, she multiplies the February 28 inventory at retail by the cost ratio found in step 2 to find the February 28 inventory at cost price.

$$\frac{\text{February 28 inventory}}{\text{at retail}} \times \frac{\text{cost}}{\text{ratio}} = \frac{\text{February 28 inventory}}{\text{at cost}}$$

$$\$10,000 \times .50 = \$5,000$$

The $5,000 figure is the ending inventory that is used on both the balance sheet and the income statement prepared at the end of February.

## Advantages of the Retail Method

The most important advantages of the retail method are as follows.

1  Interim financial statements can be prepared without having to take a physical inventory. This is a tremendous time-saver for managers who need frequent information about the cost of goods sold, gross margin, and net income or loss.

2  When a physical inventory must be taken, the retail method minimizes the chance of clerical errors. This is so because merchandise is already marked with retail prices, while taking inventory on a cost basis requires coding the merchandise, as discussed in Chapter 16, so that customers are not aware of the cost. Subsequent decoding by store personnel at inventory-taking time can result in a high rate of clerical errors.

3  Since merchandise is marked with retail prices, inventory can be taken more frequently than when coded cost prices are used. Consequently, a comparison of actual counts with estimates shown by the retail method gives management a better understanding of stock shortages as well as fast- and slow-moving merchandise.

4  In the event of damage to merchandise due to fire or some other cause, the estimated inventory computed by the retail method at the time of the loss can be used to submit insurance claims. Since merchandise comprises such a large part of a store's assets, insurance coverage is essential, as are the accompanying records to substantiate losses.

## Disadvantages of the Retail Method

The most significant disadvantages of the retail method are the following.

1  The clerical cost of maintaining records at retail prices is considerable. This arises from the need to record price changes due to markups, markdowns, merchandise returns, and so forth. A store must judge the numerous benefits of the retail method against record-keeping expenses.

2  The cost ratio in the retail method is an *average* based on the total goods available in a store for a given period. It does not account for different markups and frequencies of sales within specific departments. Consequently, the computed ending inventory may distort the actual inventory situation in particular departments. To overcome this problem, some stores apply the retail method for estimating inventory on a departmental basis.

3  Since the retail method depends on accurate sales forecasts, any significant change in retail prices distorts the estimated ending inventory.

# ACCOUNTING FOR INVENTORY ON A COST BASIS

You have already seen that when inventory records are maintained at cost prices, taking a physical inventory is an expensive and error-prone process. Nevertheless, some retailers use the cost method because of its lower record-keeping costs.

Some retailers who operate on the cost basis under a periodic-inventory system do not mark merchandise with cost figures, not even in coded form. Consequently, they are unable to specify ending inventory items by their original cost. For example, a music store that stocks all 40-inch guitar cases in one bin without regard to purchase date or cost cannot distinguish among the cases when taking inventory. Yet it must establish an ending inventory value in order to prepare financial statements.

FIFO and LIFO assumptions

The solution to the music store's problem depends on the theoretical assumption it makes with regard to the sale of the guitars. Most stores make either of the following *assumptions.*

1  **First in, first out (FIFO)**  Merchandise purchased first is sold completely before any subsequently purchased items are sold.

2  **Last in, first out (LIFO)**  The merchandise purchased last is sold completely before any earlier-purchased items are sold.

The second assumption may sound strange, but remember that it is an assumption for computational purposes *only.* Its theoretical explanation is beyond the scope of this book, but it can be found in any elementary accounting textbook. You must also recognize that since all the guitar cases are alike, it makes no difference which ones are *actually* sold.

Now let's see how the music store determines its ending inventory under FIFO and LIFO.

Suppose the store's inventory records of 40-inch guitar cases for a business year ending December 31 show the following.

| Date | Quantity | Cost per Case | Total Cost |
|---|---|---|---|
| January 1—on hand | 20 | $15 | $300 |
| April 6—purchase | 30 | 16 | 480 |
| July 14—purchase | 30 | 16 | 480 |
| November 2—purchase | 40 | 17 | 680 |

On December 31 the store took physical inventory and counted *44 guitar cases on hand.* The question is, On December 31 which 44 cases are in the inventory? Which price(s) should be used to compute the ending inventory?

# FIFO

Using the FIFO approach, the assumption is that the guitar cases on hand on January 1 were the first ones sold (first in, first out), that the next ones sold were from the April 6 purchase, and so on. Therefore, to determine which cases are on hand on December 31, we start with the ones from the last purchase of the year, that is, the purchase of November 2. This is how the computations are made.

| Date | Quantity on Hand | Cost per Case | Total Cost |
|---|---|---|---|
| From November 2 purchase | 40 | $17 | $680 |
| From July 14 purchase | 4 | 16 | 64 |
|  | 44 |  | $744 |

Using FIFO, then, the cost value of the ending inventory of 44 guitar cases is $744. Now we'll use the LIFO assumption.

# LIFO

Using the LIFO approach, the assumption is that the guitar cases from the last purchase (November 2) were the first ones sold (last in, first out), that the next ones sold were from the July 14 purchase, and so forth. Therefore, to determine which cases are on hand on December 31 we start with the ones on hand January 1. This is how the computations are made.

| Date | Quantity on Hand | Cost per Case | Total Cost |
|------|------------------|---------------|------------|
| From January 1 on hand | 20 | $15 | $300 |
| From April 6 purchase | 24 | 16 | 384 |
| | 44 | | $684 |

Using LIFO, then, the cost value of the ending inventory of 44 guitar cases is $684.

# Comparison of FIFO and LIFO

*FIFO and LIFO during inflation and deflation*

In order to understand how FIFO and LIFO affect profits and losses, refer back to the inventory cost per case on page 492. Notice that the cost of the guitar cases rose from $15 each to $16, and then to $17. In other words, since prices increased, there was *inflation* in the economy.

Now we need to examine a section of an income statement (Figure 22-5) using both FIFO and LIFO ending inventory figures. When FIFO was used, the ending inventory was $744 and the gross margin was $1144. The comparable amounts for LIFO were $684 and $1084. In other words, using LIFO during an inflationary period results in a lower gross margin. That also means a lower net income and, consequently, a lower income tax for the retailer. Of course, the reverse will be true when prices are falling, that is, during a period of *deflation*.

| | Ending Inventory at FIFO | | Ending Inventory at LIFO | |
|---|---|---|---|---|
| Net sales | | $2000 | | $2000 |
| **Cost of Goods Sold** | | | | |
| Beginning inventory (at cost) | $ 900 | | $ 900 | |
| Add: purchases (at cost) | 700 | | 700 | |
| Cost of goods available for sale (at cost) | 1600 | | 1600 | |
| Less: ending inventory (at cost) | 744 | | 684 | |
| Cost of goods sold | | 856 | | 916 |
| Gross margin | | $1144 | | $1084 |

**FIGURE 22-5**
Effects of FIFO and LIFO on gross margin.

Retailers may select either FIFO or LIFO to compute inventory on a cost basis. However, once they have made a selection they are required by the Internal Revenue Service to use that method consistently. (Exceptions are considered on a case-by-case basis.) Obviously, if inflation continues, the retailer using LIFO will have a tax advantage. Should deflation take place, however, the retailer would pay higher taxes.

## Additional Inventory Methods

There are two additional ways of computing inventories on a cost basis. They are the weighted-average method and the specific identification method.

### The Weighted-Average Method

This method is used to avoid the extremes of FIFO and LIFO caused by inflation and deflation. It is based on an average price paid by the retailer for inventory purchases. As a result, the value of the ending inventory falls between the FIFO and LIFO amounts during both inflation and deflation. Owing to the greater record-keeping demands of this method, it is not used by many retailers.

### The Specific-Identification Method

As you have seen, some merchants who sell high-priced products mark the merchandise with coded cost symbols. Since their inventories contain relatively few items, taking stock is not a burdensome process. A clerk tallies the inventory by reading from the price tag, label, or sheet. The final listing contains each stock item specifically identified.

## The "Lower of Cost or Market" Rule

After computing the ending inventory by one of the four costing methods described so far, some retailers go one step further. They determine the end-of-period replacement cost (market price) of the merchandise and match it with the computed cost. The inventory is then valued at the lower price—cost or market—so that, in keeping with standard accounting procedure, the more conservative (lower) amount will be used on the financial statements (the **"lower of cost or market" rule**). This will also result in a lower (conservative) net income. This procedure, though time-consuming, requires the retailer to check the end-of-period market prices of merchandise and renders the ending inventory more realistic. A computer is ideally suited to this purpose.

## OVERESTIMATING AND UNDERESTIMATING ENDING INVENTORY

Up to this point we have been discussing the manner in which ending inventory is determined. Whether it is derived by a perpetual or a periodic procedure or by the retail or cost method, and whether it is needed weekly or annually, the inventory on hand at a particular time is central to assessing store progress.

The question now arises as to the accuracy of the ending inventory and its effect on financial statements. In particular, we need to examine the impact of erroneous inventory estimates or counts on specific income statement items.

Figure 22-6 contains an income statement in which the ending inventory is shown in three separate ways.

1 Stated correctly

2 Overstated: Because of an error, the ending inventory is *higher* than it should be.

3 Understated: Because of an error, the ending inventory is *lower* than it should be.

The gross margins and net incomes for each of the inventory conditions in the figure are as follows.

|  | Gross Margin | Net Income |
|---|---|---|
| Ending inventory *stated correctly* | $1300 | $800 |
| Ending inventory *overstated* | 1400 | 900 |
| Ending inventory *understated* | 1200 | 700 |

**Effects of overestimating or underestimating ending inventory**

Notice that when the ending inventory is overstated, the gross margin and net income are also overstated. When the ending inventory is understated, the gross margin and net income are also understated. In other words, overstatements and understatements of ending inventory distort both gross margins and net incomes.

It should be obvious that accuracy in the determination of ending inventory is essential for retailers. Serious inventory miscalculations present false pictures of store

## INCOME STATEMENT

|  | Ending Inventory Stated Correctly | | Ending Inventory Overstated | | Ending Inventory Understated | |
|---|---|---|---|---|---|---|
| Sales | | $3000 | | $3000 | | $3000 |
| **Cost of Goods Sold** | | | | | | |
| Beginning inventory (at cost) | $1200 | | $1200 | | $1200 | |
| Add: purchases (at cost) | 1500 | | 1500 | | 1500 | |
| Cost of goods available for sale (at cost) | 2700 | | 2700 | | 2700 | |
| Less: ending inventory (at cost) | 1000 | | 1100 | | 900 | |
| Cost of goods sold | | 1700 | | 1600 | | 1800 |
| Gross margin | | 1300 | | 1400 | | 1200 |
| Operating expenses | | 500 | | 500 | | 500 |
| Net income | | $ 800 | | $ 900 | | $ 700 |

FIGURE 22-6
Effects on gross margin and net income of overstating and understating ending inventory.

achievement and interfere with proper planning. Employees who are charged with taking inventory, therefore, must exercise extreme care in the physical counting and record-keeping processes.

**NEW TERMS**

| | |
|---|---|
| assortments | new inventory |
| basic inventory | periodic inventory |
| dollar control | perpetual inventory |
| first in, first out (FIFO) | retail method |
| last in, first out (LIFO) | unit control |
| "lower of cost or market" rule | |

## CHAPTER HIGHLIGHTS

1  Inventory levels are characterized by three merchandise categories: basic inventory, assortments, and new inventory.

2  Inadequate inventory results from improper anticipation of sales, late deliveries by suppliers, insufficient funds for purchases, and unexpected customer demand.

3  Excessive quantities of stock arise from poor sales performance, overordering, and incorrect orders.

4  The type of inventory control system used by a retailer depends on the size of its inventory, the assortments within the inventory, and the information needed by top and middle management.

5  Dollar control of inventory reveals the performance of broad segments of a store. Control may be maintained by either of two inventory methods: perpetual or periodic.

6  The perpetual-inventory method tells the retailer how much stock should be on hand at any given time. Stock records are checked periodically by means of a physical count of merchandise.

7  The periodic-inventory method involves a physical count of merchandise without recourse to perpetual records.

8  Unit control of inventory involves the determination of inventory quantities rather than dollars. Control may be maintained by either the perpetual or the periodic method.

9  The retail method for estimating ending inventory is used in the development of interim financial statements. Its advantages include the preparation of financial statements without a physical count of stock, the reduction of clerical errors, the opportunity to detect stock shrinkage, and the availability of records to support inventory insurance claims. The disadvantages include the cost of maintaining records and possible distortion of the ending inventory by using an average in the cost ratio.

10  Retailers who account for inventory on a cost basis but do not list cost prices on the inventory items usually use FIFO (first in, first out) or LIFO (last in, first out) to

compute ending inventory. LIFO results in a lower ending inventory, a lower net income, and a lower income tax for the retailer during inflation.

11 The weighted-average and specific-identification methods may also be used to compute ending inventory on a cost basis. The "lower of cost or market" rule matches the end-of-period replacement cost (market price) of merchandise with its computed cost.

12 Over- or underestimating ending inventory distorts gross margin and net income on an income statement and presents an incorrect picture of the store's achievement.

# QUESTIONS

1 When discussing inventory levels, what is the significance of assortments in the development of customer loyalty?

2 Why should a store be as concerned about excessive quantities of stock as it is about inadequate inventory?

3 How does the size of the inventory affect small and large stores in the development of their inventory control systems?

4 Why is the perpetual-inventory method better suited to a business that sells high-ticket items than to one that carries low-priced products?

5 What is the basic difference between the perpetual and periodic inventory methods? What effect has the computer had on these methods?

6 What is the purpose of the reorder point on a perpetual-inventory control card?

7 How does the retail method of estimating ending inventory help the retailer assess store progress at the end of a month?

8 Why is the retail method of estimating ending inventory valuable to a merchant in filing inventory insurance claims?

9 How do FIFO and LIFO affect a store's ending inventory, gross margin, and net income during a period of inflation? During a period of deflation?

10 What is the purpose of the "lower of cost or market" rule? Why might a retailer not follow it?

11 How does an overstatement of ending inventory on an income statement affect gross margin and net income? What are the effects of understatement?

# FIELD PROJECTS[1]

1 On June 24 merchandise in L. T. Barr's specialty shop was partially damaged by fire. The owner, Larry Barr, maintained inventory records on the basis of retail prices. In order to establish an insurance claim, he decided to estimate the inventory on hand at cost price at the time of the fire.

[1]The Field Projects for this chapter involve the computation and interpretation of financial measurements used by retailers.

From a May 31 interim income statement and other records, Barr listed the following data.

| June 1 | inventory at cost | $30,000 |
|--------|-------------------|---------|
| June 1 | inventory at retail | 40,000 |
| June 1–24 | purchases at cost | 70,000 |
| June 1–24 | purchases at retail | 110,000 |
| June 1–24 | sales at retail | 88,000 |
| June 1–24 | estimated shrinkage at retail | 2,000 |

   a  Compute the June 24 estimated inventory at cost price.

   b  Explain why the cost ratio is so important in justifying the value of the June 24 estimated inventory.

2  Inventory records in the TV department of Chance's Emporium are kept on a cost basis. The store sells only one brand of 19-inch color models with remote control. The owner's financial records for this model contain the following information on December 31, the end of the store's business year.

| Date | Quantity | Cost per TV Set |
|------|----------|-----------------|
| January 1—on hand | 10 | $200 |
| May 9—purchase | 14 | 200 |
| September 3—purchase | 12 | 220 |
| November 7—purchase | 20 | 230 |

A physical count of the inventory on December 31 showed eight TV sets on hand.

   a  Compute the December 31 inventory by the FIFO and LIFO methods.

   b  Since the year was an inflationary one, how would your answers for FIFO and LIFO have affected the store's net income?

## CASES

1  Recently a men's specialty shop ran a newspaper advertisement that started as follows.

---

# CREDITOR'S SETTLEMENT
## MUST RAISE CASH!

We've been in business for a long time. In fact, we are probably the oldest and finest men's clothiers on Long Island. But, because of adverse conditions in men's retail we are forced into the position of raising cash. So, starting now, we begin a sale of our entire inventory of nationally famous brands of men's fine clothing, furnishings and sportswear! So hurry in and take advantage of our sale . . . we need the cash and you will benefit from the savings!

---

a In addition to the "adverse conditions in men's retail" mentioned in the advertisement as the reason for the sale, the store may also have had an excess of inventory. If so, what conditions may have caused that situation?

b How can a store avoid an excessive inventory?

2 George Mador is planning to open a children's-wear store with a substantial investment in merchandise. He intends to employ fifteen salespeople in four separate departments.

Since he expects to carry only high-priced goods, he is anxious to develop an efficient inventory control system. He has sufficient funds to purchase a small computer with tie-ins to six cash registers.

Mador hires you as an inventory consultant and asks you to respond to the following questions.

a Should he maintain inventory records on a retail or a cost basis? Why?

b Should he develop a perpetual or a periodic inventory system? Why?

3 Despite increasing criticism by well-known management consultants like Peter F. Drucker, many businesses continue to follow the FIFO method of computing ending inventory. The criticism arises from the fact that the use of FIFO results in higher taxes during an inflationary period. Drucker contends that significant tax savings are lost when LIFO is not used.

A further argument for LIFO is made by J. C. Penney Company and Federated Department Stores, which suggest that because it matches the latest inventory costs against revenues, LIFO is more representative of the effects of inflation.

Retailers who continue to use FIFO do not dispute the criticism. They contend, however, that FIFO results in higher net incomes and that stockholders are impressed by that fact when they study the firm's income statements.

Another reason for the persistent use of FIFO is the fear expressed by retailers who are thinking of selling their stores. They reason that the higher net incomes caused by FIFO are more attractive to potential buyers.

Some retail managers are comfortable with FIFO because it follows the way merchandise is received and sold; that is, the first products to arrive are the first ones sold. LIFO, of course, works the other way round and unsettles some managers who view it as an illogical system.

a If you were in top management at a store that uses FIFO, would you consider switching to LIFO (assuming that the IRS has granted permission)? What arguments would you use in support of making the switch?

b If you were starting a retail business this year, which method would you use, FIFO or LIFO? Why?

# REFERENCES

"Inventory Control at Ski Market," *Stores,* 63 (August 1981), pp. 52–53.

Meyer, J. S., *Dollar and Unit Merchandise Planning and Budgeting* (New York: National Retail Merchants Association, Merchandising Division, 1960).

"More Data, Faster," *Stores,* 63 (March 1981), pp. 56–58.

Moscarello, L. C., "The Pros and Cons of LIFO," *Retail Control,* 43 (August 1975), pp. 13–14.

National Retail Merchants Association, Store Management Division, *400 Ways to Reduce Expenses* (New York, 1964).

Rothman, B. R., "Expanding the Concept of Inventory Management," *Stores,* 61 (June 1979), pp. 30–34.

Rothman, M. B., "POS Poses Special Problems for Jewelry Retailing," *Stores,* 62 (April 1980), pp. 45–47.

Shipp, R. D., Jr., *Retail Merchandising, Principles and Applications* (Boston: Houghton Mifflin, 1976).

Smith, S. B., "Automated Inventory Management for Staples," *Journal of Retailing,* 47 (Spring 1971), pp. 55–62.

Sweeney, D. J., "Improving the Profitability of Retail Merchandising Decisions," *Journal of Marketing,* 37 (January 1973), pp. 60–68.

Walter, C. K., and J. R. Grabner, "Stockout Cost Models: Empirical Tests in a Retail Situation," *Journal of Marketing,* 39 (July 1975), pp. 56–60.

# chapter 23
# CREDIT

After completing this chapter, you should be able to:

1. List the advantages of credit to retailers and customers.
2. Identify credit plans commonly offered by retailers to customers.
3. List the criteria that retailers use for granting credit.
4. Identify techniques for gathering credit information.
5. Explain billing and collection procedures used by retailers.
6. Identify major federal credit laws and explain the major reasons for each.
7. Explain why there are credit bureaus and identify the two types of credit bureaus.

In Chapter 21 you saw the following items listed in the "Current Assets" section of a retail balance sheet.

Cash

Accounts receivable

Merchandise inventory

Supplies

The definition of accounts receivable indicated that it represents money owed by customers. In other words, these debts arise from sales made to customers on the basis of credit, not cash. In this chapter we discuss why credit is important to retailers, the types of credit offered by merchants, store credit systems, why stores must be careful about extending credit, and laws that deal with credit.

# EXTENDING CREDIT

To be successful, the process of doing business by credit must appeal to both the retail and the customer. Let's examine the advantages to both.

## The Retailer's Point of View

Why retailers extend credit

Retailers know that offering credit increases a store's sales. This arises from a number of factors.

1   The opportunity for shoppers to buy even when they don't have ready cash.
2   The greater attraction by credit customers to impulse buying and attractive promotions.
3   The ease with which credit customers can make telephone and mail purchases.

In addition, the availability of credit creates good will for the store. Customers often respond to credit service by continuing their patronage (loyalty) at the store. Another factor is that the ability to buy on credit enables customers to make purchases at any time. As a result, the retailer avoids the tendency of sales to be concentrated around paydays, when customers have more cash to spend. Instead, sales are spread out more evenly.

Studies have shown that shoppers who buy on credit are less concerned about prices than those who purchase with cash. Consequently, retailers are able to sell to such customers with less difficulty and in greater volume. Finally, though some merchants would prefer to sell on a cash basis only, they extend credit because their competitors do so. Significant sales can be lost by adhering to a no-credit policy in a trading area where credit arrangements are popular (see Figure 23-1).

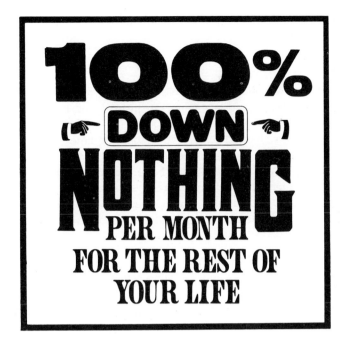

## The Customer's Point of View

Why customers like to buy on credit

Many credit customers believe that they receive better service than cash customers do. They point to the relative ease of returning merchandise as well as the special announcements of sales that are mailed to them. Another important factor is that credit customers need not carry substantial amounts of cash when shopping. This relieves them of the risk of loss due to theft and enables them to shop for high-priced items more easily.

"Buy now, pay later" is a slogan that is dear to the hearts of credit customers. The ability to satisfy immediate needs without immediate payment is a great convenience to them. Furthermore, credit transactions provide customers with a record of their purchases. The combination of sales receipts, credit memorandums, personal checks, and the store's statements of account comprises an organized system for personal budgeting and income tax preparation.

## CREDIT PLANS OFFERED BY RETAILERS

Most retail credit sales are transactions that do not use cash, but retailers offer several forms of credit. Basically, credit is handled either by merchants themselves or by merchants in association with outside organizations.

# Credit Offered by Merchants Themselves

### Open Charge Accounts

In an **open charge account,** after establishing a limit, the store permits the customer to make purchases without a down payment. Instead, the customer is given a specific period—usually thirty days after receiving the bill—within which to make payment. Though no interest is charged if invoices are paid on time, some stores charge interest on unpaid balances after the stipulated period.

Since stores really finance open charge accounts on their own (i.e., they don't generally charge interest), this form of credit is expensive for retailers. Stores that still maintain open charge accounts do so either because their customers are accustomed to this service or because the maintenance of this type of credit gives them a competitive advantage.

### Revolving Charge Accounts

Revolving charge account plans are common

In **revolving charge** accounts, too, the store establishes a credit limit for the customer. The latter then has a specific period within which to make full payment without an interest (finance) charge. Though thirty days is the most common period, some stores permit longer periods, such as sixty or ninety days. Still others use twenty-five-day periods.

At the end of the period the customer has the following choices.

1   To pay all current charges in full without a finance charge.
2   To pay a minimum amount. For example, Macy's requires a minimum payment of $15. The remainder is due in the following period and carries a finance charge.
3   To pay part of the amount due without a finance charge, with the remainder of the bill due in the next period, but subject to a finance charge.

Finance charges are normally 1½ percent per period on amounts up to $500 and 1 percent on amounts over $500. These are equivalent to annual rates of 18 percent and 12 percent, respectively. However, during inflationary times retailers attempt to increase these rates.

A typical store statement contains the following summary columns.

| Previous Balance | Charges | Payments and Credits | Finance Charge | New Balance | Minimum Payment Due |
|---|---|---|---|---|---|
| .00 | 40.60 | .00 | .00 | 40.60 | 15.00 |

The major advantages of revolving credit plans to retailers are the money they earn through finance charges and the increased sales generated by the popularity of the plan with consumers. Customers like this type of credit because it offers them sufficient repayment options for personal budget planning. Revolving credit is now more widespread than open credit, and its use is increasing.

### Installment Credit

**Installment credit** is generally extended in the sale of high-ticket items like appliances, cars, and furniture. It involves a written contract in which the customer usually agrees to

1 Make a down payment.

2 Make periodic payments (including principal and interest) until the total invoice price has been paid.

Some installment sales contracts give the buyer title to the merchandise while others, known as **conditional sales contracts,** permit the retailer to maintain title until the final payment has been made. Because the computation of finance charges in installment contracts is complicated, retailers are required to state the actual annual interest rate.

Since the financing of high-ticket items is expensive, retailers generally arrange for banks or other lending agencies to lend money to the customer. In effect, the lending institution owns the installment contract while the retailer does the necessary paper work. The association with the lender allows the retailer to make money on the sale itself and on a portion of the finance charges.

## Credit Offered by Merchants in Association with Outside Institutions

Credit cards are
sometimes called
plastic money

It's hard to believe that relatively few people used **credit cards** prior to 1960. However, the decade of the 1960s witnessed an enormous increase in the use of such cards, to the point where many people now refer to them as "plastic money." There are several types of crdit cards in use, each with a different sponsor.

### Bank Credit Cards

The *best*-known **bank credit cards** are Visa and MasterCard. A retailer who wants to affiliate with either or both arranges to do so through a local bank or banks. In return for paying the bank a percent of the customer's purchase price (usually 3 to 6 percent, depending on the arrangement), the bank collects from the customer and assumes responsibility for delinquent accounts.

There are approximately 150 million Visa and MasterCards in circulation presenting retailers with excellent opportunities for sales. Before joining a bank card plan, however, a retailer must assess its costs and benefits. For example, a merchant whose markup is 15 percent must judge what bank card rate he or she can afford to pay and still stay in business. (The rate is negotiated between the bank and the retailer and depends on the nature of the business and the trading area.)

Though banks have always levied finance charges on unpaid credit card balances, until 1981 they did not require annual membership fees for use of the cards. However, during that year many banks changed their policy and instituted an annual fee of $15. In addition, finance charges were raised significantly, with some banks charging as much as 19 percent. Nevertheless, the public continues to use bank cards in increasing numbers.

**GREEN CARD**

The American Express card is a type of travel/entertainment credit card.

## Travel/Entertainment Credit Cards

American Express, Carte Blanche, and Diner's Club

Since 1950 another type of credit card has been available to people who desire to charge their travel and entertainment expenses. Of particular use to business people and tourists, these **travel/entertainment credit cards** include American Express, Carte Blanche, and Diner's Club cards. For an annual fee ($35 is typical), a member can charge purchases at motels, airlines, restaurants, and the like up to a predetermined limit. At the end of a billing period unpaid balances become subject to finance charges.

Businesses that accept travel and entertainment cards pay the sponsoring card company a percent of sales, usually 4 to 6 percent. As with bank credit cards, the responsibility for billing customers and assuming delinquent-account risks rests with the card company.

Though such cards were, and to a large extent still are, used largely for the purchase of services, increasing numbers of retailers have begun to accept some of them for sales of merchandise. As the cost of bank cards begins to approach that of travel and entertainment cards, we may see both types of cards in general use by retailers.

## Store Credit Cards

Most department stores and large specialty shops issue their own credit cards (**store credit cards**) for use in their establishments. Many shoppers always carry cards issued by their favorite stores in their wallets or purses for convenience in making cashless purchases. Customers pay only a finance charge on balances that are unpaid after a specified period. Unlike bank and travel/entertainment cards, store cards contribute to customer loyalty and serve as reminders of past patronage.

## Company Cards

Many companies issue credit cards for use in purchasing their products or services. Businesses that issue **company cards** include oil companies (Gulf, Mobil, etc.), hotels, and even telephone companies. Since customer billing is handled by a central office, the individual retail outlet is spared major clerical costs. Though customers do not pay an annual fee for these cards, they are charged on unpaid balances after a specified time. Company cards are responsible for heavy sales volume, with more than 100 million of them in circulation.

# STORE CREDIT SYSTEMS

Before examining the specifics of store credit systems, it should be emphasized that retailers have great leeway in determining who will be granted store-sponsored credit. Retailers are not as concerned about people who use bank or travel/entertainment cards, since outside organizations are responsible for collections and delinquencies. Our concern here, then, is with procedures for the establishment and implementation of a store's own credit plans.

## Criteria for Granting Credit

Though retailers strive constantly to increase sales, they try to do so at minimum risk to themselves. Selling for cash, of course, involves little or no risk. The success of credit selling, on the other hand, depends largely on the degree to which credit customers pay their bills. It is crucial, then, for retailers to extend credit only to those who are likely to meet their obligations.

*Questions about extending credit*

How does a merchant determine who should or should not receive credit? What safeguards can be used to minimize the possibility of poor credit risks being approved? What strategic and procedural differences exist between small and large retailers in their design and handling of credit policies?

### Credit and the Small Retailer

Many small stores sell on a cash-only basis and follow a strict no-credit policy. Others adopt a variety of credit practices to meet the needs of their customers or to sustain sales. For example, a neighborhood merchant may allow credit because it is a long-standing practice in the trading area. A convenience store owner who knows customers by name may extend credit as a way of strengthening their loyalty to the store.

Whatever the reason, small stores that allow credit must develop and maintain adequate accounts-receivable records. They must also establish policies for the collection of debts as well as procedures for the disposition of delinquent accounts.

Millions of consumers use bank and store credit cards.

tained and effective collection methods applied, but sensible criteria must be developed for deciding who is a worthy credit risk. Let's examine those criteria.

**The Applicant's Personal Qualities** Stores are not very different from individuals when they are judging personal characteristics. They look for such qualities as reputation, honesty, and industry. They are concerned with the person's job history, recognizing that someone who moves from job to job or has periods of unemployment is a greater credit risk than one whose employment is steady and confined to a few employers. They are also impressed with an applicant's community status, showing greater favor to homeowners and civic-minded individuals than to uninvolved, temporary residents. Most important of all, however, is the individual's history of debt payments. It has been demonstrated countless times that those who pay their financial obligations on time are much more likely to continue to do so than those who have an erratic payment record.

*An individual's history of debt payments is crucial*

**The Applicant's Ability to Pay** This criterion refers to an individual's earning capacity. Stores are much more likely to extend credit to people with secure, well-paying positions and other sources of steady income than to people with low wages or unsteady jobs. Callous as this policy may sound, stores will point out that they are in business to make money and must therefore screen applicants carefully.

One of the unfortunate consequences of this policy is the inability of some young people—single or married—to secure credit. Without a history of credit experience or a favorable employment record, many retailers are reluctant to accept them as credit risks. It should be noted, however, that a decision in a specific case depends on the strictness of the store's policy and current attitudes about the extension of credit.

**The Applicant's Wealth** In addition to earning capacity, retailers are interested in the applicant's accumulated assets. For example, they place emphasis on size of savings accounts; extent of investments in stocks, bonds, and other securities; and possession of real property such as a house. In some instances specific assets may be pledged by the applicant as security for a credit purchase.

In addition to knowing an individual's assets, retailers also need to know the applicant's liabilities. You will remember that assets − liabilities = owner's equity, or net worth. Therefore, the amount on which retailers rely as a measurement of capacity to pay is the owner's equity.

## Assessing Criteria for the Granting of Credit

*Screening criteria vary among retailers*

It should not be thought that all retailers follow the same strategy and procedures in screening customers for credit approval. On the contrary, each store sets its own priorities for selecting credit risks. For example, store A may be more concerned with an individual's personal characteristics, while store B may stress the person's job history. With experience, store executives who are responsible for administering credit programs recognize which criteria best suit their needs and make decisions accordingly.

## Techniques for Gathering Credit Information

The usual methods for obtaining information from applicants for credit are to have them submit application forms and/or respond personally to questions by store interviewers. The required data include the applicant's (or family's) employment history, salary, bank account details, assets, liabilities, references, and so forth. Written questions are designed for brief responses, while interview inquiries are handled tactfully and tastefully. Under no circumstances is an interviewer permitted to be abusive or inconsiderate, since the store recognizes that a turned-down applicant can still use cash or bank credit cards to make purchases.

Application blanks should be easy to complete, unoffensive, and attractive. As a means of judging their adequacy, some retailers have store personnel complete the forms. Credit managers frequently fill out the blanks, too.

Having secured personal information from the customer, the store needs to verify certain facts. Since doing so on its own is a costly process, it enlists the help of organizations known as **credit bureaus.** In effect, a credit bureau gathers personal information about shoppers from stores, employes, banks, and so forth, and develops summary reports for use by stores that request them. However, the bureau does not make recommendations about applicants; rather, it leaves decisions to the individual stores.

*Cooperative and entrepreneurial credit bureaus*

Credit bureaus are of two types: cooperative and entrepreneurial. The first type is formed by a group of stores through a retail association or a chamber of commerce. Its costs are defrayed by membership fees charged to the retailers. The second category consists of private businesses to whose services interested stores subscribe.

### Techniques for Securing New Accounts

Retailers have devised a variety of techniques to persuade shoppers to apply for credit. Some use a welcome wagon, personally visiting newcomers to the community. Others encourage shoppers to fill out credit application forms by offering them free gifts. Still others use attractive in-store displays as a means of coaxing customers to visit the credit department. Whatever the method, good taste and friendliness must accompany the approach.

## Billing Procedures

Every retail credit system involves periodic notification of customers regarding the status of their accounts. Both small and large stores must develop careful procedures so that both they and their customers are clear about amounts due, payments made, and finance charges. Three billing methods are in general use by retailers.

### Descriptive Billing

**Descriptive billing** makes use of a computer printout of each customer's account for a monthly period. It lists information about the customer's purchases, including the following.

Dates

Departments in which purchases were made

Descriptions of transactions

Prices charged

Payments

Credits

In addition, the statement contains summary financial information about finance charges and the balance due.

### Cycle Billing

Instead of billing all customers at the same time, stores that use **cycle billing** stagger their customer statements. That is, they mail statements in batches at different times of the month, with each batch arranged as an alphabetic group (e.g., A–C, D–F, etc.). Stores that lack data-processing equipment may use cycle billing, omitting detailed information about customer purchases, while those with computer capabilities combine descriptive with cycle billing (Figure 23-2).

### Country Club Billing

To save time and clerical work, some retailers use **country club billing.** They mail sales slips to customers at the end of a billing period, including a simple statement listing the end-of-period balance owed by the customer. Copies of the sales slips remain with the store and substitute for more formal bookkeeping records.

There are still retailers who send detailed statements to customers at the end of a month. Though it is restricted to small stores, this method affords customers the opportunity to examine a month's activities on a transaction-by-transaction basis. The clerical work involved, however, is considerable.

# Collecting from Credit Customers

If a store's screening process is effective, most credit customers will pay their bills on time. Contrary to what some cynics think, most people do not become delinquent payers intentionally. Instead, it happens either because of circumstances beyond their control or because of forgetfulness on their part. Consequently, the retailer's role is to institute an organized collection system that encourages customers to make payments on time.

*Handling delinquent accounts*

No matter which credit plan is offered, collection procedures should include a series of specific steps. Suppose a customer's account is past due. The store might send a form letter simply reminding the individual about the unpaid bill. If no reply is received within a reasonable time, a second letter is sent, one with a slightly more compelling tone. Neither of these letters should be threatening. On the contrary, they should stress the store's appreciation of the customer's patronage and its desire to be of help. In the event that the second letter does not produce results, the store may either call the customer or, in special cases, send a telegram. When an account is truly delinquent, stores resort to one or a combination of the following actions: Send a personal collector to the customer's home; engage a collection agency; or sue. In the case of small amounts, however, a store may write off the account as a bad debt, that is, take the delinquent amount as a loss. Delinquency in installment credit occasionally results in repossession of merchandise.

Collection policies vary among retailers. Some are stricter than others, with the approach depending on the store's image, the affluence of its customers, and its collection experience. In general, stores try to collect from customers on time because delinquent accounts tie up funds and increase overhead. While high finance charges minimize such costs, seriously delinquent amounts are a drain on a store's assets.

### Additional Payment Information

Payments, accompanied by payment stub, received at the P. O. Box listed on the stub for payments by 2:00 p.m. on any Monday through Friday that is not a holiday, will be posted as of the day of receipt. Although payments made elsewhere may not be posted on the day received, they will be posted promptly within 5 days thereafter.

17-3000

### Information Applicable to Both Purchases and Advances

A minus sign (−) preceding any amount indicates a credit (including a Payment) or a credit balance. If the total New Balance is a credit balance, it will be applied to future amounts you owe us or refunded to you upon request. Send these refund requests to the address for receiving inquiries about your account appearing on the face of this statement.

You must make the required total Minimum Payment to avoid delinquency.

The Minimum Payment will be applied in the following order: any **FINANCE CHARGE**, Late Charges, Insurance Premium Charges, principal of Advances incurred before the Conversion Date, principal of Purchases incurred before the Conversion Date, principal of Advances incurred on or after the Conversion Date, principal of Purchases incurred on or after the Conversion Date.

If you wish, you may make additional payments. You may instruct us as to how to apply these additional payments. In the absence of your instructions, 50% of any additional payment will be applied in the reduction of the principal of Advances incurred before the Conversion Date, if any, and 50% in reduction of the principal of Purchases incurred before the Conversion Date, if any. If any portion of the additional payment remains unapplied to balances incurred before the Conversion Date, it will be applied to the principal of Advances incurred on or after the Conversion Date, if any, and next to the principal of Purchases incurred on or after the Conversion Date.

Any **FINANCE CHARGE** At Periodic Rate is computed for the periodic statement only through the Bill Date, but it continues to accrue daily until payment is posted. Any **FINANCE CHARGE** which accrues after the Bill Date will appear on your next statement. YOU MAY AT ANY TIME PAY YOUR TOTAL INDEBTEDNESS. Under the average daily balance method we use the earlier payments are received during a billing cycle the lower the **FINANCE CHARGE** for that billing cycle will be.

### Information About Each Finance Charge At Periodic Rate On Purchases And The Balance Upon Which Each Is Computed

Each Purchases Finance Charge Balance is an average daily balance. To compute each one, we add up all the applicable daily principal balances in the Billing Cycle and divide the sum by the Number Of Days In Billing Cycle. We get the daily principal balance for Purchases incurred before the Conversion Date as follows; each day we begin with the applicable opening principal balance for the Billing Cycle and add all New Purchases And Other Debits incurred before the Conversion Date and posted to principal since the start of the Billing Cycle (including any posted that day) and subtract all Payments And Other Credits applied to Purchases incurred before the Conversion Date and posted to principal since the start of the Billing Cycle (including any posted that day). We get the daily principal balance for Purchases incurred on or after the Conversion Date as follows: each day we begin with the applicable opening principal balance for the Billing Cycle and add all New Purchases And Other Debits incurred on or after the Conversion Date and posted to principal since the start of the Billing Cycle (including any posted that day) and subtract all Payments And Other Credits applied to Purchases incurred on or after the Conversion Date and posted to principal since the start of the Billing Cycle (including any posted that day). However, there is no "purchases finance charge balance" for purchases incurred either before or on or after the Conversion Date in any billing cycle in which you have no previous balance for any purchases or all your payments and other credits applied to purchases for that billing cycle at least equal your previous balance for all purchases for that billing cycle.

A **FINANCE CHARGE** At Periodic Rate is computed for Purchases incurred both before and on or after the Conversion Date by (i) multiplying each portion of the applicable Purchases Finance Charge Balance by the Number Of Days In Billing Cycle, (ii) applying to the resulting products the applicable Daily Periodic Rates, and (iii) adding these products together.

### Information About Each Finance Charge At Periodic Rate On Advances And The Balance Upon Which Each Is Computed

Each Advances Finance Charge Balance is an average daily balance. To compute each one, we add up all the applicable daily principal balances in the Billing Cycle and divide the sum by the Number Of Days In Billing Cycle. We get the daily principal balance for Advances incurred before the Conversion Date as follows: each day we begin with the applicable opening principal balance for the Billing Cycle and add all New Advances And Other Debits incurred before the Conversion Date and posted to principal since the start of the Billing Cycle (including any posted that day) and subtract all Payments And Other Credits applied to Advances incurred before the Conversion Date and posted to principal since the start of the Billing Cycle (including any posted that day). We get the daily principal balance for Advances incurred on or after the Conversion Date as follows: each day we begin with the applicable opening principal balance for the Billing Cycle and add all New Advances And Other Debits incurred on or after the Conversion Date and posted to principal since the start of the Billing Cycle (including any posted that day) and subtract all Payments And Other Credits applied to Advances incurred on or after the Conversion Date and posted to principal since the start of the Billing Cycle (including any posted that day), and adding a per item charge of $.25 for each Advance made on the account which will increase the **ANNUAL PERCENTAGE RATE** for any monthly billing cycle in which an Advance is included.

A **FINANCE CHARGE** At Periodic Rate is computed for Advances incurred both before and on or after the Conversion Date by multiplying each Advances Finance Charge Balance by the Number Of Days In Billing Cycle, and applying to the resulting products the applicable Daily Periodic Rates.

**FIGURE 23-2**

Finance terms under cycle billing.

# CREDIT LEGISLATION

In previous chapters we discussed the effects of consumerism on certain retail practices. We saw how consumer advocates have succeeded in minimizing or eliminating the dubious behavior of unscrupulous retailers. We also took note of the salutary effect of state and federal legislation on retailer–consumer relations.

A significant aspect of the consumer movement has been the passage of legislation to regulate credit. All states have passed laws whose purpose is to protect consumers in their credit dealings with retailers, but the legislation varies too greatly from one state to another to permit discussion here. However, several federal credit laws are particularly important to both merchants and consumers.

## The Truth-in-Lending Act

The Truth-in-Lending Act has two goals:

1  To inform consumers about the credit terms of sales transactions.
2  To specify the manner in which finance charges are determined.

Prior to passage of this law, customers were often confused by the language of their credit contracts as well as the details listed on monthly statements. Truth-in-Lending is an attempt to clarify matters for consumers by requiring retailers to state pertinent credit facts. For example, the law requires the retailer to state finance charge rates in annual percentages even when they are already stated in monthly ones. Thus, a monthly finance charge of 1.65 percent must also be listed as a 19.8 percent annual charge. The logic behind this requirement is that it is easier to understand and compare finance charges as annual rates than as monthly ones.

Figure 23-3 contains information provided to consumers as directed by the Truth-in-Lending Act.

## The Fair Credit Reporting Act

In our discussion about investigations of credit applicants, the retailer's need for thorough and reliable information was stressed. No mention was made of the consumer's rights and prerogatives. The Fair Credit Reporting Act, however, allows credit applicants to review information in their files for the purpose of determining its accuracy. It also prohibits use of the information for any reason other than credit or employment. The law makes credit bureau files available to applicants if they are denied credit. Except for bankruptcy data, information that is damaging to a consumer may not be maintained by a retailer or a credit bureau for more than seven years.

**EAB European American Bank**

Important Information in Case of Errors or Inquiries About Your Bill

Thank you for banking with us. If you have a question about your bill, or think we made an error, you're protected by the Federal Truth in Lending Act.

The Federal Truth in Lending Act requires prompt correction of billing mistakes.

1. If you want to preserve your rights under the Act, here's what to do if you think your bill is wrong or if you need more information about an item on your bill:

   a. Do not write on the bill. On a separate sheet of paper write the following: (you may telephone your inquiry but **doing so will not preserve your rights under this law).**
      i. Your name and account number (if any).
      ii A description of the error and an explanation (to the extent you can explain) of why you believe it is an error.
         If you only need more information, explain the item you are not sure about and, if you wish, ask for evidence of the charge such as a copy of the charge slip. Do not send in your copy of a sales slip or other document unless you have a duplicate copy for your records.
      iii. The dollar amount of the suspected error.
      iv. Any other information (such as your address) which you think will help the bank to identify you or the reason for your complaint or inquiry.
   b. Send your billing error notice to:

      Mail it as soon as you can, but in any case, early enough to reach the bank within 60 days after the bill was mailed to you. If you have authorized the bank to automatically pay from your checking or savings account any credit card bills from the bank, you can stop or reverse payment on any amount you think is wrong by mailing your notice so the bank receives it within 16 days after the bill was sent to you. However, you do not have to meet this 16-day deadline to get the bank to investigate your billing error claim.

2. The bank must acknowledge all letters pointing out possible errors within 30 days of receipt, unless the bank is able to correct your bill during that 30 days. Within 90 days after receiving your letter, the bank must either correct the error or explain why the bank believes the bill was correct. Once the bank has explained the bill, the bank has no further obligation to you even though you still believe that there is an error, except as provided in paragraph 5 below.

3. After the bank has been notified, neither the bank nor an attorney nor a collection agency may send you collection letters or take other collection action with respect to the amount in dispute; but periodic statements may be sent to you, and the disputed amount can be applied against your credit limit. You cannot be threatened with damage to your credit rating or sued for the amount in question, nor can the disputed amount be reported to a credit bureau or to other creditors as delinquent until the creditor has answered your inquiry. **However, you remain obligated to pay the parts of your bill not in dispute.**

4. If it is determined that the bank has made a mistake on your bill, you will not have to pay any finance charges on any disputed amount. If it turns out that the bank has not made an error, you may have to pay finance charges on the amount in dispute, and you will have to make up any missed minimum or required payments on the disputed amount. Unless you have agreed that your bill was correct, the bank must send you a written notification of what you owe; and if it is determined that the bank did make a mistake in billing the disputed amount, you must be given the time to pay which you normally are given to pay undisputed amounts before any more finance charges or late payment charges on the disputed amount can be charged to you.

5. If the bank's explanation does not satisfy you and you notify the bank **in writing** within **10** days after you receive its explanation that you still refuse to pay the disputed amount, the bank may report you to credit bureaus and other creditors and may pursue regular collection procedures. But the bank must also report that you think you do not owe the money, and the bank must let you know to whom such reports were made. Once the matter has been settled between you and the bank, the bank must notify those to whom the bank reported you as delinquent of the subsequent resolution.

6. If the bank does not follow these rules, the bank is not allowed to collect the first $50 of the disputed amount and finance charges, even if the bill turns out to be correct.

7. If you have a problem with property or services purchased with a credit card, you may have the right not to pay the remaining amount due on them, if you first try in good faith to return them or give the merchant a chance to correct the problem. There are two limitations on this rights:

   a. You must have bought them in your home state or if not within your home state within 100 miles of your current mailing address; and
   b. The purchase price must have been more than $50.
      However, these limitations do not apply if the merchant is owned or operated by the bank, or if the bank mailed you the advertisement for the property or services.

230/0609 June 80

**FIGURE 23-3**

Consumers' rights under the Truth-in-Lending Act.

# The Equal Credit Opportunity Act

Consumerism and the women's movement resulted in the passage of the Equal Credit Opportunity Act. This law prohibits retailers from denying credit on the basis of sex, marital status, religion, race, or national origin. Among other things, it protects widowed and divorced women against discrimination for lack of a credit history, since during the time that they were married their family credit was listed under the husband's name.

# The Fair Credit Billing Act

This law provides protection for consumers in cases of inaccurate billing by retailers. It gives customers sixty days in which to report billing mistakes. The retailer than has thirty days in which to acknowledge receipt of the customer's letter and sixty more days in which to resolve the problem. If the problem is not solved after ninety days, the retailer may take legal action.

# The Holder in Due Course Act

One of the ways in which a business can secure immediate cash is to sell part or all of its accounts receivables to another party. Suppose a retailer does so. Who is liable for defects in a credit customer's product? Against whom does a customer press complaints regarding a credit sale, the retailer or the third party? Prior to passage of the Holder in Due Course Act, the customer had no rights against the third party—the owner of the contract. Today, however, the third party assumes the retailer's responsibility for credit contracts and is liable to customers for product defects and complaints. Thus, consumers are protected despite any special arrangements that exist between retailers and third parties (holders in due course).

# RETAIL CREDIT— A LOOK AHEAD

Though economic predictions are usually fraught with uncertainty, most retailers, economists, and financial analysts believe that the volume of retail credit will expand. The enormous increase in the use of credit cards—bank, travel/entertainment, store, and company—shows no sign of abating. Alert retailers, large and small, capitalize on the trend and seek new ways to utilize contacts with credit customers for additional sales. For example, the Gulf Oil Corporation maintains a shop-by-mail direct marketing operation through its Gulf Consumer Services Company, a Division of Gulf Oil Corporation. Customers are introduced to the mail merchandise service as soon as they become Gulf Oil card holders.

The ways of profiting from credit customer contacts are limited only by the imagination of aggressive retailers. For their part, credit customers benefit through the convenient availability of information about new products and services.

Selections from promotional advertisements sent to active Gulf Credit Card accounts as part of the company's shop-by-mail, direct marketing program.

**NEW TERMS**

bank credit card

company card

conditional sales contract

country club billing

credit bureau

credit card

cycle billing

descriptive billing

installment credit

open charge account

revolving charge account

store credit card

travel/entertainment credit card

# CHAPTER HIGHLIGHTS

1  To a retailer the advantages of offering credit are increased sales and customer loyalty, more evenly spread out sales, and less difficulty in making sales.

2  To a customer the advantages include the ease of returning merchandise, the fact that it is not necessary to carry substantial amounts of cash, the ability to satisfy immediate shopping needs, and the availability of records for personal budgeting and income tax purposes.

3  Credit plans offered by merchants themselves include open charge accounts, revolving charge accounts, and installment sales.

4  Credit plans offered by merchants in association with outside institutions include bank credit cards, travel/entertainment credit cards, store credit cards, and company cards.

5  The criteria used by retailers for granting credit include an applicant's personal qualities, ability to pay, and credit history. The importance assigned to each criterion by individual retailers varies.

6   The techniques used by retailers to gather credit information about applicants include application forms, personal interviews, and credit bureau reports. Credit bureaus are either cooperatively owned by retailers or entrepreneurial.

7   Billing procedures used by retailers include descriptive billing, cycle billing, and country club billing.

8   Collection techniques employed by retailers include letters, telephone calls, telegrams, personal collectors, collection agencies, and lawsuits.

9   The most important federal credit laws are the Truth-in-Lending Law, the Fair Credit Reporting Act, the Equal Credit Opportunity Act, the Fair Credit Billing Act, and the Holder in Due Course Act.

10  Retailers, economists, and financial analysts agree that the volume of retail credit will expand.

## QUESTIONS

1   Why does its policy of selling on credit enable a store to increase its sales?

2   In your opinion, what is the main advantage to a consumer of buying on credit? Explain.

3   What options does a revolving charge account customer have upon receiving a monthly statement?

4   How do bank credit cards differ from travel/entertainment cards in terms of their use at retail establishments?

5   In your opinion, which of the criteria used by retailers for granting credit is most important? Why?

6   What is the difference between a cooperatively owned credit bureau and an entrepreneurial one?

7   How does descriptive billing differ from country club billing?

8   At least in its initial stages, why is it important for a store's collection techniques to be nonthreatening?

9   As a consumer, how do you feel about the Fair Credit Reporting Act? Would you feel differently if you were a retailer?

10  From the retailer's viewpoint, do the benefits of extending credit outweigh the risks? Explain.

11  How does the Truth-in-Lending Law differ from the Equal Credit Opportunity Act?

## FIELD PROJECTS

1   This chapter emphasizes the tremendous impact of credit card use on retail sales. The number and variety of retail establishments that accept cards is astonishing. In order to assess the extent of bank and travel/entertainment credit card use in your community, visit a local shopping area.

a   Count the number of stores, travel agencies, restaurants, and so forth that exhibit the following card emblems on their windows or doors.

Master Card

Visa

American Express

Diner's Club

Carte Blanche

b   Compile a list showing which card(s) is (are) accepted by each type of retailer.

2   Secure a credit application blank from a large department or specialty store in your area. After studying the form, answer the following questions.

a   What specific items does the store ask about the applicant's employment history?

b   In what way(s) does the store try to determine the applicant's earning capacity?

c   Are there any questions that you would resent answering if you were the applicant? Which ones? Why would you be resentful?

# CASES

1   Laurel's, a women's specialty shop, had long resisted the trend toward selling by credit. Since it was a fashionable store catering to customers on a personal basis, there appeared to be no need to change its credit policy.

However, the gradual influx of young single women into the community has caused Laurel's executives to reexamine the store's policy. Many of the singles, it seems, are avid credit card users, and as a result they are shopping elsewhere. In an effort to capture this trade, Laurel's has undertaken a study to determine the possible effects of a policy change on its business.

a   If the store decides to offer credit, should it notify its present customers in some special way? If so, how?

b   What type(s) of credit plan might be appropriate for Laurel's?

2   For years, giant retailers like Sears and Montgomery Ward refused to honor bank credit cards. They relied on their own credit plans to satisfy customer needs.

However, as a result of the institution, in 1980, of federal credit controls that severely curtailed installment sales, many of the large stores took a second look at bank cards as a means of stimulating sales. Several stores, including Gimbel's, considered the use of travel/entertainment cards as well.

a   Should all large stores offer customers the option of using bank and travel/entertainment cards in addition to their own? Why?

b   Before instituting a bank credit card system, some retailers test its feasibility for a year or two. What questions would you include in a study of the system?

3   Robert Costa, the credit manager of Dubree's, a large department store, has been in charge of credit operations for twenty years. He was responsible for the overall design of the current credit system, including criteria for granting credit, the construction of the

credit application form, and collection procedures. From the moment he took charge, Costa instituted a no-nonsense approach to securing new credit customers and dealing with delinquent accounts. He views his department as the store's protector, not as something to be used for promotional or sales activities. By and large, the owners of Dubree's have been satisfied with their credit operations, and they have commended Costa for his work on numerous occasions.

Lately, however, one of the store's vice-presidents has criticized the loose ties between credit operations and merchandising activities. He points out that a store's credit function is an adjunct to sales, not an end in itself, and that many of Dubree's customers view its credit department as controlling the merchandising departments. The vice-president is also critical of the stern image conveyed by the credit department, unlike the more friendly approach taken by buyers and sales personnel. Finally, he feels that a store's credit operations should enhance sales in particular departments on a flexible basis, as dictated by the store manager.

Assume that you, an outside consultant, have been asked by Dubree's owners to evaluate the role of the store's credit operations. You have been given the authority to interview *all* personnel and to review forms, reports, and the like.

a What questions would you ask the vice-president? Costa?
b How do you feel about the points the vice-president has raised? Explain.
c Do you see a way of reconciling the two points of view? Explain.

# REFERENCES

Arthur, E. M., *Checking and Rating the New Account* (New York: National Retail Merchants Association, Credit Management Division, 1960).

"Bank Cards: A Terminal Disease?," *Clothes Etc* (May 1, 1978), pp. 64–69.

Bergmann, J., "Here Comes the Crunch!" *Stores,* 62 (May 1980), pp. 10, 64.

Burge, W. L., "Credit Card Economy," *Retail Directions,* 127 (November–December 1973), pp. 19–20.

Cole, R. H., *Consumer and Commercial Credit Management* (Homewood, Ill.: R. D. Irwin, 1980).

Fonseca, J. R., *Consumer Credit Compliance Manual* (Rochester, N.Y.: Lawyers Co-operative, 1975).

National Retail Merchants Association, Credit Management Division, *Effective Collection Methods and Control* (New York, 1962).

Naumann, C. F., *Credit in the Branch Store* (New York: National Retail Merchants Association, Credit Management Division, 1960).

Ringel, L., "Reinforcing the Image by Design," *Stores,* 63 (February 1981), pp. 51–52.

Rothman, M. B., "Credit-Ability," *Stores,* 62 (September 1980), pp. 20, 24, 26, 88, 90.

————, "One Byte at a Time," *Stores,* 62 (March 1980), pp. 41–43.

————, "Third Party," *Stores,* 63 (September 1981), pp. 41–42, 46–47.

Walker, G., *Credit Where Credit is Due* (New York: Holt, Rinehart and Winston, 1979).

# part six:
# MAKING
# DECISIONS

**T**he last part of this book deals with the nature and scope of retail decision making. Chapter 24 is concerned with the place of research in the field of retailing. After distinguishing among the retail information system, marketing research, and retailing research, the chapter explains the research process and identifies the sources of primary and secondary data. We note the advantages and disadvantages of several research methods and identify some groups that are involved in retailing research. As an afterword, we speculate on retailing in the future.

Chapters 25 and 26 are devoted to the details and problems of going into a retail business. In Chapter 25 we identify the personal characteristics of successful retailers and stress the importance of technical skills, knowledge, and interest in ownership. After listing sources of investment funds for prospective retailers, we explain the roles of lawyers and accountants in the establishment of a new business. Finally, we note the advantages and disadvantages of sole proprietorships, partnerships, and corporations as well as the cautions one should consider before going into business.

Chapter 26 completes our discussion of going into a retail business. In discussing franchises we indicate sources of information for potential franchisees. After listing the major provisions of franchise agreements, we analyze the costs of franchise ownership and explain the purposes of franchise disclosure statements. Our treatment of franchising ends with the rights of franchisees and a list of major franchise categories. The chapter concludes with a discussion of retail businesses that offer services only and those that offer both merchandise and services.

# chapter 24
# RESEARCH FOR RETAILERS

After completing this chapter, you should be able to:

1 Distinguish among the terms *retail information system*, *marketing research*, and *retailing research*.

2 Describe the major areas in which retailers use marketing research techniques.

3 Explain the research process.

4 Identify the sources of primary and secondary data.

5 List the advantages and disadvantages of the following research methods: survey, observation, and experimentation.

6 List the names of four private research organizations and identify other types of groups involved in retailing research.

7 Identify expected changes in the market, downtown revival, store development and operation, personnel and employment, and merchandising and promotion.

Practically all types of retailers have been faced with escalating costs, accelerating inflation, and a changing business environment. The challenge to remain profitable appears to be greater than ever before, with some of the nation's great retailers no longer in business. One of the oldest and largest variety chains, W. T. Grant, is gone. So is Korvette's, once considered the most innovative discounter in the country. And Food Fair, once among the largest supermarket chains, has also disappeared as a result of bankruptcy.

Merchants need answers to their questions about handling customers, meeting competition, and making a profit. At one time retailers relied on intuition and "gut" feelings to answer these questions, but today the risks are too high to trust in "hunches." Consequently, retailers use the tools of retailing information systems and market research to provide information for decision making.

# RETAIL INFORMATION SYSTEMS (RIS)

The use of computers and electronic data processing has made possible the development of the **retail information system (RIS).** This ongoing system of data collection is designed to process and retain information so that it is available to management immediately for decision making.

*Types of input*

The major element of an RIS is a central **data bank** that stores information. Through the use of terminals such as computerized cash registers, data are entered into the data bank and retrieved as needed. The information placed in a typical retail data bank includes records of sales, inventory, purchasing, consumer data, accounts payable, accounts receivable, personnel, and other items.

To implement this system, the retailer places all required files and records in the data bank. This becomes the core of information, which is reviewed, updated, or changed when necessary. Updating, which refers to additions, deletions, or changes in the data bank, is important if the information is to be useful. New information is obtained from such sources as sales, inventory, and personnel records.

Data are made available to managers through terminals placed in various stations, departments, and offices. These terminals are connected to the data bank and allow information to be displayed on video screens. As a result, management has access to information throughout the day without waiting for reports to be printed. However, a variety of printed reports are available as needed (Figure 24-1).

# Advantages of RIS

*Advantages and disadvantages of RIS*

Among the advantages of RIS are the following.

- Information is collected continuously.
- Data are available at all times.
- Specific information can be utilized when and where it is needed most.
- As problems arise, management has an opportunity to make decisions early.
- Research can take place continuously.

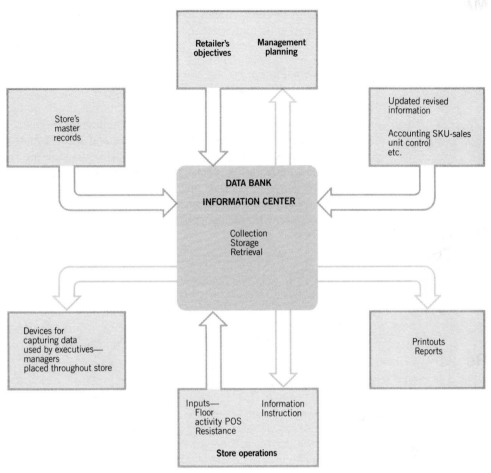

**FIGURE 24-1**
A retail information system (RIS).

* The retailer's objectives provide basic guidelines as to what information is needed and collected.

## Disadvantages of RIS

An RIS does have some disadvantages. These include the following.

* It is costly.
* It is difficult to develop without using specialists.
* Large quantities of data can create complex decision-making problems.

Retailing information systems are helpful in planning for efficiency and for controlling day-to-day activities. Nevertheless, frequently problems and questions arise that require in-depth research studies to uncover the real causes of concern. In such cases the tools of marketing and retailing research are needed.

# MARKETING RESEARCH

**Marketing research** involves the investigation and systematic gathering, recording, and analysis of data that are pertinent to a specific marketing problem. Marketing research studies institutions like wholesalers and retailers and the activities involved in moving goods and services to the consumer. These activities include the buying and selling of goods as well as advertising, packaging, and transporting them to the various markets. Manufacturers generally conduct major research studies about products, consumers, and competition. Wholesalers usually investigate markets and the costs of distributing goods. To a lesser degree, wholesalers conduct important research in the areas of display and sales incentives.

# RETAILING RESEARCH

**Retailing research** applies the techniques of marketing research to the investigation of problems related to retail activities. Such problems include merchandise selection, customer behavior, store location, pricing policies, and promotional costs.

## The Benefits of Retailing Research

Computers and point-of-sale transactions

The benefits of research techniques, once limited to large retailers, are now available to smaller merchants. As mentioned in the preceding section, the computer and other electronic machines used by retailers have paved the way for collecting valuable information in many areas. For example, in point-of-sale (POS) transactions stores are equipped with specially designed cash registers that do much more than merely ring up sales (Figure 24-2). For each customer, the salesperson records such information as product number, product description, unit price, number of units sold, amount of cash tendered, and department number. In stores that grant credit, the customer's charge account number is also recorded. Besides producing a customer sales receipt, the register transfers the sales information electronically to a remote computer containing a data bank. In turn, the computer

- Records sales by product.
- Keeps a record of how much inventory is still on hand.
- Signals reorder points to maintain sufficient stock.
- Indicates how quickly each product is being sold.
- Lists sales by department and salesperson.
- Maintains records of customer charge accounts.

This information becomes available to management within hours and enables store executives to make timely decisions. Periodically—daily, weekly, monthly, semian-

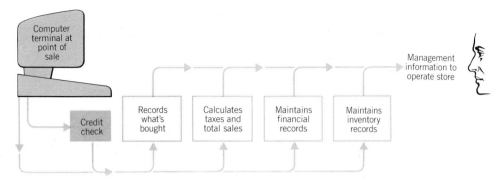

**FIGURE 24-2**
A POS computer tie-in generates management information. (Reproduced by permission of the J. C. Penney Company.)

nually—the computer prints reports about strong- and weak-selling items, the volume of returns by customers, the performance of each store, and comparisons with sales in previous periods. In some cases computers produce purchase orders based on preset reorder points. Information generated by computers regarding the purchasing habits and lifestyles of customers helps retailers determine customers' merchandise and service needs.

Through a shared-time arrangement, small retailers that cannot afford data processing equipment can also benefit from a computer's capabilities. Through computer service companies, these retailers can become involved in research activities that would otherwise be closed to them.

# The Scope of Retailing Research

Research covers a wide range of areas

The major areas of retailing research are customers, store location and layout, advertising and promotion, merchandise selection and pricing, personnel, and competition.

## Customers

Retailers are concerned about improving their stores and offerings in order to attract more customers. Studies on how to win increased patronage and how to satisfy customers are a constant challenge to merchants. In fact, consumer motivation and behavior have probably received the greatest attention from researchers in retailing.

Broadly speaking, consumer research involves an analysis of how people live, as well as the study of demographic and psychographic information. As discussed in Chapter 5, demographic studies are concerned with such characteristics as age, sex, income, and education. On the other hand, psychographic data involve personality traits, habits, perceptions, attitudes, motivations, and values. The study of this kind of information helps merchants develop customer profiles and match the store's image and total offerings with the customers they are trying to attract.

## Store Location and Layout

Selecting the right site is a critical decision that entails the investigation of population growth, shopping habits, traffic patterns, parking needs, competition, and cost of prop-

Advertising specials can be tracked by computer to measure the effectiveness of advertisements.

erty. Retailers use a variety of research techniques to determine store location. For example, they study the pattern of competitive stores in a trading area to determine the viability of a new outlet. They also study the economic stability of a trading area to measure the short- and long-term chances of success.

In order to determine the most effective store layout, in-store customer traffic patterns are studied. Retailers constantly look for new ways to increase the productivity of space as well as its convenience to customers.

### Advertising and Promotion

To create more effective advertising and promotion procedures, merchants study their experiences with media, types of ads, special promotions, and advertising costs.

*Research provides answers to specific questions*

Research can assist in answering such questions as Should we engage in promotional or institutional advertising? Which special event was most successful? Which medium is best suited to the store's customers?

Merchants measure the effectiveness of an ad campaign by store traffic, immediate sales response, returned coupons, and the like. Sales data are also used in evaluating in-store display locations.

### Merchandise Selection and Pricing

Merchandise research involves studying the buying, selling, and pricing of goods. Specifically, it is concerned with the collection and interpretation of data on markups, markdowns, profits, and sales turnover. This information is relatively easy for retailers to gather, since data processing provides internal statistics quickly.

## Personnel

Personnel research is concerned with the finding, hiring, training, compensation, and evaluation of employees. Some of the important personnel areas that require ongoing evaluation are the effectiveness of training and testing, employee turnover, compensation relative to productivity, and incentive programs.

Many retailers use consulting firms to "shop" their employees and rate their salespeople. Others use sales volume as a basis for evaluation. In any case, information regarding the effectiveness of employees is important for making wise personnel decisions.

## Competition

Market share studies help retailers recognize their relative positions in terms of the total market. They provide comparative information regarding the competition. Figure 24-3 contains data from a market share study conducted by Lowe's Companies, Inc., a retailer of home-building materials.

# THE INFORMAL APPROACH TO RESEARCH

Retailers often use informal measures to gather information or analyze a situation. When they hesitate to spend money on research because of limited funds, or are ignorant of the benefits of research, decision errors are likely. Merchants who do not utilize research rely on intuition or use old methods of doing business. Still others merely imitate the competition.

Cases in which research was lacking

In today's market it is increasingly difficult to make good business decisions without appropriate information. A case in point involves a retail office furniture dealer whose store was located in a business district. Over time the trading area changed from one composed of office buildings and factories to a predominantly residential community. In an attempt to sell to this new market, the retailer changed his merchandise offering to a largely household furniture line. He invested a great deal of money in home furnishings and stocked very traditional furniture. Unfortunately, the new line sold poorly and the retailer lost a major part of his investment.

Had the merchant investigated the situation in some depth, he could have learned more about the residents and their lifestyles. He would have found that this group consisted largely of young singles and marrieds and that they furnished their homes with modern, nontraditional items.

In another case a merchant selected a location for a toy shop on the basis of the size of the store, its low rent, and the sparse competition in the immediate area. The shop was stocked with the newest merchandise and was arranged attractively for self-service. The opening was timed to take advantage of the Christmas season. The mer-

## THE PENETRATION OF LOWE'S

| (Millions) | 1972 | 1975 | 1979 | 1980 | 1972–80 CGR† |
|---|---|---|---|---|---|
| Annual Sales of Lumber building materials, hardware— Southern region* | $8,188 | $10,636** | $17,912** | $17,757** | 10.2% |
| Lowe's annual sales*** | $ 235 | $ 388 | $ 905 | $ 884 | 18.0% |
| Lowe's sales as % of total LBH in South | 2.9% | 3.6% | 5.1% | 5.0% | |

*LBH figures for 1972 & 1975 are unrevised and include farm equipment.
**LBH figures for 1979 & 1980 also include mobile home sales.
***1972 Lowe's annual sales are based on fiscal year ending 7-31-72.
†Compound Growth Rate

### MARKET PENETRATION

In the South, where Lowe's is located, annual sales of lumber, building materials, and hardware supplies have grown. Lowe's annual sales growth has resulted in a near doubling of market share since 1972, from 2.9 percent of total sales of lumber, building materials, and hardware to 5 percent for 1980.

### COMPANY PROFILE

Lowe's Companies, Inc., is a specialty retailer of building materials and related products for the home construction and home remodeling markets. It operates a total of 214 retail stores in 19 states.

FIGURE 24-3
Data from a market share study. (Reproduced by permission of Lowe's Companies, Inc.)

chant decided to use the store window and some local posters as a means of attracting customers.

The retailer's strategy proved unsuccessful for several reasons: first, failure to recognize that a large percentage of the trading area population was middle-aged or older; second, lack of awareness that the young marrieds did a great deal of shopping outside the area; and third, ignorance of the fact that older people are less informed about toys than consumers in other age groups and generally need greater assistance. Overall, the merchant was unaware that **outshoppers** (people shopping outside their area) generally consult media sources for information.

These cases indicate that *some* research was required to minimize risks. Research may be as simple as determining whether customers like a certain gift wrap or as complicated as selecting a store location. The procedures and tools for conducting research are similar even though the problems or types of stores differ.

# THE RESEARCH PROCESS

The research process consists of five basic steps:

1 Identifying and defining the problem
2 Collecting the data: secondary and primary
3 Compiling and tabulating the data
4 Analyzing and interpreting the findings
5 Preparing the final report

## Identifying and Defining the Problem

It is important that the retailer develop a clear statement of the problem so that the research can be organized for the collection of the necessary information. Defining the problem correctly yields useful information for a solution. For example, a manager of a department store chain noticed a significant increase in the number of refunds compared to the past year. He became even more concerned after reading a report issued by a retail trade association stressing the rising trend in refund abuse and fraud.

Though there are several facets to the problem of refunds, the need to reduce refund transactions is clear. The question is, How can this be accomplished? The answer leads to the second step of the research process: collecting the data.

## Collecting the Data

*Secondary and primary data*

**Secondary data** are data that are already available; that is, information that was collected previously for other projects, such as the U.S. Census Reports. Secondary data are obtained from company records, libraries, the U.S. Government Printing Office, schools, private research firms, organizations, trade publications, and other sources. The main advantage of collecting secondary data is the *savings of time and money*.

The disadvantages are as follows.

• The information may be outdated.
• The data may be derived from unreliable sources.
• The information may be unsuitable for the project.

If secondary data provide sufficient information for problem solving, then it is unnecessary to collect additional data. Primary data are collected only if secondary data will not solve the problem at hand.

**Primary data** are collected firsthand for the particular problem under study. There are three basic data collection methods.

- Survey
- Observation
- Experimentation

## Survey

**Surveys** involve the questioning of people. This is the most widely used of the three methods. It may be accomplished by means of mail, telephone, or personal interviews. Surveys are often used to reveal customer attitudes, opinions, and shopping habits. The following illustrations demonstrate the use of the survey method.

In assessing the effectiveness of a merchandising program, the retailer could research the repeat purchase pattern (use-up rate) of a particular product. It would be necessary to study how many times the customer returns to the marketplace to rebuy.

The merchant could use several techniques for collecting the necessary information. A questionnaire could be developed for use in mail, telephone, or personal inter-

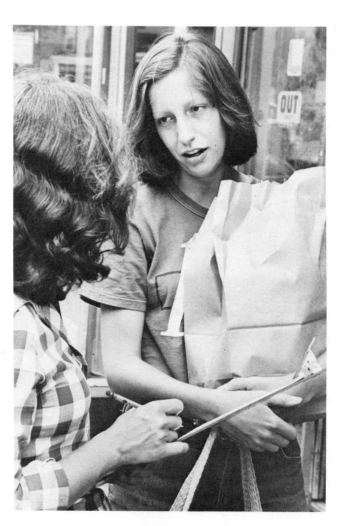

Personal interviews are useful for compiling important information about consumers.

views (Figure 24-4). *Mail* is most suitable when the study involves a large group or one that is widely dispersed geographically. Though it is relatively inexpensive, the rate of return is low and returns require considerable time. *Telephone* interviews are effective for short questionnaires. This method is fast and relatively inexpensive, and allows for some flexibility in questioning. The disadvantages include unlisted telephone numbers, households without phones, and the difficulty of reaching people who refuse to answer questions by phone. *Personal* interviews are most suitable for long questionnaires. This is the most flexible technique because it provides an opportunity for the interviewer to elicit lengthy responses. The disadvantages are possible interviewer bias (distortion of facts), the difficulty of recruiting trained interviewers, and expense.

## STUDENT QUESTIONNAIRE

Name: Mr. Mrs. Miss _____

College or University_____

Home City & State_____ Reside at School: At School ( )
At Home ( )

**1a** AGE
(Circle One)

**b** SCHOOL YEAR
(Circle One)

**c** MARITAL STATUS
(Check One)

| | | |
|---|---|---|
| **1** 17 | 1 | **1** Single ( ) |
| **2** 18 | 2 | **2** Engaged ( ) |
| **3** 19 | 3 | **3** Married ( ) |
| **4** 20 | 4 | |
| **5** 21+ | | |

Employment while at School:

**1** None ( )          **2** Part Time ( )          **3** Full Time ( )

**2** When at school, where do you buy most of your toiletries and/or cosmetics?

**1** Campus Book Store ( )          **2** Other Store ( )

**3** When at home, where do you buy most of your toiletries and/or cosmetics?

**1** Drug Store ( )     **3** Supermarket ( )
**2** Department Store ( )     **4** Discount Store ( )     **5** Other (SPECIFY)_____

**3b** What kind of eye makeup do you use?

**1** Mascara ( )     **3** Eye Liner ( )
**2** Eye Shadow ( )     **4** Other ( )     **5** None ( )

**3c** What brand of Cold Cream do you use?_____

**4a** Please list on the chart below the product and brand of samples you have obtained recently and indicate the following:

**4b** How or where did you receive the sample? (CHECK BELOW)

**4c** Degree of usage. (CHECK BELOW)

**4d** Which brands of regular size (i.e., nonsample) have you purchased since obtaining the sample pack? (RECORD BELOW)

| 4a<br>Product &<br>Brand of<br>Sample<br>Received | 4b<br>How or Where<br>Sample Received | | 4c<br>Usage | | | 4d<br>Brands<br>Purchased<br>Since<br>Receiving<br>Sample |
|---|---|---|---|---|---|---|
| | Campus<br>Bookstore | Other | Have<br>Used | Now<br>Using | Haven't<br>Used | |
| _____ | ( ) | ( ) | ( ) | ( ) | ( ) | _____ |
| _____ | ( ) | ( ) | ( ) | ( ) | ( ) | _____ |
| _____ | ( ) | ( ) | ( ) | ( ) | ( ) | _____ |
| _____ | ( ) | ( ) | ( ) | ( ) | ( ) | _____ |
| _____ | ( ) | ( ) | ( ) | ( ) | ( ) | _____ |
| _____ | ( ) | ( ) | ( ) | ( ) | ( ) | _____ |
| _____ | ( ) | ( ) | ( ) | ( ) | ( ) | _____ |
| _____ | ( ) | ( ) | ( ) | ( ) | ( ) | _____ |
| _____ | ( ) | ( ) | ( ) | ( ) | ( ) | _____ |

**5a** How often do you use a Hand Care product?

| | In Winter | | In Summer | |
|---|---|---|---|---|
| | Hand<br>Lotion | Hand<br>Cream | Hand<br>Lotion | Hand<br>Cream |
| 1 Occasionally—not every day | ( ) | ( ) | ( ) | ( ) |
| 2 Every day, once or twice | ( ) | ( ) | ( ) | ( ) |
| 3 Every day, three times or more | ( ) | ( ) | ( ) | ( ) |
| 4 Do Not Use | ( ) | ( ) | ( ) | ( ) |

**5b** What type of container do you prefer, for a Hand Care product?

| Hand Lotion | | | Hand Cream | | |
|---|---|---|---|---|---|
| 1 Glass Bottle | ( ) | | 1 Glass Jar | ( ) | |
| 2 Plastic Bottle | ( ) | | 2 Plastic Tube | ( ) | |
| 3 Aerosol can | ( ) | | 3 Aerosol can | ( ) | |
| 4 No preference | ( ) | | 4 No preference | ( ) | |

**5c** Please rank (1, 2, 3, 4) in order of importance to you the following qualities of a hand care product: ("1" for most important, "2" for next most important, etc.)

| | Hand Lotion | Hand Cream |
|---|---|---|
| Spreads easily, absorbs quickly | ( ) | ( ) |
| Doesn't leave hands feeling sticky or oily | ( ) | ( ) |
| Pleasant, distinctive fragrance | ( ) | ( ) |
| Creamy consistency, not too thick or thin | ( ) | ( ) |

**FIGURE 24-4**

Example of a research questionnaire for students regarding their preferences, opinions, and purchasing decisions about product categories.

A recent addition to the interview technique is the "pushbutton questionnaire," an automatic machine that is as easy to use as a calculator. One such machine, known as Tellus, embodies a new concept for monitoring and measuring customer opinions. It is less expensive than other questionnaire procedures and provides immediate responses. It takes little time to use, requiring only thirty seconds for the completion of a set of eleven questions. Tellus gathers customer input on the spot and avoids interviewer–interviewee confrontations. Some companies feel, in fact, that customers regard this type of survey as a sincere attempt by management to solve problems.

## Observation

Some problems can be solved simply through **observation.** For example, a retailer that is looking for a new location for a branch store might conduct a traffic study to learn how much automobile or pedestrian traffic passes a proposed site. Or a store buyer might determine the types of rainwear that customers use by conducting a fashion count. The "counter" uses a form to record the styles, shapes, or colors worn by customers or pedestrians. The advantages of the observation method are that observations are relatively simple to implement, that they do not require cooperation from the people

Some information can be obtained through observation. Pedestrian traffic is studied to determine what fashions are being worn.

being studied, and that observers do not have to be experienced. It should be noted that observation can also utilize mechanical means, such as mirrors, or films. A disadvantage is that the attitudes of the people being observed cannot be determined.

## Experimentation

A researcher can also set up an **experiment** utilizing a control factor. For example, a retailer might be interested in learning whether assembled toys sell more than those in KD (knockdown) condition. She might want to investigate the effect on sales if several large toys are sold assembled rather than boxed. The merchant might then advertise a special promotion for assembled toys at a slightly higher price than toys to be assembled by the purchaser. The control factor would be the use of the same product in assembled and unassembled forms. The variables would be the price and service. If sales of assembled toys proved to be greater in spite of the charge, the retailer might assume that her customers are willing to pay more for convenience.

Experiments can make use of surveys or observation. The methods used depend on the type of data needed.

Another type of experiment is the computer-based simulation. A model is created to represent all the factors a retailer would face in a real situation. It is similar to a computer game that involves actions and reactions to different inputs. In this situation the retailer can act as both consumer and merchant. This method can be very helpful in decision making because it is possible to determine cause and effect without the customer's participation and without the risks involved in actual situations. However, it is a very expensive and sophisticated method that requires tremendous expertise. Consequently, it is used infrequently by retailers.

## Sampling

In conducting primary research, it is important to gather data from a sample of the population. A **sample** is a representative group of the entire population being studied. The reseacher telephones, interviews, or surveys the sample to secure answers to specific questions. When composed correctly, samples provide valid information, are less costly, consume less time, and are easier to work with than the entire population.

For example, a merchant considers opening a clothing shop for men up to 5 feet 8 inches tall. The prospective owner feels that short men are neglected by stores because of limited merchandise selection and lack of true-fitting clothes. In fact, many people in this group ordinarily shop in boys' departments. The would-be retailer devises a questionnaire to determine the feasibility of opening the store.

Obviously, it would be very expensive and difficult to survey the 500,000 males in the trading area, especially since the merchant has been told by statisticians that approximately 150,000 of them would probably represent the target market. If the retailer's sample is limited to a small part of the 150,000—say, 1,000—he will probably secure sufficiently valid answers to avoid surveying the entire 150,000.

Many researchers have devised techniques that enable them to work with small samples. For example, Information Resources, a research company, has found a way to monitor the grocery purchases of a representative sample of 4,000 households; it measures how these consumers react to various marketing strategies, such as coupons, free samples, TV commercials, newspaper ads, point-of-purchase displays, and price changes. Known as Behaviorscan, the system contains 2,000 households in two test markets. An identification card is presented at the grocery store each time a member of one of these households makes a purchase. The card alerts the point-of-sale terminal to send an item-by-item accounting of the customer's purchases to a data bank in Chicago. The universal product code is read by a scanner so that researchers can pinpoint a family's purchases by price, brand, and size. This information is then correlated with the promotional stimuli to which the family was exposed.

## Compiling and Tabulating the Data

*Percentages are useful for comparative purposes*

In this stage the data are collected, organized, and processed for analysis. Data are collected and counted manually or with data-processing equipment. During this step the information is counted systematically, enabling the researcher to develop *percentages* to be used in arriving at meaningful conclusions.

For example, in a recent study a merchant noticed that out of a total of 200 shoppers in the store's cosmetics department, 38 men shopped by themselves. Stated as a figure, the number 38 is not particularly useful. When the number is stated as a percentage (19%), however, it is more useful for comparative purposes. Continuing the example, if during the same period in the previous year the comparable finding was 14 percent, the retailer might have concluded that the 5 percent increase warranted further investigation.

## Analyzing and Interpreting the Findings

This step involves studying the research findings and translating them into summary information for the final report. Interpretation is very important because it results in recommendations that usually influence decisions.

The following are examples of findings from retailing research studies.

- Store loyalty was found to be closely related to consumers' styles of shopping.
- A survey of leading practitioners and observers of food retailing revealed a consistently held opinion that supermarket management would find it profitable to give direct attention to the elderly.
- A study of teenagers' responses to retailing stimuli indicated that the mass media play an important role in the formation of young people's attitudes and knowledge.
- Selecting the most effective advertising medium is vital in getting the most from a store's ad dollars. According to one survey, stores reported that an average of 74 percent of all ready-to-wear and accessories ads are placed in newspapers. Radio and television rank second, capturing an average of 17 percent, and direct mail and catalog advertising are third, with 9 percent.

## Preparation of the Final Report

Reporting the results of the research project is the last step. The report may be presented in writing or given orally. In either case, the report should bring the data and analyses into permanent form so that they are always available for reference. Effective reports often stimulate action and result in important management decisions.

When a retailer implements the recommendations of the final report, it is not uncommon for him or her to undertake an evaluation to study the results.

# CONDUCTING RETAILING RESEARCH

In order to carry out retailing research, some firms hire research directors to conduct in-house studies using internal staff. Others employ consultants or commercial research companies. Sometimes merchants assign sales or office personnel to undertake simple studies based on internal records. Such research includes things like fashion counts or sales analyses. When the problems to be researched are complex, the retailer may choose to hire a commercial research agency.

Large retailing organizations have special departments devoted to research. They generally employ small staffs trained in the development and conduct of research studies. They prepare questionnaires, conduct interviews, and develop surveys. They deal with such matters as customer information, the effectiveness of advertising and promotion, customer attitudes regarding services, and employee morale. They collect information for specific problems and maintain appropriate records. The research department pro-

Simple studies can be based on internal records of fast and slow moving fashions.

vides up-to-date information to management, including studies and reports from trade associations, professional groups, and government agencies. Retailers who do not have their own research departments or trained employees may need to consult with private research organizations. These firms specialize in the conduct of research and the sale of information to clients such as retailers and wholesalers. Some of the better-known ones and their specialties are included in the following list.

- A. C. Nielsen specializes in studies dealing with shelf turnover; it prepares retail indexes on products sold in food and drug stores. It conducts observations on shelf distribution, prices, displays, and the like.
- Market Research Corporation of America studies consumer purchasing habits through the use of consumer panels.
- Audits and Surveys specializes in the conduct of store audits of merchandise, using field people to do the physical counts.
- Dun and Bradstreet specializes in providing credit information to clients.

Other groups are also involved in retailing research.

- Research consultants are outside experts who provide research expertise in areas of interest to retailers. For example, fashion consultants are available to aid the small retailer with purchasing problems; accounting experts are called upon to improve the fiscal health of some businesses; individuals who specialize in site research are involved when new locations are considered.
- Trade associations publish a great deal of information, conduct studies, and make the findings available to their members. The National Retail Merchants Association is the largest of the retail professional groups, most of which conduct research, hold seminars, and provide current data to their members.
- Consumer panels provide services for the study of consumer purchasing habits. They are composed of nationwide households that regularly report their purchases of selected foods, household items, and clothing by logging them in diaries. These diaries are summarized in reports that help manufacturers and retailers plan more efficiently for new products, better packaging, and so forth (Figure 24-5).
- Graduate schools often participate with businesses in joint research efforts. They provide academic expertise and personnel that can be used in conducting market research.

# AFTERWORD—
# RETAILING IN
# THE FUTURE

Retailing must respond to all kinds of social and economic changes in order to meet the needs of the consumer. Retail institutions have adapted to changes in demographics, lifestyles, and the environment. Therefore, it is no surprise that merchants seek organizations and individuals to conduct retailing research in order to gain insight into future

| DATE BOUGHT | BRAND | PRODUCT DETAILS | QUAN-TITY | WEIGHT (SIZE) | PRICE PAID | SPECIAL? COUPON? ¢ OFF? DESCRIBE | WHERE BOUGHT |
|---|---|---|---|---|---|---|---|

**MARGARINE** (OLEOMARGARINE)  ☐ None

| | | Do the words below appear in larger print on the label? Yes— Check as many as appear | | | | | | Check HOW PACKAGED | | | | | | | | How many pkgs or items of each kind | Of each can, jar, pkg, bottle, item (lbs., ozs., pts., qts., etc.) | Don't include taxes | | Describe if a special price, coupon, sale, cents off label or other offer | Name of store or delivery company |
|---|---|---|---|---|---|---|---|---|---|---|---|---|---|---|---|---|---|---|---|---|---|
| | | Corn Oil | Soft | Whipped | Diet | Unsalted | No (✓) | Four (4) Sticks | Six (6) Sticks | Two ½ lb Tubs/Cups | 1 lb Tub | 1 lb Solid | Squeeze Bottle or Tube | Other | | | | For each | Total if more than one | | |
| 8/4 | (Brand) Sweet Corn | | ✓ | ✓ | | | | | | | | | ✓ | | | 2 | 1 lb. | .47 | .94 | | Mills |
| | | | | | | | | | | | | | | | | | | | | | |

**BUTTER**  ☐ None

| | | Does Label say "Unsalted"? (✓) | | Check HOW PACKAGED | | | | | | | | |
|---|---|---|---|---|---|---|---|---|---|---|---|---|
| | | Yes | No | Four (4) Sticks | Six (6) Sticks | Other | | | | | | |
| 8/4 | (Brand) Bossert's Farm | | ✓ | ✓ | | | 1 | 1 lb. | .89 | | Mills |

**JAM, JELLY, PRESERVES, MARMALADE, FRUIT BUTTER, ETC.**  ☐ None

| | | Write KIND (Jam, Jelly, Preserves, Marmalade, Fruit Butter, Conserves, etc.) | Copy FLAVOR FROM LABEL (Strawberry, Grape, Black Raspberry, Mint Apple, Orange, etc.) | Is it Low Calorie or Dietetic? (✓) | | | | | | |
|---|---|---|---|---|---|---|---|---|---|---|
| | | | | Yes | No | | | | | |
| 8/4 | (Brand) Fruit Fresh | Jelly | Grape | | ✓ | 1 | 18oz | .49 | | Mills |
| 8/4 | Fruit Fresh | Jelly | Cherry | | ✓ | 1 | 18oz | .49 | | Mills |
| 8/4 | Pantry Delight | | Strawberry | | ✓ | 1 | 24oz | .79 | | Mills |
| | | | | | | | | | | |

**MARSHMALLOWS**  ☒ None

| | | Check SIZE | | KIND | | | | | | |
|---|---|---|---|---|---|---|---|---|---|---|
| | | Miniatures | Regular | White (✓) | Other— Describe Color or Flavor | | | | | |
| | (Brand) | | | | | | | | | |

**CARAMELS**  ☐ None     (Do Not Include Toffee)

| | | WHAT IS IT CALLED ON LABEL? (Vanilla, Chocolate, Mixed, etc.) | Check HOW PACKAGED | | | | | | | | |
|---|---|---|---|---|---|---|---|---|---|---|---|
| | | | Plastic or Cellophane Bag | Paper Bag | Box | Can | Other | | | | |
| 8/4 | (Brand) Cherry Delite | Mixed | ✓ | | | | | 1 | 10oz | .25 | 5¢ OFF | Mills |

**FIGURE 24-5**

Example of a diary page used by consumer panels.

retailing practices. Following are a number of factors that will probably affect the retail environment in the 1980s.

## The Market

Changes in population and age groups are important to retailers because as people move into different age categories, their buying power, wants, and needs change.

The maturing of America

- Since the older population is growing, the group of people age 65 and over will continue to increase in importance because of their size and affluence. Retailers that cater to this group will have increased opportunities, since it will represent approximately 12 percent of the population in 1990.
- A significant portion of this group will continue to move to the Sunbelt area. For these areas in particular, therefore, the shift in population will call for changes in retail strategy.
- Young middle-agers (35–44) will be the fastest-growing market, with high incomes to spend.
- The very young market (14–17) will decrease in numbers, together with the 18–24-year-old group, while the 25–34-year-olds will represent the largest group of adults.

Income

- Modest economic growth will enhance living standards substantially. By 1990 two families out of five may qualify as upper income earners. The most explosive growth of all during the 1980s will be in high-income groups: The number of families with incomes over $50,000 will more than double. Catering to these well-to-do consumers should prove lucrative.

Birthrate

- The increased number of women of childbearing age poses a question—Do they intend to raise families? If they do, a "baby boom" is a strong possibility in the mid-1980s.

Education

- By 1985 more than half the working population will have completed high school. The higher overall level of education should add to the sophistication of consumers and their purchase decisions.

Working wives

- Increases in the number of working women will swell this group to over 45 percent of the labor force by 1990. It is expected that 57 percent of all women will be employed at that time.
- Nontraditional lifestyles will become more common. These include one-person domiciles, unmarried couples living together, one-spouse households, and female-headed households.

## Downtown Revival

The outlook for downtown retailing is improving as significant numbers of consumers move back to the cities and municipalities rebuild their downtown areas. Another plus for downtown centers is the growing number of young "quick-spending" professionals living there. As a result, many large cities have experienced a local renaissance. Recent examples of successful downtown operations include Woodward & Lothrop in Washington, D.C.; Macy's, 34th Street, and the Albee Square Mall in New York City; and Faneuil Hall Market Place in Boston.

# Store Development and Operation

Shopping center slowdown

- Changes in shopping centers and malls are expected. This is due to the susceptibility of suburban mall developments to the energy crisis as well as the excessive number of large shopping centers. The rate of construction of new centers is expected to decline, while new space will be added through the upgrading and modernization of existing centers.

Productivity

- The concentration on increased productivity and cost relationships will dictate the allocation of space in stores. Areas and merchandise that do not yield sufficient profits will be eliminated. For example, service areas in department stores, such as snack bars, restaurants, theatres, and travel agencies, will be studied as to their profitability and power in attracting customers. The allocation of space in supermarkets will also undergo change as service areas such as rest rooms, luncheonettes, or snack bars are added.

Expansion

- High interest rates plus increased land and construction costs will affect retailers' expansion plans in the 1980s. Consequently, some retailers will remodel rather than build new structures, while others will diversify into other types of opportunities.
- Retailers will place great emphasis on control as a means of improving profitability. Stores will rely on greater use of electronic devices to curb store theft, as well as on electronic funds systems to reduce the number of bad checks and the amount of credit card abuse.
- The increased use of self-service areas, store renovations, space reallocations, and operational efficiency are expected to reduce costs and increase sales per square foot.
- To help reduce costs, more retailers will adopt energy management systems to monitor power usage and power shedding (the reduction of power use).
- Inflation may result in a cutback of store hours. In addition, there will probably be a move toward later openings and greater emphasis on afternoon, evening, and weekend shopping to accommodate working people.
- The dental clinics established in retail stores will increase in importance and will probably extend to podiatrists, optometrists, and chiropractors. In fact, retail store dentistry has already become a $100 million business.

# Personnel and Employment

- Staffing will still remain a problem for retailers as young businesspeople become more demanding and seek faster advancement, increases, and recognition. In fact, many are unwilling to accept company-imposed hardships such as transfers to other locations. (A recent study showed that one out of ten employees declines transfers.)
- The continuing popularity of the four-day work week will create problems of employee scheduling.
- A more scientific approach to recruitment, selection, and training will become a must as retailers face high turnover rates.

# Merchandising and Promotion

- Preselling of merchandise via advertising will increase as self-service merchandising expands.
- The number of items carried by department stores will decrease as the specialty concept within department stores increases.
- The 1980s will see an increase in both department and specialty stores turning to private labels in order to strengthen store identity and decrease dependence on designer labels.
- Store buyers will be able to view potential merchandise via video computer hook-ups. As the regional buying trend continues to grow, the use of computer terminals and TV for buying will increase.
- As noted earlier, regional apparel markets will attract increasing numbers of buyers from all over the country. These markets have become vital trade centers because

---

## The Brothers Bloomingdale
### LIKE NO OTHER STORE IN THE WORLD

Of all the successful department store chains in this country, probably none is better known or more exciting than Bloomingdale's. Its slogan, "Like No Other Store in the World," is familiar to shoppers, tourists, and international travelers.

The store was started in New York City in 1872 as Bloomingdale's Great East Side Bazaar. Its owners, Joseph B. and Lyman G. Bloomingdale, decided to sell ready-to-wear clothing, small personal items, and textiles. Concentrating heavily on advertising, they offered low prices and attractive merchandise assortments. This strategic combination proved an immediate success, and the brothers spent the next fifteen years in frenzied expansion.

One of Bloomingdale's early innovations was the escalator, now found in virtually all multistoried retail establishments. The two merchants also stressed customer service and custom-made clothing. But perhaps their most insightful decision involved the heavy use of advertising to popularize the name "Bloomingdale's." Despite the store's location in a nonretailing section of the city, the cleverness and persistence of its ads drew people from widely separated areas.

Though it had started as a soft-goods business, by the late 1890s Bloomingdale's had been transformed into a department store. Despite an occasional attempt to appeal to wealthier consumers, the store's basic customers at that time were drawn from middle- and low-income groups.

Bloomingdale's eventually merged with Abraham & Straus, another department store chain, and today is under the ownership of Federated Department Stores. It was also to become a major trend setter among retailing giants, known by millions as "Bloomie's." To a large extent, these and other events were foreshadowed by the brother merchants whose tenure with the store ended in the early 1900s.

they draw many designers and manufacturers to show their merchandise. Buyers can examine a variety of offerings at these marts, with the major ones located in Dallas, Atlanta, Miami, and Los Angeles.

- Many small stores will move to mini computers to control all phases of their merchandise programs.
- As the number of working women increases, preselected shopping is expected to become more popular through the use of catalogs, phone orders, and mail orders.
- The price-conscious consumer will build discounters' sales volume to 25 percent of general merchandise sales by the mid-1980s.
- Electronic funds transfer will become commonplace. This is already happening with gas stations in California where drivers are able to gas up without cash, credit cards, or attendants. Bank computer terminals connected to the gas pumps enable motorists to have their gas charges deducted automatically from their checking account balances.
- Consumers looking for service will find many retailers that are willing to provide conveniences and help simplify their shopping experiences.
- Nonstore retailing will increase in importance as the in-home shopper accepts the concept of interactive television. Shoppers will view products in their homes and order by telephone or directly via a two-way system.

### NEW TERMS

| | |
|---|---|
| data bank | retail information system (RIS) |
| experimentation | retailing research |
| marketing research | sample (in a research study) |
| observation | secondary data |
| outshopper | survey |
| primary data | |

# CHAPTER HIGHLIGHTS

1 The retail information system (RIS) processes and retains information for quick decision making by management.

2 In an RIS, managers have access to data through terminals placed in store stations, departments, and offices.

3 Marketing research is the gathering, recording, and analysis of data related to a specific marketing problem.

4 Retailing research utilizes marketing research techniques to analyze retail activities.

5 Retailing research focuses on the following areas: customers, store location and layout, advertising and promotion, merchandise selection and pricing, and personnel.

6 Though research in retailing may be simple or complex, the procedures and tools used are similar in either case.

7 The research process consists of identification and definition of the problem, col-

lection of secondary and/or primary data, compilation and tabulation of the data, analysis and interpretation of the findings, and preparation of the final report.

8  Primary data may be secured through surveys, observation, and experimentation.

9  The development of percentages from tabulated data is valuable for comparative purposes.

10  The interpretation of research findings results in recommendations that usually influence decisions.

11  Retailing research is conducted by store research departments, outside consultants, commercial research companies, and sales or office personnel.

12  Changes in retailing are expected in the following areas: market, downtown revival, personnel and employment, and merchandising and promotion.

# QUESTIONS

1  What type of information is usually placed in a retail data bank?

2  What are the three disadvantages of an RIS?

3  In conducting major research studies, with what areas are manufacturers generally concerned?

4  What kinds of information does a computer produce from point-of-sales transactions? How is this information helpful to retailers?

5  What two consumer aspects have received the most attention from retail researchers?

6  Why do merchants evaluate their experiences with media selection, ad types, special promotions, and advertising costs?

7  What are some personnel areas that require ongoing evaluation?

8  How do secondary data differ from primary data? When should each type of data be used?

9  What are the three basic methods used to secure primary data? How do they differ?

10  What are the three techniques used in the survey method of securing primary data? For what type of situation is each most suitable?

11  Why are percentages more valuable to retailers than pure numbers in the computation of comparative statistics?

12  What is the last step in the research process? Why is it of great importance to retailers?

13  What are the functions of store research staffs?

14  What changes in the field of retailing are expected in the 1980s?

# FIELD PROJECTS

1  A local shop that specializes in the sale of jeans is considering enlarging its merchandise line to include accessories. In particular, the owner wants to determine the

advisability of stocking fold-away rain boots, rain hats, and umbrellas. Unsure of how to proceed, he asks you to develop a research plan. The merchant is willing to commit $300 to the project and has specified the 16–22 age group as the target population. He wants to restrict the study to the trading area served by his store, a neighborhood shopping district. Design a plan to help the merchant. Be specific about the research methods and techniques you would use.

2  The purpose of this project is to determine the advertising and promotion factors that influence young adults to shop at certain stores. You are to interview twenty students and tabulate their answers to the following questions.

> **Part I**   In what types of stores do you usually purchase clothing, shoes, sporting goods, and record albums?
>
> **Part II**   Which media influenced you to shop in these stores?

In order to organize your work, use the following form to arrange the students' responses.

**PART I**

| Type of Merchandise | Type of Store | | | |
|---|---|---|---|---|
| | Discount | Department | Specialty | Other |
| Clothing | | | | |
| Shoes | | | | |
| Sporting goods | | | | |
| Record albums | | | | |

**PART II**

| Type of Store | Type of Media | | | | | |
|---|---|---|---|---|---|---|
| | Newspaper Advertising | Radio Announcement | TV Commercial | Window Display | Information from a Friend | Other |
| Discount | | | | | | |
| Department | | | | | | |
| Specialty | | | | | | |
| Other | | | | | | |

> a  What percent of the students who shopped in discount stores were influenced by newspaper advertisements?
> b  What percent of those who shopped in department stores were influenced by information from friends?
> c  What overall conclusions do you draw from your findings?

# CASES

1  Styles and Buys, a men's discount clothing store, has been in business at the same location for thirty-one years. The owner, Phil Glass, has watched the recent deterioration

of the neighborhood with misgivings. Torn between loyalty to his customers and the possible need for relocation, Glass decides to undertake a study to help him determine the store's future.

Since Glass knows little about the methods and procedures of retailing research, he is at a loss as to how to proceed. Though he is willing to commit some funds to the project, he wants to take an active part in the study. He has even considered reading about research methodology in the local library.

a Would you advise the owner to contact a private research organization to conduct the study? Why?

b In what ways might Glass be useful to a research organization in the conduct of the study?

c What questions should Glass seek to have answered?

d What method(s) would be used to conduct this research?

2 A large department store with its flagship store in a downtown shopping center and four branches in outlying suburban areas has always relied on consultants to conduct its major studies. However, top management is thinking of establishing a research department with a director at its head and a small staff of assistants as support.

On the horizon, management sees the need for studies of

- Inventory control
- Personnel policies
- Security problems
- Innovations in data processing

In addition, the store president wants an in-depth study of long-term needs in order to keep ahead of the competition. He is unsure about the ability of an in-house research department to conduct such a study.

a What are your arguments for and against establishment of the research department?

b Might an outside consultant or private research organization be a wise choice to conduct the long-term studies? Why?

c In what format might a study of this nature be conducted?

3 A retail home center customer is a consumer who performs his or her own home repair and remodeling jobs instead of hiring a professional contractor. The number of such consumers has risen significantly in the last ten years, primarily because of the high cost of contractor services. This trend appears nationwide and shows no signs of abating.

The Homebuilding Mart, a twelve-store chain specializing in home-building products, wants to capitalize on the increased interest in home repair by attracting additional customers. The executives at Homebuilding Mart also want to determine *why* people are switching to do-it-yourself practices. In this way they can plan their advertising, sales promotion, and merchandise strategies to increase customer patronage.

With the aid of outside consultants, the firm designed and conducted a research study to learn the nature and demographics of retail home center customers in two major trading areas. The study included the following features of home center customers.

- Their approximate number in relation to the total population of the trading area
- Their ages
- Their educational backgrounds
- Their income levels

The study revealed the following data.

### Number of Home Center Customers in Trading Area Population

| | |
|---|---|
| Trading area no. 1 | 60,000 |
| Trading area no. 2 | 45,000 |

### Home Center Customer Ages

| | Trading Area No. 1 | Trading Area No. 2 |
|---|---|---|
| Over 70 | 6% | 8% |
| 50–69 | 18 | 21 |
| 30–49 | 46 | 43 |
| 20–29 | 26 | 26 |
| Below 20 | 4 | 2 |

### Home Center Customer Educational Backgrounds

| | Trading Area No. 1 | Trading Area No. 2 |
|---|---|---|
| College degree | 47% | 51% |
| High school diploma | 31 | 36 |
| Less than high school | 22 | 13 |

### Home Center Customer Income Levels

| | Trading Area No. 1 | Trading Area No. 2 |
|---|---|---|
| $50,000 or more | 6% | 10% |
| $40,000–49,999 | 12 | 16 |
| $30,000–39,999 | 18 | 18 |
| $20,000–29,999 | 29 | 27 |
| $10,000–19,999 | 18 | 16 |
| Below $10,000 | 17 | 13 |

a Are there differences between the customer populations of the two trading areas that might affect Homebuilding Mart's plans? If so, what are the differences?

b Unfortunately, the study did not address itself to why customers are increasingly resorting to self-repair practices. What additional research techniques would you use to secure the necessary data?

c With regard to the demographic data, how might the company determine the most effective means for communicating with the potential market?

# REFERENCES

Anson, C. J., *Profit from Figures: A Manager's Guide to Statistical Methods* (New York: McGraw-Hill, 1971).

Barmash, I., "And a New and Growing Role at Retail for Research," *Stores,* 63 (April 1981), pp. 19–24.

Bergmann, J., "What Does Research Mean to You?," *Stores,* 63 (April 1981), p. 18.

Braverman, J. D., and W. C. Stewart, *Statistics for Business and Economics* (New York: Ronald Press, 1973).

Clover, V. T., and H. L. Balsley, *Business Research Methods,* 2nd ed. (Columbus, Ohio: Grid, 1979).

Crane, R. R., "Operations Research in Retailing" (New York: National Retail Merchants Association, Retail Research Institute, 1958).

Gelb, G. M., and B. D. Gelb, *Research at the Top: Better Data for Organizational Policy Making* (Chicago: American Marketing Association, 1975).

Gillespie, K. R., and J. C. Hecht, *Retail Business Management* (New York: McGraw-Hill, 1977), chaps. 37, 38.

Green, P. E., and D. S. Tull, *Research for Marketing Decisions* (Englewood Cliffs, N.J.: Prentice-Hall, 1975).

Mason, J. B., and M. L. Mayer, "Retail Merchandise Information Systems for the 1980's," *Journal of Retailing,* 56 (Spring 1980), pp. 56–76.

McLoughlin, W. G., *Fundamentals of Research Management* (New York: American Management Association, 1970).

Stark, M. S., "Where Retailing Will Expand," *Stores,* 62 (January 1980), pp. 50–54.

# chapter 25
# ENTREPRENEUR-SHIP: GETTING STARTED

After completing this chapter, you should be able to:

1 Identify the personal characteristics that contribute to the success of retail ownership.

2 Explain the importance of technical skills, knowledge, and interest in ownership of a retail business.

3 Assess the part played by location in the selection of a new retail business.

4 List the sources of investment funds available to prospective retailers.

5 Explain the roles of lawyers and accountants in the establishment of a retail business.

6 List the advantages and disadvantages of sole proprietorships, partnerships, and corporations as forms of retail business organization.

7 Identify factors that one should investigate before purchasing or buying into an established business.

While most of this book has been devoted to a description and analysis of the practices of large retailers, we have occasionally referred to small retail operations. We have identified the functions that are common to both, as well as the differences between them. Emphasis was placed on the need for all merchants to adhere to sound retailing principles if they are to be successful.

In this chapter and the next we examine the concerns and problems of going into a retail business. We discuss the similarities as well as the differences between starting a new business and buying an established one. We also explore the opportunities and cautions in purchasing a franchise, and study the special problems of retailing a service. The Appendix at the end of this chapter contains a checklist for starting a retail business.

# GOING INTO BUSINESS: RETAILING VERSUS OTHER FIELDS

*Many opportunities for retail ownership*

In probably no other field are there as many opportunities to own one's own business as there are in retailing. An examination of any trading area will demonstrate why this is so. For example, stores in a neighborhood shopping district usually range from convenience outlets to specialty shops; strip centers feature a variety of retail outlets, from auto stores to supermarkets; regional shopping centers contain numerous stores, large and small, that cater to consumers' diversified needs. Additional opportunities for ownership exist in central shopping districts, secondary shopping areas, community shopping centers, and highway outlets. Needless to say, one may also own a nonstore retail business.

# SHOULD YOU GO INTO A RETAIL BUSINESS?

Anyone who contemplates ownership of a retail business should possess the personal characteristics, knowledge, skills, interest, and financial means for success. There is little doubt that failure usually results from the lack of one or more of these requisites.

## Personal Characteristics

We have all met a variety of retail owners, ranging from the proprietors of a mom-and-pop store to the owner–manager of a specialty or small department store. Thinking about them, are you able to list the personal characteristics that distinguished the successful ones from the unsuccessful ones? Can you identify particular behavior patterns among them that captured your patronage loyalty? Let's examine some traits that appear to be necessary for success.

### Ability to Make Decisions

Retailers are required to make decisions about many matters: merchandise, money, customers, personnel, and so forth. In many instances decisions must be made quickly, as with an irate customer who is dissatisfied with a store's service. At other times decisions may require careful research, for example, when deciding whether to make additional capital investments in the business. An effective retailer takes timely and decisive action even in unpleasant circumstances, while an ineffective one hesitates or procrastinates.

## Ability to Organize

Whether one is considering inventory levels, sales campaigns, or some other business need, one must be able to organize one's work for smooth operations. One must be patient and pay attention to details. One must also appreciate the need for planning and recognize the danger of haphazard preparation.

## Willingness to Accept Responsibility

*Responsibility is burdensome—but rewarding*

An effective retailer likes to be in charge of things and is the type of person who takes responsibility for his or her actions. While the retailer recognizes the burdens of authority, he or she shows little or no reluctance in accepting them. In fact, part of the pleasure such a person feels in assuming responsibility is the ultimate excitement of achievement in addition to the potential profits.

## Ability to Lead

Retailers who employ others must be able to motivate them to perform well. This is not to imply a situation in which employees feel compelled to act. Instead, it calls for the type of leadership that causes workers to feel a commitment to their jobs. Through example and understanding, owners must get employees to go along willingly with store policies and procedures.

## Capacity for Hard Work

Almost all retail owners acknowledge the need to work hard and maintain long hours. The very nature of retailing—its concern with planning, stocking goods, selling, and so on—makes constant attention to details a necessity. The individual who contemplates owning a retail outlet, therefore, must be willing to commit much time and effort to the venture. At the risk of losing his or her capital investment, the new owner must be prepared for physical and mental stress as well as the inevitable emergencies. Early retailers like Simon Lazarus, Morris Rich, and John Bullock built successful stores through hard work.

## Ability to Get Along with People

*Poise, sureness, and tact are needed when dealing with people*

In general, business owners must be able to relate well to other people. For retailers, this is a major requirement. Whether dealing with customers, employees, or vendors, the proprietor of a retail business should have the ability to act with poise, sureness, and tact. To a large extent these attributes require a liking for people and a desire to please them. On the other hand, the owner must be firmly committed to basic business principles and store policies. Weak application of established procedures inevitably cuts into earnings.

In concluding our discussion of personal characteristics that are helpful to a retail owner, it should be noted that few people possess them all in large quantities. What is important is a blend of these traits that is sufficient to make the owner effective. In addition, awareness of the value of these characteristics improves the owner's chances of success.

# Knowledge, Technical Skills, and Interest in Retailing

To the uninitiated, managing a small retail business appears simple. "After all," they reason, "it's all a matter of selling something to a customer. There doesn't seem to be much more to it." Having read earlier chapters of this book and discussed a variety of retail topics, you realize that such an assessment is incorrect. The myriad activities that retailing comprises call for a variety of technical and management skills as well as an interest in retailing itself. The extent of these needs is often surprising to new retail owners. As indicated earlier, a large number of business failures are due to poor management techniques.

## Knowledge

The operation of a retail outlet requires the owner to possess technical information about the products or services it sells. In order to offer salable merchandise or services, the owner must understand the needs of the target population. For example, stores located in college or senior-citizen communities must cater to the requirements of those vastly different populations.

*Retailing requires different levels of expertise*

Some retail endeavors require a different level of expertise than others. For example, product knowledge is probably more important in a hardware store, where customers often ask technical questions, than in a convenience store. In the case of service retailers, the type and quantity of information needed by the owner of a travel agency is more complex than that needed by the proprietor of a laundry store. Whatever the type of business, however, a thorough knowledge of the commodities carried or services offered is important.

Retailers also need an understanding of correct selling techniques, with an appreciation of the likes and dislikes of their target populations. Where appropriate, the owner should know how to display merchandise attractively and how to promote both product and store image effectively. In addition, proprietors should be acquainted with personnel management techniques, record-keeping procedures, and inventory control.

## Technical Skills

In some retail businesses owners must possess specific skills. Such businesses include service establishments like haircutters, dry cleaners, and repair shops. They also include merchandise–service operations like jewelry stores, photography outlets, and gasoline stations. Merchants who possess the requisite skills are able to satisfy customer needs as well as evaluate and help their employees.

## Interest in Retailing

Since there is a wide variety of retail businesses among which to choose, a new owner should consider personal interests in making a selection. For example, someone who likes fashion items may enjoy operating a women's-wear specialty shop. An individual who takes pleasure in repairing mechanical items may use those skills in a repair service business. Owning a business centered on the products or skills that one enjoys allows one to "have one's cake and eat it, too."

Certain retail businesses call for technical skills.

Nevertheless, a person who is contemplating retail ownership should ask questions like the following:

- Is the field in which I'm interested overcrowded?
- Is there a new service that people may need?
- Do I have the necessary experience to do well?
- Do I need formal training?
- Should I secure advice from people in the field before making a decision?

Honest and reliable answers to these questions may accomplish one of the following.

- Fortify one's determination to go into business
- Cause one to do more investigating before starting a business
- Help one decide not to become an owner

Because a negative conclusion arrived at after thorough research can be as valuable as a positive one, a prospective owner should answer basic questions of this nature. There are other important questions that should be asked, too. Being certain of one's basic interests is vital to success.

# LOCATING A RETAIL BUSINESS

In Chapter 11 we discussed the importance of location in measuring the effectiveness of a retail outlet. We examined the factors in selecting a location as well as the various types of shopping areas. Finally, we listed several criteria that one should consider when choosing a site, and highlighted the differences between buying and renting an outlet.

Location, of course, is related to other considerations, such as type of store, competition, and economic factors in a trading area. In addition there are personal needs that may enter the picture: willingness to move one's household from its present location, desire to do business in a surburban setting, and so forth.

*Clock mechanisms are used to record pedestrian traffic*

A common technique employed by prospective store owners is to count the number of people who pass an intended retail location, either acting alone or hiring someone to make the count. A clock mechanism is used to record pedestrian traffic. With further analysis of the composition of the traffic (age, sex, etc.), a fairly accurate determination can be made of the number and types of potential customers. With this information, a conclusion can be reached regarding the type of store that would be appropriate.

# ECONOMIC ASPECTS OF GOING INTO BUSINESS

In previous chapters it was pointed out that a major reason for business failures is inadequate investment of capital. Not only must the new owner be concerned with this problem; he or she must also have a reliable source of funds on which to draw.

While it is true that many service businesses can be started with little money, virtually all merchandise outlets require modest funds at least. Few new owners can secure beginning inventories on **consignment,** that is, paying only for items that are sold. Most must secure credit to finance some of their initial purchases.

In addition to outlays for merchandise, plans must provide for the payment of store equipment and fixtures such as counters, shelves, lighting, cash registers, and office machines. If a store requires decorating, money must be available for carpeting, floor tiles, wall coverings, and the like. Supplies like bags, twine, register tapes, and postage are also needed. The extent to which any of these things is needed depends, of course, on the size and character of the store.

Having your own money is the easiest way to finance the start of a retail store. This is because you need not depend on anyone else for financing and the required funds may be used at your own discretion. Care must be taken, of course, to leave a reserve for business needs as well as for personal use. Suppose, however, that the prospective retailer lacks the necessary funds. Are there other sources, personal and otherwise, that can be tapped? The answer is that there are, though securing the money usually takes considerable effort.

## Borrowing from Personal Sources

Some people are fortunate enough to have relatives or friends who are both willing and able to lend them money. Successful retail businesses have been developed from such borrowing, and prospective owners may want to investigate this avenue. Two very successful retailers, Isaac Merritt Singer, who started The Singer Company, and Rowland Hussey Macy, founder of R. H. Macy Co., did exactly that!

In some cases a relative or friend may want to invest in a retail business without the burden of active ownership. The investor becomes a limited partner, contributing funds but little or no time to the business. In return for making the investment, the limited partner shares in both the profits and losses of the business. The advantages to a new retailer of taking on a limited partner are the immediate infusion of cash as well as the partner's limited role in running the business. In return, of course, the active owner must share profits.

Some life insurance policies can serve as a source of funds. For example, if a certain type of policy has been in effect a few years, the insured party can use it to secure money by either cashing it in or borrowing against it. Borrowing against the cash value of the policy provides funds while the insurance protection remains in force. Insurance companies, of course, charge interest for the privilege of borrowing from the cash value.

## Borrowing from Business Sources

Additional sources of funds for starting a new business include manufacturers, vendors, banks, the U.S. Small Business Administration, and venture capital operators.

## Manufacturers and Vendors

If prospective owners can demonstrate creditworthiness through past experience or the possession of sufficient assets, it is possible—but not probable—that equipment and fixture manufacturers will sell their products on credit to them. This holds true for vendors of merchandise and supplies as well. However, anyone who is starting a retail business should have no illusions about the ease of securing credit without a "track record." Manufacturers and wholesalers are loath to extend credit to beginning merchants for fear of nonpayment.

## Banks

Banks, of course, are the main source for business borrowing. However, securing a bank loan to start a retail business can be as frustrating as tapping friends and relatives. Why is this so?

Banks are conservative institutions and avoid risks like the plague. They are particularly averse to lending money to untested businesses. Their reasoning is as follows: Why expend funds on new ventures when low-risk investments in such areas as government securities, blue-chip corporate securities, and loans to long-established, reliable businesses are available?

Despite their reluctance to make small loans to new enterprises, banks may do so under the following conditions.

* The proposed venture is based on sound business practices.
* The new business shows strong promise of success.
* The new owner demonstrates a capacity for conducting a successful retail business.
* The new owner presents a credible plan for repaying the loan.

In terms of time for repayment of loans, banks accept both short- and long-term notes. **Short-term loans** are for less than a year; **long-term loans** run for a year or more. In order to secure a loan—especially a long-term loan—a borrower often has to supply collateral. This requires the borrower to give the bank some security for the bank's protection, such as shares of stock, bonds, or other valuables. When the loan is repaid, the bank returns the collateral.

Banks sometimes lend funds to promising retailers.

Borrowers should understand the significance of bank interest rates

A borrower should understand the meaning of loan interest rates because of their serious impact on ability to repay. Though banks use charts to demonstrate interest payments to borrowers, the new retailer should have a grasp of the practical effects of rates on amounts borrowed. The formula for the computation of interest on loans (called **simple interest**) is fairly easy to use. It states that

$$\text{Interest} = \text{principal} \times \text{rate} \times \text{time}$$

where principal is the amount borrowed, rate is the annual interest percent charged, and time is the length of the loan expressed as part of a year (using a 360-day year).

Here are some examples of interest payments on short-term loans using the preceding formula.

| If the amount borrowed is | and | The bank interest rate is | and | The time of the loan is | then | The interest payment is |
|---|---|---|---|---|---|---|
| $ 6,000 | | 15% | | 90 days | | $  225 |
| $10,000 | | 20% | | 6 months | | $1,000 |
| $20,000 | | 10% | | 1 year | | $2,000 |

Though it is too complex to discuss here in detail, banks usually deduct interest in advance, that is, at the time a loan is made. Consequently, the actual interest rate is higher than the one the bank quotes. Not only that; the borrower receives less than the amount requested as a loan. For example, if a person borrows $1000 and interest of $90 for six months is deducted in advance, the borrower receives only $910 at the time the loan is made; the borrower repays $1000 six months later.

As part of a loan agreement, banks frequently require the borrower to acquire property as well as liability insurance. In addition, a borrower may have to take out personal life insurance, with the bank listed as beneficiary.

## Small Business Administration (SBA)

If someone who wants to start a business has exhausted the possibilities of a loan from private or business sources without success, it may be possible to secure a loan from (or with the participation of) the **Small Business Administration,** an agency of the federal government. While SBA loans are not easy to secure, certain categories of applicants have more opportunities than others.

*The SBA Loan Guarantee Plan and Economic Opportunity Loan Program*

Under the **SBA's Loan Guarantee Plan,** a successful borrower receives a bank loan which is guaranteed up to 90 percent by the SBA. While there are federal restrictions regarding principal, interest rate, and time, the bank specifies the conditions of the loan.

The **SBA's Economic Opportunity Loan Program** is designed for economically disadvantaged entrepreneurs. While the law contains guidelines regarding "disadvantaged" status, it requires applicants to put up part of the capital, as in the Loan Guarantee Plan.

In order to secure an SBA loan, an applicant must complete elaborate forms containing projected operating and personal financial statements. The new merchant is required to estimate the first year's sales, expenses, and net income.

In addition to supporting loans, the SBA provides counseling for prospective owners. It has trained personnel who help businesspeople analyze their plans in realistic terms. It also sponsors seminars on topics that are of specific interest to owners of small businesses.

## Venture Capital Operators

A **venture capital operator** is an individual or corporation that invests money in someone else's business. For a substantial share of the profits—sometimes even more than half—the venture operator provides sufficient funds to get a business started. Long negotiations usually precede an agreement, after which the new retailer is in legal or de facto partnership with the venture operator.

# PROFESSIONAL HELP WHEN GOING INTO BUSINESS: LAWYERS AND ACCOUNTANTS

Some people start a retail business without seeking professional advice, but those who recognize the pitfalls of doing so seek guidance and direction from lawyers and/or accountants. These experts can save a new owner much time and trouble.

The Small Business Administration provides help to retailers and would-be retailers.

Lawyers, also called attorneys, are valuable in helping the retailer conform to local, state, and federal laws. They identify zoning codes (regulations that specify local restrictions on certain business operations), indicate license requirements where applicable, prepare partnership contracts when two or more entrepreneurs are involved, and file the necessary documents when the business is organized as a corporation. In addition, lawyers suggest appropriate insurance coverage and offer general advice on how to avoid legal problems.

**A lawyer's role in a small retail business**

A word of caution is in order regarding a lawyer's role in a small business enterprise. Since lawyers are usually not entrepreneurs, their knowledge of business practices may be limited. While the retailer should consider their opinions, they should question them closely on both the legal and business sides of an issue. Only then should the owner make a decision, weighing the lawyer's judgments as one element of the business mix.

Accountants help new owners of retail businesses by developing systems for the maintenance of their financial records. In this capacity, they suggest tests and measurements by which the success of the business may be determined. While after their initial input lawyers are usually called upon only when needed, accountants serve retailers on a regular periodic basis: monthly, quarterly, and so on.

Among an accountant's specific contributions are the following.

- Preparation of payroll, sales, and income tax reports.
- Preparation of income statements and balance sheets, followed by analysis and recommendations.
- Development of billing procedures.
- Design of procedures for the control of accounts receivable and accounts payable.
- Development of forms and procedures for the control of inventory.
- Analysis of cash flow, followed by recommendations.

Like lawyers, accountants may not be good merchants. Consequently, the new owner should accept the judgments of the accountant that seem logical and sensible in light of the financial or retail problems under consideration.

# CHOOSING A TYPE OF BUSINESS ORGANIZATION

In Chapter 6 we identified the characteristics of the three basic types of business organization: sole proprietorship, partnership, and corporation. Many people believe that the corporate form of organization is applicable only to large businesses. This is not so. In fact, many small businesses are organized as corporations, with quite a few states requiring only one person as an incorporator. Before deciding on the appropriate form for the operation, the new retailer should consider the main advantages and disadvantages of each.

## Advantages of Sole Proprietorship

1 Ease of starting and dissolving the business
2 All profits belong to the owner
3 Relatively little governmental control
4 Decision making controlled by the owner

## Disadvantages of Sole Proprietorship

1 Unlimited liability for business debts
2 The business has a limited life
3 Difficulty of securing funds when needed
4 Unavailability of help or advice from co-owners

## Advantages of Partnership

1 Ease of starting and dissolving the business through partnership contract
2 Talents and skills of partners are combined
3 Relatively little governmental control
4 Shared management responsibility

## Disadvantages of Partnership

1 Unlimited liability of each partner for business debts
2 The business has a limited life because it is terminated by the death or withdrawal of a partner

3  Profits are shared among partners

4  Each partner is responsible for acts of other partners

5  Division of authority frequently creates problems

## Advantages of Corporation

1  Stockholders (owners) have limited liability

2  Business has an unlimited life

3  Funds may be secured through sale of stock or bonds

4  Ownership may be transferred without permission of other stockholders

5  Owners need not take active part in business operations

## Disadvantages of Corporation

1  Complexity of starting the business

2  Business operations limited by corporation charter

3  Business pays income tax; stockholders pay additional tax on distributed profits. (If a corporation meets certain requirements under Subchapter S of the federal Internal Revenue Code, the corporation does not pay income taxes. Instead, the stockholders pay taxes individually on their proportionate shares of the corporation's taxable income. This means that stockholders avoid double taxation while receiving the benefits of corporate ownership.)

4  Governmental control through regulations and taxes

Before leaving the topic of types of business organization, it's of interest to note that Richard Sears started as a sole proprietor, then formed a partnership with Alvah Roebuck, and finally formed Sears, Roebuck and Co., a corporation. Sears' experience has been duplicated many times by other retailing figures.

# BUYING AN ESTABLISHED BUSINESS

Instead of starting a new business, a prospective merchant may decide to purchase or buy into an existing one. In this case several aspects of the enterprise should be considered.

## Reasons for Sale of an Established Business

Though it is not always possible, the buyer must try to determine why the merchant wants to sell the business. Since the seller is trying to get the highest possible price for the enterprise, the buyer must be wary of the seller's explanations. Common reasons advanced by sellers include health, change of family location, and age. However, behind these avowed reasons may lurk some damaging aspects of the business itself. These may include the following.

Negative aspects
of an established
business

- A deteriorating neighborhood
- A changing trading area population
- An impending steep increase in rent or expiration of a lease
- Poor management
- Mounting debts
- Falling profits or steady losses

As you can imagine, this list can be extended considerably. In order to determine the truth, the prospective merchant should talk to other local retailers, bank officials, and local chambers of commerce. Without question, he or she should—with the aid of an accountant—examine the seller's recent financial statements carefully and thoroughly.

## Examining Business Records

A prospective owner should examine the financial records of the seller's business, including ledgers, financial statements (especially income statements), income tax reports, sales tax reports, and insurance policies. If possible, the examination should be done with the help of an accountant.

## Checking Inventory, Supplies, and Equipment

When purchasing a merchandise business, a thorough evaluation should be made of the seller's inventory. This includes stock on shelves, in stockrooms, in warehouses, and on order. In addition, all types of retail outlets should be checked for office, store, and maintenance supplies.

## Miscellaneous Items to Consider

In addition to those mentioned earlier, the number of specific items to investigate depends on the nature and complexity of the business. Among the more common ones are the following.

- The level of employee salaries and benefits
- The operational status of the equipment
- The condition of the furniture and fixtures
- The existence of lawsuits or liens against the business
- The present discount policy, if any, of the business

- If the store is rented, the terms and duration of the existing lease
- The amount attributed to good will in the purchase price. **Good will** is an intangible asset of a business that is derived from the reputation of its owner, products, or services. The specific monetary value of good will, when claimed, is always a debatable item between buyer and seller.

# BUYING INTO A BUSINESS

Virtually all of the concerns connected with purchasing an existing business apply to buying *into* a business. The buyer becomes a partner, assuming rights and obligations under the partnership contract. Since the new partner is responsible for the debts of the partnership, he or she must examine the reliability and trustworthiness of the other partners with great care.

### NEW TERMS

| | |
|---|---|
| consignment | Small Business Administration (SBA) |
| good will | SBA Economic Opportunity Loan Program |
| long-term loan | SBA Loan Guarantee Plan |
| short-term loan | venture capital operator |
| simple interest | |

# CHAPTER HIGHLIGHTS

1 Effective retailers are good decision makers.

2 Retail owners should possess organizational ability and willingness to accept responsibility.

3 Ability to lead, capacity for hard work, and ability to get along with people are important attributes of retail owners.

4 Ownership of a retail business calls for the possession of knowledge, technical skills (in some instances), and an interest in retailing.

5 Many new owners of retail stores check traffic movement in front of or near prospective locations to determine the number and types of potential customers.

6 Sources of funds to start a retail business include the owner's personal resources, loans from friends or relatives, credit provided by manufacturers and vendors, loans from banks and the SBA, and venture capital operators.

7 Banks are reluctant to loan money to start a new retail business. When they do make loans in these circumstances, they insist on the owner's meeting certain specific conditions.

8 Banks charge simple interest on loans and usually deduct the interest from the principal at the time that the loan is made.

9   In certain cases new retailers can secure loans from the Small Business Administration, a federal agency that administers a Loan Guarantee Plan and an Economic Opportunity Loan Program.

10   A venture capital operator invests money in someone else's business and becomes a partner in the business.

11   A new owner of a retail business should seek the help of lawyers and accountants in the formation of the business.

12   Before deciding on a specific form in which to organize a business, a new retailer should consider the advantages and disadvantages of sole proprietorships, partnerships, and corporations.

13   When considering the purchase of an established retail business, a buyer should talk with other local retailers, bank officials, and local chambers of commerce—in addition to the seller—before making a decision. The same concerns hold true for buying *into* an established business.

# QUESTIONS

1   Why is the ability to make decisions an important characteristic of an owner of a retail business?

2   Why do successful retailers accept responsibility with little or no reluctance?

3   Why is it important for retail owners to balance their ability to get along with people with a strong commitment to basic business principles and store policies?

4   Cite some examples of retail businesses to demonstrate the different levels of expertise required to operate them.

5   After investigating the advisability of starting a specific retail business, what are the possible conclusions to which a prospective owner may come?

6   In connection with assessing the value of a prospective retail location, what is meant by "checking traffic movement"?

7   How can a life insurance policy be used as a source of funds for starting a retail business?

8   What conditions must usually be present for banks to agree to make a small-business loan to a new enterprise?

9   If someone needs exactly $20,000 to start a retail business, why is it probably necessary to borrow more than $20,000 from certain banks to secure the $20,000?

10   In what ways is the Small Business Administration helpful to new retailers?

11   In what ways can an accountant be of help to an owner of a new retail business? Are there any conditions that should be placed on the advice of such an expert?

12   Why might an owner of a new retail business decide on the corporate form of business organization?

13   Why should someone who is seeking to buy an existing retail outlet be skeptical about the reasons advanced by the owner for wanting to sell?

# FIELD PROJECTS

1 You probably know someone who owns or has owned a retail business.[1] Talk to that person about his or her experiences in connection with getting started in the business. Try to determine the following.

   a The type of business it is (was).

   b Where and how funds were secured to get the business started.

   c The extent to which the location of the outlet played a part in the decision to buy or get started.

   d How much (if any) technical skill on the part of the owner is (was) required.

   e From whom he or she sought advice before deciding to become an owner.

2 Visit a local commercial bank to discuss its policies regarding loans to new retail businesses. Introduce yourself to one of the executives as a student and explain the nature of this project. The major purpose is to learn whether local residents who aspire to retail ownership have an opportunity to finance a new enterprise with a bank's participation.

Here are some questions that you might ask.

   a Does the bank lend money to new retail owners? If not, what caused this policy?

   b If the answer to (a) is affirmative,

      Under what conditions might a loan be made?

      Must a new owner invest some of his or her own money? If so, what percent of the total?

      For what periods are loans made?

      Is collateral required?

   c Has the bank been involved with the Small Business Administration?

# CASES

1 In 1975 Recreational Retail Builders of El Segundo, California, developed Old Chicago, a combination shopping center and amusement park. The basic business strategy was to attract both shoppers and fun seekers to the mall, expecting that some members of each group would visit the other area.

Unfortunately, the project proved unsuccessful and the owner company declared bankruptcy in 1976. Most analysts felt that the mall's image was confusing to customers, so much so that they were unsure of why they were supposed to go there. In any event, only 280 of the 400 available retail spaces were rented, and the mall drew less than half of the traffic expected by its developers.

   a If you had contemplated renting one of the retail spaces before the mall opened, what questions would you have asked the developers?

   b If you had been a newcomer to retail ownership, would you have considered opening a store in the mall? Why?

[1]If you don't know anyone who owns or has owned a retail business, ask your friends or relatives if they can introduce you to someone.

2   Hattie Grace is a 32-year-old single woman who is a buyer in a prestigious women's-wear specialty shop. Over the years she has displayed leadership qualities and gained respect in the retail trade. In fact, some retailers consider her a future top executive.

Despite these expectations, Grace's secret wish is to own a boutique that carries high-quality merchandise. Her hope is that her background and personal qualities will make the store a success. Her long-range plans include the development of a chain of similar shops.

Grace has saved enough money to enable her to open a modest boutique shop employing three people. She also has solid contacts with designer–manufacturers and fashion merchandise vendors. In the past her banker has reacted favorably to the idea of making her a loan to start a business.

a   What personal characteristics do you think Grace possesses that make her such a popular buyer? How would these characteristics be valuable to her as an entrepreneur?

b   In your opinion, should Grace leave the specialty shop to open her own boutique? Why?

3   For some years Lou Fried, a 29-year-old married man, had wanted to open a retail appliance store in the community in which he lived. Knowing the composition of the trading area, Fried spent a good deal of time looking for an attractive location in certain sections of the community. He narrowed his choice to two possibilities and then directed his attention to financing the business.

Though Fried had some money of his own, it was insufficient to enable him to open the store. After unsuccessful attempts to borrow money from relatives, friends, and banks, and learning that he was not eligible for a Small Business Administration loan, he heard of someone who was in the business of investing money in new enterprises— in effect, a venture capital operator.

Introducing himself to the potential investor, Frank Lerner, Fried found him friendly and interested, although uninformed about the appliance business. Fried was not concerned about that aspect since he (i.e., Fried) had worked in the appliance department of a large store for five years.

After several discussions, Lerner agreed to invest 40% of the required funds if Fried would meet the following conditions.

1   Lerner was to become Fried's partner.

2   The two partners were to share profits and losses equally.

3   Fried was to be involved in the business full time; Lerner was not required to devote any time to the business.

4   Lerner was to have veto power over major decisions made by Fried.

5   Lerner was to decide the actual location of the store.

6   Fried was to make daily operational decisions, including those related to purchasing, selling, hiring, firing, and the like.

7   In any additional investment of funds in the business, Lerner was to supply 40 percent and Fried 60 percent.

    **a**  Of the seven conditions specified by Lerner, which appear unfavorable for Fried? Why?

    **b**  Should Fried have agreed to the partnership with Lerner? Why?

# REFERENCES

Baumback, C. M., *How to Organize and Operate a Small Business* (Englewood Cliffs, N.J.: Prentice-Hall, 1979).

Bunn, V. A., *Buying and Selling a Small Business* (Washington, D.C.: U.S. Government Printing Office, 1979).

Burstiner, I., *The Small Business Handbook: A Comprehensive Guide to Starting and Running Your Own Business* (Englewood Cliffs, N.J.: Prentice-Hall, 1979).

Buskirk, R. H., *Managing New Enterprises* (St. Paul, Minn.: West, 1976).

Cahill, J., *Can a Smaller Store Succeed?* (New York: Fairchild, 1966).

Fram, E. H., *What You Should Know About Small Business Marketing* (Dobbs Ferry, N.Y.: Oceana, 1968).

Frantz, F. H., *Successful Small Business Management* (Englewood Cliffs, N.J.: Prentice-Hall, 1978).

Greene, C. G., *How to Start and Manage Your Own Business* (New York: McGraw-Hill, 1975).

Gross, H., *Financing for Small and Medium-Sized Businesses* (Englewood Cliffs, N.J.: Prentice-Hall, 1969).

Lane, M. J., *Legal Handbook for Small Business* (New York: AMACOM, 1977).

Mancuso, J., *How to Start, Finance, and Manage Your Own Small Business* (Englewood Cliffs, N.J.: Prentice-Hall, 1978).

Mullin, T., "SBA Sizes Don't Fit!" *Stores,* 62 (August 1980), p. 55.

Taetzsch, L., *Opening Your Own Retail Store* (Chicago: Contemporary Books, 1977).

Tate, C., L. C. Megginson, C. R. Scott, and L. Trueblood, *The Complete Guide to Your Own Business* (Homewood, Ill.: Dow Jones-Irwin, 1977).

# APPENDIX

### Checklist for Starting a Retail Business

  **I**  Selecting a Retail Business

    **A**  Store

    **B**  Nonstore

    **C**  Buying an established business

    **D**  Starting a new business

    **E**  Franchise

    **F**  Location: shopping center, in town, etc.

    **G**  Zoning laws

II  Personal Considerations
 A  Interests
 B  Experience
 C  Capabilities
 D  Knowledge

III  Capital Requirements
 A  Starting capital
 B  Working capital
 C  Contingency capital
 D  Banks and loans
 E  Small Business Administration

IV  Type of Business Organization
 A  Sole proprietorship
 B  Partnership
 C  Corporation
 D  Tax advantages and disadvantages
 E  Services of an attorney

V  Record-Keeping Requirements
 A  Management needs
 B  Inventory control
 C  Tax considerations
 D  Payroll system
 E  Financial statements
 F  Budgeting
 G  Forecasting
 H  Filing business documents with the government
 I  Services of an accountant

VI  Office Requirements
 A  Furniture
 B  Equipment
 C  Supplies
 D  Filing system
 E  Personnel

VII  Exterior and Interior Considerations
 A  Store façade
 B  Window design
 C  Parking
 D  Lighting
 E  Displays
 F  Showcases and other furniture
 G  Storage
 H  Receiving, marking, distribution of merchandise
 I  Traffic flow

VIII  Insurance Coverage
 A  Selecting an insurance company

**B** Services of an insurance broker
**C** Types of insurance
    **1** Liability
    **2** Plate glass
    **3** Fire
    **4** Water damage
    **5** Worker's compensation
    **6** Life
    **7** Other
**D** Cost of insurance coverage versus ability to pay premiums

**IX** Credit Policies
  **A** Cash, credit, or both
  **B** Type(s) of credit
  **C** Checking customers for creditworthiness
  **D** Billing procedures
  **E** Delinquent account procedures
  **F** Knowledge of credit laws

**X** Personnel (Sales)
  **A** Assessing personnel needs
  **B** Sources of personnel
  **C** Hiring
  **D** Training
  **E** Compensation scales and plans
  **F** Employee benefits
  **G** Grievance policies
  **H** Unions

**XI** Selling Considerations
  **A** Types of selling
  **B** Advertising
  **C** Sales promotions
  **D** Incentive plans for salespeople

**XII** Dealing with Shrinkage
  **A** Prevention of shoplifting
  **B** Prevention of employee theft and pilferage
  **C** Control of stock
  **D** Protecting cash

**XIII** Management Concerns
  **A** Organization chart
  **B** Decision making
  **C** Delegating authority
  **D** Basic management principles

# chapter 26
# FRANCHISES AND OTHER SMALL BUSINESSES

After completing this chapter, you should be able to:

1 Identify sources of information about franchises.

2 List questions to ask franchisees about specific franchises.

3 Explain how franchise advertisements, meetings, and shows provide valuable information about franchising.

4 List the major provisions of franchise agreements.

5 List the initial costs of owning a franchise.

6 Explain the purpose of a franchise disclosure statement.

7 List the legal rights granted to franchisees by the Federal Trade Commission.

8 List major franchise categories identified by the U.S. Department of Commerce.

9 List retail businesses that offer services only and businesses that offer both merchandise and services.

In Chapter 25 we discussed the procedures for starting a retail business. We examined several personal characteristics required of retail owners and explored the means of financing a business. In addition, we stressed the importance of involving lawyers and accountants in the startup process, and studied the advantages and disadvantages of sole proprietorships, partnerships, and corporations. Finally, we looked at the problems of purchasing or buying into an established business.

As you learned in Chapter 6, there are other types of retail ownership besides the independent retailer. We mentioned franchising as a recent addition and listed its advantages and disadvantages. It was pointed out that a basic reason for the popularity of this form of ownership is the instruction and guidance provided by franchisors to franchisees. Though it is not without risks, a franchise does give a franchisee some protection against inexperience and adversity.

In this chapter we examine franchising in greater depth, with emphasis on this form of ownership as a way of getting started in retailing. In addition, we study the opportunities and problems associated with the ownership of service types of retail businesses—both independent and franchise.

*Franchisors provide instruction and guidance to franchisees*

# INVESTIGATING A FRANCHISE

All of the cautions about going into a retail business as an independent mentioned in Chapter 25 pertain equally well to purchasing a franchise. In fact, there are additional factors to consider because of the significant relationship between franchisor and franchisee.

## Sources of Franchise Information

Because so much interest in franchising has been generated during the last twenty years, a good deal of helpful literature about the field is available. Anyone who is interested in purchasing a franchise should read these publications for both general and specific information. Among the better-known ones are the following.

Finn, Richard P. *Your Fortune in Franchising.* Chicago: Contemporary Books, 1979.

Nedell, Harold. *The Franchise Game.* Houston, Tx.: Olempco, 1980.

Seltz, David D. *How to Get Started in Your Own Franchised Business.* Rockville Centre, N.Y.: Farnsworth, 1980.

Vaughn, Charles L. *Franchising.* Lexington, Mass.: Lexington Books, D. C. Heath, 1979.

*The Franchise Opportunities Handbook lists data about major American franchisors*

Additional publications or help may be secured from the U.S. Department of Commerce, the Small Business Administration, and the International Franchise Association. The Superintendent of Documents, U.S. Government Printing Office, publishes the *Franchise Opportunities Handbook*, which lists the major American franchisors with important aspects of their operations.

# Visiting or Calling Franchisees

One of the best ways to learn about a particular franchise is to visit a franchise location or telephone its owner. A visit provides an opportunity to see how the business operates and ask specific questions, while a call sometimes yields valuable information. Whether you are calling or visiting, it is essential to make an appointment beforehand.

*Questions to ask a franchisee*

The questions that one asks during a visit or call should deal with the following areas.

- The profitability of the franchise (this is a delicate topic, and reliable answers may not be forthcoming).
- The honesty and reliability of the franchisor.
- The aid and services provided by the franchisor.
- The extent of the franchisor's involvement in the selection of a franchise location.
- The amount of competition from other outlets within the franchise.
- The amount of time the franchisee spends in the business.
- The conditions under which the franchise may be sold.

# Advice from Relatives, Friends, Professionals, and Businesspeople

While the final decision on whether to invest in a franchise rests with the prospective franchisee, valuable advice can sometimes be secured from others. A person's immediate family, for example, may have insight into his or her ability to handle the problems of a franchise. Relatives and friends may supply helpful perspectives on business ownership. Professionals such as lawyers, accountants, and chamber of commerce officials can offer technical guidance. Businesspeople, whether they are experienced in franchising or not, can offer advice on location, inventory control, employee relations, cash flow, and so forth. The aspiring franchisee must sift the significant information and opinions from the unimportant or damaging suggestions to arrive at a sensible decision.

# Franchise Advertisements, Meetings and Shows

Some franchisors solicit potential franchisees through newspaper and magazine advertisements. Before considering a respondent as a serious prospect, however, the franchisor may require a written indication of ability and willingness to finance an outlet.

Franchise meetings are held periodically in various parts of the country at which participants receive information and literature about franchising. After listening to a speaker, the audience usually asks basic questions such as

- What are a franchisee's rights and obligations?
- What kind of training does the franchisor provide?
- Does the franchisor help the franchisee with financing?
- What share of advertising costs do franchisees bear?
- How much help does the franchisor provide in the selection of a location?
- Is the franchisor available when things go wrong?

In addition to meetings, some private organizations sponsor business shows at which different franchisors maintain exhibit booths. This arrangement gives attendees an opportunity to investigate a variety of franchise businesses and to speak personally with franchise representatives.

# FRANCHISE AGREEMENTS

A thorough investigation of a possible franchise affiliation should provide solid evidence for a decision. If the decision is affirmative, the future franchisee must be approved by the franchisor. In the case of established and successful franchises, acceptance comes after two or more interviews during which specific matters of concern to both parties are discussed. A would-be franchisee is well advised to be accompanied by an attorney on these occasions.

In addition to the interviews, the franchisor will require some indication of the franchisee's financial capabilities. While some franchises may be purchased for as little as $1000, most cost more and really desirable ones sell for amounts in five or six figures. Consequently, anyone who is contemplating owning a franchise must have some ready cash and a reliable source for additional borrowing. As indicated earlier, some franchisors offer financing help.

When an agreement has been reached by the franchisor and the prospective franchisee, the two sign a contract called a **franchise agreement** or a **license agreement** (Figure 26-1). Most franchise contracts contain the following major sections.

*Major features of franchise agreements*

- Identification of the parties. The franchisor is sometimes called the company or distributor; the franchisee is known as the owner or franchisee.
- The purpose and duration of the agreement.
- Obligations of both parties.
- Location of the franchise.
- Startup and renewal fees; additional payments to the franchisor.
- Sale or transfer of the franchise.
- Operational standards.
- Purchasing of inventory, supplies, equipment, and so forth from the franchisor and others.
- The locale for settling disputes between the franchisor and the franchisee.
- Accounting and record-keeping provisions.
- Insurance requirements.

THIS LICENSE AGREEMENT, made this _____ day of _____, A.D., 19 _____, between THRIFTY RENT-A-CAR SYSTEM, INC., an Oklahoma corporation with principal offices at The Exchange Center, Box 35250, Tulsa, Oklahoma 74135, party of the first part, hereinafter called "Licensor", and

_____               _____

of _____
                    (Address)                              (City)                (State)            (Zip Code)

party of the second part, hereinafter called "Licensee":

WITNESSETH:

WHEREAS, Licensor is the exclusive owner of, has the right to use and to license others to use, plans or systems for conducting the businesses of Vehicle Rental and Leasing, Vehicle Parking, Travel Agency, Hotel, Equipment Renting, Equipment Leasing and Automobile Sales. Licensor is the exclusive owner of, has the right to use and to license others to use, the names and service or trade marks "Thrifty Rent-A-Car System", "Thrifty System", "Thrifty Rent-A-Truck System", "Thrifty Car Leasing", "Thrifty Truck Leasing", "Thrifty Parking", "Thrifty Travel Agency", "Thrifty Hotel", "Thrifty Auto Sales", and the name and service or trade mark "Thrifty" when used in conjunction with any of the above or similar businesses. These plans or systems consist of, among other things, uniform methods of operation, accounting, advertising service and publicity, identification and credit card service, kind and amount of insurance protection, method of procuring insurance protection, equipment, style and character of equipment, furnishings and appliances used in the conduct of said businesses, and methods of procuring business. Each of the above businesses constitute a part of said Systems, which Systems are generally known as "Thrifty Rent-A-Car System". For the purposes of this License Agreement, "Thrifty Rent-A-Car System", "Thrifty" or "System" is in reference only to the business of Vehicle Rental and Leasing.

WHEREAS, the Licensee is desirous of obtaining a license to use that part of the Systems, including the name "Thrifty", in the conduct of the business of Vehicle Rental and Leasing.

NOW, THEREFORE, in consideration of these premises, it is agreed by and between the parties hereto as follows:

1.   **GRANT OF LICENSE.**

Upon acceptance of this License Agreement and in consideration of the sum of $_____ as a Franchise Fee, and in consideration of the mutual covenants herein, Licensor hereby grants to Licensee, subject to the terms and conditions hereof, an exclusive license to use the System and the service mark "Thrifty" in respect to the business of Vehicle Rental and Leasing, subject to all the terms and provisions of this License Agreement. "Exclusive License" shall be construed to mean the only entity licensed to maintain Thrifty Vehicle Rental or Leasing outlets within the licensed territory. It is understood and agreed that the use of vehicles in the licensed territory that are rented from Licensor or other Licensees from their licensed territory, shall not be deemed as infringement. The use, delivery or return of leased vehicles in the licensed territory by Licensor or other Licensees, shall not be deemed as infringement. This license covers operation of Licensee's business only in:

for a non-expiring term commencing herewith, and terminating only in accordance with the terms and provisions of this License Agreement.

2.   **LICENSOR'S RIGHTS IN SYSTEM.**

Licensee recognizes and acknowledges Licensor's interest in and exclusive right to the Systems as described above and to all parts thereof, including, without limitation, all bulletins or procedures and supplements thereto and all forms set forth or described from time to time therein and all forms, advertising matter, devices, marks, service marks, trademarks, trade names and slogans from time to time used as a part of, in connection with, or applicable to, said Systems. Licensee further recognizes and acknowledges Licensor's interest in and exclusive right to all copyrights, service marks, trademarks, service mark registrations, trademark registrations, trade names and patents now or hereafter applied for or granted in connection therewith in the United States or any other country and also the exclusive right of Licensor to use and/or grant the right to others to use the name of "Thrifty" in connection with any of the aforementioned businesses. Licensee further recognizes and acknowledges the exclusive right of Licensor to grant this license and Licensee does hereby accept this license and does covenant and agree to conduct said business of Vehicle Rental and Leasing only within the territorial limits above stated and only in accordance with the methods,

**FIGURE 26-1**

Thrifty Rent-A-Car's franchise agreement.

The cost of a franchise ranges from low to very high figures.

In addition to these features, some franchise contracts include such items as protected franchise territories, advertising rights and obligations, termination features, and rules of employee conduct.

## COSTS OF A FRANCHISE

One of the major causes of retail business failures is insufficient capital. Often new retailers see their investments disappear as a result of poor or unrealistic financial planning. This is true of franchises as much as it is of independently owned businesses. If there is an advantage to franchising, it is the willingness of *some* franchisors—but far from all—to help franchisees during times of financial stress.

In addition to paying a franchise fee and (usually) a percent of gross receipts to the franchisor, the franchisee must be prepared to absorb the following initial costs.

Initial costs of
starting a
franchised outlet

- Beginning inventory
- Rent
- Design and construction of store interior and exterior, if required
- Store and office supplies
- Fixtures, furniture, and equipment
- Payroll
- Accounting and legal fees

- Grand opening promotions
- Miscellaneous and emergency

Take a good look at the last item in this list. It is the least specific of the costs, yet it can cause panic and grief if it is not provided for sufficiently. For example, unexpected incidents and price rises during construction and preparation can cause a run on available funds. Unanticipated legal problems may cost additional money. Although no sure-fire contingency fund can be planned, some provision should be made for emergencies. On the basis of their experience, most franchisors can provide guidance in this area.

# FRANCHISE DISCLOSURE STATEMENTS

In the early days of franchising, many investors were seriously damaged by ignorance of the risks of franchising and unrealistic expectations regarding its rewards. After numerous legal confrontations between franchisors and franchisees, as well as political pressure exerted by irate franchisees, the Federal Trade Commission (FTC) issued a trade regulation requiring franchisors to supply prospective franchisees with **franchise disclosure statements.** Also known as offering circulars or prospectuses, these statements contain information about the franchisor's business experience and key personnel; franchise fees; territorial protection for franchisees; and many other items of importance to franchisees. The statements enable readers to judge the value of particular franchises and to assess them. Figure 26-2 contains a more complete list of the types of information required in disclosure statements.

Evaluating a franchise disclosure statement

Having secured a copy of a disclosure statement, a franchisee should evaluate it in two ways.

1 By matching it against disclosure statements issued by other companies to estimate its *apparent* value.

2 By interviewing other franchisees in the same franchise to estimate its *actual* value.

A word of caution is in order here. Questions to be addressed to other franchisees should be prepared in advance so that all important areas are covered. Furthermore, the franchisees interviewed should have owned their franchises for various periods so that they represent both short- and long-term experiences.

# LAWYERS AND THE LEGAL RIGHTS OF FRANCHISEES

Since franchise agreements contain items of legal import to franchisees, it is essential that the latter retain lawyers for their protection. One look at the legal terminology of a franchise contract is enough to convince the reader of this need (see Figure 26-1). In

1 Information identifying the franchisor and its affiliates, and describing their business experience.

2 Information identifying and describing the business experience of each of the franchisor's officers, directors, and management personnel responsible for franchise services, training, and other aspects of the franchise program.

3 A description of the lawsuits in which the franchisor and its officers, directors, and management personnel have been involved.

4 Information about any previous bankruptcies in which the franchisor and its officers, directors, and management personnel have been involved.

5 Information about the initial franchise fee and other initial payments that are required to obtain the franchise.

6 A description of the continuing payments franchisees are required to make after the franchise opens.

7 Information about any restrictions on the quality of goods and services used in the franchise and where they may be purchased, including restrictions requiring purchases from the franchisor or its affiliates.

8 A description of any assistance available from the franchisor or its affiliates in financing the purchase of the franchise.

9 A description of restrictions on the goods or services franchisees are permitted to sell.

10 A description of any restrictions on the customers with whom franchisees may deal.

11 A description of any territorial protection that will be granted to the franchisee.

12 A description of the conditions under which the franchise may be repurchased or refused renewal by the franchisor, transferred to a third party by the franchisee, and terminated or modified by either party.

13 A description of the training programs provided to franchisees.

14 A description of the involvement of any celebrities or public figures in the franchise.

15 A description of any assistance in selecting a site for the franchise that will be provided by the franchisor.

16 Statistical information about the present number of franchises; the number of franchises projected for the future; and the number of franchises terminated, the number the franchisor has decided not to renew, and the number repurchased in the past.

17 The financial statements of the franchisors.

18 A description of the extent to which franchisees must personally participate in the operation of the franchise.

19 A complete statement of the basis for any earnings claims made to the franchisee, including the percentage of existing franchises that have actually achieved the results that are claimed.

20 A list of the names and addresses of other franchisees.

**FIGURE 26-2**

Information required in franchise disclosure statements. (U.S. Department of Commerce, Bureau of Industrial Economics and Minority Business Development, *Franchise Opportunities Handbook*, Washington, D.C., July 1980, pp. xxv–xxvi.)

addition, attorneys are needed to clarify vague clauses in the contract. For example, a contract term reading, "The franchisee will take such steps as are necessary to increase service capabilities" is certainly in need of review. What does "such steps" mean? Who determines the adequacy of the steps? A lawyer can be of great service to the prospective franchisee in this and similar instances.

As in the case of going into business as an independent retailer, starting a franchise operation involves the probable study of pertinent government regulations and the filing of business documents: local, state, and federal forms; local zoning and building codes; permissible labeling; business agreements; and so forth. A lawyer is helpful in analyzing the documents.

Though the contents of disclosure statements are regulated by law, their authenticity must be reviewed by the franchisees. While the FTC has procedures for the redress of franchisee grievances arising out of disclosure statements, it is usually advisable for a franchisee to retain a lawyer. While the franchisee may be knowledgeable about business, it is the lawyer who knows the law.

Another important FTC regulation gives franchisees vital legal rights. Basically, they refer to periods for examining disclosure statements and franchise agreements, the right to receive substantiation of earnings claims made by franchisors, the right to receive refunds from franchisors under certain conditions, and the right to rely on items listed in disclosure statements. Figure 26-3 contains a synopsis of these rights.

---

**1** The right to receive a disclosure statement at your first personal meeting with a representative of the franchisor to discuss the purchase of a franchise; but in no event less than ten business days before you sign a franchise or related agreement, or pay any money in connection with the purchase of a franchise.

**2** The right to receive documentation stating the basis and assumptions for any earnings claims that are made at the time the claims are made; but in no event less than ten business days before you sign a franchise or related agreement, or pay any money in connection with the purchase of a franchise. If an earnings claim is made in advertising, you have the right to receive the required documentation at your first personal meeting with a representative of the franchisor.

**3** The right to receive sample copies of the franchisor's standard franchise and related agreements at the same time as you receive the disclosure statement, and the right to receive the final agreements you are to sign at least 5 business days before you sign them.

**4** The right to receive any refunds promised by the franchisor, subject to any conditions or limitations on that right which have been disclosed by the franchisor.

**5** The right not to be misled by oral or written representations made by the franchisor or its representatives that are inconsistent with the disclosures made in the disclosure statement.

---

**FIGURE 26-3**

Legal rights of franchisees. (U.S. Department of Commerce, Bureau of Industrial Economics and Minority Business Development, *Franchise Opportunities Handbook*, Washington, D.C., July 1980, pp. xxvii–xxviii.)

# SELECTING A FRANCHISE FIELD

With franchising claiming an increasingly larger share of the retail market, more and more pioneer entrepreneurs are settling on this mode of business operation. After all, they reason, there must be great opportunities in a field that accounts for close to $400 billion in annual sales and represents almost 35 percent of all retail sales.

As the aspiring retailer contemplates ownership of a franchise, he or she has a wide selection from which to choose. Recognizing the limitations posed by one's personal and financial abilities, the range of fields is still considerable. A list prepared by the U.S. Department of Commerce includes the following franchise categories.

Franchise categories and sample franchisors

| Franchise Category | Sample Franchisors |
| --- | --- |
| Automotive products/services | AAMCO Transmissions, Inc. <br> B. F. Goodrich Co. |
| Auto trailers/rentals | Budget Rent A Car Corp. <br> Hertz System, Inc. |
| Beauty salons/supplies | Command Performance <br> Roffler Industries, Inc. |
| Business aids/services | H & R Block, Inc. <br> General Business Services, Inc. |
| Clothing, shoes | Mode O'Day co. <br> Pauline's Sportswear, Inc. |
| Construction, remodeling—materials/services | Davis Caves, Inc. <br> General Energy Devices, Inc. |
| Educational products/services | Barbizon Schools of Modeling <br> Image Improvement, Inc. |
| Employment services | Acme Personnel Service <br> Management Recruiters <br> International, Inc. |
| Foods—grocery/specialty stores | The Southland Corp. <br> Tiffany's Bakeries, Inc. |
| Foods—ice cream, yogurt, candy, popcorn, beverages | Baskin-Robbins, Inc. <br> Mister Softee, Inc. |
| Foods—restaurants, drive-ins, carry-outs | Burger King Corp. <br> McDonald's Corp. |
| General-merchandising stores | Ben Franklin <br> Coast to Coast Stores |
| Maintenance, cleaning, sanitation—services/supplies | Roto Rooter Corp. <br> Servpro Industries, Inc. |
| Motels, hotels | Holiday Inns, Inc. <br> Ramada Inns, Inc. |
| Real estate | Century 21 Real Estate Corp. <br> Gallery of Homes, Inc. |
| Soft drinks, water—bottling | Cott Corp. <br> Double-Cola Co. |

Tools, hardware

Mac Tools, Inc.
Snap-On Tools Corp.

Additional categories include campgrounds, cosmetics—toiletries, foods—dough-nuts, lawn and garden supplies, pet shops, and printing. As you can see, someone who is truly interested in starting a franchise should have little difficulty finding an available field. Once a choice has been made, the next step is investigation of a specific franchise.

# RETAILING A SERVICE

Much of the material in this book has been devoted to a discussion of retail *merchandising* businesses. From time to time we have referred to the retailing of services. To conclude our exploration of the process of going into business, we will examine several important aspects of starting a retail service business, with reference to specific opportunities.

Before proceeding, it should be understood that a retail service business may be a sole proprietorship, a partnership, or a corporation. In addition, it may be independently owned or franchised.

There are many types of retail service businesses in operation. Some (e.g., insurance agencies) have been with us for many years. Others, such as computer service bureaus, are relatively new. The list continues to grow as people's needs and desires change and creative entrepreneurs develop new types of retail businesses.

In Chapter 25 we stressed the personal characteristics that are of value to retail owners. We also indicated the importance of knowledge and technical skills in certain types of retail businesses. Most service-type outlets require specialized information and ability on the part of either the owner or employees, or both. For example, tutoring, flower arranging, and photography call for high degrees of expertise and face the certainty of failure when that expertise is absent or limited.

There is a caution that should be noted by would-be service retailers who are also skilled in a specialized area; such people include, among others, craftspeople, artists, writers, and typists. Experience demonstrates that there is no automatic transfer of talent from technical skill to business acumen. The two are separate and distinct talents; sometimes they mesh in successful entrepreneurship; more often, unfortunately, they do not. The lesson, of course, is that skilled people should think long and hard before committing themselves to retail ownership.

# RETAIL SERVICE BUSINESSES

Retail merchandise and service functions sometimes overlap

In order to provide a closer look at the diversity of retail service businesses, this section describes a selection of such businesses. Brief comments about the nature of each business are included. These indicate the opportunities in service retailing as well as the need for sound research before entering the field.

The first businesses to be discussed are those in which services *only* are offered;

they are followed by a sampling of businesses in which merchandise *as well as* services are sold. The second group is included not only because the businesses are partially service oriented but also to demonstrate the overlapping of merchandise and service functions in many retail stores. For example, jewelry stores sell watches and repair them, too; home furnishings stores sell a variety of products, and usually do installation as well; and many department stores provide interior decorating services along with the sale of furniture and related items.

# Retail Businesses: Services Only

### Telephone Answering Service

This type of business receives incoming calls for clients who are away from their telephones. Messages are subsequently relayed to the clients. The necessary equipment is secured from a telephone company. The service requires someone who can handle phone calls in a businesslike manner. Unless one is buying a large, established service, the investment is usually moderate.

### Painting Service

Many homeowners, apartment dwellers, and business establishments contract with painting services to paint their premises. The owner of the service works alone or with employees. Skill at mixing paints and painting various types of surfaces is important. The investment is minimal.

### Laundromat

The owner installs coin-operated washing machines, dryers, and (occasionally) dry-cleaning equipment for use by customers. Some laundromats provide personal services for a fee. The equipment is usually located in a neighborhood store or apartment house. The owner must be able to repair the machines, or a repair service may be used. The size of the investment depends on the quantity and quality of machines installed.

### Music Studio

In this business, which operates out of rented quarters or the owner's home, students receive instrumental or voice instruction. Teachers, of course, must have musical skills and may conduct group or individual lessons. Unless the owner already possesses them, musical instruments and furniture are the main investments.

### Haircutting Shop

Catering to male and/or female customers, the owner provides haircutting and related services. Since high degrees of skill and safety are required, most states require that the owner undergo instruction, an examination, and apprentice training before granting him or her a license. The size of the investment depends on the number of chairs and the elegance of the shop.

### Tutoring

This business can be conducted in one's own home, in rented facilities, or in the student's home. Instruction is usually in elementary or high school subjects, although specialized tutoring exists in such subjects as preparation for Scholastic Aptitude Tests, bar examinations, and certified public accounting examinations. Whatever the subject, instructors must be knowledgeable, patient, and helpful. The investment is minimal, consisting of outlays for books and advertising. If rented quarters are involved, furniture, fixtures, and partitioning are required.

## Car Wash Outlet

Car owners bring their automobiles to a car wash facility for washing and cleaning. Since the owner cannot service the cars alone, employees must be used for drying, vacuuming, and so on. Neither the owner nor the employees must have special skills. However, some arrangement must be made for repair of the washing equipment. The investment for equipment and a building is considerable. Incidentally, coin-operated, self-service car wash outlets are usually very risky ventures owing to the possibility of adverse weather conditions and vandalism.

## Game and Amusement Center

Called penny arcades some years ago, these enterprises are located primarily in large shopping centers, tourist areas, and beach facilities and consist of a number of coin-operated games. Employees are required to make change, supervise customers, and make light repairs. The owner need not possess special skills, but a reliable equipment maintenance program is necessary. The investment in equipment, fixtures, and furniture can be considerable.

## Travel Agency

A travel agency arranges transportation, hotel and car reservations, tours, and cruises. In addition to the owner, virtually all agencies have personnel who deal with customers,

Customers rely on travel agents for travel information and arrangements.

arrange itineraries, process documents, and so forth. In order to gain the approval of the International Association of Travel Agents (IATA) and the Air Transport Association (ATA), and thereby earn commissions on air sales, an agency must have one or more staff members with at least one year's experience in reservations and ticketing and the promotion and selling of air transportation. Though travel agencies are often located in shopping centers, they are also found as freestanding stores and in office buildings and hotels. Unless decor is important, the investment in furniture, fixtures, and incidentals is fairly low. However, the travel organizations require a minimum capitalization, which in 1981 was $15,000.

### Interior Decorator

An interior decorator designs the interiors of homes, apartments, offices, and other buildings. In addition, he or she arranges for the purchase of furniture and appointments on behalf of clients. Knowledge of color, design, layout, and furnishings is required. Many decorators operate out of their homes. Investment in this type of business is minimal.

### Display Installation Service

This type of business specializes in window trimming and interior displays for stores, showrooms, and trade shows. A good deal of skill is involved, since displays call for intelligent use of props, mannequins, space, color, and themes. An owner can work alone or with employees. Stores often supply material items, while the display service designs and does the physical work. Depending on the size of the business, the investment is usually low to moderate.

### Dog Grooming

Many dog owners are either unable or unwilling to groom their pets. They turn to dog groomers for cutting and washing as well as nail clipping. The work is done in the customer's or owner's home or in rented space. Skill is required, especially in the cutting of hair. The investment is minimal, consisting of an outlay for tools. Of course, the need to furnish rented space would increase the investment.

## Retail Businesses: Services and Merchandise

### Equipment Rental

Equipment owned by this type of business is rented to customers. The equipment carried may range from small tools in some outlets to heavy machinery in others; and from party furniture to medical devices. The business may also sell supplies and goods related to the rented items. Ability to repair equipment is essential. The size of the investment depends on the type and quantity of equipment carried.

### Jewelry Store

These stores sell jewelry and related merchandise. Some stores carry high-priced lines while others concentrate on more modest items. In addition, most stores repair watches, brooches, necklaces, and the like. The owner must be knowledgeable about jewelry, and either the owner or an employee must be capable of doing repairs. The investment is usually considerable and depends on the quality of merchandise carried.

## Motel/Hotel

The basic income in this business is derived from the rental of rooms to travelers. In some instances parking fees comprise another source of revenue. Many motels and hotels maintain restaurants and shops for the sale of food, drink, clothing, toiletries, and miscellaneous items. The owner must be knowledgeable about the industry and, except in the case of small motels, must hire employees. The investment is usually considerable and depends, of course, on the size, quality, and location of the enterprise.

## Hobby Center

Depending on the extent of its inventory, a hobby center sells such items as model boats, cars, planes, and trains; doll house supplies; stamps; coins; miniature furniture; and chemistry kits. It usually repairs a wide variety of hobby equipment. The owner and/or employees must be capable of repair work. Because of the varied inventory, the investment required for a hobby center is considerable.

## Printing and Duplicating

Unlimited quantities of printed matter are produced according to customer specifications. Final copy includes brochures, announcement cards, invitations, programs, and the like. In addition, the business duplicates copies of printed matter submitted by the customer. Skill in equipment operation is required, and knowledge of printing and layout techniques is essential. Many printing shops carry stationery supplies for sale. Because of equipment and supply requirements, the investment is considerable.

## Gardening and Lawn Care

This type of business services people's gardens and lawns—planting, trimming, mowing, and landscaping. Much of the work is skilled and requires a knowledge of growing patterns, insect control, and landscape design. Bushes, plants, trees, grass, and pesticides are sold. The investment required for equipment, a vehicle, and inventory runs from modest to considerable.

## Photography

The owner can operate this business from home or rented space. Photos are taken on the premises or at another location. The customer specifies the photos required and the photographer plans and executes the job. Skill in photography and knowledge of equipment capabilities are required. The owner usually sells film, flashes, cameras, and accessories. The largest item of investment is inventory, and it can be modest or considerable.

## Electric Motor Service

This type of business repairs and rebuilds electric motors. It handles generators, hoists, pumps, and similar equipment. Obviously, the owner must be skilled in electrical services. Parts are usually sold to supplement income and accommodate customers. The investment is usually considerable because of the equipment needed for repairs; the quantity of inventory depends on the variety of motors serviced.

Florists must be knowledgeable about floral arrangements as well as the merchandise they sell.

## Florist

Flowers and plants are provided for all occasions. Knowledge of the products is required, and skill is needed for creating bridal, party, and funeral designs. Some florists grow plants in their own greenhouses while others purchase their inventory and maintain it with refrigeration. Gift items are often included as merchandise. The investment is modest unless a sizable greenhouse is involved.

## Dog and Cat Boarding

For pet owners who want to leave their animals in reliable hands when they are out of town, dog and cat boarding facilities are ideal. These businesses provide indoor and outdoor runs, sleeping quarters, dietary consultation, and veterinary supervision. Knowledge of animal needs and habits is essential. Some facilities sell animal food and accessories. The investment is small, since the construction of animal quarters is not costly.

## New-Car Dealership

A new-car dealership is a franchised operation that sells new cars produced by one car manufacturer, such as Ford or General Motors. Salespeople should be knowledgeable about the cars they sell. The repair shop generates a substantial part of the dealer's revenue and requires skilled personnel. Some new-car dealers also sell used cars. The investment required for equipment, showroom furnishings, and inventory is considerable.

## Locksmith

Because of the current high rate of crime, locksmiths are doing a substantial volume of business. They install locks, pulls, security steel bars, master key systems, panic devices, and the like. A high degree of skill is required for installation and repair services. Locksmiths also sell safes, locks, alarm systems, and related items. The investment is largely for repair equipment and inventory and runs from modest to considerable.

# NEW TYPES OF RETAIL BUSINESSES

For the most part, the businesses listed in this chapter have been around for many years. However, the creativity and imagination of the American people bring forth a continuous stream of new, exciting retailing opportunities. Some develop into profitable ventures, while others obtain little response from consumers.

An example of the available material regarding new types of retail businesses is the *Business Catalog* published by the American Entrepreneurs Association. It contains descriptions of new opportunities as well as a list of additional materials that can be obtained by interested readers.

The following list contains a sampling of recently developed retail businesses.

| Type of Business | Description |
|---|---|
| Storefront post office | Sells stamps, does mailings, wraps and accepts packages, rents locked mailboxes, answers phone calls, forwards mail |
| Used-carpet store | Sells used carpets to hotels, motels, hospitals, restaurants, offices, schools, etc. |
| Tanning center | Bathes customers in ultraviolet light to produce "suntans" |
| Hobby computer store | Sells desktop minicomputers for personal use |
| Dressy–casual specialty men's-clothing store | Sells limited types of men's clothing, such as slacks, dressy sport shirts, and some accessories |
| Earring shop | Sells earrings, does ear piercing |
| One-stop wedding shop | Provides all items and services needed for weddings: bride's dress and trousseau, rings, music, invitations, photography, etc. |

### NEW TERMS

franchise agreement

license agreement

franchise disclosure statement

## CHAPTER HIGHLIGHTS

1 Information about franchising may be obtained from books and publications of the U.S. Department of Commerce, the U.S. Small Business Administration, and the International Franchise Association.

2 Visiting or calling franchisees may provide valuable information about particular franchises.

3 Relatives, friends, certain professionals, and businesspeople can sometimes be of help to someone who is investigating a franchise.

4 Anyone who is interested in franchising can learn about the field and about specific franchises through newspaper and magazine advertisements, regional franchise meetings, and business shows.

5 Franchise agreements contain the terms of the contract between a franchisor and a franchisee.

6 The initial costs of owning a franchise include the franchise fee; beginning inventory; rent, design, and construction of store interior and exterior; supplies; furniture; equipment; payroll; accounting and legal fees; promotions; and miscellaneous.

7 A franchise disclosure statement contains information about a franchisor's experience, key personnel, and franchise fee; territorial protection for franchisees; and training programs. It includes a list of names and addresses of other franchisees and other items of importance to franchisees.

8 A Federal Trade Commission regulation gives franchisees certain legal rights regarding periods for examining disclosure statements and franchise agreements, franchisor earnings claims, refunds from franchisors, and the truthfulness of disclosure statements.

9 Franchising accounts for almost $400 billion in annual sales and almost 35 percent of all retail sales.

10 Most service-type retail outlets require specialized knowledge and skills on the part of the owner, the employees, or both.

11 Service retail businesses sell only services or carry merchandise in addition to providing services.

12 New types of retail businesses are constantly emerging.

## QUESTIONS

1 What types of information may be secured by visiting or phoning a franchisee?

2 How might a businessperson be of help during an investigation of franchising as a means of ownership?

3 Why might a response to an advertisement by a franchisor seeking franchisees not elicit a favorable reaction from the franchisor?

4 What are some of the major features of franchise agreements?

5 Why is it important to set up a reasonable contingency fund as part of the initial cost of starting a franchise?

6 Why is it essential for a prospective franchisee to evaluate a franchise disclosure statement before deciding to purchase a franchise?

7 What are the basic legal rights granted to franchisees by the Federal Trade Commission?

8 Why are increasing numbers of people who aspire to retail ownership selecting franchise operations? What are the advantages and disadvantages of doing so?

9 List four types of retail businesses that offer services only; list four that offer both merchandise and services.

10 Do people with specialized skills usually make successful entrepreneurs? Why is this so?

# FIELD PROJECTS

1 Using the latest copy of the *Franchise Opportunities Handbook* published by the Bureau of Industrial Economics of the U.S. Department of Commerce, prepare a list of franchisors covering three different categories. Select one franchisor from each category and supply information for each under the following headings.
Name of franchisor
Description of operation
Number of franchisees
Length of time in business
Capital needed
Financial assistance available
Training provided
Managerial assistance available

2 Using your local Yellow Pages, prepare a list of five types of businesses that sell services only and five types that sell merchandise as well as services. For each business listed, indicate the services you believe it offers. *Do not* use any of the businesses mentioned in this chapter.

# CASES

1 In 1980 there were conflicting reports from analysts regarding the progress of the fast-food industry. Some pointed to stagnant profits as an indication of trouble, while others felt that some "breathing space" was needed before the field expanded again.

One analyst suggested that certain fast-food franchisors were confusing the public by overly diversifying their product offerings. Another asserted that consumers were shifting from hamburger consumption to ethnic-type foods like those sold by Pizza Hut, Taco Bell, and similar chains. Significantly, some franchise food chains were doing better than others. On the whole, however, sales were weak and the outlook for substantial recovery in the near future was questionable.

a If you were considering ownership of a fast-food franchise in 1980, what questions would you have asked a franchisor in addition to those that are ordinarily asked?

b On the basis of the facts just presented, was 1980 a good year to purchase a fast-food franchise? Why?

2   There is a general belief that when our economy is in a recession all businesses suffer. Nothing could be further from the truth! For example, dealers in diamonds and art objects do better, as do retailers that sell distress merchandise at high discounts. Included in this list are certain service-type retailers, such as employment agencies and counselors.

Obviously, economic conditions have a profound effect on how we earn money. The enterprising person seeks ways to capitalize on people's needs, in many cases developing new types of salable services.

a Assume that the economy is in a recession. List two types of service-only retail businesses (excluding those already mentioned) that might be profitable.

b In the same type of economy, would it be wiser to buy a franchise or to go into business as an independent operator? Why?

3   The rising franchise fees and startup costs for product franchises like Burger King, Big T Family Restaurant Systems, and Hardee's Food Systems have caused increasing numbers of aspiring retail owners to purchase franchise service outlets instead.

Iris Glar, who seeks to change her working status from personnel manager to entrepreneur, is torn between product and service franchise ownership. Though she has accumulated enough funds to consider the purchase of a well-established fast-food franchise that promises immediate and lucrative returns, she realizes that her background is more suited to a service-type business such as a personnel agency.

After detailed research and soul searching, Glar committed the following facts and thoughts to paper.

| Franchise name | Eat-'Em-Hot Emporium, Inc. | Efficiency Personnel, Inc. |
| --- | --- | --- |
| Description of operation | 24-hour fast-food restaurant specializing in hamburgers. Indoor and outdoor seating. Capacity 40 to 125 people. Food, equipment, layout, and procedures are standardized. | Supplies clerical, secretarial, bookkeeping, computer, and word-processing personnel to business firms. Full- and part-timers. Qualified applicants only. |
| Number of franchisees | 260 in 18 states of the West and Southwest | 40 in 23 states of the Northeast and Midwest |
| Length of time in business | Since 1974 | Since 1962 |
| Funds needed | Total capital needed: $120,000. Includes franchise fee of $40,000, remainder for construction and equipment. $70,000 cash required, must be able to finance the rest. | Total capital needed: $40,000. Includes franchise fee of $15,000, remainder for startup expenses and office furnishings. $10,000 cash required, franchisor helps finance the rest. |

| Training provided | Complete operational training. 2-week course at no cost except for living expenses. Update training periodically at franchisee's expense. | One week orientation at company headquarters. 2-week training at franchisee's office prior to opening. |
| Managerial assistance | Startup and continuing supervision and help. Unannounced visits to check on operations. | Complete service to ensure smooth start and continuing efficient service. Help with office procedures, public relations, forms, staffing, ideas. |

Glar's personal considerations are as follows.

- She enjoys mild weather, is uncomfortable in cold areas.
- She wants to make a lot of money as quickly as possible.
- She is concerned that she knows little about the fast-food business.
- She enjoys working with people, especially helping them.
- She is not certain that she can secure a bank loan for investment in the franchise.
- She learns quickly, but has difficulty with mechanical and arithmetic matters.
- She loves to work with ideas, is creative.

   a  What are the major items that should help Glar make a decision?
   b  Which franchise appears more promising, considering her background and aspirations? Why?
   c  What advice would you offer her? Explain.

# REFERENCES

Clark, L. W., *How to Make Money with Your Crafts* (New York: Morrow, 1973).

———, *How to Open Your Own Shop or Gallery* (New York: St. Martin's Press, 1978).

Finn, R. P., *Your Fortune in Franchises* (Chicago: Contemporary Books, 1979).

Friedlander, M. P., Jr., and G. Gurney, *Handbook of Successful Franchising* (New York: Van Nostrand Reinhold, 1981).

Kahm, H. S., *101 Businesses You Can Start and Run With Less Than $1,000* (West Nyack, N.Y.: Parker, 1968).

Norback, P. G., and C. T. Norback, *The Dow Jones-Irwin Guide to Franchising* (Homewood, Ill.: Dow Jones-Irwin, 1978).

Scott, W., *How to Make Big Profits in Service Businesses* (West Nyack, N.Y.: Parker, 1977).

Seltz, D. D., *How to Get Started in Your Own Franchised Business* (Rockville Centre, N.Y.: Farnsworth, 1980).

Upah, G. D., "Mass Marketing in Service Retailing: A Review and Synthesis of Major Methods," *Journal of Retailing*, 56 (Fall 1980), pp. 59–76.

Vaughn, C. L., *Franchising: Its Nature, Scope, Advantages, and Development* (Lexington, Mass.: Lexington, 1974).

Witt, S., *How to Make Big Profits in Service Businesses* (West Nyack, N.Y.: Parker, 1977).

# GLOSSARY*

**Abandoned Goods** Unclaimed merchandise at post offices, customs offices, shippers' store-houses, and the like; sometimes sold in sealed shipping cartons. (7)

**Advance Dating** The practice in which a merchant arranges to have the credit date based on a date later than the invoice date. (14)

**Advertising** Any paid form of nonpersonal presentation and promotion of ideas, goods, or services by an identified sponsor. (19)

**Advertising Budget** A means of determining and controlling advertising expense and dividing it among departments, merchandise lines, and services. (19)

**Advertising Plan** A strategy for advertising that reflects the store's objectives, the budget, and the types of media to be used. (19)

**Anticipation** An extra discount for retailers when bills are paid before the expiration of the cash discount period. (14)

**Apparent Self** How others see an individual. (4)

**Application Form** A form completed by a prospective employee to provide important data regarding education, work experience, and references. (10)

**Area Display** A display set up for special merchandising needs, such as model rooms or seasonally used sports equipment. (18)

**Armchair Shopping (In-Home Shopping)** Purchasing done at home through the use of computers, brochures, and catalogs. (2)

**Assets** Things of monetary value that are owned by a business (i.e., land, buildings, stock, and cash). (2)

**Assistant Buyer** An individual who assists the buyer by performing assigned duties in areas with less responsibility. (2)

**Assistant Department Manager** An individual who assists the department manager by performing assigned duties in areas with less responsibility. (2)

**Associate Buyer** A person who assists the main store buyer with reorders and follow-up orders. (13)

**Associated Resident Buying Office (Cooperative Resident Buying Office)** A buying office that is owned and managed by a group of stores. (13)

**Assortment** The variety of items within a basic inventory. (22)

**Assortment Display** A display that shows a complete line of merchandise in depth, including colors, sizes, styles, and prices. (18)

**Assortment Plan** A strategy that aims to achieve merchandise balance, composed of lines of goods that are suited to the demands of customers. (14)

**Average Turnover Days** A figure that is arrived at by dividing the number of days in the accounting period by the turnover rate. (21)

**Average Collection Period** The relationship of year-end receivables to an average day's sales; the approximate time it has taken to collect a store's debts. (21)

**Backup Stock** Merchandise that a vendor will reserve without any obligation on the store's part to purchase it. (14)

*Numbers in parentheses indicate chapters where a fuller discussion may be found.

**Bait-and-Switch Advertising**   The practice of luring a customer into a store with the intention of selling something other than the merchandise advertised. (3)

**Bait-and-Switch Pricing**   The practice of luring a customer into a store with the intention of selling higher-priced merchandise than that advertised. (15)

**Balance sheet**   A statement of the financial position of a business at a particular time. (21)

**Bank Credit Card**   A type of credit card with which a customer charges merchandise, the retailer pays the bank a percentage of the purchase price, and the bank collects from the customer. (23)

**Bantam Store (Convenience Store)**   A small neighborhood store carrying inexpensive, easy-to-sell merchandise that is consumed daily or frequently. (7)

**Bargain Store (Barn Store)**   An outlet that specializes in selling factory seconds, distressed and salvage goods, closeouts, manufacturers' overruns, and abandoned goods at low prices. (7)

**Barter**   To trade by exchanging one commodity for another. (1)

**Basic Inventory**   Items that a store always stocks. (22)

**Bin**   A receptacle used to hold incoming merchandise. (16)

**Biogenic Motive**   One that is related to physical needs, such as the need for food, sex, drink, or comfort. (4)

**Blind Ad**   A type of advertisement that does not identify the store and provides only a post office box number as an address. (10)

**Blind Checking (Indirect Checking)**   A type of merchandise checking that requires a thorough check; instead of invoices, special forms are used. (16)

**Blue-Collar Worker**   An individual who works in a factory or trade, or as a laborer. (5)

**Box Store (Warehouse Store)**   A cross between a limited-assortment store and a supermarket; stocks several thousand items, including nonfood products, limited lines of perishables, and meat; customers mark and bag their own items. (2)

**Branch Store**   A scaled-down version of an established store operating at a separate location. (7)

**Breadth (Width)**   The number of product classifications that a merchant stocks. (14)

**Broad and Shallow Plan**   An approach to retailing in which the merchant carries a few items in many styles in a product class. (14)

**"Brood Hen and Chick"**   A system of organization in which the main store operates the branch by performing functions both for itself and for the branch. (9)

**Bulk Checking**   A form of direct checking of incoming cartons, but not contents; used when bulk units are received. (16)

**Buyer**   An individual who is responsible for the purchasing and selling of merchandise in one or several departments. (2)

**Buyer's Commitment System (BUYCOM)**   A system that provides a buyer with facts so that the buyer can respond immediately to the store's merchandise needs. (13)

**Buying Motive**   An emotional, rational, biogenic, or psychogenic motive that causes consumers to act or buy. (4)

**Canvassing**   A method of soliciting orders for goods by calling on people in a certain area. (8)

**"Cargo Prices"**   Another term for low prices. (19)

**Carrier**   Shipper. (16)

**Cash Budget**   An estimate of cash receipts and payments for a given period. (21)

**Cash Discount**   A reduction of purchase price offered in return for prompt payment. (14)

**Catalog Retailing**   A nonstore retailing method whereby selling is done through catalogs. (8)

**Catalog Showroom**   A store where merchandise samples are displayed and consumers place orders from a catalog. (7)

**Catchall Display**   A large container that holds large quantities of one kind of merchandise. (18)

***Caveat Venditor***   "Let the seller beware." (3)

**Central Buying**   A system in which the buyers make all the decisions regarding selection, quantities, and distribution of merchandise to all the stores in a retailing concern. (13)

**Central Distribution Plan**   A plan in which buyers make all the purchasing decisions but individual store managers have control over depth of stock. (13)

**Central Shopping District (Downtown Shopping District)**   A large collection of department stores and specialty shops located in the central or downtown area of a city. (11)

**Centralization**   An arrangement in which the major store functions are controlled through a home or regional office. (9)

**Chain Store**   One of a group of centrally owned retail stores that carry merchandise of the same type. (1)

**Checkout Counter Display**   A display located close to the cashier and featuring "impulse items" like candy, gum, or cigarettes. (18)

**Classic**   A style that remains in fashion for a long time. (3)

**Closed Display**   A display in which valuable items are protected behind glass and are handled by a salesperson. (18)

**Closeout**   Discontinued merchandise of stores that have closed or gone into bankruptcy. (7)

**Cognitive Consonance**   The feeling experienced by a consumer who has continued satisfaction, without conflict, after making a purchase. (4)

**Cognitive Dissonance**   The experience of a consumer who is not convinced that a purchase was a wise one. (4)

**Cognitive Theory**   A theory founded on the individual's ability to learn, through a thought process based on logic, to arrive at a solution. (4)

**Combination Advertising**   An approach that combines the advertisement of a specific item with an attempt to build a favorable image of the store. (19)

**Combination Plan**   A compromise between narrow and deep, and broad and shallow, breadth-and-depth plans. (14)

**Combination Store (Combostore)**   A store that offers one-stop shopping with a full line of food products, substantial quantities of nonfood items, and some services. (7)

**Commissionaire**   A foreign resident buying office. (13)

**Community Shopping Center**   A shopping center whose largest tenant is either a scaled-down department store or a specialty store; smaller than a regional shopping center. (11)

**Company Card**   A card issued by a large company for use in purchasing its products or services. (23)

**Comparison Shopper**   An individual who checks competitors' prices, assortments, and services. (15)

**Competition Research**   Studies that enable a retailer to recognize its relative position in terms of market share. (24)

**Conditional Sales Contract**  An arrangement under which the retailer maintains title to the merchandise and may repossess it if the buyer fails to make a payment. (23)

**Connectionist Theory**  The concept that learning takes place through the repeated action and association of a stimulus and a response. (4)

**Consignment**  An arrangement under which the retailer must pay only for items that are sold. (25)

**Consignment Buying**  An arrangement in which the vendor permits the retailer to pay only for goods that are sold. (14)

**Constant Dollars**  Income calculated by reference to a base year (real income). (5)

**Consultive Appointment**  A method of selling in which the salesperson consults with consumers to determine products and services that fulfill their needs. (8)

**Consumer Advocate**  An individual, often well known, who gains political awareness and support for consumer causes. (3)

**Consumer Behavior**  The process whereby consumers decide whether, what, where, when, and how to buy goods and services. (4)

**Consumer Cooperative Association**  A type of retail business in which consumers own shares, decide store policy, and share profits. (6)

**Consumer Movement**  The demand by consumers for the establishment of economic fair play through laws protecting the public against unfair trade practices. (3)

**Consumerism**  The activities of individuals and organizations that are involved in safeguarding the buyer in the marketplace. (3)

**Control Department**  The department that is responsible for protecting the store's finances. (2)

**Convenience Goods**  Items that consumers buy to meet immediate and pressing needs. (7)

**Convenience Store (Bantam Store)**  A small neighborhood store carrying inexpensive, easy-to-sell merchandise that is consumed daily or frequently. (7)

**Conveyor Mechanism**  A mechanism that carries goods from receiving areas to stockrooms or selling spaces. (16)

**Cooperative Advertising**  An arrangement whereby retailers share the costs of advertising with manufacturers, suppliers, or other merchants. (19)

**Cooperative Chain**  A group of independent retailers organized to combine orders so as to secure volume discounts for the purpose of competing with large retailers. (6)

**Cooperative Resident Buying Office (Associated Resident Buying Office)**  A buying office that is owned and managed by a group of stores. (13)

**Corporate Resident Buying Office**  A division of a parent company that buys and distributes merchandise for all of its stores. (13)

**Corporation**  A form of business ownership that is chartered by the state and recognized as a business entity separate from its owners; ownership is represented by shares of stock. (6)

**Counter Display**  A special arrangement of merchandise at a store counter. (18)

**Country Club Billing**  A time- and work-saving system in which the retailer mails sales slips and a simple statement listing the balance owed by the customer at the end of the period. (23)

**Coupon**  A form of promotion that allows a specific reduction in the price of an item. (20)

**CPM (Cost per Thousand)**  A formula that is commonly used to assess a medium's impact on a desired audience. (19)

**Creative Selling**  Selling that involves the use of selling techniques to help solve customers' problems. (17)

**Credit Bureau** An organization that gathers personal information about shoppers from stores, employers, banks, and the like, and develops summary reports for use by stores that request them. (23)

**Credit Card** A plastic or metal card bearing the owner's name and identification number, used for the purpose of charging a purchase to the customer's account. (23)

**Current Ratio** The relationship of a company's current assets to its current liabilities. (21)

**Cut-Case Display** A display in which packing boxes are cut and folded to create the display unit. (18)

**Cycle Billing** A method used by stores to stagger their customer statements throughout the month instead of billing all customers at once. (23)

**Data Bank** A storage unit for information such as sales records, inventory, purchasing, consumer data, accounts payable, accounts receivable, and personnel. (24)

**Dating** The period allowed by vendors to buyers for the payment of bills. (14)

**Decentralization** An arrangement under which store functions such as selling and sales promotion are decided by the individual store. (9)

**Delivery Receipt** A form supplied by a carrier and used by a receiving clerk to indicate that delivery has been made. (16)

**Demographics** The breakdown of the population into statistical categories such as age, education, sex, occupations, income, households, and marital status. (5)

**Department Manager** An individual who supervises a merchandise department and is responsible for service and merchandise activities. (2)

**Department Store** A large retail institution that offers a variety of carefully selected merchandise organized into specific departments. (1)

**Depth** The number of styles or brands within a product classification. (14)

**Descriptive Billing** A system whereby a computer printout of a customer's account identifies transactions by date, department, description of transaction, price charged, payments, and credits. (23)

**Direct Checking** A method of comparing numbers and markings on incoming items directly against the manufacturer's invoice. (16)

**Direct Mail** The medium that retailers use to send catalogs and brochures to customers. (19)

**Direct Premium** An item that is given to a customer free with a purchase, at the time of purchase. (20)

**Direct Sales (Door-to-Door Selling)** Selling in which the salesperson contacts customers and demonstrates merchandise by going from door to door. (8)

**Discharged** Dismissed from the company (''fired''). (10)

**Discount Department Store** A store that sells well-known brands below the suggested retail price, offers wide variety and one-stop shopping, but lacks personal service. (7)

**Discount Store** A retailing institution that offers a wide variety of merchandise at low prices with few customer services. (1)

**Discretionary Income** Money that a person or household has available to spend or save freely after payments for fixed commitments have been deducted. (5)

**Display** A nonpersonal approach to the selling process through the use of windows, signs, and fixtures. (18)

**Display Stand** An attractive, permanent, self-service display that comes in various sizes, occupies little space, and stores a great deal of merchandise. (18)

**Disposable Income**   The amount of money a person has to spend after taxes have been deducted. (5)

**Distressed Goods**   Items that have been damaged or soiled in shipping or handling. (7)

**Dividend**   The distributed profits of a corporation. (21)

**DOI (Date of Invoice)**   A system in which the credit period starts on the invoice date. (14)

**Dollar Control**   A system for gathering information about inventory using the retail dollar value of merchandise. (22)

**Door-to-Door Selling (Direct Sales)**   Selling in which the salesperson contacts customers and demonstrates merchandise by going from door to door. (8)

**Downtown Shopping District (Central Shopping District)**   A large collection of department stores and specialty shops located in the central or downtown area of a city. (11)

**Drawing Account**   A compensation arrangement that allows salespeople to take or "draw" a set amount each payday regardless of their sales. (10)

**Dump Display**   A display in which merchandise is heaped in a pile. (18)

**Electronic Article Surveillance (EAS)**   The use of electronic devices to control shoplifting. (16)

**Electronic Data Processing (EDP)**   The use of computers to amass large quantities of information, process the data at electronic speeds, and turn out reports quickly. (3)

**Electronic Funds Transfer (EFT)**   A system for making deposits and withdrawals electronically, thereby eliminating most of the paper work involved in sales and banking transactions. (3)

**Electronic Retailing**   A method of selling using two-way cable television communications, videophones, and personal computers. (8)

**Emotional Motive**   A motive that is not based on logical thinking, such as love or vanity. (4)

**End-Aisle Display**   A display in which merchandise is placed in a vacant area at the end of an aisle in a supermarket or variety store. (18)

**Engel's Laws**   Economic "laws" that show that as household income increases, there are decided shifts in the manner in which that income is spent. (5)

**Ensemble Display**   A display in which the item to be promoted is combined with related merchandise for a total effect. (18)

**EOM (End of Month)**   A system in which the discount period starts at the end of the month in which the invoice is dated. (14)

**Equal Store**   An organizational approach in which buying is done through a central or regional office and the branches are responsible for sales and promotion. (9)

**Expense Budget**   An estimate of expenses over a specified period based on past experience and future plans. (21)

**Experimentation**   A method of gathering information in which a researcher sets up an experiment whereby one or more factors are controlled in the situation being studied. (24)

**Extra Dating**   An extension of the cash discount period. (14)

**Factory Seconds**   Imperfect merchandise with manufacturing flaws. (7)

**Fad**   A fashion that is adopted and discarded within a short period. (3)

**Fashion**   The prevailing manner in which people live, dress, work, and play at a given time and place. (3)

**Fashion Cycle**   The movement of a style through the phases of introduction, acceptance, and peak of popularity to eventual decline. (3)

**Fashion Goods**  Items that are popular at a particular time. (7)

**Fashion Trend**  The direction in which different styles move according to consumer demand. (3)

**First In, First Out (FIFO)**  A method of accounting for ending inventory in which merchandise purchased first is assumed to be sold completely before any subsequently purchased items are sold. (22)

**Flea Market**  A retail outlet composed of a collection of independent retailers selling different lines of goods, old and new, at bargain prices. (2)

**Flexible Pricing (Variable-Price Policy)**  A method of selling that enables customers to bargain with retailers. (15)

**FOB ("Free on Board") Destination**  A system in which the seller pays transportation costs to the buyer's location and retains title to the goods while they are in transit. (14)

**FOB ("Free on Board") Shipping Point**  A system in which the seller delivers the merchandise to the starting point of shipment; the buyer pays transportation costs and has title from that point on. (14)

**Formal Communication**  The use of employee handbooks, manuals, house organs, bulletins, and meetings to keep employees informed. (9)

**Forward Stock**  Merchandise that is stored in drawers, bins, or racks in or close to a selling area. (16)

**Franchise**  The exclusive right to perform a service or sell a product. (6)

**Franchise Agreement (License Agreement)**  A contract signed by a franchisor and a prospective franchisee. (26)

**Franchise Disclosure Statement**  A document that contains information about a franchisor's experience, key personnel, and franchise fee, and other items of importance to franchisees. (26)

**Franchisee**  A company or individual that receives a franchise. (6)

**Franchisor (Licensor)**  A manufacturer, wholesaler, or service company that gives a franchise to another company or individual. (6)

**Freestanding Store**  A retail outlet that stands by itself. (11)

**Full-Service Wholesaler**  A merchandise resource that provides many services to retailers, including storage, credit, and market information. (13)

**General Merchandise**  An assortment of products in several unrelated merchandise lines. (7)

**General Store**  A retail outlet that maintains a limited but varied stock of merchandise; the first authentic American retailing institution. (1)

**Gestalt Concept**  A view of personality as the total outcome of an individual's interaction with his or her environment. (4)

**Good Will**  An intangible asset of a business that is derived from the reputation of its owner, products, or services. (25)

**Grapevine**  An unofficial communication network. (9)

**Gross Margin (Maintained Markup)**  The final markup on an item. (15)

**Guaranteed Sales**  An agreement by the vendor to take back merchandise that the retailer cannot sell. (14)

**Hard Goods**  Merchandise such as cameras, jewelry, furniture, and appliances. (1)

**Highway Outlet**  A store located on a main road, apart from other businesses, that offers easy access and convenient parking. (11)

**Horizontal Price Fixing** A conspiracy by retailers, wholesalers, or manufacturers to fix prices in such a way as to stifle competition. (15)

**Hypermarket** An extremely large self-service retail outlet in a warehouse setting. (7)

**Ideal Self** What an individual would like to be. (4)

**Importer** A wholesaler that brings goods from foreign markets for resale to retailers. (13)

**Impression Management** A store's attempts to present a distinct image that distinguishes it from its competition. (12)

**Income Statement** A summary of the income and expenses of a business over a specific period. (21)

**Incoming Trend** Styles that are just becoming popular. (3)

**Independent Resident Buying Office** A buying office that charges fees based on the types of services performed and the volume of merchandise purchased. (13)

**Independently Owned Store** A retailing institution that is controlled by its own individual management. (6)

**Indirect Checking (Blind Checking)** A type of merchandise checking that requires a thorough check; instead of invoices, special forms are used. (16)

**Informal Communication** Verbal communication through vertical and horizontal channels. (9)

**In-Home Shopping (Armchair Shopping)** Purchasing that is done at home through the use of computers, brochures, and catalogs. (2)

**Initial Markup (Original Markup)** The first markup on an item. (15)

**Installment Credit** Credit that is extended in the sale of high-ticket items. The buyer is required to sign a contract, make a down payment, and make periodic payments (including principal and interest) until the invoice price has been paid. (23)

**Institutional Advertising** Attempts to sell the entire concept of the store and its image rather than a particular type of merchandise. (19)

**Institutional Display** An attempt to build good will by permitting charities, schools, or the arts to become the central theme of a store display. (18)

**Interior Display** An arrangement of merchandise within a store whose purpose is to create product awareness and stimulate sales. (18)

**Internship Program** A method of testing future employees through on-the-job evaluation. (10)

**Invoice** A bill for merchandise that usually specifies the time of shipment and terms of payment. (16)

**Job Analysis** A detailed study of the duties and abilities needed to perform a job efficiently. (10)

**Job Description** A written description of a job based on information from a job analysis. (10)

**Job Rotation** A system in which employees are moved from one area to another so that they can view the total business operation prior to permanent assignment. (10)

**Job Specification** The type of person and qualifications needed to fill a job description. (10)

**Job Transfer** The assignment of an experienced worker to another job within the store or to a branch store (10)

**Last In, First Out (LIFO)** A method of accounting for ending inventory in which merchandise purchased last is assumed to be sold completely before any earlier-purchased items are sold. (22)

**Lay-Away Plan** A system in which the customer gives the store a deposit on merchandise, which is held until a later date. (12)

**Layoff** The temporary or permanent termination of an employee because of an economic slowdown or problems within the firm. (10)

**Leader Pricing** Pricing in which a retailer sells one or more products at lower than usual prices in order to attract shoppers. (15)

**Learning** Any change in an individual's response or behavior resulting from practice or experience. (4)

**Liabilities** The debts or obligations of a business. (21)

**License Agreement (Franchise Agreement)** A contract signed by a franchisor and a prospective franchisee. (26)

**Licensor (Franchisor)** A manufacturer, wholesaler, or service company that gives a franchise to another company or individual. (6)

**Lie Detector (Polygraph Instrument)** A device used to indicate whether answers to questions are lies or the truth. (10)

**Limited-Function Wholesaler** A merchandise resource for retailers that offers few services and low prices. (13)

**Limited-Item Store** A store that carries fewer than 1000 products, with few perishables and a limited number of brands. (7)

**Limited-Line Merchandise** Goods within a particular classification. (7)

**Limited-Line Store (Specialty Store)** A retail store that features a full line of a particular type of merchandise. (1)

**Line-and-Staff Organization Chart** A chart that combines the lines of delegated authority with specialists (staff) who provide expertise in certain areas. (9)

**Line Organization Chart** A chart that shows each worker's position with relation to his or her immediate superior or supervisor. (9)

**Listing Plan (Price List Agreement)** A plan that gives store managers responsibility for selecting merchandise from lists and catalogs supplied by the central buyer. (13)

**Loading Dock (Receiving Dock, Loading Platform)** A large area that can accommodate trucks or other vehicles for the unloading of merchandise. (16)

**Long-Term Loan** Credit terms that require repayment in a year or more. (25)

**Loss Leader** Merchandise that is sold by a retailer at or below cost. (15)

**Low-Margin (Low-Profit) Operator** A retailer that offers a minimum of service and low prices. (2)

**"Lower of Cost or Market" Rule** The policy of matching current replacement cost (market price) of merchandise against its computed cost; the ending inventory is valued at the lower price. (22)

**Mail Order House** A retail institution that sells through the mail. (1)

**Mail Order Retailing** The sale of goods and services to customers through the mail. (8)

**Maintained Markup (Gross Margin)** The final markup on an item. (15)

**Manufacturer** A firm that makes products that people buy. (1)

**Mapping** The process of determining the locations of departments and merchandise within a store. (12)

**Markdown** A reduction in selling price. (15)

**Market Segmentation** The process of dividing the total market into smaller sections based on a shared characteristic. (5)

**Marketing Research**  The investigation and systematic gathering, recording, and analysis of data that are pertinent to a specific marketing problem. (24)

**Marking**  The recording of a retail price on an item of merchandise. (16)

**Markup**  The difference between selling price and cost. (15)

**Maslow's Hierarchy of Needs**  A theory to explain why consumers are motivated to satisfy their needs and desires. (4)

**Mazur Plan**  A plan that divides all retail store activities into four major areas: merchandising, publicity, store management, and control. (9)

**Merchandise Budget**  Estimates of the factors that affect merchandise activities. (21)

**Merchandise Display**  An interior display that creates product awareness and stimulates impulse buying. (18)

**Merchandise Turnover (Stock Turnover)**  A measure for determining how quickly merchandise has been sold. (14)

**Merchandising Department**  The department that is responsible for buying and selling all goods and keeping merchandise records. (2)

**Middleman (Wholesaler)**  An individual or firm that purchases merchandise for resale to retailers. (1)

**Minimum Price Law (Unfair Trade Practices Law)**  A law that requires retailers to charge a minimum price for goods based on the cost of the merchandise plus a percentage for overhead. (15)

**Misses Merchandise Line**  Clothing for mature women. (15)

**Mobile**  A display that hangs from the ceiling and moves, thereby attracting attention. (18)

**Motivation**  The force that causes people to behave the way they do. (4)

**Movable Table (Portable Table)**  A table used to wheel incoming goods from the checking room to the marking room and then to the stockroom or selling floor. (16)

**Multiple-Price Policy**  A policy in which the retailer sells two or more items of the same merchandise at a unit price that is lower than the unit price if only one item is bought. (15)

**Narrow and Deep Plan**  An approach to retailing in which only a few selections are offered, but they are stocked in depth. (14)

**Neighborhood Shopping Center ("Strip Center")**  A small group of stores located alongside each other in a residential area. (11)

**Neighborhood Shopping District**  An area that contains a selection of convenience stores (e.g., a variety store, a bakery, a hardware store, a drug store, a grocery, and a laundromat), as well as an occasional specialty store. (11)

**Net Worth (Owner's Equity)**  The difference between the assets of a business and its liabilities. (21)

**New Inventory**  Items introduced by a store for the first time. (22)

**No-Frills Operator**  A retailer whose facilities are minimal and whose prices are low. (2)

**Nonmarking**  A policy in which prices are not marked on merchandise. (16)

**Objective-and-Task Method**  A budget technique that relates the advertising budget to the sales objectives for the coming year. (19)

**Observation**  A method of gathering information that consists of observing and recording consumer behavior in a particular situation. (24)

**Odd Price**   A price just below an even dollar or cents amount. (15)

**On-the-Job Training**   Training in which a new employee is assigned to a more experienced person until he or she has learned the job. (10)

**On-the-Shelf Display**   A device that utilizes shelf space as a basis for displaying merchandise. (18)

**One-Price Policy**   A policy in which all customers pay the same price for the same product. (15)

**Open Ad**   An advertisement that supplies all the information about a job as well as the name, address, and telephone number of the employer. (10)

**Open Charge Account**   An account in which, up to a specified limit, a customer may charge purchases to the account and pay for them at a later date. (23)

**Open Display**   A display in which merchandise is shown on tables, carts, and baskets designed for easy access and handling by the customer. (18)

**Open-to-Buy (OTB)**   The difference between planned purchases and stock already ordered; the dollar amount of merchandise that a buyer can order for a particular period. (14)

**Operations Department**   The department that is responsible for maintaining the store's physical plant and receiving and protecting merchandise. (2)

**Opinion Leader**   A member of a group who exerts influence on consumer decision making. (5)

**Optical Character Recognition—Font A (OCR)**   A classification system used in Universal Vendor Marking. (16)

**Order Taking**   A routine form of selling in which a store clerk fills a request, accepts payment, and wraps items. (17)

**Organization Chart**   A diagram that clearly indicates the lines of authority and responsibility in an organization. (9)

**Orientation Training**   New-employee instruction covering such topics as the history of the firm, procedures and policies, rules and regulations, promotions, and fringe benefits. (10)

**Original Markup (Initial Markup)**   The first markup on an item. (15)

**Outgoing Trend**   Styles that are experiencing reduced consumer demand. (3)

**Outshopper**   A person who is shopping outside his or her usual shopping area. (24)

**Overhead**   Business expenses such as rent, salaries, and advertising. (15)

**Overrun**   A quantity of custom-made articles in excess of retailers' orders. (7)

**Owner's Equity (Net Worth)**   The difference between the assets of a business and its liabilities. (21)

**Ownership Group**   A parent organization that owns a group of stores. (6)

**Partnership**   A form of business ownership in which two or more people invest time and money in the business. (6)

**Party Plan**   A direct-sales method of retailing in which a salesperson enlists the aid of one consumer in selling to others. (8)

**Patronage Motive**   The reason a consumer chooses one place to shop rather than another. (4)

**Peddler**   A person who hawks or sells goods. (1)

**Percentage-of-Sales Method**   The most commonly used method of preparing an advertising budget, basing it on a percentage of a sales figure such as past sales, anticipated sales, or a combination of past and anticipated sales. (19)

**Perception**   A personal interpretation of information. (4)

**Periodic Inventory**  A method of finding the value of merchandise at a particular time only by taking a physical count of the stock. (22)

**Perpetual Inventory**  A method for knowing the value of an inventory at any given time. (22)

**Personal Income**  All the moneys an individual receives from wages, salaries, investments, interest, and dividends. (5)

**Personal Selling**  A form of selling in which face-to-face methods are used to help customers with their buying problems. (17)

**Personality**  The sum of attributes that cause an individual to behave in a distinctive manner. (4)

**Personnel Department**  The department that is responsible for employee selection, training, advancement, and welfare. (2)

**Personnel Research**  Studies concerned with the finding, hiring, training, compensation, and evaluation of employees. (24)

**PM (Push Money, Spiff)**  A premium, prize, or extra commission offered to salespeople as an incentive to increase sales of a particular type of merchandise. (10)

**Point-of-Purchase (P-O-P) Display**  Devices or structures sponsored by vendors that are used in, on, or adjacent to a point of sale. (18)

**Point-of-Sales (POS) System**  A specially designed cash register system that is connected electronically to a computer. (3)

**Polygraph Instrument (Lie Detector)**  A device used to indicate whether answers to questions are lies or the truth. (10)

**Portable Table (Movable Table)**  A table used to wheel incoming goods from the checking room to the marking room and then to the stockroom or selling floor. (16)

**Postdating**  An extension of the cash discount period for an additional month when the invoice is dated on or after the twenty-fifth of the month and end-of-month terms are given. (14)

**Premarking (Source Marking)**  A policy in which the vendor marks the goods before delivery to the store according to the merchant's specifications. (14)

**Premium**  An article of merchandise that is given to a shopper free or at a reduced price as an incentive to buy a particular product. (20)

**Preretailing**  A policy in which buyers are required to list retail prices on purchase orders. (16)

**Press Release**  A formal statement prepared by a firm for submission to the media for publication. (20)

**Price Lining**  Carrying several lines of a given product, each with a different price. (15)

**Price List Agreement (Listing Plan)**  A plan that gives store managers responsibility for selecting merchandise from lists and catalogs developed by the central buyer. (13)

**Price War**  Action engaged in by retailers to underprice competitors. (15)

**Primary Data**  Information collected for the particular problem under study. (24)

**Private Label (Store Brand)**  Merchandise that is sold only in the retailer's own store. (13)

**Private Resident Buying Office (Store-Owned Resident Buying Office)**  A buying office that is owned by the firm it serves. (13)

**Problem-Solving Theory**  A view of retailing that holds that the salesperson must uncover and fully understand the customer's buying problem and attempt to solve it by presenting the appropriate merchandise. (17)

**Profit Sharing**  A plan that gives employees an opportunity to share in the profits of the firm. (10)

**Promotion**  Moving an employee to another position that carries greater responsibility and an increase in salary. (10)

**Promotion Calendar**  A calendar used by stores to pinpoint special events, local and national events, holiday promotions, advertising, and so forth. (20)

**Promotional Advertising**  Routine advertising that attempts to sell specific items or services by bringing customers into a store. (19)

**Promotional Display**  An attempt to sell merchandise directly and dramatically. (18)

**Psychoanalytic Concept**  A view of personality as controlled by the mind. (4)

**Psychogenic Motive**  A motive that stems from psychological needs such as the need for satisfaction, protection, or enhancement of the ego. (4)

**Public Relations**  A continuing program designed to encourage positive public attitudes toward the firm. (20)

**Publicity**  Free space and time given by newspapers, magazines, radio, and TV for newsworthy events. (20)

**Purchase Order**  A form that specifies the kind of goods ordered, their price, the date, shipping instructions, and terms. (16)

**Purchase Privilege Offer**  A promotion offered on a limited-continuity basis and designed to build traffic over a longer period. (20)

**Push Money (PM, Spiff)**  A premium, prize, or extra commission offered to salespeople as an incentive to increase sales of a particular type of merchandise. (10)

**Quick Ratio**  The relationship of a company's quick assets (current assets less inventory and supplies) to its current liabilities. (21)

**Rack Jobber**  A wholesaler that is allowed by a retail store to install, stock, and replenish selected items on display racks. (7)

**Rail Interview**  An initial screening that takes place before a prospective employee is asked to fill out an application form. (10)

**Rational Motive**  A motive that involves judgment and logical thinking; examples are security and durability. (4)

**Real Income**  In measuring an individual's purchasing power, the figure that determines the actual number of dollars available. (5)

**Real Self**  What the consumer is as a person; his or her physical, mental, and emotional characteristics. (4)

**Receiving Book**  A record of pertinent information about incoming goods. (16)

**Receiving Dock (Loading Dock, Loading Platform)**  A large area that can accommodate trucks or other vehicles for the unloading of merchandise. (16)

**Reference Group**  A group that is influential in shaping the attitudes, opinions, and lifestyle that an individual chooses. (5)

**Referral Premium**  A gift that is awarded to customers who send in the names of potential new customers. (20)

**Regional Shopping Center**  A combination of many small specialty shops and two or more major stores, usually in an enclosed mall, designed to service a large geographic area. (11)

**Related-Merchandise Display**  An arrangement of products with matching items (e.g., cheese and crackers), usually found in supermarkets and drugstores. (18)

**ReMarking**  Showing a markdown or markup by crossing out the old price and writing or stamping in the new one. (16)

**Reserve Stock**   Merchandise that is stored in a central stockroom or in a stockroom adjoining a department. (16)

**Resident Buying Office**   A service organization that helps retailers buy merchandise on a fee basis. (13)

**Retail Merchandise Management System (RMM)**   A system that tracks the performance of merchandise, reordering "hot" items and identifying the "cold" ones, enabling store buyers to make timely decisions. (13)

**Retail Method**   A method for estimating the cost of the ending inventory on the basis of a ratio of the cost of the goods available for sale to the retail price of the goods available for sale. (22)

**Retailer**   An individual or firm that sells goods and services directly to the ultimate consumer. (1)

**Retailing**   The selling of goods and services to the ultimate consumer. (1)

**Retailing Information System (RIS)**   An ongoing computer-based process for collecting both internal and external data. (3)

**Retailing Research**   Research that applies the techniques of marketing research to the investigation of problems related to retailing. (24)

**Return on Investment (ROI)**   The relationship of a corporation's net income to stockholders' equity. (21)

**Revolving Charge Account**   An account that enables a customer to charge purchases up to a specific amount; the customer has a specific period within which to make full payment without an interest (finance) charge. (23)

**Robinson-Patman Act**   An act that imposes restrictions on both manufacturers and retailers in the setting and receipt of prices that discriminate against other retailers. (15)

**ROG (Receipt of Goods)**   A system in which the cash discount period begins when goods are received by the buyer. (14)

**Route Selling**   A method of door-to-door selling used by retailers that sell frequently purchased convenience items. (8)

**Salary Supplement**   Money or prizes offered to salespeople as an incentive to increase sales of a particular type of merchandise. (10)

**Sales Forecasting**   Estimating future sales volume on the basis of current sales figures and information from manufacturers, wholesalers, accountants, economists, and bankers. (3)

**Sales Promotion**   Methods used by a merchant to generate sales, attract customers to the store, build customer loyalty, and promote good will. (20)

**Sales Promotion Department**   The department that is concerned with communicating the store's message to the public through advertising, display, and public relations. (2)

**Salvage Goods**   Goods that have been damaged in transit or storage. (7)

**Sample (in a research study)**   A representative group of the entire population studied. (24)

**Sample (offered as a premium)**   A trial size of a product that is provided by the manufacturer as an inducement to shoppers to try new items. (20)

**SBA Economic Opportunity Loan Program**   A program designed to counsel economically disadvantaged entrepreneurs and assist them in obtaining low-interest financing. (25)

**SBA Loan Guarantee Plan**   A program that enables a qualified businessperson to receive a bank loan guaranteed up to 90 percent by the Small Business Administration. (25)

**Scrambled Merchandising**   Increasing the types of goods that have traditionally been carried by a store. (7)

**Seasonal Merchandise**   Products that are in demand at a certain time of the year. (7)

**Secondary Data**   Information that is already available, having been collected previously for other projects. (24)

**Secondary Shopping Area**   An area that is smaller than a central shopping district and serves a specific part of a city. (11)

**Self-Concept**   An individual's perception of himself or herself. (4)

**Self-Image**   How the consumer views himself or herself. (4)

**Self-Liquidator Premium**   An item of merchandise sold (usually at cost) to a shopper after he or she has bought a product or tried a new service. (20)

**Semiautomatic Stock Control System (SASC)**   A system that replenishes the stocks of non-seasonal merchandise in stores quickly and almost automatically. (13)

**Semiblind Checking (Semi-Indirect Checking)**   A type of merchandise checking in which checkers use invoices whose quantities are omitted. (16)

**Shopper's Report**   A method of evaluating a salesperson's performance by means of observation and written reports. (10)

**Shopping Goods**   Products that consumers buy after spending time and effort to evaluate them. (7)

**Short-Term Loan**   Credit terms that require repayment in less than a year. (25)

**Shrinkage**   Merchandise losses due to shoplifting, internal theft, damage, and the like. (12)

**Simple Interest**   The formula used for the computation of interest on loans: Interest = principal $\times$ rate $\times$ time. (25)

**Single Pricing**   A policy in which the retailer sells all the merchandise in the store at one price. (15)

**Small Business Administration (SBA)**   An agency of the federal government that provides small businesses with advice and assistance in obtaining low-interest financing, and offers numerous other services. (25)

**Social Class**   A homogeneous division within a society in which a family or individual can be classified for comparative purposes. (5)

**Soft Goods**   Merchandise such as apparel, linen, and bedding. (1)

**Sole Proprietorship**   A business owned by one person, who invests time and money in it. (6)

**Source Marking (Premarking)**   A policy in which the vendor marks the goods before delivery to the store according to the merchant's specifications. (14)

**Special-Event Display**   An approach to display that is used by department stores and mass merchandisers for thematic storewide promotions. (18)

**Specialty Goods**   Particular brands for which a consumer shops. (7)

**Specialty Shopping Area**   A group of limited-line stores that sell similar merchandise. (11)

**Specialty Store (Limited-Line Store)**   A retail store that features a full line of a particular type of merchandise. (1)

**Specification Buying**   A system in which buyers develop product specifications for their purchases rather than selecting from what is available in the market. (13)

**Spiff (PM, Push Money)**   A premium, prize, or extra commission offered to salespeople as an incentive to increase sales of a particular type of merchandise. (10)

**"Split Run"**   A method that magazine publishers use to divide their national circulation into smaller sections at a lower cost to advertisers. (19)

**Spot Checking** A method of merchandise checking in which only one or a few cartons of a shipment are checked at random against the invoice or purchase order. (16)

**Staple Goods** Products that are constantly in demand and infrequently influenced by fashion changes. (7)

**Stationary Table** A table in the receiving area on which goods are laid out, counted, and ticketed. (16)

**Step Theory** A view of retailing in which a customer's decision to buy or not to buy follows a pattern of steps: attention, interest, desire, action. (17)

**Stimulus–Response Theory** A view of retailing in which a salesperson attempts to provide the "right" stimulus so that the customer responds positively. (17)

**Stockkeeping Unit (SKU)** One item of inventory that has distinct characteristics. (13)

**Stock Option** A plan that allows employees to purchase company stock at prices below the stock's market value. (10)

**Stock Turnover (Merchandise Turnover)** A measure for determining how quickly merchandise has been sold. (14)

**Stockholders' Equity** The net worth of a corporation. (21)

**Store Brand (Private Label)** Merchandise that is sold only in the retailer's own store. (3)

**Store Credit Card** A card issued by a department store or large specialty shop for use in its establishment. (23)

**Store-Owned Resident Buying Office (Private Resident Buying Office)** A buying office that is owned by the firm it serves. (13)

**"Strip Center" (Neighborhood Shopping Center)** A small group of stores located alongside each other in a residential area. (11)

**Stuffers** An advertising piece that accompanies a billing statement. (19)

**Style** A distinct feature or concept that makes a product different from others within the same classification. (3)

**Substitute Selling** Selling in which the salesperson offers the customer an alternative item when the store does not carry the specific brand asked for. (17)

**Suggestion Selling** Selling in which after a sale has been made, the salesperson suggests additional items that are related to the original purchase. (17)

**Supermarket** A self-service, cash-and-carry store that offers a wide variety of food and nonfood products in large quantities. (1)

**Superstore** A store that offers one-stop shopping with a full line of food and nonfood products; it carries a greater proportion of food products than combination stores; some services. (7)

**Survey** A method of obtaining information directly from individuals by using mail, telephone, and personal interviews. (24)

**Tearsheet** An actual copy of an advertisement. (19)

**Telephone Selling** Selling in which customers use the telephone to order goods and services from retail stores and mail order houses. (8)

**Theme Display** A display designed with an idea as a selling theme to stimulate the interest of consumers. (18)

**TO (Turnover)** Selling in which the salesperson turns the customer over to someone in authority or with particular expertise when it appears that the sale will not be closed. (17)

**Trade Discount** A reduction in list price given by vendors to volume purchasers. (14)

**Trading Area**  A geographic area from which a store draws the bulk of its customers. (11)

**Trading Post**  A place where trade may be carried on, by barter or cash, usually in a sparsely populated area. (1)

**Trading Stamps**  Stamps that are given to shoppers who spend a specified dollar amount; they are accumulated and traded for a variety of merchandise items. (20)

**Trading Up**  Selling in which the salesperson persuades the customer to buy a more expensive item or a larger quantity than originally intended. (17)

**Trait Concept**  A view of individuals as composed of characteristics such as seriousness, aggressiveness, sociability, and adaptability. (4)

**Travel/Entertainment Credit Card**  A card that can be used to charge purchases at motels, airlines, restaurants, and the like up to a predetermined limit; now accepted by some stores. (23)

**"Trending Service"**  A series of information bulletins on current fashion trends issued by a resident buying office. (13)

**Trickle-Across Theory**  The theory that each social class has opinion leaders who can influence others to accept a new style; thus, the style moves horizontally. (3)

**Trickle-Down Theory**  The theory that styles are introduced by the upper class and passed down to the masses in a vertical flow. (3)

**Twig**  A small department store branch that stocks only one kind of merchandise or several similar lines. (7)

**Type Concept**  A view of individuals that places them into groups according to physical or psychological characteristics or basic values. (4)

**Unfair Trade Practices Law (Minimum Price Law)**  A law that requires retailers to charge a minimum price for goods based on the cost of the merchandise plus a percentage for overhead. (15)

**Unit Control**  A system for gathering information about inventory by recording the stock in terms of units of merchandise. (22)

**Unit-of-Sales Method**  A method of preparing an advertising budget on the basis of the unit (number) of sales rather than dollar amounts, with a fixed sum set aside for each unit expected to be sold. (19)

**Unit Pricing**  Labeling merchandise with unit prices as well as total prices. (15)

**Universal Product Code (UPC)**  A system in which sensitized lines on product labels serve as symbols for numbers that can be "read" by a scanner and indicate the manufacturer, type of product, weight, and size. (3)

**Universal Vendor Marking (UVM)**  The premarking of merchandise by manufacturers in language that can be read by people and machines. (16)

**Variable-Price Policy (Flexible Pricing)**  A method of selling that enables customers to bargain with retailers. (15)

**Variety Store**  A retailing institution that sells a wide assortment of novelty items at low prices. (1)

**Vending Machine**  A piece of automated equipment that dispenses a wide variety of goods and services. (8)

**Venture Capital Operator**  An individual or corporation that invests money in someone else's business. (25)

**Vestibule Training**  Training in which a store uses its own classrooms to train employees prior to assignment. (10)

**Voluntary Chain**  A group of independent retailers that sell a wholesaler's products and use the wholesaler's name. (6)

**Warehouse Outlet**  A no-frills retail store that specializes in a particular line of nonfood merchandise, such as furniture, toys, or sporting goods. (7)

**Warehouse Store (Box Store)**  A cross between a limited-assortment store and a supermarket; stocks several thousand items, including nonfood products, limited lines of perishables, and meat; customers mark and bag their own items. (2)

**Warranty**  A written guarantee of a manufacturer's or retailer's responsibility. (3)

**Wheel of Retailing**  A theory to explain the institutional changes that take place when innovators enter the retail arena. (2)

**White-Collar Worker**  An individual who earns a living as a professional, in an office, or in a service occupation. (5)

**Wholesaler (Middleman)**  An individual or firm that purchases merchandise for resale to retailers. (1)

**Width (Breadth)**  The number of product classifications that a merchant stocks. (14)

**Window Display**  The use of store windows to attract customers by showing the quality of merchandise handled, price lines, and store image. (18)

**Zoning Law (Zoning Code)**  Regulations restricting the type of building that may take place in a community. (11)

# PHOTO CREDITS

**Part Three Opener:** Courtesy Dallas Market Center.

**Chapter 13** Page 259: Joel Gordon. Page 272: Courtesy Dallas Apparel Marts. Page 273: Top, Joel Gordon; bottom, courtesy Telisman Sales.

**Chapter 14** Page 282: Sybil Shelton/Monkmeyer. Page 286: Ray Ellis/Rapho-Photo Researchers. Page 293: Courtesy Dayton's.

**Chapter 15** Page 306: Courtesy Waldbaums. Page 308: George E. Jones/Photo Researchers. Page 310: Marilyn Schrut.

**Chapter 16** Page 329: Sybil Shelton/Monkmeyer. Page 336: Ellis Herwig/Stock, Boston. Page 339: Courtesy Soabar. Page 340: Courtesy Kimball Systems, Division of Litton Industries. Page 344: Courtesy Sensormatic Electronics Corporation. Figure 16-6: a,d, & f, Courtesy Kimball Systems, Division of Litton Industries.

**Part Four Opener:** F. B. Grunzweig/Photo Researchers.

**Chapter 17** Page 358: Courtesy Sears, Roebuck. Page 360: Top left, Lew Merrim/Monkmeyer; top right, Alan Carey/Image Works; middle left, Ken Karp; middle right, Peter Southwick/ Stock, Boston; bottom left, Eric A. Roth/The Picture Cube. Page 369: Courtesy Dayton's.

**Chapter 18** Page 381: Joel Gordon. Page 382: Top left, Beryl Goldberg; top right, Alan Becker/Photo Researchers; bottom left, Beryl Goldberg; bottom right, Marilyn Schrut. Page 383: Courtesy Saks Fifth Avenue. Page 384: Courtesy J. C. Penney. Page 387: Top left, Courtesy Sears, Roebuck; top right, Sybil Shelton/Monkmeyer; bottom, Courtesy Myers Modular Showcase Systems. Page 388: Courtesy The Colombus Showcase Company. Page 389: Ken Karp. Page 390: Les Mahon/Monkmeyer. Page 391: Courtesy J. C. Penney.

**Chapter 19** Page 403: Courtesy Henri Bendel. Page 404: Courtesy Strawbridge & Clothier. Page 405: Courtesy Zeller Tuxedos. Page 406: Courtesy Filene's. Page 413: Courtesy Bolton's Dress Shops. Page 414: Printed with permission of Lane Bryant, Inc. The trademark "Nancy's Choice" is a property of Lane Bryant, Inc. Page 418: Courtesy Bonwit Teller. Page 419: Courtesy WKJF Radio. Page 420: Copyright 1982, Condé Nast Publications. All rights reserved.

**Chapter 20** Page 432: Courtesy A & P Food Stores. Page 433: Courtesy Matsuri Bicycle. Pages 437, Bottom, and 439: Ken Karp. Figure 20-3: Courtesy Strawbridge & Clothier. Page 444: Courtesy Macy's. Page 445: Courtesy Lazarus.

**Part Five Opener:** Courtesy Burroughs Corporation.

**Chapter 22** Page 483: Sperry Univac, a division of Sperry Corporation. Figure 22-1: Courtesy Kimball Systems, Division of Litton Industries. Page 487: Courtesy MSI Data Corporation.

**Chapter 23** Page 506: Courtesy American Express. Page 507: Kathy Bendo. Page 515: Courtesy Gulf Consumer Services Company.

**Part Six Opener:** Courtesy May Centers.

**Chapter 24** Page 528: Courtesy MSI Data Corporation. Page 532: Esaias Baitel/Rapho-Photo Researchers. Page 535: Cary Wolinsky/Stock, Boston. Page 538: Courtesy MSI Data Corporation.

**Chapter 25** Page 555: Donald Dietz/Stock, Boston. Page 558: Sybil Shelton/Monkmeyer. Page 560: Courtesy Small Business Administration.

**Chapter 26** Page 576: Courtesy Burger King Corporation. Page 583: Robert Goldstein/Photo Researchers. Page 586: Peter Southwick/Stock, Boston.

# index